third edition

SELF-ASSESSMENT AND CAREER DEVELOPMENT

third edition

SELF-ASSESSMENT AND CAREER DEVELOPMENT

James G. Clawson

Colgate Darden Graduate School
University of Virginia

John P. Kotter

Graduate School of Business Administration
Harvard University

Victor Faux

Management Consulting Service
London

Charles C. McArthur

Career Ventures
Cambridge

Prentice Hall, Englewood Cliffs, NJ 07632

Library of Congress Cataloging-in-Publication Data

Self-assessment and career development / James G. Clawson . . . [et al.].—3rd ed.
p. cm.
Includes bibliographical references.
1. Career development. 2. Vocational guidance. 3. Self-evaluation. 4. Job hunting. I. Clawson, James G.
HF5381.S473 1992 90-14191
331.7'02—dc20 CIP

Acquisition Editor: Alison Reeves
Production and Copy Editor: Joanne Palmer
Cover Designer: Lundgren Graphics, Ltd.
Prepress Buyer: Trudy Pisciotti
Manufacturing Buyer: Bob Anderson
Supplements Editor: David Scholder
Editorial Assistant: Lioux Brun

Case material of the Harvard Graduate School of Business Administration is made possible by the cooperation of business firms and other organizations which may wish to remain anonymous by having names, quantities, and other identifying details disguised while maintaining basic relationships. Cases are prepared as the basis for class discussion rather than to illustrate either effective or ineffective handling of an administrative situation.

The authors are pleased to acknowledge the support for this work provided by the Sponsors of the Colgate Darden Graduate School of Business Administration, the University of Virginia, through the School's Case Research Program. The text and cases from this source are copyrighted by the Sponsors and are used here by permission.

Printed in the United States of America

10 9 8 7 6 5 4 3 2 1

ISBN 0-13-803180-0

Prentice-Hall International (UK) Limited, *London*
Prentice-Hall of Australia Pty. Limited, *Sydney*
Prentice-Hall Canada Inc., *Toronto*
Prentice-Hall Hispanoamericana, S.A., *Mexico*
Prentice-Hall of India Private Limited, *New Delhi*
Prentice-Hall of Japan, Inc., *Tokyo*
Simon & Schuster Asia Pte. Ltd., *Singapore*
Editora Prentice-Hall do Brasil, Ltda., *Rio de Janeiro*

Contents

Preface

In 1975, a new second-year MBA elective being taught at the Harvard Business School was awarded the EXXON award for the most creative course in business management. In 1978, Prentice Hall published the first edition of *Self-Assessment and Career Development,* which summarized major features of that course. The first edition was the result of six years of work and involved the creative and administrative input of a number of people, including Rod Hodgens, Warren Wilhelm, Eileen Morley, Frank Leonard, Allen Froman, and the creative force that launched the book, Tony Athos. Since the first edition, the course as it was taught at the Harvard Business School underwent a great deal of development—first by Victor Faux, then by Jim Clawson, by Jeffrey Sonnenfeld, and by Shoshana Zuboff as each of these have had responsibility for the development and direction of the course.

Meanwhile, an increasing number of faculty at schools around the country were beginning to teach courses on career management. Many of them used this book. This interest was built on two contributions of the text: first, a relatively comprehensive approach to introducing and becoming facile with a self-assessment process and the topography of the corporate job search; and second, a rigorous development of the broadly useful managerial skill of inductive logic. In my experience, few other courses provide MBAs the opportunity to gather multiple pools of disparate data, practice inductively identifying patterns that occur in them, make strategic plans on those observed patterns, adjust the plans to fit emerging realities, make high-stakes decisions, and then follow through over a lengthy period of time. The issues in the course are not solved in one-hour or three-hour class sessions, but extend over the course of at least two years. In this regard, the book and the course distinguish themselves from the concern of some faculty colleagues who discount such courses as "Personal Finance" as being inappropriately individualistic for schools of management. For me, the personal component is a by-product of the more central issue of managerial thinking skills, useful because it heightens students' willingness to engage the inductive skill set.

The personal aspect of the course spills over into society. Every year dozens of students, friends of students, families of students, people who have read about the course, and a variety of public media have contacted the teaching faculty to inquire how they might participate in exercises similar to those outlined by the course. The first edition was constructed more for use in a graduate level university course and did not lend itself well to these individual inquiries. The second edition was an attempt to begin making the textbook more useful to the public. Although the career management process outlined in the book was more fully explained in this edition, it's complexity made it difficult for individuals to persist in it without the support of a course.

A common concern among students midway through the course has been that although they had developed a powerful and detailed self-assessment, they could not find comparable materials on job offerings to guide them through the second half of the course—career development, including job search and joining up. The desire to address this need produced *An MBA's Guide to Self Assessment and Career Development* by Jim Clawson and David Ward. This volume consolidated and summarized student research projects on more than 50 MBA entry-level jobs and occupations. The reports were listed first by function and then by job title. The goal was to provide data on jobs and occupations that roughly matched the kinds of data students had been able to develop on themselves, including cognitive style, interpersonal style, professional demands and skills, and life style. The salary data and listings of companies that hire in each job title have become somewhat old; that volume, although useful for generic comparisons, needs to have its specific information updated.

This third edition of *Self-Assessment and Career Development* seeks to make the process more broadly available by incorporating new features—several new instruments and updated case materials. The process remains rigorous and demanding, though, so the casual buyer should know that this is not a weekend exercise.

The focus of the third edition continues to be on graduating MBAs. This focus on graduate business students does not reduce the applicability of the approach to undergraduates or job hunters in other occupational areas. The process, we believe, is broadly applicable. The examples, however, are specific to the graduate business student.

We also continue the two perspectives developed in earlier editions of looking at career management from both the individual's and the corporation's points of view. The book asks individuals to do as careful an analysis of the organizational context as they do of their own careers. Without both analyses, first the individual and second the organizational, it is impossible to develop a complete and carefully thought-out choice that will match the strengths and weaknesses of both the individual and the organization.

We believe that this matching process is essential in making well-informed and accurate career decisions, both by the individual and the recruiter or manager, who each must weigh the appropriateness not only of the applicant's managerial style, but also of his or her overall personal style and the demands and requirements of the job in the organization.

The book will outline in basically chronological order the steps in a self-assessment and career development process that one is likely to encounter in life. We believe the process to be cyclical and ongoing, in the sense that although one will not be continuously generating self-assessment data as intensively as one will be while working through this book, there will come times in life when a reassessment of one's basic life themes and motivations will be appropriate. If former students' comments are any indication, the procedures and approach outlined in this book will serve those who use it well throughout a lifetime of self-assessment and career development.

Jim Clawson
Charlottesville, VA

Reader Feedback

We want to continue to revise and update *Self-Assessment and Career Development* so that it will continue to meet reader needs. If you have *specific* suggestions for how the book might be improved in its next edition, please write them below, tear out this page, and send it to

Mr. James G. Clawson
Colgate Darden Graduate School of Business
University of Virginia
Box 6550
Charlottesville, Virginia 22906

1. What, specifically, did you like about the book and feel should not be changed?

2. What, specifically, did you not like about the book and feel should be changed?

3. What, specifically, do you think should be added to the book?

Your name and address (optional):

third edition

SELF-ASSESSMENT AND CAREER DEVELOPMENT

1

Introduction

> "Cheshire Puss," she began, rather timidly, as she did not know whether it would like the name; however, it only grinned a little wider. "Come, it's pleased so far," thought Alice, and she went on. "Would you please tell me, please, which way I ought to walk from here?"
>
> "That depends a good deal on where you want to get to," said the Cat.
>
> "I don't much care where," said Alice.
>
> "Then it doesn't matter which way you walk," said the Cat.
>
> "—so long as I get somewhere," Alice added as an explanation.
>
> "Oh, you're sure to do that," said the Cat, "if only you walk long enough!"
>
> —*Alice in Wonderland*

A sign beside a freeway in the middle of a large desert in southeastern Idaho reads

ARE YOU LOST?
Keep on going. You're making good time!

These two notes reflect, unfortunately, the kind of thinking that goes into career planning for many of us. Given the press of time and economic circumstance, we often plunge ahead into a job or a "career" without giving much thought to whether or not it is right for us or where it will lead us. We fail to anticipate where our career decisions, both small and great, will take us. And worried by the uncertainty of knowing ourselves and the future, we forge on—hoping that if we just keep going we will get somewhere, and the sooner the better.

Later, many of us find ourselves in jobs, places, and careers that we did not imagine. In some cases, that is good—we are happy with the result. In other cases, the realization is accompanied by remorse and the wish for a chance to do it over again. What we needed—what we still need—is a systematic way to think about the career decisions we make so that in both the short and the long runs, the result will be what we more or less anticipated and worked toward. Furthermore, this systematic way should not preclude flexibility in the face of changing circumstances. If the opportunities of the future change, our method of thinking about our career decisions should help us compare who we were, who we are, and who we are becoming in the midst of those environmental changes; and help us make decisions that will be appropriate for us and the times.

This book has been written for people who, for whatever reason, wish consciously and explicitly to manage their careers. Our experience has been that people who have already decided on a career (or a job), as well as people who are uncertain about what to do next, have benefited greatly from the process outlined here. The self-assessment process will leave you with a very specific and detailed profile of the things that matter most to you in life and in work. The career development process will help you generate skill at using that profile not only to make reasonable job- and career-related decisions, but also to know what facets of the decision present potential danger areas and what facets will fit you naturally. The process will also help you develop skill in assessing job and career opportunities in dimensions that are specifically relevant to you. Your career planning and activities will be based on information that will help you to develop a greater sense of direction and purpose and alert you to what to look for along the way.

The purpose of the book is to help you develop concrete skills for managing your career—skills at assessing yourself, assessing opportunities, making career- and job-related choices, and managing this process in both the short and long run. The examples and the situations we rely on to present and discuss our approach come primarily from the business world, but the approach is as useful for someone considering a nonbusiness career as it is for someone in business. The book is intended for use in formal courses, but if you are serious about wanting to make a career or job decision that is appropriate for you, and if you have the self-discipline to work on your decision carefully, then this book can help you a great deal.

When we speak of job- and career-related decision making, we are talking about a wide range of important choices that people make during the course of a lifetime. Such decisions include:

1. The selection of type of career
2. The selection of what job to seek next
3. The selection of a strategy for getting a particular type of job
4. The selection of a job offer from alternatives
5. The selection of assignments, locations, and so on within a job when options are offered
6. The selection of an approach to a job
7. The selection of career goals or a sequence of desired promotions
8. The selection of a life style that surrounds and influences a career
9. The relationship between one's partner and all these choices

It is our observation that people often make these decisions with considerably less care and expertise than they use in the selection of a television or a vacation. Even people who have professional training in analysis and decision making often spend a great deal of time making decisions that, in the context of their lives, may be of little significance, while slipping semiconsciously into major life decisions whose implications are not at all clear to them. Compared to less important decisions, their data-collection methods tend to be less thorough, their analyses more superficial, and their choice processes more random.

There are undoubtedly many reasons why people behave in this way. For most people, assessing something "outside" themselves is a great deal easier, psychologically, than assessing themselves. The latter creates discomfort, which people often deal with by avoiding. At the same time, our educational institutions have historically provided courses for helping us learn how to make "good" management decisions, legal decisions, engineering decisions, financial decisions, medical decisions—but not career and job decisions.

Some people, of course, manage to go through life quite happily without ever seriously assessing themselves or their opportunities, or making explicit job and career choices. Whether because of luck or very good intuitive decision-making capabilities, they do very well. Many other people behave that way but find the results highly unsatisfying. They often slip into boring or frustrating careers. They sometimes find themselves faced with conflicting job and family demands that are unreasonable. Many discover, to their horror, that they will never achieve the position or professional reputation they had been seeking for years. Some go through the trauma of being fired. Others find themselves securely locked into a job and life style that is no longer satisfying, but from which escape seems impossible. In the words of one forty-nine-year-old: "I woke up one day and just sat in bed thinking, how in the hell did I ever get myself into this mess?"

Although this book offers no easy answers, it does try to bring to bear the best technology and insight that exists today on the subject. Like any management task in which the manager does not have absolute control of all the relevant variables, success is not guaranteed. Nevertheless, our experience over the past fifteen years with the materials and approach presented in this book has convinced us that they are effective, and that they can be of significant help to most people in a variety of ways. The comments of some who have worked through the process may help you anticipate what you can expect to get out of the effort:

> This has been the most valuable course I've taken. I maintain that the lack of skills/abilities taught by this course is more often the cause for lack of success than any other subject or skill.
>
> I do know that I will take with me (from this course) a set of tools and a level of self-awareness and sensitivity that will undoubtedly have a profound impact upon my life.
>
> Understanding now that everyone has strengths and weaknesses due to cognitive style, value systems, etc., I've become less judgmental of myself and others in

areas of intelligence, and put more emphasis on what a person would be good at doing because of the person's (or own) cognitive style, values, etc.

I gained a fantastic understanding of the *criteria* upon which I will make my job decision. I learned a great deal about what I *really* want out of a job. I learned a great deal about the potential pitfalls of the job hunt and later career development.

I have been forced to formalize a previously semiconscious awareness of myself. This has forced me to acknowledge certain characteristics as important enough to choose a career around. Before taking this course I was boxed into a narrow idea of what were acceptable courses, and viewed incompatible characteristics as sources of tension and discontent that I would just have to live with. Now I've reassessed my priorities, and am taking a much more imaginative approach to finding a job.

I feel like I've gained a whole lot from the course. I was very confused and worried about the job-hunting process at the beginning of this year. Now, I feel I have a good focus and a lot more *self-confidence* in dealing with the whole career selection process.

This course was a lot of work but it was worth three times the work it demanded.

Who Can Use the Book

This book was written primarily for graduate students of business administration, so many of the examples and cases are set in circumstances relevant to that group. The process of self-assessment and career development outlined and developed here, however, is applicable to a much broader audience. In fact, you will probably find these exercises and readings useful regardless of the career area you have decided to pursue or of the point in your career—early, middle, or late.

UNDERGRADUATES: Undergraduates will be able to use the self-assessment exercises in virtually the same way that MBA students do. The details of the job search process may be somewhat different, but the ways in which undergraduates can use self-assessment materials to guide their job search and decision-making activities are not different from those described here. If you have not worked full time before, you may not be able to draw on your work experiences as much as older people, but if you take into account the career stage theories and the tasks associated with them as outlined in Chapter 38, you will be able to get a perspective on how your own goals, values, and career inclinations will evolve over the next few years. An introduction to this material now will better prepare you to make sense of your first experiences.

Again, the process will be helpful even if you are not interested in a career in business. Students considering any career area who work through the book carefully will gain greater insight into the kinds of work, work settings, colleagues, and organizations that would suit them best.

PEOPLE MAKING CAREER CHANGES: If you have been working for some time and are considering a major career change, the process outlined here can be of enormous help. We have found that many people leave one job because they are somehow dissatisfied with the work, the people, or the organization, but, *lacking a sufficiently clear and detailed self-assessment,* often put themselves in new situations no better suited to their interests, skills, and desires. In a sense this is like trying to find what one wants by knowing what one doesn't want. That takes a lot of trial and error. It is much more efficient to begin with a vision of the kind of work you *should* be seeking, given who you are, and to avoid getting sidetracked by "interesting" opportunities that do not really fit you. This book will help you to do that. We will not spend any time discussing the significant emotional issues of leaving a job in which you may have invested a great deal of time and energy. If you are in this category, you may be interested in the work of Meryl Louis. See, for instance, "Career Transitions: The Missing Link in Career Development," published in the Spring 1982 issue of *Organizational Dynamics*.

DUAL CAREER COUPLES: If you are trying to make career decisions in tandem, this book can be a great help. We have found that many of our students ask for copies of the materials and work through them with their spouses or close friends. The process can be even more exciting when you work through it with someone and can talk at leisure about the things you will be learning and doing. The book is organized primarily as a self-assessment exercise for individuals, but there are a few explicitly couple-oriented exercises. In addition to these, we encourage couples to compare their findings on each of the instruments and the implications of those findings for work and to discuss the meanings for their joint relationship, job search, and career development activities.

One of the basic premises of this book is that people are multidimensional and that the various dimensions are closely connected. If working through the exercises with another person will help you to keep in mind the other, noncareer aspects of your life and to make decisions that will balance those aspects in a way that is most appealing to you, then working together can be very beneficial.

One word of caution: Sometimes in discussing very personal data with other people, even those we have known for a long time and with whom we feel very comfortable, we may try to be to those people what we have come to know that they expect. In other words, we may distort our own data or our interpretations of those data for the sake of the relationship and the roles we play within it. This is a manageable danger if you are aware of it and are willing to look at yourself and your relationship openly and honestly. If you plan to work through the book with another person, we advise you to analyze each instrument and exercise alone first, perhaps making notes that you can keep in reserve and do not feel compelled to share with the other person. Then you can compare your private notes with the feedback you get from the other person and note any differences. If there are differences, you may want to think about how, if at all, and in what ways you would like to address those differences in your relationship.

Organization of the Book

The first part of this book deals with the process of self-assessment. It is designed to help you learn how to assess yourself effectively for career and job decision-making purposes, and to help you produce a usable self-assessment. The second part focuses on career development. It is designed to help you assess job and career opportunities, get a job, and deal with the challenges and problems encountered in different stages of a career.

The book was intended primarily for use in a classroom setting, but has been organized to help individuals who want to attack the self-assessment process on their own. This process will require a great deal of discipline and time, so whether you are approaching it in a class or alone, you should plan to spend ample time and energy. Self-assessment should not be rushed. The quick answers are often neither the most valid nor the most useful.

The self-assessment portion of the book will help you to generate a great deal of data. We encourage you to purchase a 2-inch three-ring binder and a set of colored index tabs with which to organize your data. The pages of this book are perforated so that you can tear them out and put them in your notebook.

Since our approach is one of self-assessment, we've asked *you* to manage the data-generation process. We will guide you through that process, but at this point we advise you to *not skip ahead* in the book. Proceed sequentially. The next chapter will outline the self-assessment process we will use more carefully and help you prepare to begin.

Your Expectations

Before you begin, however, we ask you to pause for a moment and write down your expectations for this self-assessment and career development project/course. This brief exercise will help you to clarify your goals and also provide an interesting means of reviewing your progress later on. Please be as explicit and specific as you can as you consider the following questions:

Why did you select this course/book?

What do you want to get out of the course/book?

What do you think we will be doing in this course/book?

What do you expect from the faculty/authors?

How does this course fit into your present and future plans?

Any other expectations, feelings?

2

The Self-Assessment Process

The self-assessment method presented here is a systematic process designed to generate the type of accurate self-awareness needed to make rational job and career decisions. This approach is similar to that used by many professional career management consultants, with one important exception. The process described here is not just a human assessment process, it is a self-assessment process. You will not only acquire skills in assessing other people for career decision-making purposes, you will learn how to assess yourself.

Our underlying philosophy here is that with some guidance and understanding of the process, any careful and thoughtful person can generate personal information, assess its usefulness, and draw conclusions from it that will be helpful, even extremely helpful, in making career-related decisions. Professional counselors could no doubt interpret any single instrument with a greater degree of skill than we will develop here, and if you have access to them, we encourage you to seek their assistance. *You*, however, will be making the decisions and living with them. We believe that since the consequences of your decisions will affect you, you should maintain the primary responsibility for generating, evaluating, and using the data that affect those decisions. Hence, our focus on *self*-assessment.

We realize that your lack of professional training in career counseling and your own biases and preconceptions about who you are may leave you uneasy as you contemplate a self-assessment process. We have taken these things into account and have provided ways of compensating. First, we will explain in nontechnical terms the strengths and weaknesses of the process and the instruments we will use so that you can make an informed and conservative use of the data. Second, we will provide a way of allowing for the impact of your preconceptions. Third, we will use a variety of instruments so that we will not have to rely on any single data-generating device, but rather will be able to take a view that is multifaceted and therefore less susceptible to distortion.

We also expect that you may become impatient with this process. In our graduate program, we spend a full semester working through this book. Our experience has been that at first the data-generation process seems disjointed and unconnected. Do not let that disturb you. Before long it will begin to come together, and you will understand more clearly what is happening. It *is* a rigorous process, though, so you should be committed to following through. You can learn something by doing bits and pieces of the self-assessment, but the real strength of the process lies in the integration of the various exercises we will ask you to do. We promise you, as did some of *our* students in the introduction, that it will be worth your time and effort.

The Basic Approach

We will utilize a five-step approach to each of the exercises in the self-assessment process. As you go through the first part of this book, you will be repeating the following cycle a number of times:

1. First, you will use some data-generating device.
2. Then you will be asked to record your reactions to the exercise in a Feelings Record or journal.
3. You next will read the chapter that explains how to score and interpret the scores from that device.
4. You will then practice interpreting the data supplied by that instrument, using data from one or more cases.
5. Finally, you will do an initial interpretation of your own data.

The fourth step in the cycle is particularly important. Developing your skills at assessment requires practice. The case material in the first part of the book is carefully chosen with that requirement in mind.

Generating Useful Data

Rational assessment, of necessity, begins by generating or gathering information. This book contains and describes a number of different mechanisms that can elicit potentially useful information about a person. These include devices we have created for use here, as well as some standard psychological instruments. None of these methods alone can come close to capturing all there is to know about a person. But as a group they will provide a rich and diverse pool of data tailored for our purposes.

Throughout the first stages of the self-assessment process, you will be asked to use the devices in the book to generate useful data about yourself. Most of these exercises will require only thirty to sixty minutes of your time. (One exception is the written interview, which will require considerably more time and effort, and which we will explain later.) You will probably find some of the exercises fun, or at least interesting. And you will probably find some of the exercises boring, or anxiety-producing. These feelings can be useful data too, and we will ask you to record them as well.

One of the reasons people often feel anxious while using these devices is because they assume these mechanisms are evaluating them. They consciously, or more often unconsciously, believe that the devices will tell them if they are "dumb" or "smart," whether they have any chance at all of becoming a CPA, or whether or not they are "sane." As a result, they approach these devices with ambivalence, and they find using them to be somewhat anxiety-producing.

It is very important for you to recognize at the outset that these data-generating mechanisms *do not analyze you.* They do not tell you what you can or cannot do with your life or how good a person you are. All they do is supply potentially relevant information that *you* can use to create a self-assessment, which then can help you make better job- and career-related decisions. *You* have to make sense out of the information. *You* have to do the analysis. *You* are in charge. That's what self-assessment is all about.

Recording Your Feelings

Despite what we have just said, you will no doubt have a variety of emotional reactions to the various instruments in the self-assessment process. These reactions will be in large part due to the nature of the instrument, but other things will affect your feelings as well. The way the instrument is introduced to you, your physical and emotional state when you receive the instrument, what you were doing before you received it, interruptions while you are taking the test, and many other factors will influence your response to each instrument.

A careful recording of your reactions to each device can help in several ways. First, since each of the instruments is different in some way, a Feelings Record will help you to analyze your responses to different kinds of situations. This will help you anticipate your responses to similar situations on the job. Second, since there are so many different factors that influence your reaction to any particular data-generating device, a record of the most salient will help you to sort out any distortions you feel have occurred in your test results. Finally, since you will be doing the analysis and will draw conclusions based only on data in which *you* have confidence, a detailed Feelings Record can help you to calibrate the validity a particular set of test data has for you. Your notes will remind you of your concerns about an instrument and to put its results in a reasonable perspective.

Understanding the Data-Generating Devices

In order to utilize the information supplied by any data-generating device, it is crucial that you understand the strengths and weaknesses of the device. Your data are only as good as the instrument used to generate them. The *kind* of information, the *accuracy* of the information, and the *use* of the information will all be affected by the nature of the instrument.

We have provided chapters that will give you some insight into the instruments we will be using.

These chapters are not designed to make you an expert in measuring techniques; instead, they are designed to provide you with enough information so that you can reasonably and intelligently interpret the output of those devices. Remember, *do not read these chapters before you have completed the test or exercise associated with them.* If you do, your responses may be distorted by your knowledge of the scoring system and your beliefs about what constitutes a "desirable," "right," or "socially acceptable" response.

Practicing Interpretation

Once you have taken a test or exercise and read the note accompanying it, you will be asked to practice interpreting someone else's data—in most instances a case included in the book. This will give you a chance to develop some skill in using each set of data before you begin working on your own.

Our approach is fundamentally a process of inductive logic. That is, it starts by focusing on specifics (data generated by the various devices) and from that slowly develops generalizations (themes). This is in contrast to a deductive process, in which we would begin with a set of generalizations (a model) about the behavior of all human beings, and then use them to generate more specific generalizations about a specific person. (For example, if a model says that "all people with red hair are temperamental" and Joe has red hair, we would *deduce* that Joe is temperamental.[1])

This inductive process of thematic analysis is, in a sense, systematic detective work. It involves sifting through large amounts of information looking for clues (to potential themes), drawing tentative conclusions (about what the themes might be), and then testing those conclusions against still more data. And like detective work, it can be fun.

When you make observations from another person's data (the cases), strive to be conservative and to keep your inferences closely connected to the data. It is easy to let your own values, beliefs, habits, and views of the world color what we might say about another person—and what we might conclude about ourselves. One of the major objectives of the "practicing interpretation" step is to develop skill in drawing simple, conservative inferences from the data. We will have more to say about this later on, but be sure to keep it in mind as you begin.

You might ask: "How do I go about generating conservative inferences?" Generally, you will be asked to do two things. First, you will be asked to *observe* and *cite* a specific bit of evidence (a score on a test, for example) and then to draw an *inference* about what that datum might mean. These inferences are very simple, tentative statements, closely connected to the datum, that attempt to clarify the meaning of the datum. The note that accompanies each instrument will help you make these observations and inferences.

We also encourage you to think carefully about the strengths and weaknesses of each data-generating device. Ask yourself what kind of data it is producing. How accurate is it? To what kinds of distortions is it susceptible? What does it add to what I already know (or suspect about myself?) How might I use the data in conjunction with the other data I have generated? The answers to these questions will help you put the data you generate from each instrument into perspective.

If you are working through the self-assessment process alone, we encourage you to work through the case too. Somehow it is much easier to be "objective" about someone else's data than it is about your own. We would also encourage you in your discussions with friends or spouses or counselors to seek feedback that will add to and complement your conclusions rather than that which will only confirm your views of yourself.

Interpreting Your Own Data

Now, once you have generated some data, read the note, and practiced interpreting a case, you will be asked to begin drawing inferences from your own data. Again, the principles of conservatism, tentativeness, and careful, logical connection should hold. Do not be concerned about drawing sweeping generalizations early in the process. The broader conclusions will come later. This we call "identifying themes."

Identifying Themes

Gradually, as you generate and sift through more and more data, you will begin to see inferences that

---

[1]It would be nice if we could use a deductive approach to self-assessment, particularly because most of us have been educated more in deduction than induction. Unfortunately, however, we cannot. There exists today no single model of human behavior that is of the quality necessary for our purposes. The very best psychological or behavioral models are very limited in their scope and applicability. The behavioral sciences might some day create a truly general-purpose model of human behavior, but it most certainly does not exist now. An alternative method that would still allow deduction would be to study *all* the current models of human behavior and how and when each can be useful. But that is a task far beyond our scope here.

recur or bits of data that seem to be connected in some way. These connections may be reflections of central themes that are characteristic of your life.

Keep in mind that our purpose is to use a self-assessment as an aid in making career and job decisions. That is, we seek to create a product that can help to discriminate among a set of potential or real career- and job-related options. We need something that can be used to help "predict" what might happen if a person chooses one career or job option over another: Will the individual be happier with job 1 or job 2? Will she be promoted faster at company A or company B? Will he be more likely to succeed with option 1 or option 2? Will she feel more family/job conflicts with offers 1, 2, or 3?

A self-assessment that can help answer these questions must focus on a person's central and stable characteristics. An assessment which says that an individual likes X, or tends to behave like Y, is not very useful if both X and Y can change within a month. Although human beings do change rather drastically in some ways in a short period of time, all people tend to change slowly or not at all in other ways. It is this latter set of characteristics that one searches for in the data.

To get at these more stable, central, and important aspects of a person that in daily conversation we often call "interests," "values," "skills," or "motives," we will be helping you develop skills at thematic analysis. In this type of analysis, we sort through data and inferences from the various devices looking for recurring ideas (themes). The underlying logic is straightforward and compelling: If evidence pointing to a particular theme ("likes to be in charge," for instance) is found a significant number of times in data generated from numerous devices, then it is probably justifiable to conclude that the evidence is saying something important about the person. With the systematic use of this type of analysis, you can find most of the important themes in your life and be well on your way toward a sound self-assessment.

Identifying Implications

The final step in the process is to identify the basic job, career, and life style implications of the themes you have located. This step involves translating that which you have found in the data into a form and format that is not only accurate, but easy to use in job or career decision making. We will help you as you make that translation.

Some Caveats

The process we will repeat with each instrument is outlined in Exhibit 2–1. The self-assessment checklist included at the end of this chapter is provided as a guideline to help you follow the procedure and track your progress.

Human beings are incredibly complex. You could spend your entire life learning about yourself. With varying degrees of awareness, you probably will. To undertake a self-assessment like the one presented here is an opportunity to learn a great deal about yourself in a relatively short time, and in a structured and carefully guided way. It requires a significant commitment of time and energy. Perhaps at no other time in your life will you take or make the opportunity to do what you are about to do. But there are some things you should think about before beginning.

Learning self-assessment is as intellectually demanding as learning marketing, or finance, or art history. But unlike most other subjects, self-

Exhibit 2–1

The Self-Assessment Process

1. Complete the test or instrument without understanding its intent or objectives so as not to bias or distort your responses.
2. Record your reactions in your Feelings Record. How did you *feel* about taking the test? Where and when did you take it? How did that influence your results?
3. Read the accompanying note. Find out as much as you can about the instrument. How was it constructed? What is it trying to measure? How are the responses scored? What are the instrument's strengths and weaknesses?
4. Practice interpreting a sample case. Note a piece of data (a score, for example) and then draw a *simple, conservative, tentative, and logically connected* inference from it. "This is a person who. . ." may help you get started.
5. Interpret your own data using the principles and skills developed in item 4.

LATER

6. Use all the data (including your Feelings Record and your inferences) to *inductively* identify themes that run through the data.
7. Develop a set of *implications* for job- and career-related decisions.

assessment can also be *emotionally demanding*. It is useful to recognize this aspect of the process from the beginning. It is relatively easy to be objective and calm when we are asked to evaluate someone else's strengths and weaknesses. Assessing ourselves is quite a different matter. Virtually everyone finds engaging in self-assessment difficult. It is only natural to worry about how the assessment will turn out. It is normal to find yourself occasionally angry about one of the data-generating devices or cases. It is also common for people sometimes to see nothing but "good" or nothing but "bad" things in their data, and to feel either very high or very low. That is just the way we are. Again, we encourage you to resist the evaluative posture and to adopt a descriptive one. Do not allow yourself to be always judging. Rather, *describe* and then use that description to make decisions.

Second, self-assessment can be very time-consuming. Sometimes, anxiety pushes people to spend inordinate amounts of time in the pursuit of the "final answer" or of every nuance in the "full story" of their lives. No known process can do that for you. You will not be able to "know all" as a result of this experience. Consequently, we urge you to think carefully about your schedule, your other responsibilities, and your self-discipline as you approach this process. Plan to spend enough time to allow you to work through the exercises, but also discipline yourself to say "Enough is enough." At every step, we will suggest assignments and activities to guide you through the process. These will generate enough data and enough skill in using the data to develop a personal profile that will identify most of the relevant themes in your life. You may feel compelled to go further. We caution: Be reasonable.

You should also know that there are no magic answers to the career-related questions that face you. We offer no crystal balls or predictions about "the perfect job" for you. We do offer a time-tested approach to generating and using extremely useful career data. But you must do the analysis. Do not expect miracles; expect instead an intense and very rewarding exercise in learning or articulating or confirming some important things about you.

This course is also not therapy. You should not consider the book or the process outlined in it to be a substitute for professional counseling. If it is feasible, we encourage you to take the course under the guidance of a trained faculty or in conjunction with other forms of career counseling. If you feel a need for in-depth, personal counseling, seek it. This book will not replace the benefits of that kind of assistance.

Consider these caveats carefully. Remember too, that as of December1990, more than 2,500 of our students and hundreds of students in other settings have successfully carried out this self-assessment process and have utilized it productively. Seldom has anyone found the process too demanding emotionally. Most have felt that the process, though intense and demanding, yielded extremely useful information about themselves, about jobs in business management, about making career-related decisions, and about the impact of those decisions on their lives and on the organizations for which they work.

First Assignment

With this background, we hope you are eager to proceed. If so, we would like to introduce you to the data-generation part of the self-assessment process by asking you to read the case material that follows. The Dan and Mandy case which follows will help you to think about the *kinds* of information you will want to generate in your self-assessment process. As you read, ask yourself the following questions, and then note your answers on a piece of paper:

1. What decisions do Dan and Mandy need to make?
2. What *kinds* of information do Dan and Mandy need in order to make their decisions? (Consider not only data relating to them as individuals and as a couple, but also to the specific options they face.)
3. Assuming that Dan and Mandy have been able to collect the information you identified in question 2, *how* should they make their decision(s)? What *process* should they use to decide?

DAN AND MANDY

Dan and Mandy were second-year students at the Harvard Business School. On April 15 they were sitting in Mandy's living room discussing the decisions that were facing them. They had met in the first year of the MBA program and in the fall of the second year had become engaged to be married. They faced several different career and life style options and were wrestling with the choices they had to make.

Dan's Background

Dan was raised in an upper middle-class suburb of Philadelphia. His father had an M.D. and was a teaching doctor at a prestigious university. His mother had earned a Ph.D. in Social Research. Dan was the middle child of three boys. He had attended an exclusive boys' prep school from the third grade through his high school graduation and gone on to Harvard College, taking a year off to "find himself" while working off and on as a short order cook. Dan worked for several years as a teacher of Transcendental Meditation, most recently to professional sports teams. After an attempt to write a book, Dan had decided to attend the Harvard Business School to gain more professional business education and to broaden his skills. He was 31 when he was graduated.

Dan's Options

In April, Dan had several job options.

NON-PROFIT DATA SERVICES: NPDS, a relatively new Boston firm engaged in fundraising for nonprofit organizations and direct mail marketing for private sector companies, had offered Dan the position of Marketing Manager for Sports. Dan's responsibilities would be to work with professional sports organizations to develop computer-assisted means of generating income from alternatives to paid gate attendance at sporting events.

ATLANTIC ASSOCIATES: The AA offer was in Washington, D.C., where Dan would be working with public sector clients as a salesman and trainer/consultant. Dan expected that he would be traveling to visit clients at least two or three days out of every week.

NEW ENGLAND CONSULTING: NEC offered Dan a position in Boston in their Organizational Development and Executive Education group. Dan was to be a consultant, traveling about 50% of the time.

EXECUTIVE EDUCATION: Dan had also received an offer from another business school to be an assistant program manager for a series of executive education courses conducted by the University. Implicit in the offer was the understanding that after six months to a year of experience Dan would be made the Program Manager. It was also understood that the job would probably not extend beyond five years. The school was located within an hour's drive of Boston.

A MAJOR BROADCASTING COMPANY: One of the major TV-radio networks had offered Dan his choice of two positions, one in sales and one in advertising and promotion, both located in New York. The jobs held the promise of a possible move into sports in the future.

SOLAR ENERGY CORPORATION: Dan's last offer came from SEC. The firm was young, comprised of engineers working on problems associated with the large-scale generation of solar produced electrical energy. The small firm wanted Dan to be its Business Manager. The firm was located in a rural setting west of Boston.

Mandy's Background

Mandy was born and raised an only child in a blue collar neighborhood "15 miles geographically but 850 million light years culturally" removed from New York City. Mandy's parents both worked in public education—her father as an administrator and her mother as a teacher. After she graduated from high school, Mandy went to Barnard College and in her second year married her high school boyfriend. After giving birth to two children, Mandy was divorced from her hus-

This case was prepared by Assistant Professor James G. Clawson as a basis for class discussion rather than to illustrate effective or ineffective handling of a career-related situation. Harvard Business School case 9-481-016.

band and left school to work on Wall Street for a well-known stockbroker. She rose very quickly in the organization and received large salary increases beyond her expectations. Working at night, she finally completed her undergraduate degree when she was 28. Then, with the financial support of the company, she applied to the Harvard Business School and was admitted.

Mandy's Options

Having met Dan and become engaged, Mandy faced several career options as well.

WALL STREET: Mandy's first option was to return to the Wall Street firm where she had been employed before coming to the MBA program at a greatly increased salary but to work for the same supervisor she had had when she left.

HOUSEWIFE AND MOTHER: Alternately, Mandy could stay at home while Dan worked and attend to raising her two daughters and to managing the household affairs. This alternative would provide her children with a "traditional home life" that they had not yet experienced.

UNIVERSITY ADMINISTRATION: Mandy also had received an offer to work as an Assistant Director of Admissions at a Boston university, a position that would include the supervision of the processing of thousands of applications on an annual basis.

Additional Issues and Concerns

In the midst of their career decision making, Dan and Mandy also faced some other major questions.

MARRIAGE: Dan and Mandy had set May 30 as the date for their wedding. Aside from the significant time and energy required to plan the event, they were thinking about adjusting to their new life style—indeed, about *shaping* it. Questions about family finances, education for the two children, friendship networks, commuting and travel time, recreation, and others bubbled up frequently in their conversations.

HOUSING: Since at the outset their marriage would involve four people, they had thought seriously about purchasing a home. Interest rates at the time were rising, and it seemed economically wise to invest in a house as soon as possible. Mandy, given her background, had had a childhood dream of living in a well-groomed, suburban neighborhood. An opportunity had arisen in a community 30 minutes west of Boston to purchase a home which seemed to meet both of their life style interests, and in fact, they had signed a purchase and sale agreement with a probable closing date of May 30. The house had over an acre of land and was set in a thickly wooded area.

The home was 10 minutes from SEC's offices and about 45 minutes each from Atlantic Associates and Dan's Executive Education offer. It took an hour to reach Boston's Logan Airport.

Making Their Decisions

As Mandy and Dan talked, the options that faced them raised a complex set of decisions that had to be made. They wrestled with their decision to purchase the house, with which of the job opportunities would make the most sense as a family, and with the kind of life style that they would like to forge out of their new marriage, their new family, and their new career opportunities.

3

The Written Interview Assignment

The intent of the Dan and Mandy assignment was to get you thinking about the *kinds* of information that will be useful for you to generate in your self-assessment experience. This will be helpful to you as you begin the next assignment, the written interview.

When an individual begins career counseling, the usual first step is a lengthy, in-depth discussion about the person's background. This interview provides a context and typically generates rich data about topics important to consider in making career decisions.

Since we are unable to have this interview with you personally, we have designed a means to simulate the interview and to generate that data. We have constructed some questions that will lead you through a typical background career counseling interview. Writing your answers to the questions will take a good deal of time—how much will depend on you. If you write too much, you may feel overwhelmed in the analytic stage. How much is too little or too much? That's up to you. Our experience has been that somewhere between twenty-five and seventy-five handwritten pages is a useful amount. That may seem like a lot, but it will become apparent how easy it is to talk—or, in this case, write—about yourself.

If you would rather dictate your answers, feel free to do so, but we strongly encourage you to make arrangements to have a written or typed transcript made. This written copy will be invaluable later on. You will need to be able to go back and read your answers.

If you decide to type your answers, don't worry about typographical errors or neatness. Going back to correct or to tidy up will tend to break the flow of your thoughts—and the natural flow is important.

There are eleven questions, one each on the eleven pages that follow. The point of using separate pages is that our dialogue is going to proceed in stages, as a good dialogue should. The natural development of your interview and the purity of your answers will be enhanced if you do *not* look ahead. Read the contents of each page only after you have responded completely to the previous question we, your interviewers, have posed. The point is not to spring any great surprises, but to facilitate an interview-like sequence in your ideas. To do that, we have to provide a series of cues, one at a time, so that the effect is one of question, then reply, then question, then reply.

Your replies will be much longer than the questions, of course. As is the case with any good data-generating interview, this one is going to consist of much more of *your* talk than of our talk. When you have finished what you have to say in response to each of our questions and are ready to go on, turn to the next page. We will get a few remarks of our own into the conversation, and then ask another question.

Do not feel that you have to complete the written interview in one sitting. In fact, after Question 4 we encourage you to leave it for a day or so. Feel free to leave your writing at *any* point and then to come back and resume.

Occasionally the questions may seem a bit redundant. That really depends on what you've said in response to the previous questions. If you come to a question you have already answered completely, then go on.

When you have set aside some time for your first sitting and are ready to start this "interview," please turn the page to Question 1. Relax, and write as you "talk" in reply to the question.

NOTE:
DO NOT SKIP AHEAD IN THE INTERVIEW.
READ THE FOLLOWING PAGE FIRST, AND THEN ANSWER EACH QUESTION SEQUENTIALLY.

Question 1

The goal you and we now share is to generate good data from which you can make valid inferences about your own career. In the end it is you who will make the inferences, so in one sense, all through this exercise or even all through this course, you will be talking to yourself. We are, however, going to listen in. Our presence may enable you to talk to yourself in a more useful way. We will try to steer your soliloquy away from running around in circles. Which direction its tangent should take is not, however, something we intend to dictate or direct. Our job is to show you how to generate good information about yourself, for yourself.

What you are going to need is an account of your life more structured than free association, more personal than a résumé or vita. The level of discourse will be that of personal history—an overview of all those years' diaries that you didn't keep (or at least the parts suitable for public consumption).

Just let it flow. If you belatedly realize you've left something out, put it in when you think about it. This is a *rough* manuscript! Order and method come later.

How long should your story be? As long as it takes to tell. Although an autobiography is usually book length, you may be able to tell your story in the equivalent of a chapter or two.

Tell away!

[1]This material was revised by Assistant Professor James G. Clawson. Copyright © 1980 by the President and Fellows of Harvard College. Harvard Business School case 9-481-012.

Question 2

How late did you start your story? Most people get themselves born and then jump to age twenty when they began their official "career." In a résumé you would lump all the distant past into a few lines under "miscellany." But if you want to collect the facts you'll need later to analyze your own career path, you should fill in some of the things that happened before you were an adult.

Not that we care if you fell in love with your rocking horse at the age of four. But if your story begins with "I graduated at Michigan," it probably leaves out some facts that are both public and pertinent. What do you remember about primary school or before? How about secondary school? What were your hobbies and avocations? What were the things you had to do but didn't like? What about. . .well, you tell us. This is your life.

What else went on long ago?

Set aside your rambling account of your life from Question 1, and go ahead and write some more about the beginning of your life story.

Unless you've already said all that need be said. If so, go on to the next question.

Question 3

Now, what about the unaccounted-for times? Perhaps there are none in your answers so far, but that would be unusual. Most people leave out little bits and pieces here and there. What went on during your summers? Was there a two-month gap between graduation and a first job? Did those four years at school include one spent abroad? Were there jobs that filled your evenings or weekends?

These odds and ends of living often teach lessons that matter. They often contain data you can use now even though you saw no relevance in the experience back then.

Set aside Question 2 and write some bits and pieces about the little odds and ends of living that got tucked in between the major activities you already have described.

Of course, if you have already covered everything, you won't have much work to do for this step in our conversation.

Question 4

What about the jobs you have had so far, both the full-time and the part-time ones? You may have mentioned most of them already. Think back and tell us what it was that you liked and disliked about those jobs. Was it the people? The location? The daily tasks? The pay? Or something else?

If you've already done that carefully, go on. Otherwise, take some time with this one. It can help later.

When you've completed your answer to this question, take a break. Don't go on to the next one just yet. Let it all sit for a day, and then come back to Question 5.

Question 5

Hi again! Last time we asked you about your life and the jobs you've had to this point. Today we'd like to get a little more personal. Talk a little, if you already haven't, about the people in your life. At least the public facts. Who were you closest to, and why? Who used to bug you? What did each of your parents do? Tell us about other members of your family. Were there any major changes in your family structure? What about marriage? And your friends, who are they? What is it that draws you together? In other words, who are the people in your life, and how have you arranged your life around them?

We'll make good use of all these data later on. We ask no judgments of these people, only description. They were there in your life. They're a part of the picture. Tell us about them.

Question 6

Now, what about the future? Of course, that's the question we're working on in this course, so you may not have any clear answers. But sit back and try to imagine what your ideal future would be like and write it down. What's the happy ending?

Maybe there is more than just one dream. If so, tell us about them. Or if the future is too unclear, tell us about the uncertainties you see, the tradeoffs, the dilemmas.

Question 7

If we read back over the exchanges in your written interview, we can surely find a series of points when your situation changed. You left secondary school to go to college, college to go to graduate school. You may have entered one or another of the armed services from which you subsequently departed, presumably making a decision not to stay when your hitch was over. Perhaps during your college years you transferred, took a year elsewhere, or dropped out. Or simply changed major field. At the very least, you picked a summer job or school or vacation spot.

Before we go on with our written interview, please go back over your story and pick out these points of change. Make a list of them. Add some others that we haven't discussed if others now occur to you. This list will be the backbone of our discussion as we continue our written interview.

Question 8

You may have already said something about the turning points you've just listed, but there is much to be learned by talking at greater length and in a more systematic way about them. Please go back and tell us a couple of things about each turning point.

First, what were the other options? Even in situations in which you thought you had no choice at all, in all likelihood you did. Maybe you applied only to one college; even so, what others did you consider? Did you have more than one acceptance? One's major field is not usually the one and only possibility ever thought about. Tell us about these other paths you did not take.

Second, tell us about the pros and cons of each of these options. It would be useful to know what the criteria were, the formal ones, the ones other influential people in your life were citing, and the real ones that determined which way you went.

Third, tell us how you arrived at your decisions. Were they easy choices? Perhaps some were made in large part for you? How long did they take? Did you talk to lots of other people? Maybe none? As you look back now, how did you wind your way through each of those turning points to where you are now?

Question 9

Your life changed in some ways after each of these turning points. After the turning point, what new things had importance? How was living different than it had been before? What new things stood out for you?

External circumstances presumably differed in obvious ways. A dormitory is not the same as your own home. But the point is, what changed *for you*? Was there in some ways a new you? More subtly, was there a new texture of living? How did you react to it?

As a part of your response, you might also want to reflect on which parts of your previous life are still with you, which have withered away, and which are locked up in a "wait until later" mode. Maybe electronics was a high school diversion, or skiing, or drama. Is it still? What effect did these turning points have on those interests?

Question 10

Again thinking about the turning points, what disillusionments did you suffer? Can you recall your expectations about college, or the army, or a job, and how these expectations contrasted with the event? Perhaps you were utterly realistic in advance—if so, that is a datum about you well worth recording.

Try to recall what you thought each situation was going to be like before you confronted it and then how it in fact turned out. Perhaps your expectations were dead wrong, perhaps they were right on target. Probably there were aspects of the new situation that would never have occurred to you even in your wildest imaginings!

At any rate, please try a little retrospection on the before-and-after view of each listed event. Perhaps even a table is indicated—As Seen Before and After—but a little narrative will serve too.

The emphasis here is on cognitive awareness, not on values. Did you know the facts?

Question 11

By now you must be aware of some repetition in what you've been saying. There probably are themes. What patterns do *you* see? In the past you have been basing your actions on certain kinds of considerations. Do they still hold true? Were the same criteria used in several decisions? Were your choices derived from similar processes? Can you see trends over time?

If you want to be systematic, you can make some tables showing the plus and minus factors, and perhaps also their weight, in each decision. What factors recur? Can you conceptualize a common factor that underlies apparently distinct events? If you arrange the decisions chronologically, do the choices evolve with time?

This last point is of special interest, since being able to observe yourself acting as if you held consistent values and beliefs is one thing and deciding to base your next decision on these same considerations is quite another. There are two sides to a career: where it has been and where it is going.

Can the array of ins and outs of your actions in the past reveal to you something of the direction of time's arrow?

When you have completed this reply, you are done with the interview. Put your replies together here in your notebook. It's been an exhausting experience, but we hope a very interesting one so far. We've enjoyed helping you generate this rather detailed and lengthy account of your life.

We'll both be referring to this written interview over and over again as the course progresses, so before you put it in your notebook, please go back and number each paragraph sequentially. You may have as much as sixty or seventy pages, with four or five paragraphs per page. That's over three hundred paragraphs. It will take a few minutes to do this, but it will really help later on. When you've numbered the paragraphs, you've completed your written interview.

We appreciate the time and effort it has taken to write it and trust that it will serve you well.

Upon Finishing the Written Interview

Now that you have completed your written interview, you probably are a little tired of it—even though it has no doubt generated a lot of fond (and maybe not so fond) memories and feelings. In order to get some distance from the written interview and to let your emotions settle a little, we ask you to set it aside for a while. We will go on with other parts of the self-assessment process and then come back to the written interview data.

Before we leave it, however, we would like to have you begin your Feelings Record. This will be a journal of your experiencing of the self-assessment process that will help you think more clearly—now and later—about what you are doing. It will also provide some valuable data later on.

Take a few minutes and write down on the following page your reactions to the written interview. Did you enjoy it? Why or why not? How did you feel while you were writing it? How do you feel now?

Along the way, we will remind you to make note of your reactions to each instrument, but we encourage you to make notes of your feelings at any point in the process. Feel free to expand upon our reminders as much as you like.

We also encourage you to collect your entries in one place in order to make them easier to use later on. If you are using a three-ring binder, we suggest you make a separate index tab for the Feelings Record.

When you're done making your Feelings Record entry and have set aside an hour or so, turn the page and begin working on our next data-generating device, Sorting Life and Career Values.

Feelings Record—Written Interview

4

Sorting Career and Life Values

You will need from one to two hours to complete this exercise. *Please make sure that you will not be interrupted,* for although the exercise is relatively simple it will require careful concentration. Select a space that is quiet—no music please—and that has a minimum of visual stimuli. The intent here is to reduce all external stimuli as much as possible so that you are left with your thoughts and feelings as your primary focus.

You will also need a large flat table or countertop the size of a large desk. A card table is about as small a surface as will function well. You will also need a pencil, an eraser, several sheets of 8½″ × 11″ typing paper, and maybe some 3 × 5 cards, scissors, and cellophane tape.

The pages at the end of the book contain two kinds of cards—"aspect" cards and "values" cards. Remove these pages from the book and cut them apart along the dotted lines. Note that there are several blank aspect cards and several blank values cards.

Sorting the Aspect Cards

Your first task is to arrange the aspect cards at the top of your table from left to right in descending order of their importance to you now. As you sort the cards, you may feel that two or more are equally important. Think carefully about such groups of cards and try to rank them. If you cannot, cluster the two or more equally important cards together by leaving a space between them and the next card or cards.

An alternative method is to cluster cards within three groups—Most Important, Moderately Important, and Least Important. But do not feel any pressure to use this division. If you have sorted the cards into clusters, go back to each cluster and force yourself to set priorities *within* each cluster. This may be difficult. Nevertheless, *do it.* Ask yourself the question: "If I could have everything I wanted in just *one* of these categories, which one would I choose?" Then, having chosen one aspect card and placed it on the left-hand side of that cluster, ask yourself the same question for the cards remaining in that cluster.

If you think of aspects of your life that are not included in the aspect cards, feel free to label a blank card and include it in the exercise.

As you sort the cards from left to right, use the width of the table to provide a rough guide of importance. If one value or cluster of values is much more important than the next value or cluster, separate them by a wider space than the space between two equally important values.

Once you have carefully sorted the aspect cards, note their order and relative spacing at the top of the long side of a piece of typing paper. Your diagram may look something like this:

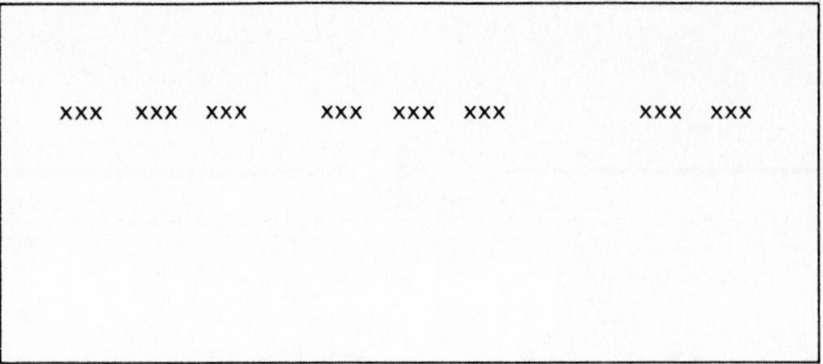

If the paper is not long enough, tape another sheet to the right-hand edge and continue.

Sorting the Values Cards

Now that you have the aspect cards arranged in order of importance, sort the values cards beneath them, toward you from top to bottom, in descending order of importance. This exercise is intended to help you identify both *what* is important within each aspect of your life and *how important* those things are. We have provided a number of values cards to help you get started, but we encourage you to write in your own answer to the question:

WHAT IS IT ABOUT THIS ASPECT OF MY LIFE THAT IS IMPORTANT TO ME?

At first, do not worry about sorting the values cards in order of importance. Rather, just stack them (using either our printed cards or your own written ones) beneath each aspect card. Some values may seem to relate primarily to one aspect or another. Other cards may seem to apply to several aspects. Feel free to duplicate cards in more than one stack if you choose.

Once you have what is a relatively complete stack of things that are important to you in *each* aspect of your life, you are ready to sort each stack in order of its importance to you. Do so for each aspect, placing the most important value at the top just beneath the aspect card and the least important value closest to you at the bottom of the column. Again, use spaces to reflect the relative strength of the values you have selected. Try to be strictly honest with yourself. Do not order the cards according to what you think you *should* value, but what you *do* value. Think about choices you have made, the way you spend your time, your language, your emotions, your private thoughts—and what they tell you about the values you now hold.

When you have finished, your table will look something like this:

aspect cards

value cards

The cards will be sorted according to this value structure:

We have included copies of the values structures of two individuals, Steven Taylor and Carrie Baugh.

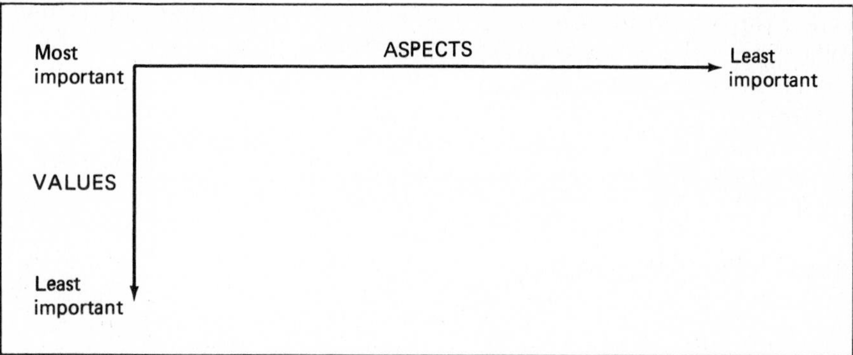

Now *write down* the arrangement you have on the sheet where you recorded your aspect values. The values in the upper left-hand or northwest quadrant will be your most important values, while those in the lower right-hand or southeast quadrant will be your least important values. You are now ready to begin interpreting your values structure.

Interpreting Career and Life Values Structures

> NOTE:
> DO NOT READ THIS UNTIL YOU HAVE COMPLETED THE CAREER AND LIFE VALUES CARD SORT.

Identifying and ranking personal values is one of the most difficult tasks in making career decisions. The task is difficult because values shift in peripheral ways from day to day, and in moderately deep ways from chapter to chapter in one's life. Furthermore, it is often hard for us to sort out our deeper values except as they are confronted in demanding, behavioral situations; sometimes we think we hold a certain value, but when it is put to the test we find that another value supplants it. At the core, many of our values are remarkably stable over the years. A few core values may change, some with dramatic effect on our lives, but most will continue to guide our choices and activities throughout our lives. Our intent in this exercise is to help you gain a clearer picture of your own value structure in terms of the aspects of your life you value most highly and of the values you hold in each of them.

Steve and Carrie were MBA students who took this course recently. We have their data for most of the instruments we will be using in the book, so you can practice on their data and talk about what they mean in class without revealing your own results. This is Step 4 in our self-assessment process (summarized in Exhibit 2-1 on page 8). If you are careful in your attempts to understand Steven's and Carrie's data as we go along, your ability to analyze will be much better developed by the time you get to your own data. (We have included a male's and a female's data so you can compare your results with either or both.)

Before you look at Steven and Carrie's structures, though, remember Step 2 in our self-assessment process, and make an entry in your Feelings Record. Do that now while your experience of the instrument is still fresh in your mind. There is space for you to do this on the next page, if you like.

When you have finished your Feelings Record entry, you can begin practicing to interpret the values data by answering the questions below for both Steven and Carrie. Use your answers in your class discussion. After you have worked through Steven and Carrie's data alone and in class, then go on and draw inferences about your own results. We encourage you to write these down, as Carrie has, so that later on you won't have to reconstruct your thinking; that will save you valuable time as you begin to write your self-assessment paper.

Step One. First notice the array of aspects across the top of the page. Is there a pattern? Are the "personal" aspects clustered? If so, are they higher or lower than the "professional" or the "family" aspects? Or are the various aspects mixed in a seeming attempt to find a relatively even balance among them all? How are the aspects spaced? Where are the gaps? What inferences could you draw from these data about this person? Write these inferences down on the Career Values Sort Inferences sheet.

Step Two. Next, look at the values cards *horizontally* across aspects. Which ones appear most often? Which ones least often? What does this tell you? Write down your inferences.

Step Three. Finally, look at the vertical columns of values. Where are the gaps? Where are the most values listed? Which ones are at the top of each column? What do these things tell you about this person?

Feelings Record: Career and Life Values Sort

Steven Taylor's Life and Career Values Card Sort

Most Important Value Cluster

A1. Familial

Accepting others
Relaxing
Looking back
Helping people

A2. Marital

Feeling intimate
Looking ahead
Laughing together
Sharing risks
Admiring the beauty
Being able to voice my uncertainties
Having spouse's support
Encouraging spouse

A3. Professional

Creating new things
Taking risks
Tackling a challenge
Planning ahead
Using energy and resources wisely
Teaching people
Being independent
Helping people
Working on broad issues

B5. Physical

Moving quickly
Concentrating on one thing
Achieving a goal

B6. Emotional

Lonesome for Sandi
Trying to show more, let it out
Learning to let the hurt out especially

Very Important Value Cluster

B1. Parental

The product of our love
Creating the future
Raising confident, independent thinkers

B2. Home

Building things
Independence at last
Finishing a task
Continuity (distinct from workplace)

B3. Identity

Accentuating the positive
Wrestling with self-criticism
Regular check-ups

B4. Intellectual

Enjoying the activity
Tackling a challenge
Looking ahead (trying)

Important Value Cluster

C1. Financial

Deciding what to do next
Planning ahead
Seeking independence

C2. Social

Meeting people
Variety
Questioning the role of alcohol
Why are some large gatherings uncomfortable?

C3. Recreational

Admiring the beauty of it all
The tranquility
Being free
Relaxing

C4. Spiritual

Growing importance
Accepting others
Opening up
Voicing uncertainties

C5. Societal

Organizing things
Helping people
Building things

C6. Political

Creating new things (slowly)
Expanding influence

C7. Ecclesiastical

On and off participation
Frustrated by dogma and pomp

Prepared by Lori Wilson and James G. Clawson. Copyright © 1989 by the Darden Graduate Business School Foundation, Charlottesville, VA. UVA-PACS-046.

Carrie Baugh's Value Card Sort

First-Tier Aspects

A1. Marital

Growing together
Keeping the passion
Continuing to appreciate his wonderful self
Making time for each other
Feeling happy
Feeling loved
Being praised by spouse

A2. Familial

Being close to others
Keeping a strong tie, open community
Being able to help, protect
Watching them grow, enjoying life
Being praised by parents
Feeling loved

A3. Balance

Admiring beauty of it all
Enjoying life's variety of activities
Using energy and resources wisely
Planning ahead, where want to be
Learning new things, having variety
Working on the broad issues

A4. Identity

Integrity
Continual growth, learning
Being independent
Being carefree
The tranquility

Second-Tier Aspects

B1. Professional

Enjoying work for sake of it
Keeping integrity
Still thinking as an individual
Achieving a goal
Expanding influence
Praise by work colleagues
Teaching people
Move quickly
Tackling a challenge
Being encouraged
Planning ahead
Finishing a task
Taking risks
Changing activities monthly
Working on details

B2. Spiritual

Faith in a being, force greater than oneself
Being a caring, loving, understanding person
Being grateful for gifts, abilities

B3. Financial

Security
Getting rewarded fairly for efforts
Getting ahead

B4. Recreational

Relaxing
Variety
Building things/hobbies
Teaching skills

Third-Tier Aspects

C1. Physical

Staying healthy
Being in good shape

C2. Emotional

Keeping perspective
Keeping stable, even outlook

C3. Material

Living comfortably

C4. Intellectual

Being challenged

C5. Societal

Helping people
Making a real difference in my community

Fourth-Tier Aspects

D1. Social

Enjoying friends, company
Meeting people
Part of group? (low)

D2. Ecclesiastical

Renewing strength through active, consistent worship

D3. Political

Understanding the complex issues
Voting

D4. Parental

Having children
Focus on well-being and happiness of children
Providing a happy, loving, and accepting home environment
Watching children grow up

NOTES:

1. Marriage and Family are first and second most important aspects.
2. Identity is in first tier of aspects.
3. Balance aspect card added; included in first tier.
4. Professional attributes in second tier.
5. Social, Political attributes in fourth tier.
6. Feeling loved, being praised in both Marital and Familial aspects.
7. Integrity mentioned under Identity and Professional aspects.

INFERENCES:

Carrie is a person who:

1. Values family and marriage above other aspects of her life.
2. Seeks to balance her lifestyle.
3. Sees professional life as important, but subordinated to Family, Marriage, and Identity.
4. Will probably spend less time on social and political activities relative to personal goals.
5. Wants to be loved and praised by her husband and family.
6. Values integrity, especially as an individual and in her professional life.

Inferences from the Career and Life Values Sort

	This is a person who	*Data*
Carrie Baugh		
Steven Taylor		

5

Survey of Behavioral Characteristics

Survey of Behavioral Characteristics

Researchers have identified a number of behavioral characteristics in managers that likely influence managerial learning and productivity. The purpose of this survey is to help you to consider your own behavioral characteristics and the influence they might have on you as a manager. Please rate the items on the following pages in terms of how much a word or sentence describes you. When you complete the items, go on to the scoring and interpretation section.

NOTE:
DO NOT READ THE INTERPRETATION SECTION BEFORE YOU COMPLETE THE ITEMS.
IT MAY INFLUENCE THE WAY IN WHICH YOU COMPLETE THEM.

Part I. The items in this section contain two words or combinations of words on each end of a scale. Please circle the number that most accurately describes you and your behavior.

habit bound	3	2	1	0	1	2	3	open minded
talker	3	2	1	0	1	2	3	listener
practical	3	2	1	0	1	2	3	innovative
exploratory	3	2	1	0	1	2	3	procedural
receptive	3	2	1	0	1	2	3	directing
factual	3	2	1	0	1	2	3	intuitive
organization person	3	2	1	0	1	2	3	entrepreneur
risk taker	3	2	1	0	1	2	3	risk averse
ritualistic	3	2	1	0	1	2	3	experimental
uninhibited	3	2	1	0	1	2	3	inhibited
leader	3	2	1	0	1	2	3	follower
poet	3	2	1	0	1	2	3	accountant

Part II. In this section, each item contains a sentence on each end of the scale. Please circle the number that most accurately describes you and your behavior.

I develop new ideas.	3	2	1	0	1	2	3	I use others' ideas.
I like to influence other people.	3	2	1	0	1	2	3	I am influenced by other people.
I like to know how things will work out before starting something.	3	2	1	0	1	2	3	I don't mind uncertainty in a project
I like for plans to emerge based on what a situation may demand.	3	2	1	0	1	2	3	I like to plan in advance and stick to it.
In problem solving, I enjoy finding the one right answer.	3	2	1	0	1	2	3	In problem solving, I like to consider several possible answers.
I like doing things in new ways.	3	2	1	0	1	2	3	I like doing things in old ways.
I am attracted to change.	3	2	1	0	1	2	3	I am resistant to change.
I like to design objects.	3	2	1	0	1	2	3	I like to assemble pre-made kits.
I read one book or less a year.	3	2	1	0	1	2	3	I read twenty books or more a year.
I prefer logical step-by-step methods.	3	2	1	0	1	2	3	I prefer open-ended methods that allow unexpected outcomes.
I don't mind uncertainty.	3	2	1	0	1	2	3	I prefer predictable happenings.
I act on objective information.	3	2	1	0	1	2	3	I act on intuitive hunches.
I seek the "status quo."	3	2	1	0	1	2	3	I seek change.
I do detail work best.	3	2	1	0	1	2	3	I do creative work best.

The Theory

You have just completed survey items that measure some aspects of creativity. The idea of creativity is important because the extent to which an individual is creative can have an impact on individual, small group, and organizational productivity. We also believe that it is a significant component of one's ability to generate vision for an organization. If one is bound by historical views of an organization's capacities and directions, then one is less likely to be able to lead the organization through the inevitable changes of the future.

In the past decade or so, numerous researchers and practitioners in business have studied creativity or have created models for developing creativity in managers. The models vary considerably but there are common concepts that surface in all of them.

SEEKING SEVERAL POSSIBLE EXPLANATIONS: Historically, we have been educated to seek the one right answer instead of looking to several possible explanations. Consider secondary and higher education. Throughout our educational careers, we take many exams and quizzes for which we are expected to produce the right answer. The ambiguous world does not always lend itself to one simple answer. Thus, to be innovative in our thinking we must be open to different approaches.

TAKING RISKS: The creative person is one who is comfortable in risk taking. In business, for example, this is a person who may make decisions that may run counter to group opinion or to standards of the industry. Such actions, while not always successful, may ultimately prove useful in developing ideas in business.

CONSIDERING AMBIGUITY IN SITUATIONS: People who are creative are comfortable with uncertainty. They are comfortable with plans that emerge based on the situation rather than needing to anticipate a project completely before it begins. While ambiguity can be devastating in some situations (giving directions for example, or creating legal documents) there are other situations in which ambiguity can foster creativity. Ambiguity forces one to consider different meanings and alternate interpretations in a creative process.

CONSIDERING THE ILLOGICAL: Have you ever been in a situation in which you proposed a seemingly foolish alternative? What happened? People probably laughed or discounted your suggestion. They might have said: "That's not logical." But it often happens that the illogical suggestion becomes a viable strategy. In situations where new ideas are being generated, if you consider all possible alternatives and quickly eliminate them due to lack of "logic" then you forego potential options. Depending on the situation, the creative thinker must consider the illogical.

The instrument that you just completed was developed to awaken you to your inner creative abilities and to stimulate some thinking about how these abilities can have an impact on your personal and professional life. We'll outline some of the possibilities later, but first, let's score the data that you have generated.

Scoring Procedure

Step 1. Remove pages 47 and 48 from this packet. Place page 47 alongside page 49 and page 48 alongside page 50.

Step 2. The answers that you gave on pages 47 and 48 can be scored by circling the numbers *in the same positions* on the scales on this page and on page 50. For example, if you circled a 2 on the left for the first item on page 47, then you would circle a 2 on the first item below. If you circled a 3 on the right for the first item, you would circle a seven for the first item below. Please note that in the items below some of the scales are purposely reversed.

Step 3. After scoring all of your items calculate the subtotal for each page. Add your subtotals to derive your total creativity score.

Scoring Template for Page 47

habit bound	1	2	3	4	5	6	7	open minded
talker	7	6	5	4	3	2	1	listener
practical	1	2	3	4	5	6	7	innovative
exploratory	7	6	5	4	3	2	1	procedural
receptive	1	2	3	4	5	6	7	directing
factual	1	2	3	4	5	6	7	intuitive
organization person	1	2	3	4	5	6	7	entrepreneur
risk taker	7	6	5	4	3	2	1	risk averse
ritualistic	1	2	3	4	5	6	7	experimental
uninhibited	7	6	5	4	3	2	1	inhibited
leader	7	6	5	4	3	2	1	follower
poet	7	6	5	4	3	2	1	accountant

Page 49 Subtotal ___________

Scoring Template for Page 48

I develop new ideas.	7	6	5	4	3	2	1	I use others' ideas.
I like to influence other people.	7	6	5	4	3	2	1	I am influenced by other people.
I like to know how things will work out before starting something.	1	2	3	4	5	6	7	I don't mind uncertainty in a project.
I like plans to emerge based on what a situation may demand.	7	6	5	4	3	2	1	I like to plan in advance and stick to it.
In problem solving, I enjoy finding the one right answer.	1	2	3	4	5	6	7	In problem solving, I like to consider several possible answers.
I like doing things in new ways.	7	6	5	4	3	2	1	I like doing things in old ways.
I am attracted to change.	7	6	5	4	3	2	1	I am turned off by change.
I like to design objects.	7	6	5	4	3	2	1	I like to assemble pre-made kits.
I read one book a year or less.	1	2	3	4	5	6	7	I read twenty books a year or more.
I prefer logical step-by-step methods.	1	2	3	4	5	6	7	I prefer open-ended methods that allow unexpected outcomes.
I don't mind uncertainty.	7	6	5	4	3	2	1	I prefer predictable happenings.
I act on objective information.	1	2	3	4	5	6	7	I act on intuitive hunches.
I seek the "status quo."	1	2	3	4	5	6	7	I seek change.
I do detail work best.	1	2	3	4	5	6	7	I do creative work best.

Page 50 Subtotal ________

Total Score (from pages 49 and 50) ________

Interpreting Your Score

The Survey of Behavior Characteristics is a twenty-six-item instrument with scores on each item that range from one to seven. Total scores (derived by adding up scores for *all* items) range from twenty-six to 182. A high score on this instrument means that overall you perceive yourself as a creative person. (Since the instrument is still new, "high" and "low" have not yet been specifically defined.) You probably enjoy such activities as brainstorming and experimentation and situations that are open-ended and somewhat ambiguous. As a person, you probably desire change in your personal and professional life, think intuitively, and work innovatively.

If your score is low (and this is not necessarily bad) you might be less exploratory and more procedural. In the workplace, for example, you could be more interested in following procedure, less interested in exploring new options. In problem solving, you might be more inclined to rely on tried-and-true methods than to act intuitively (on a hunch). If your score is moderate (high seventies or low eighties), this means that you have some creative tendencies, but not in all areas. For example, you may consider yourself an entrepreneurial person but feel some resistance to change and somewhat habit bound.

If you wish to learn more about individual creativity, innovation in groups, or organizational creativity, you may use the following list of resources to get yourself started.

SELECTED BIBLIOGRAPHY ON CREATIVITY

ADAMS, J. L. *The Care and Feeding of Ideas.* Reading, MA: Addison-Wesley, 1986.

GHISELIN, BREWSTER (editor). *The Creative Process.* The New American Library: New York, 1952.

HICKMAN, C. R., and M. A. SILVA, *Creating Excellence.* New York: New American Library, 1984.

MAY, ROLLO. *The Courage to Create.* New York: Bantam, 1976.

PETERS, T., and A. AUSTIN. *A Passion for Excellence: The Leadership Difference.* New York: Random House, 1985.

RAY, M., and R. MYERS, *Creativity in Business.* Garden City, NY: Doubleday, 1986.

VON OECH, R. A *Kick in the Seat of the Pants.* New York: Harper and Row, 1986.

VON OECH, R. *A Whack in the Side of the Head.* Menlo Park, CA: Creative Think, 1983.

Steven Taylor's Survey of Behavioral Characteristics*

When Steven took this survey, these were the results he received:

Part 1	Part 2	Total
72	85	157

Carrie Baugh's Survey of Behavioral Characteristics*

When Carrie took this survey, these were the results she received and the notes she made:

Part 1	Part 2	Total
63	73	136

NOTES:

1. As compared with the class average of 122, Carrie scored a 136 (11.5% greater than average).

INFERENCES:

Carrie is a person who:

1. Might be more creative than her classmates.

Developing Your Creativity

by Charles Thompson

(After taking the preceding instrument and getting one measure of your creativity, you may wish to consider some ideas for developing your creative insights. Chic Thompson, a private consultant to industry on developing creativity in business, is writing a book, *Ready, Fire ... Aim!* (Copyright © 1990 by Creative Management Group, to be published by Blue Jeans Press, Charlottesville, VA), that explores the creative process. Mr. Thompson worked formerly for Gore & Associates and Disney Productions and is presently the founder and president of Creative Management Group, Charlottesville, VA. This chapter is an adaptation from Mr. Thompson's new manuscript.)

> We need to make the world safe for creativity and intuition, because it's creativity and intuition that will make the world safe for us.
>
> —Edgar Mitchell, Apollo Astronaut

Consider this excerpt from a common cookie recipe and one reaction to it:

> Add ¼ teaspoon of baking soda
> for each batch of two dozen cookies.

> One quarter teaspoon! What do you do with the rest of the box? The box just sits around on our shelf, next to the spices, until it ... until it begins to smell like oregano? By Joe, the stuff absorbs odors!
>
> Hmmmm. Let me think now. Where in our lives could we use a little of this odor-absorbing ability of baking soda? Car ashtrays, perhaps, running shoes, the cat's litter box, underarms, the refrigerator. Baking soda in a refrigerator. The whole box, not just a measly ¼ teaspoon.

Imagine what that great idea did to the sales of baking soda at Arm & Hammer. Consumer needs just expanded from ¼ teaspoon to the whole box. No, make that two boxes—one for the vegetable tray and one for the ice cream bin. How about a third box in the golf locker? Now, we're on a roll!

This little chronology of thought demonstrates my favorite Creative Rule of Thumb:

> The best way to get great ideas is to get
> lots of ideas and throw the bad
> ones away.

*Prepared by Lori Wilson and Jim Clawson. UVA-PACS-037 and UVA-PACS-051. Copyright ©1989 by the Darden Graduate Business School Foundation, Charlottesville, VA.

We just don't often come up with the best idea right out of the starting gate. So, we need to figure out how to come up with lots of creative ideas. But then, what *are* creative ideas? And what personality traits, if any, prompt us to come up with such ideas? Do some people just naturally have this talent for creativity? Or do people follow a process? If so, what process? Here are our answers to these important questions.

What is Creativity?

Unless we know what it is, how will we know when we have it? Although "creativity" is difficult to define, we can begin with the notion of "creative thinking":

> Creative thinking is the ability to look at the same thing as everyone else but to see something different.

With this approach, anyone who is able to see things differently from the rest of the pack is expressing some creativity. That doesn't mean that different ideas are necessarily better than other ideas, just that by virtue of being unusual, out of the norm, nonstandard, *different,* they are creative. Of course, what we're looking for are creative ideas that are helpful, productive, applicable, and relevant to our situations. Yet, if we impose those filters too soon, we often discount or ignore "different" ideas that could really be helpful.

Now the question is, "Who can do this?" This is where people begin to part company.

Creativity and the Idea Person

Many people look with envy at "Idea People" and marvel at the seemingly endless flow of ideas they churn out without any apparent effort. Many people wish that they could be more creative but feel resigned to a fate of mundane thinking and existing. The Idea People, after all, they say, were just born that way.

I want to destroy that myth.

Creative thinking is not a trait monopolized by a few fortunate souls. Every person is creative, for creativity is the single trait that makes us all human. Creativity is just another way to describe adaptive intelligence and hard work. *YOU* have the capacity to be more creative than you are now. *YOU* have the ability to see things differently, to strengthen your unusual insights, to recombine your knowledge, and to create new thoughts, new theories, new concepts, and new ideas. This is a mental and behavorial skill that you can develop if you work at it. This chapter will give you some ideas about how to generate ideas. But creativity is more than idea generation.

The Creative Process

The greatest idea on earth is worthless unless acted upon. Somebody must evaluate the quality of the idea. Somebody must "take the idea and run with it." Somebody must develop the necessary systems of people, machinery, finances, packaging, distribution, service, and marketing to have the idea become a reality. Those systems need ongoing management. Idea People alone are just not enough for "creativity" to be realized in the world.

To be creative is to have intelligence, to be able to gather information, to "see" the data in ways different from before, and to make decisions based on those insights. To be creative is to be able to perceive and recognize the world around us, to figure out what is not working well, to recombine the facts we see in new ways, and then to set about making those recombinations a part of a new world. To be creative is to find a niche or an approach no one else has found and to go about capitalizing on that newly discovered opportunity.

I hope you begin to see that creativity really isn't just a personality trait or a talent. It's also a dynamic process with identifiable steps and stages. I think of creativity as a process that includes these subprocesses:

Generation . . . Promotion . . . Design . . .
Implementation . . . Evaluation

Earlier I said that anyone can develop and improve his or her creative thinking, the generation part of this process. I called creative thinkers Idea People. As we consider the process of creativity from left to right, we can identify other types of people, each of whom has skills vital to that stage of the creative process.

The Idea Generator must generate the idea. *The Idea Promoter* must see an array of applications of the idea and set in motion the forces that can try out some of the more promising ones. *The Idea Systems Designer* must create the necessary organizations of people, machines, space, and money and get them rolling toward the perceived goal. *The Idea Implementer* must set about accomplishing the routine tasks necessary for successfully reaching that goal. And all along the way, the *Idea Evaluator* must constantly question the quality and effectiveness of the way things work—and don't work.

Look around you and you'll undoubtedly see the hat or hats that you, your subordinates, your bosses, and your colleagues wear or have worn in the process of creativity. Idea Generators are typically the people whose main focus is on ideas themselves, not organizational advancement or status. One of their main drives in life is to deal with ideas and concepts. Sometimes they are individuals who choose not to develop other skills, including social skills, because their focus is so overwhelmingly on concepts and ideas. Their strengths primarily include their brilliance, insights, dedication, and consuming passion for discovery. These are the inventors, the tinkerers, the discoverers.

Look around and you'll see the Idea Promoters. They often take the idea of the Idea Generator, recognize its application and potential, and begin to put the wheels in motion for implementation. On the up side, the Idea Promoters are enthusiastic, resourceful, charismatic, and positive. They refuse to succumb to defeat. If something doesn't work, they'll try something else. They willingly take risks, whether the stake involves their own or someone else's fortune. On the down side, the Idea Promoters can be so single-minded that they fail to recognize reality. Often, they won't listen to opposing, negative views and won't hesitate to break institutional rules in pursuit of their dreams. Their enthusiasm can be exhausting and often overwhelming to other people.

Look around and you'll see the Idea Designers. Upon receipt of the idea from the Idea Generator and its application and vision from the Idea Promoter, the Idea Designer can see how to assemble the financial, human, manufacturing, or other resources necessary to make the idea work. These are the planners and the designers—the ones who can picture what's needed to accomplish a desired end. They can paint the broad strokes. They can picture what the organizational chart should look like. They can predict and plan each needed step along the way toward idea realization.

Look around you for the Idea Implementers, who relish making a thing work according to the design set up by the Idea Designer. They would rather "go by the book" than question the way things are. They want to know what the rules are, what the policy is, what the required procedures are. Given those rules, policies, and procedures, they will meticulously follow all necessary steps toward idea realization. Are they creative? Maybe not in the way that you originally defined creativity. Are they essential to the process of creativity in an organization? Absolutely.

Finally, when you look around, not far away you'll find an Idea Evaluator. Evaluators have an opinion about everything. They're supposed to. That's what they do. They look at the way things work (or don't work) and form an opinion about *why* they work or not. They have their standards, whether dictated to them by the organization or created by them according to their own opinions. Whatever the source of these standards, they will apply them uniformly and consistently. They rarely accept things the way they are, but are always assuming that a flaw is just around the corner waiting for their discerning eye. They are always looking for a better way.

You might see yourself in many of these roles. Or perhaps you'll see that you do best primarily in just one. You may even see that you shy away from some roles altogether. If you're an Idea Implementer, you may resent the Idea Evaluator, envy the Idea Generator, and tolerate the Idea Promoter. If you're an Idea Generator, you'd probably rather do anything else rather than implement the nitty-gritty details of your own idea.

The Idea Generator is easily termed "creative." We've thought that all along. The Idea Generator just has the knack of coming up with great ideas. But what about the Idea Promoter? The Idea Designer? The Idea Implementer? The Idea Evaluator? Mustn't they be creative as well? Indeed, won't each participant in this creative process be more creative if each tries to develop the characteristics of others involved in the process? Certainly the Idea Implementer who takes on the characteristics of the Idea Generator will come up with some great ideas on improving the implementation process. And the Idea Generator who understands the ins and outs of implementation will become a generator of better, more workable ideas—ideas that are likely to be more efficient and more realistic than they otherwise would have been.

In this chapter, we will address some ideas relating to the first two stages of the creative process, generation and promotion.

Creative Generation

THREE KEYS TO INCREASED CREATIVITY: I firmly believe that the keys to developing great personal and organizational creativity are as follows: first, the ability to recognize that all these types of people are necessary to the creative process; second, the ability to see yourself as you are and as other people most likely see you; and third, the desire and willingness to try other creative roles, to practice them, and to become more proficient at them. As we develop and mature, we see those areas in the creative process that naturally attract us. If we are to become more creative, we must try out the skills needed in the other areas. We need to flex, to stretch, to exercise unused creative muscles. We need to trust the words of Oliver Wendell Holmes:

> The human mind once stretched to a new idea never goes back to its original dimensions.

If he was right, then trying to be creative will stretch our minds in ways that will leave us forever different, more creative. This chapter will help you do some mind-stretching; it will teach you some techniques for coming up with new insights and ideas, ideas that are not light-years ahead of their time, but fifteen minutes ahead. For in the words of Woody Allen:

> The best idea is the one that's fifteen minutes ahead of its time. Those that are light-years ahead just get ignored.

When and Where Do Ideas Come From?

The most commonly asked question in my workshops on creativity is, "Where do ideas come from?" And the answers that thousands of seminar participants have given when asked the same question is "while showering," "while hiking," "while running," "while driving," "while walking," "while falling asleep," "while dreaming," "while daydreaming." All are examples of what I call "divergent thinking." These are the times when we are not focused on solving a problem, but are allowing our minds to drift free of concentrated, conscious effort. When freed up in this way, often at unsuspecting times, our minds, being the wonderful entities that they are, ebb and flow and suddenly hit on a neat idea. We can recognize, develop, and use this phenomenon; we can use this free-form thinking. As a process to be used on command, I call it

Ready, Fire . . . Aim! thinking.

Traditionally, many people would say that ideas come from "brainstorming," but, as it is often used in companies, brainstorming by itself is not enough. It is sometimes too scattered and unfocused, sometimes too forced or structured, as if the discussion leader were saying, "Okay, folks, *now* we're going to be creative!" Ready, Fire . . . Aim! thinking is similar to brainstorming, but different. It follows a one-two-three process.

1. Define the problem (Ready),
2. Come up with as many ideas as possible without criticizing them (Fire), and
3. Sift, synthesize, and choose (Aim).

Creativity begins with coming up with tons of ideas, not just that one great idea. At the outset, these ideas are typically not focused. They are not, in a word, "aimed." They don't come from clenched-tooth concentration. They don't require a lot of effort in their creation. The technique of idea making, then, requires the Idea Person to get ready, fire away, wait for the smoke to clear, and then look around and see if anything worthwhile was hit. Then she looks at all the bullet holes (ideas) and sees whether any is worth consideration. If none is any good, she reloads, gets ready, fires again, and then . . . aims. Maybe this time the Idea Generator will hit something.

The divergent thinker often thinks in terms of opposites and differences. Instead of concentrating inwardly on a problem or goal, divergent thinking looks elsewhere for solutions: up, down, under, over, far away, backwards, inside out, outside in, downside up. The divergent thinker looks for the vision that sees the problem solved. The divergent thinker plays mental "what if" games and is likely to imagine a refrigerator in dire need of two boxes of baking soda.

Many people, on the other hand, use a convergent-thinking method of idea making. They look at what's wrong with their situations, their environments, their companies, their bosses, their organizations, their spouses. By focusing on the current state of affairs, they tend to limit their views of the possibilities. Convergent thinkers tend to focus on similarities rather than on differences. The convergent thinker, for instance, would try to find new ways to use baking soda in cooking, never thinking about noncooking applications. By trying to come up with immediate, satisfactory, short-term solutions, they often actively prevent myriad solutions. By using only analytical and deductive reasoning, they force themselves down what can be a rigid path of linear reasoning. Convergent thinkers follow the pattern, Ready, Aim, Fire.

The better way is "Ready, Fire . . . Aim!"

FIRST, GET READY: Before coming up with ideas to solve a problem, you must describe what your problem is. Sure, this step is obvious, but you would be surprised at the number of people who won't take the time to articulate what the problem is. Not everyone views a given situation in the same way. Some look at a situation and don't see any problems at all. So task number one becomes problem articulation.

Are there creative ways to articulate just what the problem is? Of course! For instance, I encourage my workshop participants to write a "Dear Abby" letter describing a particular problem that needs their own or their organization's attention. The letter should read just like a "Dear Abby" letter you find in the newspaper. It should state what the problem is and should include as many concrete examples of the problem as possible. This device works wonders because it forces people to simplify the problem in order to be able to explain it to others.

Furthermore, as mentioned above, to be ready for creative thinking the mind must be relaxed, not tightened up and overly tense with concentrated focus. As with a muscle that cramps after too much exertion, the best preparation for additional effort is to relax. There are many ways to do this: closed-eye exercises, physical exercise, meditation, listening to music, and so on. Interestingly, many of these methods are seen as "weird," "soft," "irrational," "unprofessional," or "unanalytic." Yet preparation that releases the mind for divergent thinking, for seeing things differently, is essential to being able to think in this way.

Note that participating in activities that relax the mind does not mean that you are permanently giving up a controlled, analytical way of thinking; you are simply learning a new skill. If you are successful, you will have an expanded repertoire of abilities to apply to the problems that confront you. It's like adding another club to your golf bag rather than playing with the same one all the time regardless of the course terrain.

NOW FIRE! The most productive way to fire is to reframe the problem. It's really quite a simple process, and creative people have been using it throughout history. Dr. Jonas Salk, for example, when contemplating the mysteries of the polio virus, began thinking about it this way:

> I entered into a dialogue with nature and asked, "Is it possible?" I put it to nature in the form of an experiment and nature replied, under these conditions, yes, it would work.

This perspective, this reframing of the problem as a dialogue with nature rather than a more traditional attempt to overcome nature, set Dr. Salk on the path toward discovering the vaccine for polio.

The reframing device breaks down into three precise techniques you can begin to use right now to come up with some great ideas:

1. Envision the future,
2. Create a metaphor,
3. Challenge assumptions.

These approaches are different manifestations of the same thing—taking a problem, turning it inside out, upside down, or downside up, and completely changing the way you look at it. Let's examine each technique.

TECHNIQUE #1: ENVISION THE FUTURE: I was playing golf with sports psychologist Bob Rotella one afternoon and started to become tentative in my putting, invariably failing to reach the hole. After four-putting a hole, I asked for advice. He shared with me a trick he'd used with various PGA champions: "Don't putt until you know you can make it."

I replied, "But Bob, I'll be here all day waiting for that moment." He laughed and said, "Just picture yourself as making the putt. You're picturing yourself missing the putt. Make the putt. Make the putt in your mind." Well, I didn't make the putt that time and still don't make every putt I attempt, but using Bob's method helped me recover from a bad hole and par the next one.

Managers are finding out that the same method works to help solve problems. The device can be one of the most effective sources of ideas. Whatever problem you have, picture it solved; whatever goal you have, picture it already achieved. Under this circumstance, what does your future world look like? What does the future business or work environment look like? What does the solution look like? What features does it have? How did it get there? How did it come into being? What had to take place for the problem to be solved, for the goal to be reached?

The visualizer then works back incrementally to the present, to try to envision what steps were taken to produce that image. The Envision-the-Future approach thus breaks down into four easy steps:

Step 1: Identify the Problem or Goal. The most effective way, I believe, is the "Dear Abby" Approach. To get different perspectives, it's often a good idea to ask colleagues and subordinates to do the same thing.

Step 2: Fix a Solution or Achievement Date. Decide when the problem must be solved or when the goal should be achieved. The goal or problem might be a long-term, (desirable sales levels to reach in a five-year plan for example) or short-term, (perhaps current problems or organizational miscommunication).

Step 3: Visualize the Problem Solved or the Goal Reached. Close your eyes and picture what things will be like when the problem is solved or the goal is reached. Don't picture "near misses" or "maybes." Picture only success. If the goal is a certain sales level in five years, what is the precise mix of sales required to achieve the goal? What do prices look like? What steps have your competitors taken to react to your success? What is the news media saying right now about your company's or organization's performance? Did it make Eyewitness News? If so, what did the news anchor say?

Step 4: Come Back from the Future. Now return from the future incrementally, one step at a time. Try to picture all the motions you or the organization had to make to reach the desired result. Executives of Apple Computer call this technique "Back to the Future" Planning. They envision what the industry will be like, what consumers will be demanding, what the competition will be doing. They identify a desirable and reachable goal for Apple's participation in this future computer industry and then work backward, step by step, to the present day, all the while, keeping track of the precise steps needed for goal achievement.

TECHNIQUE #2: CREATE A METAPHOR: In the late 1980s Jack Welch, CEO of General Electric, declared war on "junk work," those unnecessary reports, approvals, meetings, measurements, and policies that often burden workers in a bureaucracy. His stated goal was to put speed, simplicity, and self-confidence into his employees' work. To get his ideas across, Mr. Welch used a most effective metaphor to describe the need for speed. He asked a group of top managers how many had moved their residences within the past ten years. Most raised their hands. He then asked how many had moved half-full cans of paint and pairs of stained sneakers as part of their relocation. Most raised their hands. He then asked how many had ever used those cans of paint and sneakers ever in their new homes. Only a few hands appeared.

Mr. Welch then pointed out that the same thing happens when people change positions. They take previously necessary reports, measurements, memos, plans, and policies with them to their new jobs. It was these, Mr. Welch believed, that slowed people down. What was needed instead was a healthy "spring cleaning." The General Electric spring cleaning then constituted a ten-year plan to speed up performance and foster a new mindset of constant improvement. By focusing people's minds on the metaphor of half-full paint cans, stained sneakers, and spring cleaning, the General Electric CEO worked to create an environment of speed and self-renewing innovation.

As you can see, the Create-a-Metaphor approach to idea making can be quite effective. The process is simple. Using General Electric as an example:

Step 1. Describe your problem. (We need to be more productive to compete. People spend too much time doing junk work.)

Step 2. Distill the problem down to a single word or phase. (Junk work.)

Step 3. Dream up some metaphors by completing this sentence: [the problem area from step 2] is like a . . . (Junk work is like half-full cans of paint. You keep moving them and you don't ever use them.)

Step 4. Use the metaphorical image and try to solve the metaphorical problem. (What do we do with old, half-full cans of paint?)

Step 5. Act. (If they're not being used to good advantage, throw them out!)

All sorts of ideas will emerge from the process, and the best part of it is that by using a common metaphor, all levels of your organization will understand the problem and the intended action plan. People can understand and remember well-chosen metaphors much more easily than they can a dry description of the underlying concept.

TECHNIQUE #3: CHALLENGE ASSUMPTIONS: Once I was served the wrong dinner entree. When I mentioned the problem to the waiter, he gave the expected response and apologized. When he brought my new entree, the waiter also brought back the menu and asked me to select a free dessert. I found myself thanking the waiter. I thanked the waiter for his mistake!

It then dawned on me what the restaurant had done. I asked him how they had come up with the idea of giving away free desserts. "Simple," he said. "We had a meeting about mistakes that give customers a hassle. We wanted to come up with some ideas on reducing that hassle. We all agreed we should apologize. Someone then said, 'Why not get the customer to thank us? If our mistakes hassle the customers, let's make it up to them and give them something for that hassle. That way, they'll end up thanking us.' We tried it," the waiter said. "It's unbelievable—now our customers thank us when we make mistakes. And our performance has actually improved, because we're thinking about customer service, not worrying about screwing up an order."

This restaurant used a terrific device for thinking up great ideas—it challenged ingrained assumptions. The original assumption was that if the restaurant made the mistake, the customer would be angry and nothing the restaurant could do would undo the mistake; by then, it would be too late. The customer was simply hassled, and no apology could take that hassle away. The assumption was that we would make mistakes, the customer would complain, and we'd just have to accept that. Challenging that assumption, believing that there was something to be done, led to trying to find ways to transform the customer's complaint into gratitude. The great idea of the free dessert did the trick.

The Challenge-Assumptions Approach is quite simple:

Step 1. Challenge the normal assumptions one makes when dealing with such problems or defining such goals.

Step 2. Write down all the assumptions you would ordinarily make.

Step 3. Challenge each of these assumptions by stating their opposites or by assuming the reverse.

Step 4. After studying the challenged assumptions, write down suggestions to solve the problem or achieve the goal.

These three approaches to idea making share a common element—they all require you to reframe the problem and look at it in a different way. The Envision-the-Future approach requires you to picture the problem already solved. The Create-a-Metaphor approach enables your mind to expand by looking at your problem as something that it clearly isn't. The Challenge-Assumptions approach teaches you to turn normal rules upside down, to identify all operative assumptions, and to challenge each one head-on. Changing your point of view will change and improve the quality and quantity of your ideas.

TECHNIQUE #4: IDEA MAPPING: When I go through airports and take my seat in planes, I notice the unbelievable waste of time going on around me. People will thumb through *Flight Lines,* read a novel, or just snooze. I notice this unproductive time especially on commuter flights. Recently, I've concluded that air travel time is the ideal time to create great ideas. The time is confined, the space is limited, and there isn't much else to do.

Of course, some business travelers use the time wisely. They haul out their $5,000 laptop computers or dictaphones. Here's what I do. I reach for a plastic ball point pen and a cheap legal pad. My favorite "Fire" technique is called Idea Mapping, a form of pre-outlining. Idea Mapping relies on word association as the idea-generating device.

Say you have five minutes to come up with a memo. You have to organize your ideas fast. With Idea Mapping, you write the central topic in the middle of the page, circle it, and then allow yourself to free associate. Remember, it takes preparation to do this; you must *release your mind* from the forced-concentration mode, perhaps by napping or daydreaming for five minutes. Once you've written down the central idea in the middle, you write down words or ideas all around the central word. You can circle them for clarity's sake if you like. Don't prioritize, don't judge words, just write anything that comes to mind. Quantity counts! A sample idea map about stress appears in Exhibit 1.

Exhibit 1

A Sample Idea Map

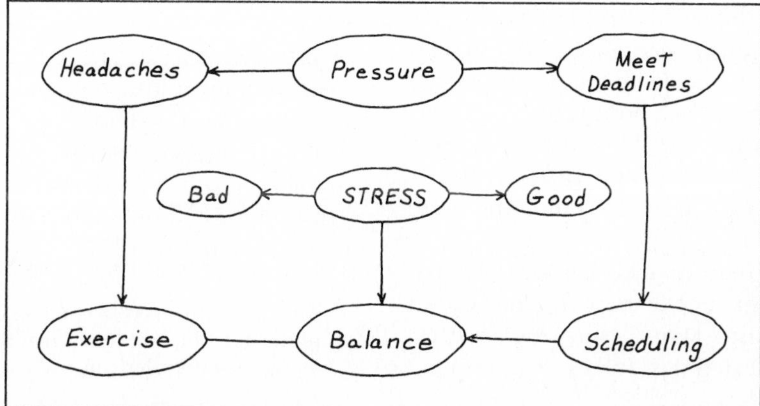

After two minutes or so, a certain order emerges on paper; your mind will begin to see the connections between your ideas. The ideas can be tied together with arrows. After you've made line links between the related word-balls, then number your words according to how you think they are important. Which ones are critical? Which ones less so? Don't be too hasty here. Think about how each might be important. Your freely wheeling mind will teach you some amazing things! Finally, you can make a linear outline from your map, which is where most convergent or traditional thinkers *begin*.

Think back to when you were in school, writing a term paper. You were supposed to write a linear outline first, then write the paper. Most of us wrote the paper first, then the linear outline! Linear outlines such as

I.
- A.
- B.
- C.

II.

don't generate ideas, they only organize them. Idea Mapping generates them. I use this approach in seminars all the time, and most people, given ANY topic, can outline a very good extemporaneous five-minute talk in less than five minutes.

USES OF IDEA MAPS: You can take this technique of Idea Mapping and expand its use to cover a host of situations and to serve as a catalyst for positive organizational change. Consider the following variations of Idea Mapping:

Team Mapping: Use huge Idea Maps on flip charts or markerboards as a means of eliciting ideas from a group in a meeting.

Vision Mapping: Put your five-year-plan goal as the focus word in the center of a large Idea Map, surround it with empty circles, hang it for all to see, and challenge your staff to fill up the circles.

Comparison Mapping: If you want to synthesize the views of differing management perspectives, draw a quick Idea Map for each perspective and then look for interrelationships. This device works wonders when you are comparing reports, or dealing with conflicting regulations or competing uses of limited resources.

The Living Map: Create an ongoing Idea Map to elicit suggestions from staff or department heads. Position the Living Idea Map in such high-traffic areas as snack rooms, cafeterias, and exercise rooms.

Idea Promotion

Suppose that now that you've got a great idea. You know it's a good one. No one else has thought of it, it's yours, and it looks good. It has all sorts of potential, all sorts of applications, all sorts of positive "impacts" on your organization. So now what?

IT'S TIME TO "AIM.": You know that no idea is any good unless somebody does something with it. Somebody has got to adopt it, accept it, put it into action, run with it. That somebody, of course, is often someone other than you. Implementing great ideas, as we discussed before, requires a team effort.

Step 1. *Tell somebody else about your idea.* It's time for your idea to make its grand entrance, but if you've ever tried to bring up new ideas to other people, you know that your great idea will be met with either thunderous applause or derisive laughter, or perhaps just a shoulder shrug.

Two things can happen to your great idea—either it succeeds or it fails. What, then, determines success or failure? Three things: the quality of the idea, the quality of its promotion, and the timing.

BEWARE OF KILLER PHRASES: If the idea is a poor one, then you want failure. You want the idea to fail and fail fast. If it doesn't fail fast, count on it eating up precious time and resources. Assuming your idea is a good one, however, you want it to succeed. What out there might make it fail despite its worth? What might shoot it down before it has the slightest chance to stretch its wings and soar? Somebody may shoot down your great idea with one of those well-known responses that I call Killer Phrases. Somebody, somewhere, at some time, will come up, gun loaded, aim carefully at your head, and say:

"It's not in the budget."
"We don't do it that way around here."
"We've tried that before."

Bang! Zap! Blast! The Killer Phrase can not only do in your great idea, it might even kill your interest in generating any more new ideas.

From conception to fruition, successful ideas tend to follow a path of grudging but ultimate acceptance. This is not a new difficulty to overcome. Machiavelli, in 1513, noted that

> The innovator has for enemies all who have done well under the old, and lukewarm defenders in those who may do well under the new.

And think of all the changes that have occured since 1513! All along the way, Killer Phrases dive in from all angles, seeking to obstruct, demean, diminish, counteract.

They have been around since the dawn of time. They are uttered by seers, pundits, pessimists, naysayers, doomsayers, leaders, bosses, husbands, wives, siblings, coaches, writers, teachers—indeed, everyone around you. They've become part of our history, part of our culture, and part of our language. As we look back on many Killer Phrases, they seem ludicrous:

> Consider what the director of the United States Patent Office said in 1899: "Everything that can be invented has been invented."
>
> Consider President Grover Cleveland's astute observation in 1905: "Sensible and responsible women do not want the right to vote."
>
> Consider what Harry Warner, president of Warner Brothers, said in 1927: "Who the hell wants to hear actors talk?"
>
> As I sit here in my home and compose this article on my Mac II computer with 40-meg hard disk and five megabytes of memory, I consider the words of Ken Olsen, president of Digital Equipment spoken in 1977: "There is no reason for any individual to have a computer in his home."

Killer Phrases are part of our culture, part of our upbringing, part of our language. All around us, practically from the first breath we take, we are bombarded by Killer Phrases. They make up our history, our home life, our school life, and they accompany us to work. One study showed that negative, no-can-do statements are all around us, outweighing positive, can-do statements by substantial margins. At home, parents say, on average, eighteen negative statements for each positive one, usually to a naturally inquisitive child trying to find out how something works. "Don't touch." "Don't play with that." The same study showed that teachers display a 12-to-1 ratio of negative to positive statements, perhaps to students eager to answer or ask a question. "Be still." "Don't talk." "Don't do that." In the national media, the ratio of negative statements to positive ones is thought to be lower than in most conversations, but it still weighs in at 6 to 1—murder, corruption, scandal. Bad Press, it's called. What about the good news?

Exhibit 2 shows my list of the "Top Forty"Killer Phrases.

Exhibit 2

Common Killer Phrases

1. "Yes, but '. . .' "
2. "We tried that before."
3. "That's irrelevant."
4. "We haven't got the manpower."
5. "Obviously, you misread my request."
6. "Don't rock the boat!"
7. "The boss (or competition) (or spouse) will eat you alive."
8. "Don't waste your time thinking."
9. "Great idea, but not for us."
10. "It'll never fly."
11. "Don't be ridiculous."
12. "People don't want change."
13. "It's not in the budget."
14. "Put it in writing."
15. "It will be more trouble than it's worth."
16. "It isn't your responsibility."
17. "That's not in your job description."
18. "You can't teach an old dog new tricks."
19. "Let's stick with what works."
20. "We've done all right so far."
21. "The boss will never go for it."
22. "It's too far ahead of the times."
23. . . . laughter . . .
24. . . . suppressed laughter . . .
25. . . . condescending grin . . .
26. . . . dirty looks . . .
27. "Don't fight city hall!"
28. "I'm the one who gets paid to think."
29. "What will people (the board) (the boss) say?"
30. "Get a committee to look into that."
31. "If it ain't broke, don't fix it."
32. "You have got to be kidding."
33. "No!"
34. "We've always done it this way."
35. "It's all right in theory, but. . ."
36. "Be practical!"
37. "Do you realize the paperwork it will create?".
38. "Because I said so."
39. "I'll get back to you."
40. " . . . " (Shocked or unbelieving silence).

Killer Phrases can serve a useful function. They can force us to reexamine both our ideas and our resolve to implement them. John Stuart Mill noted, for instance, that "Truth emerges from the clash of adverse ideas." More often, though, they simply kill the idea and the Idea Generator's motivation for creative thinking. Killer Phrases squelch good ideas, retard progress, inhibit innovation. They often stem from our natural reluctance to change. They come from an organization's preference for doing things in established patterns, using known procedures and habitual policies. They come from society's tendency to cling to the known and to fear the unknown, the untried, the new.

WHEN WILL KILLER PHRASES MOST LIKELY EMERGE?: Killer Phrases can occur throughout the idea-generation process. Even while an idea is cooking, the Idea Generator is often filled with self doubt. How often, during the course of a scheme or plan, have you said, "It'll never fly," or "I'll look stupid," or "I'm too young," or "I'm too old," or "Somebody has already done it," or "I don't have time."

We might call these Internal Killer Phrases. How often have you had a great idea but failed to follow through? How often have you put off writing that memo needed to change a system or try a new strategy? When was the last time you started working on a project but talked yourself out of it?

HOW TO OVERCOME KILLER PHRASES: You, however, like many who have gone before you, can resist and thwart Killer Phrases. And when you do, the sequence will probably look something like this:

1. It's irrelevant to this situation.
2. Ok, it's relevant, but it's unproven.
3. It's proven, but it's dangerous.
4. It's safe, but it's not sellable.
5. It'll sell—what a simple idea!

"Simple!" you say. "I'll show you 'simple.' " And you get your gun! The first weapon against Killer Phrases is the focus on its opposite. If self-doubt nags at you, write down all the negative Killer Phrases that get in the way of your creativity. Put your list in the left-hand column of a sheet of paper. Then write down the opposites of these negative statements in the right-hand column. For example,

"Too young."........................"Too old."

The process is designed to make you realize that in reality you're neither, for instance, "Too Young" nor "Too Old." You're somewhere in between. Now ask yourself how you would submit an idea if you were "Too Old." You might have someone else write it down for you and then co-sponsor it. Wouldn't this also work if you were "Too Young"?

After you get over the hurdles you erect with your Internal Killer Phrases, you must then be prepared to encounter and overcome External Killer Phrases. Successfully overcoming these Killer Phrases requires a systematic approach.

Step One. *Identify the typical Killer Phrases around you—the chances are that they have been institutionalized.* By knowing in advance what the negative responses will be, you can devise a plan of counterattack or accommodation.

Step Two. *Determine if the person is simply asking a question.* For example, the Killer Phrase, "It's not in the budget," might be the disguised question, "How much will it cost?" The Killer Phrase, "We've tried that before," might be the disguised question, "What's new and different about your approach?" If the Killer Phrase is really a question, the strategy is simple: Answer it.

Step Three. *Determine its source.* Who are the stakeholders who might be agreeing with the Killer Phrase? Do you need to sell your idea upward, downward, or outward? Successful selling requires you to marshal your political forces, to seek the input and assistance of others, to capture their imaginations with the idea, and to anticipate their concerns and potential objections.

Step Four. *If the Killer Phrase is coming from a terminal pessimist, the strategy is to agree, ignore, and proceed with your idea.* (If the pessimist is your boss, proceed on your own time.)

Smart Questions To Ask Before You Sell Your Idea

YES	NO	
_____	_____	Do the facts support my idea or eliminate some of my uncertainty?
_____	_____	Can I fall out of love with my idea or am I hopelessly lovesick?
_____	_____	Have I described my idea to anyone? Sometimes painting the picture will make things clearer.
_____	_____	Is there a second right answer to the problem? If so, what is it?

NOW, IT'S TIME TO SELL: If you've generated a new idea, introduced it, fought off the Killer Phrases, and still find yourself convinced and courageous enough to proceed, now you need to find support for it. So, how do you capture imaginations? How do you get your department behind your new idea? The best approach in our over-communicated environment is to simplify your message. "Less is more" or, as Lee Iacocca says,

> Effective communication is talking to them plain and simple.

To accomplish this you need to concentrate on your end users' perceptions. You need to sell your ideas as if your audience were purchasing them. Indeed they are, since your ideas require the time and effort of others to blossom. You need to get others to fall in love with your idea. Therefore,

- Show it off to everyone.
- Display it everywhere.
- Brag about its creators.
- Use it yourself.

SELL UPWARD: To communicate your new idea to your boss, team, or board:

- Encourage them to offer input to your idea. Send drafts with wide margins, allowing room and permission to edit.
- Anticipate their concerns and make them feel comfortable with your idea.
- Make your idea easy to grasp. Paint a picture of how your idea blends into a vision of the future. Use a metaphor or an Idea Map.
- Portray the idea as a winner. Create a fast test for your idea. Then show through initial analysis how your idea fits into the organization's strategic plan.
- Make your idea strong. Be positive by eliminating all "but . . . "s from presentations.

SELL DOWNWARD: To communicate your idea to your employees:

- Make your idea open for employee suggestions. Publish it in a newsletter and request reactions. Listen to how others think your idea will affect them, then modify it.
- Make your idea part of the work environment. Show your idea in photos or posters. Hang them on the walls of your office and meeting areas.
- Make employee buy-in possible by assigning implementation of the idea to key staffers.

SELL OUTWARD: To communicate to your consumers:

- Get news editors excited about your idea. Create a unique press release that gets noticed. For example, include a packet of tea or instant coffee in the mailing and suggest that the editor take a break while reading your release.
- Make your community aware of your idea by supporting a local cause that ties into the philosophy of your idea.

If you're uncomfortable selling your newly generated idea because you feel selling is like bragging, remember:

> The peacock that sits on its tailfeathers is just another turkey.

The Importance of "Word of Mouth"

Most people judge an innovation by subjective evaluation from other individuals who have already adopted the innovation. It has been shown that innovations really take off after word-of-mouth communications have spread the positive subjective evaluations.

Conclusion

Creativity is a process. It has several steps, and each demands a different set of skills. Beginning with creative thinking, you can practice these skills and learn to be more creative. You can recognize your own creative abilities and develop them. You can recognize the value of creative (divergent) thinking in others and learn to manage it without fearing that it will take you over. And you can begin to promote your ideas with a greater confidence than you now may have. I hope that this chapter will have helped you realize these things and given you a head start in becoming more productive by being more creative.

6

Survey of Managerial Style

Managers constantly identify desirable behavior, both in themselves and in others with whom they work. Much of this behavior takes on a characteristic pattern. Knowing something about these different patterns may help us to become more productive professionals. This instrument measures an aspect of managerial style. Please complete all items, and then score and interpret them according to the instructions that follow.

If you are taking this as a student, reflect on your last job as you answer these questions. Note that people will often rate questions like those included in this instrument in terms of how they think they should answer them or in terms of the way that they would like to be. This is not what is wanted here. Please answer the items in terms of how much you agree with a statement as it applies to what you actually do. Give careful thought to your answers and remember that your results are only valuable to the extent that they reflect what you do, not what you think you should do.

You will probably note that some of the items on the survey seem similar. Do not let this bother you—it is a necessary outcome of statistical technique. Please rate each item independently without regard to your responses on previous items. There are no right or wrong answers.

Section I: Management Style Items

Directions: For the 30 items below, read each item and decide how much you agree that the item describes you.

	Strongly Agree	*Agree*	*Slightly Agree*	*Slightly Disagree*	*Disagree*	*Strongly Disagree*
1. Managing company progress toward a vision represents a major portion of what I do in my job.	( )	( )	( )	( )	( )	( )
2. I am methodical in the way that I carry out my job responsibilities.	( )	( )	( )	( )	( )	( )
3. Most of my work-related activity involves thinking about the future of my organization.	( )	( )	( )	( )	( )	( )
4. I am a real "take charge" type of person.	( )	( )	( )	( )	( )	( )
5. Garnering commitment in people toward meeting some organizational goal represents a major portion of what I do in my job.	( )	( )	( )	( )	( )	( )

Prepared by James G. Clawson. Copyright 1989 by the Darden Graduate Business School Foundation, Charlottesville, VA 22901. UVA-0B-358. Reprinted with permission.

	Strongly Agree	*Agree*	*Slightly Agree*	*Slightly Disagree*	*Disagree*	*Strongly Disagree*
6. I am very decisive. When I must make a decision, I stick to it.	( )	( )	( )	( )	( )	( )
7. Whenever I must present information to a group, I typically speak without notes or outlines.	( )	( )	( )	( )	( )	( )
8. I focus my professional energies on envisioning the future of the organization.	( )	( )	( )	( )	( )	( )
9. Whenever I must present information to a group, I write out the speech, then read it to the group.	( )	( )	( )	( )	( )	( )
10. I am self confident.	( )	( )	( )	( )	( )	( )
11. I focus my professional energies on getting people in my organization to build their commitments to our organization and its goals.	( )	( )	( )	( )	( )	( )
12. I learn best by diving in and seeing if something works or doesn't work.	( )	( )	( )	( )	( )	( )
13. Most of my work-related activity is in carrying out day-to-day management responsibilities.	( )	( )	( )	( )	( )	( )
14. I spend most of my professional time considering views of what my organization can become.	( )	( )	( )	( )	( )	( )
15. Most of my work-related activity is in pulling people together to attain an organizational goal.	( )	( )	( )	( )	( )	( )
16. I think that the most important aspect of my job is preparing for future needs of the organization.	( )	( )	( )	( )	( )	( )
17. I manage my professional time efficiently.	( )	( )	( )	( )	( )	( )
18. I think that the most important aspect of my job is persuading people to accept my vision for our organization.	( )	( )	( )	( )	( )	( )
19. I make an effort to participate in group activities.	( )	( )	( )	( )	( )	( )
20. I focus my professional energies on managing and monitoring my organization's progress toward a goal.	( )	( )	( )	( )	( )	( )
21. Thinking about what my organization might look like in the future represents a major portion of what I do in my job.	( )	( )	( )	( )	( )	( )
22. I am a predictable person. I think that people know what to expect of me.	( )	( )	( )	( )	( )	( )
23. At work I try to foster close personal relationships with my coworkers.	( )	( )	( )	( )	( )	( )
24. I spend most of my professional time managing my company's progress toward a vision.	( )	( )	( )	( )	( )	( )
25. Solving problems in unstructured situations is an important part of what I do.	( )	( )	( )	( )	( )	( )
26. I would rather do something myself than delegate responsibility to someone else.	( )	( )	( )	( )	( )	( )
27. I learn on my own first, then apply what I have learned.	( )	( )	( )	( )	( )	( )
28. I spend most of my professional time convincing others in my organization to carry out a plan.	( )	( )	( )	( )	( )	( )
29. Whenever I must present information to a group, I speak while using an outline as a reference.	( )	( )	( )	( )	( )	( )
30. I think that the most important aspect of my job is looking at how my company is performing and determining what it is that it needs to do to stick to the company plan.	( )	( )	( )	( )	( )	( )

> NOTE!
> DO *NOT* READ THE REMAINDER OF THIS PACKAGE UNTIL YOU HAVE COMPLETED THE SURVEY!

Scoring and Interpreting Your Data

The Theory

This questionnaire was designed to measure aspects of your leadership style and preferences. Measuring leadership is not easy. Social scientists have been arguing for decades, even centuries, about the answer to the question, "What makes a good leader?" Out of this debate have emerged numerous theories about what makes a good leader. But these theories are often contradictory and confusing. We believe, in spite of the controversy about what the concept of leadership comprises, that a practical, immediate model of leadership would help focus the developmental efforts of managers on things that they can begin doing now.

Given our reading of leadership studies and our observation of leaders in the world, we have concluded and suggest that leadership includes three fundamental clusters of skills and abilities: creating vision, garnering commitment to that vision, and monitoring and managing progress toward the realization of that vision.

Vision. Powerful leaders have a clear vision of where they want their organization to go. Vision is the view a person holds about what the organization will look like and what it will be doing in the future. Obviously, some people have greater vision than others, and some have vision that extends further into the future than others. And some have vision that doesn't work or come to fruition. All managers can, and, we believe, ought to, have a vision of their organization, what they think it can become, where they think it is going, how it should be operating, and what the experience of working within it should be.

Vision is an essential part of leadership. Having vision requires creativity; one must be able to think and see beyond the present time frame and beyond the usual options. The ability to see ahead, to see nontraditional alternatives, is a creative part of leadership. So is the ability to frame the context of a business problem in broader terms that question current assumptions. The ability to incorporate these often unusual thoughts into a cohesive vision of the future of the company defines the first set of leadership skills.

COMMITMENT: The ability to garner the commitment of others to one's vision is a key cluster of leadership skills. A leader may have a vision of what an organization can become, but unless others receive and become committed to that vision it is unlikely to be realized. Leaders can create visions, but commitment, on the other hand, is offered by followers. It is this commitment of a group of followers that allows leaders to build their visions into organizational realities. A key task of the leader, then, is to garner commitment from those people who are critical to his or her success.

Leaders may foster commitment in a variety of ways: public communications, one-on-one interactions, involving others in the decision-making process, and modeling commitment to an idea, to name a few. However the successful leader goes about it, he or she is able to develop and maintain strong commitments from others to his or her vision for the organization.

MONITORING AND MANAGING PROGRESS TOWARD THE VISION: The third cluster of skills that we see in leadership is the ability to monitor and manage progress of the organization toward the vision. For us, this is the bulk of "management" education today: ascertaining what are the right measures to monitor and the techniques and tools for getting those indicators to yield the right results. This aspect of leadership focuses on the details of the business. That we place monitoring and management as a subset of leadership does not denigrate it. Rather it points out that while managers can indeed be leaders, in our view they need to augment their skills with the visionary and commitment-building skills outlined above. To us, management is a component of leadership. Ensuring that deadlines are met, objectives are achieved, and budgets are appropriately used are valuable and necessary—but not sufficient—leadership skills.

Leadership and the Survey of Managerial Style (SMS)

Although some writers have drawn a provocative and dichotomous distinction between leadership and management, we believe that they are closely related and that a consideration of the fluid relationship between them is more productive. Hence, we assert that leadership is not so much a question of whether someone is either a manager or a leader, but rather how much emphasis one places on the component skills of leadership—of which management is one. Knowing something about how one tends to emphasize creating vision, garnering commitment, and monitoring and managing progress toward the vision can help one in several ways. We'll outline some of those, but first, let's score the data you have generated.

Parts I and II of the SMS are designed to gather general information about you and to measure your self-perception of your work behavior with regard to each of the three clusters mentioned above. From these data, you can begin to construct a picture of your leadership profile, that is, how much you emphasize leadership overall and how much you emphasize the three different clusters of leadership as outlined previously. With these data, you can begin to consider how strong your desire to be a leader is and how your behavior is distributed across the three dimensions of leadership.

Scoring Your Data

Step 1. On the Section II Scoring Form that follows, you will see that values are associated with each point on the scale used in Section II of the survey: Strongly Agree - 6, Agree - 5, Slightly Agree - 4, Slightly Disagree - 3, Disagree - 2, and Strongly Disagree - 1. For each section of the scoring form, indicate the score for each of the items listed. For example, if you checked "slightly agree" for item 3 and "agree" for item 8, your scores for these items would be 4 and 5, respectively. Please note that in Section II scoring not all items are scored. The extra items in Section II of the survey are included to control measurement error and are not included in the individual scoring procedure.

Step 2. Sum the scores in each column to derive scores for vision, commitment, and management.

Step 3. Sum the scores for vision, commitment, and management to derive your total score.

Step 4. Compute proportional values for vision, commitment and management by dividing the scale score by the total score.

Step 5. Next, complete the SMS Profile on page 00. The concentric circles on the next page represent varying strengths of leadership; the larger the circle, the greater the leadership. The letters associated with each circle correspond to the total score obtained in Section II of the survey. Find the circle that corresponds to your total score in Section II and trace the circle with a heavy marking pen.

Step 6. In the score profile, there are 48 segments that can be divided up according to your personal scores. To determine the number of segments that correspond to each of your Section II scale scores, multiply 48 by each of the proportional values in Section II and round the result to the nearest whole number. For example, if your vision proportional score in Section II were .30, you would multiply 48 by .30 (which equals 14.4) and round the result to the nearest whole number (14 in this case). After you have determined the number of segments that correspond to your scale scores, count off the number of segments on the pie for each scale. (Note: You can start at any point on the pie.) For each scale indicate the beginning and ending point with a heavy marking pen. Finally, for each of these areas, draw lines to the center dot and label the pieces of the pie with their corresponding V, C, or M: V for vision, C for commitment, M for management.

Note: When you have finished scoring your data, you should have a pie chart with three divisions. The size of the pie reflects your overall strength as a leader. The size of each of the three wedges, one each for creating vision, garnering commitment, and monitoring and managing progress toward the vision, indicates the relative strength of each leadership area. When you have completed the profile, proceed to the interpretation section.

Section II Scoring Form

Instrument Scale Values

Strongly Agree	- 6	Slightly Disagree	- 3
Agree	- 5	Disagree	- 2
Slightly Agree	- 4	Strongly Disagree	- 1

Source	Score	Source	Score	Source	Score
Item 3	_____	Item 5	_____	Item 1	_____
Item 8	_____	Item 11	_____	Item 13	_____
Item 14	_____	Item 15	_____	Item 20	_____
Item 16	_____	Item 18	_____	Item 24	_____
Item 21	_____	Item 28	_____	Item 30	_____
Total Vision	_____	Total Commitment	_____	Total Management	_____

Maximum Scale Score - 30 Minimum Scale Score - 5

Total Score Section II

(Vision + Commitment + Management) - ____

Proportional Values for Section II

(Vision ÷ Total Score) - ____
(Commitment ÷ Total Score) - ____
(Management ÷ Total Score) - ____

Interpreting Your Profile

The first thing to note is that it is not necessarily good or bad to desire to be a leader. Leadership roles place demands on individuals just as all positions in life do; some people enjoy that set of demands, while others do not. Regardless of how superficially attractive the recognition and apparent influence of leaders may be, unless one's personal skills and interests fit the demands of a particular leadership position, one is not likely to be happy or successful in that position. Thus, the size of your leadership pie is not a value judgment about you or your worth in your organization or in society. Rather, it is a description of your preferences and as such can be used by you to make more sound decisions about you and your work.

Survey of Managerial Style
Profile

A = 15-29 B = 30-44 C = 45-59 D = 60 - 74 E = 75-90

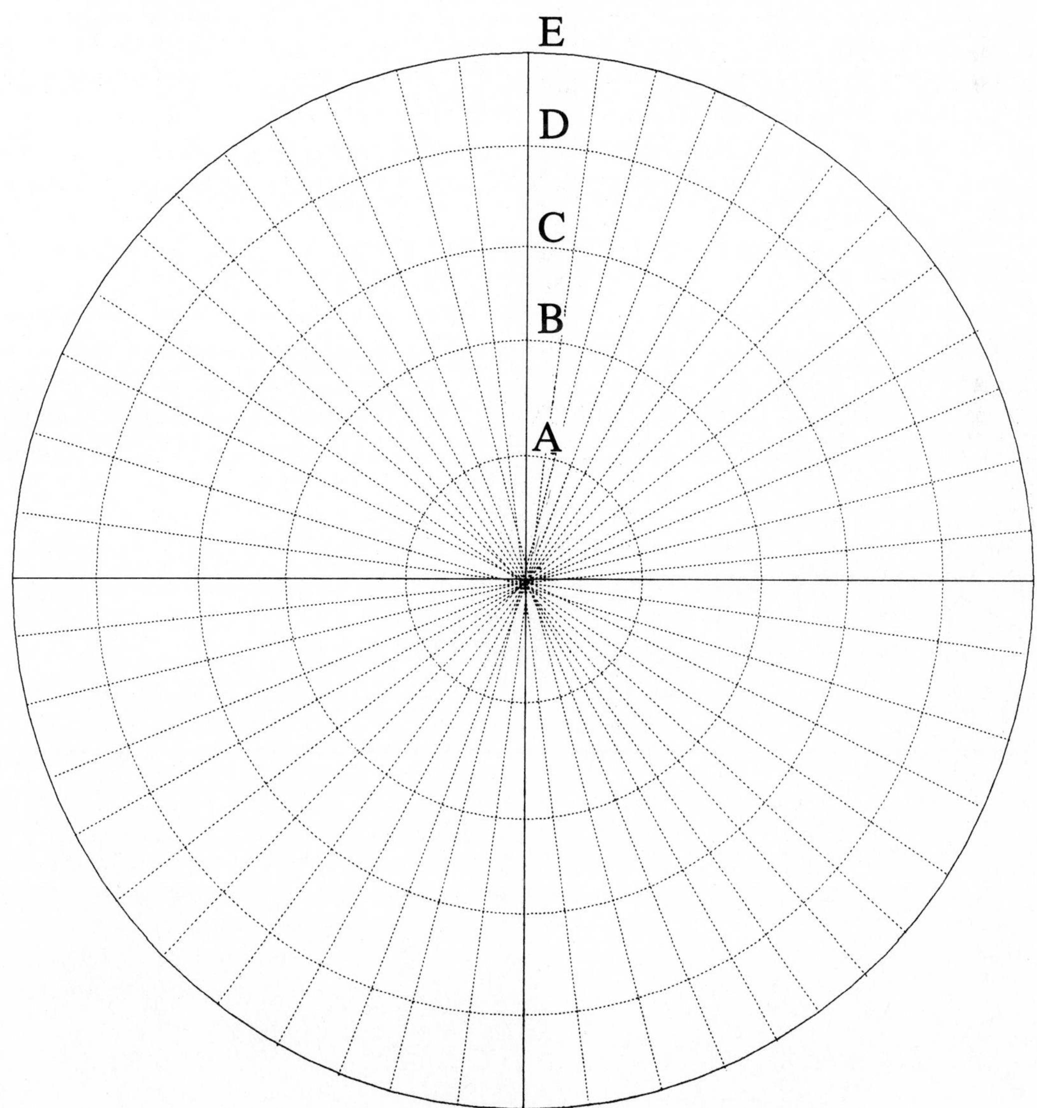

The same can be said of the relative strength of the three basic areas of leadership as proposed in this document. Knowing something about your relative position in the areas of vision, commitment, and management can certainly help you to elaborate your leadership skills and may serve to guide you as you make career and educational decisions. We encourage you not to treat these three clusters of leadership skills as fixed and equally desirable. It is quite possible that one can be fairly evenly balanced among these skills. Alternatively, one might obtain a moderate score in one area and higher scores on the others.

We expect that scores in these leadership areas can change depending on context and the demands of your job. Patterns of response such as these remain to be researched. For now, the important thing to note is that we are talking about general leadership functions and that strength or weakness in one area is not necessarily desirable or undesirable.

Interpretive Alternatives

Write your interpretation of what each of the alternative profiles below might mean to the individuals or corporations that have them.

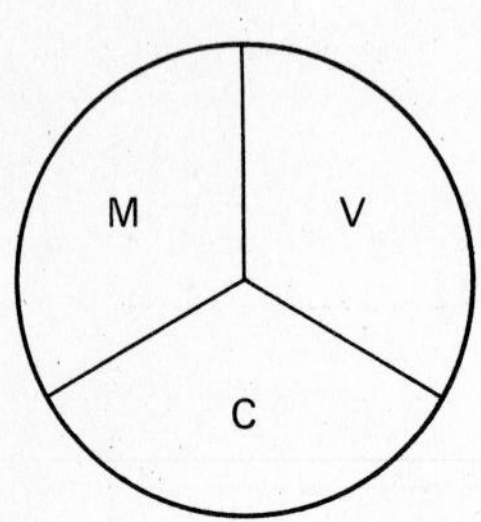

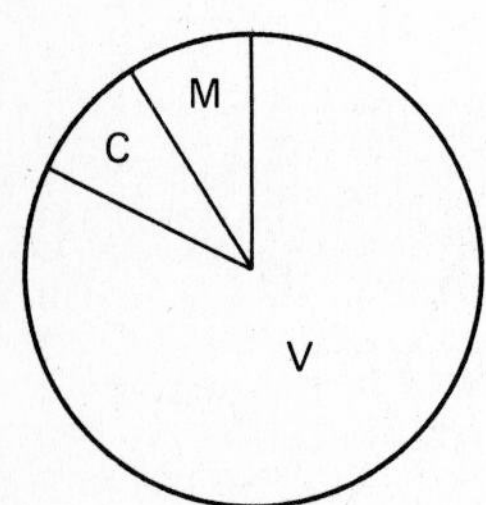

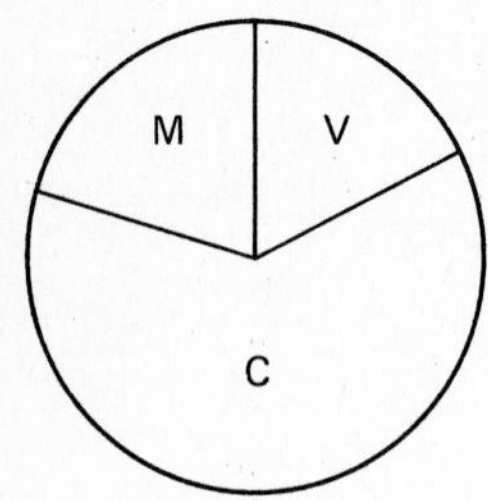

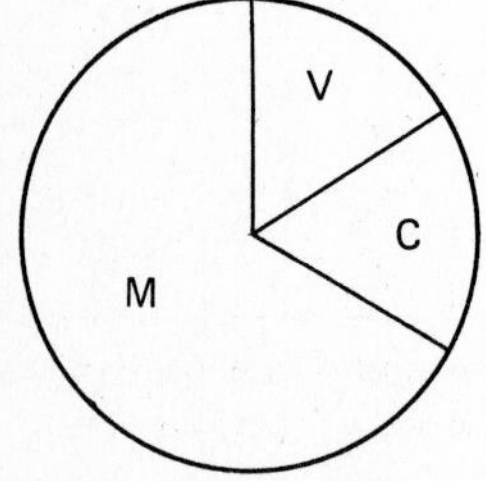

Assignment

Consider Steve Taylor's and Carrie Baugh's Survey of Leadership Style. What inferences do you make about them from these data?

Steven Taylor's Survey of Leadership Style

These are Steven's scores and score graph on this instrument.

Vision: 24 Commitment: 19 Management: 5
Total: 48

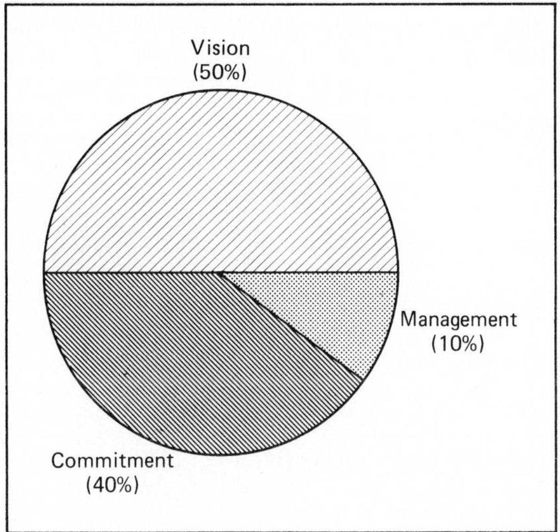

Carrie Baugh's Survey of Leadership Style

Carrie's scores on this instrument were

Vision - 28 Commitment - 2 Management - 18
Total - 48

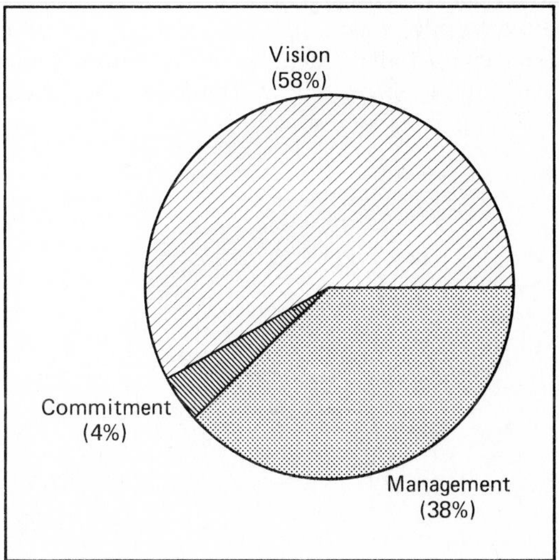

SELECTED BIBLIOGRAPHY ON LEADERSHIP

You may be interested in the following additional resources on the topic of leadership.

BASS, BERNARD A. *Stogdill's Handbook of Leadership.* New York: Free Press Revised Edition, 1981.

BENNIS, WARREN, and BURT NANUS, *Leaders.* New York: Harper and Row, 1985. (For summary see "The Four Competencies of Leadership," *Training and Development Journal,* August 1984.)

BRACHE, ALAN. "Seven Prevailing Myths about Leadership," *Training and Development Journal,* 37: 6 (June 1983), p. 120.

BURNS, JAMES MACGREGOR. *Leadership.* New York: Harper & Row, 1978.

FIEDLER, FRED E. *A Theory of Leadership Effectiveness.* New York: McGraw-Hill, 1967.

FREW, DAVID R. "Leadership and Followership," *Personnel Journal* 56: 2, (February 1977) p. 90.

GARDNER, JOHN W. *Leadership Papers,* a series of 6 papers prepared for Independent Sector, beginning January 1986, 1828 L. Street NW, Washington, D.C., 20036.

HILL, NORMAN. "Self-Esteem: The Key to Effective Leadership," *Administrative Management* (August 1976).

HOUSE, ROBERT J., and TERENCE R. MITCHELL. "Path-Goal Theory of Leadership," *The Journal of Contemporary Business* 3, (Fall 1974) p. 81.

TANNENBAUM, ROBERT, and WARREN H. SCHMIDT. "How to Choose a Leadership Pattern," *Harvard Business Review* No. 73311 (May–June 1973).

TICHY, NOEL M., and MARY ANNE DEVANNA. *The Transformational Leader.* New York: John Wiley & Sons, 1986. (For a summary see Tichy, Noel M., and Noel M. Ulrich "The Leadership Challenge—A Call for the Transformational Leader," *Sloan Management Review* (Fall 1984) or "The Transformational Leader" by Tichy and Devanna in *Training and Development Journal* (July 1986).

YUKL, GARY A. *Leadership in Organizations.* Englewood Cliffs, NJ: Prentice Hall, 1981.

ZALEZNIK, ABRAHAM. "Managers and Leaders: Are They Different?" *Harvard Business Review* 77312 (May–June, 1977).

7

Myers-Briggs Type Indicator

NOTE:
DO NOT READ THIS UNTIL YOU HAVE COMPLETED
THE MBTI
DISTRIBUTED SEPARATELY

At this point, you should have already completed the Myers-Briggs Type Indicator (MBTI) and received scoring instructions from the booklet or your instructor. This scoring procedure will give you a four-letter classification such as ENTJ or ISTP. If you have not already done this procedure, please do so before you read on. The instrument is available only to qualified test administrators and only through Consulting Psychologists Press of Palo Alto, California.

Background

The Myers-Briggs Type Indicator is arguably the assessment instrument most commonly used in American industry today. Many companies conduct seminars and, indeed, many consultants have built their entire practices around this particular instrument. This level of activity means that new versions of the instrument continue to be developed and that training seminars on how to use the instrument are growing in number. Given the instrument's unique history, this development is significant.

Before World War II, Katherine Myers and her daughter, Isabel Myers Briggs, became increasingly interested in the behavior of Isabel's husband, Clarence G. Myers. In the midst of their affection for him, they found that he started to behave differently than what they, as mother and daughter, were used to. This observation and the family interactions surrounding it, along with an interest in the then-recent (1921) publication of a theory of psychological types by Carl Jung, stimulated their interest in understanding human behavior, particularly the differences in human behavior. This mother-daughter team embarked on what was to become a remarkable professional stream of research that has thus far lasted over forty years. That such a work should begin in large part out of the desire to understand a son-in-law and husband illustrates how significant insights often grow out of "ordinary" people's reflections on "simple" daily events. This underscores our fundamental thesis that you, while not trained in psychological assessment, can understand the theoretical underpinnings of the various instruments that we will use and can make reasoned, conservative conclusions from data generated by them.

Carl Jung

Carl Jung was a student of Sigmund Freud's. Theirs was a close relationship, one often reviewed as an

Prepared by James G. Clawson with acknowledgment of John Pickering for his helpful comments and editing.

example of mentor-protegé relationships. After a highly publicized break with Freud, Jung continued to develop and establish his own reputation in the field of psychology. He proposed and then spent much of his career refining a theory of psychological types, suggesting that human behavior was not so random and chaotic as it seemed, but, given the proper framework for viewing it, really quite regular and predictable. His work grew largely from his studies of his patients in psychotherapy over many years.

Jung's theory, in brief summary, said that, in a person's conscious mental activity, there were four fundamental psychological processes: Sensing (S), Intuition (N), Thinking (T), and Feeling (F). These "functions," as Jung called them, were distinct and unique from each other. The four formed two bipolar dimensions, S–N and T–F. People used all these activities or processes but not all in predominant ways, and these characteristic patterns endured over time and across situations. This patterned use of each mental activity gives rise to a certain predictability in a person's behavior that allows an observer to categorize the individual according to a relatively simple classification scheme.

Furthermore, one can observe distinct variations in these patterns depending on an individual's orientation to life, or "attitude" (in the sense of posture) toward the outside world. People seemed to attend more either to things outside them (which Jung called the extraverted world) or to the inner world of thoughts and ideas (the introverted domain). This distinction provided a third dimension, E–I. These three dimensions allowed Jung to categorize people according to eight fundamental types: extraverts with a dominant sensing activity, introverts with a dominant sensing activity, and so on.

Myers and Briggs added a fourth "preference" dimension to Jung's theory by noting that some people are generally open to new information while others are more interested in reaching closure. They termed the "open" characteristic Perceptive and the "closure" characteristic Judging.

These four dimensions can be summarized as shown in Exhibit 1. The E–I scale relates to a person's orientation to the outside world. The S–N dimension has to do with focus of data collection and the perception of information. The T–F dimension has to do with decision making, and the J–P scale relates to openness to the outside world. In Myers-Briggs parlance, the S–N and T–F are referred to as functions or mental processes and the E–I and J–P dimensions as attitudes. From a broad perspective, the functions on the left are "outer" functions and the ones on the right are "inner." This perspective is important to note because as individuals develop over time, they usually build complementary strengths in the outer and inner functions.

EXHIBIT 1

Myers-Briggs Type Dimensions

Extraversion	---------------------------	Introversion
Sensing	---------------------------	Intuition
Thinking	---------------------------	Feeling
Judgment	---------------------------	Perception

Each of the four function/preference dimensions and the categories formed by them are *descriptive*, not prescriptive, in nature. That is, each process has its strengths and weaknesses, and none is preferred, in a general sense, to another. Of course, the strengths and weaknesses associated with each will affect a person's ability to function in various jobs. Therefore, the types may suggest better fits to one job over another, but, by themselves, one type is no more preferable or socially acceptable or *good* in any broad sense than another. In fact, as you will see later, the diversity in types allows for greater strength in a variety of social settings.

Let's examine each of the four dimensions more carefully. Note that Jung did not use the labels of his dimensions in just the same way as lay language would suggest. One cannot read the labels and immediately know what they mean. Look, for instance, for the distinction between what Jung meant when he used the term "sensing," and what the common English meaning might be.

Extraversion–Introversion

Jung's definition of extraversion was that one's attention was centered on things outside, on people and objects external to the individual. Extraverts deal directly with the things around them and are often more given to action than are introverts. They process information externally, often "thinking out loud" and actively using others around them. One way to think of this is as a flow of energy from the outside to the inside; extraverts absorb energy from what is happening around them.

Introverts, in contrast, generate energy internally. In a crowd, introverts typically lose energy and are drained by the experience. This feature is not necessarily one of shyness; it is one of focus of attention. Introverts take in and process internally, often in silence. The silence does not mean that they are uninterested or shy, only that their mental processes are private and inward. Crowds force attention to the external world and pull energy out of the introvert. The flow of energy and information is from the inside out. John Pickering, an experienced MBTI trainer, notes that extraverts and introverts have the same proportion of good and bad ideas, but everyone *knows* about the extraverts' ideas.

Another way to think about the E–I scale is to ask: From where does an individual get energy? What causes one to lose energy? If being in a crowd is draining, then one is probably an introvert. If being in a crowd is exhilarating and energizing, then one is probably an extravert. Another useful question is: Where does one prefer to process ideas, inside or outside? And a third useful discriminating question is: Is one more action-oriented, or more reflective?

Sensing–Intuition

Sensing relates to data collected through the five physical senses, sight, smell, touch, taste, and hearing. Our physical senses do not deal with the future; they yield information on the present and have offered data to be recorded in the past. Hence, those who use the sensing process predominantly are, by definition, focused on the present.

Intuitive types rely on a sixth sense, intuition. They focus more on possibilities, what could be, relationships among things; on concepts, theories, and alternative meanings. Rather than describing a thing, they will imagine its connections with the future, with other things in the past or present. Jung thought that the subconscious, rather than the outside, tangible, sensory world, informed the intuition.

Thinking–Feeling

Thinking relates to the connections between ideas and concepts. As Jung used it, thinking meant seeing logical, analytic, impersonal, and objective links from one thing to another. Thinking types make judgments about the truthfulness of something, always asking, "Is it true or false?" They tend to use impersonally held and "objectively" applied moral principles to make decisions, and they tend to focus on events, on facts, and on things.

To Jung, on the other hand, feeling was a subjective activity, based on value strength. People who use the feeling process are sensitive to their own values and priorities and to the values of others. This process is more personal than thinking. It is not just the emotional side of a person, although values may give rise to emotions. Rather it comes from what an individual holds to be important. Feeling types make judgments about the worth of something, asking, "Is it good or bad?" They tend to be people and relationship oriented, using personally-held values and moral principles, "subjectively" applied, to make decisions. These values may not necessarily be "good" in the eyes of society; the point is that they are personally and tightly held by the feeling type.

Judging–Perceiving

Judging types desire organizing and concluding activities. They want to accomplish something and move on. It is not that they are 'judgmental' in the usual sense of the word; rather, they just do not want to linger over the alternatives and possibilities. Judging types need control; they like to have plans, make decisions, reach conclusions, and work to schedules and lists. They feel time pressure early on in a project or situation and press for wrapping things up. Judging types want to control not only their own lives but the lives of those around them and to control all the things that affect them. It would be difficult, for instance, for a J to accept the prayer "Lord, grant me the strength to work on the things I can do something about, the courage to avoid worrying about the things I can't do anything about, and the wisdom to know the difference." They are impatient and often implement the process of "Ready, fire, aim" or even just "Fire, fire, fire."

Perceivers are looking for new information. They are receptive, open, adaptable, willing to bring in additional data. Perceiving types need information, options, flexibility. They resist control, plans, decisions, conclusions, closures, and schedules. They feel time pressures only very late, often too late. They are loathe to make decisions too early, or even at all. In the early stages of a decision-making process they are useful and productive because they are not likely to close down the data-collection process too soon. On the other hand, they often implement the process "Ready, aim, aim, aim . . . "

A Developmental Model

Jung's type theory is a developmental one. Born with a proclivity for one type, and shaped by one's environment, individuals continue to develop skills in their chosen type over their lifetimes. Jung taught that developing skill in one type precluded the development of skill in another type. Some find this limitation disconcerting and prefer to believe that people can be or should be expert in all types and their attendant behaviors. To Jung, such an effort would be the mark of a less developed mentality. The maturing adult, he argued, has chosen a type and become confident and at ease in it. Trying to develop superior skill in all types would leave one underdeveloped in all. So, to Jung, people have dominant functions and subordinate functions. This was not to say people were totally inept in their subordinate functions, but rather that the well-developed personality was in part a result of having made an implicit choice of type and of having developed skill and confidence in it.

As an individual developed a type in life by choosing to be involved in one setting above another, Jung observed that the dominant process or function (S–N or T–F) was usually played out in the preferred orientation (extraversion or introversion). For example, a dominant Sensing type with a preference for extraversion would play the sensing function out in the external world. At the same time, most people would then develop a counterbalancing subordinate function to be played out in the *other* preference. The sensing extrovert was likely to develop a complementary set of "inner" functions. In this way, people were not completely incompetent in settings that played to their subordinate functions but were able to develop abilities that allowed them to function quite well in various situations. Jung believed, however, that mature individuals functioned more easily, more competently, and more naturally in settings that played to their dominant functions.

On the other hand, John Pickering, for one, believed that "maturity" meant that people developed skills in their nonpreferred styles over their lifetimes that allowed them to function in various settings.

Interpreting Type

The four-letter summary of your scores on the MBTI is your type. The numbers associated with the letters indicate the clarity and consistency of your answers to the items on the instrument. A high E score, for example, means that your answers were consistently clear in favor of the Extraversion-related items on the test. Your type will be arranged by function in the order E–I, S–N, T–F, and J–P—for example, your type might be ESFJ.

One way to begin interpreting your type is to look at the numbers associated with each letter. The larger number determines which function is noted in your type. The larger that number is relative to its opposite, the stronger that function is in you. These numbers can be displayed on a continuous scale in several ways. One way is to consider the midpoint between them as zero and plot the difference between the scores as Steven Taylor and Carrie Baugh did in the cases that follow. Plotting your scores on such a chart will help you visualize the consistency of your answers on each scale. The scores you receive will depend in part on the version of the instrument that you used; there are long forms and short forms of the official Myers-Briggs Type Indicator and many other instruments that purport to measure the same dimensions.

The next thing to do is to recognize the dominant and auxiliary behavioral patterns that your type suggests. Myers and Briggs have outlined an approach for identifying dominant and auxiliary functions; while this is a useful exercise, it is one that probably should be left to those who wish to pursue the understanding of type much further than we can in this context. The procedure for doing this makes several assumptions, including the one that the J–P dimension is an indicator of the dominant function and that it "points" to the second function, S or N.

For our purposes, without wrestling through the technique of determining dominant and auxiliary functions, we shall just note that four predominant temperaments emerge from the Jungian types—SPs, SJs, NTs, and NFs. Keirsey and Bates (see reference list on page 77) describe how other psychological theories throughout history can be melded with Jung's to describe, in remarkably consistent fashion, these four broad temperamental behavioral types. Here is a brief overview of these temperaments.

The SP Temperament

Relying on their senses and eager to take in rather than close out, SPs are impulsive, tuned to the moment. They want to be free, able to respond to whatever the current situation will suggest. SPs resist preparing for doing, for they would rather be doing, NOW. They are quite happy to engage in activities with unknown outcomes. Tools are their forte; they love using tools so much that they become experts with them. Charming, impulsive, lighthearted, cheerful, SPs make acquaintances easily, yet people often note years later that they have learned little more about them than what they knew the first time they met. Having little goal orientation. SPs display amazing endurance in the face of hardships; because they are living in the present, worrying about the future does not weigh them down and they carry on. SPs, spontaneous and engulfed in the excitement of the moment, become great performers, artisans, and athletes. Their practicing is doing. While the other types practice for the performance later, SPs are performing constantly. For the SP, whatever is now, *is*, and that's what life is about. SPs are relatively common, comprising about thirty-eight percent of the population of the United States.

The SJ Temperament

SJs are about as common as SPs. Their behavior is focused around the concept of duty, especially duty to the group. For them, loyalty is a central value. Loyalty brings with it obligation and acceptance of rules. SJs learn the rules, obey the rules, and live by shoulds and oughts. SJs save, prepare, plan for the safety of the group. SJs believe, in fact, might have written Murphy's Law, the belief that if something can go wrong, it will. They work to prevent violations of law and social order. They maintain and build institutions of social order. Their devotion to the group and to orderliness leads them to professions where service is required—they teach, they nurse, they serve, they care for others. They are the repositories of culture and tradition.

The NT Temperament

NTs are more rare than their SP and SJ cousins, only about twelve percent of American society. Thus, they often feel like minorities in an alien world. For them, power is the dominant drive, gaining and exercising power over their surroundings. NTs value knowledge, learning, intelligence, improvement understanding, and perhaps above all, competence. NTs are highly self-critical, holding themselves and others to high standards of insight and understanding. They make lists of things they should do and should be able to do. NTs are less willing to accept authority, especially in matters of intelligence, preferring instead to understand the primary rationale of a conclusion and sort it out for themselves. NTs fear failure and are driven to prove to themselves and others that their competence will overcome any such probability. Like the central theme for the other temperaments, this need to express competence for the NT is not an issue that is ever resolved; rather, it must be demonstrated daily. NTs get caught up in work and have a hard time playing or relaxing. Others find NTs discomforting and demanding; consequently, this temperament is often isolated from others. NTs speak concisely and without elaboration. They say what they mean, say it once, and often wonder that others should find it at all interesting since after all their study, things begin to seem obvious to them and therefore uninteresting. At the same time, others often see what the NTs have to say as abstract and difficult to follow. NTs gravitate to the sciences, engineering, and mathematics. They focus on the future and forget about the past. Having understood one set of phenomena, they move on to another.

The NF Temperament

NFs find in searching for themselves the meaning of life. To the other three temperaments, this is a frustrating and inexplicable activity around which to organize a life. For the NF, the process of becoming one's self is what it is all about. About as rare as the NTs, NFs exert unusual influence on society through such commonly chosen professions as writers, playwrights, journalists, and teachers. They are constantly searching for deeper and higher meanings, insights that will shape and help society. NFs question themselves, their being, their values, their beliefs, their roles. NFs often become overwhelmingly committed to their search, sacrificing virtually everything else in their lives in favor of their quest. They search from one intellectual group to another, hoping for answers, discovering inevitably shallow ones, and moving on. They focus on people and their relationships, especially their relationships with themselves. It is in the exploration of these relationships through intense and continuing interactions that the NFs find daily sustenance.

With this introduction to the four dimensions and the four temperaments that provide a first level of analysis of type, we can move one step deeper, to consider each of the sixteen types themselves.

Characteristics of Types

The four dimensions outlined above can be arranged in a variety of fashions. If we arrange them according to the four temperaments we have just discussed, we can see a matrix of individual types as shown in Exhibit 2.

While our primary focus here is on the use of the MBTI for individual analysis, a large version of this matrix can be effectively used with small groups by having each member of the group mark his or her type on it and then opening a discussion of what the resultant pattern means for the group's ability to work together.

Each intersection on this matrix represents a type,

Exhibit 2

Myers-Briggs Types Arranged by Temperaments

SP	SJ	NF	NT
ISFP	ISFJ	INFJ	INTJ
ISTP	ISTJ	INFP	INTP
ESTP	ESTJ	ENFP	ENTP
ESFP	ESFJ	ENFJ	ENTJ
SP	SJ	NF	NT

with broadly predictable patterns of mental and related behavioral activity. Although mental and behavioral indicators for each cell are not constrictive in reality, they can help us to understand why people behave the way they do and therefore help us to be better able to manage or deal with them. In the context of making career decisions, these indicators can help us identify patterns in our lives that will help us to choose the careers, industries, companies, and specific jobs that will allow us to utilize our strengths rather than forcing us to play to our lesser developed sides. Figures 4 and 5 give some simple preliminary indicators of the characteristics of each type. For more detailed information on each, consult the test booklet from which you took the instrument, or any of the many publications that deal with the MBTI listed in the references at the end of this note. A particularly good and readily available one is *Please Understand Me* by David Keirsey and Marilyn Bates.

Using Your Type

There are many ways you can use the information about yourself that the MBTI provides. First, an understanding of both your type and that of people close to you can help you relate to and understand these people. If, for instance, your spouse is an ENTJ and you are an ISTP, you can anticipate that there will be times when the overt animated discussion of ideas in which your spouse wants to engage will be overwhelming to your desires to more quietly gather some hard facts at hand and reach a more solid conclusion. You share an interest in the logical connections of things, but your spouse will want to process that with you while you are likely to want to do that alone or in silence. These insights can help you talk logically and effectively about how you deal with each other and to improve your relationship. Obviously, this is also true of working colleagues, peers, bosses, and subordinates. For this reason, the MBTI is widely used in industry.

For this course, the main use of your type will be to use it in conjunction with other data to develop themes that describe you and will help you formulate implications for the kind of work you should be seeking. To the extent that sales requires one to focus on the values and feelings of others, clear ISTJ types may find selling activities stressful since that is not their natural style. For ISTJs there is a logical answer dictated by the strength of present facts. The natural tendency to interact with others to see what they want or help them see the "truth" of the facts is not as available to them as it is to ENFPs, for instance. That is not to say ISTJs never make good salespeople. In certain kinds of environments, perhaps research labs or engineering companies, they may indeed have the right kind of chemistry with the people with whom they would be working.

BEWARE! This brings us to a major caveat. The MBTI is often misused. With its increasing popularity and use comes some unfortunate superficiality. The MBTI is a seemingly simple yet very complex instrument. The more one delves into the meaning of mental functions and orientations and how they dynamically affect each other, the more powerful the model becomes. And it is not the final answer to human behavior in career choosing or organizational life. It is one tool, a tool, which, if used with other data, can provide useful insights.

Some MBTI seminar participants have gone back to the workplace and begun using the MBTI type as a form of greeting or labeling, as in, "Hi, you old ISTJ! Feel like talking today?" This kind of misguided boxing of others and overuse of the type indicators offends both business colleague and those who have worked long and hard to develop and understand the power of this mode. Psychologists trained in several psychological theories are perhaps best able to appreciate the usefulness of the MBTI as well as its limitations. Yet, to the credit of Mrs. Myers and her daughter, Mrs. Briggs, the instrument has been made available to trainers and instructors in a variety of educational settings. We encourage you to be responsible in your use of the data you receive about yourself and others during your discussion of the MBTI. Further, if you encounter the instrument again in your career, we hope you will lend to the discussions a sensitivity to the deeper implications of the theory and encourage others to work at getting beyond the superficial interpretations of the four types.

Exhibit 3

Sensing Types

ISTJ Quiet, thorough, logical, organized, conventional thinkers, managers	*ISFJ* Friendly, quiet, loyal, stable, conscientious.
ISTP Reserved, detached, humor flashes, logical connections and principles	*ISFP* Sensitive, kind, modest, avoid contention, followers, not so achievement oriented, not hasty
ESTP Problem solvers, enjoy the moment, sports, adaptable, tolerant, action	*ESFP* Easygoing, see the positive and fun, joiners, eager, facts not theories, common sense
ESTJ Practical, head for business, like to manage, can forget others' feelings, leaders	*ESFJ* Talkative, popular, committees, need harmony, doing nice things, like to affect peoples' lives

Exhibit 5

Intuitive Types

INFJ Persevering, do what's necessary, quiet, forceful, clear convictions	*INTJ* Original thinkers, skeptical, independent, determined, maybe stubborn
INFP Seldom talk, loyal, like to learn, try to do too much, absorbed	*INTP* Reserved, like theories and science, problem solvers, not good at small talk, focused, multiple interests
ENFP Imaginative, capable, quick solutions, improvisors, persuasive, unrealistic, unfocused	*ENTP* Quick, stimulating, talkative, resourceful, overlook routine and details, multiple interests
ENFJ Responsible, concerned about what others think, comfortable discussion leaders, sociable, responsive	*ENTJ* Hearty, frank, leaders, public speakers, like to learn, may be overconfident

Assignment

Before you attempt to analyze your own data, look at the cases that follow. What inferences can you draw about these people from their types? What implications do your inferences have for the kinds of work these people should be seeking?

Once you have finished practicing on the cases, answer the same questions for your own type.

REFERENCES

MYERS, ISABEL BRIGGS, and MARY H. MCCAULLEY. *Manual: A Guide to the Development and Use of the Myers-Briggs Type Indicator*. 1985: Palo Alto, CA: Consulting Psychologists Press.

JUNG, C. G., *Psychological Types* (Trans. by H. G. Baynes, revised by R. F. C. Hull). Volume 6 of *The Collected Works of C.G. Jung*. Princeton, NJ: Princeton University Press. (Originally published in 1921.)

metheus Nemesis Book Company, Box 2082, Del Mar, CA 92014.

KIERSEY, DAVID and MARILYN BATES. *Please Understand Me*. 1984, Gnosology Books, Ltd., distributed by Pro-

STEVEN TAYLOR'S PERSONALITY TYPE INDICATOR

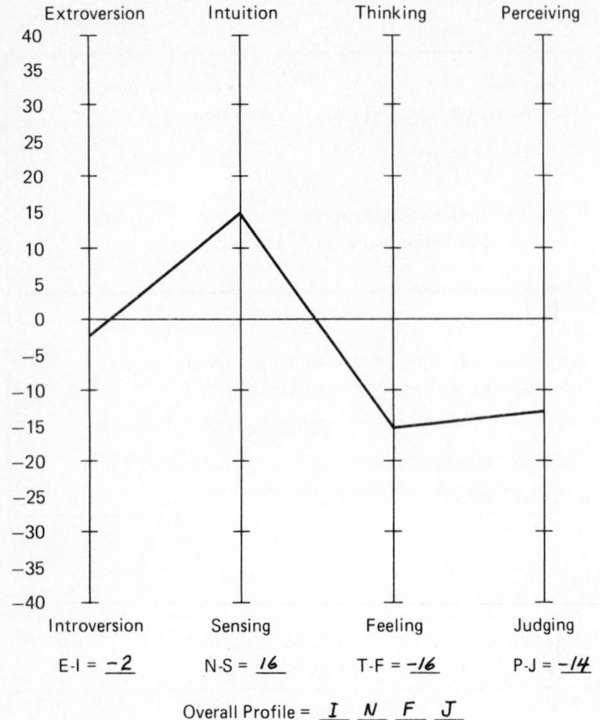

CARRIE BAUGH'S PERSONALITY STYLE INDICATOR

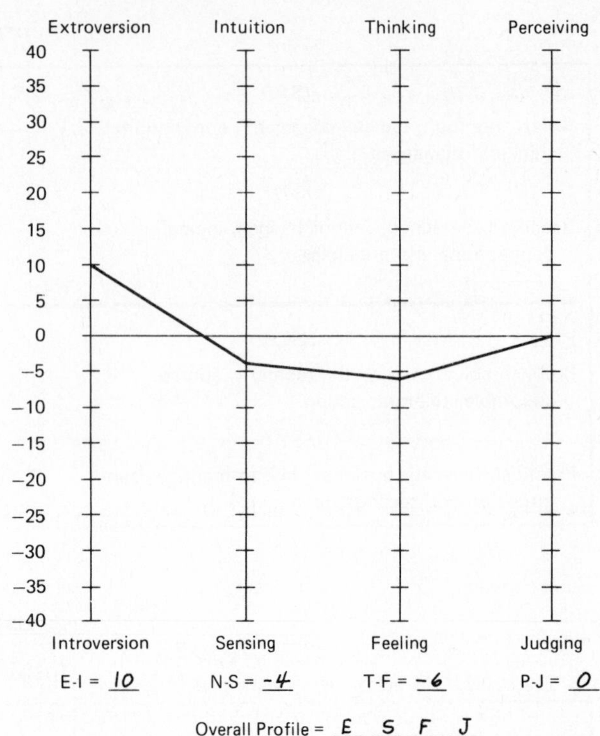

NOTES:

1. Final classification is Extroverted, Sensing, Feeling, Perceiving and Judging (Perceiving and Judging received same score).
2. More sensing than intuitive by only 4 points (10%).
3. More feeling than thinking by only 6 points (15%).
4. More extroverted than intraverted (25%).

INFERENCES:

Carrie is a person who:

1. Is outgoing; relates well to people.
2. Prefers concrete, structured, "here and now."
3. May get frustrated with theory; is practical.
4. Is empathetic.
5. Relies on gathering information before making a decision, but is decisive after gathering facts.
6. Might be action oriented.
7. Is flexible and adapts well to different situations.
8. Might like to plan.

8

FIRO-B

> NOTE! DO NOT READ THIS UNTIL AFTER YOU HAVE COMPLETED TAKING THE FIRO-B QUESTIONNAIRE!!

Scoring FIRO-B

FIRO-B comes in two forms, self-scoring and questionnaire only. If you have the self-scoring form, you can follow the instructions on the instrument to generate your scores. If you have the questionnaire only, you will have to send your answers to Consulting Psychologists Press in Palo Alto, California, to be scored. Test booklets are available to qualified administrators from CPP. Once you have calculated your scores, you may read on to learn how to interpret your scores.

What Is FIRO-B?

FIRO-B, *Fundamental Interpersonal Relations Orientation—Behavior,* is a questionnaire designed by Will Shutz, formerly of Stanford University, and distributed by Consulting Psychologists Press of Palo Alto, California. FIRO-B measures people's selfperception of how they characteristically relate to other people. In addition to giving information about how individuals see themselves behaving in interpersonal relationships, the instrument can also be used to facilitate effectiveness in those relationships. For this reason, FIRO-B has been used widely in a variety of settings including the study of individual personality dynamics, sensitivity training, marriage counseling, personnel selection and assignment, team building, and, significantly, managerial relationships.

FIRO-B addresses three dimensions of human relations: Inclusion, Control, and Affection. Mr. Shutz describes these dimensions through the analogy of a boat ride: Inclusion concerns who you would like to take a boat ride with; Control has to do with who is operating the engine and rudder; and Affection has to do with close relationships that may develop between individuals on the boat.

In more formal terms, the *Inclusion* scores reflect behavior of "moving toward" or "moving away from" people. Some might call this "extroversion" or "introversion." In some ways, this scale is a reflection of a person's general social orientation. The *Control* scores reflect the degree to which people perceive themselves assuming responsibility, making decisions, or dominating others; in some ways, it is a reflection of leadership behavior. The *Affection* scores indicate the degree to which people see themselves becoming emotionally involved with others, a tendency toward deep rather than superficial relationships.

For each of these three dimenions, FIRO-B produces two scores, one an indication of *expression* and one of *want*. Thus, in looking at one's own scores, one can consider six elements of one's interpersonal behavior:

expressed Inclusion (eI),	wanted Inclusion (wI),
expressed Control (eC),	wanted Control (wC),
expressed Affection (eA),	wanted Affection (wA).

Expressed scores reflect what we think we do with others in relationships with them. Wanted scores reflect what we want from others in relationship. Expressed scores are reflections of outward-bound behaviors, while wanted scores are reflections of desired incoming behaviors. Exhibit 1 presents some simple statements that summarize the dominant perspective of each of these six basic FIRO-B categories.

Interpreting Your FIRO-B

A good first step in interpreting your FIRO-B scores is to understand the magnitude of the scores. Each of these six scores may range from zero to nine. The higher your score, the more you indicated that you believe that the statements in Exhibit 1 reflect your behavior. You can think of the strength of your scores as ranging from extremely weak to extremely high as indicated below:

0-1	extremely low, compulsive
2-3	low, noticeably characteristic
4-5	borderline, may be a tendency
6-7	high, noticeably characteristic
8-9	extremely high, compulsive

As you compare the strength of your scores with their verbal indications above, you might ask yourself with each one how that particular tendency might affect your ability to work with individuals in your organization.

Next, we can compare the Expressed and Wanted scores on each of the three basic dimensions. If your scores are similar, you might conclude tentatively that you tend to give as much or as little as you expect. If the scores are divergent, you might conclude that you tend either to give more than you expect or that you want more than you give on that particular dimension. For example, a high wI (wanted Inclusion) score coupled with a low eI (expressed Inclusion) score would indicate someone who wants to be involved in social activities but who does not express this desire to others. This person may be perceived as being distant, aloof, or not interested, while in reality the person may be feeling resentful for having been left out. Wide differences in scores can lead to conflict and frustration in relationships. Again, thinking about what your particular pattern might mean for you in your organizational relationships, dealing with superiors, peers, and subordinates, is where the real benefit of this exercise comes.

The third step in interpretation is analyzing how your orientations in the three areas may help or hinder each other. For example, a person with a high wA (wanted Affection) score wants to establish close personal relationships and may be able to do this, given the opportunity. If he/she also has a low eI (expressed Inclusion) score, he/she may not be engag-

Exhibit 1

Scoring and Interpreting FIRO-B
FIRO-B Scoring Categories

Expressed Inclusion (eI)	*Expressed Control (eC)*	*Expressed Affection (eA)*
I make efforts to include other people in activities and to get them to include me in theirs. I try to belong, to join social groups, to be with people as much as possible.	I try to exert control and influence other things. I take charge of things and tell other people what to do.	I make efforts to become close to people. I express friendly and affectionate feelings and try to be personal and intimate.
Wanted Inclusion (wI)	*Wanted Control (wC)*	*Wanted Affection (wA)*
I want other people to include me in their activities and to invite me to belong even if I do not make an effort to be included.	I want others to control and influence me. I want other people to tell me what to do.	I want others to express friendly and affectionate feelings toward me and to try to become close to them.

ing in enough social contacts to meet people with whom he/she can become close.

A sample interpretation of a set of FIRO-B scores for you to consider follows. See if you can make the connections between the individual's scores and the comments made by the interpreter.

An Example of FIRO-B Interpretation

Jack, an executive, age 42:

	I	C	A
e	3	8	1
w	1	1	0

INCLUSION: Jack is somewhat uncomfortable around people and will tend to move away from them. He is very selective about the associates he chooses, and tends to have an "I'll call you, don't call me" attitude. He is neither a "joiner" nor a meeting lover. He prefers autonomy for himself and his subordinates.

CONTROL: Jack can and does take on the responsibilities of leadership. His self-concept is one of confidence and adequacy, so much so that he may walk into areas where most angels fear to tread. He has a strong need for recognition and is driven to do well. He may be overcompensating for some real or imagined inferiority by compulsively taking on large amounts of responsibility to gain the recognition he desires. Since he avoids anxiety by maintaining superiority, he's attracted to others who give him the recognition he needs and also to those who do not desire to control him or try to make decisions for him.

AFFECTION: Jack is very cautious about the development of close, intimate relationships and is very selective about those with whom he forms these deep relationships. Low scores here don't mean he cannot form such close, personal relationships, but that it is unusual for him to do so. Thus, close relationships are few and far between, developed only after he develops trust for the person over time. The reason for this may stem from being deeply hurt at some time in the past.

He is most comfortable when other people do not attempt to become emotionally involved with him, even to the extent of being suspicious of affection shown him. He's reserved about his inner feelings, and exhibits little warmth or consideration for others' feelings. He may, because of this, seem much more critical than complimentary while he is merely exercising objectivity in interpersonal issues.

GENERAL: As mentioned above, in managerial roles Jack prefers autonomy for himself and his subordinates. His strong desire for recognition may, however, cause him to drive his "troops" unduly in order to achieve. Coupled with his low scores in the affection area this might indicate that he comes across as cold and domineering.

An Exercise in Interpreting FIRO-B

Here are some FIRO-B scores reported by individuals. Examine them carefully and draw what careful, tentative inferences you can about them. Be sure to note carefully the exact data that you use to draw your implications.

		I	C	A
Lyle				
	e	1	0	2
	w	6	4	9
Joe				
	e	7	6	7
	w	8	8	8
Don				
	e	7	9	2
	w	1	5	5
Alanna				
	e	3	4	2
	w	1	5	5

Steven Taylor's FIRO-B

Steven Taylor's FIRO-B scores were as follows:

	I	C	A
e	5	4	4
w	5	0	8
sum	10	4	12
dif	0	4	4

Carrie Baugh's FIRO-B

Carrie Baugh's FIRO-B scores:

	I	C	A
e	4	1	3
w	4	3	5

NOTES:

1. No score above 5 for any category.
2. Scores range from 1 to 5, with most at 3 or 4.
3. Inclusion expressed and wanted both a 4.
4. Affection wanted a 5, expressed a 3.
5. Possible score ranges from 0 to 9. The higher the score, the more one believes the statement reflects her behavior.
6. Below class average for all categories.

INFERENCES:

Carrie is a person who:

1. In general, has only borderline belief that any of the statements reflect her feelings about Inclusion, Control, or Affection.
2. Perhaps wants more affection than she expresses.
3. Feels comfortable with her degree of Inclusion in groups.

9

Interpersonal Style Inventory

The following test will help you to learn more about your interpersonal style, an important dimension in a social world.

Administration

First, complete the Current Self report form by circling the number that most describes you as you see yourself now on each dimension. Then complete the Desired Self report form by circling the number that most describes you as you would *like* to be.

When you have completed both forms, select five people from among your acquaintances. It is preferable that these people be colleagues at work, or, if you are a student, people who know you reasonably well from class. Do not choose total strangers or more than two or three of your closest friends. The objective is to select a group of people who have interacted with you or observed you frequently, but who are also willing to be very honest with you.

Next, select a person who is willing to collect the data from the five people in your interpersonal sample. This is important to insure a degree of anonymity for your chosen respondents. This person might be one of the five. Give the "data collector" a list of the names of the people you have selected.

Fourth, give each person in your sample a copy of the Acquaintance's Report and ask him or her to circle the number by each dimension that best describes you as you are now. Explain that it will only take five minutes to complete. *Be sure that you have written your name and the name of the data collector at the top of the page.* Ask the person to give (send) the completed form to your data collector. Explain that the data collector will assemble the data and pass it on anonymously to you in a set of five. Or, you may ask your respondents to mail the completed forms to you.

Interpersonal Style Inventory
CURRENT SELF

Circle the number beside each dimension that you feel best describes you as you are now.

	Never		Average		Always
Takes the lead	1	2	3	4	5
Needs support	1	2	3	4	5
Seeks recognition	1	2	3	4	5
Works alone	1	2	3	4	5
Helps others	1	2	3	4	5
Follows the rules	1	2	3	4	5
Listens well	1	2	3	4	5
Is willing to learn	1	2	3	4	5
Trusts others	1	2	3	4	5
Gets defensive if criticized	1	2	3	4	5
Discusses emotions	1	2	3	4	5
Discusses personal things	1	2	3	4	5
Is easy to talk to	1	2	3	4	5
Is docile, self-effacing	1	2	3	4	5
Gives praise	1	2	3	4	5
Is consistent	1	2	3	4	5
Is conceited	1	2	3	4	5
Can adapt to different social settings	1	2	3	4	5
Is competitive	1	2	3	4	5
Makes *own* decisions	1	2	3	4	5
Is calm	1	2	3	4	5
Is mechanical	1	2	3	4	5
Is tolerant of others	1	2	3	4	5
Is patient	1	2	3	4	5
Keeps promises	1	2	3	4	5
Is cheerful	1	2	3	4	5

Interpersonal Style Inventory
DESIRED SELF

Circle the number beside each dimension that you feel best describes you as you would like to be. (Note this is not** necessarily **different from the Current Self answers.)

	Never		Average		Always
Takes the lead	1	2	3	4	5
Needs support	1	2	3	4	5
Seeks recognition	1	2	3	4	5
Works alone	1	2	3	4	5
Helps others	1	2	3	4	5
Follows the rules	1	2	3	4	5
Listens well	1	2	3	4	5
Is willing to learn	1	2	3	4	5
Trusts others	1	2	3	4	5
Gets defensive if criticized	1	2	3	4	5
Discusses emotions	1	2	3	4	5
Discusses personal things	1	2	3	4	5
Is easy to talk to	1	2	3	4	5
Is docile, self-effacing	1	2	3	4	5
Gives praise	1	2	3	4	5
Is consistent	1	2	3	4	5
Is conceited	1	2	3	4	5
Can adapt to different social settings	1	2	3	4	5
Is competitive	1	2	3	4	5
Makes *own* decisions	1	2	3	4	5
Is calm	1	2	3	4	5
Is mechanical	1	2	3	4	5
Is tolerant of others	1	2	3	4	5
Is patient	1	2	3	4	5
Keeps promises	1	2	3	4	5
Is cheerful	1	2	3	4	5

Interpersonal Style Inventory

AQUAINTANCE REPORT 1

This brief exercise is intended to collect some descriptive information on ______________________, an acquaintance of yours. Please CIRCLE the number by each item that you feel best describes this person and then hand (or send) the completed form to ______________________, who has agreed to collect several forms and return them anonymously to your acquaintance. Thank you for your assistance.

	Never		Average		Always
Takes the lead	1	2	3	4	5
Needs support	1	2	3	4	5
Seeks recognition	1	2	3	4	5
Works alone	1	2	3	4	5
Helps others	1	2	3	4	5
Follows the rules	1	2	3	4	5
Listens well	1	2	3	4	5
Is willing to learn	1	2	3	4	5
Trusts others	1	2	3	4	5
Gets defensive if criticized	1	2	3	4	5
Discusses emotions	1	2	3	4	5
Discusses personal things	1	2	3	4	5
Is easy to talk to	1	2	3	4	5
Is docile, self-effacing	1	2	3	4	5
Gives praise	1	2	3	4	5
Is consistent	1	2	3	4	5
Is conceited	1	2	3	4	5
Can adapt to different social settings	1	2	3	4	5
Is competitive	1	2	3	4	5
Makes *own* decisions	1	2	3	4	5
Is calm	1	2	3	4	5
Is mechanical	1	2	3	4	5
Is tolerant of others	1	2	3	4	5
Is patient	1	2	3	4	5
Keeps promises	1	2	3	4	5
Is cheerful	1	2	3	4	5

Interpersonal Style Inventory

ACQUAINTANCE REPORT 2

This brief exercise is intended to collect some descriptive information on ________________________, an acquaintance of yours. Please CIRCLE the number by each item that you feel best describes this person and then hand (or send) the completed form to ________________________, who has agreed to collect several forms and return them anonymously to your acquaintance. Thank you for your assistance.

	Never		Average		Always
Takes the lead	1	2	3	4	5
Needs support	1	2	3	4	5
Seeks recognition	1	2	3	4	5
Works alone	1	2	3	4	5
Helps others	1	2	3	4	5
Follows the rules	1	2	3	4	5
Listens well	1	2	3	4	5
Is willing to learn	1	2	3	4	5
Trusts others	1	2	3	4	5
Gets defensive if criticized	1	2	3	4	5
Discusses emotions	1	2	3	4	5
Discusses personal things	1	2	3	4	5
Is easy to talk to	1	2	3	4	5
Is docile, self-effacing	1	2	3	4	5
Gives praise	1	2	3	4	5
Is consistent	1	2	3	4	5
Is conceited	1	2	3	4	5
Can adapt to different social settings	1	2	3	4	5
Is competitive	1	2	3	4	5
Makes *own* decisions	1	2	3	4	5
Is calm	1	2	3	4	5
Is mechanical	1	2	3	4	5
Is tolerant of others	1	2	3	4	5
Is patient	1	2	3	4	5
Keeps promises	1	2	3	4	5
Is cheerful	1	2	3	4	5

Interpersonal Style Inventory

ACQUAINTANCE REPORT 3

This brief exercise is intended to collect some descriptive information on __________________________, an acquaintance of yours. Please CIRCLE the number by each item that you feel best describes this person and then hand (or send) the completed form to __________________________, who has agreed to collect several forms and return them anonymously to your acquaintance. Thank you for your assistance.

	Never		Average		Always
Takes the lead	1	2	3	4	5
Needs support	1	2	3	4	5
Seeks recognition	1	2	3	4	5
Works alone	1	2	3	4	5
Helps others	1	2	3	4	5
Follows the rules	1	2	3	4	5
Listens well	1	2	3	4	5
Is willing to learn	1	2	3	4	5
Trusts others	1	2	3	4	5
Gets defensive if criticized	1	2	3	4	5
Discusses emotions	1	2	3	4	5
Discusses personal things	1	2	3	4	5
Is easy to talk to	1	2	3	4	5
Is docile, self-effacing	1	2	3	4	5
Gives praise	1	2	3	4	5
Is consistent	1	2	3	4	5
Is conceited	1	2	3	4	5
Can adapt to different social settings	1	2	3	4	5
Is competitive	1	2	3	4	5
Makes *own* decisions	1	2	3	4	5
Is calm	1	2	3	4	5
Is mechanical	1	2	3	4	5
Is tolerant of others	1	2	3	4	5
Is patient	1	2	3	4	5
Keeps promises	1	2	3	4	5
Is cheerful	1	2	3	4	5

Interpersonal Style Inventory

ACQUAINTANCE REPORT 4

This brief exercise is intended to collect some descriptive information on ______________________, an acquaintance of yours. Please CIRCLE the number by each item that you feel best describes this person and then hand (or send) the completed form to ______________________, who has agreed to collect several forms and return them anonymously to your acquaintance. Thank you for your assistance.

	Never		Average		Always
Takes the lead	1	2	3	4	5
Needs support	1	2	3	4	5
Seeks recognition	1	2	3	4	5
Works alone	1	2	3	4	5
Helps others	1	2	3	4	5
Follows the rules	1	2	3	4	5
Listens well	1	2	3	4	5
Is willing to learn	1	2	3	4	5
Trusts others	1	2	3	4	5
Gets defensive if criticized	1	2	3	4	5
Discusses emotions	1	2	3	4	5
Discusses personal things	1	2	3	4	5
Is easy to talk to	1	2	3	4	5
Is docile, self-effacing	1	2	3	4	5
Gives praise	1	2	3	4	5
Is consistent	1	2	3	4	5
Is conceited	1	2	3	4	5
Can adapt to different social settings	1	2	3	4	5
Is competitive	1	2	3	4	5
Makes *own* decisions	1	2	3	4	5
Is calm	1	2	3	4	5
Is mechanical	1	2	3	4	5
Is tolerant of others	1	2	3	4	5
Is patient	1	2	3	4	5
Keeps promises	1	2	3	4	5
Is cheerful	1	2	3	4	5

Interpersonal Style Inventory
ACQUAINTANCE REPORT 5

This brief exercise is intended to collect some descriptive information on ______________________, an acquaintance of yours. Please CIRCLE the number by each item that you feel best describes this person and then hand (or send) the completed form to ______________________, who has agreed to collect several forms and return them anonymously to your acquaintance. Thank you for your assistance.

	Never		Average		Always
Takes the lead	1	2	3	4	5
Needs support	1	2	3	4	5
Seeks recognition	1	2	3	4	5
Works alone	1	2	3	4	5
Helps others	1	2	3	4	5
Follows the rules	1	2	3	4	5
Listens well	1	2	3	4	5
Is willing to learn	1	2	3	4	5
Trusts others	1	2	3	4	5
Gets defensive if criticized	1	2	3	4	5
Discusses emotions	1	2	3	4	5
Discusses personal things	1	2	3	4	5
Is easy to talk to	1	2	3	4	5
Is docile, self-effacing	1	2	3	4	5
Gives praise	1	2	3	4	5
Is consistent	1	2	3	4	5
Is conceited	1	2	3	4	5
Can adapt to different social settings	1	2	3	4	5
Is competitive	1	2	3	4	5
Makes *own* decisions	1	2	3	4	5
Is calm	1	2	3	4	5
Is mechanical	1	2	3	4	5
Is tolerant of others	1	2	3	4	5
Is patient	1	2	3	4	5
Keeps promises	1	2	3	4	5
Is cheerful	1	2	3	4	5

Scoring and Interpreting the Interpersonal Style Inventory

Do Not Read This Until You Have Completed the Interpersonal Style Inventory.

Scoring

When the data collector has accumulated all five reports and given them to you, take a few minutes to write your reactions to this exercise in your Feelings Record. How did you feel about asking acquaintances for feedback? What about asking a friend to collect the data? How do you feel, having collected the data but not yet analyzed it? Any other thoughts or feelings?

Now, transfer the data to the Interpersonal Style Inventory Scoring Form. Sum the scores for each dimension and find the simple average (mean) and standard deviation for each dimension.

Then, plot your Current Self, Desired Self, and Acquaintances' Report scores on the Interpersonal Style Inventory Profile. Draw lines to connect each score sequentially, using a red line for your Current Self, a blue line for your Desired Self, and a black line for the Acquaintances' Report.

Interpretation

The interpretation of the interpersonal style inventory consists of a series of comparisons among the three profiles you have plotted. Look first at the differentials or gaps between your Current Self profile and the Acquaintances' Report. Where are the largest gaps? Which is most accurate? Where are the

INTERPERSONAL STYLE INVENTORY SCORING FORM

ITEM	ACQUAINTANCE					SUM	MEAN	S.D.
	1	2	3	4	5			
Takes lead								
Needs support								
Seeks recognition								
Works alone								
Helps others								
Follows rules								
Listens well								
Willing to learn								
Trusts others								
Defensive								
Emotional								
Discusses personal								
Easy to talk to								
Docile								
Praises								
Is consistent								
Is conceited								
Adapts								
Competitive								
Own decisions								
Calm								
Mechanical								
Tolerant								
Patient								
Keeps promises								
Cheerful								

INTERPERSONAL STYLE INVENTORY PROFILES

Note that the sequence of items has changed. Transcribe the plots carefully!

—X—X = Current Self, ——— = Desired Self, – – – – = Acquaintances' Report

ITEM	ACQ. S.D.	Never 1	2	Average 3	4	Always 5
Takes lead		•	•	•	•	•
Seeks recognition		•	•	•	•	•
Is conceited		•	•	•	•	•
Is competitive		•	•	•	•	•
Defensive		•	•	•	•	•
Works alone		•	•	•	•	•
Own decisions		•	•	•	•	•
Mechanical		•	•	•	•	•
Consistent		•	•	•	•	•
Keeps promises		•	•	•	•	•
Praises		•	•	•	•	•
Cheerful		•	•	•	•	•
Calm		•	•	•	•	•
Patient		•	•	•	•	•
Listens well		•	•	•	•	•
Easy to talk to		•	•	•	•	•
Tolerant		•	•	•	•	•
Helps others		•	•	•	•	•
Trusts others		•	•	•	•	•
Follows rules		•	•	•	•	•
Willing to learn		•	•	•	•	•
Docile		•	•	•	•	•
Needs support		•	•	•	•	•
Discusses emotions		•	•	•	•	•
Discusses personal		•	•	•	•	•
Adapts		•	•	•	•	•

smallest ones? On which dimensions did you describe yourself as being higher than your acquaintances did? On which ones lower? What do these results tell you about your interpersonal style? Write down your answers.

Then, compare your Desired Self profile with the other two profiles. Again, note the largest and smallest gaps and whether the Desired Self was higher or lower than the other profiles. What do these results tell you about growth? Write your answers.

Now look at the standard deviations of the Acquaintances' Report. Note which ones are high and which ones are low. What does this tell you about the consistency of your interpersonal style? (Remember that others do not see us perfectly accurately.)

Next, look down the list of dimensions on the profile sheet. Do the dimensions seem to be clustered in any way? Are your scores consistent for each cluster? What does this tell you about yourself?

Finally, list the ten or so clearest findings from this exercise. These should be written down in the form of descriptive statements about yourself. You might begin each inference with "I am a person who __________."

Practicing Drawing Inferences

Look at Steven Taylor's and Carrie Baugh's ISI profiles (pages 101 and 103). What inferences can you draw about them? What inferences can you draw about the kind of work they should seek?

For Couples

The ISI is an instrument that obviously can be of help to people who are working through the self-assessment exercise together. You might, for instance, discuss the differences in your profiles, in the gaps you observe, and in how other people see each of you. Then note how these observations might affect your relationship and the relationship between your relationship and the world of work.

Feelings Record: Interpersonal Style Inventory

Inferences from the Interpersonal Style Inventory

This is a person who	*Data*

STEVEN TAYLOR'S INTERPERSONAL STYLE INVENTORY

INTERPERSONAL STYLE INVENTORY SCORING FORM

Item	*Acquaintance*					*Sum*	*Mean*	*Std. Dev.*
	1	*2*	*3*	*4*	*5*			
Takes Lead	4	4	5	4	5	22	4.4	0.55
Needs support	2	2	2	2	3	11	2.2	0.45
Seeks recognition	5	4	5	3	4	21	4.2	0.84
Works alone	3	2	4	3	3	15	3.0	0.71
Helps others	3	4	3	7	4	21	3.6	1.64
Follows rules	2	3	2	4	2	13	2.6	0.89
Listens well	3	3	2	3	4	15	3.0	0.71
Willing to learn	4	4	2	5	4	19	3.8	1.10
Trusts others	3	4	3	4	3	17	3.4	0.55
Defensive	3	4	3	2	3	15	3.0	0.71
Emotional	2	3	3	1	4	13	2.6	1.14
Discusses personal	2	4	3	2	5	16	3.2	1.30
Easy to talk to	4	5	1	4	5	19	3.8	1.64
Docile	2	2	2	3	1	10	2.0	0.71
Praises	3	4	2	3	3	15	3.0	0.71
Is consistent	4	4	4	4	4	20	4.0	0.00
Is conceited	4	4	4	2	4	18	3.6	0.89
Adapts	5	5	4	5	5	24	4.8	0.45
Competitive	5	4	5	4	5	23	4.6	0.55
Own decisions	5	5	4	4	5	23	4.6	0.55
Calm	3	4	5	4	4	20	4.0	0.71
Mechanical	2	2	2	3	2	11	2.2	0.45
Tolerant	3	2	3	5	4	17	3.4	1.14
Patient	3	2	3	4	3	15	3.0	0.71
Keeps promises	5	5	4	4	5	23	4.6	0.55
Cheerful	4	5	4	4	4	21	4.2	0.45

Steven Taylor's ISI (continued)

Note that the sequence of items has changed. Transcribe the plots carefully!

o— —o = Current Self, x——x = Desired Self, •- - - -• = Acquaintances' Report

ITEM	ACQ. S.D.
Takes lead	0.55
Seeks recognition	0.84
Is conceited	0.89
Is competitive	0.55
Defensive	0.71
Works alone	0.71
Own decisions	0.55
Mechanical	0.45
Consistent	0.00
Keeps promises	0.55
Praises	0.71
Cheerful	0.45
Calm	0.71
Patient	0.71
Listens well	0.71
Easy to talk to	1.64
Tolerant	1.14
Helps others	1.64
Trusts others	0.55
Follows rules	0.89
Willing to learn	1.10
Docile	0.71
Needs support	0.45
Discusses emotions	1.14
Discusses personal	1.30
Adapts	0.45

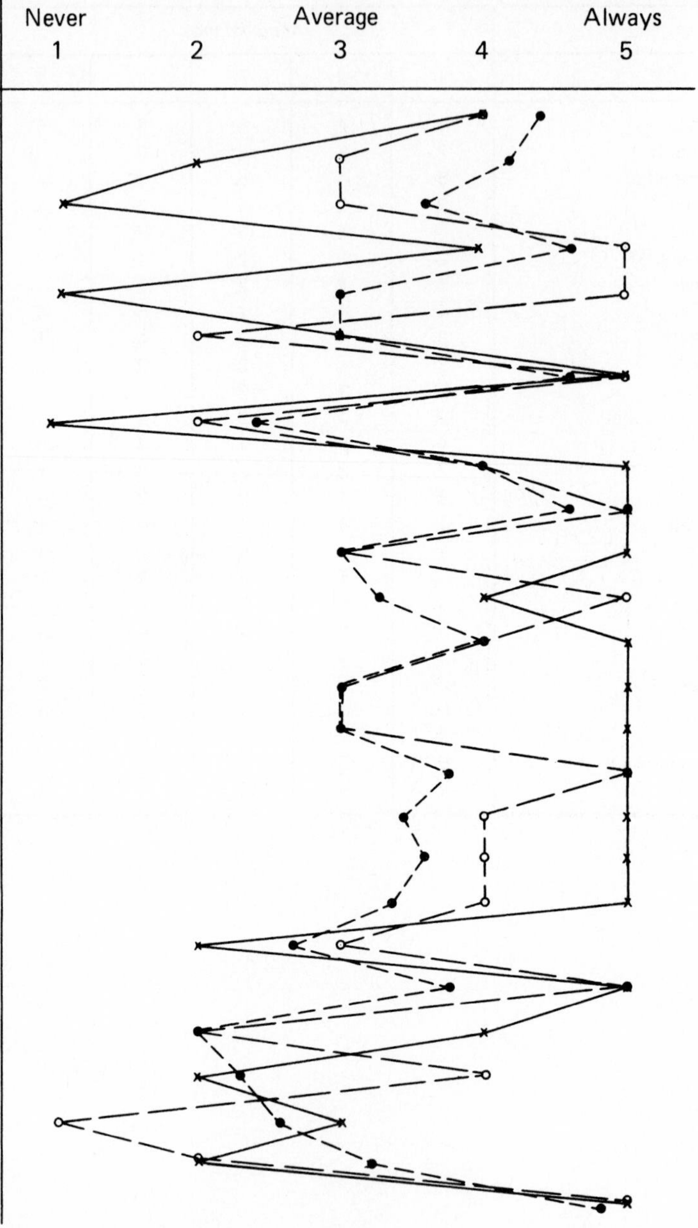

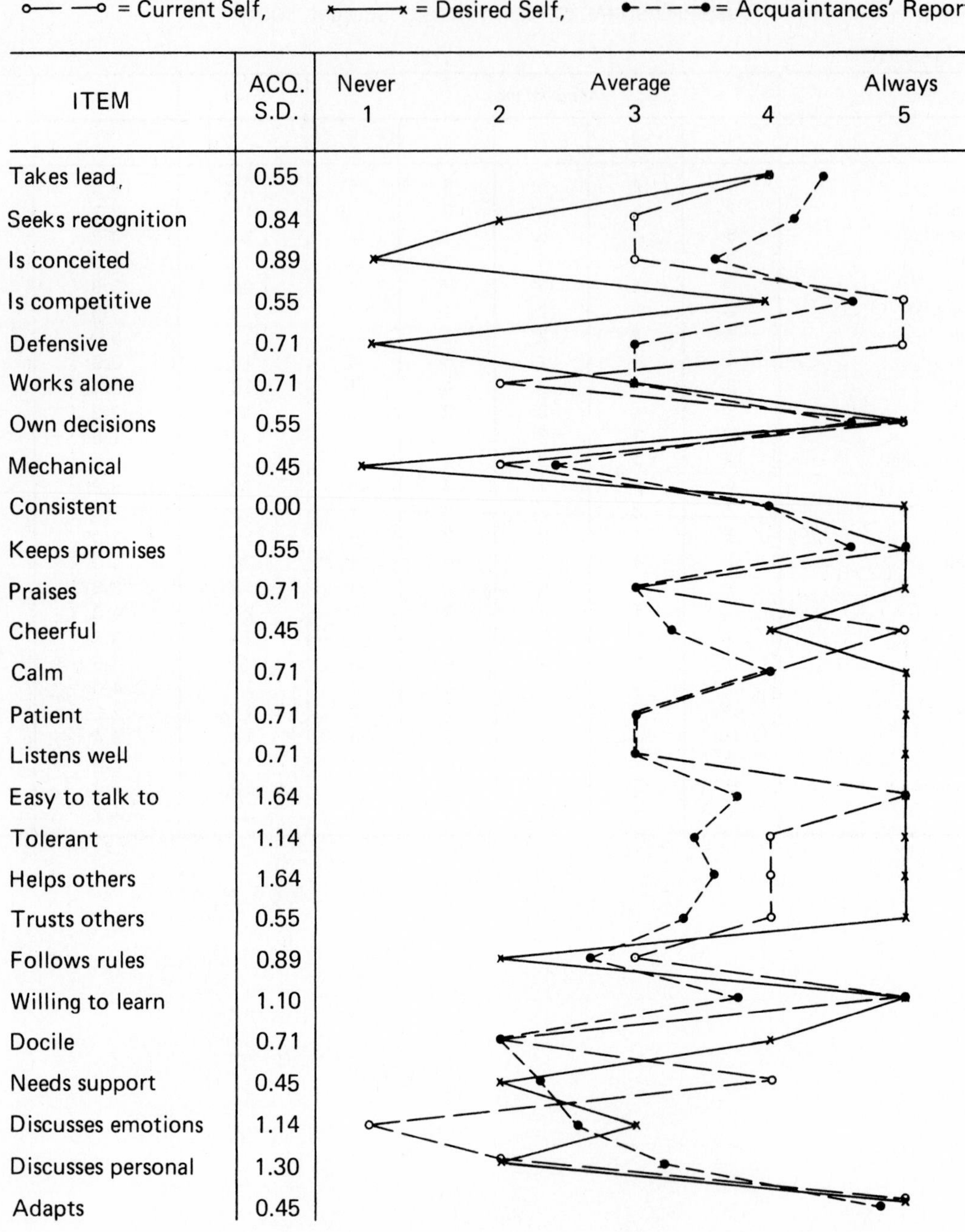

CARRIE BAUGH'S INTERPERSONAL STYLE INVENTORY

INTERPERSONAL STYLE INVENTORY SCORING FORM

Item	*Acquaintance*					*Sum*	*Mean*	*Std. Dev.*
	1	*2*	*3*	*4*	*5*			
Takes Lead	4	4	4	4	4	20	4.0	0.00
Needs support	2	2	2	5	3	14	2.8	1.30
Seeks recognition	3	1	2	5	4	15	3.0	1.60
Works alone	4	4	3	3	4	18	3.6	0.55
Helps others	5	5	4	5	5	24	4.8	0.44
Follows rules	4	5	3	3	3	18	3.6	0.89
Listens well	4	5	3	5	4	21	4.2	0.84
Is willing to learn	4	5	5	5	5	24	4.8	0.45
Trust others	3	4	4	4	3	18	3.6	0.55
Is defensive	2	2	2	2	2	10	2.0	0.00
Is emotional	4	4	3	4	4	19	3.8	0.45
Discusses personal	4	4	3	2	4	17	3.4	0.90
Is easy to talk to	5	5	4	5	5	24	4.8	0.45
Is docile	3	2	1	1	2	9	1.8	0.84
Praises	5	5	5	5	4	24	4.8	0.45
Is consistent	4	5	5	4	4	22	4.4	0.55
Is conceited	1	1	1	1	1	5	1.0	0.00
Adapts	4	4	4	5	4	21	4.2	0.45
Is competitive	5	5	3	4	4	21	4.2	0.84
Makes own decisions	3	5	4	5	5	22	4.4	0.89
Is calm	4	4	3	3	3	17	3.4	0.55
Is mechanical	2	2	4	2	3	13	2.6	0.89
Is tolerant	4	5	4	4	4	21	4.2	0.45
Is patient	4	5	4	3	4	20	4.0	0.71
Keeps promises	4	5	4	4	3	20	4.0	0.71
Is cheerful	5	5	4	5	5	24	4.8	0.45

Carrie Baugh's ISI (continued)

Note that the sequence of items has changed. Transcribe the plots carefully!

o— —o = Current Self, x——x = Desired Self, •- - - -• = Acquaintances' Report

ITEM	ACQ. S.D.	Never 1	2	Average 3	4	Always 5
Takes lead	0 4.0					
Seeks recognition	1.6 3.0					
Is conceited	0 1.0					
Is competitive	.84 4.2					
Defensive	0 2.0					
Works alone	.55 3.6					
Own decisions	.89 4.4					
Mechanical	.89 2.6					
Consistent	.55 4.4					
Keeps promises	.71 4.0					
Praises	.45 4.8					
Cheerful	.45 4.8					
Calm	.55 3.4					
Patient	.71 4.0					
Listens well	.84 4.2					
Easy to talk to	.45 4.8					
Tolerant	.45 4.2					
Helps others	.44 4.8					
Trusts others	.55 3.6					
Follows rules	.89 3.6					
Willing to learn	.45 4.8					
Docile	.84 1.8					
Needs support	1.3 2.8					
Discusses emotions	.45 3.8					
Discusses personal	0.9 3.4					
Adapts	.45 4.2					

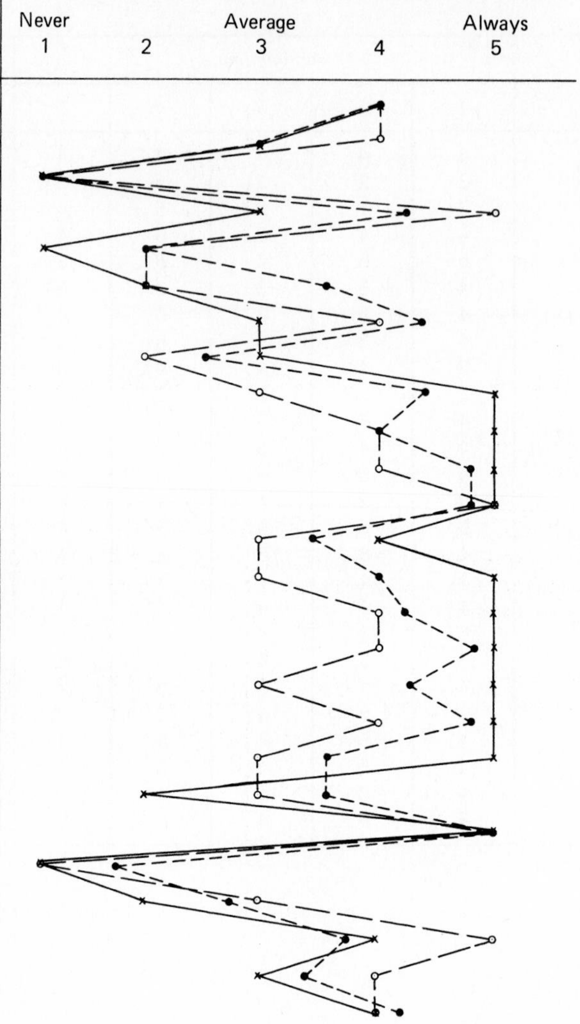

NOTES:

1. Current self, desired self, and acquaintances' reports show 1 or 2 for conceited, defensive, and docile. (1 is never)
2. Current self, desired self, and acquaintances' reports show 4 or 5 for: takes lead, praises, cheerful, calm, listens well, easy to talk to, tolerant, trusts others, willing to learn, and adapts. (5 is always)
3. Desired self is different than current self in 19 out of 26 categories. (73% of the time)
4. Acquaintance reports are at or between current self and desired self in 20 out of 26 categories. (77% of the time)

INFERENCES:

Carrie is a person who:

1. Is rarely conceited, defensive, or dociie.
2. Interacts well with people.
3. Is viewed as friendly and people-oriented.
4. Wants to improve herself.
5. Might strive for "perfection".
6. Might be too self-critical.
7. Might see life as an evolution of becoming a "better" person. (Self-improvement?)
8. Takes the lead in a variety of situations.

10

The Predisposition Test*

Next we will explore psychological predispositions. We feel this is important, because our psychological tendencies shape our behavior, especially in the workplace. Again, remember that there is no right or wrong answer. The best answer is the one that most accurately describes the way you are, not the way you want to be or the way you think you should be.

Follow the instructions carefully. When you have completed the test, as before, we will outline the dimensions measured in this exercise and explain how to record and interpret your scores.

For each of the statements below, please draw an "X" through:

DA if you *definitely agree* with the statement,
IA if you are *inclined to agree* with the statement,
ID if you are *inclined to disagree* with the statement,
DD if you *definitely disagree* with the statement.

*J. W. Lorsch and J. J. Morse, *Organizations and Their Members: A Contingency Approach* (New York: Harper & Row, 1974). Material reprinted by permission.

1. If a person is satisfied with the kind of job he has done, he shouldn't get upset if colleagues criticize it.	DA	IA	ID	DD
2. The most interesting life is to live under rapidly changing conditions.	DA	IA	ID	DD
3. One often has to be told what to do in order to do a good job.	DA	IA	ID	DD
4. It's satisfying to know pretty much what is going to happen on the job from day to day.	DA	IA	ID	DD
5. Off with the old, on with the new, even though a person rarely knows what the "new" will be.	DA	IA	ID	DD
6. One should never go with a group if the crowd means little to one.	DA	IA	ID	DD
7. Doing the same things in the same places for long periods of time makes for a happy life.	DA	IA	ID	DD
8. A person gets more satisfaction out of reading an enjoyable book than from talking to friends about their vacations.	DA	IA	ID	DD
9. Adventurous and exploratory people go farther in this world than do systematic and orderly people.	DA	IA	ID	DD
10. When planning a vacation, a person should have a schedule to follow if he's really going to enjoy himself.	DA	IA	ID	DD
11. The best work is done with some close supervision.	DA	IA	ID	DD
12. Others' thoughts of one's actions are of great importance.	DA	IA	ID	DD
13. It's better to walk along a beach alone than to sit on a beach blanket with friends.	DA	IA	ID	DD
14. Even if a man loves a girl, he ought not to marry her if his friends don't approve of her.	DA	IA	ID	DD
15. One should welcome suggestions, but resent even reasonable orders.	DA	IA	ID	DD
16. Even children know they must decide their actions; their fathers and mothers do not know best.	DA	IA	ID	DD
17. The least possible governmental and social controls are best for all.	DA	IA	ID	DD
18. A really satisfying life is a life of problems. When one is solved, one moves on to the next problem.	DA	IA	ID	DD
19. Schools which force conformity stifle creativity.	DA	IA	ID	DD
20. Teachers who force students to use prescribed methods of study make it difficult for them to learn.	DA	IA	ID	DD
21. A person usually can get a job done faster and better by working alone than with a group.	DA	IA	ID	DD

Scoring and Interpreting the Predisposition Test[1]

Introduction

Jobs have a variety of dimensions, many of which will have an effect on how much at home you feel in your work and perhaps on how well you perform. Three such dimensions are the amount of uncertainty or change, the degree of supervision, and the amount of required interaction with others. These were the underlying beliefs of a study conducted in the early 1970s by Professors Jay Lorsch and John Morse of the Harvard Business School. They wanted to understand the impact of the fit between individual characteristics and job characteristics on the effectiveness of companies.

This study represented an extension of contingency theory from its former focus on the organization–environment interface (see *Organization and Environment* by Paul Lawrence and Jay Lorsch, [Homewood, Illinois: Irving, 1969]) to include the organization-individual interface. Contingency theory, of course, is the set of ideas surrounding the notion that there is no one best way to organize, rather that the most effective organizational form depends on a variety of factors and constraints. The Lorsch-Morse study suggested that there is no one best individual employee profile, but that individual effectiveness in a job depends on the fit between an individual's characteristics and the demands made of him or her by the job.

[1]Much of this material is based on J. W. Lorsch and J. J. Morse, *Organizations and Their Members: A Contingency Approach* (New York: Harper & Row, 1974). It was prepared by Mark P. Kriger, research assistant, and revised by Ellen Porter Honnet, research assistant, under the direction of Assistant Professor James G. Clawson, as the basis for class discussion. Harvard Business School case 1-480-017.

The Development and Scoring of the Predisposition Test

As part of this study, the researchers designed a questionnaire that measures personality predispositions along three dimensions:

1. Tolerance for ambiguity
2. Preference for autonomy
3. Predisposition toward solitude in a work situation

All three dimensions are what psychologists call *personality predispositions*—that is, they are tendencies for you to think and act in certain ways that arise from your own particular personality development. For example, if your parents encouraged you as a child to make your own decisions rather than to look to them for the final say in all matters, then you may be predisposed to solving problems on your own and might prefer to work in jobs with less, rather than more, supervision. Likewise, if you were raised an only child or in such a way that you spent a good deal of your time alone, you may be predisposed to working alone more than with others. Or the opposite effect could occur, and you may prefer to be surrounded by people constantly.

There are a variety of personality predispositions which Lorsch and Morse could have explored. These three (along with one or two others), however, seemed to offer the best way to demonstrate their thesis that organization (job)–individual fit did affect effectiveness. The next problem, the most common one in social science research, was how to measure these dimensions in individuals and in jobs.

Lorsch and Morse collected a number of statements they believed described values or behaviors relating to these personality predispositions from a variety of generally accepted personality inventories. To these they added a number of statements of their own invention. They then distilled the number of statements down to twenty-one by means of factor analysis. Each of these twenty-one statements represented one of the three dispositions (a "positive" statement) or its opposite (a "negative" statement). Respondents would mark the degree of their agreement or disagreement with each statement, and then the researchers, knowing which statements were "positive" and which were "negative", could add up the respondents' scores on each dimension. The positive statements were scored as follows:

DA Definitely Agree	*IA Inclined to Agree*	*ID Inclined to Disagree*	*DD Definitely Disagree*
4	3	2	1

They reflect one's agreement with the statement. Negative statements were scored this way:

DA	*IA*	*ID*	*DD*
1	2	3	4

These reflect one's disagreement with the statement. For example, one item in the questionnaire is, "The most interesting life is lived under rapidly changing conditions." This is a positively scored statement for tolerance for ambiguity. If you indicated that you definitely agreed with that statement by putting an X through DA, your tolerance for ambiguity score would increase by 4. There are seven statements for each dimension. After each statement has been scored, you can add the seven scores and calculate an average for each dimension. We have developed a scoring sheet that matches the dimensions and scores with the questions and your answers. Once you have identified your numerical score, you can then transcribe it onto the tally sheet under the appropriate dimension.

Interpretation of Scores

The first personality predisposition, tolerance for ambiguity, measures your preference for a more changing set of conditions as opposed to well-defined, stable, and relatively unchanging conditions. The higher your score on this dimension, the greater your tolerance for ambiguity. As you might expect, if you work in an uncertain environment, you will need a greater tolerance for ambiguity on the whole than if you work in a more certain environment. Less defined work and greater uncertainty of information will produce a higher level of ambiguity with which you must cope. Your tolerance for ambiguity will also be related to the speed and quantity of feedback you receive. When feedback is frequent, you will not require as high a tolerance for ambiguity as when feedback takes longer.

The second personality predisposition, preference for autonomy, measures your preferred ways of relating to authority. The higher your score on this dimension, the greater your disposition toward working *without* supervision. Individuals with higher scores probably will prefer to have more direct influence over defining their work roles and providing their own direction and would feel more at home in jobs that do not require subordinate relationships with strong authority figures.

The third personality predisposition, predisposition toward solitude, measures your attitude towards being alone in a work situation. A higher score on this dimension indicates that you prefer to work more individualistically and to be more alone than with others. If you have a preference for being and working alone, you will probably enjoy and be more competent in a job where little interaction with others is required. Alternatively, if you prefer spending time with others, you will prefer a work environment which requires more coordination and communication with others.

The usual way of making relative sense of scores like these is to compare them with the scores of various reference groups. For the present, scores for a wide variety of reference groups do not exist for the predisposition test. Nevertheless, after scoring your responses, you will have personal scores along three interesting and provocative personality dimensions, which you can utilize in two ways.

First, you can compare your results to the two reference groups used in the Lorsch and Morse study for which we do have data: (a) scientists and engineers working in research organizations, and (b) managers and supervisors working in manufacturing organizations. In these two organizations, chosen because they represented extremes of environmental ambiguity, Lorsch and Morse found that the employees in the jobs in the uncertain environment (R&D organizations) tended to score higher on all three dimensions than the employees working in the more certain environment (manufacturing). (See Exhibit 10–1.) If your scores for the three dimensions are closer to the scores in a more uncertain environment, such as an R&D laboratory, a consulting firm, or marketing company, you might conclude that you would feel constrained in a more structured industry, such as durable goods manufacturing. If your scores are mixed—that is, one or two of them high and the remaining score or scores low—you should consider each dimension first individually and then in combination with the other two scores.

The implications one could draw from these scores are fairly straightforward. If, for example, you scored high in tolerance for ambiguity, you *might* prefer working in an uncertain environment, but not necessarily. Your score indicates that you are tolerant of ambiguity, not that it is essential to you. If, however, you scored high on both the tolerance for ambiguity and the preference for autonomy scales, the implication might be that you *would* prefer working in an environment which is both uncertain and unsupervised. Finally, if your solitude score were low, you would probably conclude that you would feel most at home in a job in which you could work together with others in a collegial, rather than a hierarchical, way, on unusual and varied tasks with uncertain results.

Exhibit 10–1
A Note on the Predisposition Test

Personality Dimensions of Members in Research and Manufacturing Environments: Overall Means for Combined High- and Low-Performing Sites

	Research Organization	*Manufacturing Organization*
Tolerance for ambiguity	2.91	2.57
Preference for autonomy	2.83	2.17
Predisposition toward solitude	2.96	2.40

J. W. Lorsch and J. J. Morse, *Organizations and Their Members: A Contingency Approach* (New York: Harper & Row, 1974), pp. 53, 55.

Your score on the autonomy scale has implications not only for the kind of organization and the job you may want to work in, but also for the kind of person who should be your supervisor. While it is not wise to judge a whole potential career on the merits of one's first supervisor, that relationship has been shown to significantly affect young managers' success. (See *Formative Years in Business: A Long-Term AT&T Study of Managerial Lives*, by Douglas Bray et al., [New York; 1974 Wiley].) Your preference for autonomy or attitude toward authority may suggest some implications about the kind of supervisory relationship that would be most effective for you and your career development in the early years.

These comments on the implications of your scores are intentionally vague. Taken alone, these scores are not accurate enough or descriptive enough to provide the basis for a job decision. When they add to and confirm trends or patterns that run through other bits of data, these scores can help to crystallize important personal characteristics.

The second way you can use your results is to compare them to the mean scores of business school students. By analyzing your scores in relation to those of others, you can gain a further indication of the direction and strength of your own personality predispositions for these three dimensions (see Exhibit 10–2).

Exhibit 10–2
A Note on the Predisposition Test

Personality Dimension of HBS Students*

Dimension	*Your Score*	*Overall*	*Men*	*Women*	*Married*	*Single*	*USA*	*Foreign*	*Age 20-25*	*Age 26-30*	*Age 31-40*
Tolerance for ambiguity		2.84	2.82	2.86	2.77	2.87	2.82	2.91	2.86	2.80	2.84
Preference for autonomy		2.61	2.58	2.66	2.61	2.61	2.59	2.70	2.58	2.62	2.64
Predisposition toward solitude		2.62	2.60	2.64	2.65	2.61	2.59	2.78	2.60	2.58	2.71
(Number of students in group)	(1)	(120)	(75)	(43)	(40)	(79)	(102)	(17)	(51)	(42)	(26)

*This information has been taken from the average test scores of the 1978 Self-Assessment and Career Development class at the Harvard Business School.

Summary

An individual's predispositions can have a great effect on that person's sense of competence and work-derived satisfaction. While there are many predispositions in one's personality, three useful ones are tolerance for ambiguity, preference for autonomy, and preference for solitude. Although the measurement of these predispositions is imprecise, the results from the predisposition test can add to your pool of personal data and can suggest, both singly and in combination with each other, some implications for the kind of organization and job in which you would like to work and would feel most at home.

Predisposition Test Scoring Instructions

1. Tear out scoring sheet on page 111.
2. Cut or fold margins on page 111.
3. Place scoring sheet over the test on page 106.
4. Write the scores corresponding to the letters you circled on the tally sheet, page 110, under the column matching the dimension of each question.
5. Sum the scores for each dimension.
6. Divide your total scores by seven to get your average score.

Assignment

Once you have scored your Predisposition Test, turn to page 112 and read Steven's and Carrie's scores. What inferences do you draw about them from these data?

Predisposition Test Tally Sheet

	Tolerance for Ambiguity (Questions 2, 4, 5, 7, 9, 10, 18)	Preference for Autonomy (Questions 3, 11, 15, 16, 17, 19, 20)	Predisposition toward Solitude (Questions 1, 6, 8, 12, 13, 14, 21)
	______	______	______
	______	______	______
	______	______	______
	______	______	______
	______	______	______
	______	______	______
	______	______	______
Total			
	÷ 7	÷ 7	÷ 7
Average			

Predisposition Test Scoring Sheet

Ques. Number	Dimension	Score DA	IA	ID	DD
1.	Predisposition toward solitude	4	3	2	1
2.	Tolerance for ambiguity	4	3	2	1
3.	Preference for autonomy	1	2	3	4
4.	Tolerance for ambiguity	1	2	3	4
5.	Tolerance for ambiguity	4	3	2	1
6.	Predisposition toward solitude	4	3	2	1
7.	Tolerance for ambiguity	1	2	3	4
8.	Predisposition toward solitude	4	3	2	1
9.	Tolerance for ambiguity	4	3	2	1
10.	Tolerance for ambiguity	1	2	3	4
11.	Preference for autonomy	1	2	3	4
12.	Predisposition toward solitude	1	2	3	4
13.	Predisposition toward solitude	4	3	2	1
14.	Predisposition toward solitude	1	2	3	4
15.	Preference for autonomy	4	3	2	1
16.	Preference for autonomy	4	3	2	1
17.	Preference for autonomy	4	3	2	1
18.	Tolerance for ambiguity	4	3	2	1
19.	Preference for autonomy	4	3	2	1
20.	Preference for autonomy	4	3	2	1
21.	Predisposition toward solitude	4	3	2	1

Steven Taylor's Predisposition Test

	Tolerance for Ambiguity	*Preference for Autonomy*	*Predisposition toward Solitude*
Steven Taylor	3.57	3.40	3.40
Research Organization*	2.91	2.83	2.96
Manufacturing Organization*	2.57	2.17	2.40

*From J. W. Lorsch and J. J. Morse, *Organizations and Their Members: A Contingency Approach* (New York: Harper & Row, 1974). Research and manufacturing data from a working paper, "Personality Dimensions of Members in Research and Manufacturing Environments: Overall Means for Combined High- and Low-Performing Sites," pp. 53, 55.

Carrie Baugh's Predisposition Test

	Tolerance for Ambiguity	*Preference for Autonomy*	*Predisposition toward Solitude*
Carrie Baugh	2.86	3.14	3.00
Research Organization*	2.91	2.83	2.96
Manufacturing Organization*	2.57	2.17	2.40

DATA:

1. Tolerance for ambiguity is average as compared with women (2.86) and age group (2.86), but slightly greater than married people (2.77) or Americans (2.82). Class average: 2.92.
2. Preference for autonomy—3.14, as compared with 2.66 for women and 2.61 overall. Class average: 2.73.
3. Predisposition toward solitude—3.0, compared with 2.64 for women and 2.62 overall. Class average: 2.73.

INFERENCES:

Carrie is a person who:

1. Can work in undefined, changing environments.
2. Prefers to work alone?
3. Values independence.
4. Does not mind being alone or working alone.

*From J. W. Lorsch and J. J. Morse, *Organizations and Their Members: A Contingency Approach* (New York: Harper & Row, 1974). Research and manufacturing data from a working paper, "Personality Dimensions of Members in Research and Manufacturing Environments: Overall Means for Combined High- and Low-Performing Sites," pp. 53, 55.

11

The 24-Hour Diary

Your task in this exercise is to make an accurate record of your activities—what you do. You are to keep a 24-hour diary, a log of your comings and goings and doings, on at least two different days: a weekday and a weekend day. If you would like to monitor more than two days, feel free to do so, but be sure you get at least two days' worth as a minimum.

Do not wait until the end of the 24-hour period to make your diary; make your entries as the day progresses. This will alter your activities a little, but that's okay. You decide how often you will make an entry, but do not wait more than three hours before going back to make your notes.

Make your entries as complete as you can, and fill in the details and events that were significant to you.

When you have completed the diaries, insert them in your notebook and go on to the note on interpretation.

Interpreting The 24-Hour Diary

> NOTE:
> DO NOT READ THIS UNTIL YOU HAVE COMPLETED THE 24-HOUR DIARY ASSESSMENT

As social scientists have discovered over the years, one useful way to learn about a person or a group of people is to obtain information regarding what they actually do on a daily basis. What type of activities do they engage in? How do they allocate their time among job, family, entertainment, sleep, and other activities? With whom do they interact, in what ways, and how often?

Even in situations that are highly structured by others (such as the army), or on the most "atypical" days, the way in which an individual adapts and behaves says something about him or her. Regardless of the setting, we are always faced with choices regarding what to do, how to do it, and when. Patterns in those choices can tell us something about ourselves.

There are a number of different ways one can collect information about an individual's daily activities, but most are not useful for our purposes. An anthropological methodology, for example, in which a second "observer" follows the individual throughout the day, is impractical. Simply asking a person what he or she does on a daily basis is practical, but research has shown it to be not very reliable. People's impressions of what they normally do are often quite inaccurate.

A method we have found to be both feasible and reasonably reliable is to ask an individual to keep a log or diary of his or her activities throughout the day. It is not very difficult or time-consuming to pause every hour or so and to make a few notes regarding what you have been doing. (The entries do not have to be particularly lengthy.) Most people can remember in some detail what they have been doing for the past hour or two. While this method loses the "objectivity" of a second-person observer, it gains an additional type of useful information. One cannot record everything. Consequently, what a person chooses to record and how it is recorded become potentially useful information in itself.

Interpreting a 24-Hour Diary

Taking into account how and why it was created, you can examine a 24-hour diary for patterns and draw inferences from those patterns. For example, some diaries have all their entries recorded at regular intervals (perhaps every 30 minutes); others do not. Sometimes entries are given very specific times (5:47, 8:54, 10:01), sometimes not (10:00, 10:15, 11:40). Some diaries will be full of human interaction. Others will not. A few might describe each person mentioned in the diary in great detail. Some will not mention any names. Some diaries are recorded in short, cryptic phrases; others read like a novel. Some describe an incredibly fast-moving, active person. Others do not. Some describe people who sleep exactly eight hours a night (invariably 11:30 P.M. to 7:30 A.M.). Some describe people who jump from one activity to another, others describe people who concentrate on one thing until the task is completed. And so on.

To help you develop some skill in using 24-hour diaries, we have included two people's diaries. Study each of them carefully. What might those people be like? What kind of work might they like?

By identifying patterns in a diary and drawing careful inferences from those patterns, you can corroborate or contradict themes that have emerged in other sources, as well as identify new themes. All that is needed is some time, patience, and a modicum of skill.

Steven Taylor's 24-Hour Diary

TUESDAY

9:00 a.m. Woke up and ate breakfast.

9:30 a.m. Showered and shaved.

9:45 a.m. Began organizing class notes from this term to date. Reviewed Business Policy (BP) case for write-up (missed class last Friday). Called Sandi to thank her for note she left me this morning. Called garbage company to arrange weekly pickup for new house.

10:05 a.m. Got dressed, back to organizing.

10:30 a.m. Finished organizing the term to come. Made list of things to do today:

- Kinko's—100 resumes, envelopes & letterhead, 100 blanks. Copies of Interpersonal Style Inventory.
- BP write-up.
- Take Mark's keys—pick up clothes.
- Pick up Sponsor's check.
- Buy three-ring dividers.
- Get fellowship info for thank you letter!

10:45 a.m. Began Management of International Business (MIB) case for today's class (4:00 class).

12:10 p.m. Finished MIB prep.

12:20 p.m. Talked with roommate about recruiting strategies.

12:45 p.m. Drove to train station to pick up car and returned to Darden.

1:15 p.m. Lunch at Cafe Death (a local student eatery), read two chapters for Starting New Ventures (read quickly).

2:00 p.m. Usual program of notes for classmates, talked to a faculty member, meeting with staff.

2:25 p.m. Called Mark to arrange key exchange tonight.

2:30 p.m. Starting New Ventures class.

4:05 p.m. Managing International Business class.

6:00 p.m. Dinner with Joe Mason, Venture Capitalist, and Carla Baker, Entrepreneur's club.

8:30 p.m. Left for Mark's house to return keys, pick up clothes.

9:30 p.m. Returned home, played with dog, talked to Sue.

9:55 p.m. Began BP case (again)

11:10 p.m. Knocked off.

7:00 a.m. Woke up, quick breakfast and shower.

7:30 a.m. Back to BP.

9:35 a.m. Finished BP make-up. At last!!

SATURDAY

8:00 a.m. Got up, played with dog, made breakfast—my usual one grapefruit (always), cereal with bananas and milk, toast with jam—read paper while I ate.

8:20 a.m. Sue got up and made coffee; I had some while we talked and played with dog. I hardly ever make coffee for myself, but I'll usually have a bit if someone else makes it up.

8:40 a.m. Shower and a shave and a. . . . Feel great! Sat down to work on written interview about 9:10.

9:10 a.m. Intense six-page session on question #1. Almost finished! How long are the rest of the questions?

11:35 a.m. Daydreamed about 5 minutes: Am I going to work out before I go to D.C. this afternoon? Wondered why I'm inside working on a written interview when I could go for a bike ride. Debated personal priorities for a moment.

11:45 a.m. Back to the grindstone.

12:35 p.m. Andy is making lunch, think I'll have some. Downstairs. . . .

1:30 p.m. Back to work. Wonder what time I should leave house to run errands and make D.C. by 5 p.m. or so.

2:45 p.m. I gotta get outa here. Packed for overnight, headed out. Patted dog on way.

5:15 p.m. Arrived at Sandi's, not bad time! Had a couple beers, watched Olympics, debated plans for evening. We decided to take a nap (wink, wink) before heading out.

9:00 p.m. Struggled out to Chinese dinner. Food was great, but Sandi too tired to go to late show of "A Fish Called Wanda." I still want to see this movie.

11:00 p.m. We took a long walk home through Cleveland Park, checking out a group of old houses on Newark Avenue. They looked like houses at a beach resort, big porches, bright colors. Wondered if this was a place for country houses when Washington was built?

11:45 p.m. Went home and had some Ben and Jerry's before bed (in bed).

7:30 a.m. Woke up briefly, glass of water—back to sleep. . . .

10:30 a.m. Got out of bed—THE END.

Carrie Baugh's 24-Hour Diary

Week Day

9:05 a.m. Last night I had set my alarm for 7:00; I'm trying to keep on a morning schedule as though I have an 8:00 class every day, in order to have a full day to prepare for classes and work on other activities. This morning, I was lazy; I finally got out of bed at 8:00 and took my shower. I spent some time straightening up the apartment (one goal for this year is to keep the place somewhat tidy), doing the dishes, and listening to the news.

I looked at my calendar and noted today's "To Do's"—call Larry for chips for first years, make some calls for Supervised Business Study (SBS) and research at library, finish up Management of International Business case for 2:30, and write thank you cards for late wedding gifts.

11:35 a.m. Just got back from Alderman Library. Might have found some leads regarding the SBS project. I wish I had more time to devote in a single sitting. I couldn't believe I found parking on campus—but it was a 30-minute meter, so I had to keep running outside to put dimes in the meter.

I'm eating a quick breakfast/lunch so I can get to Darden. I'm gonna start tomorrow's cases and get started on a survey for my SBS project . . . assuming I can be really productive before class starts at 2:30.

2:10 a.m. Well, I was fairly productive. I got a rough draft composed on the Macintosh for my SBS survey. I'm not satisfied with the wording, but I think I included all the important concepts I was trying to get across. Hopefully, my partner Susan can help me improve it—she's good at that sort of thing. I tried to read ahead for Business Policy (BP) class, but I ran into too many people! That always happens when I go to Darden to study—so many distractions. But I got half-way through the case.

6:00 p.m. Finally out of class for the day! Whew! The New Ventures discussion was interesting—a guest speaker on venture capital. There is a lot more to that field than I had believed. An interesting, intense line of work. On the way to class, I bumped into Mr. Tuffle, who is also a venture capitalist, who spoke to our class yesterday. He's from Palo Alto, California, so we had some things in common. An interesting person; very bright and personable. He asked about my background, etc. He gets a lot of financial backing from Stanford.

My International Business class, however, was disappointing, as usual. It is so hard to get called on in that class! I swear he looks right at me but calls on someone else. But I don't want to be paranoid about it—it's a very aggressive, full class. I'll wait and see how it goes. I wish the pace of class was not so slow and deliberate. I walked home with Susan and Laura. We talked about the day's events and the upcoming weekend possibilities.

9:12 p.m. Boy, am I sleepy! It's been a long day. Right when I got home, I began cooking a real dinner for myself—raviolis and a salad. Not bad, if I say so myself. I do hate spending the time to cook an entire meal—it just means I stay up later. And I need a full six to seven hours of sleep to stay attentive. But dinner tasted great! Then, to the books! As usual, I first read both cases, then took a twenty-minute nap, then began writing them up. Both cases are interesting. I've already resigned myself that I'll have to do Career Management tomorrow before class. Just too little time.

Mark, my husband, just called. We talked about New York and the case he's working on. He's had some calls from headhunters. I think he's mildly interested. He sounds up tonight. We discussed our plans for the weekend . . . golf times, dinner, stuff like that! I really miss him.

11:45 p.m. Time for bed. I finished up my two cases as best I could. I'll polish them up tomorrow morning. I'm exhausted. Time for bed. I ended up talking with Susan on the phone for half an hour. We also talked about the BPE [Business and the Political Economy] cases and how it relates to our past retailing experience. Well, good night.

Weekend Day

10:50 a.m. Mark and I finally got ourselves out of bed, and took showers. We had fun last night. Getting caught up in what each of us had done the past week. This morning, we lounged around, planning our day and just being silly, as we do every weekend morning.

Our plans for today include golf at around noon, a block of time for me to do some work, visiting with my old study group this evening, and then just being together afterwards. Mark left a few minutes ago to do some errands, which gives me a chance to "wake up" a bit and begin working. We made pancakes for breakfast.

5:20 p.m. Well, Mark and I played sixteen holes of golf; it started pouring about halfway through, and we stuck it out until we were drenched. Bill played with us; it was really enjoyable. I played OK. I'm getting there, slowly. Plus, I only lost one ball. Pretty soon, I think I'll start keeping score. Mark played fairly well; he's never satisfied, of course.

We got back (4:30), I cooked tortellini and made a salad, and we had dinner. Mark cleaned our clubs for us while I made the meal. It was yummy. Now we're getting ready to go to see my old study group—just a little get-together.

9:00 p.m. Mark and I just got back from the study group get-together. It was actually a lot of fun, more than I thought. A fun group. I think Mark had a very good time also. We talked about all sorts of things: weddings, school, golf, and different people's summers.

The guys and girls ended up in different areas of the apartment, talking about the silliest things. I loved it. Mark and I got tired about the same time, so we left. Now, we're watching "Tin Men" on TV and reading.

11:30 p.m. Mark and I are watching the Olympics! AWESOME. We did great in women's platform diving. USA won second and third. The basketball team beat Spain. Unfortunately, the men's gymnastics team is not doing so well.

We called Jen and Paul, our friends in San Francisco, to find out how life is going. They are a lot of fun, and we really enjoy finding out how things are going back home. We haven't seen them since we vacationed together this summer. Mark and Paul discussed their jobs (they work for the same company) and different people at work. I love hearing them talk, since I worked with them before coming to business school.

1:00 a.m. Mark and I are going to bed! We're exhausted! It's been a good, full day.

NOTES:

1. Mentioned goals in 7 out of 11 entries (64%).
2. Scheduled day in morning entry both days.
3. Mentioned two Darden people on weekday entry.
4. Weekend filled with golf, small get-together with old study group, watching movie and the Olympics, and calling San Francisco friends.
5. Described both days as good, and full of activity.
6. Mentioned being exhausted at end of day in both accounts.

INFERENCES:

Carrie is a person who:

1. Finds it useful to plan her day's activities.
2. Likes to set goals to accomplish during the day.
3. Might be achievement oriented.
4. Enjoys weekend sports activities.
5. Likes weekend interaction with people.
6. Focuses on school during the weekday.
7. Enjoys a lot of activity during the day.
8. Exerts a lot of energy during the day.

12

Creating Life Style Representations

One hears a lot of talk about life style these days. People talk of liking or disliking their current life styles, of the merits of various alternative life styles, of how Mary and Tim Jones have changed their life style.

The *American Heritage Dictionary* defines *life style* as "an internally consistent way of life or style of living that reflects the attitudes and values of an individual or a culture." That is, life style is someone's way of life. It is the pattern of how one relates to key parts of external reality; how one uses time; whom one relates to, and how; how one uses or relates to objects and possessions; how one reacts to geography and space generally; what one does. Second, one's life style, insofar as there is choice in its establishment, reflects some of the things inside oneself. It is, in a sense, a mapping out of who one is into what one does, how one does it, and with whom or what.

Life style relates to our present purposes in two ways. First, career- and job-related decisions are a subset of the total life decisions that people make, whether consciously or not. It would certainly make things easier if we could treat job and career decisions independently from other life style decisions, but we really can't—they are interdependent. If one chooses to live in a cabin in Maine, that choice makes the possibility of working as a loan officer in a bank in Los Angeles impractical. If one chooses to work for a consulting firm in a job that takes sixty hours a week, one third of it out of town, one probably cannot spend seven hours a day, every day, with one's spouse and children. If one chooses to be surrounded by expensive art and yet has no independent source of funds, it is probably impractical to seek a job as the executive director of the local community chest.

Second, one's past and current life styles, in that they reflect attitudes and values, can provide us with data. No matter how constrained one is by economics or institutional requirements, one always has some choice about how to adapt to those constraints. And the form or pattern of adaptation says something about the person.

Assignment

The assignment is to produce on paper a representation, nonnarrative in nature, that will reflect your life style as accurately as you can and provide you with data useful for analysis. Your life style representation should include a consideration of your past life style, your current life style, and your desired future life style.

There are a number of alternative ways you might approach this assignment.

Open-Ended Option

This first option is open-ended. You may let your creative side run free in selecting your approach to the assignment. You may choose without restraint the shape or the form of your representation. If you choose this option, feel free to use any media, any

Exhibit 12–1

An Open-Ended Life Style Diagram

(Betsy Drake)

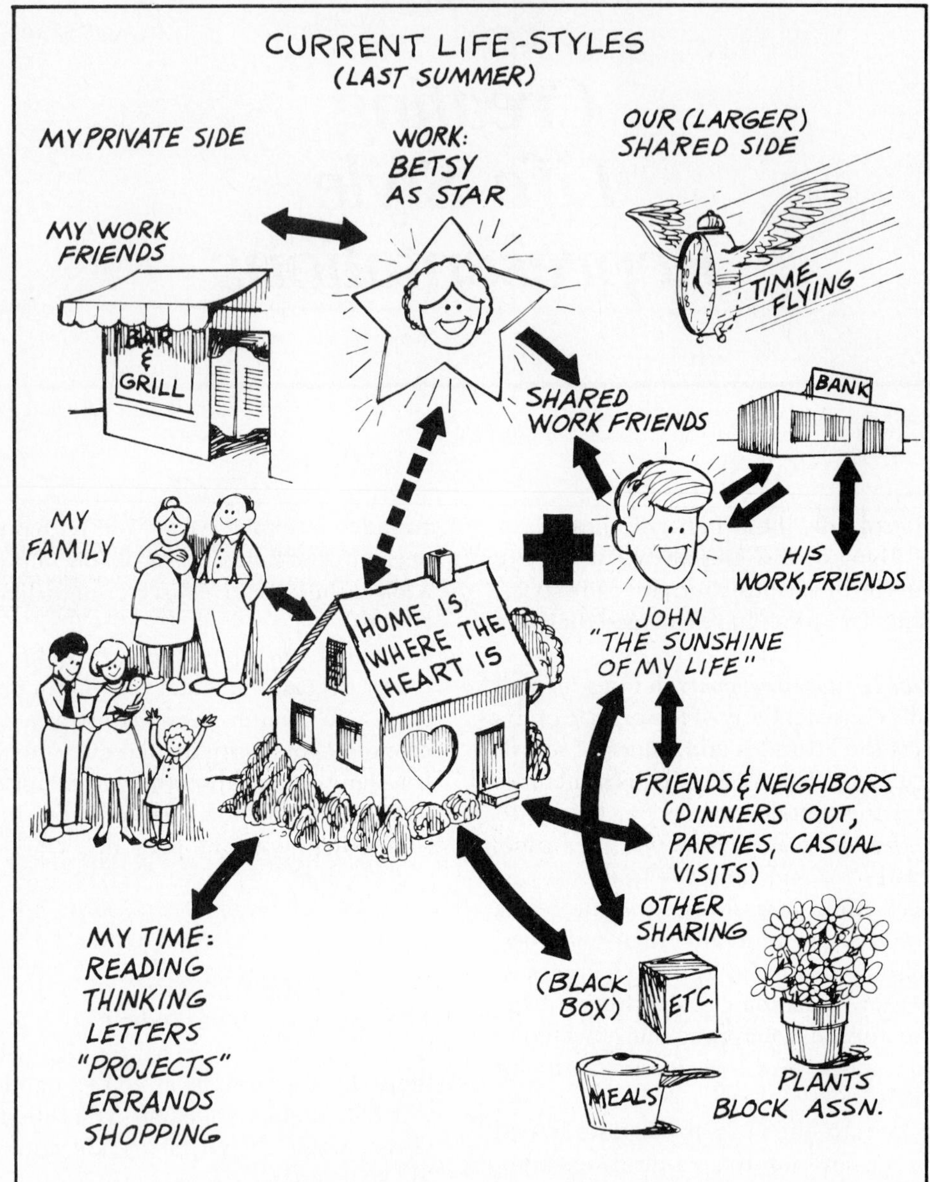

Current.

I used last summer just because it is a little more compact, a little less geographically and emotionally fragmented than my life here at school. The fundamentals are the same, and have been for as long as I've been making my own life: a place of my own, suited to my taste; John and our shared time/place/experiences/feelings/intellects; time of my own; lots of reading; work which is satisfying and visible.

In the Next Few Years.

Lots of the same elements. The only significant difference is right now a big question mark: kid or kids? If so, will I feel that I can still work?

material, and any approach that you feel captures more, rather than less, of the complexity of the detail and shape of your life style. The only constraint should be that your work can be viewed while sitting at a desk. Exhibit 12–1 is one example of a free-style life style diagram.

Time-Oriented Representations

Time-oriented life style representations begin with a consideration of the finite amount of time an individual has and attempt to reflect the personal allocations of that time. Exhibit 12–2 is an example done by a student who chose a bar graph structure. Pie charts or other graphic means are also appropriate. Exhibit 12–3 shows a life style diagram that reflects major interests and activities chronologically.

Relationships-Orientation Option

Another way to approach representing your life style is to begin with your relationships. Photograph collages; network diagrams with degrees of strength, intimacy, frequency of interaction, and other related variables indicated; or cluster diagrams are appropriate ways of using this option. You may be able to think of others.

Activities

Another way to approach this assignment is to think of the things you do and to represent those activities in ways that reflect who you are.

Aspects

Another approach is to begin with the list of aspects of our lives shown in Exhibit 12–4. This list is similar to the one we used in the Values Sort. For each aspect, write down your interests, goals, characteristics, and needs. Then use that list to devise a graphic representation of the life style (yours) that incorporates all the items on the list.

Things to Remember

Whichever option you choose, there some things you should keep in mind. Your representation should reflect the past, the present, and the future. It should

Exhibit 12–2

A Time Allocation Life Style Representation

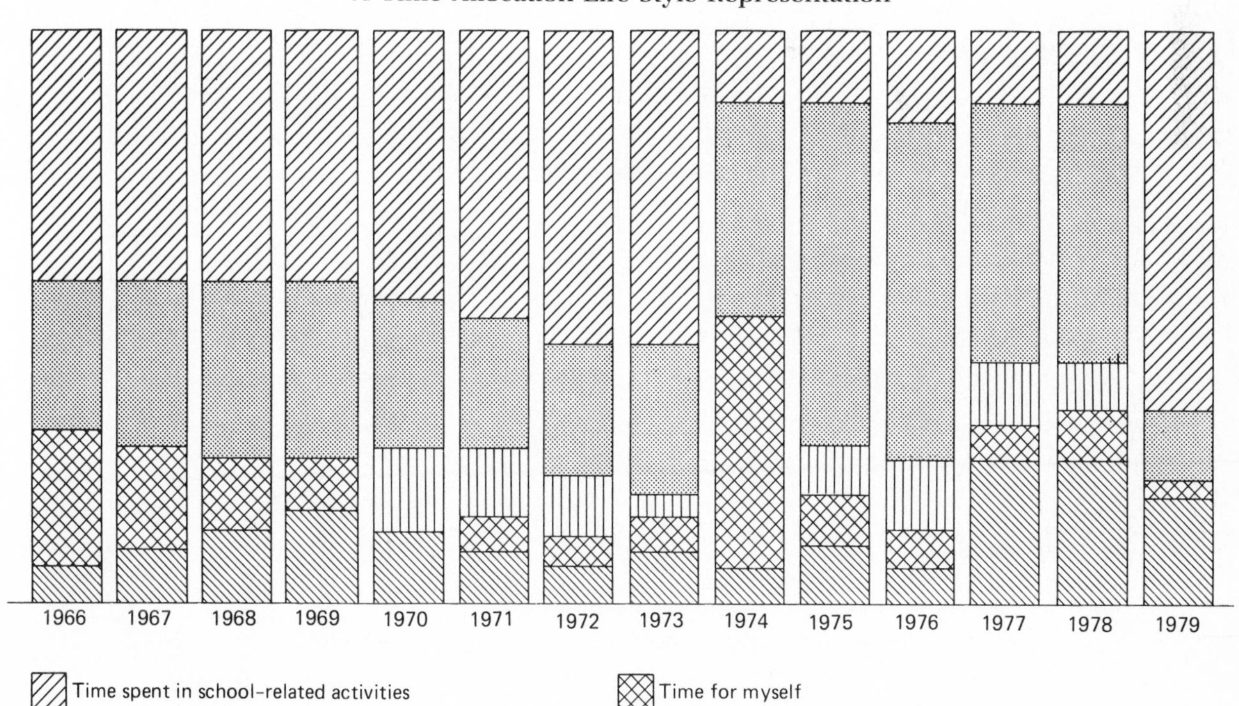

Exhibit 12–3

A Chronological Life Style Diagram

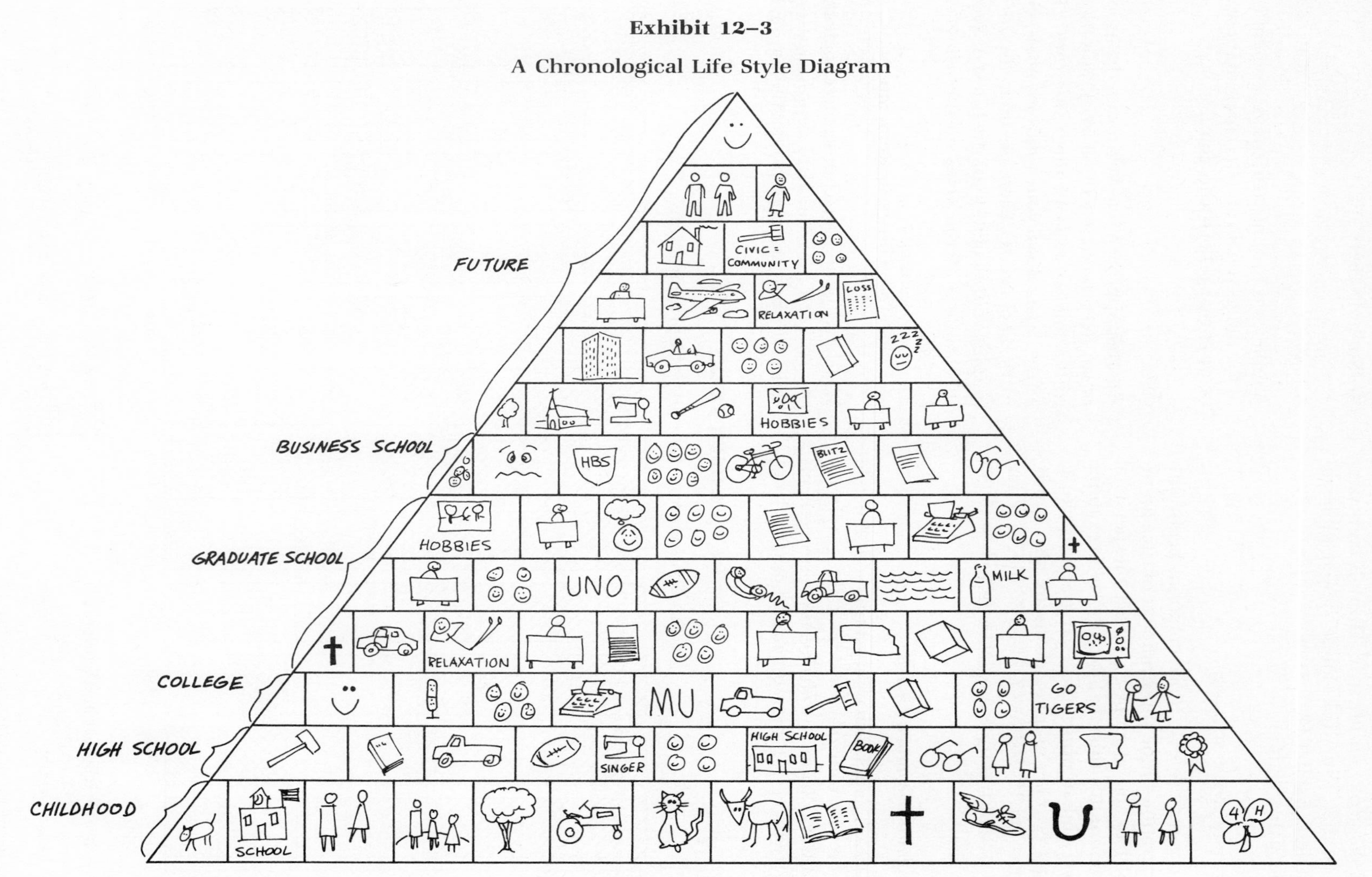

Exhibit 12–4

Aspects of a Person's Life

Physical
Material (possessions)
Financial
Emotional
Spiritual
Professional
Educational
Intellectual
Social
Marital
Parental
Familial
Societal
Political
Cultural

have some means of indicating the strength or the importance of a particular object or activity or person in your life style. It should reflect as accurately as possible the level of congestion or complexity you experience in your life. Last, it should feel comfortable to you when you have finished it. In other words, when you look at your life style representation, your diagram or representation should communicate a sense of who you are in such a way that you feel comfortable with it, that it seems to be "you," and that it reflects the major issues and aspects of your life.

Finally, remember that this is *your* exercise. Be as creative as you like. If you do not feel creative or artistic, relax. We are not expecting a work of art; what we want is a representation that says something about who you were, are, and will be.

When you have completed the Life Style Representation, make an entry in your Feelings Record. What was your reaction to the assignment? Did you enjoy it? Why or why not? What were you thinking about as you made your representation?

Feelings Record: Life Style Diagram

Exercise

Analyzing Life Style Representations

You can interpret these data by looking for patterns or relationships between parts of your lives that will provide insight into who you are and what is important to you. Look at the following two cases.

Note:

1. The relationships between things that appear in the diagram
2. The strength of those relationships
3. The sources of satisfaction and enjoyment in the diagram
4. The sources of anxiety and frustration
5. The number of people and how they fit into the diagram

Begin to draw inferences from these observations. Note the specific data that you are looking at as you write down each inference. Again, begin by asking yourself to complete the phrase, "This is a person who. . . . " When you have finished analyzing Steven Taylor's and Carrie Baugh's diagrams, go on to your own.

Steven Taylor's Life Style Diagram

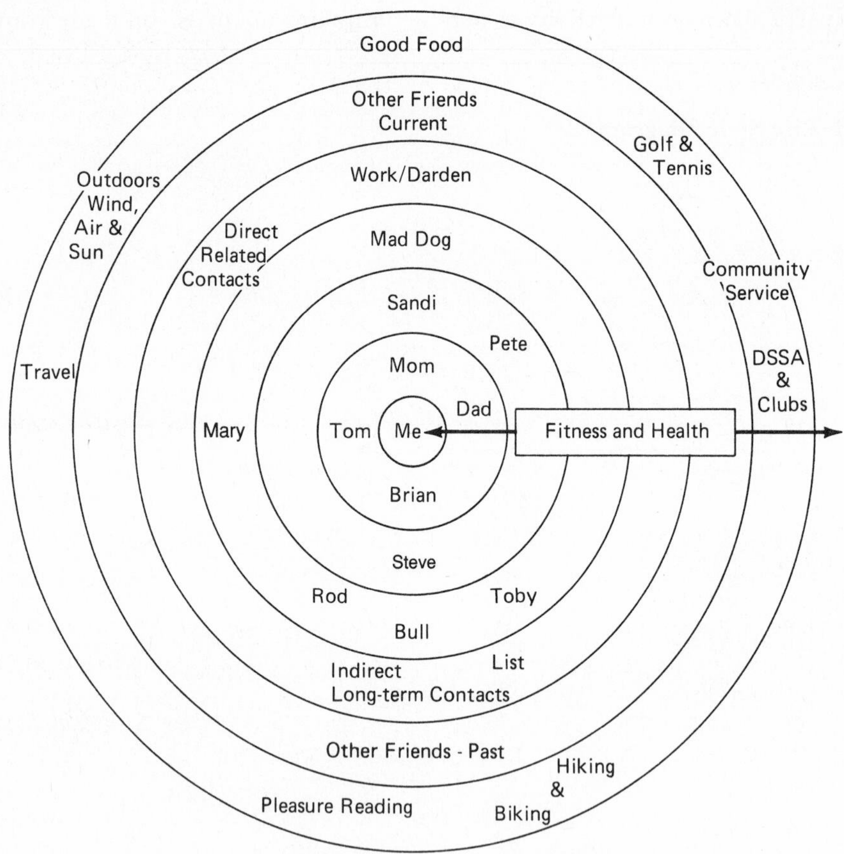

Carrie Baugh's Life Style Diagram

Carrie chose to create a three-dimensional life style diagram. Her diagram takes the form of a mobile. Five cards contain phrases cut out from magazines which pertain to Carrie's life. Each card has a central theme: Balance, Family, Company, Individual, and Leisure. Here is a replica of Carrie's mobile.

UVA-PACS-064

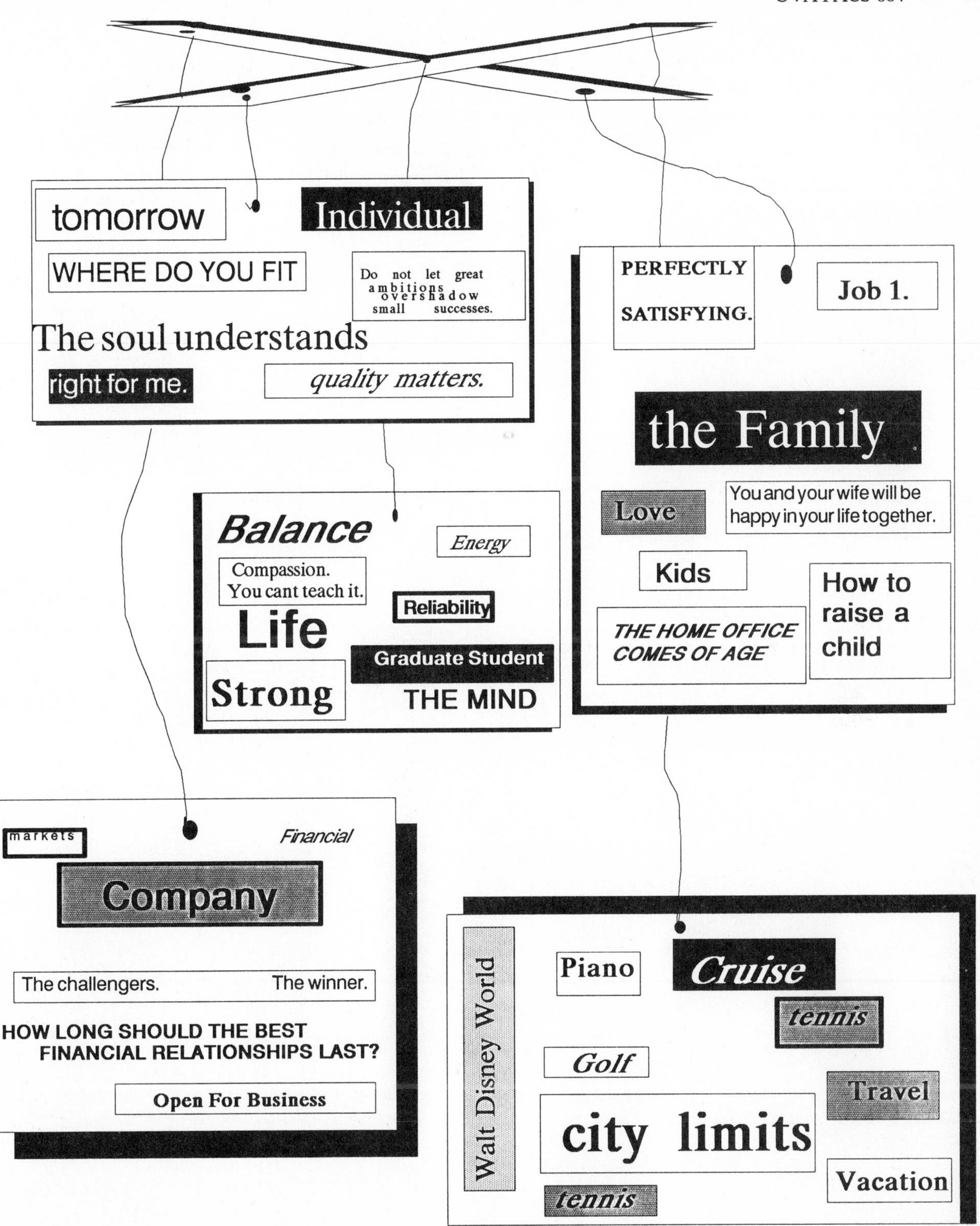

Prepared by Lori Wilson and Jim Clawson. Copyright © 1990 by the Darden Graduate Business School Foundation, Charlottesville, VA.

NOTES:

1. Areas identified: Family, Individual, Leisure, Work, Life/Balance.
2. Family is job 1.
3. Leisure includes golf, tennis, piano, and travel.
4. Family shows home office.
5. Individual shows tomorrow, quality, personal goals.
6. Company shows challenges, winners.
7. Central area is Life: compassion, strength, energy, reliability.
8. Family, Individual Development, Leisure, and Professional surround Life/Balance.
9. Created a mobile instead of drawing.

INFERENCES:

Carrie is a person who:

1. Wants to balance life style between family, career, identity, and leisure.
2. Likes athletics.
3. Enjoys the piano.
4. Considers family first priority.
5. Wants a challenging career.
6. Perhaps wants to work out of her home.
7. Values individual characteristics.
8. Seeks variety.
9. Views life as a struggle to balance different goals at different life stages.

13

The Strong Interest Inventory

The Strong Interest Inventory (SSI)

If you are using this book as a part of a course, your instructor may provide you with a SII. If you are using this book on your own, you can obtain an SII and have it scored through any reputable career counseling service (on campus or in a private business), or by sending it to:

Consulting Psychologists Press, Inc.
577 College Avenue
Palo Alto, CA 94306
415-326-4448

The SII is probably the most widely used vocational interest instrument in the world. It can reflect a lot about the similarities between your interests and the interests of people who are successful in a variety of careers, so we highly recommend that you make the opportunity to take the test.

When you have completed the test, make an entry in your **Feelings Record.** How did you react to the test? What were your feeling while you were taking it?

The SII is scored by a computer. There are two options for the scoring—a two-page profile or a more lengthy analysis. The cost of scoring a single profile was about $25 in 1990. Group rates bring the individual costs down considerably.

If you elect to get a profile, this chapter will help you to interpet the results. The more expensive and lengthier analysis tends to be more self-explanatory, but contains little information about the background and development of the instrument. Once you have received your scoring feedback, read the following chapter and follow the instructions there.

Interpreting the Strong Interest Inventory

NOTE!
DO **NOT** READ THIS CHAPTER UNTIL AFTER YOU HAVE COMPLETED THE STRONG INTEREST INVENTORY AND RECEIVED YOUR COMPUTER GENERATED PROFILE!!

The Strong Interest Inventory (SII) is the recently updated version of an enormously respected and widely used vocational guidance instrument originally developed over forty years ago. It was known earier as the Strong-Campbell Interest Inventory. The output of this instrument, generally called the Strong Profile, is a computer-generated report that provides a great deal of potentially relevant career information about a person. Indeed, our students have generally found the SII to be second only to the Written Interview in its usefulness as a data-generating device. To use the Strong Profile for self-assessment purposes, we need, as always, a fairly thorough understanding of the instrument. This chapter is intended to help you get that understanding. When you receive your computer-scored profile, you will notice that additional guidelines for interpretation are printed on the back of the profile.

The Theory Behind the Strong

The Strong is based on the career theory of John Holland.[1] In his view, the occupations of the world could be clustered together into six major groups according to common characteristics. Holland named these groups Realistic, Investigative, Artistic, Social, Enterprising, and Conventional. The Realistic or R theme, for instance, (including such occupations as forester and veterinarian) tended to involve the explicit, ordered, or systematic manipulation of objects, tools, machines, and animals. The I occupations (such as musician and reporter) involve ambiguous, free, unsystematized activities that created art forms or products. The S occupations (such as social worker and personnel director) were chosen generally by people who like to work in groups and prefer to solve problems through feelings and interpersonal relationships. The E occupations (such as realtor and investment fund manager) required strong verbal, achievement, and leadership skills and abilities. These jobs often entailed the manipulation of others to attain organizational or self-interest goals. And finally, the C occupations (such as accountant and secretary) usually entailed the explicit, ordered, systematic manipulation of data. More detailed definitions of these themes are given in Exhibit 13-1. Note, too, that in the theory, the R theme is thought to be most dissimilar to the S theme, the E theme most dissimilar to the I theme, and the C theme most dissimilar to the A theme.

Holland also believed that by the time they were of age to choose an occupation most people had developed certain predispositions toward one or more of these clusters and would naturally gravitate towards jobs and careers in those clusters. Thus, Holland's model is a fit model, a natural fit model, in which people who are successful in their careers have found jobs that match their interests, preferences, and skills. We do not assume, though, that a person is exclusively interested in one of the themes; rather, people will have some interest in each. It is the relative strength of those interests that is of interest.

As with all theories, the problem of measurement is critical to demonstrating the theory's effectiveness. The developers of the Strong took an innovative approach to testing Holland's theory in society.

The Design of the Test

The SII asks a person 325 questions that elicit preferences (likes, dislikes, or indifferences) concerning various occupations, school subjects, activities, amusements, and types of people. The test's input, therefore, is data about what we generally call interests or attitudes. The SII does not elicit information regarding intelligence, aptitudes, or skills.

The instrument uses this information about a person's interests to compute a number of scores presented in three main parts, as shown on pages 129–130, a photocopy of a blank Strong profile. These parts are the (1) general occupational themes, (2) basic interest scales, and (3) occupational scales. Each of these three sets of scores compares the taker's interests with either men and women in general, or men and women in specific occupations (bankers, advertising executives). And, as we shall see, these comparisons can be very useful data.

The data presentation in the profile is organized around Holland's six themes. Each section is marked with a word and a letter indicating these themes (R, I, A, S, E, and C). Over the years, the instrument has been administered by a couple of organizations; at present, the primary scoring license for the instrument is held by Consulting Psychologists, Inc., who use the profile format shown in here. Formerly, different formats were used, but the basic information and data reported remain the same.

The remainder of this chapter will introduce you to the various sections of data that a Strong profile provides in anticipation of your practicing interpretations on Steven Taylor's and Carrie Baugh's profiles before attempting to draw some conclusions from your own. We will begin our interpretation of a Strong profile by looking at a broad category of data often overlooked in analyzing these profiles, the Special Scores and Administrative Indexes.

Special Scores

Immediately below the individual's name on page 1 of the profile you will find a section marked **SPECIAL SCALES.** The first of these is the Academic Comfort scale. The academic comfort scale is a measure of probable persistence in the academic setting. Students graduating with a BA from a liberal arts college average 50, MAs about 55, PhDs about

---

[1]See *Making Vocational Choices: A Theory of Careers* (Englewood Cliffs, N.J.: Prentice-Hall, 1973).

Exhibit 13–1

The Six Occupational Themes

R Theme. People who score very high in this theme tend to be rugged, robust, practical individuals who are physically strong and frequently aggressive in outlook. They often have good physical skills but have trouble expressing themselves in words or communicating their feelings to others. They would like to work outdoors and they like to work with tools, especially large, powerful machines. They prefer to deal with things rather than with ideas or people. They generally have conventional political and economic options, and are usually cool to radical new ideas. They enjoy creating things with their hands and prefer occupations such as mechanic, construction work, fish and wildlife management, laboratory technician, some engineering specialties, some military jobs, agriculture, or the skilled trades. Although no single word can capture the broad meaning of the entire theme, the word "realistic" has been used to characterize this pattern, thus, the term R Theme.

I Theme. This theme tends to center around science and scientific activities. Extremes of this type are task-oriented; they are not particularly interested in working around other people. They enjoy solving abstract problems and have a great need to understand the physical world. They prefer to think through problems rather than act them out. Such people enjoy ambiguous challenges and do not like highly structured situations with many rules. They frequently have unconventional values and attitudes and tend to be original and creative, especially in scientific areas. They prefer occupations such as design engineer, biologist, social scientist, research laboratory worker, physicist, technical writer, or meteorologist. The word "investigative" is used to summarize this pattern, thus I Theme.

A Theme. Those scoring high here are artistically oriented and like to work in artistic settings where there are many opportunities for self-expression. Such people have little interest in problems that are highly structured or that require gross physical strength and prefer problems that can be dealt with through self-expression in artistic media. They resemble I Themes types in preferring to work alone, but have a greater need for individualistic expression, are usually less assertive about their own opinions and capabilities, and are more sensitive and emotional. They score higher on measures of originality than any of the other types. They describe themselves as independent, original, unconventional, expressive, and tense. Vocational choices include artist, author, cartoonist, composer, singer, dramatic coach, poet, actor or actress, and symphony conductor. This is the "artistic" theme, or A Theme.

S Theme. People scoring the highest on this theme are sociable, reponsible, humanistic, and concerned with the welfare of others. They usually express themselves well and get along well with others. They like attention and see situations that allow them to be at or near the center of the group. They prefer to solve problems by discussions with others or by arranging or rearranging relationships between others, but have little interest in situations that require physical exertion or working with machinery. Such people describe themselves as cheerful, popular, achieving, and good leaders. They prefer occupations such as school superintendent, clinical psychologist, high school teacher, marriage counselor, playground director, speech therapist, or vocational counselor. This is the "social" or S Theme.

E Theme. Those who score high here have a great facility with words, which they put to effective use in selling, dominating, and leading. These people are frequently in sales work. They see themselves as energetic, enthusiastic, adventurous, self-confident, and dominant, and they prefer social tasks where they can assume leadership. They enjoy persuading others to accept their viewpoints. They are impatient with precise work or work that involves long periods of intellectual effort. They like power, status, and material wealth, and enjoy working in expensive settings. Vocational preferences include business executive, buyer, hotel manager, industrial relations consultant, political campaigner, realtor, many kinds of sales work, sports promoter, and television producer. The word "enterprising" summarizes this pattern; thus, E Theme.

C Theme. People who score high on this theme prefer the highly ordered activities, both verbal and numerical, that characterize office work. They fit well into large organizations but do not seek leadership since they respond to power and are comfortable working in a well-established chain of command. They dislike ambiguous situations and prefer to know precisely what is expected of them. Such people describe themselves as conventional, stable, well-controlled, and dependable. They have little interest in problems that require physical skills or intense relationships with others and are most effective at well-defined tasks. Like E Theme types, they value material possessions and status. Vocational preferences are mostly within the business world and include bank examiner, bank teller, bookkeeper, some accounting jobs, financial analyst, computer operator, inventory controller, tax expert, statistician, and traffic manager. Although one word cannot adequately represent the entire theme, the word "conventional" more or less summarizes the pattern, hence C Theme.

Source: an earlier version of the profile, SVIB-SCII.

60. Students seeking advanced degrees who score low (around 40) on this scale inevitably report that they view their education as a necessary hurdle to be cleared and are usually not enchanted with the academic nature of their study. The item content for this scale (that is, the set of questions on the test that relate to this score) is heavily oriented toward science and the arts (weighted positively) and business and blue-collar activities (weighted negatively).

Below the academic comfort scale is the introversion–extroversion scale. Here, high scores (50 and above) indicate introversion and low scores (40 and below), extroversion. The item content is concerned almost entirely with working with people in social service, educational, entertainment, or business settings.

Next is an indicator of total responses. This shows how many answer marks the computer has read from the answer sheet; since there are 325 items, the score on this index should be 325 or close to it. Up to thirty-two items can be omitted without significantly affecting the results.

To the right of the total response space is the infrequent response measure. This shows the number of rare responses given. It is weighted so that almost everyone scores zero or higher; if the score is *below zero,* the person has marked an uncommonly high number of rare responses. Usually a negative score indicates some confusion, such as skipping a number on the answer sheet or random marking. If your score is above zero, you can proceed with interpreting the profile.

Administrative Indexes

The administrative indexes are found at the bottom of the second page of the profile. They simply show the percentage of like, indifferent, and dislike responses, left to right respectively, for clusters of items on the test relating to such particular topics as occupations, school subjects, activities, and so on. Although there is some variation from section to section, the average for like (left), indifferent (center), and dislike (right) responses is about 35% each, and the average standard deviation is about 16. Most of our students' percentages have been between 5 and 60.

In the Preferences section, you might note that scores above 40% in the left hand or "like" column indicate a broad range of interests that might be associated with active, outgoing individuals who deal with a range of people while lower scores (20% or less) tend to indicate the sharp focus of interest one might find in artists or scientists. Also, in the Characteristics section, the average men's scores are 55, 23, and 21, while the average women's scores are 46, 25, and 28.

Variations over these indexes can give one some interesting, if tentative, insights. A consistent HI, LO, LO pattern, for instance, might indicate a person with a wide range of interests while a consistent LO, LO, HI pattern might indicate a person who is either very focused in his or her interests or more generally negative about the various aspects of life.[2]

These two sections, Special Scales and Administrative Indexes, can often be linked up with many other bits of data we have generated in the book. Measures of introversion and extroversion appear in a number of places. Academic comfort might be compared with data generated in your Written Interview or resume. Likewise, the patterns appearing in the administrative indexes can be used to compare with data from the interpersonal style inventory, the FIRO-B, the written interview, and other instruments already presented.

Next, let's look at the three main sections of the

---

[2]A high LP response cycle (LP above 60 in several sections) will inflate your scores in the general occupational themes and the basic interest scales. If many (fifteen or more) basic interest scales are high, only the top three to five scores should be considered. High LP types might be described as overly enthusiastic and vocationally unfocused, particularly if they have none or very few "similar" ratings on occupational scales. They are often very energetic, but in a "ship without rudder" way.

If "dislike" percentages are generally high, the scores on the general occupational themes and basic interest scales will be low, and some information may be gotten from treating the relatively highest scores as "high" regardless of their absolute value. According to Campbell ["Manual for the Strong-Campbell Interest Inventory" (Stanford University Press, 1974)], high DPs tend to fall into two categories: those with such an intense occupational focus that they mark everything "dislike" that falls outside their well-defined realm of interest; and those who have few "likes" in the world and find most of everything repugnant. Those of the first type usually experience few vocational problems, unless a sudden and massive insight or external turn of events shatters their world view (as happened to many engineers in the late 1960s). The second type, however, can experience serious difficulties in career issues. One way to differentiate the two types is to check if there are at least a few occupational scales in the "similar" range. If so, chances are that this is a "type 1" profile of someone with a highly focused sense of direction.

STRONG INTEREST INVENTORY OF THE
STRONG VOCATIONAL INTEREST BLANKS

PAGE 1

PROFILE REPORT FOR: **DATE TESTED:**

ID: **DATE SCORED:**

AGE: **SEX:**

SPECIAL SCALES: ACADEMIC COMFORT
INTROVERSION-EXTROVERSION

TOTAL RESPONSES: **INFREQUENT RESPONSES:**

GOT	
R	
I	
A	
S	
E	
C	

OCCUPATIONAL SCALES

STANDARD SCORES F M — VERY DISSIMILAR (15) · DISSIMILAR (25) · MODERATELY DISSIMILAR (30) · MID-RANGE · MODERATELY SIMILAR (40) · SIMILAR (45) · VERY SIMILAR (55)

REALISTIC

GENERAL OCCUPATIONAL THEME - R 30 40 50 60 70 — F / M

BASIC INTEREST SCALES (STANDARD SCORE)

- AGRICULTURE — F / M
- NATURE — F / M
- ADVENTURE — F / M
- MILITARY ACTIVITIES — F / M
- MECHANICAL ACTIVITIES — F / M

F	M	Occupational Scale	Standard Scores F	Standard Scores M	15	25	30		40	45	55
[CRS]	RC	Marine Corps enlisted personnel	(CRS)								
RC	RC	Navy enlisted personnel									
RC	RC	Army officer									
RI	RIC	Navy officer									
R	R	Air Force officer									
[C]	R	Air Force enlisted personnel	(C)								
R	R	Police officer									
R	R	Bus driver									
R	R	Horticultural worker									
RC	R	Farmer									
R	RCS	Vocational agriculture teacher									
RI	R	Forester									
[IR]	RI	Veterinarian	(IR)								
RIS	[SR]	Athletic trainer		(SR)							
RS	R	Emergency medical technician									
RI	RI	Radiologic technologist									
RI	R	Carpenter									
RI	R	Electrician									
RIA	[ARI]	Architect		(ARI)							
RI	RI	Engineer									

INVESTIGATIVE

GENERAL OCCUPATIONAL THEME - I 30 40 50 60 70 — F / M

BASIC INTEREST SCALES (STANDARD SCORE)

- SCIENCE — F / M
- MATHEMATICS — F / M
- MEDICAL SCIENCE — F / M
- MEDICAL SERVICE — F / M

F	M	Occupational Scale	Standard Scores F	Standard Scores M	15	25	30		40	45	55
IRC	IRC	Computer programmer									
IRC	IRC	Systems analyst									
IRC	IR	Medical technologist									
IR	IR	R & D manager									
IR	IR	Geologist									
IR	[I]	Biologist		(I)							
IR	IR	Chemist									
IR	IR	Physicist									
IR	[RI]	Veterinarian		(RI)							
IRS	IR	Science teacher									
IRS	IRS	Physical therapist									
IR	IRS	Respiratory therapist									
IC	IR	Medical technician									
IC	IE	Pharmacist									
ISR	[CSE]	Dietitian		(CSE)							
[SI]	ISR	Nurse, RN	(SI)								
IR	I	Chiropractor									
IR	IR	Optometrist									
IR	IR	Dentist									
I	IA	Physician									
[IR]	I	Biologist	(IR)								
I	I	Mathematician									
IR	I	Geographer									
I	I	College professor									
IA	IA	Psychologist									
IA	IA	Sociologist									

ARTISTIC

GENERAL OCCUPATIONAL THEME - A 30 40 50 60 70 — F / M

BASIC INTEREST SCALES (STANDARD SCORE)

- MUSIC/DRAMATICS — F / M
- ART — F / M
- WRITING — F / M

F	M	Occupational Scale	Standard Scores F	Standard Scores M	15	25	30		40	45	55
AI	AI	Medical illustrator									
A	A	Art teacher									
A	A	Artist, fine									
A	A	Artist, commercial									
AE	A	Interior decorator									
[RIA]	ARI	Architect	(RIA)								
A	A	Photographer									
A	A	Musician									
AR	[EA]	Chef		(EA)							
[E]	AE	Beautician	(E)								
AE	A	Flight attendant									
A	A	Advertising executive									
A	A	Broadcaster									
A	A	Public relations director									
A	A	Lawyer									
A	AS	Public administrator									
A	A	Reporter									
A	A	Librarian									
AS	AS	English teacher									
[SA]	AS	Foreign language teacher	(SA)								

CONSULTING PSYCHOLOGISTS PRESS, INC.
577 COLLEGE AVENUE
PALO ALTO, CA 94306

STRONG INTEREST INVENTORY OF THE
STRONG VOCATIONAL INTEREST BLANKS

PROFILE REPORT FOR: **DATE TESTED:**

ID: **DATE SCORED:**

AGE: **SEX:**

OCCUPATIONAL SCALES

STANDARD SCORES: F M — VERY DISSIMILAR, DISSIMILAR, MODERATELY DISSIMILAR, MID-RANGE, MODERATELY SIMILAR, SIMILAR, VERY SIMILAR (15, 25, 30, 40, 45, 55)

SOCIAL

GENERAL OCCUPATIONAL THEME - S 30 40 50 60 70 (F, M)

BASIC INTEREST SCALES (STANDARD SCORE)

TEACHING (F, M)

SOCIAL SERVICE (F, M)

ATHLETICS (F, M)

DOMESTIC ARTS (F, M)

RELIGIOUS ACTIVITIES (F, M)

F	M	Occupational Scale	Standard Score F	Standard Score M
SA	[AS]	Foreign language teacher		(AS)
SA	SA	Minister		
SA	SA	Social worker		
S	S	Guidance counselor		
S	S	Social science teacher		
S	S	Elementary teacher		
S	S	Special education teacher		
SRI	SAR	Occupational therapist		
SIA	SAI	Speech pathologist		
SI	[ISR]	Nurse, RN		(ISR)
SCI	N/A	Dental hygienist		N/A
SC	SC	Nurse, LPN		
[RIS]	SR	Athletic trainer	(RIS)	
SR	SR	Physical education teacher		
SRE	SE	Recreation leader		
SE	SE	YWCA/YMCA director		
SEC	SCE	School administrator		
SCE	N/A	Home economics teacher		N/A

ENTERPRISING

GENERAL OCCUPATIONAL THEME - E 30 40 50 60 70 (F, M)

BASIC INTEREST SCALES (STANDARD SCORE)

PUBLIC SPEAKING (F, M)

LAW/POLITICS (F, M)

MERCHANDISING (F, M)

SALES (F, M)

BUSINESS MANAGEMENT (F, M)

F	M	Occupational Scale	Standard Score F	Standard Score M
E	ES	Personnel director		
ES	E	Elected public official		
ES	ES	Life insurance agent		
EC	E	Chamber of Commerce executive		
EC	EC	Store manager		
N/A	ECR	Agribusiness manager	N/A	
EC	EC	Purchasing agent		
EC	E	Restaurant manager		
[AR]	EA	Chef	(AR)	
EC	E	Travel agent		
ECS	E	Funeral director		
[CSE]	ESC	Nursing home administrator	(CSE)	
EC	ER	Optician		
E	E	Realtor		
E	[AE]	Beautician		(AE)
E	E	Florist		
EC	E	Buyer		
EI	EI	Marketing executive		
EIC	ECI	Investments manager		

CONVENTIONAL

GENERAL OCCUPATIONAL THEME - C 30 40 50 60 70 (F, M)

BASIC INTEREST SCALES (STANDARD SCORE)

OFFICE PRACTICES (F, M)

F	M	Occupational Scale	Standard Score F	Standard Score M
C	C	Accountant		
C	C	Banker		
CE	CE	IRS agent		
CES	CES	Credit manager		
CES	CES	Business education teacher		
[CS]	CES	Food service manager	(CS)	
[ISR]	CSE	Dietitian	(ISR)	
CSE	[ESC]	Nursing home administrator		(ESC)
CSE	CSE	Executive housekeeper		
CS	[CES]	Food service manager		(CES)
CS	N/A	Dental assistant		N/A
C	N/A	Secretary		N/A
C	[R]	Air Force enlisted personnel		(R)
CRS	[RC]	Marine Corps enlisted personnel		(RC)
CRS	CR	Army enlisted personnel		
CIR	CIR	Mathematics teacher		

ADMINISTRATIVE INDEXES (RESPONSE %)

OCCUPATIONS	%	%	%
SCHOOL SUBJECTS	%	%	%
ACTIVITIES	%	%	%
LEISURE ACTIVITIES	%	%	%
TYPES OF PEOPLE	%	%	%
PREFERENCES	%	%	%
CHARACTERISTICS	%	%	%
ALL PARTS	%	%	%

CONSULTING PSYCHOLOGISTS PRESS, INC.
577 COLLEGE AVENUE
PALO ALTO, CA 94306

Figure 1

Basic Interest Scale Bars

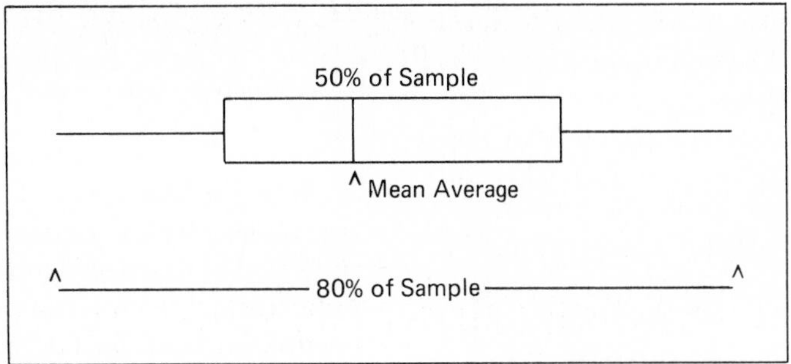

Strong; we'll take these in order of the breadth of their focus—the General Occupational Themes compares an individual's data with the general population, the Basic Interest Scales breaks down the general occupational data into job clusters, and the Occupational Scales compares one's data with smaller occupational criterion groups.

The General Occupational Themes

The General Occupational Themes scores are summarized in a box marked "GOT" at the top center of the first page of the profile. A glance here gives one a quick overview of how one's answers compare with the general population's interests in the six basic themes in Holland's theory. The general occupational scales tell you how high or low your score is relative to others of your own sex (only). And it does so in English, beside each score. Here, Very High means above the 94th percentile, High from 85 to 93, Moderately High from 70 to 84, Average from 31 to 69, Moderately Low from 16 to 30, Low from 7 to 15, and Very Low below the 6th percentile. These scores reflect your response pattern for each of the major occupational themes.[3]

In most profiles, scores across the three sets of scales (general occupational, basic interest, and occupational scales) will be roughly similar on the average for those scales related to a single theme. For example, a person whose general occupational theme score for R is very low (25) will probably also score low on most of the basic interest scales associated with the R theme (agriculture, nature, etc.), and will probably also score low on most of the occupational scales associated with R (such as occupational therapist or Air Force officer). Such a pattern simply confirms Holland's thesis and the organizational format used in the Strong Profile.

The Basic Interest Scales

The Basic Interest Scales, shown as horizontal sections of the profile on pages 129–130, break down the summary of the general occupational themes and give us more detailed information. First, the general occupational theme score is repeated immediately under the title bar of each theme, but this time we get two bars that allow us to compare our scores with those of our own sex. The shaded bar shows men's scores in the aggregate (as indicated by the "m" to the right of the bar), the plain bar women's scores, each again representing overall scores from the general population. The scores of 50% of the people sampled fit inside the thick box-like section of the bar, with the vertical line showing the average for that sex, and 80% of the sample scores lie between the ends of the bars (see Figure 1).

The six general occupational themes are broken down into twenty-three clusters of jobs in the basic interest scales. Each of these clusters are occupational activities thought to be related to that general theme. Your scores on these scales reflect your answers on ten to fifteen items on the instrument that relate to that cluster. Your score simply measures the frequency with which you said you liked, disliked, or were indifferent to certain types of activities or subjects. For example, if you said you like art as a school subject (question 136 on the SII), your score on the art scale would increase. If you said you did not like visiting art galleries (question 234), your score on the art scale would decrease. The only transformation the test makes is to set 50 as the mean

[3]That is, items were identified on the SCII that relate to each theme. Whenever you answer "like" to one of the items, your score goes up on the appropriate theme scale; whenever you answer "dislike," your score goes down. The scales were standardized so that the average person in a general sample of 600 people scored 50 on each scale, with a standard deviation of 10.

score on each scale (with a standard deviation of 10) for a random sample of 600 men and women, and to adjust your score accordingly. This allows you to compare your score to those of people in general on items selected by the instrument developers as being related to that cluster.

Because of the way these scales are constructed, it is possible for someone to score high or low on most of the scales. If a person simply chose the "like" option very often on the SII, his scores would be higher on many of the basic interest scales, while if another chose "indifferent" or "dislike" very often, her scale scores would be lower. It is also possible for a person to have a high basic interest score (65) on mathematics, and yet have a low score (10) on the occupational scales m mathematician or f mathematician. In this case, the person has reported on the SII a high liking for mathematical subjects and activities, but has not reported many of the somewhat unique interests that characterize the people *in the mathematics profession* (which may have nothing obvious to do with mathematics.).

The Occupational Scales

The Occupational Scales break the basic interest scale data down even further by considering specific jobs rather than clusters of jobs. Here, an individual's scores are compared with the scores of occupational criterion groups. Since the scoring and interpreting of the occupational scale scores is significantly different from those of the GOT and BIS sections, we will consider carefully how these scores are created. Developers of the SII took the following steps for each of the 106 occupational criterion groups represented on the instrument under the column titled "Occupational Scales" on the right hand half of both pages of the profile:

1. A group of about 150 to 450 men or women were identified as being **happily** employed in an occupation, as being **successful** in that occupation, and as having been in that occupation for more than **three** years (average tenure was usually 10 to 20 years). Thus, tenure, competence, and satisfaction were the three basic criteria for inclusion in the sample.
2. These people were asked to answer the 325 questions on the SII.
3. Whenever these people expressed some particular preference much more or less frequently than a large sample of "people in general," that alternative was used in creating the scale for that occupational group. This produced a set of items and answers from the instrument that were idiosyncratic to that occupational group.
4. The scale was then normed so that the average person in the occupational group scored 50 on the scale, while two-thirds of the group scored between 40 and 60.

As a result of this scale construction procedure, the more often a person using the SII expresses preferences that distinguish a particular occupation, the greater the score he or she will receive on that occupational scale. For example, suppose you indicated in response to question 217 that you liked "living in the city." Suppose also that the criterion group of male architects happened to choose that option much more often than most other people and therefore it was one of the items included in the cluster associated with male architects. In that case, your score on the **m** architect scale would go up a notch. If time and time again you chose an option that had been chosen by male architects (liking, disliking, or being indifferent to an item) but not chosen by others, then your final score on the **m** architect scale would be high (high is usually considered to be a score of 45 or above). You and the criterion group of architects are indicating shared attitudes. You have something in common. You express the same preferences they do.

Sharing a large number of preferences with people in an occupation is important because research has linked such commonalities to people's decisions to go into and stay in an occupation.[4] It would ap-

---

[4]For the previous version of this instrument, Strong verified the predictive values of the occupational scales for the eighteen years after the test was taken (E.K. Strong, Jr., *Vocational Interests 18 Years After College* [Minneapolis: University of Minnesota Press, 1955]); McArthur showed they predicted for fourteen years (C. McArthur, "Long-Term Validity of the Strong Vocational Interest Test in Two Subcultures," *Journal of Applied Psychology* (1954), pp. 346–533). These and other research efforts have found that the odds that the following statements will turn out to be true range from 2 to 1 up to 5 to 1, with 3.5 to 1 being the most common result.

1. People continuing in occupation X obtained a higher interest score in X than in any other occupation.
2. People continuing in occupation X obtained a higher interest score in X than other people entering other occupations.
3. People continuing in occupation X obtained higher scores in X than people who changed from X to another occupation.
4. People changing from occupation X to occupation Y scored higher in Y prior to the change than in any other occupation, including X.

pear that, given an appropriate level of ability, those who tend to share the same preferences as other occupational members—those who "talk the same language"—are also more likely to get on, to be readily accepted, to enjoy the work, and to be successful.

The occupational scales on some profiles will be relatively flat; there will be few if any high scores. The raw data here indicate that the test taker's values and attitudes have not crystallized around any of the occupational types for which the instrument is scored. The most common reason for this relates to culture. Flat profiles sometimes occur when the test taker was raised in an environment that was different from the white, middle-class American culture from which virtually all criterion groups come.

You may also notice one-, two-, or three-letter designations just to the left of each occupational criterion group. These simply give the developers' perspectives on what general occupational themes that occupational group draws. For example, because YMCA directors demonstrate leadership and management skills along with abilities and interests in dealing with a variety of types of people, an ES appears next to that occupational criterion group. In general, the first letter indicates the most dominant of the themes for that group and the groups are clustered under the basic interest scale and general theme that are dominant for them. Hence, all of the occupational criterion groups that rely heavily on the R theme are clustered under the realistic general theme near the top of the first page of the profile on pages 129–130.

To be able to use your scores on the occupational scales effectively, it is sometimes useful to have some supplementary information about the scale's occupational group, the criterion group used to construct the scale, or the type of people who tend to score high on the scale. Some of this information is given in Exhibit 13–2, so you can see the kind of criterion groups against which individual scores are compared. You should be aware of the general nature of these criterion groups when examining the profile. For example, in interpreting a high or low score on the male banker scale, it is important to recognize that the scale was based on a national sample of bank presidents and vice presidents, many of whom were employed in small commercial banks in small towns. One would suspect that such a group of people is significantly different from, say, a group of New York investment or commercial bankers. High scores (45 or above) on the occupational scales on most profiles will have a high number compared with both male and female occupational groups.[5]

Using the Strong

A good assessor can usually learn a considerable amount from a Strong Profile by treating it as we have treated data from all other data-generating instruments: that is, by making sure he or she understands the instrument and then looking for patterns. The Strong profile can and should be used both to identify new patterns or ideas, and to test themes and patterns that have emerged from other data.

To facilitate identifying new patterns you may find the following procedures helpful. First, on a separate sheet of paper list all your occupational scores above 45. If you have only one or two scores above 45, list all the scores above 40. Also, list all your scores less than 20. Then look for patterns within and across the lists. Ask yourself, "What do these occupations have in common? What activities do they share? What tasks do they share? What lifestyle patterns do they share? What demands do they make on a person? What do they give to a person?" These questions may help you to identify the characteristics of your cluster of highs and lows and thereby help you to generate tentative conclusions about the kind of work you should or should not be seeking.

Now the scores on the occupational scales, in addition to presenting you with the insight that you have interests and attitudes much like people in those occupations, can give you additional data. This listing and interpreting of high scores and low scores is a natural extension of the inductive logic process developed throughout the book. Most of the higher and lower occupational scores from two Strongs are shown in Exhibit 13–3. (Two or three scores in each case are omitted so that it is easier to see the patterns.) In the first profile, the high scores all seem to relate to the relatively high-level management of

[5]Profiles returned to individuals show the individual's scores computed for comparison with both female and male criterion groups, but only the same sex score is plotted by an asterisk on the line graph to the right. To the extent that the opposite sex criterion group may reflect more accurately an individual's relevant group, you may plot that score as well. For example, female MBA students in the 1990s may have more in common with male commercial bankers than with the female banker criterion group from the 1960s.

Exhibit 13–2

Supplemental Data on Occupational Scales

Scale/Sample	*N*	*Year Tested*	*Mean Age*	*Mean Years Education*	*Mean Years Experience*	*Composition and Comments*
Army Officer (f)	285	1979	32.2	16.8	7.9	57% completed BA degrees, 35% MA. Rank: warrant officer (4%), lieutenant (19%), captain (59%), major (14%), lt. colonel (3%), colonel (1%).
Army Officer (m)	309	1979	36.8	16.9	13.5	See women's sample above. 11% had some college education, 42% completed BA degrees, and 44% MA. Rank: warrant officer (12%), lieutenant (3%), captain (31%), major (23%), lt. colonel (23%), colonel (7%), higher (1%).
Art Teacher (f)	359	1967	46.0	16.6	10.0	From names supplied by the National Art Education Association, plus certified teachers in Iowa Educational Directory.
Art Teacher (m)	303	1978	40.2	19.2	14.9	Members, National Art Education Association. 15% completed BA degrees, 64% MA, 19% PhD.
Artist, Commercial (f)	123	1979	35.2	16.1	11.0	Artists working for agencies and studios listed in The Creative Black Book 1979, a national directory of art services. 26% had taken art courses not leading to a degree, 50% completed BA degrees, 10% MA. 41% were freelance artists, 22% were employed by a studio, and 17% worked for a combination of employers.
Artist, Commercial (m)	199	1979	38.8	16.2	15.5	See women's sample above. 27% had taken art courses not leading to a degree, 47% completed BA degrees, 6% MA. 39% were freelance artists, 23% were employed by a studio, 10% by an advertising agency, and 15% worked for a combination of employers.
Artist, Fine (f)	247	1979	44.4	17.6	17.0	Names selected from Who's Who In American Art, 1978. 18% had taken art courses not leading to a degree, 25% completed BA degrees, 42% MA. 58% were freelance artists, 15% were employed by educational institutions, and 22% worked for a combination of employers.

Source: Reproduced by special permission of the distributor, Consulting Psychologists Press, Inc., Palo Alto, CA 94306, for the publisher, Stanford University Press, from The Manual for the SVIB-SII Third Edition by David Campbell and Jo-Ida C. Hanson. Copyright 1933–1981 by the Board of Trustees of the Leland Stanford Junior University. Further reproduction is prohibited without the publisher's consent.

Exhibit 13–3

High and Low Occupational Scores from Two Strong Profiles

PROFILE #1

High Scores		Low Scores	
Department Store Manager m	52	Skilled Crafts m	10
Sales Manager m	50	Physical Education Teacher f	7
Navy Officer m	48	Vocational Agriculture Teacher m	3
Public Administrator m	48	Instrument Assembler f	1
Advertising Executive m	42	Farmer m	3

PROFILE #2

High Scores		Low Scores	
Guidance Counselor m	62	Math Science Teacher	19
Psychologist m	60	Army Officer m	8
Psychologist f	58	Police Officer m	6
Physical Therapist f	57	Department Store Manager m	4
English Teacher f	50	Agribusiness Manager m	4
Social Worker m	48	Army Officer f	1
Social Worker f	47		
Life Insurance Agent m	42		

people. They do not include all the high-level people management scales, but they include most of them. The lowest scores, on the other hand, are almost all blue-collar trades. None are managerial jobs. The latter contrasts sharply in socioeconomic terms with the high-score occupations. And, interestingly, none of the high-score managerial occupations involve supervising the types of occupations included in the low scores. One might tentatively conclude from these scores that a theme labeled "manager of white-collar and professional people" is appropriate.

In the second profile, the high scores generally seem to be in "helping" professions. That is, they all involve providing another person or persons professional help of some type. The low scores, however, seem to relate to occupations that put a person in the position of having to manage and perhaps discipline other people. In each case, the occupation in this grouping gives the person formal authority, and expects him or her to use it to accomplish some institutionally set objectives. Possible themes that emerge from these scores might be labeled "helping professions" and "dislikes relations based on formal authority."

Of course, the tentative themes we have identified in these profiles should be checked out with both other Strong data and data from other devices.

A second way in which one can go about looking for patterns in a Strong profile is by looking at the high and low scores within each of the theme-related groupings. For example, in Exhibit 13–4 we show scores from two profiles. All of the scores from Profile #1 are from the I theme occupations, yet there is clearly a difference in the higher and lower scores within that theme category. The higher-scored occupations are much more applied, pragmatic, and concrete than the lower-scored ones are. This suggests a theme we might label "applied and concrete: not abstract."

The scores from the second profile in Exhibit 13–4 are all from the S theme occupations. But the higher score occupations are obviously different from the lower ones. The higher are all jobs that require one to organize and manage others. The lower-scored occupations involve giving help to others on a one-on-one basis. The pattern suggests a theme related to the organization and management of others.

Still a third way one can look for patterns in a Strong profile is to look for high scores on the basic interest scales or the general occupational themes that automatically suggest and label a theme. That is, if the E theme score is very high (67), then "enterprising" is obviously a potential theme. Likewise, if the nature scale has a very high score, then "nature" is a likely candidate for a theme, or for part of a theme.

Exhibit 13–4

Examples of Higher and Lower Scores within Theme-Related Grouping of Occupational Scales

PROFILE #1

High Scores		**Low Scores**	
Engineer f	8	Chemist f	20
Medical Technician f	39	Physical Scientist m	18
Pharmacist f	30	Mathematician f	15
Dentist f	42	Mathematician m	19
Physician m	29	Physicist f	10
Dental Hygienist f	37	Biologist f	12
Physical Therapist f	35	Social Scientist m	19
Medical Technician m	32	College Professor m	12
Optometrist m	38	Psychologist f	19
Computer Programmer f	30	Psychologist m	20
Optometrist f	40		

PROFILE #2

High Scores		**Low Scores**	
Personnel Director m	36	Guidance Counselor m	13
School Superintendent m	25	Nurse f	14
Public Administrator m	41	Social Worker m	19
YMCA Staff f	32	Physical Therapist m	8

To test themes or patterns that have emerged in other data with the Strong data, one can simply go over all of the profile, asking questions like these:

1. Is this scale or score relevant to the theme in question?
2. If yes, does its score support or not support the theme?

For example, if "artistic" is a theme that has emerged from the written interview, one would want to examine *at least* the A theme score, the art basic interest scale, and the artist (f, m) occupational scales for support or disconfirmation. Likewise, if "political" was a theme identified in other data, you would definitely want to look at the law/politics basic interest score and the public administrator, school superintendent, and chamber of commerce executive occupational scores.

There are, of course, still other approaches one can take using a Strong profile. And as long as they include a basic understanding of the instrument and an orientation toward testing and developing themes, they too are appropriate.

Exercise

To help you practice interpreting a Strong, consider Steven's and Carrie's profiles that follow. Try to do a complete analysis of one or the other. Allow yourself some time, since interpreting a Strong is much more complex than interpreting a 24-hour diary.

Steven Taylor's and Carrie Baugh's Strong Interest Inventories

Copies of Steven Taylor's and Carrie Baugh's Strong Interest Inventory appear on the following pages.

STRONG [redacted] INTEREST INVENTORY OF THE
STRONG VOCATIONAL INTEREST BLANK

UVA-PACS-032

PAGE 1

PROFILE REPORT FOR: Steven Taylor
ID:
AGE: 28 **SEX:** MALE
DATE TESTED: 09/01/88
DATE SCORED: 09/18/88

SPECIAL SCALES: ACADEMIC COMFORT 62
INTROVERSION-EXTROVERSION 40

TOTAL RESPONSES: 325 **INFREQUENT RESPONSES:** 8

GOT	
R	MOD. LOW
I	AVERAGE
A	HIGH
S	HIGH
E	MOD. LOW
C	VERY LOW

REALISTIC

GENERAL OCCUPATIONAL THEME - R (30 40 50 60 70; F, M)
MOD. LOW (48)

BASIC INTEREST SCALES (STANDARD SCORE)

AGRICULTURE — AVERAGE (49)
NATURE — MOD. HIGH (58)
ADVENTURE — MOD. HIGH (59)
MILITARY ACTIVITIES — VERY LOW (41)
MECHANICAL ACTIVITIES — AVERAGE (48)

INVESTIGATIVE

GENERAL OCCUPATIONAL THEME - I (30 40 50 60 70; F, M)
AVERAGE (56)

BASIC INTEREST SCALES (STANDARD SCORE)

SCIENCE — AVERAGE (48)
MATHEMATICS — AVERAGE (52)
MEDICAL SCIENCE — MOD. HIGH (59)
MEDICAL SERVICE — AVERAGE (50)

ARTISTIC

GENERAL OCCUPATIONAL THEME - A (30 40 50 60 70; F, M)
HIGH (59)

BASIC INTEREST SCALES (STANDARD SCORE)

MUSIC/DRAMATICS — HIGH (61)
ART — MOD. HIGH (52)
WRITING — HIGH (60)

OCCUPATIONAL SCALES

F	M	Occupation	Standard Score F	Standard Score M	Very dissimilar (15)	Dissimilar (25)	Moderately dissimilar (30)	Mid-range	Moderately similar (40)	Similar (45)	(55)
REALISTIC											
[CRS]	RC	Marine Corps enlisted personnel	(CRS)	8	*						
RC	RC	Navy enlisted personnel	17	10	*						
RC	RC	Army officer	33	16		*					
RI	RIC	Navy officer	27	24		*					
R	R	Air Force officer	20	14	*						
[C]	R	Air Force enlisted personnel	(C)	9	*						
R	R	Police officer	30	19		*					
R	R	Bus driver	24	21		*					
R	R	Horticultural worker	30	27			*				
RC	R	Farmer	16	16		*					
R	RCS	Vocational agriculture teacher	23	12	*						
RI	R	Forester	39	36				*			
[IR]	RI	Veterinarian	(IR)	30				*			
RIS	[SR]	Athletic trainer	32	(SR)							
RS	R	Emergency medical technician	20	16		*					
RI	RI	Radiologic technologist	22	17		*					
RI	R	Carpenter	31	20		*					
RI	R	Electrician	34	11	*						
RIA	[ARI]	Architect	32	(ARI)							
RI	RI	Engineer	32	21		*					
INVESTIGATIVE											
IRC	IRC	Computer programmer	28	22		*					
IRC	IRC	Systems analyst	27	25			*				
IRC	IR	Medical technologist	22	28			*				
IR	IR	R & D manager	33	26			*				
IR	IR	Geologist	33	32				*			
IR	[I]	Biologist	32	(I)							
IR	IR	Chemist	25	30				*			
IR	IR	Physicist	15	22		*					
IR	[RI]	Veterinarian	34	(RI)							
IRS	IR	Science teacher	26	29			*				
IRS	IRS	Physical therapist	38	40					*		
IR	IRS	Respiratory therapist	31	39				*			
IC	IR	Medical technician	16	18		*					
IC	IE	Pharmacist	33	27			*				
ISR	[CSE]	Dietitian	30	(CSE)							
[SI]	ISR	Nurse, RN	(SI)	32				*			
IR	I	Chiropractor	33	50						*	
IR	IR	Optometrist	36	49						*	
IR	IR	Dentist	37	41					*		
I	IA	Physician	46	47						*	
[IR]	I	Biologist	(IR)	41					*		
I	I	Mathematician	24	24		*					
IR	I	Geographer	37	32				*			
I	I	College professor	45	47						*	
IA	IA	Psychologist	48	46						*	
IA	IA	Sociologist	36	47						*	
ARTISTIC											
AI	AI	Medical illustrator	38	38				*			
A	A	Art teacher	12	36				*			
A	A	Artist, fine	41	40					*		
A	A	Artist, commercial	32	45						*	
AE	A	Interior decorator	13	33				*			
[RIA]	ARI	Architect	(RIA)	36				*			
A	A	Photographer	44	45						*	
A	A	Musician	51	54						*	
AR	[EA]	Chef	44	(EA)							
[E]	AE	Beautician	(E)	34				*			
AE	A	Flight attendant	31	45						*	
A	A	Advertising executive	35	51						*	
A	A	Broadcaster	42	46						*	
A	A	Public relations director	33	39				*			
A	A	Lawyer	48	58							*
A	AS	Public administrator	36	50						*	
A	A	Reporter	45	44					*		
A	A	Librarian	20	43					*		
AS	AS	English teacher	23	47						*	
[SA]	AS	Foreign language teacher	(SA)	45						*	

CONSULTING PSYCHOLOGISTS PRESS
577 COLLEGE AVENUE
PALO ALTO, CA 94306

STRONG INTEREST INVENTORY OF THE
STRONG VOCATIONAL INTEREST BLANK

UVA-PACS-065

PAGE 2

PROFILE REPORT FOR: Carrie Baugh
ID:
AGE: 25 **SEX:** FEMALE

DATE TESTED: 09/01/88
DATE SCORED: 09/18/88

SOCIAL

GENERAL OCCUPATIONAL THEME - S	
MOD. HIGH (57)	F / M

BASIC INTEREST SCALES (STANDARD SCORE) 30 40 50 60 70

Scale	Result
TEACHING	MOD. HIGH (59)
SOCIAL SERVICE	MOD. HIGH (60)
ATHLETICS	HIGH (60)
DOMESTIC ARTS	AVERAGE (53)
RELIGIOUS ACTIVITIES	AVERAGE (51)

ENTERPRISING

GENERAL OCCUPATIONAL THEME - E	
AVERAGE (44)	F / M

BASIC INTEREST SCALES (STANDARD SCORE)

Scale	Result
PUBLIC SPEAKING	MOD. HIGH (58)
LAW/POLITICS	MOD. HIGH (56)
MERCHANDISING	AVERAGE (47)
SALES	AVERAGE (51)
BUSINESS MANAGEMENT	AVERAGE (53)

CONVENTIONAL

GENERAL OCCUPATIONAL THEME - C	
AVERAGE (51)	F / M

BASIC INTEREST SCALES (STANDARD SCORE)

Scale	Result
OFFICE PRACTICES	MOD. LOW (41)

OCCUPATIONAL SCALES

F	M	Occupation	Standard Score F	Standard Score M	Very Dissimilar (15)	Dissimilar (25)	Moderately Dissimilar (30)	Mid-Range	Moderately Similar (40)	Similar (45 55)
SOCIAL										
SA	[AS]	Foreign language teacher	28	(AS)			*			
SA	SA	Minister	37	48				*		
SA	SA	Social worker	34	48				*		
S	S	Guidance counselor	39	44				*		
S	S	Social science teacher	49	44						*
S	S	Elementary teacher	22	15		*				
S	S	Special education teacher	33	36				*		
SRI	SAR	Occupational therapist	31	35				*		
SIA	SAI	Speech pathologist	42	39					*	
SI	[ISR]	Nurse, RN	36	(ISR)				*		
SCI	N/A	Dental hygienist	25	N/A			*			
SC	SC	Nurse, LPN	9	23	*					
[RIS]	SR	Athletic trainer	(RIS)	12						
SR	SR	Physical education teacher	16	8		*				
SRE	SE	Recreation leader	49	52						*
SE	SE	YWCA/YMCA director	46	46						*
SEC	SCE	School administrator	48	39						*
SCE	N/A	Home economics teacher	11	N/A	*					
ENTERPRISING										
E	ES	Personnel director	45	45						*
ES	E	Elected public official	45	42						*
ES	ES	Life insurance agent	34	33				*		
EC	E	Chamber of Commerce executive	26	40			*			
EC	EC	Store manager	34	38				*		
N/A	ECR	Agribusiness manager	N/A	6						
EC	EC	Purchasing agent	40	35					*	
EC	E	Restaurant manager	36	37				*		
[AR]	EA	Chef	(AR)	27						
EC	E	Travel agent	45	45						*
ECS	E	Funeral director	29	16			*			
[CSE]	ESC	Nursing home administrator	(CSE)	46						
EC	ER	Optician	18	14		*				
E	E	Realtor	27	41			*			
E	[AE]	Beautician	18	(AE)		*				
E	E	Florist	22	26		*				
EC	E	Buyer	26	39			*			
EI	EI	Marketing executive	49	54						*
EIC	ECI	Investments manager	50	44						*
CONVENTIONAL										
C	C	Accountant	33	34				*		
C	C	Banker	33	45				*		
CE	CE	IRS agent	35	34				*		
CES	CES	Credit manager	22	26		*				
CES	CES	Business education teacher	13	26	*					
[CS]	CES	Food service manager	(CS)	33						
[ISR]	CSE	Dietitian	(ISR)	38						
CSE	[ESC]	Nursing home administrator	28	(ESC)			*			
CSE	CSE	Executive housekeeper	21	31		*				
CS	[CES]	Food service manager	22	(CES)		*				
CS	N/A	Dental assistant	14	N/A	*					
C	N/A	Secretary	24	N/A		*				
C	[R]	Air Force enlisted personnel	15	(R)		*				
CRS	[RC]	Marine Corps enlisted personnel	21	(RC)		*				
CRS	CR	Army enlisted personnel	26	9			*			
CIR	CIR	Mathematics teacher	20	13		*				

ADMINISTRATIVE INDEXES (RESPONSE %)

OCCUPATIONS	27 L %	35 I %	37 D %
SCHOOL SUBJECTS	58 L %	17 I %	25 D %
ACTIVITIES	57 L %	22 I %	22 D %
LEISURE ACTIVITIES	54 L %	26 I %	21 D %
TYPES OF PEOPLE	50 L %	29 I %	21 D %
PREFERENCES	30 L %	37 = %	33 R %
CHARACTERISTICS	64 Y %	7 ? %	29 N %
ALL PARTS	42 %	28 %	30 %

CONSULTING PSYCHOLOGISTS PRESS
577 COLLEGE AVENUE
PALO ALTO, CA 94306

STRONG [redacted] INTEREST INVENTORY OF THE
STRONG VOCATIONAL INTEREST BLANK

UVA-PACS-065

PAGE 1

PROFILE REPORT FOR: Carrie Baugh
ID:
AGE: 25 **SEX:** FEMALE

DATE TESTED: 09/01/88
DATE SCORED: 09/18/88

GOT	
R	AVERAGE
I	AVERAGE
A	HIGH
S	MOD. HIGH
E	AVERAGE
C	AVERAGE

SPECIAL SCALES: ACADEMIC COMFORT 57
INTROVERSION-EXTROVERSION 37

TOTAL RESPONSES: 325 **INFREQUENT RESPONSES:** 7

REALISTIC

GENERAL OCCUPATIONAL THEME - R (30 40 50 60 70; F / M)
AVERAGE (45)

BASIC INTEREST SCALES (STANDARD SCORE)

AGRICULTURE — AVERAGE (46)
NATURE — AVERAGE (47)
ADVENTURE — MOD. HIGH (57)
MILITARY ACTIVITIES — VERY LOW (41)
MECHANICAL ACTIVITIES — AVERAGE (46)

OCCUPATIONAL SCALES

F	M	Occupation	Standard score F	Standard score M	Very dissimilar (15)	Dissimilar (25)	Moderately dissimilar (30)	Mid-range	Moderately similar (40)	Similar (45)	(55)
[CRS]	RC	Marine Corps enlisted personnel	(CRS)	19							
RC	RC	Navy enlisted personnel	25	13			*				
RC	RC	Army officer	37	16				*			
RI	RIC	Navy officer	41	26					*		
R	R	Air Force officer	31	16				*			
[C]	R	Air Force enlisted personnel	(C)	12							
R	R	Police officer	25	13			*				
R	R	Bus driver	22	25		*					
R	R	Horticultural worker	22	23		*					
RC	R	Farmer	17	11		*					
R	RCS	Vocational agriculture teacher	12	6	*						
RI	R	Forester	24	20		*					
[IR]	RI	Veterinarian	(IR)	7							
RIS	[SR]	Athletic trainer	20	(SR)		*					
RS	R	Emergency medical technician	12	7	*						
RI	RI	Radiologic technologist	14	12	*						
RI	R	Carpenter	24	11		*					
RI	R	Electrician	29	13			*				
RIA	[ARI]	Architect	35	(ARI)				*			
RI	RI	Engineer	31	14				*			

INVESTIGATIVE

GENERAL OCCUPATIONAL THEME - I (30 40 50 60 70; F / M)
AVERAGE (51)

BASIC INTEREST SCALES (STANDARD SCORE)

SCIENCE — AVERAGE (44)
MATHEMATICS — AVERAGE (52)
MEDICAL SCIENCE — AVERAGE (48)
MEDICAL SERVICE — MOD. LOW (41)

F	M	Occupation	Standard score F	Standard score M	Very dissimilar (15)	Dissimilar (25)	Moderately dissimilar (30)	Mid-range	Moderately similar (40)	Similar (45)	(55)
IRC	IRC	Computer programmer	27	20			*				
IRC	IRC	Systems analyst	33	28				*			
IRC	IR	Medical technologist	22	18		*					
IR	IR	R & D manager	31	24				*			
IR	IR	Geologist	22	18		*					
IR	[I]	Biologist	20	(I)		*					
IR	IR	Chemist	21	21		*					
IR	IR	Physicist	9	14	*						
IR	[RI]	Veterinarian	16	(RI)		*					
IRS	IR	Science teacher	13	9	*						
IRS	IRS	Physical therapist	22	23		*					
IR	IRS	Respiratory therapist	27	24			*				
IC	IR	Medical technician	16	3		*					
IC	IE	Pharmacist	26	21			*				
ISR	[CSE]	Dietitian	26	(CSE)			*				
[SI]	ISR	Nurse, RN	(SI)	17							
IR	I	Chiropractor	22	33		*					
IR	IR	Optometrist	32	33				*			
IR	IR	Dentist	28	14			*				
I	IA	Physician	26	33			*				
[IR]	I	Biologist	(IR)	25							
I	I	Mathematician	18	18		*					
IR	I	Geographer	33	30				*			
I	I	College professor	33	37				*			
IA	IA	Psychologist	36	45				*			
IA	IA	Sociologist	26	42			*				

ARTISTIC

GENERAL OCCUPATIONAL THEME - A (30 40 50 60 70; F / M)
HIGH (64)

BASIC INTEREST SCALES (STANDARD SCORE)

MUSIC/DRAMATICS — MOD. HIGH (61)
ART — HIGH (62)
WRITING — MOD. HIGH (60)

F	M	Occupation	Standard score F	Standard score M	Very dissimilar (15)	Dissimilar (25)	Moderately dissimilar (30)	Mid-range	Moderately similar (40)	Similar (45)	(55)
AI	AI	Medical illustrator	24	35		*					
A	A	Art teacher	11	36	*						
A	A	Artist, fine	29	33			*				
A	A	Artist, commercial	42	41					*		
AE	A	Interior decorator	37	43				*			
[RIA]	ARI	Architect	(RIA)	43							
A	A	Photographer	41	48					*		
A	A	Musician	38	41				*			
AR	[EA]	Chef	25	(EA)			*				
[E]	AE	Beautician	(E)	41							
AE	A	Flight attendant	36	51				*			
A	A	Advertising executive	55	59							*
A	A	Broadcaster	48	50						*	
A	A	Public relations director	49	50						*	
A	A	Lawyer	50	52						*	
A	AS	Public administrator	56	56							*
A	A	Reporter	45	46						*	
A	A	Librarian	43	50					*		
AS	AS	English teacher	37	51				*			
[SA]	AS	Foreign language teacher	(SA)	41							

CONSULTING PSYCHOLOGISTS PRESS
577 COLLEGE AVENUE
PALO ALTO, CA 94306

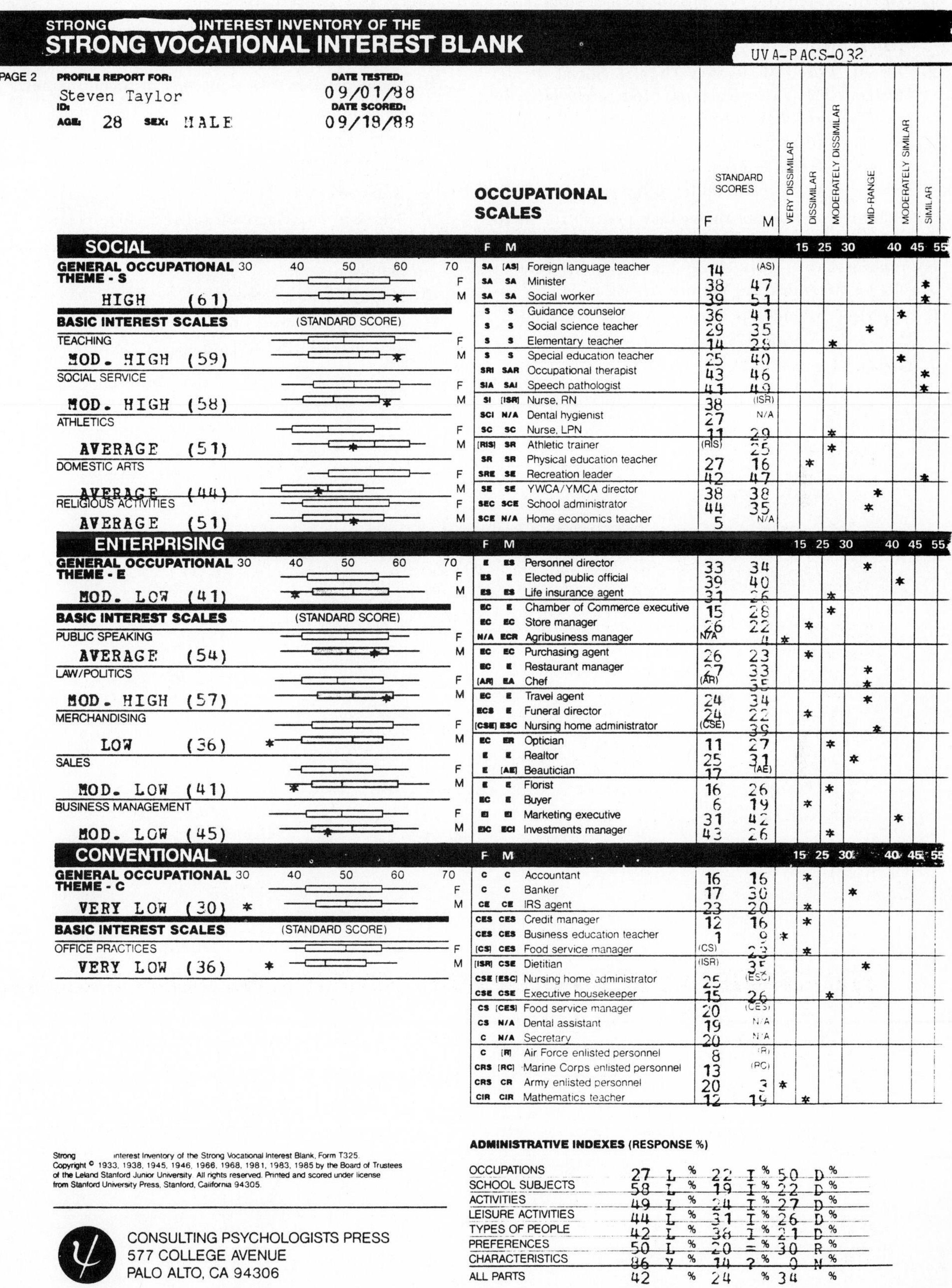

STRONG INTEREST INVENTORY OF THE
STRONG VOCATIONAL INTEREST BLANK

UVA-PACS-032

PAGE 2

PROFILE REPORT FOR: Steven Taylor
ID:
AGE: 28 **SEX:** MALE

DATE TESTED: 09/01/88
DATE SCORED: 09/18/88

SOCIAL

GENERAL OCCUPATIONAL THEME - S (30 40 50 60 70; F / M)
HIGH (61)

BASIC INTEREST SCALES (STANDARD SCORE)

TEACHING
MOD. HIGH (59)

SOCIAL SERVICE
MOD. HIGH (58)

ATHLETICS
AVERAGE (51)

DOMESTIC ARTS
AVERAGE (44)

RELIGIOUS ACTIVITIES
AVERAGE (51)

ENTERPRISING

GENERAL OCCUPATIONAL THEME - E (30 40 50 60 70; F / M)
MOD. LOW (41)

BASIC INTEREST SCALES (STANDARD SCORE)

PUBLIC SPEAKING
AVERAGE (54)

LAW/POLITICS
MOD. HIGH (57)

MERCHANDISING
LOW (36)

SALES
MOD. LOW (41)

BUSINESS MANAGEMENT
MOD. LOW (45)

CONVENTIONAL

GENERAL OCCUPATIONAL THEME - C (30 40 50 60 70; F / M)
VERY LOW (30)

BASIC INTEREST SCALES (STANDARD SCORE)

OFFICE PRACTICES
VERY LOW (36)

OCCUPATIONAL SCALES

F	M	Occupational scale	Standard score F	Standard score M	Very dissimilar (15)	Dissimilar (25)	Moderately dissimilar (30)	Mid-range	Moderately similar (40)	Similar (45)
SOCIAL										
SA	[AS]	Foreign language teacher	14	(AS)						
SA	SA	Minister	38	47						*
SA	SA	Social worker	39	51						*
S	S	Guidance counselor	36	41					*	
S	S	Social science teacher	29	35				*		
S	S	Elementary teacher	14	28			*			
S	S	Special education teacher	25	40					*	
SRI	SAR	Occupational therapist	43	46						*
SIA	SAI	Speech pathologist	41	49						*
SI	[ISR]	Nurse, RN	38	(ISR)						
SCI	N/A	Dental hygienist	27	N/A						
SC	SC	Nurse, LPN	11	29			*			
[RIS]	SR	Athletic trainer	(RIS)	25			*			
SR	SR	Physical education teacher	27	16		*				
SRE	SE	Recreation leader	42	47						*
SE	SE	YWCA/YMCA director	38	38				*		
SEC	SCE	School administrator	44	35				*		
SCE	N/A	Home economics teacher	5	N/A						
ENTERPRISING										
E	ES	Personnel director	33	34				*		
ES	E	Elected public official	39	40					*	
ES	ES	Life insurance agent	31	26			*			
EC	E	Chamber of Commerce executive	15	28			*			
EC	EC	Store manager	26	22		*				
N/A	ECR	Agribusiness manager	N/A	4	*					
EC	EC	Purchasing agent	26	23		*				
EC	E	Restaurant manager	27	33				*		
[AR]	EA	Chef	(AR)	35				*		
EC	E	Travel agent	24	34				*		
ECS	E	Funeral director	24	22		*				
[CSE]	ESC	Nursing home administrator	(CSE)	39				*		
EC	ER	Optician	11	27			*			
E	E	Realtor	25	31				*		
E	[AE]	Beautician	17	(AE)						
E	E	Florist	16	26			*			
EC	E	Buyer	6	19		*				
EI	EI	Marketing executive	31	42					*	
EIC	ECI	Investments manager	43	26			*			
CONVENTIONAL										
C	C	Accountant	16	16		*				
C	C	Banker	17	30				*		
CE	CE	IRS agent	23	20		*				
CES	CES	Credit manager	12	16		*				
CES	CES	Business education teacher	1	9	*					
[CS]	CES	Food service manager	(CS)	23		*				
[ISR]	CSE	Dietitian	(ISR)	35				*		
CSE	[ESC]	Nursing home administrator	25	(ESC)						
CSE	CSE	Executive housekeeper	15	26			*			
CS	[CES]	Food service manager	20	(CES)						
CS	N/A	Dental assistant	19	N/A						
C	N/A	Secretary	20	N/A						
C	[R]	Air Force enlisted personnel	8	(R)						
CRS	[RC]	Marine Corps enlisted personnel	13	(RC)						
CRS	CR	Army enlisted personnel	20	3	*					
CIR	CIR	Mathematics teacher	12	19		*				

ADMINISTRATIVE INDEXES (RESPONSE %)

OCCUPATIONS	27 L %	22 I %	50 D %
SCHOOL SUBJECTS	58 L %	19 I %	22 D %
ACTIVITIES	49 L %	24 I %	27 D %
LEISURE ACTIVITIES	44 L %	31 I %	26 D %
TYPES OF PEOPLE	42 L %	36 I %	21 D %
PREFERENCES	50 L %	20 = %	30 R %
CHARACTERISTICS	86 Y %	14 ? %	0 N %
ALL PARTS	42 %	24 %	34 %

CONSULTING PSYCHOLOGISTS PRESS
577 COLLEGE AVENUE
PALO ALTO, CA 94306

NOTES:

1. Overall, scored High in Artistic theme: Moderately High in Music/Drama, High in Art, and Moderately High in writing.
2. Overall, scored Moderately High in Social theme: Moderately High in teaching, Moderately High in Social Service, High in Athletics, Average in domestic and religious activities.
3. Scored Moderately High in other basic interests: Public Speaking, Law/Politics & Adventure.
4. Administrative Index shows Like or Indifferent to 80% of different types of people.
5. Administrative Index shows Like or Indifferent to 80% of Activities and Leisure Activities.
6. Academic Comfort 57: Strong interest in school. Extroversion Scale 37: Strong extrovert.
7. High percentage of Dislike in Occupations (37%).

INFERENCES:

Carrie is a person who:

1. Shows a strong interest in artistic themes.
2. Enjoys athletics.
3. Shows a fairly strong interest in social themes.
4. Likes most activities.
5. Tolerates different types of people.
6. Enjoys learning.
7. Is extroverted.
8. Seems to enjoy activities that involve people.
9. Shows interest in performance, or being in front of people.
10. Might like attention.
11. Likes opportunities for self-expression.
12. Sees herself as independent yet people-oriented.

14

Analyzing the Written Interview

NOTE:
DO NOT READ THIS UNTIL YOU HAVE COMPLETED THE WRITTEN INTERVIEW ASSIGNMENT.

Now it's time to come back to your written interview. Most people who engage in individual assessment as a vocation (such as career counselors) begin data collection with a long interview of the person to be assessed. In one way or another they say "Tell me about yourself," and then they shut up and take notes, usually intervening only when the interviewee stops talking. Usually this open-ended background interview turns out to be the most important source of information for the assessment.

We began the self-assessment process with a written version of such a background interview. The written interview exercise is very similar to a good introductory counseling interview. And like such an interview, it will be our most important data source.

The Interview Output

To use the responses to the written interview for assessment purposes, we need first to consider what types of information those responses provide. But stop and think for a moment; the most obvious answer is not correct.

If a person claims to have been born March 26, 1948, and to have one sister, it is probably reasonable to assume that these assertions are true. That is, they are probably verifiable "facts." But if you examine a typical written interview, you will find that only a small percentage of its content represents clear-cut "facts" about the person's background. More important, if you examine the interviews of three or four people, you will find considerable variety in the types of "facts" presented. Unlike a more directive interview, in which a person is asked a series of very specific "fact-eliciting" questions, this type of interview allows the interviewee great latitude in deciding what to talk about—which is, of course, the whole idea.

In talking about one's background, any person, given the time, could quite literally write at least one book. (Some autobiographies stretch across three or four volumes.) But because of the context in which the written interview is conducted, one gets instead the equivalent of one or two chapters. And the task of selecting what goes into those chapters is left to the interviewee.

Of course, people being interviewed do not sit down and visualize their history and then develop conscious criteria for editing. They just talk or, in the case of our written equivalent, write. The result, however, is hardly a random selection. Two written interviews produced by the same person a month apart will look remarkably similar (and quite different from most other people's written interviews).

This type of data-generating instrument assumes that, given considerable latitude in responding to questions, a person must consciously or unconsciously choose what and how to answer, and that those choices tell us something important about that individual. What is said, what is not said, how it is said, the order in which it is said—all is potentially useful information about the individual.

Potentially is the key, for some of these data may say more about the manner and the context in which they were generated than they do about the person. Be sure to keep in mind the caveats outlined in Chapter 2 regarding contextual influence (see page 8).

Interpreting the Output

To make sense of this "potentially useful information," to decide what, if anything, the data tell us about the more central aspects of the interviewee, let us return to a more careful consideration of the technique we often use to "interpret" information in our everyday lives: drawing inferences based on patterns we see in the data.

Drawing inferences is something literally everyone engages in almost constantly. We see or hear something, compare, often unconsciously, that perception with our assumptions about the nature of the world and of society, and then draw a conclusion that is to us "logical" or appropriate or consistent with that comparison. This mental process has been recognized for thousands of years. Epictetus, the Greek Stoic philosopher, noted that "Men are not disturbed by things, but by the views which they take of them." In other words, two people may observe the same event and draw entirely different conclusions. This is because of the differences in their assumptions about the way the world operates. Thus, the conclusions people draw reveal something about their assumptions. If we focus on those assumptions, we can learn more clearly what they are and, if they seem unrealistic, perhaps modify them. In self-assessment, this introspective process of examining our own assumptions will help us to draw conclusions or inferences that are more "logical" to others as well as to ourselves.

Consider an example or two. When Mr. Jones arrives at his new boss's home (which he has never seen before) for dinner, he notices that it has a circular driveway, a six-car garage, tennis courts, and a stable. He preconsciously makes a number of assumptions (about the cost of such a home and its upkeep, his boss's salary, his boss's previous work history, and so on) and quickly concludes that his new boss (or his wife) comes from a wealthy family. When Ms. Johnson is introduced to the manager of the Chicago office, she notices that he has a slide-rule tie clasp, a calculator on his desk, and a set of proceedings of an electrical engineering society on his shelf. She infers privately that he has a technical background and orientation.

Although we all are, in some sense, familiar with this technique for making meanings out of data, few people consciously think about the process and about how they tend to engage in it. And most of us often use it in a casual and sloppy manner in dealing with the more inconsequential aspects of our daily activities. For purposes of self-assessment, such casualness is inappropriate. In order to achieve as accurate an assessment as possible, we need to be very careful about how we make inferences.

Drawing Inferences

Exhibits 14–1 and 14–2 display some of the tentative inferences two people independently drew after studying the written interview of a third person (Ms. Jones), along with the data on which those inferences were based. Look at each carefully and see if you can see how they are different.

Most people would agree that the analysis in Exhibit 14–2 seems a lot more sound than that in Exhibit 14–1. That is not to say that the inferences in Exhibit 14–1 are wrong or the inferences in Exhibit 14–2 are correct. We really do not have enough information to make that judgment. But there are a number of differences between Exhibits 14–1 and

Exhibit 14–1

Some Inferences Made from Written Interview Data

Data	*Inferences*
Ms. Jones graduated from Stanford with honors.	She is clearly very intelligent.
Ms. Jones's writing style is very loose.	She is probably an unorganized person.
Ms. Jones is an only child.	She is probably achievement-oriented, socially withdrawn, and very tense.
Ms. Jones talks a lot about the people in her life.	She is a very people-oriented and popular person.

Exhibit 14–2

Some Inferences Made from Written Interview Data

Data	*Inferences*
The five periods in Ms. Jones's life which she says were the most "dull and boring" (see page 2, paragraph 2; page 10, paragraph 1; and page 14, paragraph 2) all have one thing in common—she is not in contact with any or many people.	Interacting with people is probably an important source of stimulation for Ms. Jones.
The only "hard" quantitative subject Ms. Jones says she took in high school or college was math, and she says she didn't like it at all (see page 5, paragraph 1; and page 16, paragraph 2).	Ms. Jones does not have strong quantitative skills.
The four people Ms. Jones lists as being "the most influential" in her life are: her father, her tenth-grade teacher, one of her summer job bosses, and her grandmother (page 20).	Ms. Jones probably relates well to authority figures and can be influenced by them.
Ms. Jones grew up in a middle-class family and twice makes references to "not wanting to be poor" (see page 1, paragraphs 3 and 4; and page 30, paragraph 1).	Money is not unimportant to Ms. Jones.

14–2 that tend to give one more confidence in Exhibit 14–2.

First of all, the "data" in Exhibit 14–2 are a lot clearer and more specific than those in Exhibit 14–1. Exhibit 14–2 states, with some precision, exactly what it is in Ms. Jones's written interview that has led to such inferences. Exhibit 14–1 is more vague in this regard. One is left wondering how much "a lot" of talk about people is, and what is meant by a "very loose writing style." Is it not possible that Ms. Jones's writing style is fairly typical, but that the person who created the inference in Exhibit 14–1 has a very structured writing style—so what is perhaps typical looks "loose" to such a person?

It is easy to lose sight of the actual data in a written interview and end up analyzing instead your own impressions of the data. We've seen people who, after expressing a strong belief in the validity of a set of inferences, were unable to point to a single specific piece of supporting information in the written interview. They had been performing a reasonably interesting analysis—but it was based mostly on their own impressions, not on the specific information provided by the other person. So it is important that you have specific data clearly in mind when you are drawing an inference. When you are trying to communicate your logic to another person, it is essential that you reveal not only your conclusions or inferences, but also your data. Otherwise, the other person may not be able to understand how you got from a set of data (which he or she may see very differently) to a set of inferences, and decide that you "have jumped to conclusions."

A second obvious difference between Exhibits 14–1 and 14–2 relates to a number of questionable assumptions. All inferences are based on one or more assumptions; some inferences are more reasonable than others. Exhibit 14–2's inferences seem more reserved and conservative (and reasonable!) because they assume less. Assumptions are like icebergs, in the sense that at first we may only see their tips (in the conclusions we draw). We encourage you in your self-assessment and in your discussions with others to be continually on the alert for iceberg assumptions and to challenge them to make sure the conclusions and inferences you reach are conservatively logical. As you move now into a more intensely inductive phase of the self-assessment process, practice careful consideration of the relationship between data, assumption, and inference.

To get from "Ms. Jones is an only child" to "She is probably achievement-oriented, socially withdrawn, and very tense," one has to assume a great deal. Of course, the inference could be true, but only if a large number of implicit assumptions are also true.[1] Even the first inference in Exhibit 14–1, which assumes a great deal less, is still based on at least the following assumptions:

1. That Ms. Jones really did graduate from Stanford *with* honors.
2. That "intelligence" is a definable, measurable human attribute.
3. That one's "intelligence" is fairly stable over time—it doesn't go up or down drastically in a month, for example.
4. That the "intelligence" one displays does not vary greatly from situation to situation or task to task.
5. That to graduate with honors from Stanford, one *must be* intelligent. That is, that all the other possible explanations as to why one could graduate with honors (work hard, bribe the dean) are impossible.

People often feel rather uncomfortable when forced to look at the assumptions implicit in their inferences. We often treat our inferences as if the assumptions were known truths, when they seldom are. All five of the assumptions implicit in the inference concerning Ms. Jones's intelligence have some probability of being accurate, but that probability is significantly less than 1.0.

The more assumptions that are not known truths that one makes, and the lower the probability that each of those assumptions is correct, the more one engages in what we might call an "inferential leap." Starting with the datum about Ms. Jones graduating from Stanford, inferential leaps of various sizes are shown in Exhibit 14–3.

As the diagram implies, the larger the "leap," the further it takes you from the data. Getting too far away from one's data can be dangerous in self-assessment. Throughout the book, we will remind you to stay close to the data—to let the data do the talking—so that your inferences are clearly connected to the data. We mean "clearly connected" not only to you, but also to another reasonable person who might look at the data you have generated and the inferences you have drawn. In fact, getting someone else whom you trust and respect to look at your data and inferences is an excellent means of checking your own logic and of uncovering large inferential leaps that may be based more on your biases, desires, and "unfounded" assumptions than they are in the data you generated. We will talk more about how to go about getting someone else to look at your data and inferences later.

A third difference between Exhibits 14–1 and 14–2 can be found in the nature of the data used. Exhibit 14–2 never starts with a single "observation" (such as "Ms. Jones is an only child"), but with a number of observations that possibly identify a pattern. And by keeping the patterns relatively simple, the author was able to draw nontrivial inferences

Exhibit 14–3

Inferential Leaps

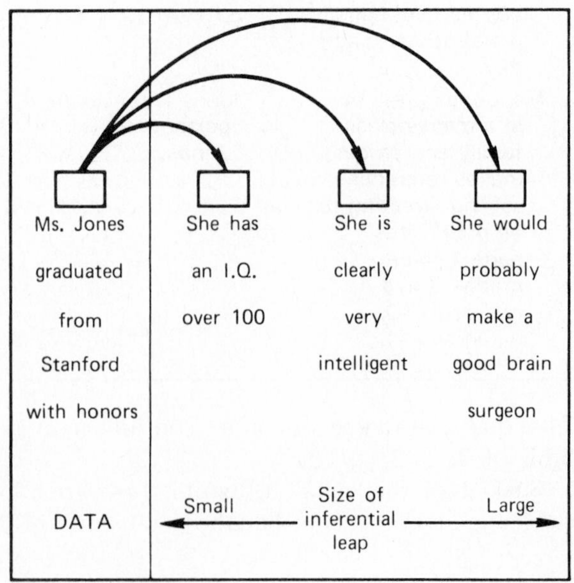

---

[1]Very often when people develop inferences that seem to be based on a lot of assumptions, the reason is that they carry a "model" (often preconsciously) around with them based on their own experiences or something they were taught in school. For example, the person who inferred that because Jones is an only child she is socially withdrawn, tense, and achievement-oriented could have been applying a model of child development learned in school. Such a model might be represented as:

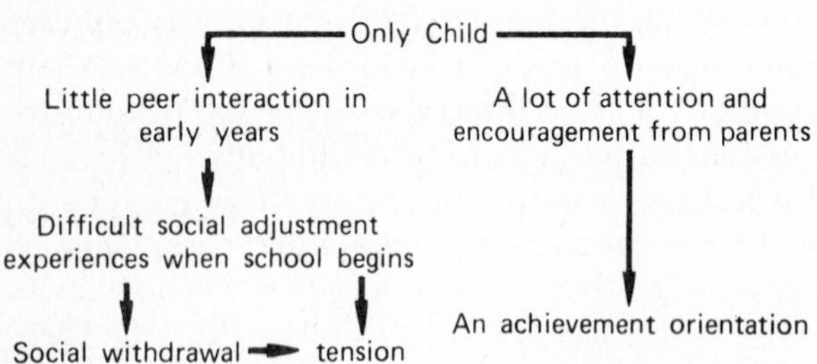

Such a simplified model of a complex phenomenon may be approximately true in some cases, but certainly not in all. Or then again, our data analyst might well have been an only child who had grown up socially withdrawn, tense, and achievement-oriented! That is, the analyst could have been identifying with the data and projecting onto them without even being aware of what was happening. In either case, it would not be unusual for the analyst to believe the inference was "obviously true" and to vigorously defend it until forced to identify the assumptions implicit in the logic that led to the inference.

without making a large number of questionable assumptions.

Perhaps the single most important part of analyzing a written interview involves looking for relatively simple patterns. Does the author of the interview repeatedly talk about any particular subject or person? Does the author always (or never) quantify things that can be measured? Does the author repeatedly use a certain type of verb or adjective? Does the author always (or never) go into great detail in describing people? Objects? Events?

Through the identification of patterns, we can start to sort the peripheral and trivial from the more central and important. As any scientist recognizes, an event that occurs once tells us very little. But one that occurs again and again, in some pattern, may well tell us something central about whatever is being studied.

Identifying Patterns

Most people just "see" patterns—that is, the process of identification often occurs unconsciously. However, there are ways in which one can facilitate one's own preconscious processes.[2] Understanding these can be helpful.

Perhaps the easiest technique to facilitate pattern identification is to underline or write on a separate sheet of paper anything that catches your attention when you read through the interview. On a second reading, you can begin more systematically to check whether some pattern is associated with any of those items.

Developing inferences from single bits of data can also help you to identify patterns. If you select a single datum, draw a conservative, tentative inference from it, go on to the next datum, and so on, you can then go back and look at your inferences to see if any of them seem related. If they are, the bits of data from which you generated those inferences may also be related. With a little rewording, you may be able to phrase an inference that captures the essence of several bits of data—and in so doing, identify a pattern. In the end, using a single datum as support for a pattern or theme will be logically weak, but it is a useful way to get started drawing conservative inferences and identifying patterns.

Simple counting can be an important tool. If something seems to occur "a lot," count exactly how many times it does occur. You may find your "sense" was very accurate, or very inaccurate. In a similar vein, if something "seems" never to occur, carefully check that out. Does it really *never* occur?

Very speculative inferences (those based on lots of questionable assumptions), although not very useful as the *product* of an analysis, can occasionally be useful in the *process* of analysis. The major value of a highly speculative inference lies in its occasional capacity to point out an unseen pattern. Having made the inference, for example, that Ms. Jones is socially withdrawn, one might then notice *for the first time* how little she talks about her relationships with people in her written interview, and that she doesn't mention belonging to student organizations of any kind in high school or college. Or you might find just the opposite. In either case, the speculative inference led you to useful data that were previously unseen.

You will undoubtedly develop still other techniques yourself. Just keep in mind that pattern finding, like most good detective work, requires a combination of instinct, disciplined search, and time. And do not be surprised if at first you have some difficulty finding patterns. People often feel they don't know what to look for in the data, or that they need a list of "typical patterns" to guide them. But this is not possible. There are literally an infinite variety of patterns that could be developed from a written interview. Because most of us are better versed in deductive than inductive processes, such a response is natural in the beginning.

Guidelines

In analyzing a written interview:

1. Stick closely to the data. Make sure you don't end up analyzing something you've manufactured in your own head. Let the data do the talking.
2. Search for patterns. Remember that one datum alone tells you virtually nothing. But be willing to start small and build slowly. Don't leap to conclusions without going back to check the data carefully to be certain that the conclusions are supported.
3. Be careful and explicit with your inferences. Try to be aware of your assumptions.
4. Treat all inferences as tentative rather than hard conclusions.
5. Try to be patient. Good analysis takes time.

[2]By "preconscious processes" we mean things that are a part of our mental activity that are not usually in our awareness, but which, if focused on with moderate effort, can be consciously thought about. We contrast this to "subconscious processes," which are more difficult to bring into awareness.

Exercise

In the following cases, you will find Steven Taylor's and Carrie Baugh's responses to the first four questions of the written interview. These interviews are typical of most written interviews we've seen.

Now, to give you some practice in analyzing this kind of data before you begin work on your own, we would like you to answer the following questions about Taylor's and Baugh's first four responses:

1. What tentative, conservative inferences do you make about them?
2. What data do you cite to support your inferences?

As you try to answer these questions, we suggest that you try the following:

1. Read the questions and responses, underlining or making notes of things you think or feel are important as you go along.
2. List several of the data points you identified as potentially important on the Drawing Tentative Inferences Worksheet (next page). Then write down a tentative, conservative inference based on that datum. An example is given on the worksheet.
3. Clarify as well as you can the assumptions you were making that led you to the conclusions/inferences that you drew. An example is given on the worksheet.
4. After you have written a few inferences from single data points, go back through the first four responses and your inferences and attempt to collect evidence related to a single inference. Try to find as much evidence for the inferences you chose as you can.

Finally, stop and consider the strengths and weaknesses of the written interview as a data-generating device. Write these down and note the impact they have on the credibility of the data to you. Be prepared, if you are in a class setting, to discuss these strengths and weaknesses and their implications for your use of the data.

STEVEN TAYLOR'S WRITTEN INTERVIEW (PART A)

Question #1—An Account of My Life (Open-Ended Question)

1. I guess we ought to start at the beginning. I was born in Akron, Ohio, in June of 1960. I was trouble right from the beginning, refusing to come forth after thirty-seven hours of labor. I was the first for my mom, so the doctor wanted to hold off as long as possible, but they finally gave up and cut me out. I was ten pounds at birth and reputedly could be easily located by the volume of my vocalizations. My family moved often in my early years, and in fact, my father moved us while my mother and I were recuperating from our first ordeal together. So I went home to my first home in Newark, Ohio, where my father worked for the B & O Railroad as a management trainee. I have very few memories of Newark—glimpses of the breakfast area in the house and the backyard of my friend Sean's house. Sean lived on a stream filled with smooth round rocks which made the water burble and laugh as it went by. The banks were filled with all sorts of creatures to inspect and examine: frogs, grubs, nightcrawlers, and all manner of things. It was a wondrous place for two small boys to wander about, and I'm reminded of that stream whenever I'm near running water even today. I wonder whether my interest in the outdoors began all the way back then? Memories of Newark are very pleasant, even if they are mostly fuzzy now.

2. We moved next to Baltimore, although we only stayed there a short time. My mother told me about my soon-to-be brother Brian while we lived in Baltimore. We shared a red-brick, two-family house there with a middle-aged lady who had lots of crystal and glass things in her house. I remember the way the light sparkled in all directions when I was in her living room. But it was also too bright in her house, sort of a harsh light. Our house always seemed very warm and cozy. My mother has always collected primitive American furniture, and all of our houses have been decorated with wood floors (sometimes stone) with throw rugs and antique chairs and tables. I was always surprised as a boy at how other people were always afraid of hurting their furniture or staining the carpet or protecting something or other. How did these people get through the day if they were so worried about getting dirty or breaking the china or whatever? It wasn't until much later in my life that I came to realize

---

Prepared by Lori Wilson and Jim Clawson. UVA-PACS-033.

that having a mother who didn't mind if we ate pizza sitting on the floor or put our feet on the coffee table was a rare privilege! We always used china plates and sterling silver just like it was what most people called "everyday" dining. My parents just used what they had gotten as wedding presents, figuring it wasn't of much use sitting in a cabinet somewhere. I'm forever grateful to them for running the house like that. I think it made my brothers and I truly aware of the value of practical beauty and elegance. If you only use the "good" china and silver with guests, what kind of commentary are you delivering about your family and the friends who come around all the time and make up the fabric of your life? But where was I?

3. Baltimore. We didn't stay there too long; in fact, by the time Brian (Bubby, to me) was born, we had moved to Silver Spring in Maryland, and Dad was working in Washington. I was three when we moved to Silver Spring, and I found two good friends, Sally Johnson and Danny Frederick, who lived across the fence in back of our house. Sally was a lot of fun and liked to play all kinds of games in spite of her being a girl. Most of the other girls in the neighborhood thought there was something special about being a girl, that they should hang out with girls or do different things because they were girls, but Sally knew better. She and I were great pals, and played on the trampoline, and built forts, and went sledding in the winter. Danny Frederick (I always think of him with both names) lived next door to the Johnsons, or maybe two doors down, but it's not important. Danny was more of a thinker, and I remember him being sick a lot. He wore a hearing aid and thick glasses, but I'm not sure I really noticed until I thought back to him just now. His father was a real health nut before such a thing was fashionable. (We're still around 1963–64 here.) His father had grown up in Maine, I think, and he knew all kinds of things about plants and animals that my parents could never explain to me. The Fredericks had the world's biggest leaf and compost piles in their back yard, and Mr. Frederick was forever out there turning it or putting this or that layer on to help the process along. And, boy, did the Fredericks come up with some different things to eat! Mr. Frederick once made a dandelion salad when I was at their house. Weeeird! Mr. Frederick was a crabby man, but he was fascinated by plants and gardening, and if I talked to him about those things, he was a great teacher. I think Mr. Frederick was the first person to show me (without intending to, of course) that if you could just get the conversation around to something he liked to talk about, he was a lot nicer to be around and he just seemed happier. A lot of other people in the neighborhood thought the Fredericks were just too weird to deal with, but even though they were odd, I had a lot of fun with them. The Fredericks never seemed to be a happy bunch, though, and at times the melancholy would get to be too much for me, and I'd just go back home and not see Danny for a couple of days.

4. I went to museums a lot with my mom. Washington is a great place for that, and we went all the time. Museums are wonderful places; no matter where you turn, there is something completely new to learn about. I think when I get around to raising kids, museums are places where I'd like to spend time with them. Learning about the evolution of the earth and how big the dinosaurs were gives a child a perspective on just how small mankind is in the greater scheme of things. While I couldn't fathom how long a time millions of years was (I don't think I can now either), I remember an exhibit showing the age of the dinosaurs, and the Ice Age, and various eras, with the appearance of homo sapiens way down in a little two-inch strip at the end of the exhibit, and a sign at the other end of the room marking where the formation of the earth would lie on the same timeline. It was also in Washington that I first learned about Thomas Jefferson and Abraham Lincoln and George Washington, and of course John Kennedy. I don't rememeber much about Kennedy being shot except that my father came home from work, or maybe he stayed home from work the next day. It was a very quiet day, very sad and gloomy. I remember watching Jack Ruby shooting Oswald, though, and how confused everyone was over whether that was a good thing or a bad thing.

5. I also started school in Silver Spring. Kindergarten was a very short experience for me. The principal came down (kindergarten was on a lower floor from the rest of the school) in the first week or so and gave me all these tests to take. I can't recall what the tests were, except that they involved matching up shapes and colors, I think. Anyhow, after a very short time, it was announced that I was moving into the first grade. This was a terribly traumatic move. I didn't know anybody in the first grade, and to this day I can't recall any individuals or teachers from that school, which I attended through first and second grades. In first grade, the class spent a lot of time learning to read, but I already knew how to read, so I had a little spot over at the side of the room where I sat by myself and read books. There were all kinds of books to read, and I read about all kinds of exotic foreign places. My little spot was nice; it was sunny, and nobody bothered me much, and I had plenty to do. I must have taken math with the rest of the class, but I don't remember a thing about it. I did have Sally, of course, who I think was a grade ahead of me, but my memory is that mostly I hung out by myself at school. I remember the scariest part about moving to first grade was eating lunch in the cafeteria. I went in there for the first time, and I didn't know anybody, but there were hundreds of kids in there running around and talking and making an amazing din. As I recall, I cried through lunch the first couple of times, but then it was all right.

6. We moved again just before second grade 1966—this time, to St. Paul, Minnesota. I walked to school in St. Paul, which was great fun, and it was *very* independent! We could even stop on the way to or

from school and buy bubble gum or squeeze pops (whatever happened to squeeze pops?) at the little store on Cosmos Avenue. I went to Grover Cleveland School, and Mrs. Bund was my teacher. St. Paul was different than other places, because everyone was so bundled up in the wintertime and each class had its own changing room. I met Alex Bell in St. Paul. Alex and I got special treatment at school because we were able to work on our math lessons on our own. We went on ahead of the class at our own speed in our own math workbooks, which was great. It was so boring to have to listen through the teacher explaining really simple problems to the rest of the class. Alex and I became great pals and played together a lot of afternoons after school. We never played organized sports together, though, because like most of my friends throughout all of school, Alex was a year and a half older than me. That fact, coupled with the fact that I inherited my father's growing pattern and developed physically much later than most guys, left me the equivalent of two or even three years behind my peer group at school in terms of physical development. I didn't fully grasp that as the reason for my difficulty in making sports teams until I was in college, and I was continually frustrated at my small size and strength compared to my friends. But that didn't stop me from playing sports, even though I seemed to get hurt more than most people. Before we leave Minnesota, I should add that it was there that I got my first ice skates, a pair of double runners that I would take with my dad down to the big ice rink in back of the school in the evenings. I was way behind most Minnesotans, of course—not getting started on skates until I was six years old—but it was my first taste of winter sports, which remain my favorites to this day.

7. In the spring of 1967, we moved again; this time to North Barrington, Illinois, a small town about fifty miles northwest of Chicago. I think of Barrington as where I spent my youth, since we stayed there from third grade through my junior year of high school, from 1967 to 1976. My folks built a house on a wooded lot of about two acres, and it was an idyllic life for a kid who likes to be outdoors. In back of our house, although our property only went back maybe a couple hundred feet, it was about a half-mile through the woods and fields before you came to the next house. Across the street from us was a row of houses, but right behind them was a swamp of maybe fifteen or twenty acres. The possibilities for exploring were pretty much endless, and my brothers and I (my youngest brother Tom was also born in D.C.; he's five years younger) built forts, and climbed trees, and made paths through the woods which only we knew about. In the winter the swamp would freeze, and we could ice skate on it. There was also a lake at the end of our block where we could fish and swim in the summer, and where we played hockey in the winter in an outdoor league. Pretty much everybody who lived near us had kids close to our age, so we could always get up a game of football or softball, or in the evenings, play "Kick the Can" or flashlight tag.

8. I went to North Barrington Elementary through fifth grade, but when it came time to go to middle school, Barrington Middle School was overcrowded, so I went with about 200 sixth graders to an experimental school built next door to the middle school called the Lines School. The Lines School was an experimental design, and it was round, with classrooms around the outside and a library without walls in the middle. The classrooms' inner walls were sliding partitions, so that a teacher could open the back wall of the classroom and allow students to spill out into the library whenever there was independent work to be done. Lines School also had a handpicked teaching staff and a special curriculum for sixth grade, which emphasized letting each student progress at his or her own speed. Seven of us were picked out of the group to take math and English separately from the rest of the school, and we pushed ahead with amazing speed. We went so far in math, for instance, that I didn't learn anything new in math from sixth grade until sophomore year of high school, four years later. At Lines School, I also had my first taste of politics, and was elected vice-president of the school. I didn't run for president because there was this cute (real early-developing) girl who I was sure had a lock on president. She won, and so did I, but I don't think she ever forgave me for what happened next. When the election results were announced, she was applauded, and I was hoisted onto the shoulders of my classmates and carried around the outside of the room twice. When they put me down I went over and congratulated Janet, but she didn't seem overly enthused to say the least. The experience left me confused for a long time, and I learned to be careful about what I aim for and why I aim for it, because if it's not what I really want or what I think I should do, winning out has implications for others as well as for me. Am I attributing too much to these early childhood events?

9. Lines School was different than the rest of my education in the Barrington school system. At Lines, it was OK to be inquisitive, studious, scholastic. After I moved back into the mainstream schools, Barrington Middle and Barrington High, the interchange between the cliques went way down. At those schools, you were either a jock or a freak (or a nerd), or else you were just one of the rest. Of course, there were some avowed freaks who still played sports, and there were some jocks who partook of various recreational substances, and there were even some of us who were members of one group and kept up with friends in the other group, but pretty much anybody who was "cool" was in one of the two groups. I hung around mostly with jocks, but a couple of my best friends from elementary school went with the freaks, so I did some crossing over. I should add that, although I played on the

tennis and golf teams, and played Babe Ruth baseball and Pop Warner football, when I entered high school I was only 5′2″ and weighed less than 100 pounds. I was younger than everyone in my class by a year and behind the normal growth schedule besides! I must have been an aggressive son of a bitch just to get noticed, much less to have been a class officer, athlete, and club president. I never connected my competitive spirit now with facing that obstacle before. I think we're getting into the real purpose of the written interview now.

10. I forgot to mention earlier that I also spent a good part of my time from about age five forward playing music. My parents started me on classical piano at age five or six, and I played for about four or five years. I had taken up the trumpet in fourth grade (age eight), and I played both for two or three years. It was at Lines School, or maybe in seventh grade, that I dropped the piano. I truly enjoyed playing the piano, but I was a very late bloomer physically, and I just didn't have the dexterity for piano. On the other hand, I was one of the best at the trumpet almost as soon as I picked it up, so when I started feeling pinched on practice time, the piano lessons went. The trumpet eventually fell to the bane of braces on my teeth, although I stayed at it for about a year with the braces on. After a couple of hundred days of bleeding lips after practice, and after falling from first chair to sixth or seventh, I gave up the trumpet and joined the tennis team. Maybe the sports urge was as much a factor as anything. There had been a growing conflict between playing music and playing sports throughout middle and high school, and I finally bagged the school band in my sophomore year. I kept up playing in the stage band for another year, but braces and conflicts between after-school practice schedules finally took the horn away from my lips. I always intended to take it up again, and I kept my silver horn (it was a fifteenth birthday gift from my parents) with me until it was stolen from a storage locker in New York in 1984. I still have a bugle, but even that is a struggle now. I keep saying it to myself, so I'll go on written record here: Someday, I'm going to take both of those instruments back up again. When? . . .

11. Where was I? Entering Middle School, I think. Barrington was a small town, but the school system gathered students from a wide radius. Middle School was located in Barrington, about six or seven miles from where we lived. Barrington Middle was a big school, with grades six–eight and probably (?) 1,500 students. I met the two friends who ended up being my only lifelong friends from Barrington while at middle school, Mike Harper and Rod Dollins. I also had my first kiss there, from Julie Bender. I was in seventh grade, she was in eighth (an older woman by two years, remember!), and we pecked each other a couple of timid times outside a Friday night sock hop at the community center. I wonder what happened to Julie Bender? But I digress. Mike moved to Barrington from Connecticut; his family lived near mine in North Barrington, and they were also tennis fanatics. Mike and I were buds, David Harper and my brother Brian became fast friends, and Chris and my brother Tom were also tight. Needless to say, our parents became and stayed close friends, and when I was in San Francisco last week, I found Mike's sister Meghan living at my parents' house while looking for a place to live during law school. Rod Dollins also moved in seventh grade, but from Texas. Rod was a nationally ranked tennis player, and although he and Mike never became too close, the three of us spent a lot of time together over the next few years. And I had my first beer with Mike and did my first serious (deliberate) female-chasing with Rod. I was in both of their weddings, and Mike's now a lawyer in San Diego, while Rod was a Wharton MBA who moved back to Dallas to get married and go to work. Then he was killed in a boating accident. I carried his coffin three months after I attended him at his wedding. You never know how fragile the world can be until it blows up on you a couple of times.

12. The sad times were later, though. High School was the BIG TIME for those of us who knew everybody, played a sport, and did well in classes. Barrington High had four grades and 3,000 students, so if you were somebody at Barrington, you could really get to thinking that you were a pretty big cheese. The school had had a reputation for drugs in the years before I arrived, but things had cooled off somewhat by the time my class started. It was a stereotypical midwestern town where I lived. There was a fair-sized contingent of upper-middle-class and even a few upper-class kids from Barrington Hills, but for the most part, the kids came from families who lived in tract homes in one of the developments which had sprung up all around the area. After school, a lot of kids worked in town, and weekends were spent cruising Route 14, hitting McDonald's or the bowling alley, looking for chicks, or just getting high and driving around. (Yes, this was back when smoking dope was still considered a normal activity among my peer group.) I worked as a golf caddie and as a Little League umpire in the summers, and I refereed junior hockey a couple of nights a week during the school year. I was busy at school, too, where I was in the band and on the tennis team, as previously advertised. I was also on the student council and active in the Ski Club. The Ski Club was a big deal at BHS, with about 700 members. We went skiing one night a week in the winters and raised money throughout the year for an annual trip to Indianhead/Big Powderhorn Mountain in Upper Michigan. I wouldn't go to Indianhead now if you paid me! My perspective on skiing has been warped by too many opportunities to ski up to my waist in the champagne stuff in Utah and Colorado and the Alps. (I've gotten around a little bit since Barrington.) No anec-

dotes about life in Barrington are jumping out at me just now.

13. At the end of my junior year, I was elected president of the Ski Club over my good buddy Jeff Garber, I was signed up for all the advanced placement classes, I was gearing up for a senior year at BHS as a "big man on campus," but my dad had a once-in-a-lifetime opportunity to move to Detroit and become president of a small railroad there. He and I had a long talk about whether I should stay in Barrington and live with the Harpers for my senior year, but I decided I'd rather go with the family and take my chances. Besides, a couple of the guys I'd been hanging out with were really starting to slide into some close scrapes with the law. I decided to move to Michigan, and as it turned out it was one of the best decisions I ever made. We moved the week before school started, and I actually went to school the first couple of days from a motel about a mile away from school while we were waiting for the movers to arrive and unpack our house.

14. I had become good enough at golf to make the team in Michigan, so I met those guys before the school year started, and when classes did start up, I found out that my new school was a couple of light-years ahead of Barrington High academically. I also had a crash course in self-assertiveness in my first two weeks at Andover (Bloomfield Hills Andover High School). I had to talk my way into two of the classes I wanted to take, because the prerequisites were different between the two states. And then the class ranks came out, and I was about 100th out of our class of 400 or so. At Barrington I'd been in the top five percent of my class, so this new ranking was quite a shock. I had to go through two guidance counselors, the assistant principal, and I finally ended up in the principal's office arguing that, since Andover weighted honors classes differently than Barrington had, my grade point average and class rank would need to be calculated differently than other students. Dr. Theodore didn't like the concept much, but he said he'd think it over and talk to me the next day. When he called me to his office the next day, though, he had a wide grin and told me how pleased he was to have a National Merit Scholarship Finalist at Andover High. He'd gotten the word during the night, and it changed his whole perspective on Steven Taylor. Funny how creating a little fame for somebody can overcome just about any size problem. Ol' Gene Theodore didn't know he'd created a monster, though. I was back in his office a week later after I found out that the school paper had disbanded two years earlier after he'd censored a story. I asked him whether he would agree to keep his hands off if I restarted a student paper, pointing out that a school without a student paper couldn't really be considered a top-notch high school. Dr. Theodore saw the merits of that argument, and by the Christmas break, we had a bi-weekly student paper, uncensored. I never did tell him that my "previous student paper experience" amounted to a write-up of a single basketball game for the BHS paper two years earlier. It didn't matter; the paper was a big hit, and it was self-supporting by its third issue. I ended up my year at Andover with an even bigger confidence builder (not that my already oversized ego needed any more inflating by that point). Andover held a leadership retreat for some of the top students from each of the three classes, where we went off for a weekend and talked about life, leaders' responsibilities, and our place in the greater cosmos. At the end of the retreat, the students and faculty voted on who should give the closing speech at dinner on Sunday night, and they chose me. I'd never done an impromptu speech before, especially not in front of all the student and faculty heavies at a banquet. I got through it—mentioning, of course, all the people who had helped me along the way-and got a standing ovation at the end. I was beginning to get pretty damn pompous.

15. I had made a college tour of the Ivy Leagues with my parents over spring break as a high school junior, and there was no doubt in my mind where I wanted to go to school, Cornell. It had a great academic reputation, it was in upstate New York, it owned its own ski hill and golf course, and it was the only school I visited where students I met said, "You *have* to come here, it is the *best*." Elsewhere, students seemed to list off some pros and some cons, but in Ithaca they grabbed you by the arm and said, "You've *got* to come to my next class; the professor is the *greatest*." I was sold. Unfortunately, when I applied early, I was told to wait until the regular admissions process, and then I got that awful thin envelope in the mail, and it seemed only a formality that they had bothered to keep me on the waiting list. I'd gotten into some great schools, and I even sent my deposit to Stanford, before my gloom was lifted by the arrival of the big envelope that meant I could go after all to Cornell.

16. When I got to Cornell, the Steven ego took some big hits early on. First of all, I had placed out of two terms of chemistry through taking advanced placement exams in high school, and my myopic freshman academic adviser told me I ought to move right into organic chemistry in my freshman fall term. Organic chemistry at Cornell is normally the last course in the pre-med sequence, and it was populated predominantly by sophomore and junior pre-meds. I was shark bait, and those guys chewed me up in a big way—not just in class, but in the lab, and in the dorm at night by making me a regular part of late-night beer bashes. I was a mess, and I made a big fat D in both terms for organic chemistry. Not quite up to snuff for a National Merit Finalist, you say? I was just getting started on jumping off the academic precipice. For four years in Ithaca, I experimented, I drank, I partied, I chased girls, I was a fraternity social chairman, I went to France for a term and came back and taught French, I was a disc jockey, I announced basketball games, I

ran a division of the Cornell Outing Club. I did a million things, but I rarely focused on class work, and I just ignored two whole courses and received failing grades in my major! Something was amiss, but when anybody asked, I was fine, just fine, no problems here. After all, everybody knew who I was, right? Wrong. Anyway, if I didn't always go to class, I did manage to go to some job interviews my senior year, and what do you know, these people weren't overly concerned about my grades. I had offers to come and work in advertising in Chicago, and from New York Money Center Bank to become a banker in New York. I didn't know whether either one was what "I really wanted to do." I hadn't slowed down long enough to think about that in several years. So I decided to go with New York Money Center Bank. I'd never been to New York, I thought it would be good for me to live in the big city for a while, and besides, if I didn't like it, I would have at least learned something about finance. So much for making a careful decision about my career. I remember the disappointment of the recruiter from Chicago when I called him to turn him down. One of my best friends had just called him to also reject an offer in favor of a job in New York, and he asked me to reconsider if it turned out that I didn't like banking. I also remember thinking how it seemed unfair that I had gotten these job offers with only a minimum of effort while so many of my friends had tried for these jobs and hadn't gotten them. And these were people who had done *well* in their classes at school.

17. I did graduate, in case you were wondering, and after a few weeks at home in Michigan, I went off to find my way in the world of the Big Apple. Going to work for a big bank proved to be an excellent decision. The rigorous structure and formality of the bank's nine-month training program gave me a chance to pull the rest of my life together. The training program was also a much-needed confidence builder. In spite of all my extracurricular accomplishments at Cornell, my poor academic performance had left me shaken, more so than I was to acknowledge for several years. In that way, entering a bank training program was good medicine. I was in a training group of twenty-five people, and we took classes most of every day in finance, accounting, credit analysis, international finance, economics, and business law. The work was not particularly challenging intellectually, and I found that if I applied myself in terms of putting in the hours after work, I excelled within my group. These were all strong students from good colleges, but I finished consistently in the top three or four places and was eventually one of the first three of us to be promoted to lending officer. I had always believed, even in the down days at Cornell, that I was as capable as anyone around me, even more capable than most, but doing well is satisfying, and thinking that I could do better than I was left me with a hollow feeling. Acting like I was doing better than I was proved exhausting after a time. Realizing what a toll that exacted may have been one of the great revelations of my life to that time.

18. I made some fast friends in the training program. Let me rephrase that, since I haven't talked to even one of them in a couple of years. I made a couple of close friends in the training program, but the relationships were passing. As I matured (I had been avoiding that for a while), I found that my interests were different than those of most of my associates at the bank. In any case, the training program was a chance for me to get back on my feet, and I grabbed at it. I also met a woman I was to later ask to marry me, although after a year of cohabitation, we canceled our wedding plans. I canceled our wedding plans. Looking back, I think the urge to get married was largely another attempt to stabilize my life after the wild years at Cornell. Janet was (is) a wonderful girl, and we had some great times together, but living together magnifies any differences in two people's basic priorities like no amount of talking about your differences can do. In our case, each of us was expecting the other to change attitudes on religion (Janet was a conservative Jew), lifestyle (she was ready for the suburbs; I needed more diversity, not less), and other things which just don't change as rapidly or as easily as we had naively assumed they could. We lived together from January 1983 to February 1984 in a beautiful brownstone in Park Slope, Brooklyn. I moved back to Manhattan and went on with my work, while Janet quit the bank and became an aerobics instructor at Club Med in Martinique. She has stuck with it and is now a manager of a new Club Med in Florida, with aspirations to move to the headquarters office in Paris. We didn't talk much for a couple of years, but we established contact again a couple of years later, and I think we both agree that things have worked out for the best.

19. At work, after the training program, I was assigned to the Energy Division, the hot area to be in 1982! I also was very lucky to be assigned to work for a Wharton MBA who ignored the NY Money Center Bank (MCB) tradition of handing out dollars and promotions based on seniority. Joe was a believer in rewarding your stars and dumping your dogs, and even though those terms were, I believe, from a portfolio management class, Joe applied them with singular success in his human resource management. This was a boon for me, as I worked hard and was rewarded with fast promotions and larger-than-normal raises, but it was hard to watch co-workers of six and seven years' experience told to seek positions elsewhere because they "just weren't keeping up with the program." I learned a tremendous amount about finance and deal work from Joe, but I probably learned at least as much from watching him deftly parry any political maneuvering which came at him. He had an admirable ability to ignore those attempts to undermine him which he believed would fail, but to bring the important crises out into the open for discussion.

Working in the oil and gas business was great fun while the boom lasted, but sometime in 1983–84 it became apparent that the bloom might be off the rose more than temporarily, and by 1985 I was spending a large proportion of my time working out problems with various credits. I was one of the fortunate few who, for whatever reason, had not made any big lending blunders, so I was kept on as times got leaner.

20. There were several opportunities during 1984 and 1985 for me to move to other positions in the bank, but each time I went through the interview process I was left flat by the prospect of committing to several more years in that mammoth corporate hierarchy. Each time, I came up with some other excuse not to move, but when I passed on the chance to go to Columbia or Wharton on the bank's tab, it occurred to me that I ought to consider a new occupation. The reason I didn't accept the offer of time off with pay to go to business school was that the offer was contingent on signing up for a minimum of three years' service to the bank after graduation. When I finally admitted to myself that that was my true feeling, I began a job search. It just so happened that my mother was diagnosed as having breast cancer at about the same time in 1985, and I decided that if I was going to change jobs, it made sense to look for something in San Francisco, where my parents now live. I love the Bay Area, and in the back of my mind I'd been thinking about living out there since my first visit in 1982. I also wanted to seek an opportunity to work in a private firm, where all of the hoopla over rabbit-from-the-hat quarterly earnings didn't have to be created again and again. Anyone at MCB with good common sense knew that the bank had been sliding for at least two or three years, yet every quarter the company would sell a building or liquidate a little more of the bond portfolio and announce a smooth continuation of upward-trending profits. After a while, it begins to offend your sensibilities, and you either become a tremendous cynic or you get out. I elected to pull the ripcord.

21. My first efforts at landing a job in San Francisco went nowhere, and after two trips to the area with several interviews but no victories, I was preparing to resign from MCB and just head west. I had already spoken with my immediate boss about my plans, and while he was disappointed to see me go, he was quite supportive. I spoke to him before formally resigning out of a sense of personal obligation, since he'd just promoted me to AVP and given me two analysts and a couple of big new accounts. One week before I was going to make it official, I had a phone call from one of the firms I'd interviewed with in San Francisco, who had previously told me that they couldn't hire anybody without three or four years' real estate experience. Well, things had changed, as three of their analysts had quit in the space of three months, and they were now interested in talking to me. I flew out again, we came to an agreement on a package that gave a substantial pay increase with a shot at an even bigger bonus, and we were off and running.

22. The move to San Francisco was a turning point in my life, and I sensed the possibilities as I made preparations to leave New York. At my new job, I would be working directly for one of the partners in a respected real estate investment company with a reputation for giving its employees as much freedom and responsibility as they could handle. I was moving to San Francisco, where I could expand on the mild fitness program I had begun in New York, and I was stepping out from the shelter of my group of college friends which still surrounded me in New York. I was going to be spending time with my parents for the first time in about nine years, but in many ways this was a chance to start anew with them, to abandon the thrust-and-parry relationship we had fallen into as I went through high school and college as an eldest child. For the first time, I also expected to be able to save some money and begin building toward a financial future (Darden was soon to relieve me of that notion). All of these things energized me like I hadn't been energized in years, and through leaving New York and moving to California, I was able to break back through to the entrepreneurial, confident, and happy person I'd lost somewhere in the years since high school. I was able to put a balance back into my life that had been missing for a long time, and my time in California turned out to be one of the best years yet.

23. Even though I decided to apply to business school after only four months at Bear Realty, I enjoyed the work while I was there. My decision to return to graduate school was, as much as anything else, a realization that I had never fully developed my intellectual capabilities or satisfied those yearnings at Cornell, and that I needed to have a chance to do that, before I proceeded on with the rest of my life. I had really hoped to stay in the Bay Area and go to Stanford, but both the Stanford and Harvard admissions offices told me that in spite of 99th percentile board scores, glowing recommendations, and strong personal essays, they just couldn't overcome crappy undergraduate grades. So in a sense, I owed Darden a strong performance when I arrived here. I'm sure that whatever faculty read my application had to take a deep breath and say, let's take him anyway, and I appreciated that and was grateful for their making that extra effort on my behalf. As things have turned out, I truly believe that I have been happier at Darden than I would have been at those *other* business schools.

24. Well, there you have the rough overview. I had a rough time knowing where to cut this back. For better or worse, my memory is such that I could recite verbatim hundreds of conversations I've had over the years, places I've been to, meals I've eaten, and hundreds of other experiences, many of them I'm sure as important as some of the stories I've related here. But for Pete's sake, let's get on to question #2!!!

CARRIE BAUGH'S WRITTEN INTERVIEW (PART A)

Question 1 (Open-ended Question)

1. I suppose I'll start at the beginning—usually a good place to begin. I was born in San Francisco, California, at Saint Mary's Hospital. I am the second child of three. Dad was finishing up his teaching credentials when I was born, or had just begun teaching at the high school. Mom had her hands full with my brother Jake and me. It's funny I start with San Francisco and teaching; both have been so instrumental in my life! My father's influence, especially. He is such a phenomenal teacher! His students adore him! Education was always stressed in my life; I *never* remember not considering college! And San Francisco, a city that holds such wonderful, wonderful memories, and truly a sense of love for its tolerance, beauty, and culture. Perhaps knowing my life began there explains why I am so strongly drawn to come "home" to San Francisco.

2. We moved to San Jose, California, when I was very young—and have lived there ever since. I really don't remember all that much about my early years—only trivial little events that seem so clear they could have happened yesterday. Like, Jake and I were playing catch when I was about five (he was six). He threw the ball on top of my dresser by accident. Being "Ms. I-can-do-it-all-by-myself" (a trait I still have), I climbed up to get the ball . . . and subsequently had the entire dresser crash onto my little body!! I must have been knocked out, because my next memory is of Dad holding me over the kitchen sink, splashing water on my face, and yelling, "Oh, God! Let her be alive!!"

3. So much for silly vignettes. I went to a Catholic grammar school from first through eighth grades—an important influence in my life, looking back, but how I hated it!! Going to a small school, with forty students in your class, together for eight years! Yuck! Everyone knew everything about you, and you were stuck in this *mold*. And I was one of those kids picked on—"Miss shy, homely little Italian girl with the hairy arms and legs!" Even now I shudder, thinking back.

4. I was smart, though, and good in sports. Being smart was good, 'cause Mom said "not to worry about those stupid girls in class; they're just jealous." It sounded good, anyway. What really sticks out in my mind during this time was learning! I was so fascinated by all the ideas and history of the world. And the teachers for the most part were great! Mrs. Martin, Mrs. Bilecky, Sister Maureen, Sister Theresa—I can remember them all very clearly.

5. Perhaps my most favorite teacher at this time was Mrs. Gwen. She is a lively, spunky, free-spirited woman who obviously *loved* kids. She taught sixth, seventh, and eighth grade math, science, and Spanish—all subjects I liked and had an aptitude for. Especially math—she made it all seem easy and important to know.

6. By seventh grade, I was becoming more open and talkative. My confidence level really grew. A few reasons come to mind: I was chosen to be a cheerleader, some boys had crushes on me, and I finally had begun to master the piano. The cheerleading incident seems so funny to me now—running around yelling silly little cheers and performing little dance steps around the football field or basketball court. And the nine of us girls getting together to practice, and gossip, and mostly talk about boys. It was strange, but when I got to high school, I wanted no part of it!

7. I mentioned the piano above. I had been taking lessons for the past several years, since I was seven (until college). When I was around twelve, I could start to play most things I wanted to, and my friends thought it was *so* neat that I could play songs they heard on the radio! Although Mom wouldn't believe it, I actually enjoyed my lessons and trying to master the tough classical songs. I just had a hard time finding time to practice. Mom and I had this deal, where she'd set the timer (after we ate dinner) for one hour, and I'd practice until I heard the buzz. It worked well, most of the time. (Plus, I found a system: after playing a song a few times, I could sneak into the kitchen and move the timer up five minutes, and nobody realized it! Like they didn't know. I guess even back then I needed to feel in control of my time and destiny.)

8. Thinking back to piano lessons somehow reminds me of summer. . . . How I *loved* summer! (especially during middle school and high school). My friends and I would go to the neighborhood school pool everyday and splash around, listening to the radio full blast. Even now, when I hear certain songs, it takes me right back to the pool and that place in time. Anyway I *loved* the heat and getting a great tan. . . . I was lucky, I just got browner and browner. I always teased my friends who needed tons of sunblock and

junk. I was "All Natural." We'd have tan contests, which was tough, 'cause most of my friends were Mexican, Portuguese, or Oriental. But we always joked about it and enjoyed just being so lazy!

9. I used to daydream a lot back then—something I still do on occasion. Mostly, wanting to be an actress or singer, up there wowing the audience with my dramatic entry, romantic flirtations, or sexy singing voice. Sometimes, it was to go on a daring, dangerous adventure—like an African safari or some sort of Huck Finn adventure. Then I'd snap back into reality, realizing I still had to finish up some homework for that day.

10. Although I really liked my friends, I also liked to be alone and to be with my family. I've always fought off the feeling of "group think," or feeling pressure to think like my friends or some acceptable way. Sometimes friendships can be so confining. To this day, I am this way! I have very few close friends, and tons of acquaintances whom I enjoy having fun with and kidding around with. But I'll commit to very few. It's something I'm working towards improving about myself—not letting friendships come and go.

11. Family, on the other hand, is a completely different matter. I come from an extremely tight-knit, open, intensely loving family. My parents are completely devoted to their children and have always sacrificed to give us "the best." I'll start with Dad. Dad is one of the most creative and talented persons I've ever met, and one of the most sensitive, thoughtful, and giving as well. He is definitely the stable force of our family—a wonderful listener! He is independent and an "I can do it" person. When I was young, Dad made all of us kids the most elaborate Halloween costumes you could imagine—scary witches, mummies, cats, princesses, even R2D2 for my sister one year! Prior to becoming a teacher, he was a tailor! And he always made us kids great clothes. In fact, he made my wedding gown this summer, and all six bridesmaids' dresses! I think back on my dad's life with much interest and respect: Second of nine children born to a poor Italian farmer in Madera, California. Was a self-taught tailor and opened his own shop at age seventeen. Went into the Coast Guard. Was in the Catholic seminary for two years—almost became a priest but stopped short because he truly wanted a family. Went to college on a Vet fund, decided to be an English and Latin teacher. Met my mom in college, got married during that time.

12. Dad was always really creative; his students loved him, and many still keep in touch with him! He used to advise a lot of clubs, have meetings at our house, and plan receptions. I remember the Latin club had a huge drama they put on; Dad choreographed and directed it! The students came over twice a week to practice. Later in life, when I was around fourteen, Dad decided he wanted to fulfill his lifelong dream to build his own cabin near Lake Tahoe, California. So he spent two years reading every electrical, plumbing, carpentry "How-To" book on the market and took advantage of his summers off to build it—with the help of my family and friends! We all learned how to make cupboards, nail in sheet rock, build a chimney, and put in a toilet! It was a wonderful time in all our lives, I think! So many hilarious things happened—like the practice toilet flush, which left water cascading down the stairway into the garage! Or the pan that exploded into flames, which we had to throw out the window, then chase down the hill to extinguish. Lord, we still look back and laugh about those days!!

13. For all his talents, I worry about Dad now. I think he *hates* the thought of growing old and having to depend on someone else. He has accomplished so many important things in his life, touched so many people; yet, he feels somehow that he should have done more. Sometimes he seems so sad, now that us kids are all grown and out of the house. I really hope he and Mom begin to treat themselves with trips and doing things they enjoy.

14. My mom is a great complement to my dad, and very different. Mom is quiet, almost shy around new people, yet a very strong person inside. She always supported Dad's ideas and activities, and was quite a worrier. Her family is her #1 priority. She fiercely guards it; we tease her sometimes, calling her a "shebear" (no, she doesn't particularly appreciate the comment). The point is, she felt each of our little pains and triumphs, and always pushed us toward excellence. It was very important to Mom that we all get college educations fully supported by the family. When she was growing up, she was told she didn't have to go to college, she was very pretty, and would find a good husband to support her. Mom, as a result, worked her way through school, with virtually no support from her parents, even though they paid for her brother's schooling. It was so important for me and my sister to go to good schools and improve ourselves.

15. I've heard about competitions between mother and daughter. It's incomprehensible to me, given the strong support Mom always had for most things I've done. Mom is also *extremely* stubborn!! I know I've picked up some of that myself. As a result, we've certainly had our major standoffs! Especially concerning boys: nobody was ever good enough, or treated me well enough, etc. I think we have very different ideas about certain aspects of personal relationships, even now. It is so important to me to be independent yet supported, cuddled and hugged but not babied, and respected for my accomplishments and abilities, yet also to lead a somewhat traditional life. (My dad and my husband are very different, indeed. I think I'm a lot like my dad, and Mark is actually somewhat like my mom, although *neither* would agree. Dad might, and he would definitely be amused.)

16. I remember back when I was sixteen and I broke up with my first major boyfriend—absolutely in love, so I thought, and that it would last forever. When

we did break up, I was heartbroken, and my pride was shattered! Mom was so sympathetic; I remember she just held me and cried with me. And she let me have a sip of brandy! Wow! I remember thinking that, yes, I am getting on toward being an adult and that I should handle this more maturely and philosophically! Mom was there, protecting me, until I was able to do that.

17. Now, when we talk on the phone, our relationship is so different—ever since the middle of college, actually. We sit there like best friends, giggling about things that have occurred in each other's lives, our thoughts on certain people and events! My friends would come in and think I was talking to an old hometown friend! I think our roles were so less obvious (as mom and daughter) over the phone. When I was back home, though, we always seemed to revert back into those roles.

18. My brother was another important person in my life, although we've grown apart since he moved away. We were really close through most of high school. He was one year older than I, good-looking, and popular. All my girlfriends wanted to date him! We had some fun double-dates. Jake is a very interesting person; he really loves the mountains and down-to-earth people. I think he hates the thought of me running in circles he perceives as shallow or selfish. I wish he knew how neat so many of the people I know are. But, through thick and thin, we've always stood up for each other! He said the most *beautiful* things to me and my husband in our wedding video. I was truly touched! He talked about never losing the passion, and to work really hard to make each other happy! His sincerity and love were so apparent (and his pride in me) that I was speechless when I first heard it! (and that's no small feat, believe me.) He picked up the stubbornness we all did!

19. Finally, my sister, Mary, is eight years younger than me. Although there is somewhat of an age difference, we are very close—probably closer than I am to any other woman. Although she's just eighteen, she is very mature, perceptive, and straightforward. She was the cutest kid—a real tomboy, just like me. Jake taught her how to throw one hell of a curve ball! She is the most athletic of the family and has a natural talent for tennis. We used to play together, but now she's in a completely different league.

20. Mary and I have always used each other as sounding boards or to let off steam. I feel like I could tell her anything. Yet, I also want to protect her from the world and make sure she's always happy! She is one person I really, really miss not seeing on a regular basis anymore.

21. I feel like I should go on about the important role she plays in my life. However, I think it suffices to say that I love and admire her, and I am proud to have her as my sister.

22. Boy, did I digress!! Well, my family has always been my source of strength; I go home as often as I can, now that I'm far away. And when I come back from being home, I somehow feel renewed!

23. I'll get back to my chronology. High school was one of the best times of my life. I really felt I bloomed then. Coming from a small Catholic school, I was so excited by the prospect of meeting so many new people and being able to break out of any previous molds. Looking back, it's funny. The girls in grammar school who were so important were really nobodies in high school. They had nobody to boss around. I loved the sense of freedom I felt, and the acceptance.

24. High school could have been tough for me, but it was not at all. You see, my dad was a counselor at the school, my mom was a registrar there, and my big brother was also there to watch over me. Fortunately, the kids all liked Dad a lot, and Jake kept the creeps away. Also, I think the guys were always extra respectful of me as a result. (I'm suprised anyone dared date me!)

25. It was in high school I gained my self-confidence and openness. I did very well in school and became very active in sports and extracurricular stuff. I enjoyed organizing stuff, as well as working hard to see something done. And once I started racking up accomplishments, I began to thrive on it. I think recognition and respect are very important to me. I like being in the spotlight!

26. Tennis had a lot to do with my confidence. Our school had a great coach! My freshman and sophomore years, I played volleyball and softball and badminton. But during the middle of my sophomore year, Miss Mills (the coach) convinced me to take up tennis. She gave me lessons during lunchtime . . . and I loved it!! The action, the strategy involved, and the concentration it demanded . . . also, the competition! First, it was competition against myself to get better; then it was to make the team and play singles my first year instead of doubles! I had a goal—and, as I usually do, I focused in on it!! I started playing at 6:00 before school, and at practice after school, as well as at lunch!

27. It was a game I loved to play and had some penchant for! And I made my goals. My coach got a big kick out of me; I would stomp around the court, intensely concentrating, acting as if the match was a life-or-death situation while I was playing. Our team won pennants those two years, so we had pretty good crowds watching. I played number two singles and lost only once in regular play! I thrived on the competition, sizing the player up, and trying my hardest to reach every ball I could. I beat girls I had no business beating just based on heart and willpower.

28. One particular match really stands out. I was playing Kim Henderson (I'll never forget her name); she was the girl who had beaten me during the early part of the season. I was so determined to beat her. She was

this little rich kid, "Miss blonde and proper," raised on the country club circuit (her own private coaches, etc.); she looked down on our school and its tennis players.

29. It was the last game of the season, my senior year. . . . I had to beat her. The game started out close; we each sized each other up and tried to find weaknesses. I had to keep focusing on the game, the stroke, and *not* her!!

30. During the third set, we were tied at five all. We had split sets, so this was the deciding set . . . and I saw I had her rattled. She asked for line judges, explaining it wasn't my calls or anything, but she just didn't want to have to think about calling the lines. I think it was a psych-out try. But it made me feel even stronger and more focused; I felt a rush of energy and knew I was going to beat her!

31. Then, the football team was let out of practice, and they had lined up to watch our various matches. They were pretty supportive, and I felt all the cards were in my hand. I won the next two games easily—and therefore the set!! It was a high, a great culmination to my career as a tennis player. I had so much energy I couldn't sleep that night. Boy, did that feel great!

32. My favorite subjects in high school included math and science. The teachers were challenging and obviously enjoyed their work. I was able to get ahead in math by taking a summer school course—and ended up in calculus my senior year. It was a small class, only six students. Tim Stevens, our teacher, helped us prepare for the AP exam, which could get you college credits if you scored high enough. Mr. Stevens talked up college *a lot*, about all the choices available. When I was applying, he wrote one of my letters of recommendation. Mrs. Church, my English teacher for two years, also wrote one. I *loved* her! She had gone to Stanford and encouraged me to apply. She had such a dramatic flair; when we had to read Shakespeare, she made us *act* out the scenes, in today's translation. (I remember her saying, "What did he mean by that? Say it in English, I never did understand that "to be" stuff!")

33. When I started applying for college, I really had a narrow scope, looking back. I must have had someone upstairs looking out for me; things always fell into place. I decided to apply to Stanford, UC Davis [University of California—Davis], and USF [University of San Francisco]. I didn't even *think* of going outside California. I figured I'd go to Davis, which had a strong biology/math program, and a lot of my friends went there. My senior year I visited with a bunch of them. It was sort of overwhelming—so big! I applied to USF because my dad had gone there. He always talked about it! And I *loved* San Francisco—wouldn't that be fun?

34. I applied to Stanford almost on a lark. Mrs. Church told me all about it and how much opportunity existed there. Our librarian, Kristie Powers, also had attended Stanford. She was a good friend of our family, and really funny! She thought a lot of me and decided to take me on a visit. I remember it was in March, and I took off a Friday. I was ambivalent about going, because I didn't know if I had been accepted and didn't want to fall in love with the school and then be turned down.

35. I remember that day so clearly. It was a gorgeous, blue, clear spring day! Kristie drove up Palm Drive, the grand entrance to the school, and already I knew I'd *love* it! She was more a "partier" type than I, and so she took me around to all the "good" places! Since the day was so warm, students were *everywhere*, lying out in the sun, getting together to plan their weekend. We went by the Lagunita Lake, and saw mobs of people listening to a band up there. The multitude of activity around me was so exciting! As we walked around the campus, Kristie told me stories of her and her husband's adventures while undergrads. She was always getting herself into funny circumstances. I remember feeling so good and really enjoying myself. We went to lunch at a place which was the big hangout after the football games.

36. Anyway, I came home with tee shirts for everyone and my mind made up that, if I got into Stanford and could afford it, I'd go!

37. My dad was kind of ambivalent about my desire to go to Stanford. I think he thought of it as a "rich kids" school, something I definitely was *not*; generally, people are not impressed with East San Jose, where I grew up, but I wouldn't have wanted to live anywhere else as a kid!

38. I was lucky; I had a lot of scholarships awarded to me (I entered a few writing contests and won over $2,500, applied to some through local business and educational associations, and was awarded a California grant). I had been working part-time at the local drugstore since I was fifteen, so I had a bit of my own money saved up. All in all, given the scholarship money, it would have cost my family the same to send me to UC Davis or Stanford.

39. The week before I heard from Stanford, my family was attending a wedding for one of our relatives. I remember the cousins were all sitting around at dinner. One cousin asked me where I was applying. When I told her Stanford, she said, "Oh, I don't know if you can get in there. You have to have straight As." I replied, "Well, I do have that."

Her: "But you also have to be president of the school and really active in extracurricular activities."

Me: "Well, I'm pretty involved."

Her: "I still think it's nearly impossible."

Me: (To myself) I'm gonna get in, in spite of your stupid comments. (Outwardly, I think I just shrugged and laughed about it, and said that Davis is a great school.)

40. The acceptance letter came on April Fool's Day—how appropriate! I was so excited! I immediately sent my acceptance back!! I felt like all I had worked for, all the focus on school and the discipline to avoid the parties and stuff, paid off. I'm sure the rest of the year I was walking on a cloud!

41. My senior ball was fun! My brother came down from his freshmen year at Umboldt State to go with one of my friends. We set up a third friend, and I went with his roommate, who I had a crush on. We girls cooked a big Italian meal before the prom, with red checkered tablecloths and everything! I felt pretty at the ball—all dressed up, with my closest friends, and with a cute "older" guy!! We drove out to the beach afterwards, and Mom and Dad had breakfast waiting when we got home! It was weird being out so late with Mom and Dad's approval. Normally, we had strict curfews.

42. The summer before I started my freshman year was very carefree! I played a lot of tennis and worked at the drugstore. It was probably one of my most lazy summers; I wanted to enjoy my family and friends before heading off to school.

43. The first day of Stanford orientation seems like yesterday in some ways! What a day! Mom and Dad and I loaded up a van that Dad had borrowed from a friend. We put in all my belongings! That morning, I was petrified; all my self-confidence was out the window. Usually, when I get nervous or scared, I become very talkative. I was so scared I couldn't talk. We drove the thirty miles to Stanford in absolute silence. My Mom and I look back and laugh about that day—me, sitting with the potted plant Mom had bought, in the back of the van, staring out the window. Mom and Dad later said they felt so bad for me; I looked like I was going to the hospital instead of to school. Perhaps my biggest fear was meeting my roommate, and surviving my classes.

44. Anyway, we arrived there, and I calmed way down. The dorm had a welcoming committee that helped me move in and made us feel very much at home. There were lots of nice, smiling faces around. My roommate was already there—an outgoing, friendly, fun girl named Julie; we got along immediately!

45. I forgot to mention the van incident. Once we got off Highway 101 onto Embarcadero Road, our van decided that it would stay only in first or second gear—no reverse, nothing! We ended up going fifteen miles per hour down the street and had to avoid all situations where we might have to use reverse! What a nightmare.

46. From day one, I loved college. My freshman dorm was especially close, and I felt I had so many opportunities to grow. Most everyone was bright, and each person had their special quality that added to the uniqueness of the school.

47. The workload was fairly intense (but not by Darden standards), but I remember my first quarter as being more about developing new friendships and becoming comfortable in the new setting than anything else. The football games were a big deal, as were the weekly parties around campus.

48. I liked most of my classes, except *chemistry*—it still leaves a bad taste in my mouth! I had entered Stanford with dreams of becoming a geneticist (*yes*, a geneticist)! And, yes, chemistry was a big part of the program in genetics. Well, I hated *everything* about chemistry: the students in there were more cutthroat than the average class, and the subject matter just didn't click in my head. As far as I was concerned, it was a foreign language. Well, I worked my buns off in that class! The first test, I totally blanked! I had never done that before, ever (nor again!)! I had studied until the early morning hours to prepare, and I must have overdone it! Well, let's just say each chemistry class was a chore!

49. My grades first quarter were okay; a few A's, B+'s, B's, and one B−, in chemistry. I have to tell you that I was so proud of my chemistry grade—I didn't want a C. My first-quarter grades were worse than I had ever done, but I was still rather proud of them. I also knew I had not completely applied myself, given I spent a lot of time getting to know my classmates.

50. Second quarter of my freshman year was sort of a turning point for me at Stanford, for a variety of reasons. Coming back from Christmas break, I had decided to totally apply myself to studying—go all out! I wanted to see how well I could do if I really went for it! If I did the same as last quarter, then I knew the extent of my abilities and could adjust my time accordingly, but how well could I do? Secondly, I carried 19 units that semester; besides the "normal" load, I added economics to my class list, and I had the next chemistry class.

51. As I said before, chemistry was not in my blood. It was still foreign to me; I couldn't pick up the concepts! About two weeks into the quarter, I had come to a tough realization: I really didn't want to be a geneticist, or a doctor, even though "everyone" said I'd be a great one! Now, a subject that intrigued me was economics! It made a lot of sense to me, based on my math background, and combined sociology, psychology, and math. I really enjoyed it! The nineteen credits was too much; I had to drop a class, and it came down to chemistry vs. economics. I agonized over it, talked it over with my parents, and finally realized I had to *enjoy* my work. So I dropped chemistry. I felt as though the world was lifted from my shoulders and *never* regretted it!

52. I also began to date a fellow in my dorm, Tom Walker. Tom was kind of a preppie, from Chicago. He was very nice and a lot of fun! He is probably one of *the* smartest people I've ever known. He is able to absorb concepts more easily than anyone I

know!! We dated seriously for over two years (I'll get back to that later). Anyway, Tom went to the library to study every evening after dinner, from 6 to 11. He had a set routine, and a bunch of people from the dorm went over together. He got me going with him. The library was much quieter than my room, and I could really concentrate on studying, away from the dorm distractions.

53. I plowed through, every night, and got into a steady routine—studying a few hours before dinner at home and after dinner at the library with Tom. A few times a week, we'd go get ice cream at Swensen's afterward, getting there just before it closed. The poor people who worked there probably hated us!

54. The hard, focused work paid off that semester: I pulled off one B+ and four A's. I felt that I did have the ability to excel at the school; I just had to work harder and study longer than most people! And you get smarter about what to study—what's important. I did well throughout my career at Stanford and was proud of my academic achievement. I *could* do it!

55. Tom was my serious relationship at Stanford. We dated from the middle of freshman year to the beginning of my senior year. For the most part, it was a great relationship. He is a very special person, who had a lot of endearing qualities. One thing about us that was really different was Tom's need to be part of a group and go along with their ideas, and my need to remain independent, for the most part, from our friends.

56. Tom was also a great musician; he played bass for the Jazz Band, and he and some friends started a band to play at parties around school. During freshman and sophomore years, it was mostly Tom and Mike, one of Tom's best friends. They'd sit around the dorm playing, but it wasn't a major commitment. My junior year, it became a full-fledged commitment, with five band members, etc.

57. During this time, our relationship seemed to be going stale. We had always allotted each other a lot of room, since we each had our set of friends and different things we liked to do, but the band thing got out of hand for me. By the middle of junior year, they were playing Friday night, Saturday night, and sometimes Sundays. Between the Jazz and Rock Band, our time together became very little, which was fine, except I didn't want to talk about the band all the time, or be with them. They were not my friends, really, except for Mike.

58. I also *hated* the thought of being a groupie: sitting around listening to music all night with adoring eyes just isn't my style, not at all! So after a while, I wouldn't go, because I would end up dancing with people, and Tom would get jealous and mad. Instead, I'd go with my friends to other parties, or just study, or go to movies and stuff. After a while, I just lost interest. Toward the end of my junior year, I applied to be a resident assistant (RA). I had to interview with the professors who resided in cottages near the dorms and actually were responsible for them.

59. I enjoyed the process and met a lot of people I didn't know at school. My favorite professor quickly became Arthur Isaacson, an English professor with a passion for San Francisco, and who was a very open, caring person. At the end of the first round, the professors asked some students back for second, group, interviews. Most were stuffy and very formal—but not Arthur's. He had a little party, complete with champagne.

60. That was a Friday, a busy day for me! I hadn't had a chance to eat lunch before I got to the interview at 3:00ish. People were in groups talking, and no one was drinking the champagne. So I took half a glass, my maximum. Arthur later told me he thought it was great that I went ahead and had some, even though no one else had wanted to offend anyone. I hadn't really thought about it that way, especially being Italian. I grew up with wine with dinner and never abused it.

61. Anyway, Arthur's party was fun and relaxing! Arthur, Joe (another student), and I got along well, laughing about school gossip and enjoying the warm spring afternoon! Arthur had us play this little game, where you write down a response to some questions, and they're supposed to mean something. I remember some:

62.	Favorite color: Why:	Midnight blue—mysterious, dark, soothing	(Means what you think of yourself—Ha, Ha!!)
	Name a body of water, describe:	puddle—dirty, small, wet, muddy	(Means what you think about sex! My husband will love that one!)
	Name an animal: Why?	sea otter—mischievous, silly, fun, curious, adventurous	(Means what others think of you???)

Anyway, everyone got a *big* kick out of it, and my puddle answer still comes up when I talk to those guys! Arthur chose Joe and me and Alan to help him with the dorm senior year! What a group!

63. So, my activities and focus were going toward things very different from Tom's. By beginning of senior year, we just sort of fizzled out. I don't

remember being particularly upset about it, given the length of time we had been going out (it had been a long, gradual decline, which I think made it easier). (I was more upset over my high school boyfriend!)

64. Tom and I had never really fought. I *have* tension and anger. It's funny that, late junior year, I finally expressed some of the anger I felt toward the band taking up his free time. We had driven all over town, picking up odds and ends for a show that night. I didn't want to go, but Tom insisted! Well, the band talks the whole time about this song, that chord, this move, and I'm bored and feeling left out of the conversation. After we let everyone off, I was pretty quiet, so Tom asked what was wrong. I began to tell him, and he said, "You make me mad!" . . . and I cut him off, saying, "Oh yeah, you make *me* mad! Just forget it!" I shocked him; he immediately apologized. It was the weirdest thing! I probably should have ended it then, but I still loved him.

65. Senior year was such a good time. I felt so free and independent, and actively avoided any inkling of a serious relationship. My whole life, I had always had some sort of boyfriend, since 8th grade! Now, I wanted to enjoy doing whatever I wanted to without worrying about someone else's feelings! I wanted to find a job in San Francisco; that much I knew. I was pretty dumb about the process; interviewed with investment banks and consultants, but took the first agreeable job I landed in San Francisco—with Macy's. It sounded interesting, the people were nice, and it meant I could enjoy senior year! Very, very short-term thinking!

66. Arthur took the seniors up to San Francisco one day—we went to a musical, went sight-seeing, and dancing. He was so interesting—talking about the history and excitement of the city. A very different experience than with my parents, which was always family oriented, visiting their relatives, and eating lunch in Golden Gate Park.

67. Then came graduation and being thrown for the first time into the big bad world.

68. I started work right away, having many a student loan to pay back. My roommates (friends from school) were not starting work until August, so I commuted from home the first part of the summer. It was a long commute, about one hour and thirty minutes with traffic. I took the Bart Trains from Fremont to Union Square in San Francisco, where Macy's buying offices are located.

69. The night before my first day in the management training program, I heard on the news that Macy's union had gone on strike! What a mess! The first two weeks were spent in a training class with about twenty-five fresh-faced graduates. We learned the basics of the business and got to know each other. We *hated* crossing the picket lines, being called rude names and stuff. It was not pretty. My class ended up as sales help on the floor; we learned how to ring up sales, and out we went. Very different than our expectations to work in the buying office, but it was actually fun! I got in the Revlon section, of all places—me, who didn't know *anything* about makeup! And these women would come in, asking about skin and color types and lipsticks! Oh, my!! Did I learn a lot!

70. I did have a man come in to buy makeup for his show. Obviously, he was homosexual and he played in one of the transvestite shows downtown. He was really nice and asked me to help him. What the heck!! I helped him choose, joked with him—who was I to judge. I think he sensed this and bought a ton of stuff, thanking me for my kindness. He even showed me a picture of himself, all done up—gorgeous, prettier than I'll ever be!

71. I've always tried to accept or at least be tolerant of people different than I am. Partly due to my upbringing (my dad is certainly that way). You have to try to look at each person for his or her good points and qualities—hard to do sometimes. But I have a much easier time accepting the faults of an "underdog" type than some egotistical, selfish jerk who expects everything handed to him or her!

72. After about a month on the sales floor, my training class was sent to Colma—to do customer service. What a nightmare! First, being in Colma, which is known for its graveyards! There are more dead people than live ones, honest to God! And the customer service office had virtually stopped operating since the strike. There were long lists of angry customers wanting their furniture delivered or wondering why their credit card balance was wrong. What a mess!! I've never been yelled at so much in my life! After a while, you'd promise anything to get them off your back. None of us knew what we were doing, that was for sure!

73. One good thing from this experience was our class became close; we'd laugh about each day's crisis and try to keep each other up. Eventually, after another one or two months, the strike was over, and we all got our buying office assignments. Now, we could get on with our careers!

74. Right. Out of the frying pan and into the fire. The buying office and function was *a lot* different than I had imagined. I was expecting to use both qualitative and quantitative skills at Macy's—working with people, but also with budgets, projections, and control systems! But Macy's is successful (or at least was at that time) because its buyers knew how to *buy* the right stuff. As a result, inventories piled up, no one knew which store had what merchandise! And the vendors were a breed unto their own (send you more than you ordered, different styles, or charge higher prices), and I had the job of negotiating or threatening them. Every function done in the Buying Office was so ad hoc, it was scary. And very few people had systems skills or wanted to implement controls!

75. After a few months in the Buying Office, I wanted *out*. It was time to start looking for a new job.

76. My roommate, Kim Meyers, was working for a company called Donaldson and Company, a consulting firm. It's a small, young, aggressive firm. Kim was always telling me while I was at Macy's how neat D & Co. was and how I would be so perfect for the job. I knew quite a few people from the company already, because my roommates and I had thrown a party, and Kim and I used to watch them play basketball at the local gym. Plus, I had dated one of the guys there when I had first moved to San Francisco.

77. So I talked to one of the partners, Al Tayler. We met for lunch to talk over business opportunities, and he told me to send over a resume. I interviewed right before Thanksgiving (about two weeks before) and met additional D & Co. people. After meeting the managing partner twice (a man who rarely has anything to say), I was offered a job! I started the Monday after Thanksgiving! I really was excited! The job and company sounded professional; the staff was young, smart, and aggressive; the salary was great! There also was a very obvious career path to making partner.

78. I remember my exit interview from Macy's very clearly. I was nervous to tell Mary, my buyer. She was a very nice person. We grabbed some lunch, and I explained my decision. At first she tried to convince me to stay, at least a year, in order for me to really learn something about the business, but I explained how I just knew it wasn't a fit; there was too much of a focus on the buying and fashion side and not enough on the managing the business side. Macy's was not the greatest to its employees, a point she agreed with. So, she ended up okay about it. I thought it was funny that the Personnel Department wanted me to stay but, when I told them the starting salary at D & Co., they said to go for it!

79. So, I went home for Thanksgiving, taking Kim along, and awaited the next phase of my life.

80. Donaldson & Company was one of the most interesting experiences of my life. I learned a lot about people and organizations from the firm, and also lost some naivete about work. I went in thinking: this was the life! As compared to Macy's, where I took the underground moon to Union Square and had to walk past the bums begging each day, D & Co. was located in the heart of the financial district, in a new, gorgeous building. I could take a bus in to work!!

81. This was a big deal. At Macy's, going on the underground moon was a *drag*. It seemed to always get jammed up while we were in the tunnel! It was so dark and gloomy, and the ride took half an hour to one hour ten minutes, depending on who had stalled! I hated that tremendously!! In contrast, the bus was crowded, but we always got a seat or could take one of the express buses that took fifteen to twenty minutes. And we could watch the outside activities, which I always found interesting—so many different types of people and buildings.

82. Indeed, the initial contrasts between the two experiences were great, and indeed different. At Donaldson, I had to wear suits, or look "professional." There was freedom on how you spent your day for the most part. You got paid for overtime, which you worked *a lot* of. And it was a small, growing company with only four levels: staff, senior, executive consultant, and partner.

83. During that time, my roommates and I moved closer to town—the Richmond District. Dave, Kim, and I picked up a fourth, Jerry (he worked with Dave), nice guy. And Kim developed a big crush, and they started going together. In fact, they are getting married next year. What a household we had! A nice flat, probably built for three, but what did we care! It had a fireplace, big kitchen, beautiful bay windows, and was located on the second floor. Initially, Kim and I shared the master bedroom, but eventually it practically became just mine.

84. What a group! I consider Kim one of my closest friends, but she is very strong willed and likes things done *her* way. She and Dave didn't get along very well. He was a slob around the house and kind of a nerd. But those two would get in an argument, and I'd have to listen to Kim go on and on about it . . . wah, wah, wah . . . she was an All-American gymnast, and I think she had devoted so much time to her sport that she was a little immature socially. She drove a lot of people crazy, 'cause she'd start talking about things not related to each other or get silent all of a sudden.

85. But she definitely had her good qualities: she was such a loyal friend and really guarded her friendships. She'd do anything for her close friends and was always there when I needed someone to talk to.

86. I think it was tough on Kim when I first started at D & Co. I'm very outgoing and made friends very easily. I was sort of a favorite of the firm in a lot of ways, but Kim had alienated a few with her outspokenness. But, as time went on, everything blended together just fine.

87. My first case was examining a claim for damage that occurred from cost overruns on a fixed-price contract. It was a huge power plant. I got to travel to Naja Valley for about two months. It was a lot of fun, and I enjoyed learning about construction. I was seen as the "cute little gal" on the case by the client, a title which I later began to resent, but during those days, I really loved the job, the closeness of the people, and the money. (I could start paying off all those bills!)

88. I moved on to another case. It was a pumped storage plant which provided electricity during off-peak hours. A remarkable plant, which used two lakes at different elevations to turn the huge turbines which generated electricity. Our team got to take a look at the plant, which was built inside a mountain—one in-

credible feat. Anyway, one of the dams had broken, causing incredible damage. We calculated the extent of those damages for the client.

89. I learned a lot about cost models during that project. It was a small team of four people, and I really got a good reputation as a hard worker and good team player. One of the seniors on the case was an arrogant MBA from Northwestern named John—very much a jerk, but he liked me a lot and thought I was smart. I swear, people used to ask me how I could stand working for him. Really, it was easy. After I proved I could handle the work, I took a large section of the more detailed work for myself, and told him I'd come by twice a week to give him status reports. He was more than happy to oblige: he hated detail work and instead loved to theorize about the most accurate way to calculate damages or whatever. I was the practical one who got the work done, which made me look good. All in all, the relationship worked out well. And I built myself a reputation as a real go-getter on the case. You see, I figured if I worked harder than everyone, got along, was a team player, stayed long hours, I would be rewarded for it, regardless of company politics. Unfortunately, it was true only to a point. A lot was taken for granted due to my good nature.

90. I learned to change that aspect of me as time went on. After having done well over the past year on the cases I mentioned, I moved to another case. We had to commute to San Ramon five days a week (an hour and a half drive) and worked, on average, until 10:00 p.m. It was a horrendous case. But I did what had always worked—was the one to work latest, get things coordinated, and do the dirty work as well. But the senior on the case was really laid back and did not control the case very well. After five or six months of this crazy pace, I got sick of being the one to come through but still not getting any of the credit. Enough was enough! My dad had warned me against this—always trying to please, always willing to do whatever needed to be done. "Miss I can do it!" People take advantage of it big time.

91. Anyway, there was also a woman—Laura—on the case who had been with Donaldson & Company about six months, less time than I had. She had her MBA from Berkeley, and was very aggressive, but also really dingy! She got away with murder on the case. But rumor had it she was slated for the fast track, because she was a woman, had an MBA, and three years prior work experience. Maybe so, but she did nothing!

92. Promotions were coming up in June. By then, I had been with the firm a year and a half. Most everyone takes two years to make senior, but everyone told me I had a great chance at making it in one and a half years, given the workload of the last case.

93. Well, I didn't make it that time. It was disappointing, but I understood, given most of my peers had to wait at least two years. But what burned my cookies was that *Laura* had made it in a year! None of the staff could believe it, especially those that had seen me in the office working all night on the case, not her. I was pissed.

94. But it was one of the best lessons I ever learned, and I am wiser for it. I talked with Al about it (the partner). He explained how she was older, and the company partners in San Francisco were getting pressure from Chicago to promote and *keep* women. Most made it to senior and quit soon afterwards. He admitted to me that I had held the case together, etc., etc., but I was young and had a great future with D & Co., and he said my bonus and raise (which was large) was very high to make up for the promotion. It was frustrating, because it wasn't like he told me I needed to improve anything, but just time.

95. After that, I was not so blindly dedicated. I still worked hard, but I did not do the more detailed work no one else wanted in addition. I took over office recruiting instead, and continued doing my best on the case I was working on—but forget helping out above and beyond the call of duty. I earned a lot of respect from a lot of people for standing up for myself and adjusting my behavior. It was hard to suppress saying "yes" to everything.

96. I ended up my last year at Donaldson on the big case. It had sixty to ninety people on it. By then I was supervising newer staff and enjoying the work for the most part. I think Al had given me a good part of the case and an excellent team. I was promoted in December, after two years with the firm.

97. Back in June, when I was passed over for early promotion, I began thinking about business school. I had always intended to go back and it seemed that I needed to learn more about managing and business strategies. Plus, I had begun seriously dating a man in the firm. (This I will go into detail about later). So, I started requesting applications and set about to find a good school to attend. I spent my entire two-week vacation in December filling out applications and perfecting them. It was a very exciting time for me.

98. Mark and I met at Donaldson after about seven months. He started with the company the July after me. He was from the D.C. office of Donaldson, out on the case I was also working on. I remember when he came to San Francisco. About ten came together from various offices. I said to Kim, "Don't you think he's good looking?" She definitely thought so.

99. A bunch of us went out to Chinese food, and I spent part of the time flirting with Mark, poking him in the stomach about how much he ate. We immediately got along well.

100. We found out we both played tennis and started playing together after work. He was good! And very funny! I was immediately attracted to him. The first time we played tennis, we went out for pizza afterwards and talked about ourselves; we had so much fun!

101. There was a problem, however. At D & Co., we weren't allowed to date people within the firm. The only problem was, I enjoyed him so much; the more time we spent together, going for ice cream, out dancing, etc., the more I knew he was someone truly special. I started thinking about him all the time! And he about me. So we started sneaking around, sort of to speak. At first it was kinda fun—kind of adventurous—but as time went on, it was just a pain! At work, of course, we were always professional (except the time I kissed him in the elevator), but it was irritating that D & Co. could also control our personal lives. They demanded so much!

102. And there was always the worry that Mark would be sent back to D.C. In fact, the first week of November, after we had been dating for about three months, Mark was sent back to work on a small case. Supposedly, he'd be back by Christmas. I remember being so sad. On Halloween, we carved a pumpkin together and talked about the situation. We hadn't known each other long enough to do anything about the situation; it was a "Wait & See" thing. The night before Mark left, we went to dinner in Sausalito and walked by the bay afterwards. Both sad, both wondering.

103. He came back in December, and what a wonderful Christmas we had! We began our tradition of "stocking stuffers"—lots of silly little presents in one of Mark's big athletic socks!! We really enjoyed that Christmas, going to Union Square, shopping, and enjoying all the magic of San Francisco in winter.

104. I was in love, and it never wavered. When it came time to talk about business schools, Mark was such a tremendous help. I applied to Stanford, Harvard, UCLA, Berkeley, and Darden. Mark had his MBA from William and Mary and knew a lot about the different schools. He was excited about this new adventure and incredibly supportive.

105. That December when I was doing applications was a special one. When Mark got back from his family's (in Boston) on December 29, he asked me to marry him. I was so excited! I knew Mark would make me happy forever. Our values and tastes were similar, and we enjoyed each other as *best friends* as well as lovers. In fact, that's the inscription on my wedding band! "Best Friends." I also knew we'd grow together, and I thought he was particularly sexy, especially when we're alone.

106. The engagement was complicated by work! So only our family knew until I quit on May 1. During these months, the whole situation seemed so stupid, so ridiculous. But I'll always remember D & Co. fondly, because without it, I would have never met Mark. We set the wedding date for May 28, 1988.

107. I thought about something else relating to Donaldson & Co. About a week before my last day, I was working on finishing up testimony my team had been preparing for a case. We'd been working hard, as usual. I really wanted to leave with all the loose ends tied up and worked about twelve hours a day to do so. My friends said I was crazy—I should be taking it easy, not working my buns off! But I hate being lazy on the job, and strive to always do my best. Well, this one particular day, I was at the client's meeting with an engineer to clear up some details. Apparently, Al had been trying to reach me. I went back into the office, and he roars at me, "Where have you been? Why didn't you leave me a number? I'm leaving to go to D.C. in an hour and need copies of the testimony!!"

108. I'm thinking: what am I, your secretary? I tell him that I'll make his copies for him, but I'm very annoyed at his attitude. I don't need this shit Well, I go back in my office mad! And I share this office with Mark and Jeff. So I'm letting off steam, and I tell them the story.

109. I don't get mad too often, but when I do, I'm quite hotheaded. "He needs it so fast, it's a high priority, is it?" So I make the copies, walk into a meeting he's having, and throw them on his desk with some sarcastic comment under my breath. The meeting was with the "boy's club," as we used to call it. The five guys who ran the big cases in the office—all very self-important.

110. So I was rude!! I felt better. Anyway, Mark, Jeff, and I are in my office when Al comes in. Mark kinda looked at me, then stood up. Al goes past Mark to me and apologizes for yelling at me and says he should have had his secretary do it, but I'm so reliable, etc., etc.

111. So everything's cool. I look over at Mark, and he's got this smile on his face. "I think I came close to blowing it," he said to me. "I thought Al was gonna yell at you for interrupting his meeting, and I was gonna stand over him and say, look, you little fuck, leave her alone, you shit!" (Al's this short, bald, little man, and Mark wanted to tower over him and point into his chest!) "Couldn't you see me grabbing Al by the britches and throwing him out of our office?" Mark muses. Mark and I both laughed about that for hours!

112. All in all, D & Co. was a great experience, which left a strong mark in my life. Especially, it's hard to break away from feeling a part of D & Co., even now.

113. Hearing from business schools was exciting; first was Darden. Mark was out of town on a case, so I called him that night. In fact, I opened it up over the phone! One in! I ended up getting into Darden, Harvard, UCLA, and Berkeley. Not Stanford.

114. It was hard trying to decide where to go! Harvard was so expensive—I just didn't know if it would be worth the extra investment. I had a friend there I visited, but it didn't particularly impress me. Darden did, however. The classes were engaging, the community small, the people very friendly. I had a great warm and fuzzy feeling. Plus, it was a new part

of the country to explore. For some time, I had been meaning to try a new place. If I had gone to UCLA or Berkeley, chances are I would have never left California.

115. The clincher came when Darden offered me a full scholarship, for both years. That helped so much. If we decided to have children in five years, I wouldn't feel obligated to go back to work right away to pay off my huge debt. Darden it was. Not too many people could believe that I had turned down Harvard, but I did not find it that difficult. I think even Mark was surprised. Although very supportive, Mark wanted me to make my own decision and did not pressure me one way or the other.

116. To celebrate, Mark went out and bought a new car—Toyota MR2 (with my Harvard $!). It's a great little car! I'm so glad Mark bought it! He works so hard, and he doesn't splurge too often! It's perfect for him, and I think he enjoys driving it when he comes down to Charlottesville to see me.

117. I quit Donaldson in May and took a temporary job during the summer, worked nine to five, and had a ton of free time. It was very relaxing, and Mark and I were slowly able to do things as a couple without worrying about what people said or who saw us.

118. We drove across country together, and took my car and Mark's. Mark's mom came along to help with the driving. It was a blast! I love to drive to begin with, and I felt as though I was starting a whole new life, a whole new adventure.

119. Darden has been quite an experience. I got there so excited! Back to working hard, learning a lot, becoming a star. Reaching for the top! (Ha! Ha!) I knew I'd be missing Mark terribly. He was still in San Francisco. But we both saw this as such an important experience. First year was rough—worrying so much about understanding the concepts, saying worthwhile things in class, earning the respect of your peers. It's not an easy way to learn, through the case method. It's very confusing at times, in fact. But you don't forget what you've learned, either. I suppose it's sort of like boot camp.

120. Section D was tremendous! What a remarkable group of people, in my eyes. I really enjoyed hearing the class discussions every day. My enjoyment was hampered somewhat by the worry of participation: did I talk enough, say noteworthy things, etc.? The professors are an interesting group also; who knows what they're thinking!

121. For the first time in my life, I had to deal with feeling average. Everyone worked as hard as I did, especially first semester, and I had an economics background, not accounting or finance. But about half way through the year, I hit upon something: I should care about what *I* think of what I said and how my classmates respond, *not* the professors. And I've tried to abide by that ever since. I think it's important to judge yourself by your own standards.

122. Throughout the first year, Mark was so wonderful; he kept on telling me I was special, that I was doing fine, that he loved me unconditionally. We were also planning our wedding, which is how I spent all my vacations. Mom and Dad were terrific! Since the wedding was at Stanford Church and the reception in San Jose, they did almost all of the real work, and it was a superb wedding!

123. Dad made my dress; it was absolutely gorgeous, very traditional, a lot of beading, silk, and off-the-shoulders neckline. My dad is so talented, as I mentioned before! He also made all six bridesmaids' dresses, which also turned out gorgeous.

124. The wedding turned out great. Mark and I got around to see everyone, and everyone seemed to be enjoying themselves. Mom was a nervous wreck the entire day. It was like she was throwing a big party, and she's the hostess. We had a traditional Italian Catholic wedding—very formal, but with people dancing, singing, and really being alive. People got a big kick out of my *red* silk petticoat under my wedding gown.

125. Yes, a red petticoat. It's kind of a long story. You see, when I was young, I told my parents I wanted to get married in a red dress—I love the color red, and wouldn't it be scandalous! Of course, Mom and Dad shook their heads. Well, when I first tried on my beautiful gown, Dad had me put a red petticoat underneath it—an undergarment from a prom dress he had made my sister Mary. Well, it gave the dress a beautiful sheen, and it came alive. Plus, my all-time-favorite movie "Gone With The Wind"—I love the scene when Rhett brings Mammie back a red silk petticoat from Paris. So it seemed appropriate. Finally, it let some of my personality come through—a little mischievous, but always in fun.

126. Mark and I had a wonderful honeymoon in Maui, Hawaii; we lay in the sun, went sightseeing, and relaxed from the hectic pace of the wedding.

127. Immediately upon returning to Washington, D.C., we went to work. Mark is still with Donaldson & Co. and still travels an awful lot. But miraculously, he was in town the entire summer and did not work much overtime or weekends. I was doing a summer internship at Sallie Mae in Georgetown. We got to commute in and out together! It was lovely spending our days together and being a full-fledged married couple.

128. During the summer, we took up golf, played a lot of tennis, and made a concerted effort to read a lot, eat health foods, and exercise regularly. We were pretty good, all and all. It was really special being together, even with the traffic jams and humid weather!

129. Sallie Mae was a wonderful experience. I had gone into Sallie Mae against a lot of friends' opinions: the pay was lousy, and the intern from last year's

class hated it. But I had a good feeling about Brian, the man I was to work for, and that it was in D.C. Besides I felt I was doing something inherently worthwhile—helping the student loan process run smoothly and more effectively. I see it as a worthy business and cause. The people I worked with, on a whole, were tremendous, very bright, disciplined, hard-working, helpful, and open to your opinions. They gave me enough freedom to work through my summer projects as I saw fit, yet held me accountable and questioned me as if I was a full-time employee—I loved it!

130. I was particularly impressed with the senior vice-president of the Servicing and Systems Division. She's very demanding and sort of abrupt, but very fair and positive if she thinks you've done a good job. She's good at delegating work and motivating her staff.

131. She liked my work a lot; I think I'll be offered a full-time position there and would definitely be interested. However, I would want to stay away from the accounting/budgeting function per se and move into the more operational issues that affect Sallie Mae.

132. I should write each of my co-workers at Sallie Mae to thank them and tell them how much I enjoyed my experience.

133. The end of the summer—which takes me to now: second year at Darden. I'm enjoying it so much better. My first-year grades, by the way, came on my wedding day, and I did very well, better than first semester, and than I had expected! This, coupled with the positive feedback from Sallie Mae, really helped me to regain a lot of confidence in myself. I actually look forward to speaking in class and have chosen classes I am interested in—which helps keep my motivation very high. It's also nice being supportive to the first-year students. I really want to help make a difference for them—tell them to keep their self-confidence, always question what's going on, to enjoy it as best they can. As a first-year section advisor, I am looking forward to helping my old section become integrated into Darden.

134. Classes are good, with most of the professors being quite interesting.

135. I miss Mark a lot. It's harder being apart this year, but he comes down every weekend, and we play golf together. We try to do things outside of Darden when we're together. It definitely helps me keep a perspective, especially since I don't mind working extra hard on the weekdays, knowing I'll take some time off during weekends.

136. And that just about sums up my life.

15

The Feelings Record

After each self-assessment instrument that you have been asked to take, we have asked you to make an entry in your Feelings Record. We asked you to note your mental and emotional reactions to each instrument and to record any other contextual factors that may have affected your scores, the data you generated from each instrument, or your reactions to them. Now, we want to consider how we might go about using that information.

Throughout the self-assessment process, we have used a variety of instruments. Some have been very structured, some have been very unstructured. Some have been very objective in nature, others have been very subjective. Your reactions to the structure, focus, content, and administration of these various instruments are data that are helpful to you in understanding how you respond to a variety of situations, emotionally and mentally. If, for example, you felt frustrated by the instructions for the Lifestyle Representation, which were very ambiguous, you might draw a tentative inference that you do not enjoy unstructured assignments. On the other hand, if you thoroughly enjoyed the highly structured interpersonal style inventory, you might infer that you enjoy structured situations. Both bits of evidence and their related inferences might be drawn together into a theme that might read something like this: "This is a person who prefers to work in structured situations."

The process we will use for analyzing and interpreting the data contained in the Feelings Record is very similar to that which we used in analyzing the written interview. That is, we ask you to consider the data and the context in which it was generated and look for patterns. You may find some new patterns suggested by the Feelings Record data, or you may find data that will provide support for patterns you have seen in the written interview or in the other instruments.

The written data contained in the Feelings Record provides some insight into your emotional side. Admittedly, it is not a perfectly accurate or detailed description of your emotional side, but it does ask you to consider not only how you think and how you behave, but also how you feel in a variety of situations, and that is an important part of our experiencing of our work and of our ability to function in various jobs.

The Feelings Record also provides information about contextual factors that may have biased or slanted or prejudiced the data you generated at various points along the way. This information will help you to qualify, to modify, and to clarify more accurately the inferences you draw from those various sets of data.

Exercise

To help you gain skill in analyzing your own feelings record, we have included a copy of Steven Taylor's Feelings Record and Carrie Baugh's Feelings Record (see cases, pp. 168–174). Note that Steven and Carrie used some instruments not in this book. That's okay; it's the feelings we're interested in here, not the content of those other instruments. Consider the following questions in relationship to Steven's and Carrie's Feelings Record:

1. How did Steven and Carrie respond emotionally to unstructured assignments?
2. How did they each respond emotionally to structured assignments?
3. What contextual factors relating to Steven's and Carrie's experiencing of the various self-assessment instruments may have affected their responses?
4. How should Steven and Carrie take all these things into account in interpreting their other data?
5. What new themes, if any, are suggested by Steven's and Carrie's Feelings Record?

STEVEN TAYLOR'S FEELINGS RECORD

The Figure Test

At first, a feeling of curiosity about what sort of analysis we would do on these. Then I wondered why the figures seemed to be deliberately asexual. I laughed a bit as I wrote down ideas, thinking that a couple of my thoughts would seem crazy to the class. I think I looked forward to hearing the laughter, and laughing at my imagination. I tried to think up as many as I could.

As I answered each question, I tried to take a number of perspectives.

Cognitive Test

The LSI test showed me as an active learner and someone who senses and feels his way through problems. I guess that applies, because I didn't even read the instructions carefully and rated the questions in reverse order (4 - - - 1 instead of 1 - - - 4). I was very conscious of the columnar format of the test, and I may have balanced my answers to some degree. I often think of myself as a "jack of all trades" rather than as a specialist. I think back to yesterday in a meeting of my field-project team. When my team asked me to take primary responsibility for the financial portion of the study, I made my agreement conditional on being able to assist with the study of medical approval processes in foreign countries.

I think one of the reasons I yearn to have my own business is to avoid being pigeonholed. I can't stand repetitive mental tasks.

Having now read the remainder of the McBer pamphlet, I am beginning to wonder about the direction I'm taking towards my longer term goal of owning an international business. My direction at present is to explore different industries and build personal capital ($) through a job in investment banking or venture capital. I realized toward the end of my summer work at Smith that I wanted a chance to do more hands-on problem solving. Financial modeling and negotiating with and selling to bankers and investors is abstract and removed from the operating functions of business. The course I excelled in last year was OPERATIONS. Consulting is the high-brow road to doing more operational work, but maybe I should be thinking about more truly "hands-on" jobs where I'm directly responsible for day-to-day management. That course begins to scare me off because of the big-company implications. I *will not* go back to a large, hierarchical corporation. I've been down that road and it ain't me!

Interpersonal Style

Passing out the forms felt very strange, like inviting friends to my wake. But I also felt a lot of curiosity and anticipation; I think that underneath my independent exterior I am more concerned about what others think about me than I let on. Before I look at the data, I'm particularly curious about the following items:

Needs Support	I do, but do I seek it?
Helps Others	I want to, but I'm not certain if I achieve this.
Defensive	Used to be more so—reality check.
Praises	I think I don't do this well.
Keeps Promises	I do, but Darden life is pressured; how often have I gone back and changed plans?

Special Entry

I talked on the phone today with a partner of the firm I worked for this summer. The purpose of the call was to evaluate my performance; I had not had a chance to speak with Bob before I left (he was away the last week of my stint).

Bob said he thought my performance was "overall, very strong," and that he would "strongly consider hiring me back and wanted to keep in active touch through the school year."

He said that my forte was a "great maturity—you know when to talk and when to shut up, which is unusual." He also said that I knew how to work on what was important, which was even more rare in his experience.

Bob said he didn't want to overemphasize deficiencies, but an area to work on was "technical skills." I pressed him, and he said that I needed to concentrate on more completeness and thoroughness in my work. He said that he thought my analytical skills were more than adequate, that I had the judgment and insight to see what things are missing from an analysis, whether it be my own or somebody else's that I'm reviewing.

My reaction to this was a little bit of disappointment, but followed by the thought that he actually gave me a very positive review.

I was particularly happy to hear that he thought that I knew when to "talk and when to shut up." That's a skill I've been trying to work on, so it was nice to have the encouragement.

I took the "technical" comment to mean that I'm not as focused on depth in my analysis as I need to be. That's something I've heard before, but evidently have yet to overcome. I wonder how important it is to overcome; I guess I really wonder if there is a cost to becoming more detail oriented. Having said (written) that, I feel a bit sheepish. There is certainly nothing inherently wrong with being thorough in my work!!!

Predisposition Test

I often hesitated when filling this one out! The test is worded in the third person, which caused me to think more about the answers for "people in general," as opposed to what I would do. For instance, question 17, "The least possible governmental and social controls are best for all." That situation is only best for those who are prepared for such a society, the strong and the skilled. That situation would not be best *for all,* so I disagreed, in spite of the fact that I myself might come out ahead in a truly laissez-faire world.

Once again, I chuckle at my puffed-up self-view!! At least I'm becoming more aware of it!

Survey of Leadership

I believe that I took this test last spring in a slightly different three-part version. Going through the test, in part 1 I noticed that I was setting priorities in the same manner as with the value sort, but without being able to see whether I was being consistent in my ranking. I also stopped up short a couple of times when I started to answer. Then I remembered the Vision, Commitment, and Management model from first-year Organizational Behavior! I tried not to bias the remainder of my responses, although my personal feeling is that I am much better at creating a vision and, hopefully, a vision that begins to garner commitment. Often, I think that I may be at my best when communicating a vision, rather than cheerleading or deliberately whipping up others' commitment to the vision. I take great satisfaction from those few moments when I am able to show someone a vision that they could not previously see or discern for themselves. The test was repetitive, and I definitely felt some resentment as I moved through the final part of those first fifty questions.

Survey of Management Style

I took this test after we talked about it in class today, and after taking the other version yesterday. I much preferred the scaled readings of my tendencies to the repetitive yes–no approach of the other version. I definitely blurred the line between what I have always done and what I've been trying to do more of over the past two years. That is, I have become more focused on what the firm needs to do, and what my priorities should be in order to move the firm in that direction. My work over the past two summers was the first time I have been able to influence not only my work but the direction of the enterprise, and I have been indescribably happier in my work as a result of my personal influence. I've also been much, much more motivated and much more sensible in my approach to the work. When I feel I'm making a positive contribution, office politics and what others think of me in general become less important, and I'm able to focus all the more on improving myself and improving the enterprise. If the test elicits this sort of outpouring, it is of use whether or not the data is useful on its own!

24-Hour Diary and Lifestyle Diagram

One of the most surprising elements of drawing the diagram was that I see my world almost entirely in terms of people, or at least I see the core of my world that way.

Personal Style Inventory

I took a test called Briggs-Myers when I was moving from New York to San Francisco and changing jobs. That test showed my profile as ENTJ, while this one has come out INFJ. I'm surprised that I would come out as an introvert on any test. I've always thought that my extrovert tendencies completely outweighed my more introspective tendencies. My mood is more thoughtful tonight as we wrap up a three-day weekend of golf, Foxfield (popular horse races), and then sunshine today. From here out, the pace picks up sharply with recruiting swinging into full tilt and our field project cranking up. Things to do are weighing on my mind tonight.

Sandi just called. We've been strained lately, and I'm sure that is also affecting my mood. She has asked me for some time away, which I gladly gave her, but I'm missing her more than I expected to. That leads me inevitably into exploring my feelings about our relationship and where we are headed. I think we are reaching the decision point.

No Particular Test

It's 7 a.m., and I've just woken up with a revelation about the unease I've been feeling of late. This is an entry about general feelings rather than anything inspired by a particular exercise, but I think it may help in the overall analysis.

I feel as though my life has begun to careen towards a conclusion which I'm not controlling, and rather than putting things into order, I have been avoiding the issue. Number one issue avoided has been my relationship with Sandi. I haven't made the deep personal commitment that she deserves. Instead, I've been acting as though my relationship with her is no bigger or smaller a part of the puzzle than my work, Darden, and my relationships (non-romantic) with other people. I've been justifying this by reasoning that my relationship with her needs to be balanced against her needs for independent growth and the other parts of my life. I think I've had that backwards. I can balance those other things against my relationship with Sandi, my parents, and my brothers only so long as I can also support those other relationships. In the MBA world it sounds corny, but for me my love for those people and theirs for me in return must be first in my life if I am to live a fulfilled life. I haven't been giving those people the consideration they deserve, and as a result I've felt shortchanged here.

This morning's revelation also included understanding that the reason I've felt as though Darden and my career have only received cursory attention is that I am unable to give it the maximum focus I'm capable of until I feel that I'm first giving the love that I should to those who I'm closest to. A second factor is that I've allowed the short-term Darden case mentality to block me from hitting course objectives, instead focusing on the case at hand. This approach works in the chip-shot driven world of the classroom, but it doesn't fulfill my objectives in coming here. Darden is a deliberate exercise in overassigning tasks in order to force the student into choosing his or her priorities and teaching the student to live with the chosen priorities regardless of whatever priorities the school or classmates may try to impose. Hah!! I wonder whether Darden would agree with that statement. I wonder if the administration will agree with it enough to put it in admissions materials or admit it in an admissions interview. If sorting those priorities and living my life in terms of my priorities is what I learn while at Darden, I'll be doing all right. This is a tough way to get at that basic truth, but can someone who hasn't gotten through to that truth understand that the journey is worth it, or that in many ways "the journey is the reward." (Our accounting professor quoted "an eastern philosopher" yesterday—I'm getting philosophy from my accounting professor?). End of soliloquy, class calls me!

Life Values Card Sort

I'm going through a period of enormous emotional strain right now, and I haven't been open about it. About four or five weeks ago, Sandi told me that she felt like she needed some time "at home" to catch up on fixing up her apartment and generally feeling like she actually lived there. We had spent the summer split between her place and my sublet and weekends traveling various places. Then, two weeks ago, the axe fell, as they say, and she told me that she felt that we weren't right for each other and that we should break up.

I was emotionally destabilized; it was like having a great weight descend upon me, that this had been building up and I had refused to see it developing. I fought; I told her I couldn't accept the conclusion. I still think that, in spite of the strain of the past two years of living apart, we will never forgive ourselves if we don't see our relationship through to marriage and a life together.

Writing this out is interrupting the card sort, as I began to try to sort the MARITAL, EMOTIONAL, PROFESSIONAL, and PARENTAL cards into a priority. Writing something like this also shows me what root problems lie behind my emotional strain.

The root problem here is that I am having tremendous difficulty forgiving myself for being insufficiently attentive to Sandi's needs and for having had relationships with other women during the times we've been apart. None of the others have been more than substitutes for the love and warmth of Sandi and me, but the guilt of these other associations has affected the passion of my relationship with Sandi. I think this is probably one of the root troubles.

Sandi said something last week which just came back to me. She said that I still had her on a pedestal, that I wasn't being realistic about who she was and what our lives together would be like. She thinks that my hopes for a life with her are based on an idealistic view of our relationship.

Another thing she said, although this was two weeks ago, when she told me that she wanted to break up, was that she believes that if I really thought that we should be married I would have asked her by now. I had been planning to ask her the following weekend, when we were going to be in New York together. She didn't come up to New York; instead, she went to her parents' farm to be with them. Sandi and I met in New York, and I had hoped to take her back again to the restaurant we went to the night we met, for our six-month anniversary together. But I didn't get that chance, not yet.

Her feeling that I've put her on a pedestal is probably related to my guilt over having seen other women while I've been seeing Sandi. Incidentally, she knows about these other relationships. She has also had at least one (and I think *only* one) relationship during our time together. Neither Sandi or I have seen anyone else while we've been living in the same town; it has been during the bicoastal time and when I was in London two summers ago. But our mutual guilt has now contributed to tearing us asunder. I also think that the guilt and mistrust of self has made it hard to let ourselves be happy together. *That* is what needs to be overcome!

I think that Sandi and I trust each other, and each of us believes the other to be a wonderful person and loves the other very much. It is a matter of loving ourselves as much as we love each other. I miss her in huge amounts, palpable amounts, and I find it difficult (I find it impossible) to imagine my life without Sandi next to me, as a partner in coming to understand more about the world and the role I play in that world. I'm still smitten with her like I was in the fall of 1985, for better or worse, and I pray that at the end of this difficult time she finds that she shares those feelings.

Self-Assessment Exercise

I have a difficult time finding contradictory evidence for themes I have created. This is *much* more difficult than finding supporting evidence.

I wonder how much of this comes from my "judging" nature, as shown by the MBTI, and how much comes from the strength of the themes I've found so far?

CARRIE BAUGH'S FEELINGS RECORD

The Figure Test

This was fun! I felt rather silly; so many silly, mischievous thoughts came to mind. I enjoyed just letting the ideas flow to my mind. I found myself rejecting some and not writing them down—mostly because they were pretty farfetched. I could see and hear the actions/scenarios. I enjoyed this exercise.

Inventory Test

Lots of choices—there are a lot of things I would love to do, but don't necessarily have the talent (singing, for example). But I did not necessarily provoke a strong feeling. I felt this exercise covered the range of interests I have, both inside and out of a work situation.

Cognitive Style

I feel like I'm being categorized again, just like when I took the Myers-Briggs test at Sallie Mae this summer. So much depends on WHAT I am learning, who I'm with, and the amount of creativity a task requires.

I feel great. Happy, secure with my abilities at Darden.

I wonder if I am choosing answers as a reaction to an understanding of the Myers-Briggs test. Aren't we more diverse and complicated than this? (As human beings, both thinkers and feelers?)

I wonder if my answers would change if I took this at home and was thinking about my family/husband.

Cycle of Learning

Wow! It feels right. I wish I wasn't so "lopsided," but I know I am. I am relieved to see my "feeling" side up there. It is important to me that I do not lose this aspect of myself as I get engrained in a business framework.

Value Cards

I felt I had to put all the blue cards somewhere, which was fine, since I value all of them to some degree. At first, I tried to do the same with the white cards, but there were too many I wanted to add on my own and too many that were meaningless and unimportant to me. So I included only those cards that I really valued and that would represent a potential tradeoff to me.

The orderings were relatively easy, but the entire time I could see major potential future conflicts. When push came to shove, would I still hold true to them? When I do have children, that will become my number one or two priority, and it means that many other aspects of my life I can juggle now won't be so easy then.

Overall, I didn't agonize all that much over the aspect rankings, but more so on the value rankings.

Meta-Programs

The questions were very easy for me to answer. No real reaction to any of them, except my husband is the opposite from me on trusting someone: You have to earn his trust. But he's more sympathetic to shortcomings than I am. I wish I was more like that sometimes.

FIRO-B

With most of the questions, I wanted to explain what I meant by my answer. I am funny about wanting to be friendly and open with most everyone, but I feel closely tied to very, very few. And I like group activities, but not all the time. It's a real balancing act for me. I like to be alone, but I'm certainly not a loner; I need people very much.

I was hoping I was being consistent on the questionnaire.

Predisposition Test

Many of the questions depend on what I'm doing: I think I can take on different roles depending on if I'm at home or at work or school, etc. So much of it depends on the people I'm with, and how much I value their input and reactions.

Overall, I didn't have too much of a reaction to this test. I have pretty much remained open to the potential usefulness of all the tests so far.

Interpersonal Style Inventory

I am very curious to note consistencies and differences; I wish I had marked work versus school versus old friends. I think it will prove to be very helpful and insightful. I feel very comfortable with the exercise. Many times, I'm my own harshest critic, and I am pretty open about who I am and how I feel about stuff.

24-Hour Diary

It was a great exercise. The only thing is that I knew exactly how I was going to spend my time. I am in a routine at school, focusing on school work and preparation during the weekdays, and focusing on Mark and our relationship on the weekend. I try to work extra hard during the week so I can spend little time during the weekend on school. My routine has pretty much been this way while I've been here. I do think my attitude has changed, so I spend very little time worrying about making it through Darden, as compared to last year's struggle to become one of the better students here.

Lifestyle Diagram

I did a mobile. It felt like I was back in kiddiegarden. If I had time, I wanted to do something more elaborate. All in all, however, it was interesting and a fun representation. I wanted to drive home the importance of BALANCING the key aspects of my life. During the different phases of my life, different aspects became more or less important. However, the WORK, FAMILY, and INDIVIDUAL INTERESTS groups have always been pertinent.

I wanted to illustrate balance and the important themes that have always been in my life. Wanted to choose adjectives that illustrate how I feel. My life is indeed an evolution of these same themes.

Leadership Traits and Skills

Of all the leadership tests we've taken so far, this one considers a variety of leadership areas and qualities—energy, persistence, cooperation, etc. So many of the other tests were so LIMITING about what leadership is. I think there are so many possible mixes of people's traits that make up good leadership. I am dissatisfied with all the research I've read concerning leadership. I think there are some other concepts that we're all missing, but I'm not sure what they are. This test listed more of the things I identify with than ones that talk about garnering commitment and persuasion.

Myers-Briggs

This was VERY interesting. I took the Myers-Briggs test at Sallie Mae this summer. I'm an ESTJ according to that sitting. I took it at work. Here, I took the test at home, and the questions were considered in the context of work and social life, not just work, as was the Sallie Mae test.

The outcome was quite a bit different—ESFP/J, which I think more accurately reflects my actual tendencies. In my prior field, I have had to focus more on EST attributes, but I worked at doing that. Especially as a woman, I wanted to downplay feeling and intuition, and show that I was as analytical and judgmental as any man in my field. I'm worried about the implications, especially given my Campbell Interest Survey outcome—Artist/Social tendencies. I am curious to note how much is my perception of what I had to do to become successful versus my natural abilities and tendencies overall.

Written Interview

I enjoyed going through my life story—so many neat opportunities. I feel so privileged, given all the wonderful people in my life—family, friends, even acquaintances. I really could have written more, but I think this brings out my essence.

It was an exhausting process, but very enjoyable! It also helped me see where I've been and get a perspective on what's important and achievable in your life. Sometimes, you've got to go with an option and make the best of it. You can always choose another course if it does not work out. But you have to push yourself and try new things. If you don't, you have stopped trying to improve.

Survey of Behavioral Characteristics

This tool was a lot more interesting to me than the leadership survey, mostly because the statements made were easier to relate to and to interpret. I also thought it considered a lot more areas than the narrow view some of the other tests seemed to perpetuate.

Survey of Managerial Style

This survey was interesting, although a little repetitive; again, I felt like a lot depended on the level of my job—as I get higher in a firm, my focus changes on what is important. I think that it is important to think of the different roles you *like* to play or be in when answering these sorts of questions.

Survey of Leadership Style

This was not the most useful tool by any means. I felt like this tool was obviously trying to test my interest in being a persuading, group-oriented person, someone tied to her own ideas, etc. One major problem I felt was to answer the questions given the lower level positions I've held or what I'd do as a company leader. I decided to answer as a company leader. This tool seems too repetitive, and most of the questions depend on interest and opportunity within an organization to make such decisions.

I do not lend too much importance to whatever this tool is supposed to measure, because it does not take into account different roles we play and at what level we have responsibility and involvement in the company we will join.

NOTES:

1. Found tools useful, insightful, or interesting 15/17 total (88% of the time).
2. "I have pretty much remained open to the potential usefulness of all the tests so far."

3. I think a lot of the info in my feelings records will emerge as patterns when combined with the other tools. I will reserve my other inferences until then.

INFERENCES:

Carrie is a person who:

1. Seeks to learn from different situations.

16

Developing Life Themes

Now that you have generated all your data and had a good deal of practice scoring, examining, and drawing inferences from data, it is time to begin developing full-blown themes from all the pools of data. In the last two chapters, you began drawing inferences in earnest as you read the first part of two written interviews and two feelings records. The critical principles were these:

1. Staying close to the raw data.
2. Looking for patterns that were more rather than less common.
3. Trying to be aware of your own assumptions.
4. Keeping your inferential leaps small and conservatively connected to the data.
5. Using more rather than less data to support an inference.

In this next exercise, begin in a small way to use all the data by developing a single theme from all of the data Steven and Carrie developed. We'll add first the second half of their written interviews. Once you have read these, then consider all of the data we have developed on both people to construct a single complete theme for one of them.

We encourage you to use the form in Exhibit 16–1 to develop your theme. You can use the wide right-hand column to collect data that seem connected in some way. Then you can use the narrow left-hand column to note the sources of your data citations. At the bottom there is a place to note evidence that is contradictory to the underlying thread or theme which seems to hold the mass of your data together.

If you get too much contradictory evidence, you may have identify another theme or perhaps develop two. How much is too much? Enough that it begins to make you wonder whether you are really identifying a consistent and solid life theme. Some themes may have no contradictory evidence. Others may have three or four items, but if you get more than half as many contradictory bits of data as you do supporting data, we would say that the theme is not clearly established.

Note that there is a place at the top of the form for you to begin framing your theme label. No doubt you will write, erase, rewrite, and rewrite this label many times before you are satisfied with it.

Okay, charge ahead. Choose one person and then create one theme complete with label from all of the data. And remember, you are developing your inferential skills as you go, so don't shortchange yourself. You will be glad you didn't when you begin to do the same with your own data.

Exhibit 16–1

Life Theme Development Worksheet

Theme Label: ______________________________

Sources	Data

Contradictory Evidence

STEVEN TAYLOR'S WRITTEN INTERVIEW (B)

Question #2 (Other Memories?)

1. Steven already completed question #2 while answering the first question.

Question #3 (Unaccounted for Times?)

1. In fact, I did leave out a couple of summers, so here goes.

2. I spent the summer between my first two years of college working as a machinist at a giant tractor factory in Michigan. They were hiring when I returned from college that summer, and I managed to get one of the slots. They didn't ask whether I intended to do it forever, and I didn't tell them. I also had to fudge my weight a little bit to get the job. The plant had a 150-pound minimum for machinists, as the work involved some heavy tools and machinery. I weighed about 147 when I arrived home, but three days of seven bananas and several milk shakes and hamburgers got me over the limit by the time I had to weigh in on the first day of work! I was assigned with the other new hires to the midnight to 8 a.m. shift, which did pay a fifty cent per hour premium, even if it ruined your social life. We worked on a furious schedule that summer, seven days a week and ten hours a day for one three-week stretch. I was a probationary member of the United Auto Workers, and the shift I worked on didn't think all that much about anyone who even remotely resembled an Ivy Leaguer. They didn't think all that much of me either at first, but after I dove in and busted ass with the best of them to make my quotas each shift, I was accepted into the post-work billiards and beers group. (Remember, this was billiards and beers at eight in the morning.) One of the most interesting things I learned that summer was that many of the guys who worked with me had given up more "respectable" jobs for this one because they could earn more money for their families. On my shift, there were two former state troopers, a former bookkeeper, and a former elementary school teacher. They didn't like the work as machinists at all, but they were making \$25–35K per year, which was sometimes double what they were making in their previous work. To this day I struggle with what society can do to make careers in the police force, teaching, and other essential public functions attractive to those with the best talents for them. The summer also taught me a number of invaluable lessons on labor relations, and how *not* to run an effective plant. The U.A.W. system at that time was completely slanted over to the side of labor, to the point that the foreman on our shift backed down on three separate occasions in the summer when he tried to move workers from one task to another and they didn't want to change. The worker simply called the union steward over and told him that he didn't think the new job was safe, and the foreman would have to cajole someone else into moving into the new job. The real reason that the older workers would protest job moves was that each job had an hourly quota attached to it, and if you completed an eight-hour quota in six hours, you could walk off the shop floor and read or find a hidden place to sleep until the end of the shift came around and you could punch out. That meant that the longer you worked on the same job, the less time you actually had to work each shift. Once again, the foreman could recommend quota increases, but since there was no incentive for improving speed on specific tasks and no worker participation in department, plant, or company profits, no one was willing to pick up the efficiency on any job.

3. After that summer, I spent the following semester studying on a Cornell language program in Bourges, France. I lived with a French family of four and attended classes with a group of twenty Cornell students in an I.U.T., the French equivalent of a technical school for draftsmen, surveyors, and other skilled trades. I had endless political debates with my French father, a foreman on a bridge construction crew, and with my brother Patrique, who was sixteen and headed for a career as a chef or restaurateur. I was lucky to have a family who took a sincere interest in my learning the nuances of the language and who were determined that I should appreciate France for what it was, not just for the opportunity it offered to me as a student passing through. Living abroad changed forever the way I look at my own country, and the way I react to the public actions of our political and business leaders, because I always hear Papa's voice shouting that "there go those presumptuous Americans again, simply assuming that the rest of the world would love to be just like them in every way." He was forever drilling me that I didn't have to be that way, that we could all be different yet still work

together in a civil fashion if only the Americans and the Soviets (*les Russes*) would get off their high horses for a couple of minutes and listen to what some of the rest of the world would like to see improved.

4. While in France, I fell in love for the first time as well. A good bit of advice to come out of this experience is never to travel to Paris or Florence with a member of the opposite sex unless you are already in love with her or intend to be at the end of the trip. My friend Laura and I decided to travel together for a couple of weeks at the end of the semester before hooking up with a larger group of students in Rome. We set out together more or less because we both wanted to travel within France and Italy while others wanted to undertake multicity, multicountry tours. This premise for our trip lasted for only about twelve hours after leaving Bourges, and we had a wonderful couple of weeks walking on the banks of the Seine, and then hiking in the French Alps before gorging ourselves on food and wine and shopping in Florence and finally connecting with the rest of the group in Rome. It was a passionate month-long affair, but after we returned to school, we drifted back into our two separate groups of friends, although we've stayed good friends to this day.

5. I spent another summer working in Washington as an intern on a senator's staff. In Washington, I got a firsthand education in the ponderous nature of the American legislative process. The work was exciting, without a doubt, but the underlying progress was an exercise in muddling along, compromising all but the most critical objectives to move a bill forward, allowing "unconscionable" budget increases in one program in order to preserve those which you believed were "critical" somewhere else. And the staff were underpaid and overworked. But I couldn't help thinking that if the constituents' needs weren't being met best by the senator, they certainly wouldn't keep returning him to office. In any case, my time in Washington revealed to me the seductive nature of the place, and I resolved not to return until I had reached an independent situation psychologically, socially, and financially, if I return at all to that arena.

6. I also quit my San Francisco job after being accepted at Darden and worked for a friend's start-up venture in London, England. I doubled as a sort of utility man on some of his work crews and as a business consultant when we could get time together in the office. Graeme is the managing partner of a promotions company, which began as an inflatable advertising business and now has branched into corporate events management, music promotion, and even small-scale construction. While I was there, we bought out the other partners in the construction business and acquired the assets of a graphic design firm that was already spending about seventy percent of its time designing and producing work for the company's various businesses. We also renegotiated the firm's credit arrangements with its bank, removing the partners' personal guarantees from a working capital facility which was more than adequately covered by a blanket lien on the firm's assets. As part of the deal, I also had a chance to go on tour with bands such as Genesis, Prince, U2, David Bowie, and others—great fun, and a bit of an education into the rebirth of entrepreneurial spirit in the U.K. More importantly, I saw just what a great time Graeme and his partners were having, in spite of their cramped office, hectic lifestyle, and pressures from their girlfriends to spend less time at the job. They were making their way on their own, which made all the difference in terms of being satisfied with their lives.

Question #4 (Jobs)

1. There is no question, when I look back at the various jobs I've held, that I was happiest when I was able to work independently, to show others the merits of my ideas and to get them on board to help realize those ideas, and when I was able to share in the value I created, both financially and in an ongoing way, either through managing or just advising. I have a skill at generating ideas and setting plans for implementing my ideas, but I tend to lose interest as those plans evolve into more routine activities. That's not exactly right. I like to have an ongoing role as a sort of advisor and editor of the plans, but I like to hand them off to someone else and get on to the next project. For me, the problems in a crisis situation or in a totally unexplored area seem much more interesting than the problems inherent in following a project through to completion.

Question #5 (People, Acquaintances)

1. How about my parents? You may be wondering why in the hell we kept moving all the time as I grew up. My father likes to tell people that he chose to work in an industry rather than at a profession, and his industry is railroading. Dad grew up in a small town in western Wyoming called Evanston. The town's original purpose was literally to serve as a whistle stop, a place where the east–west trains stopped to take on coal and water. Coal was brought down to Evanston from mines to the North, and westbound trains would load up before making the pull over the Wasatch Mountains to Ogden and Salt Lake City. My father's father had come over to the United States from Scotland to work in the coal mines with his two brothers. My grandfather died when my dad was only four, and he was raised by his mother, her sister, and my father's two sisters, who were 8 and 12 years older

than him. The whole family were practicing Christian Scientists, and in fact my Great Aunt Leonora (my father's mother's sister) was a renowned practitioner of faith healing until she died in her 90s just a few years ago. The entire family moved across the mountains when my dad was about fourteen to Ogden, Utah, where several of them still live. My father's first job was sweeping out passenger cars in Ogden, and the only nonrailroad job he's held since was when he waited tables in a dormitory at Stanford. But I'm not here to tell his story, so I'll be brief. My dad was chosen as the alternate candidate to Annapolis two years running, but when the Korean War came along, he elected to enlist in flight school instead of waiting. After the war, the G.I. Bill enabled him to attend Stanford, where he met my mother. She was getting a master's degree in journalism at the time, having graduated from Indiana University and taught high school for three years. My mother was two years older than my dad, but they fell in love and were married immediately after their graduation. A side note here is that for the most part, the women I have dated have been older than me. Food for thought. My father had worked during his summers as a fireman on the Union Pacific, back when the fireman actually shoveled the coal to fire the steam boiler, but when he graduated from Stanford, he entered the management training program with the Baltimore and Ohio Railway. His decision to leave the union and enter management does not sit well to this day with some of the members of his family. My father is a very humble man, but he does get a good chuckle out of the fact that he seems to get more visits from those same family members now that he lives in a home with a guest house just outside of San Francisco.

2. The paragraph structure of this thing sure doesn't make much sense, does it?

3. At the B & O, trainees learned the business by physically experiencing as many facets as possible, and for the first two years my parents were married, they only saw each other one or two days a week, since my father had to travel the railroad the rest of the time. They also tell some great stories about their economic situation at that point. The one I remember best is my father only owning one sportcoat and one pair of slacks when he started work, since he had no money left after buying a new bed for them to sleep in. He wore the sportcoat for the first few days he worked, until his supervisor finally asked him when he was going to wear a different sportcoat, or even a suit. My father replied that he would wear a different sportcoat (1) after he received his first paycheck and (2) after he had purchased two chairs for him and my mother to sit at so they could eat dinner at the card table they had bought for the living room! Between his earnings and my mother's, though, things soon improved. I've heard many stories about my father's style over the years, but what it boils down to is a deep and sincere caring for people. He is one of the fairest people I've ever met, and very even-tempered. He is also the sort who will do absolutely anything to help out a friend in need. A friend of his captured my father's essence last year when we were playing golf one day. My father's pal turned to me and said, "You know, Steve, your father is walking, breathing proof that nice guys can get ahead in today's business world."

4. I guess I shouldn't slight Mom in all this data gathering, eh? My mother is an amazing optimist and an amazing adaptor. She is a survivor—both in a figurative and a literal sense—and she seems to grow younger as she grows older. She was unusual for a woman in her generation—rising to editor of the paper at Indiana, then winning a Fulbright to go and teach in the Far East before electing to go to Stanford and graduate school. She married a younger man, too. After my brothers and I were born, she continued to write freelance pieces for newspapers and magazines, and she wrote a book while I was in high school. Lately she has been working as a radio newswriter and announcer and looking for work as a substitute newswriter for TV news. She also spent unknown thousands of hours helping my brothers and me to get a jump on the world by teaching us to read and to love books, and to appreciate the arts and music and good food. I have all kinds of good things to say about her, too.

5. I've always been close to my mother, and although I always relished the time I've spent with my father, and he put aside time for each of my brothers and me, I don't think I really knew him until the past three or four years. A lot of that coincides with my mother's cancer. Both of my parents now say that, in retrospect, the experience with cancer was probably a net benefit, because it revealed to them the wonder of their lives so far and the incredible fortune they've had in finding someone they could still be crazy about after thirty years together and with the family they've raised. Recently our family has grown much closer, partially because of the rallying around my mother when she needed us, and partially because of my brothers and I reaching an age where we can all be together as friends and equals as well as relatives. It's funny how you wake up one morning to realize that your little brother has turned into a great guy who you can hang out with and talk politics, sports, or whatever with.

6. Other friends. I tend to have a lot of friends and acquaintances, but very few truly close friends. An awful lot of people I know would probably tell you that they don't know the real Steven Taylor. Or at least that's my perception. I like it that way, or at least I've allowed that to occur, and I don't mind it. I'm pretty cautious about reaching out to others in an intimate way, although every once in a while I meet someone who I know immediately that I'm going to feel very close to very quickly. It's hard for me to put my finger

on the exact factors that go into that, but it's often someone who takes a fairly normal public profile but who is underneath a bit of a risk-taker, who is ready to play a little fast and loose with traditional customs and have some fun. Many, if not all, of my truly close friends are students of the world and of those around them. I am basically an experiential person, and I think it is that which I share with my close friends, a need to experience in order to understand. That contrasts, seemingly, with my love for books, but for me books and music are another form of experiential travel. Through books, I can go places where I can't or don't otherwise go, across time and to faraway locations inaccessible because of limits on my time or my funds, or merely because I wasn't born in the time of ancient Rome or Arthurian England. In the same way, music reveals emotions and moods that I don't see or feel or find in my everyday life.

7. I also don't need to talk to my close friends on a regular basis, although I certainly relish the time I am able to spend with them. My very close friends are scattered all over the world, yet I feel close to them. I form very lasting bonds with those I do get close to, as opposed to the many friends who come and go as I move from place to place or job to job. I expect a lot from my true friends, and maybe that is another thing that draws me to them. I would do anything in my power to help this group of people, and I expect that they would do the same for me in a crisis. Most of the people I meet in my life do not make that kind of two-way commitment, and I think I view that commitment as the only basis for a true friendship.

8. And romances. . . ? My youngest brother takes great joy in pointing out what he sees as the foibles of my romantic relationships. I remember being completely shocked about a year ago when he joked that I'd better not break up with my girlfriend because I'd be lost without one. I asked him what that was supposed to mean, and he laughed and said, "It doesn't mean anything except that you never go too long without a steady girlfriend. You evidently don't seek them for marriage, but you always have a girlfriend." I thought about that for a minute, but I had to admit he was right. Since about my junior year in college, I have had an ongoing relationship on one level or another at almost all times. Much as it is socially unacceptable to admit, more than one of those relationships overlapped. Some of the relationships ended as a result of my relocating, but I'm still close to most of the women I've dated seriously. In almost every case, I've been very close friends with women I've been involved with, as well as being lovers. I don't perceive that all or even a majority of other people's relationships operate like that, although I don't have any hard evidence to base that statement upon.

9. I'm basically a romantic, and I believe that there is someone out there that each person can find a happy life with if that is what you want. I've certainly had some wonderful and fulfilling romances, and I feel very lucky to have had those opportunities. I'm willing to go out of my way for someone I love, and in the cases where I've chosen to end relationships, it has always been because I realized that this was a person I was no longer willing to go out of my way for. I have a tremendously difficult time functioning in a relationship if I don't feel that kind of ongoing desire to do whatever I can to make my mate happy.

10. I feel as though I'm losing focus. On to question #6!

Question #6 (Future, Ending)

1. The ideal future. . . . I see a pink Cadillac . . . and a house in Fort Lee . . . . sorry, just kidding! It's getting a little late tonight.

2. The happy ending is definitely sitting back as the sun sets over the hills and thinking that it was all very much worth the effort. I think that, as long as I feel that my life has been a net benefit to the world, I'll be happy at the end. I firmly believe that is the end objective—to make life a little better for the rest of the world. I'm sure the satisfaction would be all the more personal if I can feel that I made a contribution for those who were close to me.

3. For better or worse, I believe that commerce, or business, is going to provide the path to greater world cooperation and understanding in the 1990s. We have passed through phases where treaty organizations, superpower detente, and now regional cooperation agreements have been the main thrust of international relations, but I think that, because of the shrinking of the world which has been accomplished by the telephone, satellite communication, and now through individual access to international computer networks, the path is clear for the small businessman to hawk his wares to the world. I would like to play a part in this interweaving of the world economic system by being among the few who see the opportunity of financing small and growing concerns across international borders. While we in the United States are accustomed to a well-developed system for funneling capital from institutions to the entrepreneur, that same ease of access to growth capital does not exist in many arenas, particularly in the Far East. I also believe that it is in America's interests to develop a venture-investing expertise within the Pacific Rim, because for better or worse we will increasingly be seeking financing for our ventures from outside our borders. This is not a message of doom for the United States economy, but merely the balancing of relative standards of living and pools of wealth and liquidity which is a natural outgrowth of a more balanced and interdependent world economic system. That is a very obscure way of saying that I hope to live in the Far East for a time, returning to the western United States to

seek a career as a United States venture capitalist focused on cross-border venture financing. The desired end of that is to be in a position of financial independence by age forty-five or so, with the option to take a more direct plunge into public service if I find that my chosen work is not satisfying my urge to leave the world a better place than I found it.

4. Another piece of my ideal world would be to spend the last part of my life as a teacher. I've always felt that my best teachers were those who had lived life on their own before returning to impart wisdom to me and my peers at our young and impressionable ages. I've always thought that America is missing an opportunity to put some of our best teachers, those people who have the wisdom of age and experience, into the classrooms of our children. I have this suspicion, too, that working with youth is probably the most rejuvenating experience one can have, better than taking the waters at Vichy, better even than a weekend of golf and massages at La Costa.

Question #7 (Points of Change)

Moved to Newark (one week old)
Moved to Baltimore
Moved to Silver Spring
Began kindergarten
Skipped kindergarten, began first grade
Moved to Minnesota
Moved to Barrington
Moved to Detroit
Left for Cornell
Abandoned pre-med, became government major
Went to France
Six months off to work in Washington
Graduated Cornell
Moved to New York, started work as a banker
Engaged to be married
Broke off engagement
Quit New York, moved to San Francisco
Accepted to Darden
Quit San Francisco
Spent summer in London
Began Darden
Spent summer with LBO group in Washington
Back to Darden

Question #8 (Other Options, Decision Making)

1. The first few turning points listed were beyond my control, as I was moved along with the family as we went from place to place in those years. I've talked about my decision to leave Barrington for Michigan and Michigan for Cornell at some length, but I can expand a bit on how I came to attend "the college of my choice," as Cornell's president used to be fond of describing whatever school someone attended. I talked about how I toured some of the eastern schools, but what was funny about the college application process was that I applied to Stanford and to Denison and Kenyon in Ohio while I didn't apply to the University of Michigan, in spite of the fact that I never visited any of those schools. I also elected not to apply to Harvard, Brown, M.I.T., and Princeton after visiting them. I ended up applying to Cornell, Stanford, Amherst, Denison, and Kenyon. I was intending to apply to Northwestern as well, but by the time I finished all the other applications, I decided that I didn't want to go to college in a city anyway, so I threw it out. This upset my parents at first (when I announced it a couple of days after the deadline had passed), but they came to see it with the same sense of humor as I did after a couple more days. I remember from my college tour that Harvard and M.I.T. seemed downright oppressive, Brown was so unstructured that they seemed in need of help, and Princeton was incredibly arrogant. I did meet one fellow at Harvard who was a great guy, one of the Lampoon staff, but he told me he wished he'd gone somewhere with a less ponderous approach to education, so I didn't think that was the place for me either. At Amherst, I spent a lot of time with a lacrosse player who was a big classical music fan. I figured any place that attracted people with those diverse interests must be all right. As you can see, my decisions about where to apply were largely based on who I met when I was there and what they had to say about the place. That has developed into a more conscious and deliberate process on my part. I like to rely on my assessments of other people and what they believe is right. I filter their opinions according to what I think of them, of course, but I can gain a great amount of useful information by simply asking someone who knows more about a particular topic than I do. In most cases, people love to tell you what they know or what they think about a particular issue. In cases where I don't have the ability or time to complete in-depth research of my own, I often rely on the judgments of others. In applying to colleges, I used this process instinctively, since the people I met on visits were the best indicators I had access to for information about what life was like and what the student body would be like at these various schools. In the case of the University of Michigan, for instance, it struck me that a number of my otherwise curious and intelligent friends in high school were going to Michigan without considering other possibilities, simply because it was close by, someone in their family had gone there, or because it was a good enough school and why complicate the decision. I need to be around people who are more critical than that, more discerning, more

sophisticated, if you will, and so I decided not to follow the crowd of my close friends to Ann Arbor.

2. I decided to drop my pre-med plans after taking the organic chemistry sequence my freshman year at college. I didn't do well in the class, but I had a couple of long talks with various academic advisors who seemed to feel that a poor performance in a freshman-year course could probably be overcome if I wanted to become a doctor. And there was certainly plenty of time to retake the course for a better grade if I needed to. But after long comtemplation, I decided that becoming a doctor meant spending the next eight years in school with the people I'd just gone through organic chemistry with, and then that same group would become my professional peer group. I switched to political science. Today, I probably wouldn't put the same weight on how my associates reflected on me, but I would still weigh heavily the kind of people with whom I would have to work in a job or career.

Question #9 (Major Changes)

1. One of the most important moves I've made was the move from New York to San Francisco, which coincided with a move from a large hierarchical organization to a small firm with a very flat structure. In San Francisco, I reported sometimes to a senior vice-president and sometimes to a principal. That was normal throughout the Bear organization, and even in some of the staff areas the partners would wander about quizzing people about what they were working on and what things ought to be improved around the office. In New York, my company held its annual all-officers meeting at Radio City Music Hall and nearly filled the place. In San Francisco we held a lunch for the professional staff at a local bar and grill once every two weeks or so. The new firm changed the way I felt about myself. I realized that my role was not limited to my defined job, and that my ideas really were just as good as anybody's in the entire firm, sometimes better. I also found that, if I pressed a proposal, people listened, and they respected my ideas and took them as seriously as they would expect me to take theirs in return. Most importantly, I came to see that I had allowed the organization to limit my progress and my thinking about the problems faced by the business. This feeling of being able to make a difference spilled over into my home life as well. I had begun working out, eating better, and drinking less about a year earlier in New York, but in San Francisco I came to see the fitness program as a personal challenge. How strong and fast could I become, and how would that improve the way I felt about myself? I began spending more time outdoors than I had for a number of years, and I came to appreciate how important the feel of cool air and the wind and sun were to me. In many ways, I felt like some very important parts of me had fallen away or maybe just been out of use over the years, and I was suddenly given a chance to retrieve them and rediscover the happiness that they had previously added to my life.

2. Coming to Darden was in many ways a continuation of my rebirth, but in an academic and intellectual sense rather than in a physical sense. I had buried for a long time my disappointment and frustration that I didn't take greater advantage of the intellectual opportunities at Cornell, and I felt that I was somewhat underdeveloped in terms of being a careful thinker, a critical thinker. Darden has allowed me to prove to myself that I can cut it with the big boys, and it has brought me great joy to find some intellectual kindred spirits among my best friends here in Charlottesville. I enjoy critical debate, and the case method certainly provides opportunity for that, even if occasional chip-shot barrages do break out. If there is one thing that has frustrated me most at Darden, it is professors' unwillingness to pursue loosely framed or poorly supported statements, and students' unwillingness to push themselves to become more critical thinkers and analysts. Most of my compatriots do push themselves to excel, but often it is in terms of Darden's evaluation of their performance rather than a personal desire to become better business people and better citizens generally. Too many times, students put their faith in Darden's ability to teach the right lessons rather than asking themselves how they are progressing in their education. I'm proud to be a part of the program here, but I think we need to work harder at improving ourselves and not so hard at meeting whatever parameters are specifically demanded by the MBA program.

3. Teaching and music are clearly parts of my life which are "on hold" right now. I hope to take part in a handicapped ski instruction program this winter, which should start to bring teaching back into my life, but so far I haven't managed to fit music back into my life except from the perspective that I am taking more frequent advantage of opportunities to listen to fine music. But the bottom line is that I need to reincorporate playing music into my life. We'll see, won't we?

Question #10 (Disillusionments)

1. Ha! The most obvious example of a disillusionment was certainly getting engaged to be married but having to face the music a year later and admit that I was wrong, that we were wrong about having found our life partners. The main problem in retrospect was that we each saw marriage as a force which would smooth many other problems. I think I already mentioned that I think that each of us had sufficiently inflated and myopic views of ourselves that we expected

the other person to change to suit our own desires. That is certainly a lesson that can be generalized. You'd better like somebody for what they are now, because unlike many other problems we face in life, people will decide for themselves whether they are interested in changing their lives, and in the end, they will determine their own destinies if your suggestions don't feel right. This is one of the great unspoken benefits to delegating responsibilities to others. If someone decides to back an idea or a project of their own free will, then you can work together on it in the most powerful way. If, on the other hand, you decide what someone else will or will not do, the odds are exponentially greater that you will not receive their full effort (and you may find yourself working against them), and your ability to achieve a desired end will be radically reduced.

2. It is the same with romantic relationships. If partners come together as equal individuals aiming for common goals, the power and strength and especially the potential for the relationship will be infinitely greater than if one pushes or cajoles or maneuvers the other to fulfill objectives counter to the ones which would otherwise arise of free will. This discovery has greatly improved my ability to relax and enjoy my relationships with women I have been close to.

3. For the most part, my expectations about my career choices have been a good fit with the eventually discovered reality.

CARRIE BAUGH'S WRITTEN INTERVIEW (B)

Question #2 (Other Memories?)

137. I started my story from the very beginning. I believe I covered all the pertinent points and aspects of my life in the first question.

138. The only thing that comes to mind is I don't remember a lot of details from my childhood—not until about 6th grade. I do remember that I used to daydream an awful lot—about being a missionary, a politician, a doctor. I really wanted to help people with my actions. I loved being friends with everyone, or at least nice to them. Everyone deserves to be treated with warmth and dignity. As I got older, I became more cautious, as I learned more about the bad things that are a part of the world we live in.

139. My favorite activities were sports, especially volleyball and tennis. And I loved to organize extracurricular activities—things like dances, dinners, parties, guest speakers, etc. The piano has always been an important part of my life, as well. It is an essential way for me to express my feelings and work out things in my head. Of course, family was all-important!

Question #3 (Unaccounted for Times?)

140. During high school, I worked part-time as a sales clerk in the local pharmacy. I worked a few hours each day and one weekend day, or 2 to 2½ days. I enjoyed the spending money of working, and freedom. I also liked working with customers. People really respond to a friendly hello, thank you, etc. All you need to do is extend common courtesy.

141. During college, I spent the summers as an intern/clerk at the East Side Union High School district in San Jose. Dad had originally got me the job the summer before college, and I worked there every summer until graduation.

142. They were a very nice, helpful group of people—mostly women as secretaries, me in the management roles. But people seemed to get along very, very well. It was also a very low-key working environment—8:00-4:30, and *no one* worked late. They thought I was such a hard worker, and I liked to complete a task given to me. By the third summer, they had lined up projects for me to do and let me do them as I pleased, for the most part. They knew I'd do them completely and accurately. I also improved my typing skills tremendously there, and that skill has come in handy many, many times.

143. I've always led a very busy life, one with a work component. When I was 11, I used to cut apricots at the local orchards. The spending money was exciting to have, and I met so many new people from that experience. It was more social than work.

144. In college, I held part-time jobs, to help pay my expenses. I didn't work my freshman year, because I wanted to devote myself to studying. My sophomore and junior years, I worked for the Energy Modeling Forum, part of the Department of Engineering/Economic Systems at Stanford. It was a small group

of professors, graduate students, and secretaries who did studies of the trends within energy markets. It was good pay back then, $8 an hour. Also, I was in charge of all bookkeeping and mailing activities, so I got to choose when I worked. I'd say I worked about ten hours a week. It was a nice contrast to the rigorous pace of school.

145. The R.A. experience my senior year at Stanford took up an awful lot of time; we planned a lot of social and cultural events and tried to make the dorm atmosphere like a family. People used to say I'd make a great mom. (Ha!) My favorite activities were when groups of us planned big social events, like a casino night to benefit the children's hospital, a crazy Halloween party, and a Christmas formal. There's so much involvement and excitement. However, I also enjoyed figuring the dorm out, what made them tick, how they viewed Stanford, stuff like that.

146. During my days working in San Francisco, the time spent not working (which was minimal) was spent enjoying the city life. Mark and I loved going out to dinner and finding special little neighborhood restaurants that were gems. We really splurged on this, but we both knew this time in our lives lent itself to enjoying what a big city has to offer.

147. We also used to attend the musicals that came to town, like "Cats" and "42nd Street," and even tried an opera! Since each part of the city has a unique flavor to it, we used to spend a lot of evenings and weekends exploring different shopping areas, dancing spots, parks, and stuff like that. And playing a lot of tennis.

Question #4 (Jobs)

148. I think I've pretty much answered this question, but I'll summarize it here.

149. *Part-time Jobs*: Loved having spending money, or at least contributing to my college expenses. I also enjoyed the change of pace, and diversity, brought on by working, even if the work was somewhat boring and repetitious. I always felt I was making a contribution. I've been lucky to work with very nice, almost maternal people in my part-time jobs—very supportive, very positive relationships.

150. *Macy's*: Liked the location in San Francisco, but disliked the grime and pathetic nature of parts of Union Square. So many people down and out—it made me feel very guilty.

151. The people, on a whole, I was not very impressed with. They did not seem very dynamic or smart (perceptive) about the business. I think retailing prevents a lot of top people from entering, 'cause the pay is so low.

152. The daily tasks I did were rote, clerical, and very unorganized. I never felt there was a system to the madness, which bothered me greatly. I also hated answering the phone every two minutes! It was not a very professional atmosphere—extreme, fashion-oriented dress; the offices were cramped, dingy, and very inefficient; the supervisors very unapproachable, for the most part.

153. Too "seat of the pants" for me—I need to see the reasoning behind the madness!

154. *Donaldson & Co.*: *Loved* the location—financial district in San Francisco; beautiful, spacious offices; beautiful view of the bay. The environment was conservative, professional—suit and ties, etc. People worked quite hard, and were young and aggressive. I enjoyed many of my peers, although the company as a whole is going through some growing pains and has very young middle managers.

155. The pay was very generous, especially coming from retailing. I liked getting paid for overtime, and the bonus, based on individual and company performance.

156. I also didn't mind the detailed nature of the work, as long as I had the freedom to organize and plan my part of the task, and especially as long as I could see where we were going with it and what the "Big Picture" was.

157. I also disliked that the partners were so short term and that the politics were so big. If you didn't fit in, you were put on the awful jobs. I tried to help those people if I thought they had potential.

Question #5 (People, Acquaintances)

158. I have discussed my family at length. I'm sure it's obvious that they are all important to me and my source of strength in so many ways.

159. My sister is my best friend. She's in college now, so we don't see each other as often, but we are definitely close still, writing and calling each other often. We tell each other how much we love each other a lot.

160. And my husband, Mark, is precious to me. He's an attractive mix of so many of the qualities I wanted in a spouse. He's supportive and encouraging without being wimpy; he definitely is his own person and says what he thinks; he's a very personal person; he's athletic and competitive; he's a smart-ass at times, he loves to joke and tease a lot; he's open with people; he's very humorous and can be so silly; he's sexy in a way I love, dark, handsome, quiet at times. I also like that he questions life and authority, and is protective without being overbearing. He is a person who I would delight in coming home to every night (plus, he's Italian!)

161. Also, ambitious, but wants to stop and enjoy the little things in life. I love him dearly.

162. As I mentioned, my friends tend to come and go throughout different stages of my life.

163. My best friend during childhood was Cindy Gold. A very caring, fun, sensitive person. Cindy liked everyone, almost, and never seemed to judge people. She had simple tastes and hated complications. She was an incredibly loyal, supportive friend. We spent our summers at the pool together or playing softball in the neighborhood. Unfortunately, Cindy and I grew apart after high school. She got married right away and started working at Safeway, and I left to go to college. She was so much smarter than she realized, but she always said she was happy with her lifestyle and future. She has two beautiful children now. One of the most touching moments of my wedding was seeing Cindy again—it brought back so many wonderful, sweet memories.

164. In high school, my closest friends played sports with me. One of my best friends was Karen Baker, a great tennis player with a very energetic personality. We used to play together all the time, and spent some vacations together. Karen's pretty rowdy, but always in harmless ways. She was one of a few girlfriends who didn't talk about boys all the time. I always got bored with that subject. I figured: they either like you or they don't, and there are a ton to choose from. Instead, Karen and I did things, like go to movies, to amusement parks, and swam.

165. In college, I suppose Tom was my best friend. I've already talked about him. Karen Bertol was another good friend—but much too nice. Karen was always trying to make everyone else happy, thinking of their feelings. Often to her own detriment, I think. She went out with Tom's good friend Mike, so the four of us did a lot of stuff together. When Karen and Mike broke up, it was very hard on Karen. She didn't know how to react; part of her wanted to be strong, let it go, and move on, but another part of her wanted to find a way to get him back. She got really emotionally up and down by senior year and became bitter about stuff. We grew apart in a sense, because I didn't like to party as much as she did, and she thought I was judging her, since she got drunk and there I was drinking a ginger ale.

166. Tom's roommate Ken was truly a good friend. He is a quiet, sweet guy, and we became very good friends during college. He is one of the few people I keep in touch with even now. He has a very close, welcoming family, and they're very hospitable and generous, as is Ken. After Tom and I broke up, Ken was careful not to take sides, either way, and still made an effort to do things with me. During graduation, Ken's mom and my mom were trying to figure out how to get the two of us married off. It would have been like marrying my brother! He is now married to a great gal—and seems very content. I think Ken and I will always be special friends, even if we don't see each other a lot.

Question #6 (Future, Ending)

167. The ideal future for me is one where Mark and I successfully *balance* our lives with leisure, work, and family. Balance is very, very important to me, especially because it is so easy for me to focus my energies in one direction and plow right on through. I don't want the important things in life to pass me by, meanwhile being unaware of what's important anyway. Mark and I are both very ambitious and love to work hard. But at the same time, we have strong family values and very similar basic backgrounds. We want to meld both worlds. But enough; here's a happy scenario:

168. It's five years from now, and Mark and I are living in a San Francisco area suburb (what the heck, say Palo Alto). We've both done well at work: Mark is now the managing partner at Donaldson and Company Consulting and has developed a special practice in patent infringements and lost-profits cases. As a result, he runs his area as if it was his own business. There is so much business in the Bay Area that he rarely travels more than twice a month. The overtime has also slowed down; he works ten to twelve hour days, but very few weekends.

169. I have been working for a strategic planning group at a bank. With my help, the bank has again become the leading bank in the United States. We've improved the efficiency of our system, made ourselves service- and customer-oriented, and invested wisely abroad. It's been a long, hard road—challenging, but also very rewarding. I'm being considered for vice-president in charge of our division.

170. Our home is a modest, but nicely furnished, three bedroom, with a huge deck surrounding the house. It's brightly painted and very spacious, with a lot of big bay windows. In our garage sit three cars—a Toyota MR-2, a Cabriolet, and a Jeep. We feel financially secure, even though our house payments are huge.

171. I've just turned 30, and Mark and I have decided we want children. We're at a crossroad. I've decided to give up the promotion possibility, quit, and start my own business while I'm at home raising our children. It is crucial for me to be there until they get to be school age: they are very important and deserve my attention. Therefore, I will need to start slow in my new business. It has to be something I can do from the house, like consulting or some information business. If it gets too much, I've already made the decision to hold off until the kids are in preschool, at least. This will be a hard tradeoff for me to make, but a critical and worthy one.

172. I want Mark and me to be the ones who raise our children—as did my mom and dad—and to always be there, always supporting, sharing, and giving my love. It's important they know that, at home, they receive unconditional love . . . period.

173. To keep myself apprised of the business and world events around me, I plan to read extensively—in fact, maybe I'll write a book or start a newsletter!! That's an idea, and it would be fun to plan. I also want to keep in great shape and looking good. I want Mark to smile every time he comes home!

174. We've been able to vacation extensively since we both started working. We'll probably have to cut down there, but we'll just make better use of the golf and tennis clubs.

175. Mark and I see this stage in our lives as family-oriented. He's promised to leverage out a lot of his work and work at home where possible; our kids will be paramount, and I'll take an active role in educational and social pursuits to help our community while helping my children. I'm going to teach them Italian and Spanish when they're young and get them excited about learning.

176. After the children begin first grade, I'll have time to focus much more on my business. Once the kids go to college, Mark and I will work on continuing our *personal* relationship and begin traveling together again. It will be our time, again, to enjoy each other on a more focused basis.

177. And I'll focus my energies on building a challenging, successful career.

Question #7 (Points of Change)

My points of change:

178. From small, closed grammar school to open, large high school.
179. Getting into Stanford.
180. Point at Stanford when received A's (first year, second quarter).
181. Phi Beta Kappa end of junior year—a lot of accomplished, self-confident feelings.
182. R.A. senior year (relationship with dorm, staff).
183. When decided to leave Macy's to join Donaldson and Company.
184. Relationship with Mark.
185. Business-school decision.
186. Marriage.

Question #8 (Other Options, Decision Making)

Turning Point	Other Options	Pros & Cons	How Decision Arrived At
Grammar school to high school	Private, Catholic high school	Education, financial, new people	With parents, easy decision
Stanford	USF, UCD accepted	Education potential, close to home, financial package good	With parents, but my choice, talked with teachers, set on it
Macy's	Morgan Stanley Law School Masters in Economics	Proximity to San Francisco, money, experience	Not well-thought out, a lot of discussions with friends, family
Donaldson	School, Continue with Macy's	More professional, more money, more commitment, young firm, quantitative, travel	Made myself with a lot of input from friends listed pros, cons
Business School	Continue working, Harvard, UC-Berkeley, UCLA, Darden as choices	Financial, case vs. lecture, location, prestige, opportunities	Listed pros and cons, but "just knew" it was Darden

187. Generally, my way of deciding turning points was to gather information, discuss possibilities with people who I respected and trusted, and then ultimately make my own decision. In fact, in the case of Macy's and Darden, it was against the opinion of my friends and family, but I just knew it was right for me.

188. I've always had *a lot* of options open, but I've never really had trouble deciding between them. I usually knew if one option or decision didn't pan out, I wasn't stuck in it forever. The only decisions I've made that will last forever are deciding to marry Mark and my relationship with my family. Those are decisions, conscious choices, I see as lasting.

189. Turning points are places of opportunity—only *I*, individually, can really choose the route I take. Like a big road map—if you get on a wrong street, you wait until you can make a U-turn to get back on track.

Question #9 (Major Changes)

190. I've become more independent, less naive, perhaps less accepting through my experiences. But I'm basically a people-oriented, fun-loving, energetic person who focuses on the *important, positive* aspects of my life.

191. In fact, adversity makes me very feisty—like some of the structure of Darden—how it tries to make you conform. Since I'm so stubborn, it makes me fight that much harder *not* to succumb. I have overcome most troubles, and will continue to *try*; if you don't try, then you've lost the game.

192. Actually, I'm not sure what this question is trying to get at; most stuff is in question 1.

Question #10 (Disillusionments)

	Expectations	
Turning Point	Before	After
Grammar school to high school	Thought positive, excited about new situation.	Was great!
Getting into Stanford	Life will be great,What a learning opportunity.	Was great!
Macy's	Positive location: great, great, exciting job.	Company doesn't care about their people, no recognition, depressing situation
Darden	Positive: can really shine and improve my skills. New people to know.	Mostly good. But system forces conformity, and seems very "good old boy" oriented. I think sometimes some professors tend to put down women's future contributions to the business world, so why pay attention to their abilities here?

Question #11: Patterns

Close to family, values their opinions.

Makes own decisions, with others' input.

Enjoys life and its possibilities.

Is achievement oriented, sports oriented.

Likes recognition.

17

Dyad Exercise

The dyad exercise is an exchange of data between two partners, a thorough, intensive analysis of that data, and a feedback session. It is designed to give you greater skill in inductively analyzing complex data before you write your self-assessment paper.

Preliminary Considerations

Your chosen partner will read your data and give you a preliminary written analysis of it. You will do the same for him or her. Your partner must be a student in the course. Given the importance of the assignment (many later report it to be one of the key experiences in the course), you should have a clarifying session with your partner before you agree to work with each other to discuss these issues:

1. Confidentiality
2. Level of rigor in analysis and time commitment
3. Format of written feedback
4. Timeliness of feedback
5. Level of candor and care in giving feedback
6. Other concerns you may have

You should allow eight to twelve hours of time to work on this assignment. We suggest that you schedule it during your clarifying session.

Schedule some time (one to three hours) with your partner to conduct the feedback session. In giving your feedback, let one person give *all* of his or her analysis *before* you respond or ask for clarification. The danger is that you will be so defensive or preset in your own analysis that you won't hear what is being said. Use it to learn and to get another perspective on yourself.

Procedure

1. Select someone who is also taking this course or doing a self-assessment.
2. Exchange notebooks. That is, give the person all your data.
3. Each does an assessment of the other person's data, using the methods outlined in the *Self-Assessment and Career Development* text. That is, identify as many supported themes as you can.
4. You need not write up your assessment formally. Instead, simply prepare some charts or exhibits from which you can talk.
5. Meet with your partner and take turns presenting your assessments verbally. Allow at least thirty minutes for each presentation and ten to fifteen minutes for questions afterward.
6. Insert all the materials, exhibits, and notes from your partner's assessment of you in this section.
7. Remember any reactions you may have had in the Feelings Record at the beginning of your workbook.

The written material Steven Taylor and Carrie Baugh received from their dyad partners is shown on pages 189–194. How will this information help them? What different formats can you imagine for giving people feedback on their data?

STEVEN TAYLOR's DYAD EXERCISE

Here is the feedback Steven received from his dyad partner:

1. Strives to excel; may see success as a means to be accepted.
WI - Busted ass on machine job
WI - Outstanding student in various schools
WI - Had to excel in athletics to compensate for size
WI - Hollow feeling after academic mediocrity at Cornell

2. Does not necessarily subscribe to artificial/imaginary boundaries
WI - Coffee table/good china
WI - Hung out with both freaks and jocks

3. Family is important—you seem to see yourself as a member of this large unit.

4. Needs constant learning stimulation
WI - Museums as a child
WI - Experimental school
WI - Experience at NY Money Center Bank

5. Thrives in an unstructured environment
- Experimental school
- Job in San Francisco

6. Does not indicate a tendency to view authority figures as threats
- Job at New York Money Center Bank
- Reaction to and method of addressing initial problems at Bloomfield Hills

7. Enjoys external confirmation of accomplishments/abilities
- Running for various offices (Ski Club, Student Council)
- Speech after Andover
- National Merit
- You tend to work hard for rewards (Money Center Bank, especially)

8. Enjoys change; is adaptable to change
- Interpersonal style evidence
- Adaptability after moving
- "I needed more diversity" (broke up with fiancee)
- Willing to head west without job
- Question 4 of WI—Likes to "get on to next project"

*Insight: Perhaps new projects are like new towns—CHALLENGES!

9. Needs *some* structure
- Desire for stabilization after Cornell (training program, fiancee)
- "balance back into life"

10. Can handle crisis
- Question 4
- mother's cancer a NET BENEFIT (This is an impressive outlook.)

Underlying Themes

- Wants to improve/advance. Never fully satisfied with the current product.
  - fitness mentioned several times as a goal
  - wants to play trumpet "someday"
  - wants to teach
- Self-sufficient. Has not looked to external source for livelihood.
  - Graeme and Company—respects that they "make their way on their own, which made all the difference."
  - entrepreneurial satisfaction.

I think you see corporate hierarchy as inherently weak and dependent.

- Strong values—honesty, integrity, two-way commitment, go out of your way to make mate happy.
- Pompous.
- Seeks companionship.
- Don't want to save the world—just make the world a little better for those around you (more deeply, more significant). See a strong sense that your world is small. You do not really concern yourself with all those countless bodies that populate the earth. Your world is the one you see. It extends beyond yourself, but not even as far as all the people you see around you. The opinions of others about whom you do not care one way or the other are not important to you. I do not get the impression that you've agonized too much over what the herds think about you. Evidence, overall impression of WI; "Listens well" is low.

  You are a (goes back to pompous) snob, not socially, but, Question 8 #1, not going to Ann Arbor; "Conceited" in Interpersonal Style.

- High degree of willingness to make commitments.
- Does not depend on others for support.
  - low "Needs support"; 4 in Interpersonal Style
- You want to be loved, you want to love.
  - strive for approval of others
  - always have a girlfriend
- Creative problem solver.
  (The way you dealt with your Money Center Bank job—no (or not many) bad loans)
- Class performance.
- See people as a resource, but clearly separate. You are you. Separate being. Define yourself. Listen to others, but define yourself.
- Want the glory, but need some encouragement to *do the work.* You don't naturally work hard, as in Protestant work ethic. Feelings record.
- Perhaps you don't like large organizations because you know your inherently passive nature will be tolerated. Let's face it, in the corporate world, the MINIMAL extra effort is rewarded and noticed, while in a small environment, you have to make a MEANINGFUL contribution in order to be rewarded.
- Critical of yourself in some respects. You laugh at yourself.

CARRIE BAUGH'S DYAD EXERCISE

Test	*This Is A Person Who*	*Evidence*
Figure Test (FT)	Displays a range of motivations and emotions with people	Evenness of People responses
	Considers a lot of ideas in an ambiguous situation	42 answers, little direction
	Is action oriented	40% response, environmental active
	Is very people oriented	50% People responses
Feelings Record (FR)	Feels presentation of material is important	Done on MAC laserwriter
	Sees value, finds insight in most situations	Noted learning from most tests
Card Sort (CS)	Puts marriage and family first	1 and 2 aspects
	Strongly values growth and closeness in relationships	
	Seeks balance	Added to exercise
	Values integrity	Identity and Professional
	Does not see friends as important aspect (relative to family)	Fourth-tier aspect
	Sees values/priorities changing and evolving	Feelings record
FIRO B (FB)	Equally expresses and wants inclusion	
	Rarely expresses control, but occasionally wants control	
	Maybe wants more affection than expresses	
Predisposition Test (PT)	Can adapt to changing environments	Average tolerance for ambiguity
	Is closer to Research Organization for ambiguity	
	Prefers individual challenges vs. team challenges	High preference for autonomy
	Tends to be alone	High predisposition for solitude
	Is closer to Research Organization than Manufacturing for autonomy and solitude	
	Might work well in a research environment	

(continued)

Carrie Baugh's Dyad Exercise (continued)

Test	*This Is A Person Who*	*Evidence*
Leadership Report (LR)	Might provide more vision, insight, and planning than gaining commitment from people	Feelings record indicated that this test answered as if corporate leader
	May not have had a job where gaining commitment was important	Lower C
Management Style (MS)	Has experience working at setting direction and organizing to achieve that	Equal V and M
	May not see gaining commitment as important as vision and management	Lower C
Interpersonal Style (IS)	Is seen as one who takes the lead	
	May seek recognition in some situations and not in others	High SD
	Is not seen as defensive or conceited	
	Presents self fairly consistently to others	Very few high SDs
Report Self	May be too self-critical	Acquaintance and Desired closer than perceived self
	Sees lots of room for self-improvement	Only meets Desired five times
Daily Diary (DD)	Is very expressive	Great descriptions
	Interacts with just a few people at Darden	Mentions only 2 Dardenites
	Constantly sets objectives and goals	Every weekday entry mentions something to be done in the future
	Is much more involved with people on weekends	More references
	Relaxes more when Mark is around	Weekend, last weekday reference
Strong-(SII)	Shows strong common interests with Arts and Social	
	Has high athletic interest	
	Not interested in office routines	
	Is extremely comfortable with academic challenge	
	Extroverted vs. introverted	
	Likes most activities	Administrative indexes
	Is very open-minded about people	Administrative indexes
Myers-Briggs (MB)	Is more extroverted than introverted	
	Relies equally on both perceiving and judging	
	Relies slightly more on sensing than intuition	
	Relies slightly more on feeling than thinking	
Learning Style Inventory (LSI)	Learns by doing; likes to experiment	
	Is more interested in results than methods	
	Learns from both people and logic	
Peterson (PET)	Is valued as a team player	
	Is driven	
	Can successfully tackle intellectual challenges	
	Is comfortable with technical assignments	
	Is self-motivated	
	Is a careful planner	
	Has not had an opportunity to fully test management and leadership abilities	
	Is enthusiastic	

(continued)

Carrie Baugh's Dyad Exercise (continued)

Test	*This Is A Person Who*	*Evidence*
	Prefers to do the work herself rather than delegate to others	
Life Style	Is creative	Mobile vs. flat sheet of paper
Representation (LSR)	Stresses balance in life	Center
	Sees balance between family, identity, work, future, and recreation	
	Sees job impacting family	Job included on family hanger
Written Interview (WI)	Has family and husband central to her life	
	Needs time to be alone	
	Is excited by, and looks forward to, change	
	Often succeeds through determination	
	Can set very difficult goals and attain them	
	Enjoys music in her life	
	Needs autonomy, independence	
	Enjoys an intellectually challenging professional environment	
	Likes order to things	
	Likes to be surrounded by people	
	Does not like confrontation	
	Transitions fairly easily between task-oriented and people-oriented activities	

CARRIE BAUGH'S DYAD EXERCISE—LIFE THEMES

TEST	*THEME*
	1. IS COMMITTED TO STRONG LOVING AND NURTURING RELATIONSHIPS WITH MARK AND FAMILY
CS	Marital, Familial, Growth important
	2. VALUES INDEPENDENCE AND AUTONOMY
FR	"I like group activities, but not all the time."
CS	"Still think as an individual" #3
PT	High preference for autonomy
WI	"I felt so free and independent"
	". . . Tom's need to be part of a group"
	"I also hated the thought of being a groupie"
Contradictory	
SCI	extroverted
MB	extroverted
	3. VALUES CREATIVITY AND LISTENING IN CLOSE RELATIONSHIPS
WI	"Dad . . . is a wonderful listener"
	"Dad was always really creative"
	4. HAS A HIDDEN PASSION FOR PERFORMING
FT	singing, I've got to be me, in a dramatic scene in a play
WI	"my friends thought it was so neat that I could play songs they heard on the radio"
	"Mostly wanting to be an actress or a singer, up there wowing the

audience with my dramatic entry . . . "

"I liked being in the spotlight"

"People got a kick out of my red silk petticoat . . . "

SCI High interest in Arts

LSR Creativity in mobile

5. HAS BEEN ABLE TO SET DIFFICULT GOALS AND SUCCEED

DD Sets goals throughout the day

CS Professional, achieve a goal #4

WI "trying to master the tough classical songs"

"And I made my goals"

"I felt like all I had worked for, all the focus on school and the discipline . . . paid off"

"I had decided to really apply myself to studying—go all out"

"The hard focused work paid off . . . "

6. FORMS CLOSEST RELATIONSHIPS WITHIN FAMILY; PREFERS A FEW VERY CLOSE FRIENDSHIPS AND LOTS OF ACQUAINTANCES

CS Familial, being close to others

WI " . . . sometimes friendships can be so confining" "I have very few close friends and tons of acquaintances"

"(Mom) We sit there like best friends . . . "

"(sister) . . . we are very close—probably closer than I am to any other woman"

7. LIKES ROUTINE AND PLANNNG

WI "and got into a steady routine"

"And very few people had systems, skills or wanted to implement controls"

18

Other Data-Generating Devices

The ten data-generating devices contained in the workbook should provide you with enough information to do your self-assessment. Many other possible sources of data, however, might be useful to you. You may wish to use such sources to supplement those you now have. In this chapter we will briefly describe some of those other sources.

We would offer two caveats, however, neither of which should surprise you. First, be sure you understand the nature of other data-generating sources so that you can understand the information they produce. Second, be sure you treat the supplementary data as you have treated those from the ten devices in this book. Remember that a single datum from a single source proves nothing; look for patterns.

Other Psychological Tests

Various students of ours have at one time or another used the following instruments in their self-assessments:

1. Edwards Personal Preference Schedule
2. Thematic Apperception Test
3. Rorschach Inkblot Test
4. Myers-Briggs Type Indicator
5. FIRO-B

There are numerous other instruments like these.

You may find that you cannot gain access to these tests—especially tests like the Rorschach—except through a properly trained psychologist. And this is probably how it should be. If a psychologist administers a test to you and interprets its output, be sure *you* understand the basis of his or her interpretation.

IQ and Other Aptitude Tests

A number of IQ and so-called aptitude tests exist today. No doubt you have taken at least one of these tests (such as the SAT or GRE tests you took as a part of applying to undergraduate or graduate school). A few of the more popular are these:

1. Wechsler Adult Intelligence Scale
2. Harvard Speed Alphas
3. Skills Inventories
4. Miller Analogies

Be sure to treat these devices as carefully as you do all your data-generating instruments. Sophisticated "tests" such as these look more authoritative to many people than a simple device like a 24-hour diary, and so people may be more passive, less critical, and less demanding in dealing with the output of these tests. Don't be!

Experiential Exercises and Games

In the past decade, a number of exercises and games have been created that simulate some type of real-world activity and can provide interesting data to the participant. An example is the In-Basket test, developed by Educational Testing Service and AT&T, and today available in a variety of versions. In a typical version, an individual is given the role of a manager who has twenty-five items in his or her in-basket (letters, memos, phone messages, and so on), must catch a plane in three hours, and can reach no one on the phone or in person (it is Sunday). The individual is given three hours to go through the in-basket and take any actions that seem necessary (schedule meetings, write notes, and so on); his or her behavior and decisions become the output of the exercise.

Experiential exercises and games can provide useful data for people of all ages, but we've found them particularly helpful to young people—especially those with no work experience.

The output from these exercises, which can be rather rich, should be treated just like the output of other devices. Again, it is important to understand the data-generating device to avoid misusing its output. The most common misuse of game output is to make huge inferential leaps to grand conclusions, based on the assumption that the game experience was exactly like the real experience it was simulating. (For example, Joe seems to do a much better job than other participants playing a "plant manager" in the in-basket exercise. Joe therefore would probably be a good plant manager.)

The In-Basket exercise can be obtained through Educational Testing Service, Princeton, NJ 08540. Other exercises of this type can be found in *Organizational Psychology: An Experiential Approach,* by Kolb, Rubin, and McIntyre (Englewood Cliffs, NJ: Prentice-Hall, 1974) and in *Management: An Experiential Approach* by Knudson, Woodworth, and Bell (New York: McGraw-Hill, 1973).

Other Personal or Historical Documents

Our students have occasionally used a variety of documents from their pasts as data in their self-assessments. For example, we have asked them to include their graduate school application form, since it requires them to answer a number of interesting essay questions. Some students have also used old diaries, photographs, letters of recommendation, performance appraisals, newspaper clippings, and essays that they wrote. As long as you are sensitive to the circumstances under which these personal or historical documents were generated, they can occasionally be useful additions to your data.

19

Assessing the Self-Assessment Exercise

We have outlined a rigorous and multifaceted approach to self-assessment so far in this book. If you have followed along each step of the way, you are ready to begin pulling it all together. Before you do that, we suggest that you read through a self-assessment paper or two to get an idea of what one might look like.

We have included the entire set of data for Lauren Davis and her Self-Assessment Paper. Note that she used some instruments that we did not use in the book. You, too, should feel free to add other data to your information pool.

Using your knowledge of the self-assessment process, the instruments, and the characteristics of useful theme labels, how would you judge Lauren's efforts? Is her paper reasonable? What are the strengths and weaknesses? What do you learn from this example about writing your own?

If you are using the book in a course, we encourage you to read the paper and write down the feedback you would give to Lauren, along with a grade. Be prepared to present your feedback in class.

LAUREN DAVIS' SELF-ASSESSMENT DATA

Figure Test

Lauren Davis gave the following responses to the ten figures. The question she was asked while looking at each figure was: "What might this person be doing?"

Responses to Figure 1	Category
• Looking up at clouds on a sunny day	ENV PAS
• Youngster chastised by mother and standing at attention	PEO DEP
Responses to Figure 2	
• Giving direction or telling someone to leave via that exit	PEO DIR/ PEO COMM
• Telling someone who has displeased him to leave (arm or hip might mean anger)	PEO AGG
Responses to Figure 3	
• Just got in 1st college of choice, jumping for joy	ENV ACT
• Just finished Darden; in jubiliation that it's successfully over	ENV ACT
Responses to Figure 4	
• Preparing for an attack, defensive position	PEO AGG
• Pulling back a sling shot	PEO AGG
• Nudging his neighbor playfully	PEO AFF
Responses to Figure 5	
• Smelling a flower	ENV ACT
• Waving goodbye sadly to a departing friend	PEO COMM
• Waving hello to friend coming up	PEO AFF
Responses to Figure 6	
• Leaning on a tree or post	ENV PAS
• Putting his hand on a buddy's shoulder	PEO AFF
• Picking something off a shelf	ENV ACT
• Dancing	PEO DEP
Responses to Figure 7	
• Sleeping	ENV PAS
• Diving off a high dive	ENV ACT
• Somersault	ENV ACT
• Exercises	ENV ACT
• Groaning in pain	PEO COMM
Responses to Figure 8	
• Shaking hands	PEO AFF
• Jumping exercises	ENV ACT
• Sitting down and taking someone's hand to get up	PEO DEP
Responses to Figure 9	
• Welcoming a group of relatives, friends who haven't been seen for ages	PEO AFF
• Describing something large to someone	PEO COMM
Responses to Figure 10	
• Standing with both arms on elbows	ENV PAS/PEO AGG
• Bending over from waist to touch toes	ENV ACT

Lauren's Scoring

	Total Tallies	*Percentage*
Environment		
Active	9	30
Passive	4	13
Total Environment	13	43
People		
Affection	5	17
Aggression	4	13
Communication	4	13
Dependence	3	10
Direction	1	4
Exhibition	0	0
Total People	17	57
Grand Total	30	100%

Lauren's Inferences

- highest: ENV ACT (9), PEO AFF (5), ENV PAS (4), PEO AGG (4), PEO COMM (4)
- doing things by myself (sports, emotions)
- doing things with people in which I am expressing an emotion or interest

Rorschach Inkblot Test

Lauren Davis made the following replies to four Rorschach cards:

Card Side

I 1. (W) Emblem for the medical profession. Army insignia.
2. (W) Bird flying (looking down from above). Pig about to chomp on something.
3. (W) Oriental house, pagoda—Arc d' Triomphe.
4. (W) Boat passing under a bridge.

II 1. (W) Fat ballerina on her tiptoes.
2. (W) Jet flying over dark clouds.
3. (W) Two elves with tall hats hitting hands and stomping feet.
4. (W) Same as 2.

III 1. (W) Old guy with hat and beard and overcoat and gray scarf.
2. (W) Blast shot out of space ship.
3. (W) Someone being burned at the stake.
4. (W) Monster sticking out fiery tongue.

IV 1. (W) American eagle emblem.
2. (D) Alligator head with jaws open.
3. (W) Showgirl with oriental headpiece, boa around neck and pompoms in her hands.
4. (W) Race car still moving with clouds of smoke streaming out.

Lauren's Scoring and Analysis

Card:	*I*	*II*	*III*	*IV*	*Total*	*Percentage*
	W	W	W	W		
	W	W	W	D		
	W	W	W	W		
	W	W	W	W		
Total Responses	*4*	*4*	*4*	*4*	*16*	*100%*
Total W	4	4	4	3	15	94%
Total D	0	0	0	1	1	6%
Total d	0	0	0	0	0	0%

Lauren's Inferences

- 94% W's. Big Picture Person—problems with accounting.
- Always wants to be a generalizer—everything reminds person of a concept.

Learning Style Inventory

Lauren's Scores

CE 16	RO 7	AC 17	AE 18
AC−CE = 1		AE−RO = 11	

Lauren's Inferences

This is how I see myself as a learner:

Active Experimentation: 18 (75%) "Doing" orientation; projects, homework, small group discussions; dislike passive learning situations (lectures), extroverts

Concrete Experimentation: 16 (63%) Receptive, experience-based approach to learning; relies heavily on feeling based judgements; empathetic, people oriented; theoretical approaches unhelpful; treat each situation as unique case; learn best from specific examples in which become involved, oriented more toward peers than authority in approach to learning; benefit most from feedback and discuss with fellow CE learners.

Accomodator

Strengths: carrying out plans and experiments; involving self in new experiences; more of a risk taker; excel in situations where one must adapt oneself to specific, immediate circumstances; solves problems with intuitive trial and error; relies on other people for information rather than on one's own analytic ability; at ease with people; impatient and pushy at times; action oriented jobs—marketing, sales.

FIRO-B

Lauren's Scores

	I	C	A	Sum (I + C + A)
e	3	3	4	10
w	0	2	5	7
				Total Sum
sum (e + w)	3	5	9	17
				Total Diff.
diff (e − w)	3	1	−1	3

Lauren's Inferences

1. Preference for solitude.
2. Desire for considerable amount of giving and receiving affection and interpersonal closeness.
3. Tendency toward active initiation of interpersonal behavior with others.
4. Want others to initiate behavior towards me.
5. Strong preference for considerable amount of interpersonal interaction.
6. Preference for others to initiate inclusion.
7. Preference for taking rather than giving orders.
8. Preference for receiving in contrast to initiating affection.
9. Preference for being the recipient of the initiations of interpersonal activities.

Predisposition Test

	Tolerance for Ambiguity	*Preference for Autonomy*	*Predisposition Toward Solitary Effort*
Lauren Davis	3.0	2.57	2.86
Research Organization	2.91	2.83	2.96
Manufacturing Organization	2.57	2.17	2.40

Lauren's Inferences

1. Very high tolerance for ambiguity: Don't mind a changing set of conditions; less defined work and greater uncertainty of information OK.
2. Preference for autonomy average for age group of HBS; close to my characteristics; closer to research organization than manufacturing; a bit higher preference to define work roles, provide own direction; less inclined to like subordinate relationships with strong authority figures.
3. High disposition toward solitude—prefer to work individually.
4. Scored closer to R&D environmental group: tolerate a bit more ambiguity; have less preference for autonomy; want to work alone a little more.

Life and Career Values Card Sort

Most Important Value Cluster

Marital

Tranquility
Changing activities daily
Praised by spouse

Identity

Getting ahead
Being free
Expanding influence
Achieving goals

Very Important Value Cluster

Professional

Run show
Public recognition
Feeling expert
Learning new things
Tackling challenge
Rewarded fairly for efforts
Directing next person
Changing activities weekly
Working on broad issues

Financial/Material

Being independent
Having as much as possible
Planning ahead

Important Value Cluster

Social

Close to others
Part of group
Relaxing
Meeting people

Recreation/Physical

Enjoying activity
Do better than next person
Feeling capable
Moving quickly

Intellectual

Organizing things
Using energy and resources wisely
Finishing task
Working on details

Somewhat Important Value Cluster

Parental

Looking ahead
Teaching
Watching growth
Moving slowly

Familial

Being encouraged
Being praised
Looking back

Other Considerations

Political	Emotional
Helping people	Watching people grow
Spiritual	**Societal**
Admiring beauty of it all	Involved

Lauren's Inferences

-Definite priorities here:
- -Personal (Bill & me, me)
- -Professional/Material
- -Extracurricular
- -Kids: Parents
- -Others

Lauren Davis' Interpersonal Style Inventory Data

Item	*Acquaintance*					*Sum*	*Mean*	*S.D.*
	1	2	3	4	5			
Takes Lead	4	3	2	3	3	15	3.0	.71
Needs Support	3	3	3	4	2	15	3.0	.71
Seeks Recognition	3	2	2	3	2	12	2.4	.55
Works Alone	3	3	4	3	4	17	3.4	.55
Helps Others	4	4	3	4	4	19	3.8	.45
Follows Rules	3	3	4	4	3	17	3.4	.55
Listens Well	5	5	4	4	3	21	4.2	.84
Willing to Learn	5	4	4	4	3	20	4.0	.71
Trusts Others	4	4	3	3	3	17	3.4	.55
Defensive	2	3	3	4	2	14	2.8	.84
Discusses Emotions	4	3	2	3	2	14	2.8	.84
Discusses Personal	4	3	2	3	2	14	2.8	.84
Easy to Talk to	5	4	2	4	4	19	3.8	1.10
Docile	2	4	4	3	4	17	3.4	.89
Praises	4	4	3	4	3	18	3.6	.55
Is Consistent	4	4	4	4	4	20	4.0	0.0
Is Conceited	3	2	2	3	1	11	2.2	.84
Adapts	4	4	3	4	4	19	3.8	.45
Competitive	3	3	3	3	2	14	2.8	.45
Own Decisions	4	3	2	4	3	16	3.2	.84
Calm	5	4	4	4	4	21	4.2	.45
Mechanical	2	2	3	4	2	13	2.6	.89
Tolerant	4	4	3	4	4	19	3.8	.48
Patient	5	5	4	4	3	21	4.2	.84
Keeps Promises	4	5	4	4	4	21	4.2	.45
Cheerful	5	4	3	4	5	21	4.2	.84

Lauren Davis' Interpersonal Style Inventory Profiles

Note that the sequence of items has changed. Transcribe the plots carefully!

* = Current Self, o = Desired Self, X = Average of Acquaintances' Reports

Never 1 2 3 4 Always 5

ITEM	ACQ. AVG.	S.D.
Takes lead	3.0	.71
Seeks recognition	2.4	.55
Is conceited	2.2	.84
Is competitive	2.8	.45
Defensive	2.8	.84
Works alone	3.4	.55
Own Decisions	3.2	.84
Mechanical	2.6	.89
Consistent	4.0	0.0
Keeps promises	4.2	.45
Praises	3.6	.55
Cheerful	4.2	.84
Calm	4.2	.45
Patient	4.2	.84
Listens well	4.2	.84
Easy to talk to	3.8	1.10
Tolerant	3.8	.48
Helps others	3.8	.45
Trusts others	3.4	.55
Follows rules	3.4	.55
Willing to learn	4.0	.71
Docile	3.4	.89
Needs support	3.0	.71
Discusses emotions	2.8	.84
Discusses personal	2.8	.84

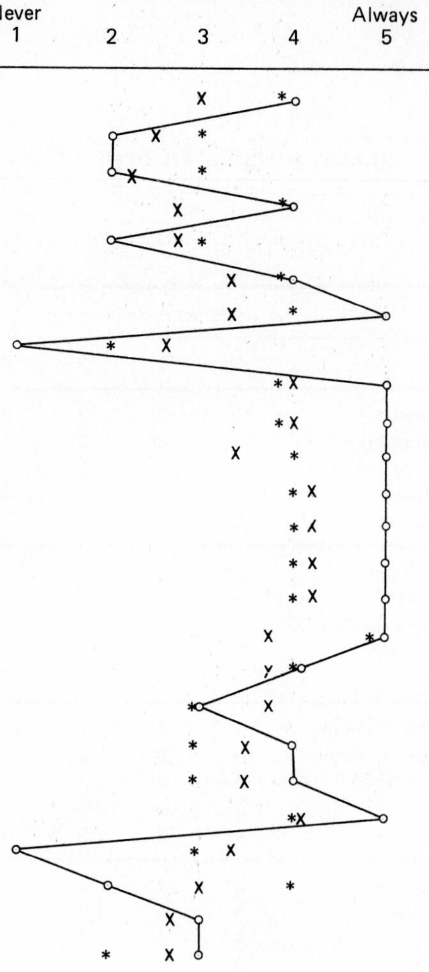

AVL Study of Values

Scale	Lauren's Score		Value Name
50			
49			
48	________	48	Social
47			
46			
45			
44			
43			
42			
41	________	41	Economics/Religious
40			
39			
38	________	38	Theoretical
37			
36	________	36	Aesthetic/Political
35			

Lauren's Inferences

1. Social very high: love of people; prizes others as ends in self-kind, sympathetic, unselfish.
2. Economic/Religious: interested in useful practical; perhaps seeing environment in ''totality''—big picture outlook?

24 HOUR DIARY

Friday

8:00 Got up reluctantly. I'm starting to get a cold, and I feel lousy. No classes today, but plenty to do—have to be at school by 9 a.m. to meet with Advertising Manager group and work on group project. Showered, breakfast, read paper.

9:00 Finally left to get over to school (which means I was going to be 15 minutes late!) When I got to School @ 9:15 only 2 other group members were there—and I thought *I* was irresponsible. I don't like to be kept waiting—so I apologized for being late—however the group member who was supposed to have organized our notes into an outline hadn't arrived, so there was nothing to do yet anyway!

9:30 Bruce and I began calling other group members in order to get going. Everyone of them was still at home or in bed.

10:20 Mary brought outline over to school and began reviewing it to clarify any questions we might have.

11:00 Decided how to organize the paper and break it up into sections for 4 of us to write individually. Planned to work individually until 12:30 and then compare writing styles. Worked on my section until then—also ate lunch in the interim. Didn't eat much because I'm feeling so sick. I wish I could go home and crawl into bed.

11:30 Met with group—but no one was very far along. Everyone seemed to be writing in a similar manner (we wanted to make the style as consistent as possible), so we split up again and planned to meet @ 12:30.

12:30 All four read and discussed each others sections, made some corrections, and broke up again to finish off the writing.

1:30 Met with "final" versions and went through same process again. Began to prepare exhibits, and discussed flaws that had popped up in some of our logic.

2:45 Went to Sponsors seminar on home computers. Wasn't too bad—I would have enjoyed it more if I didn't feel so lousy. I'm dying to learn more about computers. I think that's one of Darden's biggest weaknesses. Everyone should be urged to take a 1/2–1 semester course on programming and use of computers. We are going to *have* to be able to use and understand computers in most every business-related job. A bit shortsighted on the School's part.

4:00 Back to the group. Winding things down. Rest of members showed up to pick up where we left off. Discussed paper with them.

5:30 Left school for home. What a wasted day. I don't feel like I accomplished much. Plus cold medicines always make me spacey. It's a good feeling if you can lay back and go to sleep, but not if you need to be alert and have to fight off those side effects. Pills like those also affect my mood. I get grouchy and mad at the world.

6:30 Left to go to scuba diving class with Bill. Neither one of us feels up to swimming, so we planned to leave right after the classroom time.

8:15 Came home. Stopped and got subs at the sub shop. Ate subs and watched the World Series. I don't usually like to watch baseball, but I do like to watch the World Series. I guess I like it because something big is at stake. Same goes for the Super Bowl. Those games I can get involved in and enjoy.

9:00 Fell asleep on the couch. Pills made me drowsy. Bill and I finally woke up and went to bed about 1:00 a.m.

Saturday

8:20 Woke up about half an hour ago—don't need to get up early today, but couldn't sleep because of a bad cold and sore throat. Knew I had plenty to do today, so might as well get going. Projects, projects, projects! It's funny how some mornings it's so difficult to get up and others it's so easy. When I'm behind in my work, I'd rather put the pillow over my head and go back to sleep. But if I'm on schedule or ahead in my work, I don't mind jumping out of bed.

8:30 Showered, breakfast, read Washington Post, took some cold medicine.

10:00 Drove over to school to get started on school work. Advertising group project was supposed to be in a group member's box so the rest could give it a final review. It wasn't there. It really irritated me. Half the group worked hard on it yesterday and the others were supposed to polish it off last night. Feel a bit put-upon!

10:30 Organizing notebook in order to get started. It's hard for me to work with a messy notebook. In order to keep the workload organized in my head and in order to make sure I cover everything I need to be organized and neat.

11:00 Talked to Kevin. He's going to the game today even though he has a ton to do, too. I'm a bit envious. I don't mind working when I know everyone else is working too, but it's hard to be disciplined on a sunny football day.

11:30 Worked in the library until 1:30. Picked up Bill at home and went to Graffiti for lunch. I needed a break. This isn't going to be much of a weekend with all the work I have, so I deserve to take some fun breaks. Bill's working on his SBS, so we both need the break! Found out next World Series game is on at 4, so I'm going to try to work while I watch the game.

3:00 Back to library for more studying.

5:15 Home to see game and watch work on PACS. I wish I had more time, PACS work is beginning to pay off. The themes are really interesting. Watched the Dodgers win. Good for Dodgers, bad for my studying. That means more games on TV to distract me.

6:30 Fixed spaghetti for dinner—made it ahead so it didn't take long. Watched the rest of the game while we ate.

8:00 Went back to work. Am feeling very disorganized because I have lots of half-completed themes.

8:50 Drove to movie "Rich & Famous." Not bad—some of it was overdone, but it was good, legal entertainment. People around me probably hated me—I blew my nose constantly.

11:10 Home and to bed. I'm sick, so early to bed—getting well!

Lauren Davis: Life Style Diagram

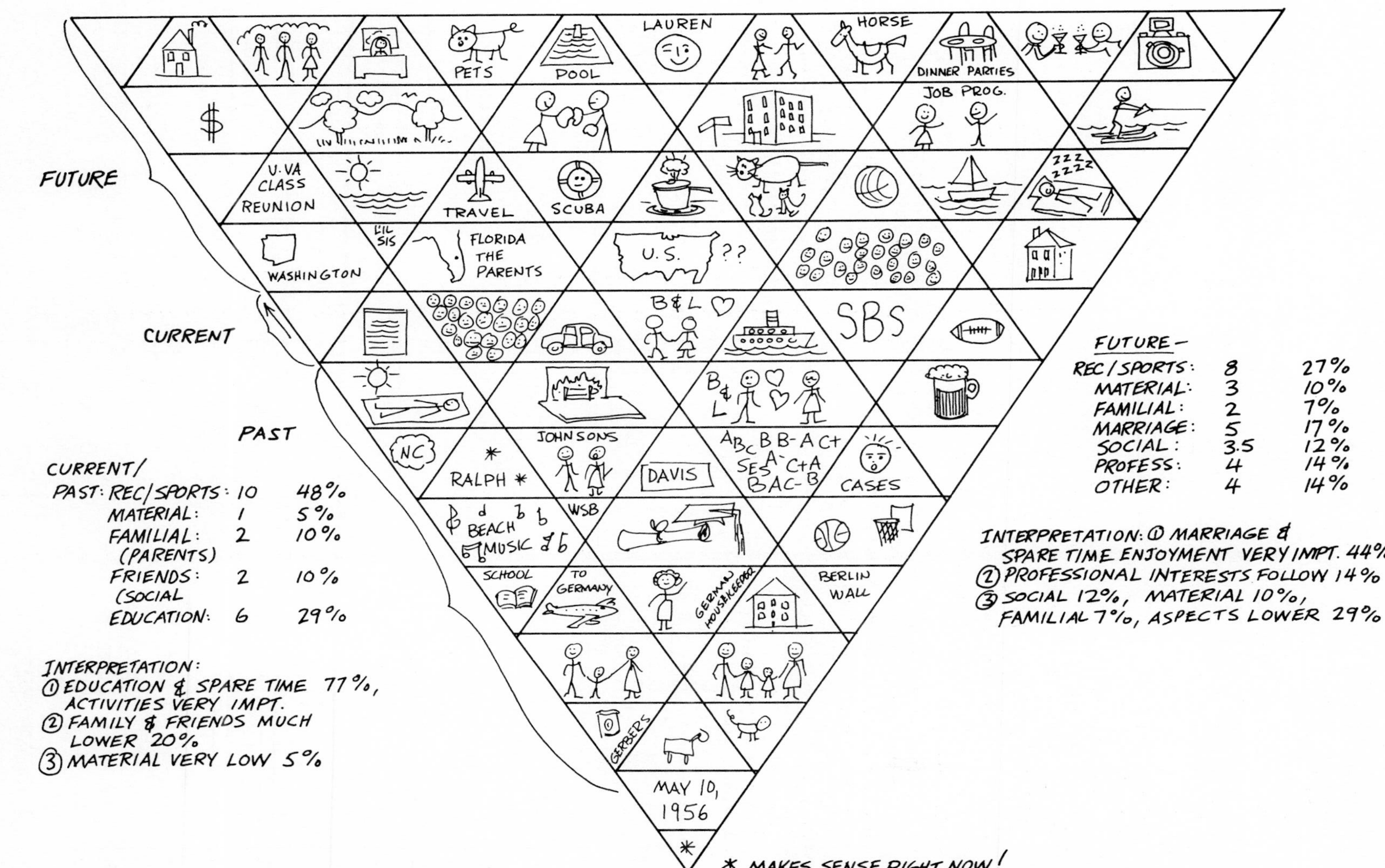

Lauren Davis: Strong-Campbell Interest Inventory Score

SCII LAUREN DAVIS FEMALE DATE SCORED 09/23/81 065 0021 1

Interpretive Scoring Systems

Division of National Computer Systems, Inc.
P.O. Box 1294
Minneapolis, MN 55440
Phone 800-328-6116

I. ADMINISTRATIVE INDICES

A. RESPONSE PERCENTAGES	L%	I%	D%
1. OCCUPATIONS	18	31	50
2. SCHOOL SUBJECTS	25	33	42
3. ACTIVITIES	47	29	24
4. AMUSEMENTS	31	31	38
5. TYPES OF PEOPLE	25	21	54
PARTS 1-5	27	30	43
6. PREFERENCES	33	0	67
7. CHARACTERISTICS	64	29	7

B. TOTAL RESPONSES =	325
C. INFREQUENT RESPONSES =	5
D. ACADEMIC COMFORT =	25
E. INTROVERSION–EXTROVERSION =	40

II. GENERAL OCCUPATIONAL THEMES

	SCALE	STD. SCR.
R	REALISTIC	37
I	INVESTIGATIVE	43
A	ARTISTIC	47
S	SOCIAL	39
E	ENTERPRISING	49
C	CONVENTIONAL	44

(Chart columns: VERY LOW; LOW INTER. 35; AVERAGE INTEREST 43–57; HIGH INTER. 65; VERY HIGH)

III. BASIC INTEREST SCALES

	SCALE	STD. SCR.
R	AGRICULTURE	46
	NATURE	33
	ADVENTURE	51
	MILITARY ACTIVITIES	41
	MECHANICAL ACTIVITIES	41
I	SCIENCE	37
	MATHEMATICS	37
	MEDICAL SCIENCE	41
	MEDICAL SERVICE	40
A	MUSIC/DRAMATICS	46
	ART	40
	WRITING	50
S	TEACHING	40
	SOCIAL SERVICE	35
	ATHLETICS	50
	DOMESTIC ARTS	46
	RELIGIOUS ACTIVITIES	35
E	PUBLIC SPEAKING	63
	LAW/POLITICS	62
	MERCHANDISING	58
	SALES	55
	BUSINESS MANAGEMENT	55
C	OFFICE PRACTICES	40

(Chart columns: VERY LOW; LOW INTER. 35; AVERAGE INTEREST 43–57; HIGH INTER. 65; VERY HIGH)

IV. OCCUPATIONAL SCALES

	FEM. CODE	MALE CODE	OCCUPATION	FEMALE SCALE	MALE SCALE
R	RC	RC	AIR FORCE OFFICER	51	21
	RC	RC	ARMY OFFICER	49	30
	RI	RI	ENGINEER	31	7
	RC	R	FARMER	32	26
	RI	R	FORESTER	28	20
	RIC		LICENSED PRAC. NURSE	-3	
	R	RC	NAVY OFFICER	49	18
	RAS	RAS	OCCUPATIONAL THERAPIST	19	15
	RE	RE	POLICE OFFICER	54	33
	R	RI	RAD. TECH. (X-RAY)	28	15
	N/A	R	SKILLED CRAFTS	N/A	9
		RI	VETERINARIAN		11
	N/A	RCE	VOC. AGRIC. TEACHER	N/A	-5
I	I	I	BIOLOGIST	17	13
	IR	IR	CHEMIST	21	0
	IRE	IRE	CHIROPRACTOR	35	37
	IA	IA	COLLEGE PROFESSOR	37	34
	IRC	IRC	COMPUTER PROGRAMMER	35	20
	IR	N/A	DENTAL HYGIENIST	25	N/A
	IR	IR	DENTIST	33	25
	I	I	GEOGRAPHER	45	27
	IR	IR	GEOLOGIST	31	19
	I	I	MATHEMATICIAN	20	16
	IRC	IRS	MATH-SCI. TEACHER	16	7
	IR	IR	MEDICAL TECHNOLOGIST	12	13
	IR	IR	OPTOMETRIST	34	27
	I	IE	PHARMACIST	40	26
	IR	IR	PHYSICAL THERAPIST	19	16
	IR	IR	PHYSICIAN	20	19
	IR	IR	PHYSICIST	3	-4
	IAS	IAS	PSYCHOLOGIST	33	34
		IRS	REGISTERED NURSE		16
	IA	IA	SOCIOLOGIST	30	21
	IRC	IRC	SYSTEMS ANALYST	37	21
	IR		VETERINARIAN	24	
A	AE	AE	ADVERTISING EXECUTIVE	56	54
	AIR	AIR	ARCHITECT	33	19
	A	A	ART TEACHER	4	16
	A	A	ARTIST, COMMERCIAL	39	34
	A	A	ARTIST, FINE	38	25
	A	AS	ENGLISH TEACHER	33	38
	A	A	FOREIGN LANG. TEACHER	32	32
	AE	AE	INTERIOR DECORATOR	31	38
	AI	AI	LAWYER	60	57
	A	A	LIBRARIAN	46	39
	A	A	MUSICIAN	33	34
	A	A	PHOTOGRAPHER	48	42
	AE	AE	PUBLIC RELATIONS DIR.	49	51
	A	A	REPORTER	49	43
S	S	S	ELEMENTARY TEACHER	34	23
	SEC	SCE	GUIDANCE COUNSELOR	30	32
		S	LICENSED PRAC. NURSE		27
	SA	SIE	MINISTER	22	21
	SR	SR	PHYSICAL ED. TEACHER	24	11
	SRE	SRE	RECREATION LEADER	45	53
	SI		REGISTERED NURSE	34	
	SE	SE	SCHOOL ADMINISTRATOR	47	33
	SEC	SEC	SOCIAL SCIENCE TEACHER	44	41
	SA	SA	SOCIAL WORKER	42	45
	S	S	SPECIAL ED. TEACHER	29	23
	SA	SA	SPEECH PATHOLOGIST	49	37
	SE	SE	YWCA/YMCA DIRECTOR	46	36
E	N/A	ERC	AGRIBUSINESS MANAGER	N/A	19
	E	EA	BEAUTICIAN	36	42
	EC	EC	BUYER	42	35
	EC	E	CHAMBER OF COMM. EXEC.	50	46
	E	E	DEPT. STORE MANAGER	58	52
	EC	ECR	DIETITIAN	47	38
	E	E	ELECT. PUBLIC OFFICIAL	48	42
	EA	EA	FLIGHT ATTENDANT	53	48
	ES	N/A	HOME ECON. TEACHER	20	N/A
	N/A	EI	INVESTMENT FUND MGR.	N/A	63
	E	E	LIFE INSURANCE AGENT	51	36
	EI	EI	MARKETING EXECUTIVE	61	63
	EC	ECS	NURSING HOME ADMIN.	46	41
	E	E	PERSONNEL DIRECTOR	58	48
	E		PUBLIC ADMINISTRATOR	55	
	EC	EC	PURCHASING AGENT	48	39
	E	E	REALTOR	52	36
	EC	E	RESTAURANT MANAGER	47	48
C	C	C	ACCOUNTANT	47	43
	CE	CE	BANKER	45	55
	CES	CES	BUSINESS ED. TEACHER	28	26
	CE	CE	CREDIT MANAGER	47	33
	C	N/A	DENTAL ASSISTANT	29	N/A
	CER	CER	EXECUTIVE HOUSEKEEPER	26	35
	CE	CE	I.R.S. AGENT	46	40
		CA	PUBLIC ADMINISTRATOR		45
	C	N/A	SECRETARY	33	N/A

(Chart columns: VERY DISS. 15; DISSIMILAR 25; AVERAGE 44; SIMILAR 54; VERY SIM.)

STRONG-CAMPBELL INTEREST INVEN RY — FORM T325

Strong-Campbell Interest Inventory of the Strong Vocational Interest Blank. Revised and expanded profile for use with Form T32[illegible]tanford University Press, Stanford, CA.

Reply 1 (open-ended)

1. I was born in Tacoma, Washington, the daughter of a lieutenant in the Army. My mother had been raised as an Army brat, married my father at 18, and I arrived when she was 20. Mom didn't work outside the home, so from pictures and what little I remember I had quite a bit of attention as a young child.

2. Kim, my younger sister, was born about 2 years after me in Fort Sill, Oklahoma. From stories, again, I am told that we adored each other. Kim was my shadow, and I was her teacher. I have a few recollections about my young life before the age of about 5–6. Our family have lived in four locations over the first 6 years of my life, and when I started kindergarten we lived with my grandparents in Champaign, IL, while my father was in Greenland.

3. I loved school from the beginning. My mom and sister would walk me to the bus each day, and every day Kim would cry because she couldn't come with me. I loved teaching her all the things I'd learned when I came home from school. Whether I was right or wrong or interesting or boring she would listen to every word I said.

4. After kindergarten my dad came back from Greenland and was reassigned to Babenhausen, Germany. My dad went to Germany over the summer, but the rest of our family had to remain in the states for the length of the summer. This was the period of the Berlin Wall Crisis, and President Kennedy had forbidden military dependents from living in Germany temporarily.

5. We finally got clearance to go and after much red tape we flew to Germany. My dad already had an apartment arranged on the Post, so we moved into a neighborhood with lots of families similar to ourselves.

6. The elementary school was just a few blocks from home, so I walked to school each day. Mom became active in outside interests and eventually was elected president of the officer wives club, so she wasn't home every day when Kim and I got home from school. (Kim was in nursery school.) Because she had to be out a few afternoons a week, Mom hired a part-time keeper who would be at the apartment when she was gone. We had several over the 2-year period we lived in Germany. They were usually middle-aged German women who were very kind to us and taught us German songs and prayers that Kim and I remember to this day.

7. School was enjoyable. I remember very little about it. It was a very structured environment with assigned readings and problems each day. I do remember how frustrated I would get because I could never finish all my work before lunch. We (the class) were competing with one another on a chart, to see who could work the fastest and most efficiently. (You got *stars* depending on your speed). Well, I couldn't stand it when some (a few) of my classmates were always finishing their work very early. The whole system was based on your *word,* so I claimed to have finished one day before I had and got caught and admonished before the class. I look back and laugh, but what a trauma at 6!

8. I adored my 1st grade teacher, but I remember very little about 2nd grade, except my effort to be in the top reading group. I had one close friend in Germany, and we were inseparable. After Germany we moved to Cherry, Washington. My dad went back to school to get a Masters Degree at Eastern Washington State University. I was in 3rd grade in a city school while Kim went to a school affiliated with the university. We lived in a large house across from university dorms, and Kim and I milked the students selling Koolaid and Girl Scout cookies.

9. I think I was a slightly above average student in school. The teacher liked me this time so I enjoyed being her pet. I was a bit of a tomboy by 3rd grade, and I preferred softball to any other activity. I was the only girl on the "team." My rough activities led to my teacher sitting me down for a talk. I quickly grew out of the tomboyishness.

10. Cherry was fun. We had a big yard and a dog and a cat. Kim and I were just beginning to get on each other's nerves.

11. I was transferred to Kim's school in 4th grade (I had wanted to go there to begin with but my class was full). The school was very progressive in both the style and the content of the teaching. We were at the stage in math where most students go through flash cards and memorization, but our math was concept-oriented "new math." We were told not to worry about the right answers as long as we understood the process. I think that today my math is so weak, but who knows.

12. By 6th grade we changed classes each period and were learning to adapt to the new routine we'd be exposed to in Jr. High. My 5th and 6th grade teachers had us learning from TVs before that became more popular. We were observed through a one-way

window (it looked black to us). The whole atmosphere was conducive to expanding your learning abilities, which normal classroom settings inhibit. We were all told we were smart—that's how we were allowed into the program—and the framework was very positive and I enjoyed it.

13. I took part in two plays that year—which I loved.

14. My father was then transferred to Washington, DC, for one year. It was difficult to try to establish many friendships in that period of time, and I wasn't sorry to leave for Ft. Leavenworth, Kansas, the next year. We spent 3 years in Kansas, and my memories of Ft. Leavenworth are the best of any of the places I've lived. My parents bought Kim and me a horse, and eventually we bought another. So I learned to ride and entered many horse shows in the area. My closest friend had been riding for several years, so with her help and the many (cheap) lessons available at the stables on Post, I got to be quite good. Leaving riding has been one of the most difficult things to accept; I'm dying to have a horse again and hope to soon in the future.

15. But back to Ft. Leavenworth. I guess in three years you become more attached to friends, and as you grow older friendships mean more—so leaving Kansas was very upsetting. We moved back to D.C. when I was in the 11th grade, so I spent two years in Northern Virginia before proceeding to college.

16. It wasn't a particularly spectacular period of time. I began realizing that my education really was important, so I worked much harder in school. That work got me into UVa in 1974. Virginia was my first choice of colleges, and I was very pleased to get in. I was very ready to get away from my parents and have a little freedom.

17. My first semester grades were a disaster because I was too undisciplined. But my second semester I came back with excellent grades and knew then that I could do it. College was a great life! I majored in English, which was a tough decision—I didn't know what I wanted to do. I didn't think any liberal arts degrees would be best for jobs. I knew I didn't want to go into business.(!!) So I majored in what I liked best and was best at. I thought at the time (and still do from time to time) that I wanted to go to law school. So after living with 5 roommates for the last two years of college in a huge old apartment, I set out to determine if law was the way to go. I took a paralegal course in Philadelphia, Pa., which was reputed (and I believe is) to be the best program around. After 3 months in Philadelphia I returned to D.C. and took a job with a legal document retrieval and publications company as a production assistant for two securities law journals. I moved up quickly in the company and took over my boss' job. (She moved up too.) The company was fairly small so I knew the vice president very well and enjoyed working for the company. It was very people-oriented from the top down. The management's philosophy was very team-oriented.

18. It didn't take long for me to hit the ceiling (as far as challenge goes) again. I knew I couldn't move up fast enough to be challenged or be compensated enough to put up with the lack thereof. So B-School was on the horizon. It didn't just pop up though. After working for a year I became interested in the stock market (I analyzed proxies and registrations all day, so I had enough exposure to know what I was getting into.) After taking 2 business classes at night, I decided it was for me and came.

19. First year was a bitch! I'd hate to think I'd have to go through anything like it again. The pressure was tough. For the first time *ever* I started to realize my capabilities were not endless. In the past I always knew that if I really tried I could do most anything well. The frustration of working hard for hours and accomplishing little was extremely unsettling.

20. Trying to manage (well) a relationship outside of Darden put an extra strain on me. The pressure turned me into a *different person* many times. Darden forced Bill and me to be together in class every morning and we were together for the rest of the day. By December we felt like we'd known each other for a couple of years. The support really helped me get through the year.

21. Over the summer I worked for an industrial manufacturing company in Atlanta. I was disappointed in my project a bit. First it wasn't SBS material and secondly it was not much of an intellectual challenge—but I did a good job and felt good about what I learned about organizational problems and politics from interacting and observing many top managers.

22. By August I was tired of my job, tired of only seeing Bill on weekends and bored with Atlanta. Back to Charlottesville to move 2 apartments into 1 in one week (ha, ha!) And the *wedding!* Then a 2 week honeymoon—which was fantastic and just what I needed in between the job and Darden. I'm very enthusiastic about the coming year!

Reply 2 (Other Memories?)

23. I've always liked getting involved in clubs and organizations, although I always wonder why I got into them after I do because they don't interest me very long.

24. When I was young, I enjoyed Brownies and Girl Scouts—but not for the "fun" things to do—more to be with friends and socialize. I also enjoy sports—particularly swimming, skiing, racquetball and volleyball (at picnics).

25. As I said before I love riding—that sport is

by far the most fun for me. I loved competing in horse shows and loved winning ribbons!

Reply 3 (Unaccounted for Times)

26. Going back to Fort Leavenworth—which starts with 8th grade—I got into more trouble during the three years—but I grew up the most then too. My summers were spent at the pool almost every day during those years—after moving back to Virginia in '71 I spent a very boring summer—knowing no one in a rented house while my parents worked and looked for a house.

27. Between 11th and 12th grades, I worked as a waitress at a restaurant nearby and hated it. I wasn't very good and got tired of nasty customers—so after graduating I worked in the receiving department of Lord & Taylors and was bored to death putting price tags on merchandise.

28. I'm one year ahead. Between 11th and 12th, I worked in a drug store as a clerk.

29. Getting back. After my 1st year in college, I worked as a secretary for an attorney to try and see what law was like. Once again, boring. I'm not a very good typist and my OB skills are not the best when I strongly dislike someone (which is not often), but the attorney and I were not sorry to part ways. (I'll bet you're waiting for the good summer to come up. Sorry, the next isn't much better.)

30. Between my third and fourth year in college I worked for the Government as a GS-4 clerk typist at the Federal Employee Appeals Authority. It was a job, and I needed the money. Again I typed and was a conscientious employee so I was well liked by my boss, a lawyer who could give me a recommendation! But I *hate* to type. I hate to take orders from people who are GS-morons. So, it was frustrating. It was also an eye opener to see some of the inefficiencies that are prevalent throughout the government!

31. The next summer was spent in Philadelphia at the Institute for Paralegal Training. All of the students in the course were bright and close to the same age, so I really enjoyed it.

Reply 4 (Jobs, Likes, Dislikes)

32. The first job I had was in a drug store. Basically all I did was work the cash register and stock shelves. I didn't find it too bad for a high school student. I worked with some real weirdos, but I was fairly independent. I did a good job. I enjoyed talking to people, although you meet a lot of grouchy people working a cash register.

33. The waitress job I abhorred. I don't like waiting on anyone. I thought the job (along with the secretarial jobs) was demeaning. Career waitresses are not the most social creatures.

34. The next job was just plain boring. I hate to sound so negative, but with most summer work you have to take what you can get, and this was all I could find. I worked with a small group of people checking in merchandise and working several machines which print price stickers. I also attached these price tags with plastic "guns" that force plastic strips through material. Neat, huh?

35. The secretarial job wasn't a bad job because it was secretarial, but because of the shyster-lawyer I worked for. He ran his own practice and worked out of a small law office. It was interesting, and I did some research for him, corrected his grammar and punctuation and wondered how he ever got as far as he did. My last summer was detailed before.

36. I haven't talked much about my only full-time job. After taking the paralegal course, I worked at the DC Associates. I enjoyed many aspects of the job and clearly detested others. During my first six months I was closely supervised by a woman one year my senior who was a Vassar graduate. Those two criteria alone mean nothing, but I picked up the job quickly and needed little supervision, so I felt very confined and stifled being hovered over.

37. I enjoyed the routine at first. It was the type of work that required a very organized individual. There were a million details involved in getting the information into print. I love organizing, so I enjoyed that part of the job. However organizing materials which you have no time to pursue becomes very dull. So my abilities were recognized, and I moved into the rewriting end of the department. (I had been working with the editor "on the sly" learning the ropes.) The job then required a different kind of detail, reading between the lines. I was working with the latest Securities & Exchange Commission interpretations of the law. I loved the currentness of the job. It was exciting to read in the papers about a case I'd been working on the day before. The thrill wore off, however. A combination of office atmosphere and ceiling bumping (I began to get bored) led me to B-School.

38. I found positive and negative reinforcement to have had more to do with my work at the company than in any other situation. I had two adversaries (for reasons I know not—competition?) who were very difficult to work with and with whom I dealt daily. And I had very good friends and supporters in two vice presidents. The adversaries were not disliked by the VPs—one adversary was very close to a VP—so I don't think rivalry in *that* respect was a factor. It was unsettling, trying to deal with individuals who wouldn't reveal why they disliked you—very moody individuals. I think I was as neutral as I could be, but it was an eye opener to me. I always thought I could "bring them around" and become friends.

Reply 5 (People In My Life)

39. My closest friend and confidant is Bill, my husband. If I were to arrange the people in my life I'd say Bill and I are closer than any of my other friends. Next to Bill, I value the friendship of my sister most highly. But this is a difficult way to answer this question, so I'll begin again in a more structured way.

40. Who was I closest to? My first very close friend was Joanne Davis. She and I went to two years of junior high and one year of high school together. I had friends before Joanne, but we moved around so much I never felt close to any of them. I suppose we were such good friends because we were very similar; we liked to do the same sorts of things. We were inseparable for a long time. We both rode horses, so we rode together after school everyday. Leaving Kansas was tough, and I never developed any close friendships with girls again until my second year of college.

41. In college I got to be friends with another girl in my dorm who, again, seemed to have similar interests. Sally and I did a lot of partying together and a lot of activities. Its hard to say why we were close—being around each other a lot, we confided in each other as is natural.

42. I had two other close friends—one boyfriend in high school and one in college. Gordon, the high school boyfriend, was very smart and good natured, so he was a pleasure to be with. Rip, the college friend, was also smart and good natured, but he lacked ambition—which really bugged me. He was lazy in his school work (although he was very capable), so I knew early on that this would be a major stumbling block to any serious relationship. Ambition and self-betterment are important to me, so I couldn't understand Rip's lackadaisical attitude. I always knew Gordon would make it, which was one reason I was attracted to him. He was very capable and intellectual while not being pretentious. (Alas, the chemistry didn't last.)

43. I had trouble getting close to spacey people. They definitely bugged me. Although Joanne wasn't brilliant, I think I was attracted to smart, commonsensible people. Dumb people are no fun to talk to and frustrate me (as friends—that is I have nothing against people less intelligent than myself—I just couldn't be around them a lot and confide in them as close friends).

44. My family consists of Mom, Dad and Kim, my younger sister. Kim is 2 years younger than I, and we carried on a love/hate relationship while we grew up. Unfortunately I was a bossy sister, which alienated Kim in a lot of ways. All in all, though, I'd say we were good friends and ran in separate circles to stay that way.

45. We have no major changes in our family structure aside from my Dad going to Vietnam for 1 year when I was in 6th grade, and to Laos when I was in 11th grade. My family lived all over, so in some ways our family structure changed every 1 to 3 years. We never lived in one place, except Kansas, for more than 2 years.

46. Marriage—what can I say? I'm hardly an old pro after one month, but it is a comfortable phenomenon. Bill is more patient and less moody (nonmoody is a better term) than anyone I know. I grew up in a very up and down household with my parents fighting a lot, so it's important that I get away from that life style. Probably the most influential characteristic about Bill is his confidence and self-assurance that he will be successful.

47. I have neglected to mention many passing friends. I guess I'm not close to many people.

48. My parents are important people in my life in a funny way. I enjoy talking with them from time to time, but they drive me up a wall if I have to be around them for any length of time. Mom is always tired and depressing, and Daddy just can't relate to my lifestyle. He is absorbed (so's Mom) in work, work, work. Hearing about work gets old and makes me mad. They should be doing more avocational and recreational things and try to be happy.

Reply 6 (Future)

49. I'm looking forward to a fun and fulfilling future.

50. I guess my idea in the short run is to move to a comfortable neighborhood in a medium-sized city. I'd want to be able to commute to work in about 15 minutes, but be in an area where I could own a horse again on property behind a house.

51. Work is fabulous at this point, but whatever I end up doing I want it to be in pursuit of developing skills that I can apply in my own business. Challenge is very important. I'd rather be overworked and challenged than underworked and bored. It's important for me to be growing in a job, so I want to work for a medium-sized company with that philosophy. Success is the key to my happiness, also. I get great satisfaction out of doing a project well—part intrinsic satisfaction but more peer recognition.

52. Part of the happy ending is also a time for fun. I'd like to travel twice a year on vacations—go to Florida or sunny places often. Vacations with other couples also sound fun at this point. Football games, plays, ACC basketball games, dancing parties—fun socially.

53. Long run doesn't look much different, except that I hope to establish a business with some partners. I also want to have 2 or 3 kids and a pool, stable, and a fair amount of land. I hope to become active in civic affairs in the area where Bill and I buy a house—but not domestic!

54. Housework, cooking and stereotyped women's roles scare me. I don't want to get sucked into those roles so my happy ending would include shared responsibilities or a maid!

55. I don't need to be rich, but I'd like to be very comfortable, and I'm willing to work hard for material comforts. I'd like to have a summer home on a beach that is big enough for lots of friends.

56. A big part of my happy ending is staying in love with my husband. It's really the center of my happy ending, because everything else will be brighter if our relationship continues to be happy.

57. Tradeoffs—where to live—NC, VA? TX?
—housework, both of us or neither of us. It won't be *just* me.
—His career vs. my career? Sacrifices upon promotion? Transfers?

58. It is unclear how these tradeoffs are going to be made. Bill and I are both fairly strong-minded, so a lot of patience is going to be required.

Reply 7 (Points of Change)

59.
0. Lived in Illinois with grandparents from birth to kindergarten.
1. Illinois to Germany (1st & 2nd grade)
2. Germany to Washington (3rd, 4th (changed schools) & 5th grade
3. Washington to Illinois (6th, Dad to Vietnam)
4. Illinois to Va. (7th)
5. Va. to Kansas (8th, 9th, & 10th, started HS)
6. Kansas to Va. (11th, 12th, Dad to Laos in 11th)
7. College (Parents moved to apartment from house)
8. Paralegal course and job hunting
9. DC Associates (Work)
10. Graduate School, Bill
11. Marriage

Reply 8 (Options, Pros and Cons, Decisions Made At Turning Points)

60. I guess most of my turning points did not involve personal choice. Since my father was in the military we moved every 1 to 3 years, so, although the moves had a major impact on me, I had few options. The only options I can see are whether or not I chose to accept the moves, and how quickly I adapted to new surroundings.

61. It was much more difficult to move from Kansas to Virginia than it was from Illinois to Germany for two reasons: first, the older I was, the more attached I became to friends, and second, the longer I lived in one area, the harder it was to uproot myself. So, my choice in the matter was the speed at which I choose to adapt.

62. The first turning point in which I had options was in my decision about college. The decision to remain in-state was made by my parents because they couldn't afford the out-of-state tuition. I suppose I *chose* not to supplement my parents' tuition payments in order to go to another school, but I had my heart on UVa anyway. I also applied to VA. Tech and got in but dreaded the thought of having to go there.

63. The pros and cons of the situation: Virginia's academic standing was far and away the most influential factor in any decision. My parents played a miniscule role in the whole process—I was influenced more by my peers. I knew the smart ones who were staying in-state were going to UVa. or to Wm. & Mary, and the airheads were on the road to Tech. I didn't want to be seen as an airhead. Or go to a school that was more a extension of high school than college. I think the "cons" in the whole process was that I didn't really *look* for a school—UVA just fell in my lap, and I was pleased with it.

64. I arrived at my decision long before I started looking for colleges. I just couldn't imagine going anywhere else, so I asked for and got no advice.

65. Turning Pt #8: What to do when I get out of school? I thought for so long that I wanted to go to Law School and then I wasn't sure. I took the boards and did OK, but nothing spectacular. I didn't want to go to a mediocre law school and have to accept a mediocre job after that, so I needed more input into my interests. I took a paralegal course immediately after graduation in order to better find a job in a law firm and then decide whether law was really what I wanted.

66. I had the choice to go out and look for a job right away, but I felt paralegal school would better prepare me (with a skill) since I was coming out of college with an English literature degree.

67. I guess the idea of the course was suggested to me by my boyfriend at that time, but the decision was really mine. My parents financed the venture, so they had some input, but not much.

68. Turning point #9: After the paralegal course I took a waitressing job while I looked for a paralegal job. I had two opportunities to work: (1) for the government as a paralegal or (2) for a legal publishing co. I took the second job, which paid less, but I really didn't want to work for the Government.

69. The cons in this decision were: I wouldn't be using my paralegal skills in the manner that I was trained. (The pay was about $2,500 less.) The pros were: the change of upward mobility were greater, the offices and people were nice, and the employee benefits were great. I think one of the most influential

variables in comparing the two jobs was that at DCA those hiring me were impressed with my background and encouraging about my future. Also, it was a team-oriented company. Everyone from the top down contributed in even the smallest project if it was necessary.

70. Turning Point #10: Graduate school or boredom were my options—or looking for another job—or confronting my boss. I didn't think my time would be best spent in another job unless I took time off to get an MBA. It's really necessary in order to be taken seriously, quickly. I found that WSB was moving me as quickly as I could hope, but I was tired of waiting. After 4 years in college and 1 1/2 more, I wanted to do something useful. The pros and cons of this: pros—better prospects for jobs after school and taken more seriously without having to start at the *very* bottom.

71. The cons—I saw none then, I was tired of the commuting rat-race, ready for something new. How I arrived at my decision? I became interested in the stock market because my paralegal training was in Securities Law and my work at WSB involved analyzing proxies and registration statements and the 33 and 34 acts. I took statistics and a finance class at night, liked it, and applied. I only applied to UVA. It's hard to say why. I guess I figured it was the best school I could get into. My boards were good, but my grades were just average. So, again I knew it would be a waste to go to just any B-school. If I couldn't get into VA, I'd just wait and regroup and do something else. (I could stay at DCA.)

72. I didn't talk the idea over with anybody but my roommate—who was also planning to apply to B-school. I guess I always knew I'd get some kind of graduate degree that was important to them. So, it was just a natural progression.

73. Turning Point #11: Marriage! That was an enormous turning point. Other options: Call it quits (sure!), wait until after graduation.

Pros —it was hard to wait
Cons—interfering with our school work
—difficult to plan while in school.

How I arrived at the decision? Who knows? Love! No, it wasn't an easy choice, and I didn't talk to anyone before deciding. Just like most other events in my life. It just came along and fell in my lap unexpectedly.

Reply 9 (Differences After Changes, What Stayed the Same)

74. Turning Point #7:—College: Going to college was one of the *most* exciting times in my life. I was very ready to get away from home. The independence was wonderful. I was ready to plan my own time and not live by my parent's timetable.

75. After college and paralegal school I was again independent in Washington DC, but although I enjoyed living alone, I realized what a hermit I was becoming. So, I sought out a roommate. It was a super arrangement, but it wasn't until 6–8 mos after moving to DC that I realized (for the first time) that I really needed friendships. I had become too cut off, too independent in my effort to establish that I could be self sufficient.

76. DCA: I changed because of the confidence that a couple of the vice presidents showed in me. That kind of positive reinforcement encouraged me to put numerous hours of overtime into my job, which I see as good. I think you have to go the extra mile to get anywhere in this world.

77. Grad School: That has changed me more than anything I can remember. I'd rather not be the person I turned into last year. The pressure turned me into a bitch around Bill. I questioned (regularly) whether I belonged at Darden. But on the other hand it also has helped to make hard work a habit, so I don't (or didn't this summer) mind it as much now.

78. Marriage: I don't feel any different, but I'm happier and more relaxed.

79. I don't understand this question. I can't think of anything that has "withered" away or is "waiting until later"—unless the withering might be my liberalism—which has turned to "conservative liberalism".

Reply 10 (Disillusionments)

80. I'm tired of turning points.

81. College required more studying than I expected. High school had been a breeze, but college was different and it took me a semester to realize that (GPA = 2.4) and one to recover (GPA = 3.6)

82.

Tables, Tables*

	Expected Before	*Realized After*
College	no study	yes study!
	freedom	freedom!
	friendships	yep!
83. Paralegal	work hard	work, but not hard
	meet people	made some very good friends—still in touch
	expect easier getting job	not quite as easy
84. DCA	challenge	developed—but not quite as fast as I wanted
	Education	yep
	Learned computer stuff	yep

(continued)

	Expected Before	Realized After
85. Grad School	Education	yep
	Social/fun	not 1/2 as much as I thought
	Extracurr stuff	not much
	Time for old school friends	nope
86. Marriage	Fun/Security	yep

87.	College	Para.	DCA	Grad. Sch	Marr*
Right place at right time (Fell into it)	x	x	x	x	x
Independence goal	x		x	x	
Ambition/Career	x	x	x	x	
Friendships	x			x	x
Social	x			x	
Friends did it	x				
No outside influence in decision	1/2x	x	x	x	x
Parents influence	1/2x	x	x	x	x

*This doesn't mean Ambition/Career and Independence are not still important—they are, they just don't apply here.

Reply #11 (Patterns)

None Given

Feelings Record

Figure Test

Wondered what good my responses would do in telling me something about myself. How did I feel—I didn't enjoy or mind it as I was taking the test I thought my reactions might have been a bit negative—what I saw in the pictures. It seemed similar to a child's game but I'm sure there must be some value if we have to take it.

Rorschach Test

Again I'm curious about what I can interpret from this type of an exercise. I found it difficult to describe the objects differently when they pointed one way or another, although they looked very different when turned upside down.

I also wonder how much my military upbringing is coming out since I saw emblems and insignias and rockets.

Learning Style Inventory

This test is interesting because although I know how I learn best—I don't always apply these rules in class. The active participation of class is most beneficial; however, I do not take advantage of that.

FIRO-B

I enjoyed this test, although its difficult to answer many of the questions because I feel differently in different circumstances. These questions are hard to answer also because my true answer isn't what I'd always like it to be.

With previous instruments I had some idea where the test was going. I was curious, although I was planning to answer "honestly," what a different answer might mean.

On many of the answers I found myself very much in the center. I like being more specific in my yes–no answers.

After scoring:

I have some doubts about the questions regarding autonomy—I would not put myself below average in this category and find some of the numerical values assigned questionable.

Life and Career Values Card Sort

This is very important in recognizing what makes me happy. By analyzing these criteria I can get a better handle on what I would be most happy doing.

These seem to be fairly obvious to me.

Creative Life Style Diagram

An artist I am not—but after "discovering" someone else's formal it was fun. It was kind of a catalog at Christmas—I could draw in all the events and situations that would make me happy in the future.

Getting past that artist's block the rest was fun.

Written Interview

What a chore. I hated it. I wasn't sure how personal to get or how professional/career inputs were more important. I really dislike reviewing my family history—a lot of it was unhappy so I'd rather leave it in the past.

It's also hard to expose yourself when you know someone else will read this. I'm very private about some aspects of my life. It's hard to open up.

I'm glad it's all over.

Dyad Exercise

Lauren's dyad partner developed the following themes after reviewing her self assessment data:

1. I have little tolerance for an environment below my intellectual ability.
2. The people I like most share my values and intellectual ability.
3. I am aspiring to the top and the people and activities I seek out are all avenues to reach that goal.
4. I want to be independent and self sufficient.
   a) own decisions
   b) marriage, own time
5. I am competitive, and I want to win.
6. Having friends is important and has become increasingly so over time.
7. One of my life objectives are material rewards.
8. I am often a victim to events in my life, things just fall into my lap.
9. In a supportive environment, I am happier and more productive.
10. I get inspired and then often lose interest.
11. I enjoy routine and organization.

The dyad partner cited the following evidence in support of the themes:

Theme 1, 2, 3: (Grouped because of similarity of themes) Written Interview (paragraphs 21, 27, 30, 33, 54, 35, 29, 30, 51, 63, 18)

Theme 4: Written Interview (32, 36, 44, 46, 47, 48, 63, 67, 72, 74, 75); Strong Campbell (highest score 49 - enterprising); Life and Career Values (Identity second only to Marital); Predisposition (preference toward solitude 2.86). Discomfirming data cited was only average preference for autonomy in Predisposition Test.

Theme 5: Written Interview (7, 8, 25, 9, 17); Learning Style Inventory (75% AE score); Life and Career Values (Professional Ranks 3rd)

Theme 6: Written Interview (8, 14, 24, 15, 75, 52, 55, 47); Figure Test (57% people - 13% affection); Learning Style Inventory (63% CE Score); Life and Career Values (Friends/Social Ranks 5th)

Theme 7: Written Interview (69, 52, 53, 55); Life and Career Values (Financial Ranks 4th)

Theme 8: Written Interview (34, 60, 64, 71, 73)

Theme 9: Written Interview (22, 75, 76, 9, 17, 78, 69); Predisposition Test (average for Tolerance for Ambiguity)

Theme 10: Written Interview (37, 23, 17)

Theme 11: Written Interview (37, 39)

Lauren Davis' Self-Assessment Paper

A little learning is a dangerous thing;
Drink deep or taste not the Pierian spring.
There are shallow draughts intoxicate the brain,
And drinking largely sobers us again.
Fired at first sight with what the muse imparts,
In fearless youth we tempt the heights of arts,
While from the bounded level of our mind
Short views we take, nor see the lengths behind;
But more advanced, behold with strange surprise
New distant scenes of endless science rise!
So pleased at first the towering Alps we try
Mount o'er the vales, and seem to tread the sky,
The eternal snows appear already past,
And the first clouds and mountains seems the last;
But, those attained we tremble to survey
The growing labors of our lengthened way
The increasing prospect tires our wondering eyes,
Hills peep o'er hills, and Alps on Alps arise!

Alexander Pope
From An Essay on Criticism

Introduction

I am approaching an important turning point. The decisions I make in choosing a profession, a job, a company, and a location will have an enormous impact on the direction of my life. This is an exciting time and a frightening time. What if I make a terrible mistake?

The themes that follow are not all-encompassing; however, they do represent many of my values. By compiling these themes, I hope to develop a better picture of myself and sort through the potential consequences of my future choices.

I have divided my themes into four groups, according to their order and magnitude of importance in my life.

1. I work best with positive reinforcement and support.
2. I enjoy being with people.
3. I enjoy change and a fast pace.
4. I am happiest when I am challenged/growing in a job.
5. I do not enjoy taking orders or working for strong authority figures.
6. I learn best by direct experience/involvement.
7. I have very few close friends and confide in few people.
8. The people I like best are smart and strive to better themselves.
9. Material comforts are important to me.
10. Independence is important to me.
11. I prefer a team-oriented environment.
12. Status and prestige are important to me.
13. Owning a horse, riding, and showing are important to me.
14. I enjoy getting organized and work better when I am organized.
15. I place a high value on reliability and honesty.
16. I enjoy teaching and persuading others.
17. I am competitive and like to win.
18. I enjoy athletics.

After each theme title, I have noted in parenthesis the number of supporting data, number of disconfirming data, and the number of instruments used.

Instruments

AVL	AVL Study of values
ESS	Darden Application Essay (2/20/80)—see "Other Data" (not included)
EVAL	DC Associates Annual Evaluation (10/14/80) (not included in DATA)
FIRO	FIRO-B
FR	Feelings Record
FT	Figure Test
ISI	Interpersonal Style Inventory
LSI	Learning Style Inventory
LCV	Life and Career Values
LSD	Life Style Diagram
PDT	Predisposition Test
REC	Darden Letter of Recommendation (not included in DATA)
ROR	Rorschach Test
SCI	Strong—Campbell Interest Inventory
24D(X)	24-Hour Diary, paragraph (X)
WI (X)	Written Interview, paragraph (X)

1. I Work Best with Positive Reinforcement and Support (14, 0, 4)

CLV	Marital: #4—Praised by spouse.
LCV	Professional: #2—Public recognition. #6—Rewarded fairly for efforts. Familial: #1—Being encouraged/praised.
ISI	Current self—"Needs support": 4 high (mean = 3.5)
LSI	Concrete experience: 63% (Second most dominant style) Interpretation: Benefit most from feedback and discussion with fellow CE learners.

This case was prepared by Kevin E. Sachs, MBA 1982, under the direction of James G. Clawson as the basis for class discussion.

WI(9)	The teacher liked me this time, so I enjoyed being her "pet".
WI(12)	The whole atmosphere was conducive to expanding your learning abilities which normal classroom settings inhibit. We were told we were smart, and that's how we were allowed into the program. The framework was very positive, and I enjoyed it.
WI(17)	My first semester grades were a disaster because I was too undisciplined. But by second semester I came back with excellent grades, and then I knew I could do it.
WI(17)	I enjoyed working for the company. It was very people-oriented from the top down. The management's philosophy was very team-oriented (supportive).
WI(20)	The support (from Bill) really helped me get through the year.
WI(38)	I found positive and negative reinforcement to have more to do with my work at the company than in any other situation. I had two adversaries who were very difficult to work with.
WI(69)	I think one of the most influential variables in comparing the two jobs was that at DCA those hiring me were impressed with my background and encouraging about my future.
WI(76)	I changed because of the confidence that a couple of the Vice-Presidents showed in me—that kind of position reinforcement encouraged me to put numerous hours of overtime into my job.

2. I Enjoy Being with People (21, 0, 6)

FIRO	Very high (17): Interpretation—Preference for a considerable amount of interpersonal interaction.
FT	People: 57%—Slightly more oriented toward people than toward the environment.
LCV	Social: #1—Close to others. #2—Part of group. Marriage: #3—Praised by spouse.
LSD	Friends increased from 10% to 20% from current/past to future.
LSI	Active Experimentation: 75% (Dominant theme) Interpretation: extrovert.
LSI	Concrete Experience: 63% (Second most dominant theme) Interpretation: empathetic, people-oriented.
WI(3)	I loved teaching her all the things I'd learned when I came home from school.
WI(4)	I guess in three years you become more attached to friends, and as you grow older, friendships mean more—so leaving Kansas was very upsetting.
WI(17)	The company was fairly small so I knew the VPs very well and enjoyed working for the company. It was very people-oriented from the top down.
WI(24)	When I was young and enjoyed Brownies and Girl Scouts but not for the "fun" things to do—more to be with friends and socialize.
WI(26)	After moving back to Virginia in 1971, I spent a very boring summer, knowing no one, in a rented house.
WI(31)	All of the students in the course were bright and close to the same age—so I really enjoyed it.
WI(32)	The first job I had was in a drug store . . . I did a good job—I enjoyed talking to people.
WI(33)	Career waitresses are not the most social creatures.
WI(56)	I would like to have a summer home on a beach that is big enough for lots of friends.
WI(75)	Although I enjoyed living alone, I realized what a hermit I was becoming—so I sought out a roommate. It was a super arrangement, but it wasn't until 6–8 months after moving to DC that I realized (for the first time) that I really needed friendships.

2. I Enjoy Being with People

		Expected Before	Realized Later
WI(82)	College	Friendships	Yep!
WI(83)	Paralegal	Meet People	Made some very good friends Still in touch
WI(84)	Darden	Time for old school friends	Not much

3. I Enjoy Change and a Fast Pace (18, 0, 6)

FT	Environmental Active = 30% Interpretation: See my environment as a Dynamic phenomenon
LCV	Recreation: Moving quickly. Professional: Learning new things. Changing activities weekly. Marital: Changing activities daily.
LSI	Accommodator — excel in situations where one must adapt oneself to specific immediate circumstances. — impatient and pushy at times.

	— involving self in new experiences. — action-oriented jobs.
LSI	Active experimentation = 75% (Dominant theme) Interpretation: "Doing" orientation Dislike passive learning situations.
PDT	Very high tolerance for Ambiguity: Interpretation: Don't mind a changing set of conditions.
SCI	Enterprising: 49—highest—adventurous—energetic Interpretations: Impatient with precise work or work involving long periods of intellectual effort.
WI(17)	It didn't take long for me to hit the ceiling again. I knew I couldn't move up fast enough to be challenged.
WI(22)	By August I was tired of my job, tired of seeing Bill only once a week, and bored with Atlanta.
WI(23)	I have always liked getting involved in clubs and organizations, although I always wonder why I got into them after I do—because they don't interest me very long.
WI(27)	I worked in the receiving department of Lord & Taylors and was bored to death putting price tags on merchandise.
WI(37)	I enjoyed the routine at first . . . I love organizing, so I enjoyed that part of the job. However, organizing materials which you have no time to peruse soon becomes very dull.
WI(37)	I loved the "current-ness" of the job. It was exciting to read in the papers about a case I had been working on the day before. The thrill wore off, however . . . I began to get bored.

3. I Enjoy Change and a Fast Pace

WI(45)	My family lived all over, so in some ways our family structure changed every 1–2–3 years. We never lived in one place for more than 2 years except Kansas.
WI(70)	It's [MBA] really necessary to be taken seriously quickly. I found that DCA was moving me as quickly as I could hope, but I was tiring of writing.
WI(71)	"The Cons"—I saw none then, I was . . . ready for something new.
WI(80)	I'm tired of turning points.

4. I Am Happiest When I am Challenged/Growing in a Job (12, 0, 2)

CLV	Learning new things #4 Tackling challenge #5 Professional
WI(18)	It didn't take long for me to hit the ceiling (as far as challenge goes) again. I knew I couldn't move up fast enough to be challenged or be compensated enough to make up for it—so B-School was on the horizon.
WI(21)	I was disappointed in my project a bit. First, it wasn't SBS material, and secondly it was not much of an intellectual challenge.
WI(27)	After graduating, I worked in the receiving department of Lord & Taylors and was bored to death putting price tags on merchandise.
WI(34)	The next job was just plain boring. I hate to sound so negative—but w/most summer work, you have to take what you can get.
WI(37)	I enjoyed the routine at first—it was the type of work that required a very organized individual. There were a million details involved in getting the information into print.
WI(51)	Challenge is very important. I would rather be overworked and challenged than underworked and bored.
WI(51)	Work is nebulous at this point—but whatever I end up doing I want it to be in pursuit of developing skills that I can apply.
WI(51)	It's important to me to be growing in a job.
WI(70)	Grad school or boredom were my options . . . I didn't think my time would be best spent in another job unless I took time off to get an MBA. It's really necessary to be taken seriously, quickly (to be challenged).
WI(70)	The pros and cons of this: pro—better prospects for jobs after school and taken more seriously without having to start at the *very* (boring) bottom.

5. I Do Not Enjoy Taking Orders or Working for Strong Authority Figures (9, 1, 5)

LCV	Run show = #1: Professional
LSI	Concrete experience 63%—Oriented more toward peer than authority in approach to learning.
PDT	2.96 High disposition toward solitude—prefer to work individually.
PDT	2.57 (Closer to research org.): Preference for autonomy. — less inclined to like subordinate relationships. — higher percentage to provide own direction.
WI(17)	I enjoyed working for the company . . . The management philosophy was very team-oriented.
WI(30)	I hate to take orders from people who are GS-morons—so it was frustrating.

WI(33)	The waitress job I covered—I don't like waiting on anyone. I thought the job (along w/the secretarial jobs) was demeaning.
WI(36)	During my first six months, I was closely supervised by a woman one year my senior who was a Vassar graduate. Those two criteria alone mean nothing, but I picked up the job quickly and needed little supervision so I felt very confined and stiffled being hovered over.
WI(69)	Also, the reason I liked it was that it was a team-oriented company. Everyone from the top down contributed in even the smallest project if it was necessary.

Disconfirming Data

FIRO	C = 5, middle range: I don't prefer to give or take orders, but will do both when appropriate.

6. I Learn Best By Direct Experience/ Involvement (14, 0, 5)

AVL	Economic 41/Theoretical 38 Practical, experience-based orientation stronger than abstract theoretical orientation.
ESS(2)	Further, the active participation encouraged in the program will enable me to more accurately determine the areas of business which will continue to interest and challenge me.
ESS(3)	Throughout my graduate years, I particularly enjoyed participating in seminars and small classes which required discussion.
FR(3)	I know how I learn best (but) I don't always apply those rules in class. The active participation of class is most beneficial.
LSI	Dominant learning style: Active Experimentation 75% Interpretation: • Doing orientation • Benefit from projects, homework • Small group discussions • Dislike passive learning situation
LSI	Concrete experience: 63% Interpretation: • Receptive to experience-based approach to learning • Theoretical approaches unhelpful • Learn from specific examples • Benefit from feedback and discussion
WI(17)	We were at the stage in math where most students go through flash cards and memorization—but our math was concept-oriented new math! We were told not to worry about the right answer as long as we understood the process. I think that is why my math is so weak.
WI(17)	My first semester grades were a disaster because I was undisciplined. By my second semester I came back w/excellent grades and knew that I could do it.
WI(17)	I set out to determine if law school was the way to go. I took a paralegal course in Philadelphia.
WI(18)	After working for a year, I became interested in the stock market (I analyzed proxies and registrations all day so I had enough exposure to know what I was getting into. After taking two business classes, I decided it (B-school) was for me.
WI(29)	After my first year in college, I worked as a secretary for an attorney to try and see what law was like.

6. I Learn Best By Direct Experience/ Involvement

WI(65)	I took a paralegal course immediately after graduation in order to better find a job in a law firm and then decide whether law was really what I wanted.
WI(77)	But on the other hand, it also helped to make hard work a habit, so I don't mind it (Darden) as much now.
WI(81)	College required more studying than I expected. High School had been a breeze, but college was different, and it took me a semester to realize that (GPA 2.4)—and one to recover (GPA 3.6).

7. I Have Very Few Close Friends and Confide In Few People (14, 0, 3)

FR(11)	It's also hard to expose yourself when you know someone else will read this. I'm very private about some aspects of my life, and it's hard to open up.
ISI	Discusses emotions 2.8. My average and median scores were 3.4. Discusses personal 2.8, so this is fairly low.
WI(8)	I had one close friend in Germany, and we were inseparable.
WI(40)	My first close friend was Joann Davis. She and I went to two years of junior high school and one year of high school together. I had friends before Joann, but we moved around so much I never felt close to any of them.
WI(40)	Leaving Kansas was tough, and I never developed any close friendships with girls again until my second year in college.

WI(47) I have neglected to mention many passing friends. I guess I am not close to many people.

WI(63) My parents played a miniscule role in the whole process (choosing a college)

WI(64) I just couldn't imagine going anywhere else (to college) so I asked for and got no advice.

WI(67) I guess the idea of the course was suggested to me by my boyfriend at that time, but the decision was really mine. My parents financed the venture, so they had some input, but not much.

WI(73) No, it (marriage) wasn't an easy choice, and I didn't talk to anyone before deciding.

WI(72) I didn't talk the idea over with anybody but my roommate—who was also planning to apply to B-school. I guess I always knew I'd get some kind of graduate degree—that was important to me—so it was just a natural progression.

WI(75) Although I enjoyed living alone, I realized what a hermit I was becoming—so I sought out a roommate . . . but it wasn't until 6–8 months after moving to DC that I realized (for the first time) that I really needed friendships—I had become too cut off.

WI(87) No outside influence in decisions: college, paralegal, DCA, grad school, marriage.

WI(87) Parents influence: half college, none in other turning points.

8. The People I Like Best Are Smart and Strive to Better Themselves (11, 0, 2)

AVL Social: 48, Economic: 41 (2 highest scores)
Interpretation: Social = love of people, economic = practical, so perhaps love of practical people.

WI(31) All of the students in the course were bright and close to the same age—so I really enjoyed it.

WI(35) The secretarial job wasn't a bad job because it was secretarial—but because of the shyster-lawyer I worked for . . . I did some research for him, corrected his grammar and punctuation, and wondered how he ever got as far as he did.

WI(36) I was closely supervised by a woman one year my senior who was a Vassar graduate (Interpretation: the snob in me is coming out by referring to her school—she wasn't smart, and I had little respect for her.)

WI(42) Rip was also smart and good natured, but he lacked ambition which really bugged me. He was lazy in his school work (although he was very capable) so I knew early on that this would be a stumbling block.

WI(42) Ambition and self-betterment are important to me so I couldn't understand Rip's lackadaisical attitude.

WI(42) I always knew Gordon would make it—which was one reason I was attracted to him. He was very capable and intellectual.

WI(42) Gordon was very smart and good natured, so he was a pleasure to be with.

WI(43) I had trouble getting close to spacey people, they definitely bugged me. I think I was attracted to smart, common-sensical people. Dumb people are no fun to talk to and frustrate me.

WI(46) Probably the most influential characteristic about Bill is his confidence and self-assurance that he will be successful.

WI(63) Virginia's academic standing was far and away the most influential factor in my decision . . . . I knew the smart ones who were staying in-state were going to Virginia and. . . the airheads were on the road to Tech.

9. Material Comforts Are Important To Me (10, 0, 5)

AVL Economic 2nd highest score:
Interpretation: interests in satisfaction of bodily needs and the accumulation of tangible wealth.

LCV Financial/Material: #2 having as much as possible.

LSD Material past/current 5%, future 10%—becoming more important.

SCI Enterprising: 49 highest occupational theme
Interpretation:
- enjoyed working in expensive settings
- like power, status, material wealth.

WI(14) I'm dying to have a horse again.

WI(50) I would want to be able to commute to work in 15 minutes but be in an area where I could own a horse again—on property behind a house.

WI(52) I'd like to travel twice a year on vacations—go to Florida or sunny places often.

WI(53) I also want to have . . . a pool, stable, and a fair amount of land.

WI(55) I would like to be very comfortable, and I'm willing to work hard for material comforts.

10. Independence Is Very Important To Me (12, 1, 5)

LCV —Run show #1 under professional
—Being free #2 identity
—Independent #1 financial/material

PDT — Preference for Autonomy 2.57
Closer to research characteristics:
- higher preference to define work roles, provide own direction
- less inclined to like subordinate relationships with strong authority figures

PDT — • Preference for Solitude 2.86—high
• Prefer to work individually

SCI — Artistic 2nd dominant occupational theme
Interpretation: • prefers to work alone
• describes self as independent

24D(5) — Decided how to organize the paper and break it up into series for four of us to write individually.

WI(16) — I was very ready to get away from my parents and have a little freedom.

WI(32) — The first job I had was in a drug store. . . . I didn't find it too bad for a high school student. I worked with some real weirdos, but I was fairly independent. I did a good job.

WI(36) — During my first six months I was closely supervised—so I felt very confined and stifled.

WI(63) — My parents played a miniscule role in the whole process (of choosing a college).

WI(74) — I was ready to get away from town—the independence was wonderful! I was ready to plan my own time and not live by my parents' timetable.

WI(75) — After college and paralegal school, I was again independent in Washington, D.C.

WI(87) — Independence goal: College, DCA, Grad School.

Disconfirming Data

WI(75) — I really needed friendships—I had become too cut off, too independent in my effort to establish that I could be self-sufficient.

11. I Prefer A Team-Oriented Environment (11, 2, 8)

FIRO — C = 5, middle range: I don't prefer to give or take orders, but will do both when appropriate.

ISI — Acquaintances reports: (mean = 3.4)

Keeps promises	4.2
Patient	4.2
Competitive	2.8

- These attributes would be positive in an environment where team-work is required.

LSI — Concrete experience: 16 or 63%
Interpretation:
- oriented more toward peers than authority in approach to learning
- benefit most from feedback and discussions with fellow CE learners

LSI — Accommodator: "relies on other people for information rather than one's own analytic ability."

PDT — Preference for autonomy: 2.57—moderate
Interpretation: less inclined to like subordinate relationships with strong authority figures.

REC(5) — Her attitude in both positions has been one of . . . cooperation . . . and a strong ability to get along with co-workers.

ROR — W-94%—Interpretation: look at the *big picture,* in an organization, of a company serving a customer. All employees working as a team to achieve a goal.

WI(17) — I enjoyed working for the company—it was very people-oriented from the top down. The management philosophy was very team-oriented.

WI(54) — Housework, cooking, and stereotyped women's roles scare me. I don't want to get sucked into those roles, so my happy ending would include shared responsibilities or a maid!

WI(57) — Housework: both of us or neither of us—it won't be just me.

WI(69) — Also, it was a team-oriented company. Everyone from the top down contributed in even the smallest project if it was necessary.

Disconfirming Data

PDT — Disposition toward solitude: 2.86—high —prefer to work individually

SCI — Artistic—47 second highest theme
Interpretation: prefers to work alone

12. Status and Prestige Are Important To Me (16, 0, 3)

LCV — Professional: "public recognition" ranked number two.

LCV — Identity: Getting ahead #1
Professional: Run show #1

SCI — Enterprising: 49, highest general occupation theme
Interpretation: "like power, status, material wealth".

WI(7) — I couldn't stand it when a few of my classmates were always finishing their work very early . . . so I claimed to have finished one day before I had.

WI(8) — I remember very little about 2nd grade, ex-

	cept my effort to be in the top reading group.
WI(9)	The teacher liked me this time, so I enjoyed being her 'pet'.
WI(9)	I was the only girl on the team!
WI(17)	I took a paralegal course in Philadelphia which was reputed (and I believe it is) to be the best course program around.
WI(25)	I loved competing in horse shows and loved winning ribbons.
WI(42)	I always knew Gordon would 'make it'—which was one reason I was attracted to him.
WI(46)	Probably the most influential characteristic about Bill is his confidence and self-assurance that he will be successful.
WI(51)	I get great satisfaction out of doing a project well—part intrinsic satisfaction, but more peer recognition.
WI(63)	Virginia's academic standing was far and away the most influential factor in my decision.
WI(63)	I knew the smart ones that were staying in-state were going to Virginia or William and Mary and the airheads were on the road to Virginia Tech. I didn't want to be seen as an airhead.
WI(65)	I didn't want to go to a mediocre law school and have to accept a mediocre job after that.
WI(71)	Again, I knew it would be a waste to go to just any B-school.

13. Owning A Horse, Riding, and Showing Are Important To Me (7, 0, 2)

LSD	My "future" drawings included one block with a horse.
WI(14)	We spent three years in Kansas, and my memories of Ft. Leavenworth are the best of any of the places I've lived. My parents bought Kim and me a horse and eventually we bought another.
WI(14)	Leaving riding has been one of the most difficult things to accept. I'm dying to have a horse again, and I hope to show in the future.
WI(25)	I love riding—that sport is by far the most fun for me. I loved competing in horse shows and loved winning ribbons!
WI(40)	We both rode horses, so we rode together after school everyday. Leaving Kansas (and my friend and horse) was tough.
WI(50)	I want to . . . be in an area where I could own a horse again.
WI(53)	I also want to have . . . a pool, stable, and a fair amount of land.

14. I Enjoy "Getting Organized" and Work Better When I Am Organized (12, 0, 8)

AVL	Economic: 41—2nd highest score. Interpretation: Interested in what is useful and practical to accomplish task (being organized helps me perform more efficiently)
EVAL	"She has a good eye for detail. She has devised production systems (organization) for the SEC NALI and S which have increased the accuracy of our supplement."
LCV	Intellectual: #1—Organizing things #2—Using energy and resources wisely #3—Working on details
LSD	Interpretation: the format I chose is very organized, with items fitting neatly into a total organized structure.
REC	"A strong organizational and analytical ability . . . have been clearly evident from her performance in this position."
EVAL	"She has a good eye for detail, which is invaluable."
ROR	94% whole 6% large part Interpretation: struggled to "organize" all of the extraneous details so that they fit into one big picture.
24D(5)	Decided how to organize the paper and break it up into sections for four of us to write individually.
24D(18)	Organizing notebook in order to get started. It's hard for me to work with a messy notebook. In order to keep the work load organized in my head and in order to make sure I cover everything I need to be organized and neat.
WI(37)	I enjoyed the routine at first—it was the type of job that required a very organized individual. There were a million details involved in getting the information into print. I love organizing, so I enjoyed that part of the job.
WI(39)	—But this is a difficult way to answer this question so I will begin again in a more structured (organized) way.
WI(73)	Marriage: Cons—interfering with our school work; difficult to plan while in school (Addition: this was a traumatic time in many ways because there were so many school and wedding details to attend to—it drained me because I couldn't deal well with so many constant loose ends. I couldn't even get my "plan of attack" on those loose ends organized.)

15. I Place A High Value On Reliability and Honesty (7, 0, 4)

ISI	Acquaintances' report:	keeps promises	4.2 (mean = 3.4)
		consistent	4
	Desired self:	keeps promises	5
		consistent	5

REC — Her attitude in both positions has invariably been one of . . . dependability.

24D(2) — I was going to be 15 minutes late! When I got to school at 9:15, only two other group members were there—and I thought *I* was irresponsible . . . so I apologized for being late.

24D(17) — Advertising group project was supposed to be in a group members box so the rest could give it a final review. It wasn't there. It really irritated me.

WI(6) — . . . so I claimed to have finished before I had and got caught and admonished before the class. I look back and laugh, but what a trauma at six! (Interpretation: this incident is one of few that stands out vividly in my memory. I learned a powerful and long-lasting lesson about the importance of honesty.)

WI(30) — Again I typed and was a conscientious employee.

WI(38) — It was unsettling trying to deal with individuals who won't reveal why they dislike you.

16. I Enjoy Teaching and Persuading Others (9, 1, 6)

APP — My present job, which requires that I address short presentations to a sales staff, has extended my appreciation and enjoyment of this type of interaction.

ISI —
- Acquaintance report
  - —"Helps others": 3.8 Relatively high, the mean for all items was 3.4.
- Current self—takes lead: 4.0 Mean is 3.5.

LCV — Identity: #3—expanding influence
Professional: #7—directing next person
Parental: #3—teaching
Political: #1—helping people

REC — . . . excellent oral and written communication skills have been evident from her performance in this position.

SCI — Basic Interest Scales: Public Speaking: 63—highest ranking of all such items.

SCI — General Occupational Theme: Enterprising—49 highest theme
Facility with words in selling, dominating, leading
Interpretation:
—Prefer social tasks where they can assume leadership
—Enjoy persuading others to my viewpoint.

WI(2) — Kim was my shadow, and I was her teacher.

WI(3) — I loved teaching her all the things I had learned when I came home from school.

WI(38) — It was an eye opener to me—I thought I could "bring them around" and become friends.

Disconfirming Data

SCI — Basic interest scales: Teaching was low (40, mean = 50)

17. I Am Competitive and I Like To Win (9, 1, 4)

LCV — Getting ahead #1 Identity
Achieving goal #3 Identity
Do better than next person #3 Recreation

ISI — Competitive: ranked myself 4 (avg = 3.5)

SCI — Enterprising 49—my dominant theme
Interpretation: prefers social tasks when they can assume leadership.

WI(7) — I do remember how frustrated I would get because I could never finish my work before lunch. We (the class) were competing with one another on a chart to see who could work the fastest and most efficiently. (You got stars depending on your speed.) Well, I couldn't stand it when a few of my classmates were always finishing their work very early . . . so I claimed to have finished one day before I had.

WI(8) — I remember very little about second grade except my effort to be in the top reading group.

WI(14) — So I learned to ride and entered many horse shows in the area. My closest friend had been riding for several years—so with her help and the many cheap lessons available at the stables on Post, I got to be quite good.

WI(25) — I love riding—that sport is by far the most fun for me. I loved competing in horse shows and winning ribbons.

WI(38) — I had two adversaries (for reasons I know now—competition?) who were difficult to work with.

WI(38) — But it was an eye opener to me—I always thought I could bring them around and (win) become friends.

Disconfirming Data

ISI — Acquaintance report:
Competitive: 2.8—low (avg = 3.4)

18. I Enjoy Athletics (16, 1, 8)

24D(23)	Watched the Dodgers win—good for Dodgers—bad for my studying—that means more games on TV to distract me.
FT	Environment active: 30% Most of my responses in this category dealt with sport activities: dancing, exercises, diving off high dive, somersault.
LCV	Recreation/Physical: 6th/Value out of 13 #1—enjoying activity #4—moving quickly
LSD	Recreation/Sports topics: past and current = 48% future = 27% *Large % of total entries.
SCI	Occupational Scale: Recreational Leader—45 "similar"
24D(12)	Left to go to Scuba Diving Class.
23D(19)	It's hard to be disciplined on a sunny football day.
WI(9)	I was a bit of a tomboy in 3rd grade, and I preferred softball to any other activity.
WI(24)	I also enjoy sports—particularly swimming, skiing, racquetball, and volleyball.
WI(25)	I love riding—that sport is by far the most fun for me.
WI(40)	We liked to do the same sorts of things . . . we both rode horses, so we rode together every day after school.
WI(41)	In college I got to be friends with another girl in my dorm who, again, seemed to have similar interests. Sally and I did a lot of partying together and a lot of sports activities.
WI(50)	I want to be in an area where I could own a horse again.
WI(52)	Football games, plays, ACC basketball games (also sound fun at this time).

Disconfirming Data

SCI	Basic Interest Scales: Athletics—50 = average.

Conclusion

The process of compiling information about myself was not enjoyable. As a result of the process, however, I have discovered data which provide insights into why the exercise was so difficult. Some of the reasons for my frustration may be found in the following themes:

1. I enjoy change and a fast pace.
   - I was very impatient with the written interview because it took so long to write.
2. I have very few friends and confide in few people.
   - I had a great deal of difficulty "opening up."
3. I enjoy "getting organized" and work better when I am organized.
   - With my Rorschach, big picture outlook, I had difficulty envisioning how all the instruments could be consolidated and organized into a useful tool.
   - I am not satisfied that I have organized the notebook to the best of my ability, or written the assessment to the best of my ability. Time constraints frustrated my efforts at more thorough organization.

Although I have noted only 18 themes, I feel that each is a strong and independent statement about my values. Some may find conflict in the themes:

> "I enjoy being with people"
> "I prefer a team-oriented environment"
> vs.
> "I have few close friends . . . "
> "Independence is important to me."

However, team-oriented environment is not necessarily an environment in which one must work together with others. Further, being with people and being very close to people are not necessarily inconsistent themes.

None of the preceding themes contradicts my image of myself. That is not to say that I recognized all of the values in myself before I began the self-assessment process. The Dyad exercise was an invaluable exercise in which several aspects of my values were brought to light:

- Theme 5—"I do not enjoy taking orders or working with strong authority figures."
  —the support for this was more emotional and more harsh than I would have anticipated.
- Theme 8—"The people I like best are smart and strive to better themselves."
  —this is phrased as a positive theme; however, there is more evidence than I would have imagined which indicated that I actually *dislike* individuals who do not measure up to certain standards.

Finally, I would like to recognize the lack of disconfirming data in several of my themes. It may very well have been an oversight on my part; however, potential themes which were weakened by substantial disconfirming data were eliminated. I attribute the lack of disconfirming data to the selection process.

20

Writing Your Self-Assessment

We believe that if you take the time to *write down* your self-assessment conclusions, they will be much more useful to you not only now, but also in the future. The writing does several things. First, it forces you to put into words thoughts, impressions, and feelings. This process causes one to think more clearly and carefully about the nuances and meanings of those thoughts, impressions, and feelings. And after all, that is what self-assessment is all about—to make explicit what is already within you in a way that is useful.

Second, once the words are on paper, you can gain some emotional distance from them and view them a bit (not a lot) more objectively than you can in your head or heart. The paper provides a means of detaching the conclusions so that you can consider them.

Third, the paper also provides a greater opportunity for you to check your self-assessment against the views of others. Spouses, partners, family, close friends, and others who know you well may provide interesting confirmations or questions about your life theme conclusions. Those conversations, based on a list of life themes, can stimulate your thinking to further clarify the labels.

Fourth, a written record of your self-assessment will help you to monitor your growth, change, and development over time. It is much easier to see those changes when you can *read* what you concluded in the past rather than when you must try to *remember* the conclusions and then compare them with a current self-assessment.

Finally, writing your self-assessment will sharpen your inductive skill greatly. As humans, we often jump (occasionally, leap) to conclusions that are not well founded in facts. Our minds race ahead so quickly that the weakness of the logical connections may not be considered or even recognized, especially when the topic is charged with emotion, as it is in a self-assessment. Slowing down enough to write out the data and the conclusions you draw from the data forces you to look at the connections between those data and conclusions and to consider their strengths. That mental, analytic skill is one which has application far beyond the self-assessment process. It will help as a person in business, in society, in relationships, in science, wherever.

Procedures and Guidelines

We encourage you to approach writing your self-assessment in two steps. First, develop a *single* theme. Choose one of the many that probably have occurred to you by now and search through the data to see if it is supported. Collect the data on cards or a piece of paper. We have provided another worksheet for you (Exhibit 20–1). If the format appeals to you, use it. If not, devise your own method for developing this theme. Note the contradictory evidence. Phrase the label. Recheck the connections between label and data. Revise the label. Recheck the data pool in light of the revised label.

Then, when you have completed a single theme and written out its name (label) and the related referenced data, show it to someone. Talk about it.

Exhibit 20–1

Life Theme Development Worksheet

Theme Label: ______________________________

Sources	Data

Contradictory Evidence

Retrace your steps. How did you go about assembling it? How long did it take? How could you be more efficient? Does the label and the process feel right to you? Why or why not? You may wish to discuss this in class if you are in one.

Having completed a single theme and taken some time to debrief that experience, you can then go on to complete your written self-assessment by repeating the process you used and revised to develop your initial theme.

The Number of Themes

After you have analyzed all available data and found all the themes you can, you may wonder whether the number of themes identified is typical or appropriate—or whether you are still missing something.

Our experience suggests that the number of themes that can be generated depends to some extent on the number and type of data-generating instruments used. Using the devices in this book, you normally will find about fifteen to twenty-five themes in a good analysis. Initial analyses based on data from only three or four devices may yield as many as a dozen "tentative" themes that, while not yet convincing, look promising. Good analyses based on more than our devices will generally not produce more than thirty well-supported themes.

Sometimes people are not able to locate more than a dozen convincing themes in their data. Usually they simply haven't looked hard or long enough, but that is not the only reason. Sometimes a person, either consciously or unconsciously, tries to find themes that are completely "independent"—that do not, in a sense, overlap. Similarly, one sometimes looks for themes that fit into a limited number of categories, such as "skills," "values," and "goals." In both cases, the underlying problem is the same: The person is imposing a model or a set of constraints on the data, thereby limiting what the data can say. As we have said before, it is essential to effective thematic development that one let the data speak for themselves.

A different set of factors is often associated with an analysis containing thirty to forty themes. Often many of these themes say almost the same thing: The degree of overlap is extreme. Or many of the themes may be supported by very few data. In either instance, many similar themes can usually be collapsed into more general and better-supported themes without the loss of any important information.

A good self-assessment does not have to contain a certain quota of themes. But our experience strongly suggests that if you end up with less than fifteen or more than thirty themes, it is wise to reexamine them carefully.

Assessing the Accuracy and Importance of Themes

Before you accept a set of themes as final, you have to judge the importance and accuracy of each theme that has been located and labeled. Judgment is required, because no rules, outside of one's own common sense, are available for determining whether the evidence supporting some theme is "enough" to ensure its accuracy, or whether the amount of evidence suggests that a theme is of great importance, moderate importance, or minor importance.

The questions one needs to raise in making this judgment are fairly obvious ones:

1. How many data seem to support the theme? A theme supported by ten data certainly has a greater chance of being accurate and important than one supported by only three.
2. Where do these data come from? Do they all come from just one of the data-generating devices, or do they come from more than one? A theme supported by data from four different instruments seems more likely to be accurate and important than one supported by data from only one source.
3. How many, if any, data contradict the theme? Any contradictory datum raises the question of a theme's validity. But a theme with ten data supporting it and one contradicting it would quite reasonably be handled differently from a theme with four data supporting it and two contradicting it.

One might suppose that, because precise decision rules are lacking, judgments about themes tend to be highly idiosyncratic. However, we have not found this to be the case. Most people, when looking at the same set of themes, tend to make similar judgments regarding the accuracy and importance of each one.

For an example of a final set of themes in a self-assessment, refer to Lauren Davis's self-assessment paper (see case, pp. 000–00). The self-assessment paper assignment that follows is one we have given to our students to guide their efforts; it may be of some help to you.

Self-Assessment Paper Assignment

Purpose

The self-assessment paper (SAP) is designed to help you develop a set of life themes from the data you have generated so that you can use those themes to establish goals and ideas for work and career. The paper is also intended to develop your skills at analyzing large and complex pools of data and at seeing the trends and patterns in that data.

Content

The SAP should stand by itself; that is, a person should be able to read it without the benefit of background information and be able to follow the logic and conclusions easily.

The paper should include the following elements:

1. A brief introduction that establishes the date, the nature of the assignment, and any background you would like to include.

2. A body containing theme labels and related data. Your logic, especially as it connects data and theme labels, should be crystal clear. We suggest putting one theme per page, with the label at the top and those data and their sources beneath. Separate supporting and contradictory evidence. Number each theme.

Quote data verbatim, then *add* any interpretation if necessary. Citing, for example, paragraph 3 of the written interview but providing *only* interpretation of that paragraph makes it difficult to assess your logic. When you use data from quantitatively scored instruments, cite the scores. Citing the Strong-Campbell without showing scores and your interpretations of those scores does not reveal your logic. Your purpose is in part to demonstrate—to communicate—the logic connecting individual data to the theme label.

Also, remember that *variety* of sources of data lend strength to a theme. A theme supported by data from eight different sources is more believable than one supported by data from two sources. Don't neglect the Feelings Record and other "less formal" instruments. Feel free to include data from sources like journals, other tests, letters, and so on. If you do, include them in your binders.

If the volume of your supporting data for a theme runs on for two pages, feel free to cite only the 10 to 20 *strongest* bits of evidence and then to summarize in one line the volume of additional data not presented.

Be *sure* to recognize and cite contradictory evidence where you find it. If the volume of contradictory evidence is large, perhaps you have two themes rather than one in that pool of data.

3. A description of things that you believe about yourself (preferably in theme label format) which are important to career decisions, but which did not emerge in your data pool.

4. A conclusion that includes a brief description of your level of confidence in the accuracy, comprehensiveness, and importance of the themes. Include a list of your themes (on one page). Include also a consideration of the dilemmas, tradeoffs, or conflicts suggested in your themes.

Format

Your SAP must be typed. *Maximum* length is thirty-five pages. Put a *copy* of your paper in your blue binder under the blue tab marked Self-Assessment Paper. Then hand in your binder (with *all* of your data and interpretations). Keep the original of your paper. You will need it in class.

Criteria for a Good Self-Assessment Paper

1. Demonstrates understanding of various instruments.
2. Clear logic between data and theme labels.
3. Sufficient volume of supporting data for themes.
4. Recognizes contradictory evidence.
5. Cites a variety of sources for each theme where possible.
6. Well-written theme labels.
7. Adequate range and volume of themes.
8. Themes grouped where appropriate and ranked.
9. Implications address a variety of dimensions.
10. Readable, easy to follow and check.
11. Reasonable length.

21

Drawing Implications from Themes

The final step in the self-assessment process involves identifying the career and job implications inherent in a set of themes. The ultimate purpose here is to translate the basic assessment into a more useful form.

It is often possible to identify some job and career implications directly from each theme. If the theme is "short attention span," then one might reasonably conclude that "a job requiring concentrated attention on one task for long periods might prove unpleasant." One could approach this final step in the self-assessment process in just this manner—by taking each theme, one at a time, and looking for what it implies regarding job or career.

Having done that, you should then look for overlaps or connections between and among themes that confirm your preliminary list of implications or add to it.

Procedure

First, group together all the themes that overlap or are strongly related. For example, suppose one had three themes that related to one's way of thinking and approaching problems and tasks: "doesn't like detail," "very systematic," and "future-oriented." These themes would be grouped together. So would the two themes "needs to be number 1" and "needs people contact," which speak to what one wants from life. And so should the three themes "dislikes crowded living," "nature very important," and "strong affiliation with family (who live in Oregon)," which all relate to life style preferences.

Some themes, of course, because they overlap a number of other themes in a number of different ways, will end up in more than one grouping. Some themes may not fit into any groups—they seem to be quite independent of the others. The overall grouping shown in Exhibit 21-1 is a sample of the typical kind of result of this process.

You can translate each grouping into an initial set of implications by writing a phrase, sentence, or sentences that seem to capture what is being expressed in the themes. For example:

Themes	Implication
1. Likes immediate feedback. 2. Prefers planning ahead. 3. Pragmatic. 4. Has disciplined responses to uncertainty.	This person should seek work that rewards systematic approaches to practical problems and that does not require initiative or creative responses to a lot of uncertainty.

Guidelines

Some people find the process of grouping themes together and identifying their implications difficult. Here is a step-by-step method that may help such people:

1. **Generate an initial set of implications, even if the process seems awkward and uncomfortable.**

Exhibit 21–1

Typical First Grouping of Themes

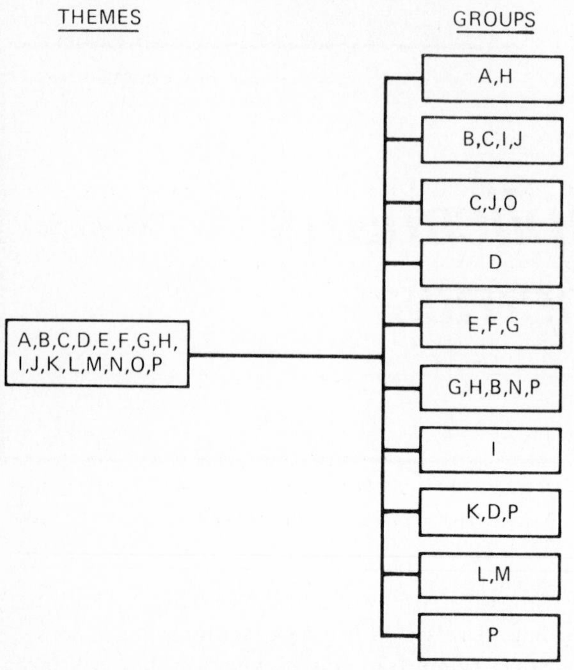

2. Evaluate your results in light of three criteria: (a) Do the implications overlap to a minimum and yet take into account the overlap inherent in the themes? (b) Do the implications speak about all the characteristics and behavior that are obviously relevant to job and career questions? (c) Do the implications take into account all the information in the themes? If your implications satisfy these criteria, your task is over. More often than not they won't, and you will have to continue in an iterative process of making modifications until they do.

3. If your implications have ignored a theme or themes correcting this is easy. Take the theme and see if it fits into any of the groupings. If it does, change the implication based on this new addition. If it doesn't fit into any existing grouping, identify and add a new implication directly from the theme itself.

4. If some implications still seem to overlap significantly, the problem probably lies in a poor grouping of themes. By going back and trying different theme groupings, you can eliminate the problem by trial and error.

5. If the implications don't seem to speak to some career and job issues, clearly identify what those issues are and then go back to see if any of the themes speak to them. If you can find one or more relevant themes, group them together and add a new implication.

To aid in assessing whether an initial set of implications speaks to all the basic job and career issues, we have found questions of the following type to be useful:

1. Does this set of implications tell us anything about what types of people (if any) this person likes to be with and work with?
2. Does it say how he or she likes to relate to people?
3. Does it tell us what types of tasks this person prefers to work on?
4. Does it suggest what types of intrinsic and extrinsic rewards he or she prefers?
5. Does it say what types of environments this person strongly likes or dislikes?

Sometimes you will identify an issue that an initial set of implications does not address, and upon checking find that none of the themes addresses it either. If the themes have been developed properly, then you can do nothing except leave this void in the set of implications. It is very important that you not go back to raw data and try unsystematically to create an implication to fill some void.

Finalizing a Set of Implications

One final task should be completed before you stop working on your implications. Insofar as possible, you want to try to differentiate the implications in terms of importance. In a typical self-assessment, some implications are more important than others. The more clearly this is specified, the more the assessment will help you to choose among different "good" job and career options.

To differentiate implication statements by importance, you need only work backward to trace the information each is based on. For example, an implication statement derived from three themes, each based on fifteen data from five different data-generating devices, probably is speaking to a more central and important issue than one derived from a single theme based on eight data from three devices. Your own judgment is crucial here, of course, and it cannot be replaced by mechanical rules.

The best test of whether you are finished writing your self-assessment, or whether it still needs some work, is your own opinion of it. If you feel that your set of implications is sound, accurate, and useful—your task is done. If you don't feel that way, you need to keep working until you do. *You are the one who will have to use your self-assessment, and if you don't believe it, you won't use it.* We have found that when people really believe in their self-assessment, not only do they use it, but their belief heightens their energy and motivation to overcome job and career obstacles that frustrate and stop many others. Accurate self-knowledge in which one has confidence can be a tremendous source of power for an individual.

Assignment

The themes that Steven and Carrie developed in their Self-Assessment Papers are listed below. Choose one list or the other and develop a set of implications for the kind of work each should be seeking.

Next, consider how this list of implications might be prioritized. What criteria could one use? Which would you use? Why?

Then reread your list to see if you have addressed the major aspects of life. Do you have implications for work? Play? Personal style? Cognitive style? Interpersonal style? Life style? Recreation? Educational activity? Family activity? Financial activity? Job tasks? and so on. Do not accept this list as exhaustive; rather consider other dimensions of life that seem important to you, and look for any implications that their themes lists may have on that dimension.

Steven Taylor's Themes List

Self-Assessment Themes (Plus Three)

Steven Taylor is a person who:

1. Requires a balance in work and personal life.
2. Plays a little fast and loose with traditional customs.
3. Thrives in an unstructured environment.
4. Is demanding of self—a drive for continuous improvement.
5. Has a need for intellectual stimulation.
6. For whom family is important.
7. Can be pompous, but is usually conscious of it.
8. Needs to spend time in outdoor activities.
9. Values independence and self-sufficiency.
10. Cares more deeply about a smaller number of people.
11. Enjoys external confirmation of success.
12. Is demanding of friends.
13. Prefers an active environment.
14. For whom playing music is missing as a part of my life.
15. Handles crises well.
16. Learns from setbacks.
17. Adapts well.
18. Is restless; likes to get on to the next project.
19. Is willing to take risks to gain greater rewards.

Plus three!

20. Would like to see more of the world and its variety.
21. Senses the emergence of a more contemplative me.
22. Would like to find a place to call home, somewhere I will always come back to.

Prepared by Lori Wilson and Jim Clawson. Copyright © 1989 by the Darden Graduate Business School Foundation, Charlottesville, VA. UVA-PACS-040

Carrie Baugh's Life Themes

A summary code word for each theme is given in capital letters after each theme and then the name of the theme cluster to which each theme belongs.

NO. THEME

1. Family is my source of strength and support. (FAMILY/Personal Identity)
2. Carrie values her independence and family over having lasting friendships. (INDEPENDENCE/Personal Identity)
3. Although independent, Carrie needs contact with people. (CONTACT/People-Oriented)
4. Carrie wants to maintain a balanced lifestyle. (BALANCE/Control)
5. Carrie wants to be seen as special and talented. (SPECIAL/Achievement-Oriented)
6. Carrie seeks to learn from new situations. (LEARN/Diversity)
7. Carrie enjoys jobs that utilize both people skills and Analytical/Quantitative analyses. (SKILLS/Diversity)
8. Carrie consults those people she trusts and respects, then makes her own decisions. (TRUST/People-Oriented)
9. Carrie strives to improve herself. (IMPROVE/Achievement-Oriented)
10. Carrie enjoys working in teams. (TEAMS/People-Oriented)
11. Carrie is practical. (PRACTICAL/Personal Identity)
12. Carrie sets goals, then works hard to accomplish them. (GOALS/Achievement-Oriented)
13. Carrie tends to make unstructured environments more structured. (STRUCTURES/Control)

Prepared by Lori Wilson and Jim Clawson. Copyright © 1990 by the Darden Graduate Business School Foundation, Charlottesville, VA. UVA-PACS-058

14. Carrie enjoys competition and thrives on challenges. (COMPETITION/Achievement-Oriented)
15. Carrie is results-oriented. (RESULTS/Achievement-Oriented)
16. Carrie likes to feel in control of her time and actions. (CONTROL/Control)
17. Carrie has a hidden passion for performing. (PERFORMING/Achievement-Oriented)
18. Carrie enjoyed living in San Francisco and likes the culture and diversity of a larger city. (URBAN/Diversity)
19. Carrie enjoys helping others. (HELPING/People-Oriented)
20. Carrie enjoys participating in sports. (SPORTS/Diversity)
21. Carrie enjoys playing the piano. (PIANO/Diversity)
22. Carrie tries to be tolerant of different types of people. (TOLERANCE/People-Oriented)
23. Carrie dislikes long commutes to work. (COMMUTING/Control)
24. Carrie is prideful. (PRIDE/Personal Identity)

Career Development

22

The Career Development Process

Over the past 30 years a fairly large number of people have studied various aspects of career development. One recent review of this literature references well over 500 books and articles.[1] Because many of these writers approached the subject with very different backgrounds and for very different purposes, the literature tends to be split into a number of camps, with little cross-referencing or building. Although there have been several attempts to synthesize these divergent approaches, as yet there is no one generally accepted theory of career development. The different camps may be characterized as having a sociological or a psychological perspective.

Perspectives

The Sociological Approach

The sociological approach tends to look at society as a structure consisting of various occupations. Careers are viewed as movement from one occupational level to another within a structure stratified by status and by the occupational role expectations of a person in a given status. The occupational level achieved in career development is seen as the result of a social process. Membership in a social class (indicated normally by father's occupation status) and socialization (the process by which individuals are trained, their expectations developed, and their values internalized) are seen as the prime determinants of occupational level. In addition, environmental factors (such as personal contracts, available financial backing, and socioeconomic conditions in society) are also relevant. Any one of these factors may be given major importance as an independent or explanatory variable, depending on the interests of the researcher in question.

The Psychological Approach

The psychological perspective is taken by those who support an individual theory of career development. Some take an intrapsychic approach, seeing unconscious forces as influencing conscious decision making. The shape of these unconscious needs or drives is often postulated to stem from early childhood experiences. Satisfying them then becomes a major determinant in job choice. Others take a rational decision-making approach to career development. Individuals are seen as testing themselves through interaction with their environment, weighing the factors and alternatives, then making conscious career choices. According to some scholars, this all occurs in a developmental process consisting of various stages through which the individual passes.

Scholars in this camp disagree particularly with respect to the relative importance of different variables. Some claim that environmental factors are most important in career development; others make the same claim for intrapsychic factors. Some believe

[1] S. H. Osipow, *Theories of Career Development* (New York: Appleton-Century-Crofts, 1973).

that most career job decisions are made consciously by individuals; others feel they are made unconsciously. Some believe that a person's experiences during the first few years of life are central to career development; others do not. And so on.

For our purposes, these disagreements need not distract us. The basic points on which most of the experts agree are strong enough to provide us with a solid base from which to proceed.

What Is a Career?

The first issue is that of career itself. The term originally referred to the speed with which a defined course was traversed by a wagon or contestant. Two interesting features of this older usage that remain today are those of speed and of defined course. We often think of a *career* as a defined course and of the success of an individual in that career as measured by whether or not the person completed the course (reached the top) and how quickly. But this view is unnecessarily limiting. Consider a broader view.

Scope: Individual, Organizational, Occupational

A person's career lies, in scope, somewhere between life style and job. A life style encompasses all aspects of a person's life. A job is a specific set of interrelated tasks in a particular context. A career may affect most or even all aspects of a person's life, but it is not all of it. Rather, a career is that part of a person's life that pertains to the work they do to sustain their lives physically and psychologically. By *work* we mean that which people do in exchange for the tangible or intangible things that sustain them. A career also consists of more than a job; it is a *series* of jobs that are related in some way.

The means we use to relate that series of jobs determines how we use the term career. We might use individual, job content, or organizational boundaries to relate a series of jobs to one another.

If we use the individual, then we may say that *everyone* has a career. We may or may not be paid for the work we do, but we all do things that are intended to sustain our lives. Homemakers bear and raise children and manage households. In return, they receive things that sustain their lives—food and shelter at a minimum, and optimally love, support, companionship, and fulfillment. Volunteer workers receive the satisfaction of contributing to society, although volunteer workers must also have some other means of support. For some, this is work; for others, it is heritage. In the latter case, where family wealth provides the support, a person's career may be almost totally in volunteer work. The *individual career* is the most comprehensive view of the term in the sense that it can incorporate the other careers we are about to mention.

Sometimes we say that so-and-so had a fine career at XYZ company. In this instance, we are using organizational boundaries to define a career. The jobs one has in an *organizational career* vary in terms of their content rather than their affiliation. A manager may be promoted or given a new assignment. A wife may have another child, or the family (the organization) may move to another location. These examples all represent changes in job content, but not in the career within the organization.

We might have said that so-and-so is pursuing a career in accounting. We then use job content to talk about *occupational careers.* Occupational careers are career courses defined by a particular set of related tasks for which one is compensated. The courses have relatively well-defined career paths. An occupational career in commercial banking, for instance, typically consists of some education in finance and a series of jobs/titles, including financial analyst/credit officer, account responsibilities (assistant vice president), industry responsibilities (vice president), regional responsibilities (senior vice president), and bank-wide responsibilities (president).

Organizations can offer at least a job and at most a career that is both organizational and occupational in nature (in the case of the person who dies while working in the same company in the same occupational area he or she began in). Usually companies offer an organizational career with a varied occupational content or a segment of an occupational career.

Perspective: Internal or External

We also can take either an external or an internal perspective to each of the careers we have discussed.[2] By *external* we mean the observable characteristics of a person's career—the salary, the title, the tasks assigned, the power wielded, the speed of promotion, and so on. When we observe a person's career progress and remark, "That person's going nowhere," we are using the ancient imagery to comment on the person's external career. The internal

[2]See Douglas T. Hall, *Careers in Organizations* (Pacific Palisades, CA: Goodyear, 1976).

perspective refers to a person's subjective experiencing of the traversing of the career course. This internal view is distinct from and not necessarily parallel to the external view. A person may, for example, have a "successful" external career by reaching the top (whatever that may be) in good time, but be very dissatisfied with the result. This evaluation grows from a comparison of career-related results with internally held values, beliefs, and aspirations.

For a long time, many employers and researchers ignored the significance of the internal view of the career. You can no doubt see the importance of taking personal reactions to external careers into account in understanding careers. The external measures of our careers occur against the backdrop of our internal experiencing of those measures, and it is the expectations, the hopes, the desires, and the values of the latter that determine in large part the sense of "integration"[3] and satisfaction we experience with the former.

Recently a number of books have been written which recognize this important distinction between the external and the internal career. Their titles are self-explanatory: *Career Success/Personal Failure,* by Abraham Korman (Prentice-Hall, 1980); *Must Success Cost So Much?,* by Paul Evans and Fernando Bartolome (Basic, 1981); *The Failure of Success,* edited by Alfred J. Marrow (AMACOM, 1972); *Tradeoffs,* by Barry Greiff and Preston K. Munter (New American Library, 1980); *Work, Family and the Career,* edited by Brooklyn Derr (Praeger Special Studies, 1980); and *Balancing Jobs and Family Life* by Haleyon Bohen and Anamaria Viveros-Long (Temple University Press, 1981). Taken together, these books are saying that it is not fruitful for individuals *or* organizations to think about career management from an external view only. Rather, to avoid potentially high personal and organizational costs, we must look at career management and development from both the external *and* the internal perspectives and understand better the dynamics between the two. Our lives are not as well compartmentalized as we might hope. The activities and events of one sphere will surely affect the other, and we should understand how.

A Conceptual Overview

So far, we have said that:

1. A career is the series of related jobs that a person does to sustain his or her life physically and psychologically.
2. Jobs may be related on at least three different dimensions—the individual, the organization, and the job content.
3. Careers have both an external (or objective) and an internal (or subjective) set of characteristics. Both need to be considered carefully.

[3]See Erik Erikson, *Childhood and Society* (New York: Norton, 1950), p. 268.

Exhibit 22–1 summarizes this conceptual view of careers. It also raises the question of time and how a career changes or "develops" over time.

Career Development

The phrase "career development" is one that has been used extensively and with a wide variety of meanings. Most of the usages of "develop" have to do with growth or progress, and yet there are many situations and cases in which the unfolding of a person's individual career can hardly be described as a progression or growth. We prefer instead the photographic connotation of *develop*—"to render visible"—because it reflects the importance of the internal as well as the external perspective on the career, and it carries with it the notion of a picture gradually taking shape. *Career development* consists of the gradual disclosure of the activities that internally and externally sustain an individual through life. This phrasing permits us to talk about the various careers in a variety of terms—not just progressive ones. We can discuss people who failed in their occupational or organizational careers but are happy

Exhibit 22–1

The Career

Individual Career	
The set and sequence of jobs that sustain life both physically and psychologically. May consist of occupational (related by job content) and/or organizational (related by organization) career segments.	
External Characteristics	*Internal Characteristics*
Title	Self-concept
Salary	Goals
Perquisites	Hopes
Prestige, status	Aspirations
Power	Values
Frequency of changes	Feelings
Location	Satisfaction
Travel	Patience
Influence	Anger
Number of subordinates	Disappointment
Career path traversed	

Exhibit 22–2

External Career Shapes

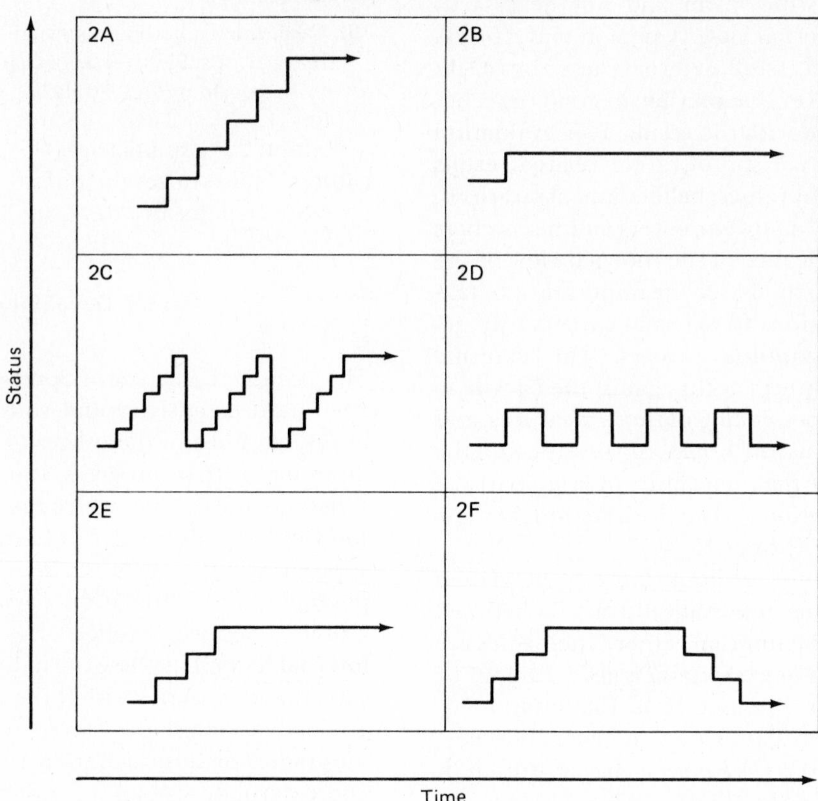

in their individual careers, as well as people who succeeded in occupational careers but "failed" in individual careers.

Time is central to the idea of career development. And when one thinks of the passage of time, one wonders about marking its passage and the changes that occur within it in some way. Several researchers have tried to characterize stages through which most people's careers pass. Super[4] and Dalton, Thompson, and Price[5] outlined the two most commonly accepted ones—about which we shall say more later. For the time being, suffice it to say that time is a key dimension in the consideration of the career development process.

We can add to time a number of other dimensions and begin to sketch out the *shape* of careers over time. Status, income, and learning rate are the most common dimensions used to develop these shapes. Consider the career shapes shown in Exhibit 22–2, which can be generated by using time and status as the defining dimensions. The first four represent common career patterns identified by Professor Michael Driver at USC. These patterns are linear, steady-state, spiral, and transitory, respectively.

The linear pattern reflects the drive of an individual to reach the top of an organization or occupation. The steady-state shape reflects careers that show little change over long periods of time. Many professional occupations fit this pattern. The spiral pattern characterizes the careers of people who for a number of reasons leave an occupational or organizational career every five to ten years to pursue something new. A desire for variety or new learning is often the motivation. Exhibit 18-2D shows the transitory pattern, in which people move from job to job relatively quickly and with no apparent long-term objective in mind.

To these four patterns, we have added two. First, in 2E, is a "plateaued" career; second, in 2F, is a declining career. Both are common in occupational and organizational careers.

---

[4]Super, D., J. Crites, R. Hummd, H. Moser, P. Overstreet, and C. Warnath, *Vocational Development: A Framework for Research* (New York: Teachers College Press, 1957).

[5]Dalton, J., P. Thompson, and R. Price, "The Four Stages of Professional Careers," *Organization Dynamics*, Summer 1977.

The notion of a person's career gradually taking shape over time makes us wonder about the factors that affect shape.

Factors That Shape Career Development

The shape a person's career takes over time is a function of several things. Let us consider these factors within the context of the job and career opportunities provided by organizations. Although we will not treat careers that are created by individuals outside organizations, there are many parallels to the organizational context.

When an individual accepts a position in an organization, there are costs and benefits to both parties. Simply put, the individual gives up time and talent and receives compensation and a job focus. The organization gives up financial resources and gains talent and time. In this arrangement, there is an explicit or implicit attempt to match costs and benefits. In reality, these costs and benefits change in various ways over time, and both parties attempt to manage the fit continuously. When changes occur, decisions are made. Both parties assess the alternatives and choose one. Thus, the career-related decisions for both sides have a direct impact on the shape of the career development of the individual. The factors that affect the career-related decisions on both sides have an indirect influence on the shape of career development.

A simplified view of this is presented in Exhibit 22–3. The self-assessment process was intended to give you a more accurate picture of your perceptions of yourself. The career development process we are about to consider is intended to help you learn a process so that you can get a more useful picture of the organization, can give the organization a more accurate picture of you, can understand more clearly how the organization sees itself, and can help both the organization and you make more productive decisions.

The Career Development Process

The first step in the individual's side of the career development process is to develop a focus. There are simply too many alternatives in society to examine them all. Next, you must begin to generate options (step 2). This will require that you make contact with organizations in your target focus, and then generate information that both you and the organi-

Exhibit 22–3

Factors That Shape Career Development

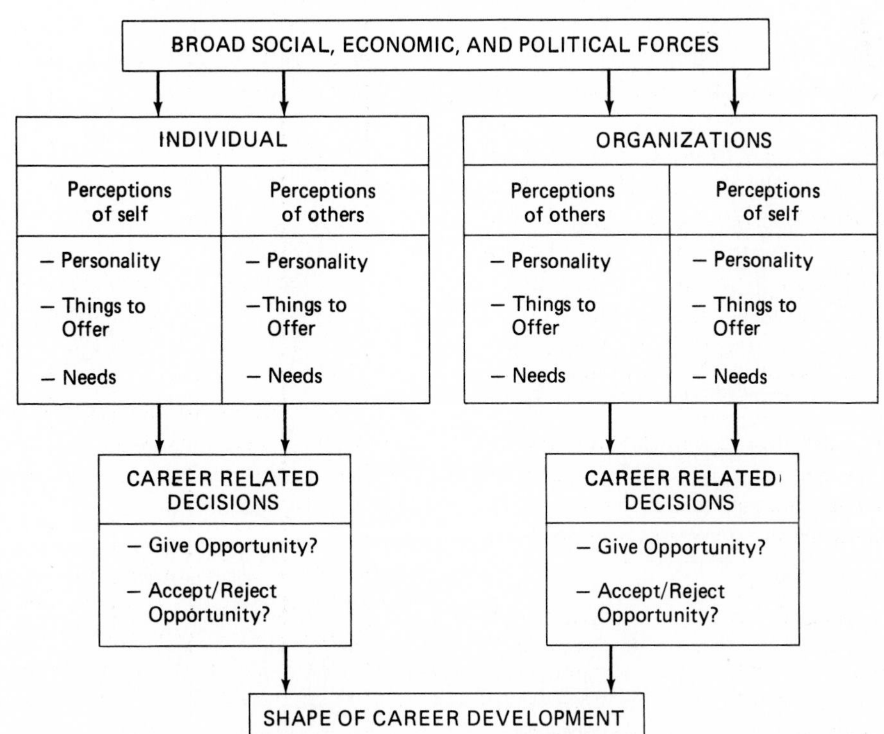

zation can use to assess the fit between you and organization. This assessment will generate career-related decisions based on the criteria both you and the organization deem important. Your experience with those decisions then becomes additional data for your ongoing self-assessment. This process (step 3) continues throughout life, and is summarized in Exhibit 22–4. It is important to note that you have as much responsibility for the accuracy of the decisions as the firm does. Every organization is not right for you. Although many people think of the job search as an exercise in selling, in fact it is also an exercise in buying.

The remainder of this book is organized roughly as follows in Exhibit 22–4. First, we will consider the job search process. The examples we use will relate specifically to people searching for jobs directly out of school, but the process is equally applicable to people about to make job or career transitions. We will help you consider the importance of developing a job search focus using your implications (step 4). Then we will consider ways of getting information about the vast array of opportunities in society (step 5). Having established a focus to your job search, you will then consider how to seek out and generate options that fit your focus. Once you have some options, you will need to assess them and choose one (step 6). We will provide some ways of thinking about and doing that. When you have accepted an offer, your transition to your new job or career will be much more effective and efficient if you manage the joining up process (step 7). Then, being up to speed in your new job, you will be starting the cycle again, reassessing continuously your fit with the job and career and adding to your knowledge of yourself (step 8). The choices that you and the organization make will then determine the shape of your career development and your satisfaction with it over time. Near the end of the book, we will help you to anticipate some career-related issues that will face you in one form or another in the future.

Exhibit 22–4

The Self-Assessment and Career Development Process

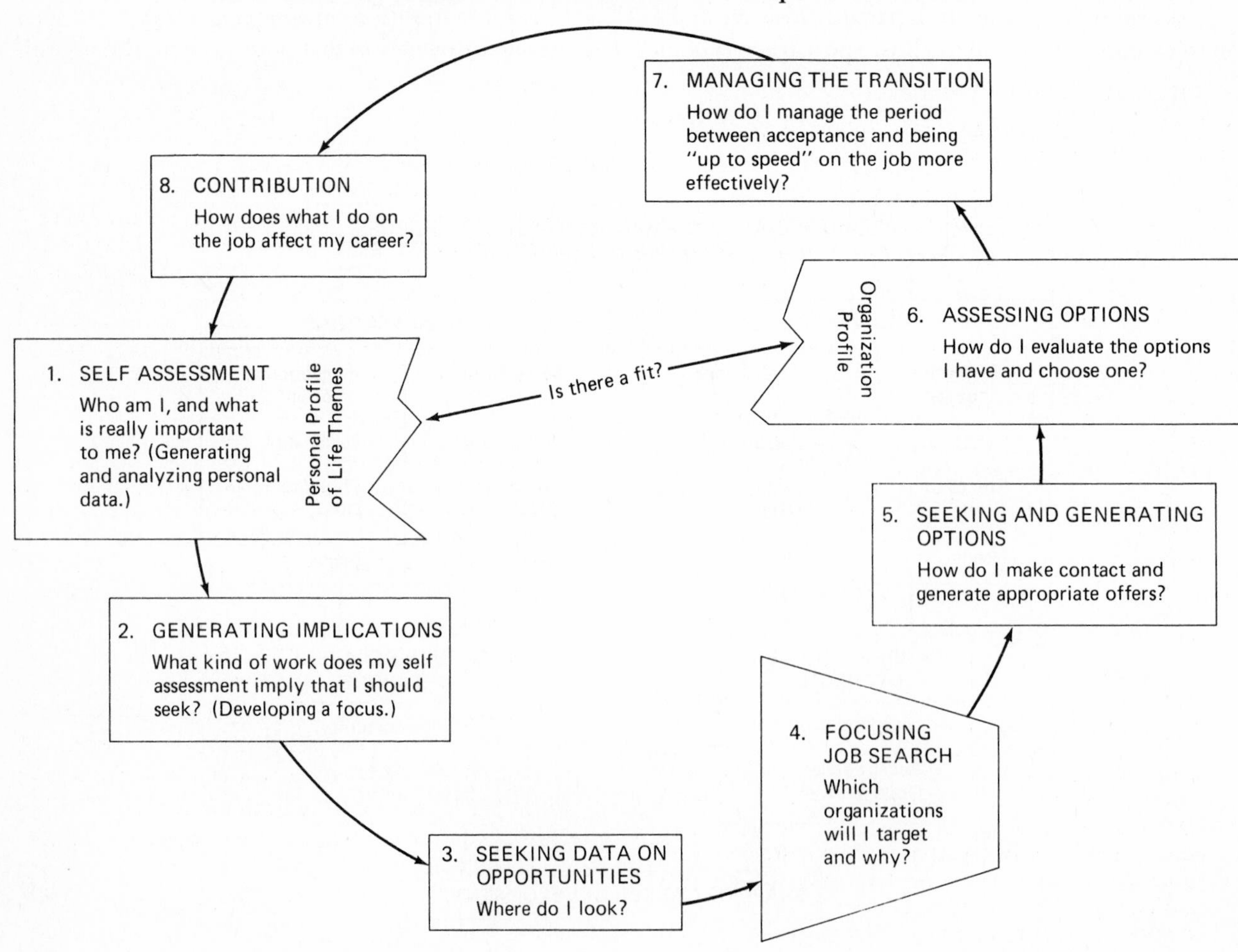

23

Some Hard Facts about MBA Job Searches

After almost two years of graduate school, John Wainwright was about to receive his MBA from a leading business school. But he was not particularly happy, nor was he looking forward to graduation. John didn't have a job.

Although this situation may seem unusual, every year many MBA graduates discover that their degree does not automatically guarantee them a job. They graduate without an acceptable offer.

General economic conditions certainly contribute to situations like John's, but we find that many job hunters do not plan for the time it takes to conduct an effective and successful job search. Some MBA candidates rely heavily on others, such as the placement office, to conduct the search for them; others merely go through the job search motions, finding false security in published statistics about the placement percentage for graduating classes. Still others, like John, continually postpone the search until, sadly, they are faced with a difficult and trying set of circumstances. Perhaps a little more information about John and his situation will help to illustrate this problem.

> John completed his first year of business school without a great amount of difficulty. He was more interested in marketing and consulting courses and, as a result, signed up for several classes in those areas for his second year. While he liked his classes, John was still not sure what he wanted to do. As Christmas approached, conversations with classmates turned more and more toward jobs. Some classmates knew exactly what they wanted, while others were still thinking about different possibilities. John was not particularly worried; others seemed to be in the same stage as he was, and there was still plenty of time before graduation in May. Besides, his attention was better directed toward classes, papers, and finals. After the semester was over, he decided to relax and enjoy vacation. January was soon enough to start his job search.
>
> Interview sign-ups began shortly after vacation ended in January. John felt awkward signing up for interviews because he still didn't know what he wanted to do. Everyone else in the class was securing interview slots, so John decided to sign up for several interviews too. Surely, he thought, at least one of the interviews would work out. Class work at this point was taking most of his time, so he picked firms that were well-known, seemed to be popular with his classmates, and offered above-average salaries. None of the interviews went particularly well, and by the time John realized that he would not get any second interviews, recruiters had stopped coming to the school.
>
> John began to set up appointments with faculty members, hoping that a few words of advice would solve his problem. When that failed, John began to write letters furiously. Much to his dismay, most companies never replied, and those that did were not offering interviews. John's worst fears had come true. He graduated without a job.

What disturbs us most about John and the others that we have observed in his situation is not that they don't have jobs, but that the majority of their problems were unnecessary. Job searching is a personally demanding and time-consuming process. We believe that many of the problems facing MBA job hunters can be foreseen and managed with effective planning.

In order to gather data that might assist MBA candidates in planning their job search, we distributed a questionnaire in the spring of 1981 to the graduating class of the Harvard Business School and to a portion of the graduating class at the Colgate Darden Graduate School of Business, University of Virginia. Approximately fifty percent of the graduating class at Harvard completed and returned the survey. The results therefore reflect the experience of a large portion of the class. The Darden survey was completed by about thirty students who took an elective course on career development in the fall of their second year. We recognize that the results of the surveys may or may not be representative of the MBA community as a whole. Our hope is that the information provides some insights into MBAs and their job searches that you will find useful in planning your own job search.

Key Characteristics of Job Searching

Time

Most MBA candidates encounter difficulties at some time during their job search directly due to lack of time. As we mentioned earlier, job hunting will demand a substantial portion of your time during the second year. The average MBA student in both surveys reported spending 150 to 175 hours on job search activities between September and April of the second year. A few students reported spending no time on job hunting, while others spent as much as 600 hours in job search activities.

Most students spend over sixty-five percent of this time during a three-month peak period from January to March. During this peak period, the average respondent devoted ten hours per week to job hunting; this is the equivalent of two full-time courses. Some MBAs even reported spending up to forty hours per week in March on job search activities. Exhibit 23–1 shows the average hours spent on job search activities by the Harvard respondents. In our experience, most MBAs who fail to plan adequately for this substantial time commitment encounter a variety of problems in their job search.

Career Choice

John Wainwright's uncertainty about the type of career he wanted was not particularly unusual. In fact, most MBAs begin their second year with an unclear idea of what they want to do. Both the Harvard and Darden respondents to the survey reported that in September they were highly uncertain in matters concerning career choice. The average MBA,

Exhibit 23–1

Hours Spent on Job Search Activities (Harvard Survey)

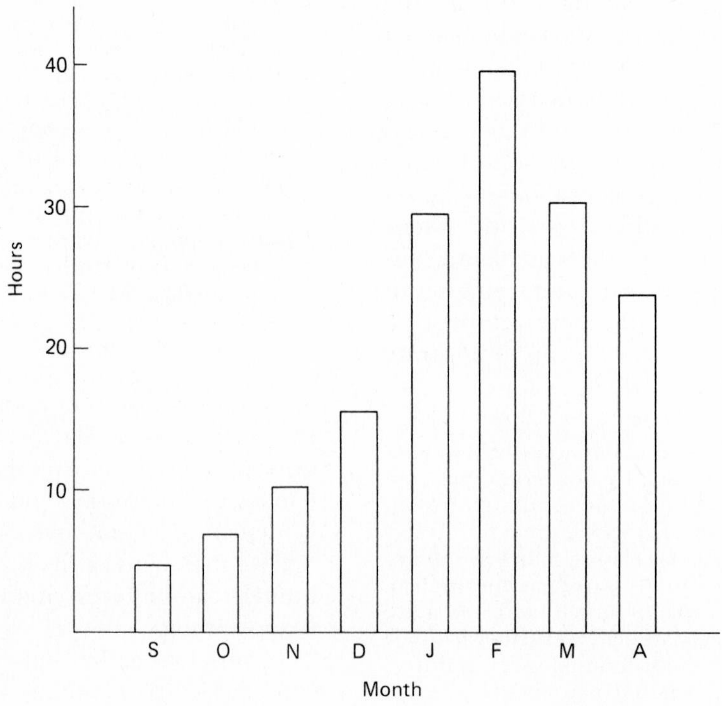

however, becomes more and more certain as the months progress. This increasing confidence is illustrated in Exhibit 23–2.

In the Harvard survey, only thirty percent of the respondents reported feeling "very certain" of what they wanted to do when school started in September. Twenty-seven percent reported that they were very uncertain. By January, forty-eight percent felt certain and only thirteen percent felt uncertain. By April, eighty-two percent felt certain that they knew what they wanted to do, while only nine percent still felt very uncertain. In our experience in working with MBA students over the years, those students who begin to sort out career choices early in the second year tend to have more productive and satisfying job searches.

Source of Contact

If you are like most MBA candidates, you will rely heavily on the school placement office to identify and contact your future employer. As measured by the sources of contact for accepted job offers, over forty-three percent of the Harvard graduates surveyed found employment through the placement office. This was over twice as many as any other source of contact. Summer job experiences and personal contacts accounted for seventeen and fifteen percent, respectively.

The high percentage of contact made through the placement office is due in part, we feel, to the effectiveness of placement office activities. We also sense, however, that MBAs are increasingly passive in conducting their job searches. John Wainwright, for example, was depending on some unknown factor reflected in placement statistics to conduct much of his job search for him.

Advice

Another indication of the increasing trend toward passivity is illustrated by the ways and stages at which MBAs seek advice. The average respondent talked to seven people about his or her job choice. A substantial number, thirty-five percent in the Harvard survey, reported not consulting with *anyone* about their job search. Like John, most MBAs do not seek advice during November, December, and January. During the early stages of the job search, our observations are that MBAs tend to rely on the placement office and to follow the crowd in signing up for interviews.

Many MBAs begin to ask for counsel late in the job hunting process. Most students talk to people about their job search only after they have received some firm offers. Students seem to hope that advisors will somehow guide them toward the "right" offer. The students who do not receive offers often

Exhibit 23–2

Student Confidence in What They Want to Do

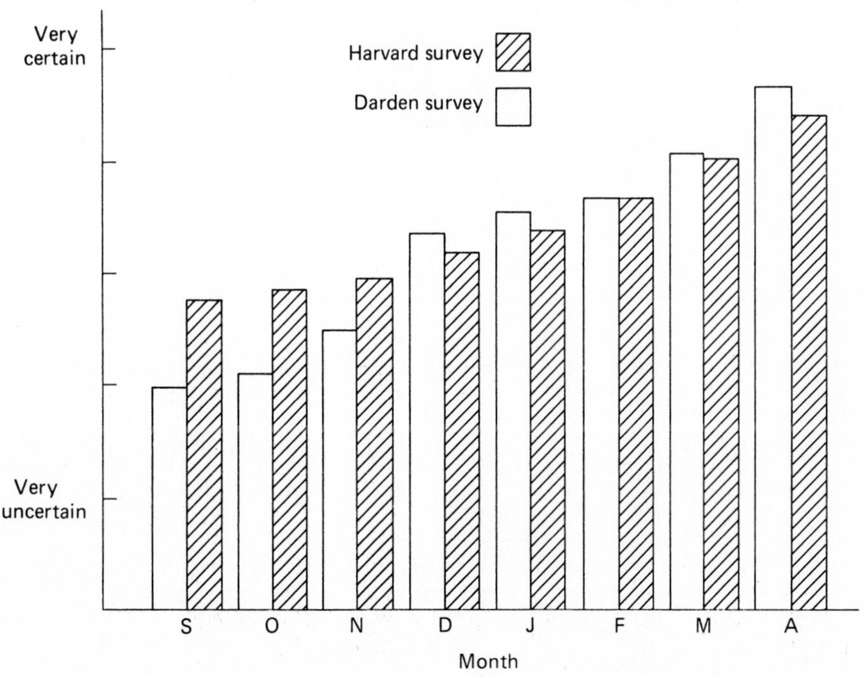

seek advice, hoping that someone else can solve the problem.

Interviews

As John's experience illustrated, having interviews does not necessarily result in having a job. While one must, almost always, have interviews to get a job, there does not appear to be any correlation between the number of interviews and the number of offers. In fact, in our experience, those students with the greatest number of interviews often are below average in the number of offers. Those students with the greatest number of offers often are those who had an average or even slightly below average number of interviews. As illustrated in Exhibit 23–3, there was no correlation between interviews and the number of offers in those surveyed at the Darden School.

The average MBA in both surveys had about twenty-five different interviews with twenty-three different companies, including first, second, and third rounds. The peak interviewing period was between January and March (see Exhibit 23–4). Students have commented to us after the interviewing season that having several "tuneup" or practice interviews was neither particularly beneficial, nor likely to increase the number of successful interviews as measured by offers. Some students even found such interviews to be detrimental because they adversely affected their interviewing attitude and approach.

Offers

The statistics certainly *are* in John Wainwright's favor. Of those we surveyed, over eighty percent had received at least two offers and over niney-four percent had received at least one offer by the end of April. The average MBA in both surveys received between three and four offers as a result of his or her efforts. The statistics show that most MBAs do indeed get jobs.

The statistics also show, however, that some students do not get jobs. Twenty-one students in the Harvard survey reported having no firm offers at the time of the survey. In the Darden survey, four students reported having no firm offers by June. For those students, published aggregate statistics are little comfort.

Job Selection

MBAs we talk to have a fairly clear picture of the factors involved and the relative importance of each factor for their own personal job selection. In the questionnaire, we asked the students to rank fourteen various factors in regard to job selection. The MBAs who responded in both surveys did not rank starting salary as particularly important. The most important factors listed by the students were colleagues and work setting, starting function, variety of job content, and geographical location. The least important factors were impact on society, travel demands, prestige of the organization, and starting

Exhibit 23–3

Interviews vs. Offers
(Darden Survey)

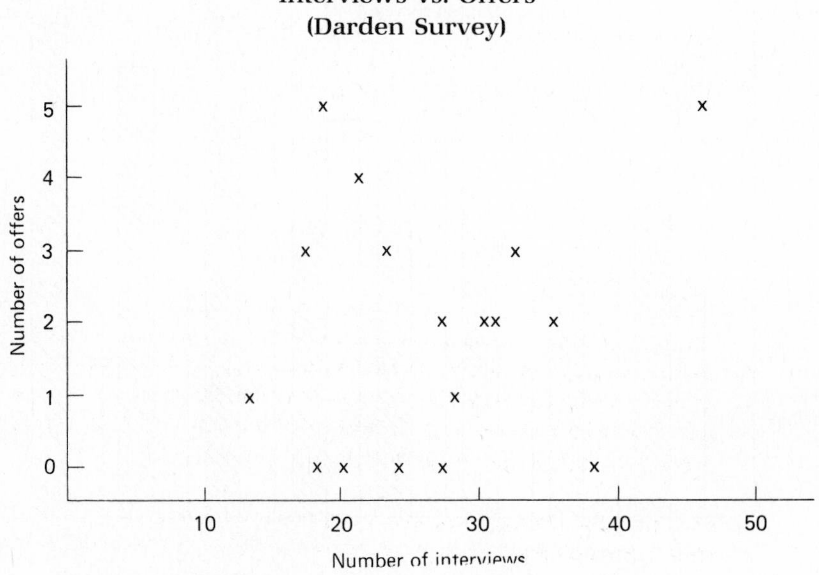

Exhibit 23–4

Average Interviews per Month (Harvard Survey)

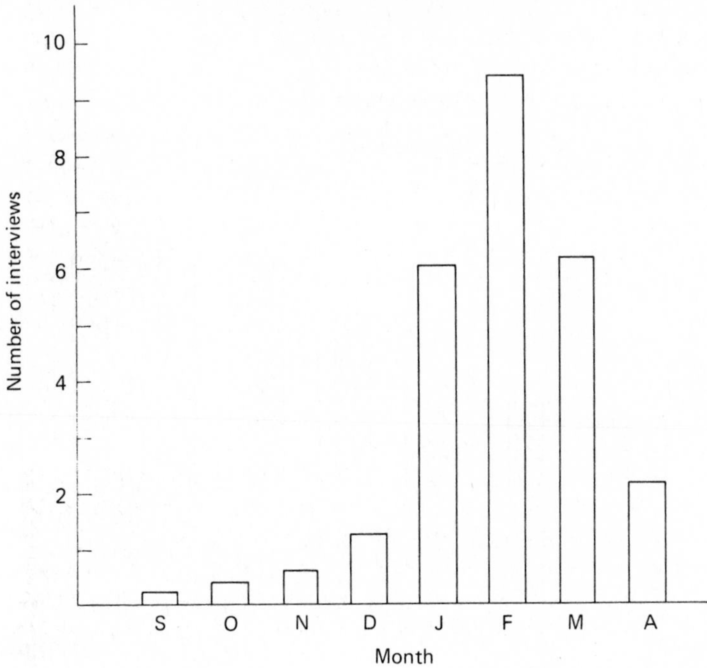

salary. The ranking of the 14 factors in both surveys is shown in Exhibit 23–5.

Anxiety

Every year we see a new MBA class go through the trauma of looking for jobs. In every class there are some students who have few problems in finding a job. Some students, like John Wainwright, have severe problems. Most students are somewhere in between. The majority of students that we know experience some type of anxiety during the recruiting process. Feeling some anxiety is natural; choosing a career is an important decision. A significant number of MBAs, however, experience a very high level of anxiety, and high levels of anxiety can interfere with the effectiveness of a job search and with the health of the job hunter. We believe the level of anxiety felt by MBA job hunters is correlated to the way in which students approach the job search process. Those students who plan for the demands and strains of a job search in an MBA setting tend to experience lower levels of anxiety.

The questionnaire we distributed asked students to rate their level of anxiety in recruiting on a month-by-month basis. A 5-point scale was used to measure anxiety, with a 5 being a very high level of anxiety. The average level of anxiety was low during the September to December period, as can be seen in Exhibit 23–6. Anxiety began to build in January and peaked in February and March. In February, sixty-five percent reported some anxiety; by March, only thirty percent reported a very high level of anxiety.

Exhibit 23–5

Relevant Importance of 14 Factors in Job Selection

Rank	*Harvard Survey*	*Darden Survey*
1	People/work setting	People/work setting
2	Starting function	Geographic location
3	Geographic location	Variety of job
4	Industry	Starting function
5	Nonfinancial prospects	Financial prospects
6	Variety of job	Nonfinancial prospects
7	Financial prospects	Travel demands
8	Independence	Independence
9	Boss/mentor	Industry
10	Starting salary	Spouse's career
11	Prestige of company	Starting salary
12	Travel demands	Boss/mentor
13	Impact on society	Prestige of company
14	Spouse's career	Impact on society

Exhibit 23–6

Level of Anxiety Experienced in Job Search Activities

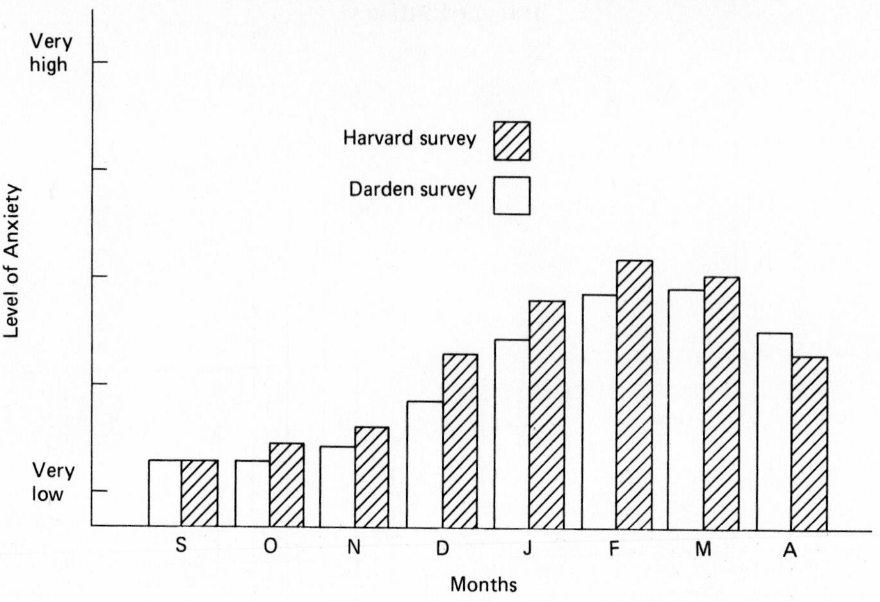

Summary

Although the outcome of John Wainwright's job search was not typical, we have found that some of the characteristics of John's search were. Many MBA students do not plan for the substantial commitment of time and energy an effective job search entails. Students especially do not plan for the extra ten hours per week of work. Most MBAs begin their search without a clear picture of what they want to do. Yet despite this, they seek limited, if any, advice from others, especially during the early stages of their job search. Many approach the task passively, preferring to allow others, such as the placement office, to plan much of the job search for them.

Given this lack of a planned approach, it does not surprise us that so many MBAs feel anxiety during their job search. The highest level of anxiety we observed appears to be connected more with the search and the uncertainty of receiving an offer than with the selection of one offer. We believe that you can reduce the level of anxiety in your job search by planning for the extensive process involved in a job hunt. You can also make your experience more pleasant and successful by anticipating this anxiety and developing ways to deal with it. If MBAs planned for their search, perhaps the experience of John Wainwright would become even more unusual.

Assignment

Job Hunting Diary

Because job hunting can be hectic and confusing, some people find that keeping a diary is very useful. Periodically reading back over the last week's or month's entries often helps one put things in their proper perspective and conduct the whole job hunting process more dispassionately.

You might wish to keep a diary yourself and write your entries in this section of the workbook. The following guidelines may be helpful to you:

1. Make entries as often as you can (preferably once a day).
2. When making an entry, ask yourself:
   a. What has happened today of importance with respect to job hunting?
   b. How has this changed my strategy and plans, if at all?
   c. How do I feel about today's events?

But before you go, take time to read Henry Rock's Job Search Diary and Life Themes. As you do, develop a Gantt chart of Henry's job search process. (A Gantt chart is a chart of the time span covered by specific activities or tasks contained in a process or project. See Exhibit 23–7.) This will help you to

Exhibit 23–7

A Simple Gantt Chart Outline

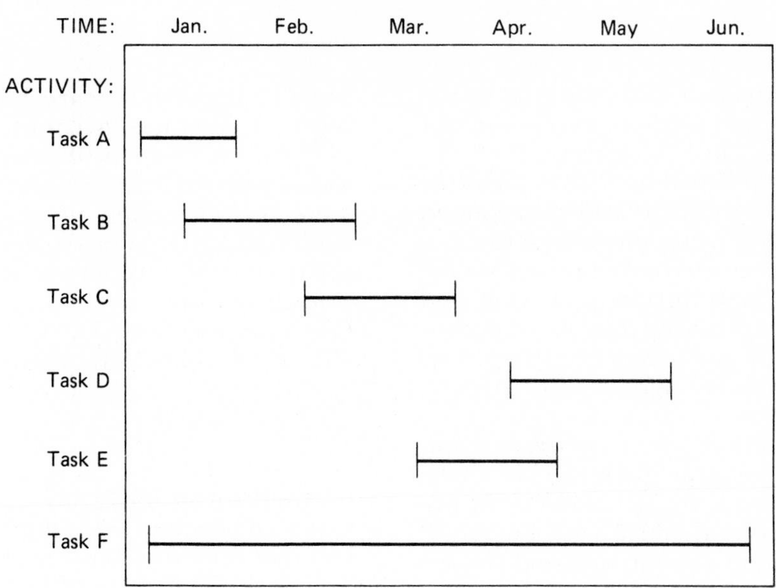

"see" more clearly the various tasks and lead times related to the job search. Note also the unexpected events Henry encountered. Note the things that Henry managed well and the things that Henry could have managed better in his job search. How, if at all, could Henry have managed his job search more effectively? Finally, note the emotional side of Henry's job search. What is the sequence of *feelings* Henry experienced? What does this tell you about the job search process?

HENRY ROCK: JOB SEARCH DIARY

October

We had our first placement office meeting in Burden. One of the things we spoke about was the writing of our résumés. The "career objective" was stressed as being very important and we were encouraged to be as specific as possible. Since my résumé was due in late October, I agonized over that portion of it for a week or so before realizing that I couldn't honestly be specific. So I put down "initial job in marketing or finance with general management as long-run objective." I hope this general statement isn't harmful.

November

Over Thanksgiving I wrote 11 letters to northern California firms that are either coming to campus this year or who had come in the past. My goal is to work in either San Francisco or Boston. Being a bachelor, I'd hate to be stuck in some dead place.

There was a lot of work involved in getting these letters off. I went through the preliminary lists of companies coming to the school and checked last year's job descriptions for job type and location. The card file (by region) also gave me some additional names. I also looked in *Sum-*

mitt's MBA employment guide and got two additional names.

December

The replies to my letters started coming in. By the end of the month I had received replies to 8 of my initial 11 letters. Three of those eight were companies who were signed up at HBS, and they thanked me for my letter and said they looked forward to seeing me when they came to campus. Of the other five, three had come in the past but were not signed up for this year. One said they would be doing no hiring this year. Another said to see them if I came to San Francisco. The third said they planned to sign up soon to interview at the school.

The remaining two letters were from companies who had never come to the B-school. One said they had no needs for someone with my qualifications. The second said to see them when I came to San Francisco. Later in the week, I even got a call from one company that was coming to interview in March.

Before Christmas break, we had to turn in our priority cards. This was easy for me, as I had already researched who was coming to campus. There were four San Francisco firms I was interested in and I assigned priorities to them. For the fifth, I chose a consultant in Los Angeles. I'm not really that interested in number 5, and it made me mildly nervous that I only had four potential interviews that really seemed desirable.

Toward the end of the month, letters from employers started coming in as the result of the résumé book being distributed. These unsolicited letters are really an ego trip. I am especially impressed by the personalized ones.

January 1–7

Received three more replies to my California letters. Two were from companies coming to HBS and were enthusiastic and thanked me in the typical way. The third was from an employer not signed up to interview. They said they couldn't match my qualifications to their needs.

Continued to get unsolicited letters. Also, on January 2, job descriptions began to be posted outside the placement office. I plan to make a daily trip to check the postings.

January 8–14

I continue to make the daily trek to the placement office boards. The office is constantly packed and it's difficult to get near the board. Everyone seems to be looking at each opportunity thoroughly.

January 16

Today I had a new career idea planted in my head. My financial accounting professor spoke of the public accounting profession and its virtues. I enjoy the issues in that class, so my eyes were opened when he said that MBAs often achieve the status of partner in 8-10 years at a salary of over $100,000. In addition, the profession allows initial flexibility in geographical location. I can interview for the San Francisco office with no problem. My interest is aroused!

January 17

I signed up to interview a Chicago firm for a financial position. I was attracted to them by the fact that they sent me a personalized letter and an impressive packet of information. They also have a reputation for paying well and are a growth company. I'm not sure that I could stand to work in Chicago, but I'd like to get an offer, especially one with a high salary, to use as leverage. It's also something to fall back on if all else fails. That seems to be the general psychology here at this time—get an offer as soon as possible. I was one of the last in my neighborhood to sign up for an interview.

January 20

I decided it would be wise to send more letters to West Coast employers, specifically those who aren't coming to school. I spent hours over at Baker Library going through *Moody's* and *Standard and Poor's.* I got a list of about 30 or 40 companies and chose to write to 10 of them based upon my interests and potential compatibility with them. By the time I had sent off these 10 letters, I had invested about 10 hours of research in them. (All were personalized, of course). To date, I haven't been too concerned about researching Boston firms, as they are right here and can be contacted easily.

January 22

I went out to dinner with my girl friend to celebrate our one-year anniversary of dating. I was sort of uptight because I had an incredible amount of work for the next day. As we went to say goodnight, she asked me where our relationship was going. She has been pressuring me lately with the end of school in sight, and it has been making me uneasy, especially since I'm uncertain about the relationship anyway. It was a bad time to ask me. I told her that I wasn't sure it was going anywhere and that we both should start to date other people. This completely blew her mind. She sat outside the apartment in her car and cried for 5 hours. I felt really bad, but also felt it was the right thing.

January 23

I signed up to speak with two of the San Francisco companies from my priority list who are coming next month. Also signed up to see a manufacturing company from New York. This is a hedge, also, against failure in San Francisco. However, like the Chicago company, they are an outstanding company and have good opportunities for MBAs. The New York company also seems fairly hot for me. They're taking me out to dinner on the 31st and have me interviewing on a closed list.

January 27

I've been trying to establish some communication with my girl friend. I didn't want to break things off altogether. She's been very hostile toward me, though. This surprises me, as I didn't think our discussion the other night was final. This hassle makes me less interested in staying in Boston. That had seemed to be a possibility before only because of her.

January 30

I had an appointment with my financial accounting professor to further investigate the possibility of working in that area. He turned me on even more and suggested three firms that he thought were the best. I discovered that one of them was interviewing on campus today. I ran home and threw on a suit and ran back, bringing my résumé to a walk-in interview at 4 o'clock. I had to B.S. my way through it, as I had done no research on the company. However, I think I was successful, and the interviewer promised to forward my résumé to the San Francisco office. I was relieved. That half-hour interview had seemed like two hours.

January 31

The dinner with the New York company was a bore. I didn't like the company representatives. They were awkward and uptight and never seemed to know what to say. Several other HBS students were there and all seemed ill at ease as the result of their bumbling. The food was good, anyway.

February 1

Right after lunch I had my interview with the Chicago company. I had consumed a couple of beers during lunch and was half gassed when I walked into the interview. Luckily, I sat pretty far away from the interviewer so he couldn't smell my breath. The interview went pretty well. I had researched them a lot and asked some good questions. The interviewer seemed tense, though. I wonder if he knew I was gassed.

A couple of hours later I had my third interview of the year with the New York manufacturer. The interviewer, whom I hadn't met, seemed obnoxious and authoritarian. His group was similar to the group I had worked for last summer (although in a different company), so I told him I thought a lot of their work might be busy work and boring. He disagreed and we talked about it, but our interview went downhill. What a disastrous experience. I'll get rejected by them but won't care.

February 2

Signed up to see two more accounting firms and another San Francisco company that I had priority for. The placement office boards remain packed all the time.

February 3–4

Nothing.

February 5–7

Checked all the postings and correspondence opportunities. I read them all, just in case. I have a routine now where I stop by the office every day about the same time.

February 8

Spoke with my second accounting firm. Liked my interviewer a lot. He seemed much sharper than the other people I've spoken with. He promised to send my résumé to San Francisco, although he promised no results. Both accounting firms I've talked with have had about five or six students wanting their résumés sent to San Francisco. They willingly do this, as they are ostensibly national recruiters. However, they are usually partners of the Boston office and would like to attract Harvard people to their own office. So it's a touchy situation. One must tread lightly.

February 9

I have thoroughly researched the San Francisco firm I'm talking to February 12. They are my number one priority. However, they have only one spot available, and my chances of getting it are slim. Perhaps I can get an edge by being well prepared.

February 10–11

This breakup with my girl friend has been continually on my mind. It has affected me in class and in my interviews. It's very upsetting. I'm getting more interested in leaving the area every day.

February 12

After being absent when called on last week, I was well prepared for class today. Directly after my second class I had an interview with my number one priority company. Although my chances of getting the job were never good, I was still very disappointed by the interview. The interviewer was a recent HBS grad, and we just didn't get along. Furthermore, he was 15 minutes late for the interview, so I was annoyed from the beginning. This was definitely one of the best jobs in San Francisco, so it is very disappointing.

However, I felt better when I went home because I had received a letter from accounting firm #1 telling me I was into phase 2 with them. That gave me a lift.

Tomorrow I talk with priority #4 from San Francisco. I am nervous about these West Coast interviews, as I am now sure I want to go to that area.

February 13

I had my interview after my first class today. The interviewer was a young, personable fellow and I liked him. He was also a skillful interviewer. I think he was impressed with me, too, so the interview was a success. Hopefully, they will invite me on a plant trip. Spring break is coming up soon (about 3 weeks), so I mentioned this to the interviewer as a convenient time to visit. I hope they come through.

February 14

I had no interviews today. However, I received two responses to my San Francisco mailings. Most of the replies to these letters have been negative. However, out of the 15 letters I've sent to companies that have no plans to interview at HBS, I've received about one-third favorable responses. I think this is a good yield. I should mention that in the letters I said I'd be in the area soon and asked if they would be interested in seeing me. This removes the barrier of travel expenses. I would guess that this has increased the number of favorable responses. If I get a good job as a result, I think the $305 plane fare is a great investment.

I had a bit of excitement today. At my Creative Marketing Strategy meeting I found out that I will be taking a trip to California. Although this will be a busy trip, I may get an opportunity to call some firms that have responded to my letters.

February 15

Today I spoke with my Starting New Ventures professor about finding a job with a small company in the control area. He got all excited and told me about two jobs he knows of. His enthusiasm is infectious. Now I'm interested in these opportunities.

Right after my appointment I spoke with another New York manufacturing firm. The interviewer was about 32 and was the head of the group I'd be in. He was very aggressive and pushy and made me very tense. He was also an extreme elitist. I knew I wouldn't like working for him.

After that interview, I went to a Pacific Northwest meeting. Only 6–8 people attended, but all spoke of their past and present efforts to get jobs in the West. No one seemed unusually successful, but I did pick up one or two ideas.

February 16

Although this was one of our Fridays off, I had a 10 A.M. interview with the Chicago firm at the Fenway Cambridge. It was my second interview with them and was an hour long. The interviewer was a soft-spoken HBS grad from 1966, whom I liked. He asked a lot of tough questions, such as "What do you consider the biggest potential problem of fit between you and our company right now?" I was very honest in the interview but wondered afterward if I hadn't been somewhat emotional and inarticulate. I sensed that he either was very impressed or very turned off, but I couldn't judge which. I would like to get a job offer from them. They are an impressive company.

February 17–18

This weekend I decided to call up my old girl friend in California. We hadn't talked to each other in about a year but had a great conversation. That evening I went to a party and talked to a friend who is also moving to San Francisco. She encouraged me to go, too. These conversations really bolstered my determination to go back.

February 19

Nothing.

February 20

Today I got two letters from San Francisco. One was a rejection from a correspondence opportunity. The other was a positive response resulting from my California letters of January 20. Apparently the chairman of the company I originally wrote forwarded my résumé to his management consultant. The consultant said he may have something for me. I became intrigued and went to Baker Library to look for information about the consultant. Found nothing.

I've felt more anxious lately about this job search, particularly with respect to San Francisco. I've heard nothing encouraging or discouraging from any of the people I've spoken with on campus, and it's been about three weeks since I had my first interview.

This nervousness made me decide to take a more aggressive tack. When I came home, I wrote two follow-up letters to companies I'd interviewed in the past week, and one letter to a San Francisco correspondence opportunity from three weeks ago. At the time I hadn't been that turned on about that opportunity, but now I'm beginning to worry about job offers there.

I'm also concerned about the San Francisco companies that haven't replied, because I hope to go to the area over spring break. I'm worried now that I might have to pay for that trip myself, as plant trip invitations are still uncertain. This is compounded by the fact that my research report is sending me to San Francisco and Los Angeles next Monday for a week. Perhaps I should just stay there, as spring break is only one week after I get back. But I'm anxious about missing two weeks of classes. I haven't spoken in any of them at all this term and can't afford to cut, too.

February 21

We had our CMS meeting at 6 P.M. One of the results of this meeting is that our California trip has been pushed back two days. I was really disappointed because I'd really been aiming for Monday. I can still go, though.

At home after the meeting, my day was made, however. I got a call from public accounting firm #2 inviting me out to San Francisco. Since this was my first firm trip offer, it really took a load off my mind. It was magnified an hour later when I got a call from my ex-girl friend in San Francisco who checked on my plans for spring break. She offered me the use of her car and apartment when I come out. That really made me feel good. I appreciate her friendship, especially in light of the recent hostilities between me and my local girl friend.

February 22

I had two interviews today, one with San Francisco priority #3 and one with public accounting firm #3 (first time for each). The first interview was disappointing. The interviewer and I just didn't hit it off and, besides, I found during the interview that the job involved living in Central or South America, and that turned me off.

The second interview was just the opposite. The interviewer and I really hit it off. He was a casual and interesting fellow. (He got his present job by impressing a partner of the Tokyo office during a conversation in a bar in the Philippines.) He appeared to like me, too, and said he'd send my résumé to San Francisco the next day, as I told him about my upcoming trip out West over spring break.

February 23

Today I called two companies in San Francisco and set up appointments for the spring break visit. Both of them were firms that had responded to my letters of November and January. It looks like I'll have about seven interviews when I go out.

At the placement office today the notice went up for my #2 San Francisco priority. It was a week and a half late. I was really glad to see it.

The placement office has been fairly dead. No notices have gone up, because spring break is three weeks away. I continued to drop by every day to check the correspondence opportunities, however.

I still haven't heard from any of the other companies I've interviewed, other than public accounting firm #2. I'm particularly anxious to hear from the Chicago company.

February 24

Some of my questions were answered today. I got two job rejections as the result of interviews, one from priority #1 in San Francisco and one from the second New York company. Neither was a surprise, although I am disappointed that the interview with the San Francisco firm didn't go well. The letter from the New York company was sort of funny because it was curt and uptight just like the interviewer had been (although it was written by a different person). I showed it to my roommates and they got a laugh out of it too.

However, I got a telegram inviting me to visit the Chicago company. This was exciting, as I've been quite interested in them. I was also unsure of my status with them. I'm very encouraged.

Later in the day I got a long distance call from San Francisco priority #2 firm talking about their upcoming visit. I was dismayed to discover that I will miss their visit to campus if I go to California next week for the research report. This, coupled with the need to find time for the Chicago trip, makes me now want to miss the research report trip.

February 25

Our research report team met and changed the California trip to spring break. Since I had a schedule conflict, two new team members were chosen. Strangely enough, I am happy not to be going. Since I'm going for sure over spring break, this trip would have only been a burden.

February 26

I set up a plant trip to Chicago for this Thursday (3 days away). This company is amazingly well prepared. There will be no need for me to send in an expense report, as they sent me a ticket and have arranged for a limousine to meet me at the airport.

At the placement office, a San Francisco company job description that I had been waiting for came in. I signed up for a position as a securities analyst, mainly because the job is in the city. I'm not sure I'm really interested in that type of work, though.

February 27

I called four of the S.F. companies I would like to see over spring break. Two accepted appointments. The conversation with one of them, public accounting firm #1, was disappointing. They were not willing to even split expenses and said they had only a few available positions at that time. In fact, the personnel director flatly told me that they looked toward Stanford for their new hires. However, it's still a visit. Of my other calls, one was lukewarm and said to call again when I got there, and anoher was enthusiastic and will talk to me more about it tomorrow.

February 28

Today was frantic as I continually tried to call Chicago to tell them what flight I was on. They had asked me to do this, as they were to arrange for a limousine to meet me. However, I couldn't get through, so I had to leave a message. Left the apartment in a rush for the airport. When I got into Chicago, the limousine was there and took me to my home. I was relieved to be there. I immediately called some friends in the area and talked for awhile. Then I stayed up until 1 A.M. reading the company material I'd only skimmed before.

March 1

Got awakened at 6 A.M. by a call from my girl friend in Boston. She wished me well on the interviews. I was glad to hear from her, although our relationship has been upsetting and confusing for the past month.

The same limousine picked me up at 8:30 and got me to the plant by 9:00. There I was met by the personnel man who had originally interviewed me at Harvard. He was extremely friendly and relaxed and seemed completely unlike the tense, businesslike man I'd spoken to at school. We chatted about various subjects and finally got around to discussing who I would talk to that day. It was at this point that I realized that I was being interviewed for a job in the treasurer's office. Until today, there had seemed to be a possibility of entering both the controller's office and marketing directly. Consequently, when he asked me if I had any questions before leaving for the first interview, I mentioned my surprise at being considered for this spot. As he had done at Harvard, the personnel man assured me that they were looking for generalists and not specialists and that this was only an entry point. This reassured me, as I'm not sure how much I would enjoy the type of work done in a treasurer's office.

During the day I spoke with the corporate treasurer, financial vice president, executive vice president, and a first-year employee who had gone to HBS. The talks were very informative, but more importantly, I liked the individuals that I spoke with personally. The style and atmosphere of the company appealed to me very much. The people are very competent, but there is still a casual approach to work. People there were friendly, and the tension level seemed low. In addition, since the company is growing so quickly, there seem to be a lot of interesting projects and a lot of appealing positions to rise to.

At the end of the day, I spoke again with the personnel man. He gave me the official company line about getting in touch within two weeks and sooner if they weren't going to make an offer, but then told me that he had heard all good things from the people I'd spoken to. What a relief his final statement was! I left very turned on about the company.

That evening I went out with some old friends from the area. I realized that I was very tense because of the day's experience. I really like the company, but I have a hang-up about returning to Chicago. This conflict was made even worse by my friends' strong encouragement to return. I got sort of depressed thinking about it and got sort of a sick feeling that the potential jobs I will see in California will not match this opportunity.

March 2

My friend took me to the airport this morning. He talked to me again about the virtues of Chicago and how much they'd like to see me come there. I still feel tense about the whole thing.

When I got home there were three letters awaiting me. A shoot-down from New York firm #1 arrived. It was expected and overdue. The other two letters were from S.F. priority #4 and accounting firm #3. Both said they enjoyed the interviews and indicated I would hear from them soon. This is discouraging, as I had hoped both would offer to split expenses on a trip to San Francisco over spring break. I'll have to call them this week and try to rush the decision. This whole interview process goes much slower than I had expected.

March 3–4

I've noticed that I've been very uptight lately. I think it's mostly because of the job situation. I have no interest in doing school work and seem to be thinking either of jobs or dates. Any distraction seems to be enough to keep me from studying. I think this is another source of my tension. Classes are still demanding and I've been behind and haven't even participated in two of them. Although this semester's grades won't mean anything, there remains a certain amount of self-induced pressure to do well and get something out of the classes.

March 5

Today was a hectic day. I was running about constantly. At 7:30 P.M. I went to the meeting arranged by S.F. priority #2. It was to be a two-hour lecture and question and answer period about the company. I was really turned off by it. The first hour was devoted to a technical demonstration of the products, complete with blackboard diagrams and technical terms. They certainly made it clear that they were looking for highly technical people. Furthermore, they surprised everyone by announcing that interviews would commence at 10 P.M. after the meeting ended, and would end at midnight. Interviews, all an hour long, would begin again at 7 A.M. the next morning and go until midnight again. Their attitude about interviews bothered me too, obviously.

In spite of this, I signed up for an appointment. Although I was turned off, I feel that I must make a strong effort at every San Francisco job. I don't want to leave any stone unturned.

March 6

Today I called S.F. priority #4 and asked them about seeing me in San Francisco and paying for part of the trip. Their recent letter said that they wouldn't be making decisions for a couple of weeks. The personnel man hesitated at first and didn't make any commitments over the phone, but called back ten minutes later with an invitation. I now have two sponsors for the big trip.

March 7

I called accounting firm #3 in San Francisco today to try to arrange for a spring break interview. I had called them twice before earlier in the week but had no response. Today they told me that the Oakland office would see me. This looks like the third paying customer. I think this is a reasonable portion for each firm to pay.

In the afternoon I had my interview with the San Francisco company that had put on the educational session the other night. True to character, the interview was conducted in a rush on the way to the airport. As we drove a rental car to the airport, the interviewer quizzed me. He was probing, and I must admit that I like him in sort of a perverse way. I took a cab back from the airport. When asked about my plans for spring break, I told the man that I would be in the Virgin Islands, because I was afraid he'd ask me to stop by if he knew I planned to be in the Bay area. I don't have time to talk to them, as I have filled all my days out there with other interviews. However, this problem may never arise, as I don't expect a plant trip invitation from them.

I'm getting excited about my trip tomorrow. Am also apprehensive about it too. It's now or never for my job plans in San Francisco.

March 8

Rushed to catch a 5 P.M. plane. Missed it. First time I've ever missed a plane. I just had too much to do today. I scheduled a direct flight for an hour later which arrived at about the same time.

My old girl friend met me at the airport. I was sort of nervous about seeing her, as I hadn't seen her in over a year. She looked great, and we really were happy to see each other. We drove right over to my ex-roommate's home where a birthday party for him was in progress. I saw several of my old friends. It really was great. I felt very tense though. I've built up this trip in my mind so much that I couldn't adjust to being here.

Went out dancing later and had a great time. I'm really happy to be back.

March 9

I had an interview today with one of the companies I'd written to. Their needs were vague and undefined. The personnel man said they'd let me know more in April, when their plans were more clear. I liked the interviewer, though, and the potential position, which was in the control area, sounded appealing. I'll be in touch with them.

Since the interview lasted only an hour and a half (a surprise to me), I had a lot of free time, so I took a cable car to the wharf and had a crab cocktail. It was a beautiful, warm, clear day. As I hung on the outside of the car, I was really turned on by the smell of the ocean air and the breeze in my face. I love this city. Everything seems alive and exciting here, there is no hustle and bustle atmosphere here, nothing like Boston driving. I must move back here.

March 10

Today my ex-girl friend and I went skiing at Squaw Valley. Really enjoyed that. When we got back, I found that the interviewer from S.F. priority #2, whom I had told I would be in the Virgin Islands, had called the apartment. I thought I was going to have a heart attack. He somehow had discovered that I lied about going to the Virgin Islands and had found out where I was.

March 11

I called home and found out that S.F. priority #2 had called my Cambridge apartment and was told of my whereabouts by one of the roommates. I could strangle him. I decided to call the fellow back as he requested. We set up an appointment starting this Friday noon, possibly going until late Friday evening. I apologized for not having a full day available, but decided not to mention the Virgin Islands lie.

March 12

I interviewed accounting firm #3 in Oakland today. I spent the morning with the managing partner in his plush office overlooking the bay. He seemed like a nice guy, but seemed somewhat awkward and nervous interviewing me. He's a local oldtimer and seems somewhat limited in his abilities. (I later found out that he may have been nervous since he's never hired or dealt with an MBA before.)

The talking lasted until about 2 P.M., when he gave me his card and asked me to call him back Friday after I'd had other interviews to ask questions and give him my impressions about the different firms. This seemed strange to me.

However, I was more concerned by the fact that I was getting ready to leave and that he'd never mentioned anything about reimbursing me for part of the trip expenses, as they had agreed to do. I asked him about it. He said he'd never heard of the arrangement, but would talk to me about it Friday when I called. All in all, a strange interview.

March 13

Talked with S.F. priority #4 today. I spoke to about eight people, who all explained their area of responsibility to me. Some of the jobs seemed marginally interesting and the flexibility of their program seemed desirable.

I liked the people too. They seemed easy going and appeared to like me, as well. In all, I think that they would do in a pinch. They said I'd hear from them in two weeks. I expect to get an offer from them.

March 14

Today was my day with accounting firm #2. I'm tense about it because I have a terrible cold and am taking all kinds of medicine to suppress it. I'm afraid it will affect my interviews.

As had been true with accounting firm #3, their offices were plush and impressive. I first talked with the personnel man, who was a pleasant and knowledgeable fellow. I was impressed by the fact that they anticipate great growth in their office in the next three years. In fact, they expect to double their size in that time, so they told me they wanted to hire potential managers now. This growth rate really appealed to me.

I was also very impressed with the managers and partners I spoke with. They were all quite young and seemed intelligent and personable. I went to lunch with two staff accountants who were about my age. They seemed OK, but I wasn't as impressed with them as I was with the managers and partners. At the end of the day, I spoke again with the personnel man, who shocked me by offering me a job on the spot. Unfortunately, the salary offer was only $14,000. He seemed embarrassed about this, as I had asked $16,500 on my application, and made all kinds of excuses about why they couldn't offer me more—e.g., cost of living, my lack of experience in accounting, Stanford nearby, etc. However, he did seem very anxious to hire me and said before I left that he would reconsider the offer if I was offered more by another San Francisco accounting firm. My opinion is that they're being cheap because they anticipate hiring 35 people. However, I'm very interested in the company and particularly in this office. This has to be my best prospect, so far.

March 15

I had been dreading this day, as I have two appointments—accounting firm #1 in the morning and a company that I contacted in the afternoon. The first interview was interesting. I didn't feel too comfortable around the people—they seemed stiff and uptight. The personnel man was the exception. He was as loose as a goose. We really liked each other. Although they left things indefinite and said they will call, I believe I will get an offer due to my rapport with the personnel officer. Frankly, though, I didn't think they compared with accounting firm #2.

I had to hustle to get to the second interview and arrived late. However, the personnel man was even later. When we finally saw each other, he was very reserved and seemed to be sizing me up. Finally, he seemed to get enthusiastic when I told him I'd like a line position in the field after some financial staff experience. Apparently that pushed his button. He arranged two interviews with financial officers for an hour later. However, when I met these men, I wasn't too impressed with them and had the impression that finance was not important and, in fact, even looked down upon in the company. Furthermore, the program they had in mind was ill-defined and vague. So, I was turned off, but politely told them that I was interested and would pursue things further at some later date.

I find that I'm becoming weary of all these interviews, and am not worried anymore about getting a good job. Perhaps the offer from public accounting firm #2 took care of that. It doesn't bother me that companies such as the one this afternoon that I aggressively pursued don't seem good at all. There seem to be a lot of good opportunities here. A couple of months ago I wouldn't have believed it.

March 16

This morning I rushed off to my interview with the consultant for one of the firms I had contacted. I was several minutes late but had to wait about an hour to see him. He was an executive search man and a skillful interviewer. I felt that I was inarticulate in the interview, but at the end of the hour he asked me if I wanted to talk to his client (the one I had originally contacted). I was surprised but pleased. The job he described sounded like a high-powered one.

As we left it, I was supposed to call back in the afternoon, and see if he were able to arrange an interview for tomorrow, Saturday, since I was leaving Sunday. This wasn't possible, unfortunately. I told him I would probably return in two or three weeks and could talk to them then.

As the interview ended two hours later than I had anticipated, I drove like a madman for San Francisco priority #2 (the Virgin Islands affair). I was a half-hour late, but ended up waiting another half-hour for an interview. The man I had spoken to on the way to the airport back at HBS took me to lunch and then gave me a plant tour and had me meet a few other people. I got way off schedule, as interviews ran over time. Furthermore, I had to take time out to call the two companies that I'd promised to call, accounting firm #3 and the consultant.

When I called the accounting firm, the Oakland partner asked me why I hadn't seen the San Francisco office as planned. Shocked, I told him I never knew of such a plan. He told me to call San Francisco to try and straighten out the mixup. I called them and said I would like to see them, but explained that it would have to be in two or three weeks when I returned, as I was leaving Sunday. They seemed to understand. The personnel man even agreed to pay their portion of my expenses after kidding me about it.

After I hung up, I thought about how badly they had screwed up my interview. They missed connections on my schedule and on my trip reimbursement. At least the reimbursement misunderstanding is straightened out. However, I'm not sure I'll see them again when I come back.

As the result of these phone calls, I missed one interview altogether, and arrived at the last man's office at 5:30 for a 4:30 interview. The fellow was a young guy out of the Stanford Business School for four years, about my age. He was very bright and intense, though personable. He took me directly to his home nearby, and he and his wife took me out to dinner at a really fine French restaurant. Although he quizzed me occasionally, the event was mostly social. The Stanford guy was very noncommittal about my status, so I don't know where I stand. The interview day at their plant was certainly a fiasco, though. I can't see how they could give me an offer. I must say that I'm not too interested in them anyway, although it would be an ego blow to be shot down by a peer.

At 10:30 I left for my friend's place. I felt relieved as I drove back. My interviews here are over. The pace has been hectic, the questions repetitive. (I've spoken with eight companies.) It's tiring to be constantly on your toes trying to impress someone. If I was able to, I'd stay on another week and interview the client of the consultant I spoke with and some of the other companies I wasn't able to see at all. However, I have a midterm Monday and am tired of all this interviewing anyway. I only hope that I can return in a couple of weeks to finish up this interviewing without having to pay for the travel myself.

March 17

I got up early today to see my ex-girl friend. We were planning to spend my last day together. Had a great time. Went into the Santa Cruz mountains for lunch, drove along the coastline and shopped in Sausalito and San Francisco. In the evening, we ate at the Blue Fox restaurant. It really has been great to see her. She's been so nice, lending me her car for the week, cooking for me, and being a great companion. I really enjoyed myself out here.

March 18

Got up early to catch an 8:30 flight to Boston. I was a little depressed to be leaving when I got on the plane, but that passed quickly. In general, I am as high as a kite. I feel very encouraged by my ten days here. I'm more relaxed and happy than I've been in a long time. In fact, my experience out here was such an enjoyable one that I realized that I've been uptight most of the time during my two years at HBS. I really used to be relaxed all of the time.

Seeing my old girl friend was also great for my ego, especially after my experiences with my girl friend in Boston. Finally, I have an offer from the company I like best. I feel great!

When I got to Boston, the scene seemed fitting. It was cold and dark and we were delayed waiting for our baggage. As I was jostled in the MTA, I thought about how much more relaxed people were in San Francisco. I must be psyching myself up to move back.

I couldn't stop talking about the trip when I got back to the apartment. My roommates hadn't gone anywhere over spring break, so they were envious. Studying for my midterm never materialized.

March 19

In the afternoon I spoke with another Bay area firm about financial jobs. I really wasn't too interested, but I hope to get another trip out West to complete all my interviewing. The fellow I spoke with was encouraging.

I felt really loose going into this interview. I'm relaxed and confident from my trip and am not nervous at all anymore. I contrast my feelings now with early in the interview season when I felt I had to get an offer in hand right away. Although I've never been really tense during an interview, every interview seemed critical. Now, some of those that seemed critical no longer seem even desirable.

Also, in contrast to my generally relaxed state of mind, I feel fairly ambitious about school this week. This is probably due to guilt feelings. I've spoken only three times all semester. It is important that I participate pretty soon, particularly if I'm going to miss some class by taking another trip West.

March 20

With my renewed vigor, I went into both classes well prepared for a change (but still didn't speak!). In the afternoon, I had my last on-campus interview of the year. It was for management consulting in Los Angeles. I really liked the interviewer. He was loose as a goose, too, so we got along pretty well. He was very positive about me and indicated an invitation to visit them might be forthcoming.

In the evening, I rushed in expense reports from the recent trip. It really caused a cash flow problem.

March 21

Today I relieved a certain burden from my mind by speaking in New Ventures for the first time. I still have that familiar feeling that I should cover myself in all classes.

The placement office is dead these days, although I continue to stop by daily, partly by habit and partly to check for new correspondence opportunities.

When I got home, I found that I had received a shoot-down letter from San Francisco priority #3, whom I had interviewed about a month ago. At that time they had seemed like a crucial opportunity, but I had forgotten about them completely as these new opportunities have come up. It's amazing how things change.

March 22

Not much happened today. These days I eagerly await the mail, hoping I'll hear something from one of the companies I'm interested in. A part of the excitement, too, is just getting a lot of mail. It's great having so much attention. I'll be sorry when this is all over.

My mood changed drastically in the afternoon when I went to the pub and talked with a friend who has decided he's going to work for an accounting firm. I was angered to find out that none of the firms pay moving expenses for new employees. I was counting on this, as I will have a cash problem in June. It really annoys me and seems really cheap. It shook my interest in accounting firms. I'm willing to pay a salary penalty, but I think this moving expense thing shows something about their attitude. Industrial firms are more generous. These accounting firms are a bit backwards with respect to new employees.

March 23

Had some great spring weather today. It made it hard to work, especially since we have no class on Fridays. Worked on my research report, however. As are most people, we're behind the eight ball with that report. We have a lot to do.

No word from my companies. However, I got an interesting letter from a manufacturer in Ohio. It was the second packet they had sent me, the first being about two months ago. They reminded me that I hadn't seen them and were giving me a second chance, as they were returning to campus for summer job interviews! They must not have had a good yield the first time. I was very flattered though.

This evening I went to a great party and met some interesting new faces. Seems like when it rains it pours. Everything is going right.

March 24

Another beautiful warm day. It puts everyone in a good mood. My roommates are really bubbly. I did some running and spent a lot of time outside.

In the afternoon I was called by accounting firm #1 in San Francisco. They offered me a job as the result of my visit. Although their salary was a guaranteed, set amount (no overtime as with others), it was still low. I'm not really that keen on this firm, but it's nice to get an offer. Besides they offered to split expenses for my trip. I appreciate this, although I think they were kind of cheap for not offering in advance.

March 25

Today I wrote letters to all the companies I visited in San Francisco. I also filled in two application forms for companies out there I have recently contacted (one via an on-campus interview). This job search takes a lot of time, especially if done aggressively.

In the evening, I was called up by the head of the Los Angeles firm I had interviewed last week. He asked me to meet him at the Fenway, Cambridge this Wednesday. I was disappointed, as I had hoped they would invite me to Los Angeles. However, this may still be in the cards.

March 26–27

Nothing much happened. The wait continues.

March 28

After class ended at 1 o'clock, I rushed over to the Fenway, Cambridge for my second interview with the L.A. firm. At the end of the hour interview, I was startled when told that I would receive an offer in the mail in two days. In addition, they were willing to pay my way to L.A. to visit the company. This put me in a super mood. This offer represents my first definite alternative from accounting and gives me some leverage that I didn't really have before. I will really consider this offer. Just being wanted again has really turned me on.

In the afternoon I had my last on-campus interview with a San Francisco firm. It went pretty well but I won't be able to take the second step for awhile. I'm not really that interested anyway.

March 29

Today I received a packet from accounting firm #2. In it was a description of a course they want me to take this summer if I work for them. We had discussed the content of the course during my visit there, trying to decide whether or not I needed to take it. Their personnel man thought I should, but I don't really want to. The reason is that the course is given only once, starting in mid-June. I had wanted to travel in Europe for a month or so before beginning work. Unfortunately, this course will not allow that. As I read the description, I was depressed to realize that I really need to take it. This really frustrates me. I really like this job the best, but I am faced with paying the price in salary and benefits, and now, in taking vacation. I'm wondering where to draw the line. I've been trading off pleasurable opportunities for career enhancement all my life, and I want to stop it. I look at public accounting as a good learning experience and a stepping stone. I just don't know what to do.

March 30

I've been thinking about who to see on my final trip to the West Coast in the coming weeks. There are a lot of people I could see. However, I sometimes wonder if I'm just making sure I leave no stone unturned, rather than acting out of interest. I doubt if the few jobs I could look into in San Francisco could interest me more than the accounting jobs. And, after all, I really don't have time to spend days interviewing people if the jobs don't have real potential. However, new opportunities are hard to overlook. It's simply hard to say no. The feeling that the next interview might uncover the "dream job" seems to be my attitude.

I'm still disturbed about this summer course I'm faced with taking with accounting firm #2. In the afternoon I spoke with my financial accounting professor about my doubts. He boosted my spirits a bit by giving me a pep talk about the great experience I'd be getting and how salary, etc., didn't matter. In addition, he told me he strongly felt that accounting firm #2 was the best. I felt better after our talk.

March 31

Today I received a call from the Chicago company I had visited about a month ago. The suspense level with them was high. I had intended to call them in a day or so if I hadn't heard from them. They offered me a job as a profit planner for $18,000. I like them a lot, but I'm not as turned on as I was when I visited them. A lot of good opportunities have unfolded since then.

April 2

Today the mail brought an offer from the L.A. firm that I spoke with last week. It was very flattering and offered a good salary. There was a certain amount of tension in the car going to school, as one of my roommates had just been shot down by them.

In the same mail, I got a rejection letter from S.F. priority #2. Although I hadn't been too excited by them, I nevertheless disliked being rejected. The letter was from the young Stanford fellow who took me to dinner. That was kind of an ego blow.

April 3

I stopped by the placement office, but the place is really dead. I also spent some time chatting with other students who are considering going with public accounting firms. I'm psyching myself up for the offer I have with public accounting firm #2. I still have a lot of questions to ask them about policies, salary, benefits, etc. I've been putting off calling them about these things. They're subjects I'd prefer to avoid.

April 4

I was called in the afternoon by the fellow I'd be working for in the Chicago company. We just chatted about the job I'd start out in. It really sounds sort of boring—one of those paper-generating staff positions.

April 5

I had a very upsetting experience this evening. I ran into another second year student who I've known for years and dislike immensely, and found out that he was thinking of working for accounting firm #2. Two weeks ago he had asked me about my plans, and since he professed no interest in accounting or finance, I told him all the virtues of that job. It turned out that he had a job offer from their New York office and now intends to transfer to San Francisco after a year. His interest is based on what I told him I hoped to do, and he concluded he wants to do the same thing. The idea of having to see this guy all the same really bothers me, and it unfuriates me that he weaseled this information out of me. I'm really considering calling the San Francisco office and telling them the situation. If he's going to be there, I'm not sure I want to go.

April 6

I called the L.A. firm that recently offered me a job to arrange for a plant trip during report writing week. The president was very enhusiastic and friendly, but asked me before I hung up what the chance was of me accepting their job offer. I was caught off guard by this question, but babbled that the chances were good, although I was talking with other companies. I feel kind of guilty about making the trip now, as I may have overstated the certainty of my acceptance. I'm really just looking.

April 7

Today I received a rejection letter from S.F. priority #4. This was a surprise, as I had felt that the interviews there had gone well. In fact, this is the first situation I've had during this entire process where I haven't correctly anticipated the results. However, my other offers in the area have overshadowed this anyway.

April 8

I spent the day in Newport, R.I., today visiting my brother. It was really a relief to get away. Constantly thinking about jobs and the Business School can get very tiresome.

April 9

Today I was utterly unprepared for class and was called on to start Urban Land. My response established an all-time personal low. This put me in sort of a bad mood. I was further annoyed by having to walk over to the Fenway, Cambridge at 4 P.M., for what seemed like the tenth time, to speak with the personnel man from the Chicago firm. However, when I arrived the recruiter bought me a couple of beers and we chatted about the position I was offered. I enjoyed it.

When I got home I called up California to arrange to see the firm I had been in contact with briefly during my spring break visit. I will journey up to San Francisco to see them and accounting firm #3 after my visit in L.A.

April 10

Today I did a thing I've been dreading doing for a long time. I called up accounting firm #2 to talk about benefits, salary, and the summer school class they want to send me to. My strategy was to get them to think I was close to accepting their offer and then ask them about time off before reporting (so I can go to Europe), and a salary increase. I had thought over my exact questions (and wording) and order of asking them for the past two weeks. Naturally, I was nervous about the results, since I would really like to work for them. During the conversation, the personnel man said it was OK to take time off before reporting, but declined to consider raising my salary offer. (My offer is $500 below some others I'd heard of in the area, and he said to tell him of this if it occurred.)

Therefore, the conversation was only marginally successful. However, a half hour after I hung up, he called back and raised my offer by $500. I was ecstatic. He paused and hemmed and hawed around, hoping I'd accept on the spot. However, I repeated to him that I'd be deciding in two weeks. He told me he'd call on the 22nd, which is less than two weeks. Not too subtle a hint. The pressure is on.

April 11

People are continually asking you who you're going to work for. Until now, I've said I don't know. However, I'm now saying that I'll *probably* work for accounting firm #2. I guess I've pretty much decided that I will work for them, but am holding off to see if a miracle occurs during my trip West next week.

April 12

Had my appointment confirmed in San Francisco with the company I had contacted in the spring. My trip is only next week.

April 13

I can't decide whether to call accounting firm #3 in San Francisco to set up an appointment when

I go next week. I told them I'd see them, since my previous meeting was only with the Oakland office. However, I wasn't too impressed by that office and wonder if I'm wasting my time. I'm influenced because several HBS friends are really turned on by accounting firm #3 in San Francisco. I have this dilemma. Will I be missing out if I don't talk to them versus would I really ever work for them anyway based on my experience to date?

April 14–15

Picked up tickets and pressed suit for trip. I'm hustling around working on my research report to justify not being around during report writing week. Luckily our project is not due at the end of the week.

April 16

I left for L.A. this afternoon for my final trip. The day was hectic. I got up at 7 A.M. and worked on my research frantically until 2 P.M. By then I had finished my part so the other fellows could work without me. Then I madly packed and rushed to the airport. I'll be glad when this all ends. On the plane I was still weighing whether I should talk to accounting firm #3 in San Francisco. I just can't decide.

April 17

I was lodged last night in a really luxurious motel. It had a fabulous view and was very impressive. I got up at 6:00 A.M. to meet the president of the company for breakfast at 7:00. However, he called up at 6:30 and said he'd be there at 7:45. Typical. It's really a hang loose company.

I spent the day touring several jobs of theirs with the president. It seemed pretty interesting, although more technically oriented than I would prefer. On the other hand, I really liked the people in the company personally. I was also favorably impressed by the location. The recent HBS grad I had interviewed with at school took me to dinner and gave me a semi-hard sell. Later he dropped me off at the airport. I had a really enjoyable day.

Ironically, it bothers me because it further complicates the job choice I must make soon.

I arrived in San Francisco at 9:30. My old girl friend picked me up and we went out dancing again. Had a great time again. I really am looking forward to coming out here.

April 18

I had scheduled no interviews today so I slept late. Unfortunately it was very windy so I couldn't lie by the pool as I had planned. Thwarted, I decided to spend part of the afternoon renewing my California driver's license. Then, having nothing to do, I finally decided to call accounting firm #3 at about 4:00. I got the secretary of the personnel man, who said he had stepped out of the office. She told me that he would call back before he left for the day. He never called. This really annoyed me and I decided to forget about them. It was really rude and typical of my experience with them.

April 19

Drove in a rush to the city this morning for an appointment with the company I'd wanted to speak to last time. Their office was unbelievably plush—oriental rugs and carved wooden doors. I was also quite impressed with the people I interviewed. However, they only had me speak to three people for a total of 1½ hours. This was disappointing. They must not be too serious about hiring anyone.

Since I finished early, I decided to call accounting firm #3 again, although I had sworn I wouldn't. I was finally able to get hold of the personnel man. He said he couldn't meet that afternoon because of meetings and that tomorrow, my last day in San Francisco, was only a half-day for them. He sounded discouraging, but I said I'd come in the next morning for a half-day.

I must still have this "mustn't leave any stone unturned" philosophy. There must be something to this firm, since at least one sharp fellow at HBS is going to work for them. On the basis of my experience with them, though, I'm crazy to pursue it. In any event, I don't have any other plans for tomorrow, so it can't hurt to see them.

I spent the rest of the day visiting friends. The pace of this visit is slower and more relaxed than the last one.

April 20

I showed up at the accounting firm at 9:30. Typically, I had a half hour wait. The personnel guy that I've had so much trouble with brought me to his office at 10:00. He's sort of a crass and arrogant fellow and I didn't enjoy talking to him. To my amazement, he pulled out a letter from the Oakland office, whom I'd spoken with during the last trip, rejecting me. It apparently had been sent after I left for this trip. However, he said the San Francisco office made its own decisions.

He then sent me on my first interview. This lasted about an hour, and I really liked the guy I spoke with. Then he and another fellow took me to lunch. The second fellow, an HBS grad of several years ago, was also a really good guy and very impressive. I spoke with two other people that day and had a similar impression of each. It's a very hang loose group and a friendly atmosphere. Only the personnel man seems like a jerk.

I ended up leaving at 3:00. At the wrap-up interview, I was told I would hear in early May! I had expected that I might get an offer on the spot. Somewhat annoyed, I objected and explained that I had a good deal of pressure to decide by Monday, April 23. He objected at first, but then agreed he would let me know on Monday.

I was so excited by the interview that I drove to accounting firm #2 to talk with them some more about their offer. I wanted to ask them some questions, as my certainty about working for them has been shaken. However, I couldn't remember exactly where their office was and by the time I did, it was too late to see them.

I must say that I am still very upset about the prospect of having the HBS grad that I dislike working at accounting firm #2. Therefore, I feel excited about firm #3, but also frustrated about having the job choice complicated.

April 21

I flew back to Boston this morning. This trip was more enjoyable than the last one. The pace was slower, and I am particularly happy to have seen accounting firm #3 after so much uncertainty. They seemed quite appealing.

When I arrived at my apartment, I gave my research report chairman a call. I was relieved to find that the report was going well and that they hadn't been working all that hard. I had been a little concerned that they would be unhappy about my skipping out during report writing week.

April 22

When I arrived home yesterday, I had received a message that the Chicago firm had called. The personnel man's message was "just tell him I called." In addition, a partner from accounting firm #2 had called. They already are expecting an answer tomorrow and he left a message that he'd call back on the 23rd. So, the pressure is on.

I decided to write letters to accounting firm #1 and the Chicago manufacturer and the L.A. firm rejecting their job offers. I spent a lot of time on them, particularly on the Chicago manufacturer, as I may want to work for them someday. I made copies of the letters for future reference.

I called a number of classmates and talked about accounting firms #2 and #3. I'm trying to get some perspective on the two. I learned a little, but both still look very good to me.

I also talked specifically about the problem of this fellow I dislike working for #2. Most of the people I talked to were surprised that I was so concerned about it. I realize that I'm making too big a deal out of it, but it is a mind-blowing thought. However, I'm beginning to disregard it as a criterion for making a choice.

I also called home and spoke with my parents about the choices. My Dad, who was a personnel man in his company, suggested I make a list of the pros and cons of each job. This seemed to be a good idea, as there seem to be a lot of areas to consider in making a choice. However, I've been sorting things out in my mind. I think one has to choose as much by feeling as by a rational "pros and cons" approach.

April 23

Today I continued to talk to students who are familiar with accounting firms #2 and #3. I'm beginning to feel more positive about #3, although their "loose" approach to everything worries me a bit. It might be excessive.

At 6:00 I called up accounting firm #3 as we had planned. The personnel man told me that I had been liked a lot, but they couldn't give me an offer because they'd had more acceptances on outstanding offers than expected. This was extremely disappointing to me. I really thought I'd get an offer from them.

However, it certainly simplifies my choice. When accounting firm #2 called an hour later, I accepted.

Although I feel bad about not getting an offer from #3, I'm quite happy to have this job business over with. It is fun and an ego trip for a while, but it also is a lot of work, time, and strain.

April 24

Today I spoke with another fellow who had the same experience with accounting firm #3. They had wanted to hire him but couldn't because of having had too many acceptances. This made me feel better, as I had been suspicious that I'd simply been shot down.

I spoke with accounting firm #2 again today. We arranged for my summer school course in accounting. In addition, we agreed that I would not start work until September 17. This will give me about two months off after the end of summer school to travel as I had wanted to. I'm happy about this.

At this point, I feel pleased but not excited about my job choice. I feel that I've done the right thing. I'm going to enjoy this summer and am looking forward to going to work.

April 25–May 2

As people continue to ask me about my job plans, I am becoming more enthusiastic about them myself. While many of my peers consider accounting the ultimate bore (to my frustration), others recognize the same advantages I see. In addition, everyone is envious of my being in San Francisco.

At this point, thinking about the job makes me a little apprehensive, but I'm fairly confident I've made the right move. I think I recognize the bad points as well as the good and feel that I have the total picture in perspective.

Looking back on the last few months I have a number of general observations. First of all, my general job objective did not hurt me at all. A general objective will hurt only in certain professions, such as investment banking, where the recruiters expect you to be interested in only their profession. Banks, consultants, accountants, and most manufacturing firms don't flinch at general objectives.

Secondly, I realized during interviewing just how much some companies value HBS graduates over all others. Whether justified or not, the mystique really seems to exist.

Thirdly, I was interested to note my own tendency to rationalize the experiences that went bad. However, I do feel that bad interviews are usually seen that way by both parties. (I had only one big surprise—S.F. priority #4.) In any event, I think it's not a bad thing to do. Remaining confident and loose is one of the most important things to do during the interview process.

Finally, I compare my job search with that of my two business school roommates. They both sat back, sent no letters and waited for companies to come to them. Their response was poor, and they spent some nervous weeks in April before finally getting jobs. In fact, one roommate panicked and arranged an interview with the placement director, who suggested he write letters expressing continued interest to those companies that had recently rejected him. He finally ended up getting a job with a firm that had earlier rejected him, largely as the result of the interest expressed in his letter.

The Life Themes of Henry Rock

1. Economic considerations influence decisions heavily.
2. Interested in quantitative and technical things.
3. Seeks new experience.
4. Social life and family are important.
5. Monetary rewards are a major motivation.
6. Prefers informal, small work environments.
7. Political considerations influence him strongly.
8. Seeks power.
9. Seeks status recognition—both from self and from others.
10. Resents people who underestimate his abilities.
11. Takes pride in achievement.
12. Works well with others.
13. But can be critical of others.
14. Is not particularly creative or esthetically inclined.
15. But desires to do things with a certain "flair."
16. Likes competition and athletics.
17. Works hard (and long hours).
18. Has a continuing interest in business.

24

Focusing a Job Campaign

Most people find themselves in the job market, by either choice or necessity, a number of times in their careers. At such times, skills in the various aspects of job hunting can play a leading role in career management. In this and the next four chapters, we focus on job hunting and the more effective ways people have found to engage in it.

The Importance of Focus

Considerable evidence suggests that one of the primary reasons some people are much more successful at job hunting than others is that they approach the job market with a clearly defined and reasonably narrow focus.[1] That is, they look not for "opportunities," but for a reasonably specific type of job and career opportunity. Instead of looking for "something exciting" or "a good-paying job," for example, they look for "an entry-level position in a large retailing organization with prospects for promotion to a general management position within seven years" or "a general management consulting job within a moderate to large established firm in the United States."

With a moment's reflection, it is not difficult to understand why a focused approach to job hunting is important. There are over 100 different identifiable major "industries" in the United States (see Exhibit 24–1 for a partial listing.)[2] Each has a large number of different kinds of career opportunities and jobs within it. Indeed, one government publication covering all industries lists over 20,000 different types of jobs.[3] And that listing, of course, does not take into account that two jobs with the same title can differ significantly in two different organizations. In the United States alone there are well over 100,000 different organizations that regularly hire people. Operationally this means the number of career and job opportunities that exist at any single point in time, even in a depressed economy, is very large—so large, in fact, that no job hunter could ever hope to pursue more than a mere fraction of the total opportunities. There just aren't enough hours in the day.

A little bit of arithmetic will help clarify this very important point. Let's assume for a moment that you wish to get a job within the next four months. Let's further assume that you can spend, on average, four hours per day, six days a week, engaged in job hunt-

[1]For example, in a survey of a sample of the 1974 MBA class at Harvard, we found that those people who reported the highest level of job satisfaction seven months after graduation interviewed fewer employers on campus, wrote fewer unsolicited letters, and pursued a smaller number of different types of organizations while job hunting.

[2]For a more detailed listing, see the *Standard Industrial Classification Manual,* U.S. Office of Management and Budget (Washington, D.C.: U.S. Government Printing Office, 1972).

[3]*Dictionary of Occupational Titles,* Vol. I: *Definitions of Titles,* U.S. Department of Labor (Washington, D.C.: U.S. Government Printing Office, 1965).

Exhibit 24–1

A Partial Listing of Industries

Advertising	Legal service
Aerospace (airframes, general aircraft, and parts)	Metals and mining (nonferrous metals, iron ore, etc.)
Airlines	Natural resources fuel (crude, oil, coal)
Appliances	Nonbank financial (brokers, investment bankers, etc.)
Auditing and consulting	Office equipment and computers
Automotive (autos, trucks, equipment, and parts)	Oil service and supply
Banks and bank holding companies	Paper
Beverages (brewers, distillers, soft drinks)	Personal care products (cosmetics, soap, etc.)
Building materials (cement, wood, paint, heating and plumbing, roofing, etc.)	Publishing (periodicals, books, magazines)
Chemicals	Radio and TV broadcasting
Conglomerates	Railroads
Containers	Real estate and housing
Drugs (and hospital supplies)	Retailing—food
Education	Retailing—nonfood (department, discount, mail order, variety, specialty stores)
Electrical and electronic	Savings and loan
Food processing (baked goods, canned and packaged foods, dairy products, meat, etc.)	Service industries (leasing, vending machines, wholesaling, etc.)
Food and lodging	Specialty machinery (farm, construction, materials, handling).
General machinery (machine tools, industrial machinery, metal fabricators, etc)	Steel
Government	Textiles and apparel
Health and medical services	Tire and rubber
Instruments (controls, measuring devices, photo and optical)	Tobacco
Insurance	Trucking
Leisure-time industries	Utilities (telephone, electric, gas)

ing activities. This adds up to a total of twenty-four hours per week, and about 400 hours over the four-month period. To identify a specific job opportunity, to go through a set of employment interviews, and to get to the point where you might get a job offer will require, at a bare minimum, about ten hours of your time. It will usually require considerably more than that. Therefore, at the very most, you can actively pursue about forty opportunities and stay within your budgeted four hundred hours.

Now, if we restrict ourselves to the United States, at any point in time the 100,000 or so organizations that actively hire people will probably have well over a million different job openings (possibly many more). If we take the conservative figure of one million, that means that you will have at most time to pursue about 40 out of one million, or one out of 25,000 job opportunities. Without a clear focus to help identify which one of 25,000 job opportunities to pursue, it is inevitable that a job hunter will waste a great deal of time and energy, and experience considerable frustration. Job hunting without a clear focus is not unlike trying to hit a target the size of a quarter from fifty yards, using a shotgun, while blindfolded.

Without clear criteria to use in screening possibilities, students often find the process of selecting companies to interview on campus frustrating and time-consuming. In their efforts to leave "no rock unturned," they waste time and experience anxiety trying to choose whom to interview, then waste still more time going through two or three times as many interviews as their friends who have a focused job campaign. It is not unusual for job hunters who have a focused campaign to send out twenty letters to a carefully chosen group of potential employers and to receive in return invitations from ten of them to have an interview. People with an unfocused job campaign sometimes "shotgun" out 100 or 200 standardized letters to a poorly screened group of potential employers and receive in return no favorable replies at all.

Exhibit 24–2

The Process of Creating a Focus for a Job Campaign Based on a Self-Assessment

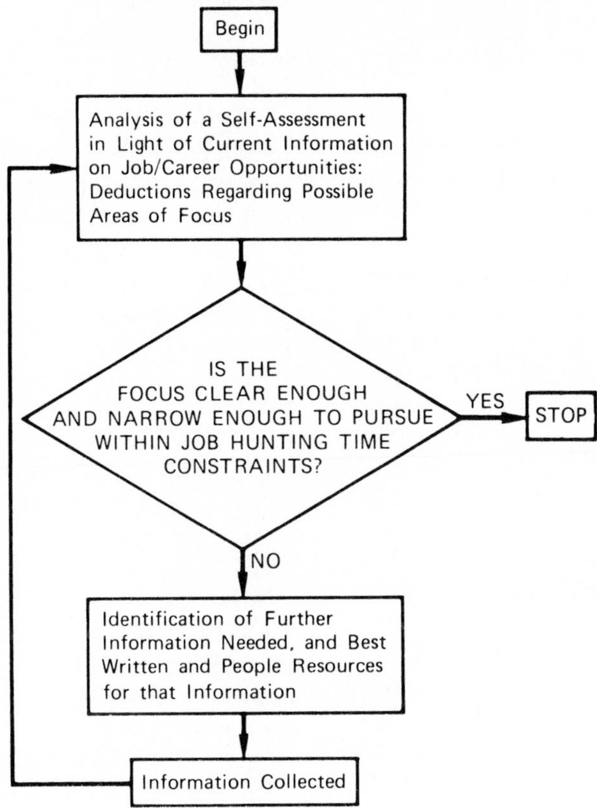

We've seen people waste hours aimlessly reading help wanted ads or talking to employment agencies because they didn't have a clear idea of what they were looking for. People who tell their friends and acquaintances they are looking for a job are more likely to get useful job leads in return if they specify in some detail exactly what they want.[4] By giving reasonably clear and tight screening criteria to professional friends and acquaintances, for example, you not only increase the chances that they will indeed "keep their eyes open" for you, but you also save yourself the time and effort of following up inappropriate leads that might otherwise be passed on to you.

In job hunting, knowing in advance what you want significantly increases the chances that you will get what you want and significantly reduces the costs associated with the process itself.

[4]Imagine yourself in the position of friend or acquaintance. How would you react if someone said he or she was in the market for a new apartment or home, but didn't specify what kind? You would probably ask for more information. What would you do if the only reply was, "I want something very nice"?

Creating an Appropriate Focus

The key to creating a useful focus for job hunting is self-knowledge. Without a clear understanding of who you are, you cannot rationally decide what kind of job and career opportunities you should pursue. A good self-assessment can be enormously helpful in this regard. The decision of whether your self-assessment is adequate probably follows the sequence shown in Exhibit 24–2. There will probably be times when you feel you need more information in order to pursue a particular focus. Gathering more is a waste of time.

Given your self-assessment—that is, your list of life themes and their implications, which describe the kind of work that would seem to fit you—the next step in the process is to use the information you have about the various job opportunities in the world to begin to develop a job search focus.

Your background knowledge of business may be extensive enough to permit you to winnow out a lot of jobs, careers, and industries that look inappropriate. One must be careful here, though, since our experience has been that many students have formed inaccurate stereotypes of jobs they have not experienced. Even students who have held very similar jobs sometimes will have very disparate views of those jobs. So we caution you to test your perceptions of job opportunities before you dismiss those jobs as being entirely inappropriate.

By carefully examining your self-assessment in light of what you currently know about job and career opportunities, you can identify a number of areas that look promising and a number that don't. For example, if one implication in a self-assessment paper is "hates to travel more than two days a month except for vacations," and if you have reliable knowledge that almost all management consultants spend twenty to seventy-five percent of their time traveling, then management consulting should be given a very low priority, if not tentatively eliminated. By systematically going through all the implications in a self-assessment in this manner, you can usually identify two or three career areas that seem very promising (banking, financial work in large manufacturing firms, auditing for a CPA firm), and a large number of areas that can be tentatively eliminated (such as all production work, all public and nonprofit work). Of course, the more information you have on what job and career opportunities are like, the more focused the output of this exercise will be.

If you do not have a lot of business experience, you may feel at a loss as to how to begin to develop a focus. Many students have expressed a nagging concern that they feel the "perfect job" is out there somewhere, but, given the realities we have outlined above, they have no hope of researching all the opportunities before making a decision becomes a necessity. First, we say there are several jobs "out there" that any one person might be well suited for, and that with any job–person match there will be some dimensions that don't fit well. So don't be overly concerned about a perfect fit. Second, there are a number of ways of finding out enough about various opportunities to make a preliminary decision whether to pursue an opportunity further.

Sources of Information

There are three basic sources of information on potential jobs and on the organizations in which the jobs are located: published documents, people, and direct observation. Each is different in the information it can supply and the cost of obtaining that information, but all three can be very useful.

Published Documents

Written sources, such as those listed in Exhibit 24–3, can be especially useful in supplying information on an organization's past financial performance, its current demographic characteristics (size, products/services offered, assets, and so on), its industry, and its major actions (bringing out a new product line, bringing in a new president, and so on). Published sources have the advantage of relative ease of access. All major libraries will have most of the sources in Exhibit 24–3. You can look over such information at your convenience, as often as you wish; you only need to allocate enough time to this task. People we have observed who have not been very successful at job hunting almost always seem to underutilize published information sources. Their time and their energy get absorbed elsewhere, in less productive activities.

Most large public libraries and university-associated libraries have considerable information about job and career opportunities. In the appendix to this chapter, we have listed the best library sources we know of for information on topics our students have typically researched.

In addition, we have utilized the research energies of our students to generate job research reports. These short reports consist of a two-page summary of vital information about various jobs. The data consist of a job description, including typical responsibilities, tasks, and routines, likely career paths, compensation patterns, and opportunities for advancement; the names of some companies who hire people in those jobs; and sources of additional information. We have found that teams of from two to four people can generate a wealth of useful information on a particular job in less than three days. At present, we have collected over eighty such job descriptions and are planning to publish in the near future a compilation of the findings to help job hunters develop a focus. A copy of the assignment sheet we use appears in this chapter for your reference (see Exhibit 24–4). You may wish to use it as a guide in developing your own portfolio of opportunities to consider in your job search.

People

People, although often less accessible than books, can be enormously useful sources of information on

Exhibit 24–3

Where to Find Written Information about Companies

A. Company and Industry Directories

Compiled by Henry Wingate,
Head Librarian, Camp Library,
The Darden School, University of Virginia,
March, 1990.

There are many published directories of companies. A few are general lists of larger companies, others are specialized, either by location (country, state, or city) or by industry or trade. Some give as much information as the first three below, others merely give address or industry. These first two directories are probably used most often as a starting point for brief information on larger U.S. companies.

- *Standard & Poor's Register of Corporations, Directors and Executives.* 3 volumes, annual Poor's Register of Corporations, Directors and Executives. Alphabetical list of approximately 55,000 U.S., and Canadian corporations, giving officers, products (if manufacturer), standard industrial classification (SIC), sales range, and number of employees. Volume 1 consists of brief information on about 70,000 executives and directors. Volume 3 consists of geographical and SIC indexes.
- *Dun & Bradstreet Million Dollar Directory.* 5 volumes, annual. Lists approximately 160,000 U.S. companies/ $500,000 or over. Gives officers, products (if manufacturer), standard industrial classification, approximate sales, and number of employees. Volume 4 lists companies geographically and Volume 5 by SIC industries.
- *Ward's Business Directory.* 3 volumes. Annual. Lists 92,000 public and private U.S. companies. Ranked by sales within SIC code categories. Gives address, chief executive officer, sales, and number of employees.
- *Marketing Economics Key Plant.* Annual. Lists 40,000 plants in the U.S. Arranged geographically. Gives address and number of employees.
- *Thomas Register of American Manufacturers.* (20 vols., annual). Volumes 1–12 list manufacturers by specific product. Volumes 13 and 14 are alphabetical lists of companies and include address, branch offices, subsidiaries, products, estimated capitalization. Volume 14 also contains a list of leading trade names (yellow sheets). Volumes 15–20 consist of product catalogs of individual companies.

1. Regional and State Manufacturers Directories

Manufacturing firms not listed in the Thomas Register of American Manufacturers may be listed in one of the state directories. For example:

- California Manufacturers Register
- Directory of New England Manufacturers
- Massachusetts Directory of Manufacturers
- MacRae's Industrial Directory for New York State.

2. Directories of Companies in Foreign Countries

- *Dun & Bradstreet Principal International Business*
- *International Directory of Corporate Affiliations*

There are also directories for individual countries and areas, such as:

- *Japan Company Handbook*
- *Dun's Latin America's Top 25,000*

3. Directories for Specific Industries or Trades

Examples:

- American Marketing Association, New York Chapter, *International Directory of Marketing Research Companies and Services*
- *Directory of Management Consultants*
- *Directory of Department Stores*
- *Davison's Textile Blue Book*
- *Franchise Opportunities Handbook*
- *Lockwood's Directory of the Paper and Allied Trades*
- *Money Market Directory.* (A directory of institutional investors and their portfolio managers)
- National Association of Real Estate Investment Trusts, Directory of Members
- *Rand McNally International Bankers Directory*
- *Rubber Red Book*
- *Security Dealers of North America*
- *Securities Industry Yearbook.* (A directory of investment banks and brokerage firms).

(continued)

Exhibit 24–3 *(Continued)*

- *Standard Directory of Advertising Agencies*
- *Venture Capital* (monthly publication)
- *World Aviation Directory*

4. Directories of American Firms with Foreign Subsidiaries

- *Directory of American Firms Operating in Foreign Countries,* 3 volumes
- *International Corporate Affiliations*

5. Guides to Directories

If you cannot find a directory for the industry or geographic area you want in any of the sources listed above, look for a bibliography of directories that may list a trade directory or a directory issue of a trade journal. One of the best bibliographies is:

- *Directories in Print*

B. Financial Information about Companies

The following documents for New York and American Stock Exchange companies also can be very useful:

- Annual reports to stockholders
- 10-K reports to the Securities and Exchange Commission
- Listing statements
- Proxy statements
- Registration statements

C. Articles about Companies

- *ABI/Inform CD/ROM Database.* (Monthly.) A compact disk database which offers abstracts of articles from periodicals about business information, including company information.
- *F & S Index of Corporations & Industries* (Monthly, cumulated annually). Indexes articles on companies and industries that have appeared in selected business and financial publications.
- *F & S International* (Monthly, cumulated annually). An index similar to the one above, for foreign companies.
- *Lotus One Source CD/Corporate Database.* (Monthly.) A compact disk database that covers all United States public companies. Includes information from annual reports and SEC filings as well as the texts of brokerage house research reports and periodical/newspaper articles on individual companies.
- *Newspaper Abstracts CD/ROM Database.* A compact disk database that indexes articles from the Wall Street Journal, the New York Times, the Washington Post, and several other major newspapers in the United States.
- *Wall Street Journal Index* (monthly, with annual cumulation). Each issue has two parts: corporate news and general news. Indexing is based on the final Eastern Edition.
- *Wall Street Transcript* (weekly). A compilation of brokerage house reports on companies and industries. Each issue is indexed, and there is also a periodic cumulated index.

D. Lists of Largest Companies

- *Business Week Top 1000.* Annual. Ranks the top 1000 United States companies by market value of outstanding shares.
- *Forbes Annual Directory.* Each May, Forbes ranks the largest 500 Unites States companies by several criteria: sales, profits, assets, market value, and so on.
- *Fortune 500 Series.* In three separate issues, Fortune magazine lists the Fortune 500 Industrials, the Fortune 500 Service companies and the Fortune 500 International companies. All three lists are arranged in rank order by sales. Includes financial information on each company.

---

specific job and career issues.[5] Our students have found that by using whatever personal contacts they have to set up meetings (often at lunch) with people who actually work in the industries, companies, types of jobs, or geographic areas in which they think they might be interested, they can get a large amount of useful information very quickly. Armed with specific questions created in conjuntion with a self-assessment paper, a person can sometimes learn more in thirty to sixty minutes from a well-informed source than from six hours in a library.

For example, Jerry Jones knows from his self-

[5]We've noticed that some of our students resist this strategy of identifying and using people because they feel they don't know any such people or because they think it would just be too cumbersome to try to find such people and convince them to talk. Once prodded into action, however, virtually all our students have found that: (a) they do know someone who in turn knows the type of person they are looking for; and (b) when asked, people are usually more than willing to talk.

Exhibit 24–4

Career Development Job Research Report

Job Description (Activities, Routines, Life Styles, Key Required Skills):

Compensation (Salary Range, Usual Benefits):

Career Paths (Future Potential, Transferability, Likely Advancement Routes):

Employers (Some Companies Likely to Hire, Sources for Finding Others):

Additional Data:

assessment, among other things, that he does not tend to work well under pressure and that he is very ambitious. In an initial analysis of his self-assessment, he decides he should look more deeply into professional auditing work. So on Tuesday he sets up a lunch with Jim Smith, a partner in a large CPA firm who is also a graduate of Jerry's college. (Jerry got Smith's name from his accounting professor.) Among the questions Jerry asks Smith are the following:

1. Do people in the CPA profession have to work with tight time and/or cost constraints? Or does it vary from firm to firm or job to job?
2. Do you feel much pressure in your job? What about most new employees you have observed—do they feel a lot of pressure?
3. How much does the average employee in your firm make after five, ten, or fifteen years?
4. Is your firm growing? How fast? Is the industry growing? How fast?
5. Out of every twenty people hired each year, how many will probably become partners? How long will that take most people?

Contrast that scenario with this one. Phil Roy has a "gut feel" that he may enjoy being a CPA. He spends his lunch hour on Tuesday asking the people who are sitting at his table in one of the university's cafeterias whether they think being an auditor is a good job. He gets two unqualified yesses, two qualified yesses, three maybes, one noncommital response, two qualified nos, and a piece of paper thrown at him (possibly an unqualified no).

It is very easy, while job hunting, to end up in Phil Roy's position—wasting his own and other people's time in endless dialogues about careers and job opportunities that do not help him focus on a limited number of rational opportunities out of the many possibilities. And the reason it is easy is because most people do not begin job hunting with a good, accurate, up-to-date assessment of themselves.

There are two types of human information sources about potential jobs: current employees of the organizations with the job openings, and others. These others might be former employees, consultants who have worked with the organization, financial analysts who have studied the organization for their own firms, and so on. A job hunter automatically gains access to some of the organization's employees while interviewing. For moderate-sized to large organizations, our students have almost always been able to find a few people who fall into that "other" category. It is a rare case, for example, in which no faculty member has ever had dealings with such an organization and no student has worked for it (if only for a summer).

In brief conversations with informed nonemployees, one can usually get reasonably candid and unbiased information of a type that doesn't tend to appear in print and that is awkward to obtain from the organization's current employees. What kind of problems does the organization have? How does it treat employees? Is it really going to be able to grow as fast as it says? If you previously worked for this organization, did you enjoy it? Why?

Inside sources can supply slightly different types of data. They can give you first-hand information on what it is currently like to work for that organization, what the potential job is really like, what the career path associated with it is really like, and what the people you would be working with are like. And possibly the easiest way to get that information is to ask these people about themselves. How long have you been working here? Why did you join up? What job did you start in? Specifically, what did you do? Whom did you work with? What did you like and dislike about that job? What job did you move to next? When did the move occur? Why did it occur? What did you do in your next job? And so on. People generally enjoy talking about themselves. When describing their own careers and jobs, they also generally give much more accurate and useful information than when they try to generalize about careers or jobs in their organization.

The third means of gathering data about job opportunities is direct observation, which we will come back to in the chapter on company visits.

The Key: Self-Assessment

By systematicaly going back and forth from analyzing one's self-assessment to gathering some more information to reanalyzing the self-assessment, one can create in a practical amount of time a rational focus for a job campaign. Hundreds of students have done just that. And the competitive advantage this has given them over those classmates who behave more like Phil Roy while job hunting is very significant.

The important things to remember here are these:

1. The importance of developing a focus so as to not dilute your job hunting efforts unnecessarily

2. To use your self-assessment as a set of criteria for making a decision on whether or not to pursue a particular opportunity

The latter point is extremely important. It would not make much sense to generate a careful self-assessment and then abandon it in favor of momentary excitement as you generate a job search focus. Consequently, we urge you to *use* your self-assessment by considering each theme and each implication to check the fit with a potential career opportunity. This process will also help you to discard with confidence opportunities that on one dimension may seem attractive, even glamorous, but that are not good fits with you.

This process of focusing is a progressive one. Your breadth of focus probably will be much wider at the beginning of your job search than it will be at the end. As you move through the job search, your focus will gradually narrow until you have accepted a single offer. Exhibit 24–5 represents this narrowing focus and the screens you will use as time goes by.

ASSIGNMENT

Here are Steven Taylor's and Carrie Baugh's life themes and the implications they drew from those themes. Use these to develop a focus for each. One of the major dilemmas here, as it will be with your own focusing, is that you are limited by your knowledge of the opportunities out in the world. For this assignment, that is okay, but you will probably want to find ways of expanding your view of the jobs available through a variety of exploration devices when you begin to develop your own focus. Be prepared to explain why you think Steven or Carrie should investigate further the options you identify. The following questions should help you in preparing for this discussion:

1. What job and career areas seem promising for this person? Why?
2. What areas can be eliminated given their themes and implications? Why?
3. What areas might be promising, although you're not sure because you don't have enough information? What additional information would you like to have?

Exhibit 24–5

The Narrowing Job Search Focus

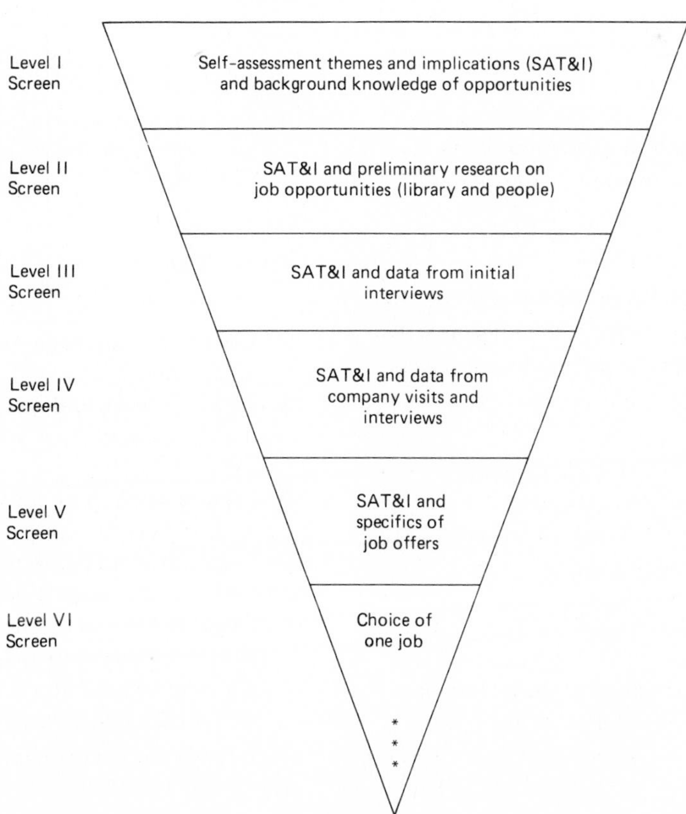

STEVEN TAYLOR'S THEMES LIST

Self-Assessment Themes (plus three)

Steven Taylor is a person who:

1. Requires a balance in both work and personal life.
2. Plays a little fast and loose with traditional customs.
3. Thrives in an unstructured environment.
4. Is demanding of self/a drive for continuous improvement.
5. Has a need for intellectual stimulation.
6. For whom Family is important.
7. Can be pompous, but usually conscious of it.
8. Needs time to spend time in outdoor activities.
9. Values independence and self-sufficiency.
10. Cares more deeply about a smaller number of people.
11. Enjoys external confirmation of success.
12. Is demanding of friends.
13. Prefers an active environment.
14. For whom playing music is missing as a part of my life.
15. Handles crises well.
16. Learns from setbacks.
17. Adapts well.
18. Is restless; I like to get on to the next project.
19. Is willing to take risks to gain greater rewards.

Plus three!

20. Would like to see more of the world and its variety.
21. Senses the emergence of a more contemplative me.
22. Would like to find a place to call home, somewhere I will always come back to.

Steven Taylor's Self-Assessment Theme Implications

Professional Aspect

Cognitive:

1. I like to balance intuitive and analytical approaches to solving problems (T4,T7,T8).
2. I enjoy a constant flow of new and challenging situations (T3,T4,T5,T17,T19,T20).

Routines:

3. Predictability of hours is not critical, but relentlessly long hours will be unacceptable (T1,T3,T6,T8).
4. I like to take a break between major projects (T1,T3,T15).
5. A varying daily routine is exciting (T2,T3,T13, T18,T15).
6. I want to commute less than 45 minutes from home to work, and I prefer not to drive (T6,T18).

Tasks:

7. I enjoy making presentations and being challenged to support the analyses (T3,T4,T5,T7,T9,T17,T19).
8. I like to travel in my work and would like to travel internationally (T3,T5,T9,T13,T17,T20).
9. I thrive on unearthing the difficult questions, the ones nobody likes to answer (T3,T4,T12,T17).
10. I want to be responsible for managing my day (T1,T2,T3,T4,T9).
11. I derive great satisfaction from getting a team to pitch in and push a project to completion (T3,T10,T15,T17).

Organizational Style:

12. If it's not a fun place, then it's not for me (T2,T3, T13,T20).
13. I want to work with people who see excellence as a goal in and of itself and worth the effort (T4,T5, T9,T10,T12).
14. I like to work in an informal environment (T2,T3, T13,T15,T19).
15. I want to work in a firm small enough that I know everyone by name (T1,T9,T10,T19).
16. I want to know if I've done well, and I want to hear about it if I haven't (T4,T11,T16,T19).
17. A little pressure in my work is exciting! (T3,T4,T13, T15,T16,T19).

Rewards:

18. I would like to have an equity interest in my work, or at least a compensation plan that returns some equity (T11,T19).
19. I would like to have enough capital seven years from now to take no salary for a year while starting a business (T2,T19).
20. I will seek at least $50,000 per year as a base salary.

Environment:

21. I would like to work in an office where I can tell whether it is day or night outside (T8).
22. It would be best if I can work with a very organized secretary or support staff (T2,T3,T13,T15,T18, T19).

Social Aspect

23. I would like to live in a place where there is a diverse and international population (T20,T22,T2).
24. I would like to have access to both the ocean and the mountains (T8,T21).
25. I would like to be close enough to theaters and music performance venues to go on a week night (T14,T5, T21,T20).
26. I like having a small group of friends to get together with regularly (T5,T10,T12,T22).

Material Aspect

27. I want to buy a home and a piano to go inside (T22,T14).
28. I would like to begin planning for acquiring a ski house with access to both downhill and cross-country skiing (T6,T8,T22).

Family Aspect

29. I would like to begin a family within the next ten years (T6,T13,T22).
30. I want to give my children the same exposure to natural beauty that I had while growing up (T6,T8, T10,T20,T21).
31. I want my children to have a place they will always think of as home (T6,T22).

Emotional Aspect

32. I need to cultivate a more conscious sensitivity to the effects of my actions on others (T2,T4,T7,T10, T12).
33. I need to come to a better understanding of my own definitions of success, and I need to evaluate myself in those terms and not as much by what others say or do in reaction to my efforts (T2,T9,T11,T17).
34. I need to allow myself greater joy in my successes, lest I exhaust myself THROUGH RELENTLESS SELF-CRITICISM (T4,T18,T19,T21).

CARRIE BAUGH'S LIFE THEMES

A summary code word for each theme is given in capital letters after each theme and then the name of the theme cluster to which each theme belongs.

NO. THEME

1. Family is my source of strength and support. (FAMILY/Personal Identity)
2. Carrie values her independence and family over having lasting friendships. (INDEPENDENCE/Personal Identity)
3. Although independent, Carrie needs contact with people. (CONTACT/People Oriented)
4. Carrie wants to maintain a balanced lifestyle. (BALANCE/Control)
5. Carrie wants to be seen as special and talented. (SPECIAL/Achievement Oriented)
6. Carrie seeks to learn from new situations. (LEARN/Diversity)
7. Carrie enjoys jobs that utilize both people skills and Analytical/Quantitative analyses. (SKILLS/Diversity)

8. Carrie consults those people she trusts and respects, then makes her own decisions. (TRUST/People Oriented)
9. Carrie strives to improve herself. (IMPROVE/Achievement Oriented)
10. Carrie enjoys working in teams. (TEAMS/People Oriented)
11. Carrie is practical. (PRACTICAL/Personal Identity)
12. Carrie sets goals, then works hard to accomplish them. (GOALS/Achievement Oriented)
13. Carrie tends to make unstructured environments more structured. (STRUCTURES/Control)
14. Carrie enjoys competition and thrives on challenges. (COMPETITION/Achievement Oriented)
15. Carrie is results oriented. (RESULTS/Achievement Oriented)
16. Carrie likes to feel in control of her time and actions. (CONTROL/Control)
17. Carrie has a hidden passion for performing. (PERFORMING/Achievement Oriented)
18. Carrie enjoyed living in San Francisco and likes the culture and diversity of a larger city. (URBAN/Diversity)
19. Carrie enjoys helping others. (HELPING/People Oriented)
20. Carrie enjoys participating in sports. (SPORTS/Diversity)
21. Carrie enjoys playing the piano. (PIANO/Diversity)
22. Carrie tries to be tolerant of different types of people. (TOLERANCE/People Oriented)
23. Carrie dislikes long commutes to work. (COMMUTING/Control)
24. Carrie is prideful. (PRIDE/Personal Identity)

Carrie Baugh's Theme Implications

Job Content

1. *I want to further develop both analytical and interpersonal skills at work.* (Balanced, People Oriented, Analytical/Interpersonal, Team Oriented)

   I most enjoy work that includes two components: financial and strategic analyses, and interaction with different groups of people. I am people and team oriented as well as analytical. One of my goals is to balance these different skills in my job.

2. *I want to have responsibility for making decisions and for implementing the results of those decisions.* (Independent, Goal-Setter, Results Oriented, Control)

   Part of being independent and wanting control includes the need to make decisions. In order to meet goals, I tend to focus on action and results.

3. *I want to be responsible for a variety of tasks.* (Competitive, Independent, Diverse)

   I enjoy being able to respond to new and different situations. I find it challenging to make decisions in a variety of different areas.

4. *I want to solve analytical problems that are intellectually challenging.* (Competitive, Analytical/Interpersonal, Results Oriented)

   I enjoy solving challenging problems and working through the implementation of potential action plans. I need to be challenged analytically. This situation makes the administrative tasks that are necessary less boring.

Organizational Style

5. *I want to work in an environment that encourages open discussions among employees.* (People Oriented, Team Oriented, Interactive, Analytical/Interpersonal, Helpful)

   I work best in an environment that supports open discussion of ideas and new solutions to problems. I appreciate the value of making decisions after having consulted knowledgeable people. I also value the opportunity to learn from others within the firm.

6. *I want to be judged on both the quantitative and qualitative results of my work.* (Competitive, Analytical/Interpersonal, Results Oriented, People Oriented)

   I want to be judged on "results" that include important management skills such as coordinating different groups, bringing in business, and cutting costs. Although I believe in the importance of the "bottom line," I also see enormous benefits in smoother cooperation among employees. In the longer term, those employees become more efficient. I would like to be judged on my contributions to both areas.

7. *I want to receive feedback on my work and career progress at least twice a year.* (Competitive, Interactive, Self-Improvement, Results Oriented, Goal-Setter)

   I need to know how I am performing over time, because improving and learning are essential to me. As a result, I need to receive both positive feedback and to be told which specific areas I can develop further. Constructive criticism allows me to focus my energies on improvement.

8. *I want to work in an environment that does not require close supervision.* (Independent, Goal-Setter, Control, Performer)

I work most effectively when I have the freedom to pursue ideas and set goals. Once I understand the problem or what needs to be done, I will follow through and get the work done effectively. Although I don't mind supervision, I am less effective if a supervisor is looking over my shoulder all day long.

Organizational Structure

9. *I want to work with different groups of people in a team environment.* (Team Oriented, Tolerant, People Oriented, Diverse)

   I work most effectively in teams, where sharing ideas, seeing other perspectives, and developing strong plans are important. I don't mind working alone, but really excel with the support of team members. My sports background also made me appreciate the role of teams in getting things accomplished.

10. *I want to work in an organization or division with no more than 300 people.* (Special, Structured, Results Oriented, Performer, Independent)

    In a smaller group, I would have a greater chance to be recognized for my achievements. I want responsibility early in my career and believe smaller groups provide that opportunity.

11. *I want to have a clear understanding of my career path and how long I can expect to be in each position.* (Self-Improvement, Goal-Setter, Structured, Control, Results Oriented)

    I want to be on the "success track" within the firm. As a result, I want to know how I'm doing relative to company expectations. One way I can measure my development is to know the career path I'm on and where I should be at specific points in time. I can then work to achieve my career goals and objectives.

12. *I want a job that leads to significant supervisory responsibility within two years.* (Goal-Setter, Control, Structured, People Oriented, Independent)

    My interpersonal skills will be an asset to me once I begin supervising others. To me, significant responsibility includes having at least three subordinates and responsibility for my group's results. Supervision also allows for control over the implementation of tasks.

Work Environment

13. *I want to have my own desk and space for organizing my work and setting up my own filing systems.* (Structured, Practical, Control, Independent)

    I like to have a place to file away my work-related information. I want to have easy access to the information I need. I almost always structure my work areas efficiently and so others can get what they need quickly. I cannot work at a completely messy desk.

14. *I want a "professional" office environment that is well lit and has comfortable, aesthetically pleasing furniture.* (Structured, Special, Practical)

    The physical office environment tells me a lot about how a company values its employees. A nice office also makes it easier for me to perform well.

15. *I want an environment that utilizes up-to-date technology and advanced financial analysis tools.* (Independent, Practical, Results Oriented, Control)

    Technological advances provide important tools to help an employee work more effectively. I think it is important to use tools that will help me provide the best service I can. Technology improvements also indicate a company's commitment to long-term results.

Routines

16. *I want to spend on average 55 hours per week or less at work.* (Family, Balanced, Control, Independent)

    In order to be happy, I need more than a successful career. I also need a strong, positive family life. I can control this aspect only through explicitly balancing the time commitment I am willing to make at work with family needs.

17. *I want to travel no more than one week per month.* (Family, Balanced, Independent, Control)

    From a practical point of view, since my family is most important to me, I need the freedom to go home at night and enjoy Mark. Travel is an outside variable that I can control up front, by avoiding jobs that require extensive travel.

18. *I want a busy work environment.* (Goal-Setter, Self-Improvement, Competitive, Results Oriented, Diverse)

    I would rather be too busy than not busy enough. One way I challenge myself is to work extra hard during the day so I can get my extensive list of "to do's" completed. I do not enjoy having to sit around during the day.

Reward Systems

19. *I want to be recognized for both team and individual achievements.* (Independent, Team Oriented, Results Oriented, Special, Competitive)

    I think team recognition is critical to accomplishing high-quality work. However, I also stay motivated when I am recognized for my individual efforts as well. I am somewhat competitive and need the recognition.

20. *I want recognition to include verbal acknowledgement of accomplishments as well as financial rewards.* (Special, Prideful, People Oriented, Interactive, Competitive)

Pats on the back do wonders to keep me motivated. The financial rewards are also important but are not enough in and of themselves.

21. *I want my promotions and raises based on merit, not time spent with the firm.* (Results Oriented, Goal-Setter, Performer, Competitive, Special)

I need to be recognized for my results and contributions. If I have new or additional goals to achieve within a job, I enjoy the challenge—but once I know the routines, I want to move on to new challenges.

Personal Lifestyle

22. *I want to live in or near a small- to medium-sized city, with a round-trip commute of an hour or less.* (City Person, Short Commute, Diverse)

I love the cultural diversity and exciting pace of good-sized cities. I can enjoy these activities if I can manage the hours I spend at work and my commute time.

23. *I want to live near tennis courts, golf courses, and a health club.* (Athletic, Balanced, Self-Improvement, Performer)

To maintain an intense lifestyle, I need several forms of exercise. Athletic activities also help me feel healthy and improve my stamina.

24. *I want to spend most weekends with Mark.* (Balanced, Family, Independent, Practical)

Time will always be stretched for both Mark and me. We are both intense and ambitious, yet we value family above work. From a practical point of view, we want to spend our weekends together so we can further develop and enjoy our life together.

25. *I want to live where we could afford to buy a pleasant home.* (Balanced, Family, Practical)

We want to enjoy our surroundings as much as possible. We would love to own a house next year, so we can begin putting down some ties.

Material Needs

26. *I want to earn a salary competitive with my peers.* (Prideful, Results Oriented, Practical, Competitive)

Salary, at least in part, reflects the value a company thinks an employee can add to the firm. Since I do have a lot of pride and want to be viewed as talented, a competitive salary provides one mechanism for me to attain this goal. It will also enable me to fill material wants as well.

Appendix to Chapter 24

Sources of Information on Selected Industries and Career Opportunities

The references listed here represent a selected set of useful information that is readily available to you. Each reference can be located in any major library. Titles are listed first according to industry or profession—"advertising," "health services"—and then by type—Directory, Book, Periodical, and so on. There are, however, four essential reference books, which should be consulted before you go on to the works listed below under a specific industry or field.

1. *Encyclopedia of Associations.* 3 Volumes. (Annual.) Detroit: Gale Research Inc.

   A detailed listing of associations in the United States. Trade associations are a valuable source of information on specific industries. A telephone call to the research department of a trade association will often result in the mailing of a package of industry information, nearly always at no cost.

2. *Predicasts F & S Index.* (Monthly, with quarterly and annual cumulations.) Cleveland: Predicasts Inc.

This reference was prepared by Henry Wingate, Darden Graduate Business School Librarian, University of Virginia.

Published in two separate sections, one devoted to industries and one to specific companies, the *F & S Index* lists articles from magazines, newspapers, and trade journals. Each bound volume covers articles for one year. Looking through the current volumes and the volumes covering the most recent five or six years will provide an extensive list of articles on any industry or company.

3. *Standard & Poor's Industry Surveys.* 2 Volumes. (Quarterly.) New York: Standard & Poor's Corporation.

   These books offer excellent overviews of specific industries. The reports, usually about fifty pages long, are very current and provide detailed analysis of industry trends. Additional sources of information are listed for each industry.

4. *U.S. Industrial Outlook.* (Annual.) Washington, D.C.: U.S. Department of Commerce.

   Similar to the *S & P Industry Surveys* listed above. Each industry chapter is written by an industry expert of the Department of Commerce. The chapters offer excellent industry overviews, with listings of additional reference sources.

ADVERTISING AND CONSUMER MARKETING

Dictionaries and Encyclopedias

1. *Ayer Glossary of Advertising and Related Terms.* Philadelphia: N. W. Ayer & Son, 1972.
2. Baker, Michael J., ed, *Dictionary of Marketing & Advertising.* Nichols Pub. 1985, p. 246.
3. Bennett, Peter D., ed. *Dictionary of Marketing Terms.* Am Mktg., 1989.
4. *Encyclopedia of Advertising,* 2d ed. New York: Fairchild Publications, 1969.
5. Graham, Irvin. *Encyclopedia of Advertising,* 2nd ed. Fairchild, 1969.
6. Shapiro, Irving J., *Dictionary of Marketing Terms.* 4th ed. Totowa, NJ.

Handbooks and Manuals

7. Barton, Roger, ed. *Handbook of Advertising Management.* New York: McGraw-Hill, 1970.
8. Worcester, R. M., and J. Downham, eds. *Consumer Market Research Handbook,* 3rd ed. Elsevier, 1986.
9. Stansfield, Richard H. *The Dartnell Advertising Manager's Handbook,* 3rd ed. Chicago: Dartnell Corp., 1982.

Bibliographies

10. Dickinson, John R., *The Bibliography of Marketing Research Methods,* 2nd ed. Lexington MA: Lexington Books, 1986.
11. Fisk, Raymond P., and Patriya S. Tansuhaj, *Services Marketing: An Annotated Bibliography,* Chicago, Ill.: American Marketing Assn., 1985.
12. "Marketing Abstracts," *Journal of Marketing.* (Quarterly.) Each issue contains an annotated bibliography covering selected articles of interest to marketers. It is arranged in 22 broad subject headings.
13. Robinson, Larry M. and Roy D. Adler, *Marketing Megaworks: The top 150 books and articles.* Foreword by Paul E. Green. New York: Praeger, 1987.

Books

14. Dirksen, Charles J., Arthur Kroeger, and Franco M. Nicosia, *Advertising: Principles and Management Cases.* 6th ed. Homewood, Ill.: R. D. Irwin, 1983.
15. Dunn, S. Watson, and Arnold M. Barban, *Advertising: Its Role in Modern Marketing.* 6th ed. Hinsdale, Ill.: Dryden Press, 1986. (The Dryden Press series in marketing).
16. Hass, Kenneth B. and John Ernest, *Principles of Creative Selling.* 3rd ed. Encino, CA: Glencoe Publishing, 1978.
17. Kotler, Philip, *Marketing Management: Analysis, Planning, Implementation, and Control,* 6th ed. Englewood Cliffs, NJ: Prentice Hall, 1988.
18. Mandell, Maurice I., *Advertising,* 4th ed. Englewood Cliffs, NJ: Prentice Hall, 1984.
19. Zober, Martin, *Principles of Marketing.* Boston: Allyn and Bacon, 1971.

Periodicals

20. *Academy of Marketing Science Journal.* (Monthly.)
21. *Advertising Age.* (Weekly.) This journal publishes several annual surveys of special interest to advertisers: (1) Marketing profiles of leading national advertisers; (2) 100 leading national advertisers; (3) U.S. agency.
22. *Journal of Advertising.* (Quarterly.)
23. *Journal of Advertising Research.* (Bimonthly.)
24. *Journal of Marketing.* (Quarterly.) Features: book reviews, legal developments, and marketing abstracts.
25. *Marketing News.* Bimonthly.

Directories

26. American Marketing Association, New York Chapter. *International Directory of Marketing Research Houses and Services.* (Annual.) Often called the "Green Book."
27. Bradford, Ernest S. *Bradford's Directory of Marketing Research Agencies and Management Consultants in the United States and the World.* (Biennial.) A list and description of reliable market research agencies in the U.S. and abroad.
28. *Commercial Atlas and Marketing Guide.* (Annual.) Skokie, Ill.: Rand McNally & Company. Lists of railroads, airlines colleges, and universities by state. Lists of largest 50 corporations: advertising agencies, commercial banks, life insurance companies, retailing companies, transportation, utilities, and industrial corporations.
29. Goldstrucker, Jac L., ed., *Marketing Information: A Professional Reference Guide,* Atlanta, Ga.: Georgia State University. Business Pub. Division, 1982.
30. *Marketing Economics Key Plants.* (Annual.) New York: Marketing Economics Institute. Directory of 40,000 plants with 100 or more employees. Useful as a statistical research tool, a prospect list, and a geographic guide to sales territories.
31. *Standard Directory of Advertising Agencies.* (Annual.) Skokie, Ill.: National Register Publishing Co. Covers 4,400 agency establishments, both national (4,000) and foreign (400). Issued three times a year, in February, June, and October.
32. *Standard Directory of Advertisers.* (Annual.) Directory of companies that advertise nationally, arranged by industry groupings, with alphabetical index. Gives officers, products, agency, advertising appropriations, media used, etc. Includes a "Trademark Index."
33. *Who's Who in Advertising,* New York: Marquis, 1989. Index to company names. Limited to United States and Canada.

Career Information and Opportunities

34. Catalyst. *Advertising Career Opportunities.* Prepared by Catalyst, the national nonprofit organization dedicated to expanding employment opportunities for college-educated women who wish to combine career and family responsibilities. A concise and simple overview of what advertising is and what opportunities are available. Good source of information for both women and men.
35. Gamble, Frederic R. *What Advertising Agencies Are: What They Do and How They Do It.* New York: American Association of Advertising Agencies. This pamphlet is also available from the AAAA at no charge.

AEROSPACE AND AIR TRANSPORTATION

Abstracts and Indexes

36. *Air University Library Index to Military Periodicals.* (Quarterly.) See "Aerospace Industry" and "Aeronautical Research." See "Airlines" for articles on companies.
37. *Applied Science and Technology Index.* (Monthly.)
38. *International Aerospace Abstracts.*
39. *Scientific and Technical Aerospace Reports.* For NASA contractors, it contains ongoing research projects and reports issued by the government.

Statistical Sources

40. *Aerospace Facts and Figures.* (Annual.) Aerospace Industries Association of America.
41. *Air Transport Facts and Figures.* (Annual.) Air Transport Association of America.
42. *Air Transport World,* "World Airline Report." (Annual.) June Issue.
43. *Aviation Week and Space Technology,* "Forecast and Inventory Issue." (Annual.) March issue.
44. United States Civil Aeronautics Board. *Handbook of Airline Statistics.* (Biennial.)
45. U.S. Federal Aviation Administration. *FAA Statistical Handbook of Aviation.* (Annual.)

Periodicals

46. *Aviation Week and Space Technology.* (Weekly.)
47. *Business and Commercial Aviation.* (Monthly.) Murdoch Magazine.
48. *Interavia.* (Monthly.) Jane's Information Group.

General Investment Services

49. Forbes. *"Annual Report on American Industry."* First issue in January each year has section on aerospace.
50. Standard & Poor's Corporation. *Industry Surveys.* (Quarterly.) Coverage is separate for aerospace and air transportation.

Census Publications

51. *Census of Transportation.* Washington, D.C.: U.S. Bureau of the Census, Government Printing Office, 1987.

52. *Current Industrial Reports.* Washington, D.C.: U.S. Bureau of the Census. Irregular. Contains pamphlets that are arranged alphabetically.

53. Miller, E. Willard and Ruby M. Miller, *Air Transportation—Airlines: A Bibliography.* Vance Biblios, 1987.

Books

54. Bailey, Elizabeth E., *Deregulating The Airlines.* MIT Press, 1985.

55. Kane, Robert M. and Allan D. Vose, *Air Transportation,* Dubuque, Iowa: 9th ed. Kendall-Hunt, 1987.

56. O'Connor, William E., *An Introduction to Airline Economics,* 3rd ed. New York: Praeger, 1985.

57. Sampson, Anthony, *Empires of the Sky.* London: Hodder and Stoughton, 1984.

58. Taneja, Nawal K., *The International Airline Industry: Trends, Issues & Challenges.* Lexington, MA: 192p. Lexington Books, 1987.

ARTS MANAGEMENT

Directories

59. *American Art Directory.* New York: R. R. Bowker, 1989–90. Museums, art schools, and art associations in the United States; includes lists of art magazines, fellowships, and scholarships, art schools abroad, and other art resources.

60. *Who's Who in American Art.* New York: R. R. Bowker, 1989–90.

Indexes

61. *Art Index.* (Quarterly.) New York: H. W. Wilson. For relevant articles check under subject headings such as Museums and Art Galleries—Administration, Art Patronage, Art and State, Art and Society, Business Committee for the Arts, National Endowment for the Arts, etc.

62. *Business Periodicals Index.* (Monthly.) New York: H. W. Wilson. For relevant articles check under subject headings such as Art and State, Museums, Performing Arts, The Arts, Art and Industry, Art Patronage, Theater, Opera, etc.

63. *PAIS.* (Weekly.) New York: Public Affairs Information Service. For relevant articles check under subject headings such as Arts Market, Museums, Theater, Opera, Art and Industry, Art and State, Art and Society, Performing Arts, Art Patronage, etc.

64. *Reader's Guide to Periodical Literature.* (Semi-monthly.) New York: H. W. Wilson. For relevant articles check under subject headings such as Art and Industry, The Arts, The Arts—Finance, The Arts—Federal Aid, Museums, Museum Directors, Theaters, Dance, Opera, Orchestras, etc.

Books

65. Baumol, William J., and William G. Bowen. *Performing Arts: The Economic Dilemma.* New York: Twentieth Century Fund, 1966.

66. Caplin, Lee E., ed. *The Business of Art.* Englewood Cliffs, NJ: Prentice Hall, 1982.

67. Dubin, Steven C., *Bureaucratizing the Muse: Public Funds and the Cultural Worker.* Chicago: University of Chicago Press, 1987.

68. Eells, Richard Sedric Fox. *The Corporation and the Arts.* New York: Macmillan, 1967.

69. Georgi, Charlotte. *The Arts and the World of Business,* 2d ed. Metuchen, NJ: Scarecrow Press, 1979.

70. Horwitz, Tem. *Arts Administration: How to Set up and Run Successful Non-profit Arts Organizations.* Chicago: Chicago Review Press, 1978.

71. Kesler, Jackson. *The Performing Arts: Guide to the Literature.* Libs Unl., 1989.

72. Moore, Thomas Gale. *The Economics of the American Theatre.* Durham, NC: Duke University Press, 1968.

73. *Nonprofit Enterprise in the Arts: Studies in Mission and Constraint.* Edited by Paul J. DiMaggio. New York: Oxford University Press, 1986. xv, 370 p.: ill.; 24 cm.

74. Reiss, Alvin H., *The Arts Management Reader.* Written and edited by Alvin H. Reiss: foreword by Kitty Carlisle Hart. New York: Audience Arts, c1979. xiv, 686 p.; ill.; 24 cm.

75. Shore, Harvey, *Arts Administration and Management: A Guide for Arts Administrators and Their Staffs.* New York: Quorum Books, 1987. xii, 218 p.; ill.; 23 cm.

76. Vogel, Harold L., *Entertainment Industry Economics.* Cambridge University Press, 1986.

77. *The Cost of Culture: Patterns and Prospects of Private Arts Patronage,* edited by Margaret Jane Wyszomirski and Pat Clubb. New York: ACA Books, 1989. ix, 102 p.; 23 cm.—(ACA arts research seminar series).

Bibliographies

78. Benedict, Stephen and Linda C. Coe, eds. *Arts Management: An Annotated Bibliography,* Rev. ed. New York: Center for Arts Information, 1980.

Periodicals

79. *Arts Management.* (5 yearly.) New York: Radius Group.

80. BCA News. (Biennial.) New York: Business Committee for the Arts.

COMMUNICATIONS

Directories

81. *Broadcasting Cable Yearbook.* (Annual.) Washington: Broadcasting Publications. List of all TV stations and AM–FM radio stations in the United States and Canada, including addresses and telephone numbers, licenses and owners, and representatives. Lists names and addresses of radio and TV commercial and program producers, news service distributors, network executives, and research services.
82. *Editor and Publisher Yearbook.* (Annual.) New York: Editor and Publisher Inc. A directory and structured guide to the newspaper industry.
83. *Literary Market Place.* (Annual.) New York: R. R. Bowker Co. A directory of publishers, literary agents, editors, etc.
84. *O'Dwyer's Directory of Public Relations Firms.* (Annual.) New York: J. R. O'Dwyer Co.
85. *Standard Rate and Data Service.* (Monthly.) Wilmette, IL: Standard Rate and Data Service, Inc. Issued in 12 parts (Radio, Television, Consumer Magazine, etc.).
86. Weiner, Richard, *Professional's Guide to Public Relations Services,* 6th ed. New York, NY: American Management Association, 1988.

Books

87. Cutlip, Scott M., Allen H. Center, and Glen M. Broom. *Effective Public Relations,* 6th ed. Englewood Cliffs, NJ: Prentice Hall, 1985.
88. Haberman, David A., and Harry A. Dolphin. *Public Relations: The Necessary Art.* Ames, Iowa: Iowa State University Press, 1988.
89. Lesly, Philip, ed. *Lesly's Public Relations Handbook,* 3rd ed. Englewood Cliffs, NJ: Prentice Hall, 1983.
90. Moore, H. Frazier, and Frank B. Kalupa. *Public Relations: Principles, Cases, and Problems,* 9th ed. Homewood, IL: R. D. Irwin, 1985.

Periodicals

91. *Broadcasting.* (Weekly.) Washington: Broadcasting Publications, Inc.
92. *Public Relations Journal.* (Monthly.) San Francisco: American Council on Public Relations.
93. *Publishers Weekly.* (Weekly.) Witinsville, MA: R. R. Bowker, Inc.

CONSULTING

Bibliographies and Indexes

94. *Management Consulting: ACME Annotated Bibliography of Selected Resource Materials.* New York: Association of Management Consulting Firms, 1988.

Directories

95. *Association of Consulting Management Engineers Directory of Members.* (Annual.) New York: Assoc. of Consulting Management Engineers.
96. *Bradford's Directory of Marketing Research Agencies and Management Consultants in the United States and the World.* (Biennial.) Middleburg, VA.: Bradford's Directory of Marketing Research Agencies.
97. *Consultants and Consulting Organizations Directory.* (Annual.) Detroit: Gale Research Company.
98. *Directory of Management Consultants.* Fitzwilliam, N.H.: Consultants News.
99. *Dun's Consultants Directory.* (Annual.) Parsippany, NJ: Dun's Marketing Services.
100. *Management Consulting.* (Annual.) Boston, MA: Harvard Business School Management Consulting Club.
101. *Who's Who in Consulting.* (Irregular.) Detroit: Gale Research Company.
102. *3rd Annual Directory of Human Resource Services, Products and Suppliers.* New York: American Management Association, 1990.

Periodicals

103. *Consultants News.* (Monthly.) Fitzwilliam, N.H.
104. *Journal of Management Consulting.* (Quarterly.) New York: Elsevier, Inc.

Books

105. Arnoudse, Donald M. *Consulting Skills for Professionals.* Homewood, IL: Dow Jones–Irwin, 1988.
106. Barcus, Sam W. and Joseph W. Wilkinson, eds. *Handbook of Management Consulting Services.* New York: McGraw-Hill, 1986.
107. Cohen, William A. *How to make it big as a consultant.* New York, NY: American Management Association, 1985.

108. Easton, Thomas A. and Ralph W. Conant. *Using Consultants: A Consumer's Guide for Managers.* Chicago, IL: Probus Publishing Company, 1985.

109. Greenfield, Wendy M. *Successful Management Consulting.* Englewood Cliffs, NJ: Prentice Hall, 1987.

110. Holtz, Herman. *Choosing and Using a Consultant: A Manager's Guide to Consulting Services.* New York: Wiley, 1989.

111. Holtz, Herman. *How to Succeed as an Independent Consultant,* 2nd Edition. New York: Wiley, 1988.

Industry Information

112. Kennedy, James H., ed. *Analysis of the Management Consulting Business in the U.S. Today.* Fitzwilliam, N.H.: Consultants News, 1990.

COMPUTERS

Industry Information

113. Standard & Poor's Corporation. (Quarterly.) *Industry Surveys.* New York: Standard & Poor's Corp. Provides basic data with current updating.

114. *U.S. Industrial Outlook.* (Annual.) Washington: U.S. Dept. of Commerce. Pertinent forecast and statistical data.

115. *Value Line Investment Survey.* (4 issues monthly.) New York: A. Bernhard & Co. Provides industry overview and stock evaluations for specific companies.

Dictionaries and Encyclopedias

116. Freedman, Alan. *The Computer Glossary.* 4th ed. New York, NY: AMACOM, 1988.

117. Meadows, A. J., et al. *Dictionary of Computing & Information Technology,* 3rd ed. New York: Nichols Pub., 1987.

118. Rosenberg, Jerry M. *Dictionary of Computers, Information and Telecommunications,* New York: Wiley, 1987.

Statistical Sources

119. *Computer Review.* (Annual.) Lexington, MA: GML Corp. Lists significant features of virtually all computers and related peripheral devices and indicates comparative prices. Updated every four months to include specifications of new equipment.

120. *Computing Reviews.* (Monthly.) New York: Association for Computing Machinery. A journal of reviews and abstracts of current publications in areas of the computing sciences.

121. *Predicasts.* (Annual.) Cleveland: Predicasts, Inc. Provides forecast data by SIC number. Sources for each forecast are given.

Directories

122. *Computers and People: Computer Directory and Buyer's Guide.* (Annual.) In addition to organizational listings, includes information on the industry as a whole: a world computer census, a comprehensive list of computer applications, and a roster of college and university computer facilities.

Periodicals and Trades Journals

123. *Communications of the ACM* [Association for Computing Machinery]. (Monthly.)

124. *Computer Decisions.* (Monthly.) Teaneck, NJ: Baetech Pub. Co.

125. *Computer Literature Index.* (Quarterly with annual cumulations.) Phoenix: Applied Computer Research.

126. *Computerworld.* (Weekly.) Framingham, MA: CW Communications/Inc.

127. *Data Processing Digest.* (Monthly.) Los Angeles: Data Processing Digest, Inc. Reviews and abstracts books and articles in the computer field.

128. *Datamation.* (Monthly.) Barrington, IL: Technical Pub. Co.

129. *PC Week.* (Weekly.) New York: Ziff-Davis.

Books

130. Athey, Thomas H. and Robert W. Zund. *Introduction to Computers and Information Systems,* 2nd ed. Glenview, IL: Scott, Foresman/Little, Brown College Division, 1988.

131. Bilissmer, Robert H. *Introducing Computers: Concepts, Systems, and Applications.* New York: Wiley, 1988.

132. Bohl, Marilyn. *Essentials of Information Processing.* New York: MacMillan, 1990.

133. Downing, Douglas and Michael Covington. *Dictionary of Computer Terms,* 2nd ed. New York: Barron, 1989.

134. Edmunds, Robert. *The Prentice Hall Encyclopedia of Information Technology.* Englewood Cliffs, NJ: Prentice Hall, 1987.

135. Sanders, Donald H. *Computer Concepts and Applications.* New York: McGraw Hill, 1986.

136. Sanders, Donald H. *Computers Today: With BASIC,* 3rd ed. New York: McGraw Hill, 1988.

Industry Information

137. *Digest of Education Statistics.* (Annual.) Washington, D.C.: U.S. National Center for Education Statistics.
138. *Projections of Education Statistics.* (Annual.) Washington, D.C.: National Center for Education Statistics.
139. *Requirements for Certification: Teachers, Counselors, Librarians, Administrators for Elementary Schools, Secondary Schools, Junior Colleges.* (Annual.) Chicago: University of Chicago Press.
140. *The Condition of Education.* (Annual.) Washington, D.C.: U.S. Department of Education.
141. *U.S. Industrial Outlook.* (Annual.) Washington, D.C.: U.S. Department of Commerce. Chapter on "Educational Services."

Directories

142. *Accredited Institutions of Postsecondary Education.* (Annual.) Washington, D.C.: American Council on Education.
143. *American Library Directory.* (Annual.) New York: R. R. Bowker. Lists public libraries, county and regional systems, college and university libraries, and private libraries. Information includes names of key personnel and addresses.
144. *American Universities and Colleges.* (Quadrennial.) Washington, D.C.: American Council on Education.
145. *Barron's Profiles of American Colleges.* (Annual.) Barron's Educational Series. Detailed profiles on 1,350 colleges. Competitive ratings listed.
146. *Barron's Guide to the Two-Year Colleges.* (Annual.) Woodbury, N.Y.: Barron's Educational Series.
147. Cass, James, and Max Biernbaum, eds., *Comparative Guide to American Colleges.* New York: Harper & Row. Descriptions of U.S. four-year colleges, with indexes by state, religious affiliation, selectivity, and number of degrees granted in selected fields.
148. *College Blue Book.* (Biennial.) New York: Macmillan.
149. *Community, Technical, and Junior College Directory.* (Annual.) Washington, D.C.: American Association of Community and Junior Colleges.
150. *Directory of Public School Systems in the U.S.* (Annual.) Association for School, College and University Staffing. Madison, WI.
151. *Handbook of Private Schools.* (Annual.) Boston: Porter Sargent Publications. Schools and academics listed by geographical districts.
152. *Hep Higher Education Directory.* (Annual.) Falls Church, VA: Higher Education Publications, Inc.
153. *Lovejoy's College Guide.* (Biennial.) New York: Simon and Schuster.
154. *Peterson's Guides to Graduate Study.* (Annual.) Princeton, NJ: Peterson's Guides, Inc.
155. *Peterson's Guide to Four-Year Colleges.* (Annual.) Princeton, NJ: Peterson's Guides, Inc.
156. *Private Independent Schools.* (Annual.) Wallingford, CT: Bunting and Lyon. Listed by state.

Bibliographies and Indexes

157. *Business Periodicals Index.* (Monthly—Cumulative.) New York: H.W. Wilson.
158. Butler, Lois. *Education: A Guide to Reference and Information Sources.* Englewood, CO.: Libraries Unlimited, 1989.
159. *Educational Administration Abstracts.* (Quarterly.) College Station, TX: University Council for Education Administration. Abstracts approximately 100 journals.
160. *Education Index.* (Monthly with annual cumulations.) New York: Wilson. The major index to periodical articles in all fields of education.
161. *Educational Resources Information Center* (ERIC). ERIC is a national information system established by the U.S. Office of Education in 1964. Its purpose is to collect, process, and make available a wide range of educational documents. These are four major parts to the ERIC system: (1) Thesaurus of ERIC Descriptors, (2) eduational documents on microfiche, (3) abstract indices to microfiche—ex. RIE (Research in Education), and (4) machinery to read and reproduce microfiche. Initially, use the topic "Educational Administration"; for more in-depth research, check with Thesaurus of ERIC Descriptors. Access to ERIC is through an on-line database service such as DIALOG or through ERIC on CD-ROM database.
162. Freed, Melvyn N. *The Educator's Desk Reference* (EDR): A sourcebook of educational information and research. New York: American Council on Education: Macmillan Publishing Company, 1989.
163. *Library Literature.* (Monthly with annual cumulations.) New York: Wilson. The major index to periodical articles for library administrators.
164. Shafritz, Jay M., Richard P. Koeppe, and Elizabeth W. Soper. *The Facts on File Dictionary of Education.* New York: Facts on File Publications, 1988.
165. Woodbury, Marda. *A Guide to Sources of Educational Information,* 2nd Edition. Arlington, VA: Information Resources Press, 1982.

Books

166. Davis, Gary A. and Margaret A. Thomas. *Effective Schools and Effective Teachers.* Boston: Allyn and Bacon, 1969.
167. Davis, Ralph M. *Leadership and Institutional Renewal.* San Francisco: Jossey-Bass, 1985.
168. Foster, William. *Paradigms and Promises: New Approaches to Educational Administration.* Buffalo, NY: Prometheus Books, 1986.
169. Hoy, Wayne K., and Cecil G. Miskel. *Educational Administration: Theory, Research, and Practice,* 3rd Edition. New York: Random House, 1987.
170. Knezevich, Stephen J. *Administration of Public Education: A Sourcebook for the Leadership and Management of Educational Institutions,* 4th edition. New York: Harper & Row, 1984.
171. McCorkle, Chester O., and Sandra Orr Archibald. *Management and Leadership in Higher Education.* San Francisco: Jossey-Bass, 1982.
172. Rausch, Erwin. *Management in Institutions of Higher Learning.* Lexington, MA: Lexington Books, 1980.
173. Rebore, Ronald W. *Educational Administration: A Management Approach.* Englewood Cliffs, NJ: Prentice Hall, 1985.
174. Silver, Paula F. *Educational Administration: Theoretical Perspectives on Practice and Research.* New York: Harper & Row, 1983.

Dictionaries and Encyclopedias

175. Dejnozka, Edward L., and David E. Kapel. *American Educators' Encyclopedia.* Westport, CT: Greenwood Press, 1982.
176. Husen, Torsten, and T. Neville Postlethwaite. *The International Encyclopedia of Education: Research and Studies.* New York: Pergamon Press, 1985.
177. Mitzel, Harold E., ed., *Encyclopedia of Educational Research,* 5th edition. New York: Free Press, 1982.

Periodicals

178. *Chronicle of Higher Education.* (Weekly.)
179. *Educational Administration Quarterly.* (Quarterly.) Columbus: University Council for Education Admin.
180. *Library Journal.* (Semi-weekly.) New York: Bowker
181. *Review of Educational Research.* (Quarterly.) Washington, D.C.: American Educational Research Association.

ENERGY AND PUBLIC UTILITIES

Dictionaries and Encyclopedias

182. *Glossary of Electric Utility Terms.* Washington, DC: Edison Electric Institute, 1970.
183. Parker, Sybil P. *McGraw-Hill Encyclopedia of Energy,* 2nd edition. New York: McGraw-Hill, 1981.
184. Langenkamp, Robert D. *Illustrated Petroleum Reference Dictionary,* 3rd edition. Tulsa, OK: Penn Well Books, 1985.

Bibliographies and Indexes

185. *EIA Publications Directory, A User's Guide.* (Quarterly with annual cumulations.) Washington, DC: U.S. Department of Energy.
186. Weber, R. David. *Energy Information Guide.* Santa Barbara, CA: ABC-Clio, 1984.

Directories

187. *Electrical World Directory of Electric Utilities.* New York: McGraw Hill. Over 3,500 investor-owned, municipal, rural cooperative, and government electric utility systems in the United States and Canada.
188. *Moody's Public Utilities Manual.* (Annual.) New York: Moody's Investors Service, Inc. Extensive company and financial information, including historical financial tables for the industry.
189. *U.S.A. Oil Industry Directory.* Tulsa, OK: Penn Well Publishing Company. Over 3,500 independent oil producers, fund companies, petroleum marketing companies, crude oil brokers, and integrated oil firms; trade and professional associations, state and federal government agencies are also included.

Periodicals

190. *Coal.* (Monthly.) Chicago: Maclean Hunter Publishing Company.
191. *Energy Journal.* (Quarterly.) Washington: Energy Economic Educational Foundation.
192. *Modern Power Systems.* (Monthly.) Kent, UK: Maxwell Business Communications.
193. *Oil and Gas Journal.* (Weekly.) Tulsa, OK: Penn Well Publishing Company.
194. *Public Utilities Fortnightly.* (Bi-weekly.) Arlington, VA: Public Utilities Reports, Inc.

Books

195. Crew, Michael A., and P. R. Kleindorfer. *The Economics of Public Utility Regulation.* Cambridge, MA: MIT Press, 1986.
196. Danielsen, Albert L., and David R. Kamersechen. *Current Issues in Public-Utility Economics: Essays in Honor of James C. Bonbright.* Lexington, MA: Lexington Books, 1963.
197. Howe, Keith M., and Eugene F. Rasmussen. *Public Utility Economics and Finance.* Englewood Cliffs, NJ: Prentice Hall, 1962.

Industry Information

198. *Basic Petroleum Data Book.* (3 times a year.) Washington, DC: American Petroleum Institute.
199. *Coal Data: A Reference.* Washington: U.S. Energy Information Administration, 1989.
200. *Electric Power Annual.* (Annual.) Washington: U.S. Energy Information Administration.
201. *Energy Facts.* (Annual.) Washington: U.S. Energy Information Administration.
202. *National Gas Annual.* (Annual.) Washington: U.S. Energy Information Administration.
203. *NPN Factbook.* (Annual.) Des Plaines, IL: National Petroleum News.
204. *Moody's Public Utilities Manual.* New York: Moody's Investors Service. 2 volumes (annual, with semiweekly supplements).
205. *NUEXCO Annual Review.* (Annual.) Denver: NUEXCO Corporation.
206. *U.S. Energy Information Administration.* (Monthly.) Washington, DC: *Energy Review.*

FINANCE AND BANKING

Dictionaries

207. Munn, Glenn G. *Glenn G. Munn's Encyclopedia of Banking and Finance,* 7th ed. revised by F. L. Garcia. Boston: Bankers Publishing Co., 1973.
208. Rosenberg, Jerry Martin. *Dictionary of Banking and Financial Services,* 2nd. ed. New York: Wiley, 1985.

Bibliographies

209. Aggarwal, Raj. *The Literature of International Business Finance.* New York: Praeger, 1984.
210. *Banking Literature Index.* (Monthly with annual cumulations.) Washington, D.C.: American Bankers Association.
211. *Foreign Commerce Handbook,* 17th ed. Washington, DC: Chamber of Commerce of the United States, 1981. Part 3 of this handbook consists of a bibliography of books and periodicals relating to international business.
212. Ryan, Cynthia C. *International Business Reference Sources.* Lexington, MA: Lexington Books, 1983.
213. *The International Executive.* (Bi-monthly.) American Management Association. An extensive bibliography of articles and books on international business.

Books

214. Altman, Edward I., and Jan McKinney. *Handbook of Corporate Finance.* New York: Wiley, 1986.
215. Bierman, Harold, and Seymour Smidt. *The Capital Budgeting Decision: Economic Analysis of Investment Projects,* 6th ed. New York: Macmillan, 1984.
216. Brealey, Richard A., and Stewart C. Meyers. *Principals of Corporate Finance,* 3rd ed. New York: McGraw-Hill, 1988.
217. Brigham, Eugene F. *Fundamentals of Financial Management,* 3rd ed. Chicago: Dryden Press, 1983.
218. Cochran, John A. *Money, Banking, and the Economy,* 5th ed. New York: Macmillan, 1983.
219. Goldfeld, Stephen M., and Lester V. Chandler. *The Economics of Money and Banking,* 8th ed. New York: Harper & Row, 1981.
220. Helfert, Erich A. *Techniques of Financial Analysis,* 5th ed. Homewood, IL: Irwin, 1982.
221. Ritter, Lawrence S., and William L. Silber. *Money,* 5th ed. New York: Basic Books, 1984.
222. Ritter, Lawrence S., and William L. Silber. *Principles of Money, Banking and Financial Markets,* 5th ed. New York: Basic Books, 1986.
223. Schall, Lawrence D. *Introduction to Financial Management,* 5th ed. New York: McGraw-Hill, 1988.
224. United States League of Savings Associations. *Savings and Loan Fact Book.* (Annual.) Chicago: United States Savings and Loan League.
225. Van Horne, James C. *Financial Management and Policy,* 7th ed. Englewood Cliffs, NJ: Prentice Hall, 1986.
226. Van Horne, James C. *Fundamentals of Financial Management,* 4th ed. Englewood Cliffs, NJ: Prentice Hall, 1980.
227. Weston, J. Fred, and Eugene F. Brigham. *Essentials of Managerial Finance,* 7th ed. Chicago: Dryden Press, 1985.
228. Weston, J. Fred, and Thomas E. Copeland. *Managerial Finance,* 8th ed. Chicago: Dryden Press, 1985.

FOOD PROCESSING AND DISTRIBUTION

Books

229. Connor, John M. *Food Processing: An Industrial Powerhouse in Transition.* Lexington, MA: Lexington Books, 1988.

Directories

230. *Progressive Grocer's Marketing Guidebook.* (Annual.) New York: Progressive Grocer Information Sales.

Periodicals

231. *Agricultural Statistics.* (Annual.) Washington, DC: US Department of Agriculture.
232. *Beverage Industry.* (Monthly.) New York: Magazines for Industry, Inc.
233. *Beverage World.* (Monthly.) East Stroudsburg, PA: Keller International Publishing Company.
234. *Convenience Store News.* (Monthly.) New York: BMT Publications.
235. *Food Engineering.* (Monthly.) Radnor, PA: Chilton Company.
236. *Progressive Grocer.* (Monthly.) New York.
237. *Quick Frozen Foods.* (Monthly.) New York: Harcourt Brace Jovanovich.
238. *Supermarket Business.* (Monthly.) New York: Fieldmark Media, Inc.
239. *Supermarket News.* (Weekly.) New York: Fairchild Publications.

Industry Information

240. *Annual Financial Review.* (Annual.) Washington, D.C.: Food Marketing Institute.
241. *The Annual Report of the Convenience Store Industry.* (Annual.) New York: Progressive Grocer Magazine Resources.
242. *The Food Marketing Industry Speaks.* (Annual.) Washington, DC: Food Marketing Institute.
243. *Progressive Grocer Annual Report of the Grocery Industry.* (Annual.) Stamford, CN: Maclean Hunter Media Inc.

HEALTH SERVICE INDUSTRIES

Books

244. Berman, Howard J. and Lewis E. Weeks. *The Financial Management of Hospitals*, 6th ed. Ann Arbor, MI: Health Administration Press, 1986.
245. Cleverley, William O. *Handbook of Health Care Accounting and Finance.* Rockville, MD: Aspen Systems Corporation, 1982.
246. Darr, Kurt and Jonathon Rakich. *Hospital Organizational & Management: Text & Readings*, 4th ed. Owings Mills, MD: National Health Publishing, 1989.
247. Dilenschneider, Robert L. *The Dartnell Public Relations Handbook*, 3rd ed. Chicago: Dartnell Corporation, 1987. With a special section on the health care field.
248. Schulz, Rockwell and Alton C. Johnson. *Management of Hospitals*, 2nd ed. New York: McGraw Hill, 1983.

Industry Information

249. "Compensation Survey" in *Modern Healthcare.* (Annual.) In October issue.
250. *Health Care Financing Review.* (Quarterly.) U.S. Health Care Financing Administration.
251. *Hospital Statistics.* 1989 Edition. Am Hospital. American Hospital Assoc. Staff.
252. *Interstudy Edge.* (Quarterly.) Excelsior, MN: InterStudy, Inc.
253. *Long Term Care Databook.* (Annual.) American Health Care Association.

Periodicals

254. *HealthWeek.* (Bi-weekly.) Emeryville, CA: HealthWeek Publications, Inc.
255. *Hospitals.* (Bi-weekly.) Chicago: American Hospital Publishing Company.
256. *Modern Healthcare.* (Weekly.) Chicago: Crain Communication, Inc.

Bibliographies

257. *Abstracts of Health Care Management Studies.* (Annual.) Ann Arbor, MI: University of Michigan. Published by Health Administration Press for Cooperative Information Center for Health Care Management Studies.
258. *Hospital Literature Index.* (Quarterly, with annual cumulations.) Chicago: American Hospital Association.
259. *Medical Group Management Association.* (Annual.) Denver: The Administrator's Bookshelf.

HOTELS/RESTAURANTS/RECREATION/TRAVEL

Books

260. Benest, Frank, et al. *Organizing Leisure and Human Services.* Dubuque, IA: Kendall/Hunt Publishing Company, 1984.
261. Egerton-Thomas, Christopher. *How to Open and Run a Successful Restaurant.* New York: Wiley, 1989.
262. Gray, William S. and Salvatore C. Liguori. *Hotel and Motel Management and Operations.* Englewood Cliffs, NJ: Prentice Hall, 1980.
263. Hodgson, Adale, ed. *The Travel and Tourism Industry: Strategies for the Future.* New York: Pergamon Press, 1987.
264. Powers, Tom. *Introduction to Management in the Hospitality Industry,* 3rd ed. New York: Wiley, 1988.
265. Shivers, Jay. *Introduction to Recreational Service Administration.* Philadelphia: Lea & Febiger, 1987.
266. Smith, William O. *Restaurant Marketing,* 2nd ed. New York: McGraw Hill, 1990.
267. Vogel, Harold L. *Entertainment Industry Economics: A Guide for Financial Analysis.* New York: Cambridge University Press, 1986.

Periodicals

268. *Billboard.* (Weekly.) New York: Billboard Publication, Inc.
269. *Broadcasting.* (Weekly.) Washington, DC: Broadcasting Publications, Inc.
270. *Cornell Hotel and Restaurant Administration Quarterly.* Ithaca, NY: Cornell University.
271. *Hotel and Motel Management.* (Monthly.) Cleveland: Edgell Communications, Inc.
272. *Hotel and Motels International.* (Bimonthly.) Boston: Cahners Publishing Company.
273. *Restaurant Business.* (Monthly.) New York: Restaurant Business.
274. *Variety.* (Weekly.) New York: Variety Pub. Co.

Directories

275. *Directory of Hotel and Motel Systems.* (Annual.) New York: American Hotel Association Directory Corporation.
276. *The Financial Times World Hotel Directory.* (Annual.) London: Financial Times Limited.
277. *OAG Travel Planner, Hotel & Motel Redbook.* (Quarterly.) Oak Brook, IL: Official Airline Guides, Inc.

Industry Information

278. *Broadcasting Yearbook.* (Annual.) Washington, DC: Broadcasting Publications.
279. *Economic Review of Travel in America.* Washington, DC: U.S. Travel Data Center.
280. *International Tourism Reports.* (Quarterly.) London: Economist Publications.
281. *National Travel Survey.* (Annual.) Washington, DC: U.S. Travel Data Center.
282. *Travel Industry World Yearbook.* (Annual.) New York, NY: Child & Waters Inc.
283. *Trends in the Hotel Industry.* (Annual.) Houston, TX: Pannell, Kerr, Forster.

MANUFACTURING AND PRODUCTION

Books

284. Buffa, Elwood, and Rakesh K. Sarin. *Modern Production/Operations Management,* 8th ed. New York: Wiley, 1987.
285. Chase, Richard B., and Nicholas J. Aquilano. *Production and Operations Management: A Life Cycle Approach,* 4th ed. Homewood, IL: Richard D. Irwin, 1985.
286. Maus, Rex and Randall Allsup. *Robotics: A Manager's Guide.* New York: Wiley, 1986.
287. Schey, John A. *Introduction to Manufacturing Processes,* 2nd ed. New York: McGraw-Hill, 1987.
288. Schroeder, Roger G. *Operations Management: Decision Making in the Operations Function.* 3rd ed. New York: McGraw-Hill, 1989.
289. Stevenson, William J. *Production/Operations Management.* 2nd ed. Homewood, IL: Irwin, 1986.
290. Tersine, Richard J. *Production/Operations Management: Concepts, Structure, and Analysis,* 2nd ed. New York: North-Holland, 1985.

Directories

291. *Fortune 500: The Largest U.S. Industrial Corporations.* (Annual.) New York: Fortune.
292. *Key Plants: Plants with more than 100 Employees.* (Annual.) New York: Marketing Economics Institute.
293. *Reference Book of Manufacturers.* (Annual.) New York: Dun & Bradstreet, Inc.

294. *Thomas Register of American Manufacturers.* (Annual.) New York: Thomas Publishing Company.

NOTE: There are many state and regional industrial directories. Every state has its own manufacturing directory. The major publishers in the field are George D. Hall, Co. (Boston) and MacRae's (New York).

Periodicals

295. *Industrial Engineering.* (Monthly.) Atlanta: Institute of Industrial Engineers.
296. *Industry Week.* (Weekly.) Cleveland: Penton Publishing Company.
297. *Iron Age.* (Monthly.) New York: Fairchild Publications.
298. *Production.* (Monthly.) Cincinnati: Gardner Publications.

MULTINATIONAL COMPANIES AND INTERNATIONAL BUSINESS

Directories

299. *Directory of American Firms Operating in Foreign Countries,* 11th ed. New York: World Trade Academy Press.
300. *Directory of Foreign Firms Operating in the United States,* 5th ed. New York: Uniworld Business Publishers, 1986.
301. *Europe's 15000 Largest Companies.* (Annual.) London: ELC International.
302. *Principal International Business.* (Annual.) New York: Dun and Bradstreet.
303. *Rand McNally International Bankers Directory.* (Annual.) Skokie, IL: Rand McNally & Company.
304. *The U.S. Industrial Outlook.* (Annual.) Washington, DC: U.S. Department of Commerce.

Dictionaries and Encyclopedias

305. *Directory of Foreign Manufacturers in the United States,* 3rd ed. Atlanta, GA: Georgia State University, 1985.
306. *Dun's Latin America's Top 25,000.* (Annual.) New York: Dun and Bradstreet.
307. *Foreign Commerce Handbook,* 17th ed. Washington, D.C.: Chamber of Commerce of the United States, 1981.
308. *Fortune's International 500.* (Annual.) New York: Time, Inc. In a July issue each year, Fortune magazine ranks by sales the 500 largest companies worldwide.
309. Hoogvelt, Ankie M. M. *Multinational Enterprise: An Encyclopedic Dictionary of Concepts and Terms.* London: MacMillian Reference, 1987.
310. *International Corporate Affiliations.* (Annual.) Wilmette, IL: National Register Publishing Company.
311. *International Corporate 1000.* (Annual.) Washington, DC: Monitor Publishing Company.
312. Isaacs, Alan. *The Multilingual Commercial Dictionary.* New York, NY: Facts on File, 1980.
313. Johannsen, Hano, and T. Terry Page, eds. *International Dictionary of Business,* 3rd ed. Englewood Cliffs, NJ: Prentice Hall, 1986.
314. Kohls, Siegfried. *Dictionary of International Economics: German, Russian, English, French, Spanish.* Leiden: Sijt'hoff International.
315. *Overseas Summer Jobs.* (Annual.) Oxford: Vacation–Work.
316. *U.S. Custom House Guide.* (Annual.) Washington, D.C.
317. *United States Importers and Exporters Directory.* (Annual.) New York: Journal of Commerce.
318. Walmsley, Julian. *Dictionary of International Finance,* 2nd ed. New York: Wiley, 1985.
319. *World Chamber of Commerce Directory.* (Annual.) Washington, D.C.

Periodicals

320. *Asian Wall Street Journal.* (Weekly.)
321. *Business International.* (Weekly.) New York, NY: Business International Corp.
322. *Columbia Journal of World Business.* (Quarterly.) New York.
323. *Euromoney.* (Monthly.) London: Euromoney Publications.
324. *Financial Times.* [London.] (Daily.) London: MacRae, Curtice & Co.
325. *International Executive.* (Quarterly.) Hastings-On-Hudson, NY. American Management Association.
326. *Multinational Business.* (Quarterly.) London: Economist Intelligence Unit.

Books

327. Baker, James C., John K. Ryans, Jr., and Donald G. Howard, eds. *International Business Classics.* Lexington, MA: Lexington Books, 1988.
328. Bartlett, Christopher A., and Sumantra Ghoshal. *Managing Across Borders: The Transnational Solution.* Boston, MA: Harvard Business School Press, 1989.
329. Belkaoui, Ahmed. *The New Environment in International Accounting: Issues and Practices.* New York: Quorum Books, 1988.

330. Cateora, Philip R. *Strategic International Marketing.* Homewood, IL: Dow Jones-Irwin, 1985.

331. Eiteman, David K., and Arthur I. Stonehill. *Multinational Business Finance*, 5th ed. Reading, MA: Addison-Wesley, 1989.

332. Fayerweather, John. *International Business Strategy and Administration*, 2nd ed. Cambridge, MA: Ballinger, 1982.

333. Holland, John. *International Financial Management.* Oxford, UK; New York, NY: B. Blackwell, 1986.

334. Jain, Subhash, C., and Lewis R. Tucker, Jr. *International Marketing: Managerial Perspectives*, 2nd ed. Boston, MA: Kent Publishing Company, 1986.

335. Kane, Daniel R. *Principles of International Finance.* London; New York: Croom Helm, 1988.

336. Kolde, Endel Jakob. *Environment of International Business*, 2nd ed. Boston, MA: Kent Publishing Company, 1985.

337. Lessard, Donald, R. *International Financial Management: Theory and Application*, 2nd ed. New York: Wiley, 1985.

338. Porter, Michael E. *Competition in Global Industries.* Boston, MA: Harvard Business School Press, 1986.

339. Rodriguez, Rita M., and E. Eugene Carter. *International Financial Management*, 3rd ed. Englewood Cliffs, NJ: Prentice Hall, 1984.

340. Rugman, Alan M., Donald J. Lecraw, and Laurence D. Booth. *International Business: Firm and Environment.* New York: McGraw-Hill, 1985.

341. Stonehill, Arthur I., and David K. Eiteman. *Finance: An International Perspective.* Homewood, IL: Irwin, 1987.

342. Terpstara, Vern. *International Marketing*, 3rd ed. Chicago: Dryden Press, 1983.

343. Walter, Ingo, and Tracy Murray, eds. *Handbook of International Management.* New York: Wiley, 1988.

PUBLIC ADMINISTRATION

Dictionaries and Encyclopedias

344. Chandler, Ralph C., and Jack C. Plano. *Public Administration Dictionary*, 2nd ed. Santa Barbara, CA. 1988.

Bibliographies

345. McCurdy, Howard E. *Public Administration: A Bibliographic Guide to the Literature.* New York: Marcel Dekker Inc., 1986.

346. *Monthly Catalog of U.S. Government Publications.* (Monthly.) Washington, DC: GPO. With semiannual, annual, and quinquennial cumulative indexes.

347. *PAIS International.* (Monthly updates.) New York: Public Affairs Information Service, Inc., 1972 to present.

Directories

348. *Congressional Directory.* (Biennial.) Washington, DC: U.S. Government Printing Office.

349. *The Municipal Year Book.* (Annual.) Washington, DC: International City Management Association. A standard listing of city and county officials.

350. *State Administrative Officials Classified by Function.* (Biennial.) Lexington, KY: Council of State Governments.

351. *U.S. Government Manual.* (Annual.) Washington, DC: GPO. The U.S. Government Manual is the directory of federal agencies, quasi-official agencies, international organizations, boards, commissions, and committees.

Periodicals

352. *Bureaucrat.* (Quarterly.) Arlington, VA.

353. Caiden, Gerald E. *Public Administration*, 2d ed. Pacific Palisades, CA: Palisades Publishers, 1982.

354. Cohen, Steven. *The Effective Public Manager: Achieving Success in Government.* San Francisco: Jossey-Bass, 1988.

355. Gawthrop, Louis G. *Public Sector Management, Systems, and Ethics.* Bloomington: Indiana University Press, 1984.

356. Gordon, George J. *Public Administration in America*, 3rd ed. New York: St. Martin's Press, 1986.

357. *Government Finance Review.* (Bi-monthly.) Washington, DC: Government Finance Officers Association.

358. Lane, Frederick S. *Current Issues in Public Administration*, 3rd ed. New York: St. Martin's Press, 1986.

359. Mercer, James L., Susan W. Woolston, and William V. Donaldson. *Managing Urban Government Services: Strategies, Tools, and Techniques for the Eighties.* New York: AMACOM, 1981.

360. Murin, William J. *Classics of Urban Politics and Administration.* Oak Park, IL: Moore Publishing Company, 1982.

361. Nigro, Felix A., and Lloyd G. Nigro. *Modern Public*

Administration, 6th ed. New York: Harper & Row, 1984.

362. *Public Administration Quarterly.* (Quarterly.) Randallstown, MD: Southern Public Administration Education Foundation.

363. *Public Administration Review.* (Bi-monthly.) Washington, DC: American Society for Public Administration.

Industry Information

364. *The Book of the States.* (Biennial.) Lexington, KY: Council of State Governments. The basic guide to statistical information on state government.

365. *Municipal Yearbook.* (Annual.) International City Management Association. Provide statistical data on U.S. cities.

REAL ESTATE

Dictionaries and Encyclopedias

366. Allen, Robert D., and Thomas E. Wolfe. *The Allen and Wolfe Illustrated Dictionary of Real Estate.* New York: J. Wiley, 1983.

367. Bagby, Joseph R., and Martha L. Green Bagby. *Real Estate Dictionary.* Englewood Cliffs, NJ: Institute for Business Planning, 1981.

368. Harris, Jack C., and Jack P. Friedman. *Barron's Real Estate Handbook*, 2nd ed. New York: Barron's, 1988.

369. McLean, Andrew James. *Real Estate Terms and Definitions.* Santa Monica, CA: Delphi Information Sciences Corporation, 1980.

Bibliographies and Indexes

370. Haikalis, Peter D. *Real Estate: A Bibliography of the Monographic Literature.* Westport, CT: Greenwood Press, 1983.

371. *Real Estate Appraisal Bibliography.* Chicago: American Institution of Real Estate Appraiser, 1940–1972, 1973–1980.

372. *Real Estate Periodicals Index.* (Annual.) New York: J.A. Munro Associates.

Directories

373. *Directory of Designated Members.* (Annual.) Chicago: Society of Real Estate Appraisers.

374. *The Directory of Real Estate Investors.* (Annual.) Wilmette, IL: National Register Publishing Company.

375. *National Real Estate Investor—Directory Issue.* (Monthly.) Atlanta, GA: Communication Channels, Inc.

376. *National Roster of Realtors.* (Annual.) Cedar Rapids, IA: Stamats Communications, Inc.

377. *Roulac's Top Real Estate Brokers.* (Annual.) New York: Deloitte, Haskins & Sells.

Periodicals

378. *Appraisal Journal.* (Quarterly.) Chicago: American Institution of Real Estate Appraisers.

379. *Journal of Property Management.* (Bi-monthly.) Institution of Real Estate Management.

380. *National Real Estate Investor.* (Monthly.) Atlanta: Communication Channels, Inc.

381. *Real Estate Forum.* (Monthly.) New York: Real Estate Forum, Inc.

382. *Real Estate Review.* (Quarterly.) Boston: Warren, Gorham & Lamont.

Books

383. Brueggeman, William B., and Leo S. Stone. *Real Estate Finance*, 8th ed. Homewood, IL: R.D. Irwin, 1989.

384. Irwin, Robert. *The McGraw-Hill Real Estate Handbook.* New York: McGraw-Hill, 1984.

385. Ring, Alfred A., and Jerome Dasso. *Real Estate Principles and Practices*, 10th ed. Englewood Cliffs, NJ: Prentice Hall, 1985.

386. Silverman, Robert A. *Corporate Real Estate Handbook.* New York: McGraw-Hill, 1987.

387. Weidmer, John P. *Real Estate Investment*, 4th ed. Englewood Cliffs, NJ: Prentice Hall, 1988.

388. Wofford, Larry E. *Real Estate*, 2nd ed. New York: Wiley, 1986.

389. Unger, Maurice. *Real Estate Principles and Practices.* Cincinnati: South-western Publishing Company, 1987.

Industry Information

390. *Dollars and Costs of Shopping Centers.* (Annual.) Urban Land Institute.

391. Harris, Laura A. *The Real Estate Industry: An Information Sourcebook.* Phoenix: Oryx Press, 1987.

392. *Roulac's Top Real Estate Brokers.* (Annual.) New York: Deloitle, Haskins & Sells

RETAIL TRADE

Directories

393. *Chain Store Age General Merchandise Edition—Top 100 Chains Issue.* (Monthly.) New York, NY: Lebhar-Friedman, Inc.
394. *The Direct Marketing Market Place.* (Annual.) Hewlett Harbor, NY: Hilary House Publishers.
395. *Directory of Department Stores.* (Annual.) New York: Chain Store Guides, Inc.
396. *Directory of Discount Stores/Catalog Showrooms.* New York: Lebhar-Friedman, Inc. 1986.
397. *The Directory of Mail Order Catalogs*, 4th ed. New York: Grey House Publishing, 1989.
398. *The Franchise Annual.* (Annual.) Lewiston, NY: International Franchise Opportunities.
399. *Franchise Opportunities Handbook.* (Annual.) Washington, DC: U.S. Department of Commerce.
400. *Mail Order Business Directory.* (Annual.) Coral Springs, FL: B. Klien Publications.
401. *Progressive Grocer's Marketing Guidebook.* (Annual.) Stanford, CT: Maclean Hunter Medias.
402. *The Source Book of Franchise Opportunities.* Homewood, IL: Dow Jones-Irwin, 1985.

Periodicals

403. *Chain Store Age Executive.* (Monthly.) New York: Lebhar-Friedman, Inc.
404. *Direct Marketing.* (Monthly.) New York: Hoke Communications.
405. *Journal of Retailing.* (Quarterly.) New York: New York University.
406. *Progressive Grocer.* (Monthly.) Stamford, CT.
407. *Sales and Marketing Management.* (Monthly.) New York: Bill Communication.
408. *Stores.* (Monthly.) New York: NRMA Enterprises, Inc.

Books

409. Berman, Barry and Joel R. Evans. *Retail Management: A Strategic Approach*, 3rd ed. New York: Macmillan, 1986.
410. Cohen, William A. *Building A Mail Order Business: A Complete Manual for Success*, 2nd ed. New York: Wiley, 1985.
411. Duncan, Delbert J., Stanley C. Hollander, and Ronald Savitt. *Modern Retailing Management: Basic Concepts and Practices*, 10th ed. Homewood, IL: R.D. Irwin, 1983.
412. Hodgson, Richard S. *The Dartnell Direct Mail and Mail Order Handbook*, 3rd ed. Chicago: Dartnell Corporation, 1980.
413. Muldoon, Katie. *Catalog Marketing: The Complete Guide to Profitability in the Catalog Business*, 2nd ed. New York: American Management Association, 1988.
414. Nash, Edward L. *Direct Marketing: Strategy, Planning, Execution*, 2nd ed. New York: McGraw-Hill, 1986.
415. Roman, Ernan. *Integrated Direct Marketing: Techniques and Strategies for Success.* New York: McGraw-Hill, 1988.
416. Seltz, David D. *The Complete Handbook of Franchising.* Reading, MA: Addison-Wesley, 1982.
417. Simon, Julian. *How To Start and Operate a Mail-Order Business*, 4th ed. New York: McGraw-Hill, 1987.
418. Stone, Bob. *Successful Direct Marketing Methods*, 4th ed. Lincolnwood, IL: National Textbook Company, 1989.
419. Webster, Bryce. *The Insider's Guide to Franchising.* New York, NY: American Management Association, 1986.

Industry Information

420. "Annual Report of the Grocery Industry." *Progressive Grocer.* (Annual.) New York: Progressive Grocer. April issue.
421. "Census of American Chain Stores." *Chain Store Age Executive.* (Annual.) New York: Lebhar-Friedman Inc. July issue.
422. *Fact Book on Direct Response Marketing.* (Annual.) New York: Direct Mail/Marketing Association.
423. *Fairchild's Financial Manual of Retail Stores.* (Annual.) New York: Fairchild Publications.
424. *Franchising in the Economy.* (Annual.) Washington, DC: U.S. Department of Commerce.

SMALL BUSINESS AND ENTREPRENEURSHIP

Books

425. Cohen, William A. *The Entrepreneur and Small Business Problem Solver: An Encyclopedic Reference and Guide*, 2nd ed. New York: Wiley, 1990.
426. Eyler, David R. *Starting and Operating a Home-based Business.* New York: Wiley, 1990.
427. Kuriloff, Arthur H., and John M. Hemphill. *Starting and Managing the Small Business*, 2nd ed. New York: McGraw-Hill, 1988.

428. Merrill, Ronald E., and Henry D. Sedgwick. *The New Venture Handbook: Everything You Need to Know to Start and Run Your Own Business.* New York: American Management Association, 1987.

429. Pickle, Hal B., and Royce L. Abrahamson. *Small Business Management*, 4th ed. New York: Wiley, 1986.

430. Stevenson, Howard H., et al. *New Business Ventures and the Entrepreneur*, 3rd ed. Homewood, IL: Irwin, 1989.

431. Timmons, Jeffry A. *The Entrepreneurial Mind.* Andover, MA: Brick House Publishing Company, 1989.

432. Timmons, Jeffry A. *New Venture Creation: Entrepreneurship in the 1990s*, 3rd ed. Boston, MA: Irwin, 1990.

433. Vesper, Karl H. *New Venture Strategies*, Englewood Cliffs, NJ: Prentice Hall, 1980.

Periodicals

434. *D & B Reports.* (Bimonthly.) New York. Dun & Bradstreet, Inc.

435. *Entrepreneur.* (Monthly.) New York: Chase Revel, Inc.

436. *Entrepreneurship Theory and Practice: ET&P.* (Quarterly.) Volume 13, No. 1 (Fall 1988), Waco, TX: Baylor University, 1988.

437. *Journal of Small Business Management.* (Quarterly.) Morgantown, WV: National Council for Small Business Management Development.

438. *Journal of Small Business Venturing.* (Bi-monthly.) New York: Elsevier.

439. *Venture.* (Monthly.) New York: Venture Magazine, Inc.

Directories of Venture Capital Sources

440. *Corporate Finance Sourcebook.* (Annual.) Wilmette, IL: National Register Publishing Company.

441. *Directory of Members.* (Annual.) Menlo Park, CA: Western Association of Venture Capitalists.

442. *Handbook of Business Finance and Capital Sources.* (Annual.) Minneapolis: InterFinance Corporation.

443. *National Venture Capital Association NVCA Directory.* (Annual.) Washington.

444. *Pratt's Guide to Venture Capital Sources.* (Annual.) Wellesley Hills, MA: Capital Publishing.

Business Plan Guidebooks

445. McGarty, Terrence P. *Business Plans that Win Venture Capital.* New York: Wiley, 1989.

446. Siegel, Eric S. et al. *The Arthur Young Business Plan Guide.* New York: Wiley, 1987.

Career Guidebook

447. Ashmore, M. Catherine et al. *Entrepreneurship as a Career Choice.* Columbus, OH: National Center for Research in Vocational Education, 1987.

25

Getting Job Leads

The last chapter was intended to help you develop a job search focus based on your self-assessment. At this stage you should have identified one or more areas of interest to which you will apply your energies. The next step in the process is to generate options—that is, job offers from which you can choose.

The process of obtaining job offers typically includes a number of key activities: getting job leads, interviewing, and follow-up. In this chapter we'll explore the first of these activities, getting job leads.

Sources of Job Leads

There are five primary sources of job leads: college-associated placement offices, unsolicited direct-mail campaigns, friends and acquaintances, ads in newspapers and journals, and profit-making placement firms (such as personnel agencies and executive search firms). A typical successful job hunter relies on one, two, or three of these sources, depending on his or her particular needs.

School Placement Offices

The placement offices of colleges and universities are generally designed to help graduating students get together with moderate to large prospective employers from the local area. (The more prestigious the school, the larger the area.) Most placement offices are very good at that limited objective. They are generally not particularly helpful if one is looking for a job in a small company, or in another part of the world, or in any type of organization that hires few of the school's graduates (for example, few hospitals interview at business schools). In addition, most placement offices are not organized to help alumni or students seeking summer jobs.

Virtually all undergraduates and most graduate students use their placement offices as a source of job leads. From our own observations, we suspect that few people who should use the placement office as their primary source fail to do so, while a considerable number who should be relying primarily on other sources instead rely exclusively on placement offices, simply because it's easier that way.

To decide how much to rely on a placement office for job leads (or whether to rely on it at all), a student needs to learn, well in advance of the recruiting season, which organizations with what types of job tend to recruit on campus. (Lists of organizations, along with job descriptions from the previous year's recruitment activities, are usually available at placement offices.) If the type of companies and jobs on which you are focusing don't usually recruit on your campus, you will need to rely on other sources for job leads. We have known many graduate students who obtained very satisfying jobs without ever using their placement offices.

Personal Solicitation

Most of our students who have not relied primarily on our placement office have gotten their job leads through direct personal solicitation. That is, they have written unsolicited letters to potential employers asking if they have any job openings. In a typical case, a student will send out ten, twenty, or thirty one- or two-page letters to carefully chosen targets. The letter, in one way or another, asks that the writer be considered for a job, and encloses a résumé. If the letter and résumé are well written and the targets well chosen, the person may expect to receive from ten to fifty percent "positive responses" (usually an invitation for an interview). Poorly written letters and résumés sent out to inadequately screened targets often net no positive responses. We've seen people send out 100 letters and receive photocopied rejection letters from twenty organizations, personal rejection letters from another three, and no response from the remaining seventy-seven.

Personal solicitation can be time-consuming and very frustrating. It takes a reasonably strong ego to withstand getting rejections in the mail day after day after day. It's both easier and less ego-deflating to look over ads in the newspaper or lists of employers at the placement office—a process in which *you* reject (screen) *them*. As a result, most job hunters probably underutilize personal solicitation as a source of leads.

Personal Contacts

The single most important source of job leads for nonstudent professional, technical, and managerial workers is their own personal contacts.

The most useful personal sources of leads include people who are looking for a similar job, former work associates, and professional acquaintances made through professional organizations. People inside an organization often know of, or can easily find out about, job possibilities that are never advertised externally. Professional associations often actively solicit job-possibility information from all their members and then make that information available to their members or to anyone who requests it. The tactic of trading leads with another similar job hunter often can net a large number of previously unknown possibilities.

Some successful job hunters spend virtually all their effort in the first month of job hunting setting up a network of contacts who are aware of their new job-hunting status as well as the exact focus of their job campaign. They then use that network as a radar screen to identify job leads.

Advertisements

A fourth source of leads job hunters often use is advertisements. Newspapers carry job ads on a daily basis for the area they serve. Professional journals and magazines sometimes include a help wanted section. Access to these sources is relatively easy, by subscription or through a library.

Almost all job seekers who are out of school use this source of leads to some degree, probably because it is easy and doesn't require much personal initiative. And ads are the most visible source of job leads. However, very few students seem to actually find jobs through this source, and a relatively small percentage of nonstudent professionals (managerial or technical) actually gain their jobs through ads.

However, job advertisements may serve a useful function beyond being a source of job leads. For the same reason that advertising in general is often useful to people who are not currently looking for a specific product, job advertisements probably help some people get a useful "feel" for the job market. That is, they can sometimes supply information to a job hunter regarding what types of jobs, at what salaries, exist in what numbers, and where. Particularly at the start of a job hunt, such information could be very useful.

Profit-Making Organizations

A final source of leads commonly used by job hunters is such profit-making organizations as executive search firms and personnel agencies. We know of no student at all who has found a job as a result of a lead from these sources. And although we have known many nonstudents who have used this source of leads, very few have actually found jobs that way.

We have personally heard many more bad stories than good about people's interactions with personnel agencies. One gets the sense that they can be helpful to nonstudents, but that there are plenty of risks involved, due to the large number of marginally competent people in those agencies.

Many of the established and larger executive search firms have a reputation of doing a competent job for their market. But that market is fairly small—managers at the upper end of the salary range.

Exhibit 25-1 summarizes this discussion. The number-one job-lead source for students is the placement office. For nonstudents, the number-one source is personal contacts. Unsolicited letter campaigns and other forms of direct application are the second most-used source for both groups.

Before you make an initial contact with an organization (through one of the five sources outlined above), we suggest that you do a little preliminary research to develop an informed first impression as to whether or not the organization seems to offer a good fit with your self-assessment. If the results of this research are completely contradictory to your self-assessment, you may decide not to waste any time on making the contact. Moderately contradictory impressions, however, probably should be followed up (especially if the company fits your focus), since your first impressions may not be completely accurate. Your research, along with your self-assessment, will arm you with specific questions that you can carry to the interview. (See the next chapter.)

Annual Reports

One of the most common sources of information on job opportunities is the annual report. If you are able to develop a framework for reading annual reports, it will help you immensely in your attempt to focus your job search and to wade through large volumes of data relatively quickly and efficiently.

Exhibit 25–1

Summary Chart: Sources of Job Leads

Sources	Comments
1. College placement office	By far the most widely used source for students. Probably overused.
2. Unsolicited direct-mail campaigns	Number-two source for all job hunters.
3. Personal contacts	By far the most widely used source for nonstudents.
4. Advertisements	Useful for job-market data. Not terribly useful for specific leads.
5. Personnel agencies and executive search firms	Best for people earning $30,000 a year or more.

We will not pay attention to financial analysis related to the balance sheets, income statements, and other financial reports contained in an annual report, since much has been written about that elsewhere. And we assume that you will use that kind of analysis in your preparation for interviews. Rather, we will ask you to focus on the nonfinancial aspects of the annual report—its composition, the photographs, the prose, the company's products, and so on.

Looking for a Fit between Organization and You

As you read through an annual report to decide whether or not to make contact, you should remember that, in a focused job search, you are looking for a fit between yourself, a particular job, and the organization in which that job is embedded. In this sense, you are looking for a fit between your personality and the organizational culture of the organization that will be employing you. The annual report can provide a number of clues and signals to help you assess the fit. As was the case in the self-assessment process, no single signal or datum is sufficient to give you an accurate, reliable view of an organization. And so our philosophy here is the same as that expressed earlier; namely, that if you can generate a variety of pools of information about potential employers, you will have a better perspective on the goodness of fit between you and the organization. The annual report will provide several signals that will contribute to that multifaceted pool of data about an organization.

Corporations are spending increasingly large volumes of money, energy, and time in preparing their annual reports. In one study of twenty-seven large corporations, it was estimated that top management spent well over a thousand hours in planning, editing, and approving the annual report. The range was from 112 to 5,760 hours. If one values senior management time at an average of $275 per hour, the average cost for management time spent on the development of those twenty-seven annual reports comes to $61,750. You can see that, from the corporation's point of view, the impression that is left by an annual report is an important one. In the same way that you as a job candidate will be trying to create an impression with your résumé and cover letter, the organization is trying to create an impression with the annual report that will be both accurate and favorable (see the alternate exercise on p. 295). When you read an annual report, the signals and characteristics we identify below will no doubt do much to create the impression that you have of that organization. We want to make those signals explicit to you so that you can use them more efficiently and effectively in assessing the fit between you and the organization.

The Cover and the President's Letter

One fundamental issue in reading an annual report is a consideration of who wrote the president's letter and the other explanatory prose contained throughout the report. In many cases, the letter and the explanation prose are written by corporate staff people who may or may not be accurately reflecting the philosophies and ideas of top management. In most cases, we assume that annual reports have been approved by top management people. Ask yourself if the president's letter seems to have been written by him or her individually or by a staff member. What does that tell you about the organization and its management? The question of authorship introduces a question of validity into your reading of an annual report. It should also caution you not to either accept or reject what is contained in an annual report as fact without further investigation.

Consider the cover. What is on the cover? Why do you think that particular cover (in many cases a photograph) was chosen? What was the company trying to say about itself by choosing that cover? What does the cover say about what is important to the company?

Next, consider the relationship of the president's letter to the financial results of the corporation. If the results were bad, who gets the blame? Does the corporation look to outside factors to explain its business results, or is the organization willing to look internally as well? What does this tell you about the management of the organization and about what it might be like to work with? If the results were good, to whom does the credit go? Are the senior managers willing to disperse credit throughout the organization, or is it again attributed to factors over which management feels it has little control?

People

Look for the attention given to people. How many people are mentioned in the annual report? In what ways? Are they described in personal or impersonal ways? How many people are there in the organization? Is the number of people growing? What does this tell you about the industry the organization is in? What is the ratio of sales to employees? What does this tell you about the efficiency of the organization? What does this tell you about what it would be like to work in this organizational culture? What about turnover in the organization? Are the reasons for turnover mentioned? If not, why? If they are mentioned, what do the reasons tell you about what it would be like to work for this organization?

What about changes in senior management? Who has gone and who has come in the past year? Where did they go? From where did they come? Outside the organization? If inside, from what areas? What does this tell you about the standards and criteria for advancement within the organization? Are senior management all of a particular age or ethnic background? What does this tell you?

Try flipping through the annual report without reading anything. Look only at the pictures. What do you see? People? Products? Neither? If you see people, what can you learn from them? Are they all the same age, same sex, same race? What are they doing? Why do you think those pictures were chosen?

Problems and Plans

Note the problems identified in the various prose descriptions of the organization's business. What kinds of problems does the company face? Are these problems you would find interesting to work on? Are they the same ones you would expect the company to be facing?

You might also look for plans for dealing with those problems. Are there any? Do they seem realistic? Are they reasonable given your knowledge of the economy and the industry? Do they seem attainable, given the resources the organization has at its command?

Consider the organization of the company. Is this outlined in the annual report? What is it? What does that imply about what it would be like to work for that company? Will there be a lot of transfers? Where are the facilities? Which parts of the organization report to whom?

Look for signals about how decisions are made in this corporation. Are many people involved, or do decisions seem to be made by a singie individual? What does this tell you about what it would be like to work for this company?

You may not be able to glean answers to all these questions from any particular annual report. That in itself is data and can provide you with questions for an interview.

Exercises

Comparing Annual Reports

Choose annual reports for two companies in each of two different industries. Then read the president's letter from each and compare and contrast the tone and content of the letters. You might, for instance, get the latest General Electric, GTE, General Mills, and General Foods annual reports. Ask yourself:

> What tentative inferences can be drawn about what it would be like to work for each of these companies?
>
> How are the annual reports similar?
>
> How are they different?
>
> Do you see any common characteristics in the two companies in the same industry? (This will give you some insight into industry characteristics that might be true regardless of the company you interview with in a particular industry.)
>
> How do these reports differ from others you have read?
>
> What seems to be most important to each company?
>
> What can you infer about the management style of each company?

This assignment will help you to calibrate the amount of variation you can expect in recruiting within and among industries. It will also sharpen your insight into the realities of corporate cultures and the ways they influence corporations and the people who work in them. This skill will be very useful to you later on when you begin interviewing and making company visits.

Alternate Exercise: Gaining Insight into the Accuracy of Written Promotional Materials

An interesting exercise that will help you see more clearly how well written promotional materials reflect the experience of living in an organization is to examine a situation in which you have both personal and written experience. Consider your school if you are taking this material in a course. It might be interesting to have the class review promotional material (brochures) published and distributed by the school. Read the brochures in advance of the class and be prepared to discuss how well the brochures match or do not match your experience and view of the school. Then consider the differences you found with the kind of differences you might expect to find between an annual report and working for a company. This may help you to calibrate the information you will glean from reading annual reports.

If you are working through this book on your own, you may wish to compare the annual report or descriptive brochure of an organization you have worked with in the past with your own experience.

26

Making Contact

Once you have decided to make contact with an organization, you must decide how to do it in a way that will make the organization receptive to you. Of the sources of job leads outlined in the previous chapter, unsolicited direct-mail campaigns and answering advertisements present the greatest difficulty, since usually the only introductions one has in those two cases are one's cover letter and résumé. In order to get an interview in which the employer is receptive to you, you must pass through an initial screening process.

Most employers have no more desire to waste their time in the labor market than you do. So they too set up some type of screening process. The key to success is to differentiate yourself from the masses and convince the decision maker that the time taken to interview you probably isn't going to be wasted.

It is not unusual for an organization to receive twenty to fifty inquiries for a job opening. Some jobs will attract hundreds of inquires. Since simply hiring a single managerial or professional person can cost an organization as much as $20,000, employers have a strong financial incentive to try to keep costs down. Interviewing everyone who inquires about a job opening can significantly increase costs.

Convincing some decision maker to take the time to interview you is not just an exercise, as many people seem to think, in making yourself look "impressive" in some ill-defined, abstract sense. What is "impressive," like beauty, is in the eye of the beholder. The beholder is an employer with particular goals, values, problems, and needs. And here lies the key not just to getting an initial interview, but to getting job offers.

The more you can put yourself in the position of the potential employer and understand that person's (or those people's) point of view, the more successful you will be in getting job offers. With respect to getting an initial interview, this means that it helps enormously to know something about the potential employer before you make your initial contact. Any person who has gone through the process of creating a rational focus for a job campaign, and who has done the little additional research necessary to screen leads, has probably learned enough about potential employers to make the type of initial contact that gets an interview. It doesn't require hours and hours of additional effort. Since so many job hunters do almost no research, doing just a little can be a real competitive advantage. Then, if you can somehow communicate to those making the screening decision that you may have the potential of meeting *their needs*, you will certainly get the interview.

You should not attempt to do this, of course, if it means ignoring parts of your self-assessment that are central to who you are. Remember that "fit" from both your and the employer's points of view is the essential factor. The point here is that what you say and how you say it will be more effective if you consider carefully the person who will be reading or listening to what you say than if you are concerned only about satisfying some personal needs.

Résumés

Consider, for example, your résumé. Most people, even those with no full-time job experience, could write a several-page résumé if coached. They could elaborate at length on their schooling, their part-time jobs, their hobbies, their health, their job objectives, and so on. Most people don't, of course. Instead, they ask someone what a résumé is supposed to look like, or for a sample résumé, and then semiconsciously select things to put into that format. The end result is seldom a great résumé.

A good résumé is nothing more than a tool that can convince employers you will be able to meet their particular needs, help with their problems, and share enough in common with them to "fit in." Creating a good résumé therefore depends on your understanding of what an employer's needs are, what the problems are, what the values are, and what you can contribute. Since books and volumes of articles have been written on how to prepare and compose résumés, we will not spend much time on the mechanics of this process. Rather, we refer you to the appendix at the end of the chapter. However, we would like to make a few comments with regard to the philosophy behind résumés and then give you a brief exercise to help you translate those philosophical comments into practical applications.

Format

Résumés have two fundamental dimensions—format and content. One might believe that the format of the résumé is unimportant. We have not found that to be the case. One recruiter, looking at a professionally composed and typeset résumé, remarked enthusiastically to the job candidate: "It really is nice to see such a well-done résumé. I could tell from the moment I saw it that you believed in high standards of professionalism in your work. We get so many résumés here that are poorly typed and photocopied or mimeographed, that it really is refreshing and reassuring to get one like this." That recruiter was responding to the format of the résumé he was looking at.

A résumé that looks as if it was typed on a cheap typewriter by a nontypist communicates a number of things about you. It says that you are a sloppy person (and who wants to hire a sloppy person?), or that you really don't care much about getting a job (and who wants to hire someone who doesn't want to work?), or that you don't really care much about the person you sent the résumé to. It's worth the time and money to *look* professional and interested.

The way your résumé is laid out on a sheet of paper is extremely important in leaving an impression with the person who reads it. We encourage you to experiment with a variety of formats and to choose the one that leaves an impression consistent with who you are and what you are looking for in a corporation. You may have a terrific résumé in substance, but if the format is poor it may leave a poor impression.

There are several aspects to format we would encourage you to keep in mind. The first is the spacing on the page. Résumés with very small margins leave the impression of a great deal of activity. But they also leave the impression of disorganization. Although it is general practice to have résumés limited to one page, crowded margins may undo whatever benefit you may get from increasing the volume. One alternative if you have too much to put on one page is to type it on a longer page with wider margins and have the entire page photoreproduced and then duplicated on an 8 1/2 by 11 sheet.

Another item is the question of parallelism in format. Recruiters read hundreds, perhaps thousands of résumés in the recruiting season. They get in a rhythm as they read, using whatever framework they have personally developed to help them quickly get the pertinent information. Some of this is conscious; some of this is subconscious. Every time a résumé format interrupts or jars that rhythm, the recruiter's impression is also interrupted or jarred. An effective résumé will pique the recruiter's attention at the places *you* want to emphasize and not at unintended or inappropriate places.

A lack of parallel construction is one way to jar or interrupt a recruiter's reading rhythm. Most résumés, for instance, begin paragraphs with a noun describing the previous job title and then the activities that it included in the lines that follow. However, a lot of people under the "Education" sections of their résumés begin those paragraphs with verbs like "Graduated" or "Received." It is our preference to maintain parallel construction by beginning the descriptive paragraphs under each job or educational experience in the same way. If, for example, you wanted to begin each paragraph with a noun, you could begin your educational paragraphs with the word "Graduate" followed by your degree and the honors and activities associated with your experience there.

Content

Format alone, of course, will not ensure a good impression. Content is also extremely important. A well laid out format that has no substance will not get you very far. As you think about the content of your résumé, keep in mind that résumés are very much like short stories. They are designed to leave a particular impression with the reader in a minimum of space. Because of their brevity, every word or phrase in a short story and a résumé counts. You cannot afford to waste space or words when you are trying to create a favorable impression on one page.

Remember that you are creating an impression. The impression must be an accurate one; it must reflect who you are and what you've done, but it is indeed an impression. The words you choose, the sentences you frame, and the format in which you package this content will create impressions in the minds of the people who read the résumé. Try to create the impression that *you want* to leave; one that accurately reflects the results of your self-assessment.

Perhaps the major feature of the content part of a résumé is the repetition with which patterns or themes appear in the material. A person who writes a résumé that includes a degree in education, teaching in an elementary school, teaching in a secondary school, a masters degree in higher education, and work for an education foundation has created a pattern that sends the signal they have selected a career in education. Applying for jobs in noneducational areas will require some additional impression-creating and selling.

In some cases, students who have not developed a focus in their job search have attempted to list all their activities and in some cases to fluff up or expand their résumés by including activities and memberships that were only marginal experiences. We find this to be more harmful than helpful. If, for instance, in the business educational section of your résumé you list membership in the Management Consultant Club, the General Management Club, the Small Business Club, the International Finance Club, and the Marketing Club, in the belief that the range and diversity of your interests will be an attractive feature to a recruiter, we believe you are mistaken. A person with a focused job search who wants a job in marketing would eliminate the other club activities from the résumé so that the impression left is that of a person who knows what he or she wants to do. Recruiters in marketing-oriented companies who read the résumé are more likely to be left with the impression that here is a person whose interests seem to match our own.

Another common characteristic of poorly written résumés is that their writers tend to use very general words to describe the activities and responsibilities of each experience or position. A well-written résumé will always contain nouns, verbs, adjectives, and adverbs which pinpoint the job focus that person is trying to create. Again, a person seeking a position in marketing will look for the words that accurately describe his or her activities and experience but that also have immediate and relevant application to careers and positions in marketing.

Summary

The point of what we have been trying to say is that like a short story, a résumé is basically an impression-creating document. When you write your résumé, you should be sensitive to this feature. Be careful with every word you use. Ask yourself if it helps to create the kind of impression you want to leave and if it is relevant to the kind of recruiter who will be reading your résumé. If you are uncertain about the impression that is being left or of how it will be received, leave the word out.

Assignment 1

Consider Kathleen Johnson's résumé (case, p. 300). What impressions does it leave with you? What do you think Kathleen's job search focus is? What inferences can you draw about Kathleen?

Cover Letters

The cover letter is a means of contacting an organization, presenting your résumé and your job focus, and of asking for a response. You may in fact write several different kinds of cover letters if you are deciding to pursue more than one focus in a particular job search. Most people write cover letters with the idea that they must sell themselves to the reader. While this is an important part of the cover letter's purpose, a more effective cover letter is one that also provides the writer with an opportunity to learn from the responses it generates.

RÉSUMÉ OF KATHLEEN JOHNSON

Chase Hall B-11
Harvard Business School
Boston, MA 02163
Phone: (617) 498-0000

Home Address:
33 Upland Road
Summit, N.J. 07901
Phone (201) 273-0000

education

1978–1980 HARVARD GRADUATE SCHOOL OF BUSINESS ADMINISTRATION

Candidate for the degree of Master in Business Administration in June, 1980. General management curriculum with emphasis on marketing and production. Member of Management Consulting, Marketing and Real Estate Clubs.

1977 AMERICAN MANAGEMENT ASSOCIATION — NEW YORK, NEW YORK

Seminars in sales management.

1969–1973 FAIRLEIGH DICKINSON UNIVERSITY — RUTHERFORD, NEW JERSEY

Received Bachelor of Science degree in Experimental Psychology, January 1973. Dean's List. New Jersey Scholar and Travelli Grant recipient. University Administrative Intern, Residential Advisor, and Counselor at a medium security prison. Extracurricular activities in sports and music.

work experience

summer 1979 NEW JERSEY BANK & TRUST — NEWARK, NEW JERSEY

Credit Analyst. Analyzed financial position of potential corporate customers and made loan development calls.

1973–1978 BABBITT PHARMACEUTICAL CORPORATION — WHITE PLAINS, NEW YORK

1977–1978

Midwest Regional Sales Manager. Brought region from last to first place with respect to quota attainment while reducing the proportion of selling expense to sales by 25%. Developed and implemented a management by objectives plan and supervised field work for a major test market. Handled all recruitment, conducted sales seminars, trained sales representatives, provided expense budgets, coordinated cooperative advertising programs, and developed key accounts for a 9 state area.

1973–1977 Sales Representative. Sales and service of a vitamin and health care product line to pharmacies. Designated 1975 "Sales Representative of the Year" for highest attainment of quota.

1973 PUBLISHERS GUILD — MORRISTOWN, NEW JERSEY

Sales Representative. Personal contact sales of dictionaries and magazines.

other experience

United States Representative to a Swiss Girl Guide International Conference. Financed college education through various part-time and summer jobs.

references

Personal references available upon request.

JIM LYDON: COVER LETTER

Dear Mr. _____:

I shall receive an M.B.A. in June 1978 and plan a career in the real estate field with a leading properties firm. My survey of the industry indicates that your firm has established an outstanding record and, therefore, it would be advantageous for me to learn more about the specific opportunities it offers and to discuss with you my objectives and capabilities.

My highest priority is to find a challenging, fulfilling environment in which to learn and work. Pursuant to this objective, I seek a firm which: (1) recognizes the need for professional management of M.B.A. caliber in this rapidly growing field, (2) gives a broad exposure to real estate and discourages overspecialization, (3) operates in an informal structure with close personal relationships among employees, (4) allows new M.B.A.'s to contribute immediately and to assume early responsibilities, and (5) measures performance and allocates compensation and advancement accordingly without regard for senority. I would like to know more about your firm with respect to these criteria.

The enclosed resume gives you a brief outline of my background but does not deal with relevant personal qualities. I have an entrepreneurial spirit, the ability to coordinate several projects simultaneously with proven results, and a "knack" for working successfully with diverse groups of people eliciting their trust and confidence. I am performance-oriented, mature, willing to travel, able to communicate effectively, and confident that the pattern of success that has characterized my past will lead me to greater achievements in the near future.

Mr. _____, if you feel that my objectives and qualifications may be compatible with your firm's opportunities and needs, please contact me to arrange a meeting that could be to our mutual benefit. I shall hope to hear from you soon.

Sincerely,

James L. Lydon

JLL/lmm

Enclosure

Assignment 2

Jim Lydon, for example, after going through an extensive self-assessment process, decided to focus his job search on real estate and banking. He signed up for twelve interviews offered by his campus placement office, and in addition decided to write to thirteen banks and twelve real estate firms.

Assume that you are Jim Lydon's roommate and that before sending out his letters, he has asked you to critique his cover letter (see above). What is the paragraph by paragraph structure he has used? How would you respond to Jim? What suggestions would you make? What predictions would you make?

Appendix to Chapter 26: Making Contact

Sources of Information on Developing Job Opportunities

CAREER STRATEGY/JOB HUNTING

1. Beatty, Richard H. *The Complete Job Search Book.* New York: Wiley, 1988.
2. Bolles, Richard Nelson. *What Color is Your Parachute?: A Practical Manual for Job-Hunters & Career Changers.* Berkeley, CA: Ten Speed Press, 1990.
3. Bostwick, Burdette E. *How To Find The Job You've Always Wanted,* 2nd ed. New York: Wiley, 1982.
4. Bronstein, Eugene, and Robert D. Hisrich. *The MBA Career: Moving on the Fast Track to Success.* Woodbury, NY: Barron's Educational Series, 1983.
5. Burack, Elmer H., and Nicholas J. Mathys. *Career Management in Organizations: A Practical Human Resource Planning Approach.* Lake Forest, IL: Brace-Park Press.
6. Clawson, James G., and David D. Ward. *An MBA's Guide To Self-Assessment & Career Development.* Englewood Cliffs, NJ: Prentice Hall, 1986.
7. Cohen, William A. *The Executive's Guide to Finding a Superior Job,* rev. ed. New York: American Management Associations, 1983.
8. Crystal, John C., and Richard N. Bolles. *Where Do I Go From Here With My Life?* New York, NY: The Seabury Press, 1974.
9. Houze, William C. *Career Veer: How to Position Yourself for a Prosperous Future.* New York: McGraw-Hill, 1985.
10. Jelinek, Mariann. *Career Management: For the Individual and the Organization.* Chicago, IL: St. Clair Press, 1979.
11. Leape, Martha P. *The Harvard Guide to Careers.* Cambridge, MA: Harvard University Press, 1983.
12. Lewis, William and Carol Milano. *Profitable Careers in Nonprofit.* New York: Wiley, 1987.
13. Lewis, William and Nancy Schuman. *Fast-track Careers: A Guide to the Highest-Paying Jobs.* New York: Wiley, 1987.
14. Morgan, Marilyn A. *Managing Career Development.* New York, NY: D. Van Nostrand Company, 1980, p. 285.
15. O'Brien, Mark. *The MBA Answer Book: A Career Guide for the Person Who Means Business.* Englewood Cliffs, NJ: Prentice Hall, 1984.
16. Petras, Kathryn and Ross Petras. *The Only Job-Hunting Guide You'll Ever Need: The Most Comprehensive Guide for Job Hunters and Career Switchers.* New York: Poseidon Press, 1989.
17. Rust, H. Lee, *Job Search: The Complete Manual for Jobseekers.* New York, NY: AMACOM, A Division of American Management Associations, 1979. p. 258.
18. Stumpf, Stephen A., Ph.D. *Choosing A Career in Business.* New York, NY: Simon & Schuster, Inc., 1984.

RESUMES AND COVER LETTERS

19. Allen, Jeffrey G. *The Complete Q & A Job Interview Book.* New York: Wiley, 1988.
20. Beatty, Richard H. *The Perfect Cover Letter.* New York: Wiley, 1989.
21. Beatty, Richard H. *The Resume Kit.* New York: Wiley, 1984.
22. Bostwick, Burdette E. *Resume Writing: A Comprehensive How-To-Do-It Guide,* 3rd ed. New York: Wiley, 1985.
23. Fear, Richard A. *The Evaluation Interview,* 3rd ed. New York: McGraw-Hill, 1984.
24. Foxman, Loretta D. *The Executive Resume Book.* New York: Wiley, 1989.
25. Holtz, Herman. *Beyond The Resume: How to Land the Job You Want.* New York: McGraw-Hill, 1984.
26. Linkemer, Bobbi. *How to Write an Effective Resume.* New York, NY: AMACOM, 1987.

Compiled by Henry Wingate, Darden School Librarian, and James G. Clawson.

INTERVIEWS

27. Hellman, Paul. *Ready, Aim, You're Hired!: How to Job-Interview Successfully Anytime, Anywhere with Anyone.* New York, NY: AMACOM, 1986.
28. Medley, H. Anthony. *Sweaty Palms: The Neglected Art of Being Interviewed.* Berkeley, CA: Ten Speed Press, 1984.
29. Moffatt, Thomas L. *Selection Interviewing for Managers.* New York, NY: Harper & Row, 1979.
30. Ryckman, W. G. *How to Pass the Employment Interview (with flying colors).* Homewood, IL: Dow Jones-Irwin, 1982.
31. Yate, Martin John. *Knock'em Dead: With Great Answers to Tough Interview Questions.* New and Expanded Edition. Boston: B. Adams, 1987.

EXECUTIVE RECRUITING SEARCH FIRMS

These selected sources provide information about executive recruiting search firms, commonly called recruiters or headhunters. They are frequently retained and paid by employers. Their job is to find qualified candidates for specific positions their clients have available. Recruiters do not hire people; they only recommend them to their clients. The two professional associations to which recruiters belong are:

Association of Executive Search Consultants (AESC), 17 Sherwood Place, Greenwich, CT 06830. (203) 661-6606.

Association of Consulting Management Engineers (ACME), 230 Park Avenue, New York, NY 10169. (212) 697-9693

32. Cole, Kenneth J. *The Headhunter Strategy: How to Make it Work for You.* New York: Wiley, 1985.
33. Cox, Allan J. *Confessions of a Corporate Headhunter.* Richmond Hill, Ontario, Canada: Simon & Schuster of Canada, Ltd., 1973.
34. *Directory of Executive Recruiters.* (Annual.) Fitzwilliam, NH; Consultants News.
35. *The Executive Grapevine: Retainer Search.* New York: Executive Grapevine, 1986.
36. Freedman, Howard S. *How To Get a Headhunter to Call.* New York: Wiley, 1986.
37. Hickson, Jacqueline M. *The Executive Grapevine: Contingency/Retainer Search.* New York: Executive Grapevine, 1986.
38. Perry, Robert H. *How to Answer a Headhunter's Call: A Complete Guide to Executive Search.* New York: NY: AMACOM Book Division, 1984.
39. Taylor, A. Robert. *How to Select and Use An Executive Search Firm.* New York: McGraw-Hill, 1982.

SALARIES

40. *The American Almanac of Jobs and Salaries.* New York, NY: Avon, 1988.
41. *Executive Compensation.* (Annual.) Princeton, NJ: Sibson & Co.
42. *Executive Compensation.* (Biennial.) New York, Financial Executives Institute.
43. Harrop, David. *America's Paychecks: Who Makes What.* New York: Facts On File, 1980.
44. Kennedy, Marilyn Moats. *Salary Strategies: Everything You Need to Know to Get the Salary You Want.* New York, NY: Rawson, Wade, 1982.
45. Krefetz, Gerald and Philip Gittelman. *The Book of Incomes.* New York: Holt, Rinehart, and Winston, 1982.
46. *National Survey of Professional, Administrative, Technical and Clerical Pay.* Private nonservice industries. Washington, DC: U.S. Bureau of Labor Statistics, 1989.
47. *Top Executive Compensation.* (Biennial) New York: Conference Board.

INTERNATIONAL EMPLOYMENT

48. Aluick, June L. *Looking for Employment in Foreign Countries,* 7th ed. New York: World Trade Academy Press, 1985.
49. *Directory of American Firms Operating in Foreign Countries.* New York: Simon & Schuster, 1988.
50. *Indexes of Living Costs Abroad and Quarters Allowances.*

(Quarterly, with annual summary.) Washington, DC: U.S. Department of State.

51. Kocher, Eric. *International Jobs: Where They Are, How To Get Them: A Handbook for Over 500 Career Opportunities Around The World*, revised ed. Reading, MA: Addison-Wesley Publishing Company, 1984.
52. Plave, Mitchell, ed. *Internships and Careers in International Affairs*, 2nd ed. New York: United Nations Association of the United States of America, 1984.
53. Powell, James N. *The Prentice Hall Global Employment Guide*. Englewood Cliffs, NJ: Prentice Hall, 1983.
54. Schuman, Howard. *Making It Abroad: The International Job Hunting Guide*. New York: Wiley, 1988.
55. Win, David. *International Careers: An Insider's Guide: Where to Find Them, How to Build Them*. Charlotte, VT: Williamson Publishing, 1987.

ESPECIALLY FOR WOMEN

56. Cannie, Joan Koob, *The Woman's Guide to Management Success: How to Win Power in the Real Organizational World*. Englewood Cliffs, NJ: Prentice Hall, Inc., 1979.
57. *Career Opportunities Series for Women*. New York, NY: Catalyst, Inc.
58. Fuchs, Lawrence H. *Family Matters*. New York, NY: Warner Paperback Library, 1972.
59. Gallese, Liz Roman. *Women Like Us*. New York, NY: William Morrow and Company, Inc., 1985.
60. Gilligan, Carol. *In a Different Voice*. Cambridge, MA: Harvard University Press, 1982.
61. Harragan, Betty Lehan. *Games Mother Never Taught You*. New York, NY: Warner Books, Inc., 1977.
62. Hennig, Margaret and Anne Jardim. *The Managerial Woman*. New York, NY: Pocket Books, 1976.
63. Josefowitz, Natasha, *Paths to Power: A Woman's Guide from First Job to Top Executive*. Reading, MA: Addison-Wesley Publishing Company, 1980.
64. Kanter, Rosabeth Moss. *Men and Women of the Corporation*. New York, NY: Basic Books, Inc., 1977.
65. Landau, Suzanne, and Geoffrey Bailey. *The Landau Strategy: How Working Women Win Top Jobs*. New York: C. N. Potter, 1980.
66. The staff of Catalyst. *Making the Most of Your First Job*. New York: Putnam, 1981.
67. The editors of Catalyst; foreword by Sylvia Porter. *Marketing Yourself: The Catalyst Women's Guide to Successful Resumes and Interviews*. New York: Putnam, 1980.
68. Moore, Lynda L. *Not as Far as You Think*. Lexington, MA: Lexington Books, 1986.
69. Neugarten, Dail Ann, and Jay M. Shafritz. *Sexuality in Organizations*. Oak Park, IL: Moore Publishing Company, Inc., 1980.
70. Rice, F. Philip. *A Working Mother's Guide to Child Development*. Englewood Cliffs, NJ: Prentice Hall, 1979.
71. Stead, Bette Ann. *Women in Management*. Englewood Cliffs, NJ: Prentice Hall, 1978.
72. Westoff, Leslie Aldridge. *Corporate Romance*. New York, NY: Times Books, 1985.
73. Williams, Marcille Gray. *The New Executive Woman: A Guide to Business Success*. New York, NY: First Mentor Printing, 1978.
74. *The Working Woman Report: Succeeding in Business in the '80s*, by the editors of Working Woman. New York, NY: Simon and Schuster, 1984.
75. Zeitz, Baila and Lorraine Dusky. *The Best Companies for Women*. New York: Simon and Schuster, 1988.

DUAL CAREER FAMILIES

76. Brothers, Joyce. *The Successful Woman: How You Can Have A Career, A Husband, and a Family—and not feel guilty about it*. New York: Simon and Schuster, 1988.
77. Gilbert, Lucia Albino. *Men in Dual-Career Families: Current Realities and Future Prospects*. Hillsdale, NJ: L. Erlbaum Associates, 1985.
78. Gilbert, Lucia A. *Sharing it all: The Rewards and Struggles of Two-Career Families*. New York, NY: Plenum Press, 1988.
79. Magid, Renee Y., and Nancy E. Fleming. *When Mother and Fathers work: Creative Strategies for Balancing Career and Family*. New York, NY: AMACOM, 1987.
80. Sekaran, Uma. *Dual-Career Families*. San Francisco, CA: Josey-Bass, 1986.

SELF, FAMILY, AND WORK

81. Cooper, Cary L. *Executive Families Under Stress.* Englewood Cliffs, NJ: Prentice Hall, 1981.
82. Derr, C. Brooklyn. *Work, Family, and the Career: New Frontiers in Theory and Research.* New York, NY: Praeger Publishing, 1980.
83. Evans, Paul, and Fernando Bartolome. *Must Success Cost So Much?.* New York, NY: Basic Books, 1981.
84. Greiff, Barrie S., M.D. and Preston K. Munter, M.D. *Tradeoffs: Executive, Family and Organizational Life.* New York, NY: The New American Library, Inc., 1980.
85. Korman, Abraham K., with Rhoda W. Korman. *Career Success/Personal Failure.* Englewood Cliffs, NJ: Prentice Hall, 1980.
86. Lee, Mary Dean, and Rabindra N. Kanungo. *Management of Work and Personal Life.* New York, NY: Praeger, 1984.
87. Machlowitz, Marilyn, Ph.D. *Workaholics: Living with them, Working with them.* Reading, MA: Addison-Wesley, 1980.
88. Marrow, Alfred J. *The Failure of Success.* New York, NY: AMACOM, 1972.

PLACEMENT DIRECTORIES

89. *Careers and the MBA.* (Annual.) Boston: Harvard Student Publications Board, Graduate School of Business Administration, Harvard University.
90. Krantz, Les. *The Jobs Rated Almanac: 250 Jobs: Ranks the Best and Worst Jobs by More than a Dozen Vital Criteria: Including Salary, Stress, Benefits, Travel and More.* New York: World Almanac, 1988.
91. Levering, Robert et al. *The 100 Best Companies to Work for in America.* Reading, MA: Addison-Wesley, 1984.
92. *The National Job Bank.* (Biennial.) Brighton, MA: B. Adams.
93. Plunkett, Jack W. *The Almanac of American Employers: A Guide to America's 500 Most Successful Large Corporations.* Chicago: Contemporary Books, 1985.
94. Salzman, Marian L., and Nancy E. Marx. *MBA Jobs: An Insider's Guide to the Companies that hire MBA's.* New York, NY: American Management Association, 1986.
95. Ulrich, Heinz, and J. Robert Connor. *The National Job-Finding Guide.* Garden City, NY: Dolphin Books, 1981.

GEOGRAPHIC AREAS: QUALITY OF LIFE

96. American Chamber of Commerce Researchers Association. *Cost of Living Index: Comparative Data for 280 Urban Areas.* (Quarterly.) Louisville, KY.
97. Bayless, Hugh. *The Best Towns in America: A Where-To-Go Guide for a Better Life.* Boston: Houghton Mifflin, 1983.
98. Bowman, Thomas F. et al. *Finding Your Best Place to Live in America.* New York: Red Lion Books, 1981.
99. Bowman, Dr. Thomas F., Dr. George A. Giuliani, and Dr. M. Ronald Minge. *Finding Your Best Place To Live In America.* West Babylon, NY: Red Lion Books, 1981.
100. Boyer, Rick, and David Savageau. *Places Rated Almanac: Your Guide to Finding the Best Places to Live in America.* New York: Prentice Hall, 1989.
101. *CPT (Consumer Price Index) Detailed Report.* (Monthly.) Washington, DC: U.S. Bureau of Labor Statistics. Provides comparative cost of living indexes for major metropolitan areas.
102. Levering, Robert, Milton Moskowitz, and Michael Katz. *The 100 Best Companies to Work for in America.* Boston, MA: Addison-Wesley, 1984.

ADULT LIFE AND CAREER STAGES

103. Gould, Roger L., M.D. *Transformations: Growth and Change in Adult Life.* New York, NY: Simon and Schuster, 1978.
104. Herr, Edwin L., and Stanley H. Cramer. *Career Guidance Through the Life Span: Systematic Approaches.* Boston, MA: Little, Brown and Company, 1979.

105. Levinson, Daniel J., Charlotte N. Darrow, Edward B. Klein, Maria H. Levinson, and Braxton McKee. *The Seasons of A Man's Life*. New York, NY: Alfred A. Knopf, Inc., 1977.

106. Sheehy, Gail. *Passages: Predictable Crises of Adult Life*. New York, NY: Dutton, 1974.

107. Sofer, Cyril. *Men in Mid-Career: A Study of British Managers and Technical Specialists*. New York, NY: Cambridge at the University Press, 1970.

108. Vaillant, George E., *Adaptation to Life*. Boston, MA: Little, Brown and Company, 1977.

109. White, Robert W., *Lives in Progress: A Study of the Natural Growth of Personality*. Boston, MA: Henry Holt and Company, Inc., 1952.

CAREER THEORY

110. Arthur, Michael B., Douglas T. Hall, and Barbara S. Lawrence. *Handbook of Career Theory*. Cambridge, MA: Cambridge University Press, 1989.

111. Blotnick, Dr. Srully. *The Corporate Steeplechase: Predictable Crisis in a Business Career*. New York, NY: Facts on File, Inc., 1984.

112. Bray, Douglas W., Richard J. Campbell, and Donald L. Grant. *Formative Years in Business: A Long-Term AT&T Study of Managerial Lives*. New York, NY: Wiley, 1974.

113. Brown, Duane, Linda Brooks, and associates. *Career Choice and Development*. San Francisco, CA: Jossey-Bass Publishers, 1984.

114. Gysbers, Norman C., and associates. *Designing Careers: Counseling to Enhance Education, Work, and Leisure*. San Francisco, CA: Jossey-Bass, Inc., Publishers, 1984.

115. Hall, Douglas T. *Careers in Organizations*. Pacific Palisades, CA: Goodyear Publishing Company, Inc., 1976.

116. Hall, Douglas T., and associates. *Career Development in Organizations*. San Francisco, CA: Jossey-Bass Publishers, 1986.

117. Hammaker, Paul M., and Louis T. Rader. *Plain Talk to Young Executives*. Homewood, IL: Irwin, 1977.

118. Jencks, Christopher. *Who Gets Ahead? The Determinants of Economic Success in America*. New York, NY: Basic Books, 1979.

119. Jennings, Eugene Emerson. *The Mobile Manager: A Study of the New Generation of Top Executives*. New York, NY: McGraw-Hill Book Company, 1967.

120. Jennings, Eugene E. *Routes to the Executive Suite*. New York, NY: McGraw-Hill, 1971.

121. London, Manuel, and Stephen A. Stumpf. *Managing Careers*. Reading, MA: Addison-Wesley Publishing Company, 1982.

122. Osipow, Samuel H. *Theories of Career Development*. Englewood Cliffs, NJ: Prentice Hall, 1973.

123. Schein, Edgar H. *Career Dynamics: Matching Individual and Organizational Needs*. Reading, MA: Addison-Wesley, 1978.

124. Sonnenfeld, Jeffrey A. *Managing Career Systems: Channeling the Flow of Executive Careers*. Homewood, IL: Irwin, 1984.

125. Stoner, James A. F., Thomas P. Ference, E. Kirby Warren, and H. Kurt Christensen. *Managerial Career Plateaus: An Exploratory Study*. New York: Center for Research in Career Development, Graduate School of Business, Columbia University, 1980.

126. Wanous, John P. *Organizational Entry: Recruitment, Selection, and Socialization of Newcomers*. Reading, MA: Addison-Wesley, 1980.

127. Zaleznik, Abraham, Gene W. Dalton, and Louis B. Barnes. *Orientation and Conflict in Career*. Boston, MA: Division of Research, Harvard Business School, 1970.

27

Interviewing

A professional person will virtually always be asked to interview with from one to twenty-five or more different members of a hiring organization. Many people look forward to these interviews, especially initial "screening" interviews, with the same ambivalence that precedes an operation—and with good reason. Interviewing, for many people, is an anxiety-arousing, painful experience in which they display little skill or common sense. Exhibit 27–1 outlines some of the common problems that arise in interviews.

The archetype of the poor interviewee is the young student. Such a person goes into an interview, especially at the beginning of the recruiting season, with an awkward feeling that is usually reinforced by his or her friends ("Hey, Jerry, is that really you underneath that suit and without any hair?"). Sometimes people have a gnawing feeling, which they know is silly, that they are basically unemployable (born in the wrong century). At some level, these young people often see the interviewer as someone with life-or-death power over them (which frightens some and enrages others). The fright, anger, and awkwardness are made even worse in the interview when the interviewer doesn't behave as the interviewee somehow expects. Trembling or hostile, interviewees exhibit defensive behaviors that even they usually recognize are not in their own best interests. As a result, some people have real difficulty getting job offers—even people who eventually go on to have splendid careers.

Much of the anxiety that accompanies a person into an interview can be reduced or eliminated by following the procedures outlined previously in this book. People who are confident in knowing who they are and what they want invariably feel more relaxed going into interviews than people who don't. Even people who spend just a half-hour or so before an interview (or a set of interviews) doing some research on the employer tend to be more confident and relaxed.

In addition, we have found that anxiety can be significantly reduced if you have a realistic understanding of the context of the job interview, the different types of job interviews, and the situation the interviewer is in. A surprisingly large number of people go into interviewing situations with very unrealistic assumptions.

For example, most job interviews are thirty to sixty minutes long. As any successful salesperson knows, it's extremely difficult to sell an expensive and complex product (and let's face it, you are an expensive and complex product) within a short time constraint without excellent preparation. Yet many interviewees do not prepare adequately.

Being prepared in a job interview has two elements: (1) anticipating what the interviewer will want from you and being ready to supply it; (2) knowing what you want from the interviewer and being ready to ask for it.

Exhibits 27–2 and 27–3 supply data on what interviewers want from an interview. When 236 recruiters

Exhibit 27–1

Common Problems in Recruiting Interviewing

Common Problems for Interviewees	Common Causes	Appropriate Action
Is unable to present self and ask questions within short time.	Does not recognize implications of *30*-minute interview.	Prepare. Polished answers to usual questions and a set of key questions to ask.
Tries to do too much in on-campus interview.	Does not recognize screening purpose of first interview.	Recognize purpose of first interview.
Behaves in calculated, guarded way. Appears to be insincere.	Assumes goals of both parties are in conflict.	Recognize *mutual* desire to find a good "fit."
Gets angry at interviewer for not conducting good interview. Anger makes it worse.	Assumes interviewer will be competent.	Understand the interviewer's frame of reference. Be prepared to make his/her job easier.
Gets angry at what appears to be incompetence. Creates poor impression.	Is unaware of organizational and situational constraints on interviewer.	Assume interviewer wants to do a good job, but is operating within unknown constraints.
Stresses wrong things in interview.	Incorrect assumptions about interviewer's criteria.	Try to get some idea in advance about screening criteria.
Highly anxious in interview. Creates poor impression.	Bad history in interviews, assumes stakes are gigantic.	Being prepared tends to relieve anxiety, as do realistic expectations. Know the company, self.
Judges and rejects interviewer quickly.	Fear of rejection.	Be aware of fear, be realistic about process.
Interview ends without discussion of relevant issues.	Interviewee either misunderstands interviewer's purpose and method or is unwilling or unable to take initiative.	Assess the interviewer's skill. If purposeful, realize importance of "fit." If unskilled, gently ask appropriate questions.
Learns nothing from interview.	Assumes the interviewer is the only one who has purpose.	Recognize your purpose to gather information. Prepare questions based on implications and be prepared to seek answers at the appropriate time.

were asked what behavior on the part of the interviewees led to the "best" interviews, they responded as shown in Exhibit 27–2. Interviewers seem generally to like interviewees who have "done their homework"—who know what they want, and who know something about the organization they are interviewing. In another survey of well-known business and industrial concerns, college recruiters were asked what types of questions they typically ask in an interview (see Exhibit 27–3). Exhibit 27–4 lists some common questions by interviewers with different styles. Well-prepared students take the time to create short (one- to five-minute) articulate answers to these kinds of questions before they begin interviewing prospective employers. These students seem to be much more successful.

Types of Interviews

When preparing for interviews and while interviewing, it is important to remember that there are a number of different kinds of job interviews.

Screening Interviews

The primary purpose of the screening interview is to save an organization and its managers time and money by limiting the number of job applications they will have to examine. The interviewer has a very limited number of more or less specific criteria that constitute the rough screen. The question he or she is addressing is simply: Does the interviewee make

Exhibit 27–2

What Made the Best Interviews?*

1. *Interviewee knew about company* (''had done homework,'' ''knows the field'')	66% (174)
2. *Interviewee had specific career goals* (''knew what he/she wanted,'' ''good fit between our needs and his/hers,'' ''well-thought-out career interests'')	41% (108)
3. *Interviewee knowledgeable* (''asked good questions,'' ''knew what to ask'')	29% (76)
4. *Interviewee socially adept* (''rapport,'' ''in tune with me,'' ''outgoing and expressive'')	28% (74)
5. *Interviewee articulate* (''able to express ideas,'' ''spoke well,'' ''good with tricky questions'')	19% (50)

*Based on questionnaire responses from 236 people who recruited at Harvard Business School in 1973; more than one response allowed.

it through the screen or not? The campus interview is typically a screening interview. So are many of the interviews in large companies with a person from "personnel."

The most common mistake made by job applicants in screening interviews is to try to get into too much depth. In many cases, especially with larger corporations, the responsibility of the individual doing the screening stops at selecting from among the interviewees the most appropriate candidates to be invited for a second interview, usually on the company's premises. The interviewer in such cases is seldom the final decision maker regarding a job offer and may not even know the specific requirements of the jobs to be filled. Consequently, an interviewee who attempts to tell an interviewer everything about him or herself, and who tries to learn everything about the company and job, as if both parties had to make a final decision regarding employment on the spot, seriously undermines a screening interview.

Decision Interviews

A second type of interview is with the person (or one of the persons) whose responsibility it is actually to make the hiring decision. These interviews sometimes conclude with the interviewer making a job offer. The question that guides the interviewer's behavior is this: Do I want to hire this person? In this type of interview, you want to make your full "sales presentation." Forgetting or not having time to tell all the major messages you have—about what you want in a job and career, why you want that, and why you think you can help the company with its needs and problems—can diminish your possibilities of getting a job offer. At this stage, it is important to go into detail.

Data-Gathering Interviews

A third type of interview is with people who will have only an input into the hiring decision, and who often will end up working with the person who is hired. Because they have less at stake in the hiring decision, they often are more casual and less prepared for the interview. The key question that tends to go through their minds is this: What's it going to be like around here if this person is hired?

Exhibit 27–3

The Most Commonly Asked Questions*: General Classification

1. Goals and purposes—Life purposes—Career objectives
2. Type of work desired—Kind of job—Job expectations
3. Reasons for selection of company—Knowledge of company.
4. Personal qualifications—Strengths and weaknesses
5. Career choice—Reasons for decisions
6. Qualifications for the job—How college education has prepared the candidate
7. Educational choices and plans—Choice of college—Choice of major
8. Geographical preferences—Willingness to relocate
9. Major achievements and accomplishments

*From the *29th Annual Endicott Report*, by Frank S. Endicott, Director of Placement Emeritus, Northwestern University, Copyright 1974 by Northwestern University.

Exhibit 27–4

Questions Frequently Asked by Interviewers with Different Styles

Stress Interview Questions:

Given your background, you don't seem to be qualified for this job.
People like you (on whatever dimension) have never done well in our firm. Why do you think you will?
We aren't hiring this year, just keeping in touch.
We only take the best people. What makes you think you measure up?
I think you're wrong. (To whatever you might say.)

Specialized Knowledge or Skill Questions:

How do you calculate ROI?
What is PIMS and how would you use it in this job?
What is the corporation's liability under Title IX?
What would OSHA (or other related regulatory agency) say about that?
How would you assess the future of this industry given the current situation?

Open-Ended Questions:

Tell me about yourself.
What do you know about our company?
What is important for us to talk about today?
What do you plan to do in this industry?
What else would you like to know? Or talk about?
What questions do you have?

Person-Job Fit Questions:

This job demands assertiveness. Are you assertive? What are your strengths and weaknesses?
What kind of person do you think would succeed in our company? Could you?

Interviewees often treat this third type of interview just like the second one; this is a mistake that can create problems. It's important in this third type of interview just to establish some rapport with the person, and not to try to make the big sale. Coming on too strong with potential peers might hurt an interviewee (few people like the idea of too much competition around them). Because the stakes are somewhat lower in this type of interview than in the second type, one can also safely allocate more time to gathering information from the interviewer (more on that in the next chapter).

Although the objectives of these three types of interviews are different, they are seldom in direct conflict with the objectives of the interviewee. Both parties want very much to find someone who can meet their needs. A job decision never works out really well unless both sets of needs are met. (If only one set is met, the employee will typically quit or be fired before too long.) For these reasons it is in the best interest of both parties to see if they have compatible resources and needs. Yet interviewees sometimes assume an adversary relationship, taking the interviewer's objectives to be in conflict with their own. They behave in a somewhat guarded and competitive way. Not only does that behavior undermine the interview, but it usually gives the interviewer a poor impression of the interviewee.[1]

An Interviewer's Perspective

> I spend nearly all my time between January and March interviewing at universities. It's a tough three months. I'm almost always on the road and away from home. The pace can be very hectic.
>
> Yesterday is a beautiful example of the difficulties involved in this job. I got in late two nights ago. Yesterday morning during breakfast I briefly looked over the résumés of the 15 people I was supposed to see that day. Three of them looked like a mistake; I couldn't imagine why they wanted an interview with us. Because I was running late I walked three blocks in the rain to flag down a cab. I managed to get to the campus a few minutes before my first interview—who didn't show up.

[1]Interviewers usually react negatively if they think the interviewee isn't being honest. This happens surprisingly often. In a 1973 survey of interviewers at Harvard Business School, 60 percent said they felt they were being more honest than the interviewees, while only 9 percent said they felt less honest than the interviewees. An interviewee who assumes an adversary stance often comes across as being not very honest.

I got some coffee and then had a good interview at 9:30. When I asked the 10:00 interviewee, shortly after we started talking, if he had worked full time before coming to school, he gave this annoyed look and said, "I sent you my résumé two months ago—haven't you read it yet?" The interview went downhill from there. My schedule had no break in it until 12:30, and for that last half-hour I thought more about my bladder than about the student I was interviewing. I think my 2:30 interviewee was just trying to kill a half-hour between the naps he takes in his classes. He didn't even know what business we were in and had no conception of what he wanted to do. What a waste of time. My 4:00 interviewee was a very impressive young man, but I can't get over the feeling that I was conned. Some of these kids are more skilled at interviewing than I am. When I got back to my hotel at 5:45, I immediately started reviewing the day and my notes. Already the interviews were beginning to blur together. You know, you end up thinking, now which one was the guy who said such and such.

Last week I came up against one of the parts of the job that really annoys me. I interviewed a young woman that I think could turn out to be a very important addition to one of our divisions. But I decided against recommending her because it was too risky. You see, in evaluating my contribution it can take years and years to determine whether the people I recommended (who eventually join the company) are a real success. But it only takes 12 months or less to determine if they are a disaster. So I tend to be evaluated more on not producing disasters. And that, of course, discourages risk taking. And hiring that woman would, I'm afraid, be risky.

I hired seven people for my department last year. I must have interviewed around 50 people. Of all the parts of my job, I feel in many ways least sure about this one. I keep thinking, there must be a better way.

Interviewing is often an intrusion on other parts of my job. As a result, I'm sure that at least some of the time when I'm interviewing someone my mind and heart are elsewhere. And I can't believe I do an effective job under those circumstances. I often wish I could spend a lot more time with interviewees, but that's just not possible.

I've read a few things on the subject of how to interview, but they haven't been terribly useful. I still wonder if I'm asking the right questions or correctly interpreting the interviewee's remarks.

I just don't know what to do with the person who doesn't really know much about us or our industry, or the one who isn't sure what he or she wants. You could spend hours talking to that kind of person trying to sort things out.

On some days when I'm tired and hassled, I wish the interviewee would run the interview. I've actually seen a few who did just that.

Some of the most common mistakes interviewees make stem from their own inaccurate assumptions regarding the interviewer and the position such a person is in. Job hunters, for example, often behave as if the responsibility for the success or failure of the interview were solely the interviewer's. They themselves assume no responsibility. They further behave as if they expect the interviewer to be extremely competent and working under ideal conditions. When the interviewer subsequently doesn't behave as he or she "should," these people get angry or annoyed, and that feeling further undermines the interview. Less-than-ideal conditions, a less-than-perfect interviewer, and an interviewee who is prepared to tolerate neither systematically produce bad interviews.

The best interviewees not only have realistic expectations regarding the interviewer, they even try to empathize with him or her. Such activity helps them develop a rapport that leaves a favorable impression, as well as helping promote the kind of information exchange that is needed to meet the objectives of the interview.

Interview Structure

Interviews occur in a variety of ways. Sometimes the candidate does all the talking; sometimes the recruiter does all of the talking. Given our basic premise that recruiting is an attempt on the part of *both* the organization and the individual to find a good fit, we believe that a balanced approach is most effective. By that we mean that since the fit is important to both parties, *both* parties in essence have a screen and need to collect data to see if the other passes the screen.

Thus, it is as important for you, the job candidate, to collect information as it is to give it. The company has to sell itself as well as you having to sell yourself. With this mutuality of purpose in mind, you will be able to approach interviews with less anxiety (since the evaluation process is two-way rather than one-way) and with greater clarity about *your* objectives for the interview. Your self-assessment provides the base from which you can develop a list of questions specifically designed to gather information related to your most prominent themes.

Given this dual purpose to a recruiting interview, a common thirty-minute interview structure looks like this:

Greetings and introductions	1–3 minutes
Recruiter's questions and candidate's responses	5–10 minutes
Recruiter's summary question or comment	1–3 minutes
Agreement on the nature and timing of the next step	1–3 minutes
Goodbyes	1 minute

Some recruiters may have so many questions to ask that they may not allow you the time to ask questions (see Exhibit 27–4). You should remember that *you* bear part of the responsibility for the success of the interview. All recruiters are not professional interviewers. Hence, you must decide how you will meet your objectives for the interview. Will you interrupt or divert the recruiter? Will you save your questions for a later interview?

Getting a Commitment

Always get a commitment from the employer before leaving an interview (or a set of interviews) regarding what will happen next, and when you will hear from them next.

Some of the uncertainty that accompanies this period in job hunting can be eliminated simply by asking the employer to clarify the process. When will you make a decision as to whether a job offer will be made? How is that decision reached? When will I hear from you next? Most employers will expect better, more confident job applicants to ask these questions.

In addition, by getting a specific date when you can expect to hear next, you put yourself in a less dependent position. The knowledge of that date allows you more accurately to plan the other aspects of your own job campaign so that you don't suddenly find yourself caught in a timing conflict. If you find that date is too far away—after, for example, you are expected to accept or decline someone else's offer—you can tell the employer so and often get it changed. And when you interview with other employers and are asked when you can reply to their offer, you can respond knowing that it will be after you hear from the places you have already interviewed.

Getting a commitment regarding the time of an employer's reply also reduces the chances that you will be strung along. Without a date, some job hunters wait for weeks or months, often afraid to call or write the employer because it will make them look impatient or desperate. The job applicant who has a commitment to a specific date can legitimately call at once if the employer doesn't respond as promised.

After the Interview

It is a good idea to record your reactions to each interview after it is over. These data will be very useful to you later during the decision-making process. When you have written your observations down, file them in the folder for that firm.

Your log of the interview may include the data, name of the organization, the name and a description of the recruiter, a list of the questions he/she asked, and an outline of your responses. Note which answers you need to think about and prepare better. Note too the data you collected and how it relates to your self-assessment. Are there still large unanswered portions of your themes and implications? What additional data will you want to get next time? Ask yourself too if you accomplished *your* objectives for the interview. Did you present yourself well?

An Interviewing Exercise

It is probably a good idea for most people to do some practice interviewing before undertaking any serious job interviews. There are any number of ways in which you can practice, (including the one we have just given you based on the Martin Taylor case), but let us also suggest the following exercise.

PARTICIPANTS: 4 people.

TIME: 3 hours.

PREPARATION:

1. Each participant should give a résumé, a brief description of a type of job he or she would like to interview for, and a description of the interviewer and the interview location to one of the other three people.
2. To prepare for being an interviewee, each participant should think about the kinds of questions that may be asked and the kinds of questions he or she may wish to ask in return. (It may be useful to write out some of these questions and answers.)
3. To prepare for being an interviewer, each participant should look over the résumé and job description he or she has been given and consider how to conduct the interview.

THE EXERCISE: The exercise will consist of four thirty-minute interviews (each involving an interviewer, an interviewee, and two observers), each followed by a fifteen-minute debriefing.

1. The interviewer should start and stop the interviews.
2. The observers should record their observations.
3. At the conclusion of each interview the observers should share their observations with the others, and everyone should discuss them.

You may find it useful to enter in this notebook any feedback you receive plus answers to common questions.

Assignment

Read the Martin Taylor case that follows and the On Campus Recruiting Interview Forms that follow it. Try to take the perspective of Martin Taylor about to interview Kathleen Johnson (see page 300 for her résumé) for a position as a commercial banker. What questions would you ask her? Why?

If you had a choice, which of the five recruiting forms would you use? Why? What do you learn from these forms about the variety of criteria used in screening interviews? If you were Kathleen Johnson, what questions would you ask of Martin Taylor? (See below for a copy of Kathleen's theme list.)

Note: If you are taking this material as part of a course, you may want to use a classmate's résumé rather than Kathleen Johnson's to role play the interview. If so, ask the interviewee (job candidate) to give you a copy of his or her résumé before class so you can prepare your questions.

KATHLEEN JOHNSON: THEME LIST

Theme Labels

1. Needs to be close to "family."
2. Needs a group of friends and time to spend with them.
3. Enjoys meeting new people.
4. Wants a job with a lot of interaction with people.
5. But doesn't want to have to get involved with social service or counseling activities.
6. Has a need for constant attention and support.
7. Will buck strict social or organizational norms but then reacts poorly to estrangement.
8. Wants things to be fair and just.
9. Enjoys roles involving leadership and responsibility.
10. Needs a standard or goal to measure myself against.
11. Needs to be a success, preferably number one.
12. Prestige is important.
13. Often needs to be motivated, needs encouragement from authority figures.
14. Is indecisive when confronted with too many options.
15. Disorganized.
16. Practical orientation.
17. Wants activity and variety.
18. Doesn't like situations that require long periods of intellectual effort or theoretical or academic approaches.
19. Uncomfortable with situations requiring creativity.

This case was prepared by Ellen Porter Honnet, research assistant, under the direction of Assistant Professor James G. Clawson for class discussion.

MARTIN TAYLOR

Martin Taylor, a corporate account manager for one of the largest commercial banks west of the Mississippi, had been asked by the bank's headquarters to make a two-day recruiting trip to the East Coast to interview second-year MBA students at a large Eastern business school. This was to be

This case was prepared by Mark P. Kriger, research assistant, under the supervision of Assistant Professor James G. Clawson as a basis for class discussion rather than to illustrate either effective or ineffective handling of an administrative situation.

the second year in a row that he would be recruiting, a task he had performed conscientiously the previous year. He was not a full-time recruiter, but looked forward to speaking with MBA graduates-to-be from his alma mater. Martin knew that, as much as he tried to plan ahead, the two days of interviewing would be an intense, energy-consuming process and that at the end of it he would be more exhausted than after two days at his regular job at the bank.

Taylor's Background and Preparation for Employment

Martin Taylor grew up in Ann Arbor, Michigan, and had a fair amount of freedom to travel and to choose his own summer activities. His mother had been the first person on either side of the family ever to go to college.

During the summer of his junior year in high school, Martin made a trip east. Upon seeing Amherst, Massachusetts, he knew that Amherst College, with its rural setting and relatively small student body, was for him. He ended up attending Amherst and doing, in his words, "reasonably well." He majored in economics, which he felt was "a pretty marketless degree."

Upon graduation, Martin went to work for the government as a bank examiner in Detroit, Michigan, for which he received an occupational deferment from the draft. Although his job with the government was relatively comfortable and his pay was better than it would have been in private industry, Martin was concerned that he might get stuck working for the government. So, two years after receiving his BA he applied to three business schools and was accepted into all three.

After Martin Taylor's first year in the MBA program of his first-choice school, Martin went back in the summer to his job as a bank examiner in Michigan because he "could live at home and earn a good salary." In addition, Martin liked what he had been doing, so he did not really try to find another summer job. In the back of his mind he could see himself directing the efforts of a small bank. However, Martin felt that he had to start out in a large bank because, as he put it, "You could go from a big bank to a small bank, but you can't go the other way around."

During the fall of his second year in the MBA program, Martin began his job search process by visiting the placement office and doing some reading. Martin mentioned to Jim Davis, one of the staff members of the placement office, that he had worked as a bank examiner. Davis, in response, made a passing reference to one of the major banks west of the Mississippi River and stated that more people always signed up for their interviews than the allotted interview slots. Martin said to himself, "Well, if everybody wants it that bad, it must be worth looking into." So he examined the material available on the bank, including the annual report, and signed up for an interview with a high rank on his preference card.

Over Christmas vacation he set up several interviews with banks in Detroit, mostly as practice for future interviews with firms that were among his top choices. He quickly concluded that his choice had to be in a large bank in a major city with a corporate banking orientation. Martin ended up flying out during spring vacation to the bank first mentioned when he was in the placement office, and eventually accepted the offer he was given.

Martin's New Job

When Martin arrived for work there was no formal training program at the bank. He was temporarily assigned to Bill Johnson, who was willing to take him on as a special projects assistant. Martin was then given a number of different tasks designed to give him exposure to a number of areas in the bank. In his words, he "spent a lot of long hours in the evening just trying to get the overall picture without a great deal of help from anyone else."

One of the line people who worked for Mr. Johnson as head of the western region in the corporate bank got a position in another part of the bank. As a result, the western territory opened up and was assigned to Martin. After just one previous business trip, Martin Taylor found himself responsible for servicing corporate customers ranging in size from about $20 million to $3.5 billion in sales. His territory expanded and shrank over the next year and a half, but generally it covered the Southwest, including the Rocky Mountains, New Mexico, and Texas. In order to service his customers Martin spent an average of one week per month on the road. Several weeks of additional travel time were required each year for special bank meetings and seminars, but since he was single he rather enjoyed the chance to move about.

Martin's Selection as a Recruiter and Preparations for Interviewing

In 1975 the corporate bank took over its own recruiting from central personnel. That year there was a graduate from Martin's alma mater who had more seniority, so he did the recruiting. However, when this person left the bank in 1976, Martin went to the corporate personnel manager and asked, "Who are you sending back this year?"

The response was, "I'm going to try to go, but I don't know if I'll have the time. Would you be interested?"

Martin was glad to have the opportunity to go back to visit his former school. He also hoped to develop some faculty connections and establish some continuity in relations that he felt had not existed in the past between the bank and his school.

The first year that he went recruiting, he had ample time to prepare. When the résumés arrived at the bank in early December, he took time out to familiarize himself with all 800. He then wrote letters in advance of Christmas to some of the people inviting them to come to the bank during the holidays if they were available. He also wrote a second set of letters in advance of his interviewing trip in February.

The next year Martin was asked to recruit once again. He was to interview only at his alma mater, even though the bank made recruiting visits to about fifteen schools. This time Martin was very busy with business obligations during the latter part of November and most of December. It suddenly occurred to him on December 20 that he had not looked at the résumés yet and the recruiting trip was only a few weeks away. He did manage to screen the résumé book with the help of the preselected list the students put their names on. Martin wrote letters to eleven people who impressed him as having more than just passing interest in the bank for which he worked. He had chosen these people by virtue of their record and their interest in locating in the West.

The Recruiting Trip

Martin's plane arrived two hours later than expected due to a snowstorm. As a result, Martin had less sleep than he would have liked. In addition, he had only a doughnut and a glass of orange juice for breakfast, since he wanted at least a half hour for reading the résumés for the day's interviews. Despite the relatively short sleep and quick breakfast, Martin was looking forward to the interviews with enthusiasm.

When Martin arrived at the Office of Career Development at 8:20 A.M. to pick up his schedule for the day and the stack of résumés, he found the place in tumult. Three additional recruiters, each from other divisions of the bank, were to have arrived. However, the snowstorm had prevented one of the members of the four-person team from coming. Martin, looking at his schedule, noticed that he had received a couple of shift-overs from the absent man's schedules. This further crowded his schedule.

Martin arrived at the interview carrel at 8:30 to spend a half hour reading over and familiarizing himself with the résumés. To his surprise Martin found the carrel without any chairs and had to go and borrow some from a classroom. He then organized the company literature and brochures he had brought with him and finally turned to reviewing the student résumés.

A few minutes before 9 A.M., Martin was smoking a cigarette while finishing reviewing the résumés of the people on his list. He wondered why some of the people were interested in interviewing with a bank since their résumés revealed no banking experience whatsoever. He felt that the preferences listed in the résumés book probably had little correlation with the positions people finally accepted. Upon reading one résumé his interest was piqued by the phrase "presented findings to management." Martin reflected, "That's relevant to us in our loan review committee work. I'll ask him about that, for sure."

Martin's objective in recruiting was to spot from the 25 interviews four or five people who would be invited west to the bank's headquarters for further interviewing. Martin would have to decide who was going to be advanced to the next step in the recruiting process based on a 25-minute interview plus a résumé. Each person invited back to headquarters would cost the bank approximately $500 to $600 in expenses.

Taylor's 9 A.M. appointment did not show up. At twenty past the hour, he was not angry but he felt he would write to the person later, saying that he missed him at the interview and hoped that he would stop by and visit the bank if he were in the area. Martin believed in offering the person the benefit of the doubt. The student for the 9:30 interview showed up on time.

For each of the interviews Martin followed pretty much the same tactics and timing. He would begin the interview by asking a few questions to try to get a feel for how interested the person was in banking. Martin would use the résumé to spot key experiences and interests. If the person had some banking experience he might ask, "What is it about banking that you like?" On the other hand, if the person had a lot of varied experience, but none in banking, he might ask, "Could you tell me how your interest in banking developed?" The second question after that often would be, "How did you learn about our bank?" or, "As you reviewed the many banks that interview here, why did you choose us?" A tougher version of this last question might be, "Could you give me your impressions or notions about what made our bank different from the other banks you have looked at and, therefore, why are you talking to me now?" After the first eight to ten minutes Martin would let the person being interviewed come back at him with some questions for about ten minutes. Next, he would go back at him or her for another five minutes, leaving time for one final question.

He used this strategy of alternately questioning the student and then allowing the student to ask questions because he wanted to meet two objectives: first, to see how the interviewee conducted himself in response to focused questioning, and, second, to give the interviewee a chance to get some basic questions answered. Furthermore, the quality of the questions asked gave him considerable insight into how well prepared the person was, as well as how seriously they were considering working for the bank. Finally, it would take two to five minutes to say goodbye, leaving Martin from three to five minutes to fill out his interview form. After each interview, Martin filled out his impressions of the candidate on the company interview form. His company had separate forms for campus recruiting and for home-office recruiting.

At noon Martin received a letter from Peter Carlson, the person who was to have been Martin's 9 A.M. appointment. The letter, which was poorly typed with a number of words crossed out, stated that the people in charge of interviews had told him that since one of the interviewers on the bank's team had not arrived, all the interviews were cancelled. The letter seemed to be sincere to Martin, and he appreciated that the student had gone out of his way to let him know what had transpired. Martin planned to get in touch with Carlson as soon as possible.

The remaining interviews Martin conducted in the morning went relatively smoothly, with Martin feeling enthusiastic and on top of the interviewing process. "For me, the best time for interviews is early in the day. But I can't remember them all. I have to rely on my brief notes."

Martin's luncheon discussion with his colleagues ran on so late that when Martin returned to his carrel, his next appointment was already waiting. Although Martin needed to visit the men's room, he did not want to keep the student waiting.

As Martin was about to go into the carrel another MBA student approached him and said, "I'm not on your list, but I'm supposed to be. Can I see you sometime? Here's my résumé."

Martin doubted that the student had done his homework because the appointment office had made no mention of any slip-up. As a result, he shunted the student off to one of the other interviewers from his bank who had had a cancellation. Martin conjectured, "Maybe he'll get in, maybe not."

After his 2 P.M. interview, Martin remarked to the casewriter, "That was a big disappointment. His résumé looked the best to me—my most promising candidate. But he was the most nervous, shy and unaggressive of all. It may be under there, but it wasn't showing today."

Martin was filling out the form from his previous interview when the next interviewee popped his head into the carrel and asked, "Do you want me to give you a minute or two?" Martin replied, "Yes, just a minute, 'til I finish filling this out." Meanwhile, Martin's colleague in the next cubicle could not get the sliding door unlocked. He and the person he had been interviewing were working on the door from the inside, while the next appointment was banging on it from the outside. After five minutes of banging, shoving, and exchanging suggestions back and forth, the door finally snapped open.

At 3 P.M. Martin was due for a half-hour break, and by this time, much needed, but Peter Carlson came by. Since Martin had been favorably impressed by Peter's effort and honesty, Martin broke his rule of not conducting interviews during the break. Breaks were important, he felt, as a chance to refresh himself mentally and physically. Martin agreed to see Peter and had no break.

Fortunately, however, the 3:30 appointment did not show up. Martin was finally able to take a break. As he and the casewriter walked down the hall, Martin commented on his interviews:

> The people don't seem so well prepared now. When I was interviewing as a student, I read every issue of *American Banker* to be up on the latest. I don't see it in these people. They're not aware of the major news in the industry. If they're sincerely interested in banking, they should be on top of all that stuff.

By 4:30 P.M. Martin had interviewed ten people (see Exhibit 27–5) and was beginning to get rather tired. He felt he was starting to fumble. With less than six hours of sleep, he thought that he was starting to lose the advantage in the interview process. He wanted to give each person interviewed an equal chance, but his mind was just not as sharp as it had been at 9 A.M. and had begun, in his words, "to turn to mush." Martin's thoughts drifted to his plans for that evening: to see an old friend, drink a couple of beers, and get some badly needed sleep before another day of the same thing. In this state of mind, Martin Taylor finished filling out the interview form, and rose to meet his last interview of the day.

Exhibit 27–5

Martin Taylor's Schedule

Arrival (Monday evening)

11:30 P.M. Snowstorm caused delay in airplane schedule; Martin's flight arrives 2 hours later than expected.
12:30 A.M. Martin arrives in hotel room.
12:45 A.M. Goes to bed.

First Day of Interviews (Tuesday)

6:30 A.M. Wakes up.
7:00 A.M. Leaves hotel without having had breakfast.
8:00 A.M. Martin has a doughnut and a glass of orange juice on campus.
8:20 A.M. Picks up résumés and schedule for the day.
8:30 A.M. Has a half hour to read résumés.
9:00 A.M. First interview does not show. Continues reviewing résumés.
9:30 A.M. Interview.
10:00 A.M. Interview.
10:30 A.M. Coffee break at a coffee machine in the hallway near the interview carrel.
11:00 A.M. Interview.
11:30 A.M. Interview.
12:00 noon Interview.
12:30 P.M. Lunch. Discussion with two other colleagues.
1:30 P.M. Interview.
2:00 P.M. Interview.
2:30 P.M. Interview.
3:00 P.M. Scheduled coffee break, but 9 A.M. appointment comes by for interview.
3:30 P.M. Appointment does not show. Takes a break.
4:00 P.M. Interview.
4:30 P.M. Interview.
6:00 P.M. Plans to meet an old friend for dinner and drinks.

Second Day of Interviews (Wednesday)

6:30 A.M.-5:00 P.M. Similar schedule expected for the second day.
6:00 P.M. Plane flight west, shortly after last interview.

ON-CAMPUS RECRUITING INTERVIEW FORMS

This case consists entirely of interview forms used by five companies for on-campus MBA recruiting. It is intended to give you a perspective of the range of complexity of forms used and a sample of the criteria used by recruiters in evaluating on-campus interviews.

Company A

One major company that interviews on campus has no recruiting interview form. Recruiters are free to make notes as they please.

This case was written by Mark P. Kriger, research assistant, under the direction of Assistant Professor James G. Clawson, as a basis for class discussion. Harvard Business School case 9-480-023.

Company B

Candidate		Previous Interview Data	
Position			
Interviewer			
Today's Schedule			

1. Please briefly summarize the major topics covered in your conversation with the candidate, including both his/her major questions about us and the major topics you raised.

2. Based on your interview, do you believe that this candidate would make a positive contribution to the morale and internal work environment of the firm? Would you enjoy working with the candidate on a project team? Why?

3. What are the candidate's major career alternatives? How does he/she currently rank them? If   should eventually extend an employment offer, what do you think the probability of acceptance is? Timing of decision?

Company B (continued)

4. What major topics should we pursue or follow up on with the candidate in subsequent interviews?

5. Please use this space for general comment and to expand on your answers to the other questions if you need to:

Signature: ______________________________

Company C

CANDIDATE:______________________ INTERVIEWER:______________________

POSITION:______________________ DATE:______________________

The purpose of this form is to aid you in your assessment of the candidate's strengths in each of the key areas listed. Consider the candidate's academic background, work and/or military experience, extra-curricular activities and personal interests. Be sure to cite the evidence behind your assessments. Also, please check one of the three symbols located to the right of each key area.

+ = Good
o = Acceptable
? = Questionable

1. ACHIEVEMENT/ACCOMPLISHMENT

(Is there a solid, consistent record of achievement? Is there evidence of clear objectives, personal initiative, perseverance, and growth?)

+ ______
o ______
? ______

Supporting evidence:

2. LEADERSHIP

(Has the candidate been an effective leader? Has he/she actively sought leadership roles? Was this candidate able to instill confidence in his/her peers and subordinates?)

+ ______
o ______
? ______

Supporting evidence:

3. THOUGHT PROCESS

(Did the candidate appear to be alert and attentive? Did he/she proceed logically from premises to conclusions? Was the candidate insightful in his/her questions?)

+ ______
o ______
? ______

Supporting evidence:

4. INNOVATIVE ABILITY

(Has he/she demonstrated an ability to think and act creatively?)

+ ______
o ______
? ______

Supporting evidence:

Company C (continued)

5. COMMUNICATION SKILLS
   (Did the candidate provide clear, concise, logical answers to questions? Is the candidate direct and persuasive? Did he/she listen well?)
   Supporting evidence:

   \+ ______
   o ______
   ? ______

6. SELF-CONFIDENCE
   (Did the candidate present himself/herself in a mature and professional manner? How has the candidate reacted to pressure situations?)
   Supporting evidence:

   \+ ______
   o ______
   ? ______

7. CAREER DIRECTION
   (Is the candidate's record consistent with his/her stated objectives? Is the candidate genuinely committed to this position?)
   Supporting evidence:

   \+ ______
   o ______
   ? ______

8. POTENTIAL
   (Does this candidate have the ability to grow and accept increasing responsibility?)
   Supporting evidence:

   \+ ______
   o ______
   ? ______

DECISION
Do you recommend this candidate for a second interview? ______ Yes ______ No

WHY?

Company D

PRIMARY EVALUATION
for
CORPORATE ACCOUNT OFFICER

CANDIDATE'S NAME: ______________________________

INTERVIEWER'S NAME: ______________________________

INTERVIEW DATE: ______________________________

SCHOOL: ______________________________

1. Rate each skill or trait in one of the following categories:

SKILLS AND TRAITS	BELOW AVERAGE	AVERAGE	ABOVE AVERAGE	EXCESSIVE
Demonstrated Initiative:				N/A
Priority-Setting Ability:				N/A
Conceptual Ability:				N/A
Analytical Ability:				
Perceptiveness:				N/A
Enthusiastic Demeanor:				
Verbal Communication:				N/A
Pressure-Handling Ability:				N/A
Aggressiveness:				

NOTE: In questions #2 – #4, please check only one answer per question:

2. Rate the candidate's composure in the interview:

☐ a. Very poised and personable.

☐ b. Somewhat nervous but could be developed.

☐ c. Poor.

3. If you were a corporate client, what would your initial impression be of this individual as a calling officer?

☐ STANDS OUT ☐ AVERAGE ☐ NEGATIVE

Company D (continued)

4. Given background and experience, how insightful was the candidate about this job?

A. AMOUNT OF BACKGROUND AND EXPERIENCE:

- ☐ Summer only
- ☐ 0 to 2 years
- ☐ Greater than 2 years
- ☐ Bank or bank-related
- ☐ Non-bank

B. INSIGHTFULNESS:

- ☐ Superficial understanding
- ☐ Some research and understanding
- ☐ Realisitic understanding

5. How do you rate the candidate's knowledge of our bank or the banking industry?

- ☐ Superficial knowledge
- ☐ Some research and knowledge
- ☐ Very good knowledge

6. Is there anything about the candidate that you feel might distinguish this person as a calling officer?

____

____

____

____

____

7. In which group will this person fit best? ______________________

8. Do you feel that this candidate should be invited back for the second interview?

☐ YES ☐ NO

Company E

INTERVIEW EVALUATION GUIDE

PURPOSE

This guide is designed to:

- Help you obtain the information you'll need to make a good selection decision.
- Be consistent with s commitment to equal employment opportunity and compliance with Federal and State EEO laws.

SELECTION CHARACTERISTICS

- The Selection Characteristics listed on the following page were judged most important by Managers surveyed.
- All characteristics listed should be scored. The most relevant to the position under consideration should have the most influence in the final decision.
- The questions provided should be viewed as aids to the interviewers. Alternative questions which help interviewers to focus on relevant experience information can be substituted.
- If a special technical or professional skill is required, use the blank space provided to describe the relevant characteristic following the guideline format.

INTERVIEW GUIDELINES

NOTE:
An Interview Evaluation Guide must be completed for each external candidate interviewed for a position.

This guide can be used most effectively if before interviewing you familiarize yourself with the questions and rating scales. In addition, you should keep in mind the following basic principles:

- Avoid questions that can be answered with a yes or no.
- Try to obtain clear and detailed responses about the applicant's experiences — what has been done.
- Satisfy yourself that the applicant's descriptions are consistent and generally accurate.
- Concentrate only on those areas that are relevant for evaluating applicants on the Selection Characteristics.
- Complete this form as soon as possible after the interview, and definitely before interviewing any other applicants.

Company E (continued)

SELECTION CHARACTERISTIC	CONSIDER	SUGGESTED PROBES/QUESTIONS
EXPERIENCE/CAREER/SKILLS SCHOOL EXPERIENCE	• Applicability of courses, studies to position • Ability to apply skills and knowledge in solving problems	• What was your major course of study in school? • What parts of your course work are most applicable to a (position) at
WORK EXPERIENCE	• Applicability of prior work to current position	• What were (are) the major responsibilities (activities) of your last (current) job? What did you do? • What was your most outstanding achievement in your last (current) job? What impact did it have on the organization? • What responsibilities have you had supervising others? How many? What did you do?
CAREER ASPIRATIONS	• Clarity and specificity of career goals and plans • Ability to assess own strengths and weaknesses in relation to career in	• What did you accomplish in your last job that was most related to your career goals? • How did you decide on your career? What characteristics do you feel you have that are most (least) suited toward a career in
TECHNICAL/PROFESSIONAL (Please complete prior to interview)	__________ __________ __________ __________	__________ __________ __________ __________
PERSONAL CHARACTERISTICS ASSERTIVENESS	• Forcefulness, ability to persist in accomplishing goals • Ability to overcome obstacles and problems in attaining goals	• What was the most challenging task/activity you've ever attempted? Why was it difficult? What happened? • Why did you try to accomplish (complete) that task/goal/activity? Who set the goal? Why?
COMMUNICATION SKILLS	• Ability to present ideas in a clear, interesting and persuasive manner — orally and in writing • Ability to sell self; persuade	• What would you consider your most outstanding success in persuading someone to do something? What did you do? What happened? • To what extent are you (have you been) involved in public speaking, debating or dramatic presentations? What did you do? What happened?
DECISIVENESS	• Appropriateness of the time and information needed to make a decision • Uncertainty about decisions; frequency with which decisions change • Ability to accurately assess risks	• What was the most challenging decision you were ever asked to make? What happened? What did you do? What effect did this have on your organization? • What was the worst decision (best decision) you ever made? What happened? What did you do? Why?
ENERGY	• Ability to work hard over extended period of time • High activity level	• Have you ever been in a situation that required long and hard work for a period of time? What was this due to? What happened? Were others in this situation required to work under the same conditions? • How often do you find yourself in this type of situation?
FLEXIBILITY	• Ability to adapt to changing situations • Alertness and sensitivity to the environment in which one is working	• Were you ever faced with a situation where you had to change the direction (nature) of your activities? (change direction on a project)? What happened? What did you do? • How did you feel about having to change direction in the middle of an activity?
INTERPERSONAL SKILLS	• Ability to establish and maintain effective working relationships • Tact, sensitivity to the feelings of others	• What was your most challenging personal encounter with someone? How did you deal with him/her? • Consider a project where you had to work with other individuals to complete some task. What happened? What was your role?
MATURITY	• Acceptance of responsibility • Ability to avoid impulsive or confusing actions • Calmness under pressure	• Tell me about an occasion when you were responsible for some major activity. What impact did this activity have on your organization? What did you do? What happened? • What was the most frustrating experience you've ever had? How did you handle it? • Have you ever worked under pressure? What happened? What did you do?
REASONING/JUDGMENT	• Ability to abstract the essential elements of a problem and develop/find an appropriate solution	• What was the most challenging (work/technical) problem you've ever encountered? What happened? What did you do? • Given the following situation . . . what would you do? Why?

Company E (continued)

	COMMENTS	EVALUATION	1	2	3	4	5
SCHOOL EXPERIENCE		Not ascertained; Don't know	Course of study not relevant to position			Major course of study directly relevant to position	
		Not ascertained; Don't know	Academic knowledge; shows little understanding of problems involved in applying skills and knowledge			Has practical experience applying skills and knowledge; understands and able to handle problems applying knowledge	
WORK EXPERIENCE		Not ascertained; Don't know	Prior work experience not relevant to skills and knowledge required			Prior work experience directly relevant to skills and knowledge required	
		Not ascertained; Don't know	Little or no supervisory responsibilities; experience mostly as an individual contributor			Has had broad management responsibilities; experience in coordinating and integrating functions	
CAREER ASPIRATIONS		Not ascertained; Don't know	Career goals vague and poorly articulated; low agreement between personal qualities and career			Career goals clear and well articulated; high agreement between personal qualities and career requirements	
TECHNICAL/ PROFESSIONAL		Not ascertained; Don't know					
ASSERTIVENESS		Not ascertained; Don't know	Easily discouraged; passive; tends to react to events; avoids challenging situations			Initiates activities; continues at tasks despite problems and setbacks; confident, seeks new and challenging situations	
COMMUNICATION SKILLS		Not ascertained; Don't know	Hesitant and uncertain; has difficulty presenting ideas clearly and logically			Poised, confident and convincing; can present complex ideas in a clear and interesting manner	
DECISIVENESS		Not ascertained; Don't know	Uncertain, ill-at-ease about decisions; frequently changes mind; takes excessive time to make decisions			Confident about decisions; accurately assesses risks and implications; makes decisions within appropriate time frame	
ENERGY		Not ascertained; Don't know	Rarely works hard; appears to have difficulty maintaining a heavy workload and performing efficiently			Frequently works hard; capable of maintaining a heavy workload while remaining efficient	
FLEXIBILITY		Not ascertained; Don't know	Unaware, oblivious of changing situations; has difficulty adapting and changing goals, directions, etc.			Sensitive to changing situations; capable of adapting to changing demands, goals, requirements, etc.	
INTERPERSONAL SKILLS		Not ascertained; Don't know	Has difficulty maintaining relationships; insensitive; lacks tact			Capable of working effectively with others; sensitive to the feelings of others; tactful	
MATURITY		Not ascertained; Don't know	Responds carelessly and impulsively; avoids assuming responsibility for own actions; panics under pressure			Carefully considers effects of potential actions; reliable; willingly accepts responsibility for handling difficult problems; calm under pressure	
REASONING/ JUDGMENT		Not ascertained; Don't know	Doesn't seek enough information; misses essentials of problem; solutions are superficial			Identifies need for and seeks relevant information; solutions have been innovative and effective	

MANAGEMENT RECRUITING / COLLEGE INTERVIEW SUMMARY FORM

RETURN COMPLETED FORM WITH RESUME TO

CANDIDATE'S NAME	SCHOOL	DEGREE / YEAR	DATE OF INTERVIEW
			/ /

SOURCE (CHECK ONE)

☐ INTERVIEWED ON CAMPUS ☐ REFERRAL ☐ WALK IN / WRITE IN ☐ CAREER DEVELOPMENT

☐ SUMMER INTERN ☐ INTERNAL TRANSFER (OTHER THAN CAREER DEVELOPMENT)

OVERALL IMPRESSION

TAKING INTO ACCOUNT ALL OF THE RELEVANT INFORMATION YOU HAVE OBTAINED IN THIS INTERVIEW, WHAT IS YOUR OVERALL IMPRESSION OF THIS CANDIDATE?

1	2	3	4	5
VERY WEAK	WEAK	CAPABLE	STRONG	EXCEPTIONAL

COMMENTS:

PLEASE COMPLETE EXPLORATORY OR FULL DAY SECTION

EXPLORATORY INTERVIEW (ON CAMPUS OR IN HOUSE)

INTERVIEW DECISION

☐ INVITE — FOR FURTHER ASSESSMENT AND EVALUATION BY YOUR GROUP

GROUP: ______________________

SUGGESTED AREA (IF APPLICABLE)

☐ REFER — RESUME AND EVALUATION TO OTHER GROUP FOR INVITE OR TURNDOWN DECISION

RECOMMENDED GROUP

☐ TURNDOWN

CORRESPONDENCE INFORMATION

SALUTATION: DEAR ______________________

☐ NO
☐ YES
INDICATE WHETHER YOU WOULD LIKE TURNDOWN LETTER SIGNED BY A PROFESSIONAL RECRUITER

FULL DAY INTERVIEW

RECOMMENDATION TO HIRE

NO ☐ YES ☐

DO NOT WRITE IN THIS BOX - FOR CRU USE ONLY

NO LETTER	TYPE OF LETTER	DATE OF LETTER
☐	A B C D E F G H I #9 #12	/ /

INTERVIEWER'S NAME TITLE (PLEASE PRINT OR USE STAMP)	INTERVIEWER'S SIGNATURE	DATE
		/ /

28

Company Visits

A major source of information on jobs is direct observation. Most professionals are invited to visit the organization itself before any job offer is extended, even if that means a long trip at the organization's expense. The four to twenty hours that are spent in the organization itself can provide an enormous amount of information beyond that obtained in interviews. All you have to do is keep your eyes and ears open.

Visual Clues

Job hunters tend to underuse direct observation for a number of reasons (chief among them is that most well-educated people do not seem to be very visually oriented). Yet this information source is very attractive in two ways. First, it doesn't require the use of the job hunter's most precious resource—time. If you visit a company for a day, you get eight hours of visual data at no extra cost. Second, it can be an incredibly rich source of impressionistic data, which you can use in checking out your conclusions about the company and its people derived primarily from what people were saying.

Ignoring visual data, or not being alert to cues provided by direct observation, can get a job hunter into trouble. The following story, related by a very bright and capable young man, illustrates the point rather clearly:

> While job hunting, I found this small firm that built the most beautiful modern lighting that money can buy. I spent a full day there and yet I just didn't pay attention to all the visual clues that suggested I might not get along with the boss. I was so enchanted by the job, and by what he said, that I didn't see the obvious signs.
>
> You see, I recognize that I have a fairly large need for autonomy, and a fairly large need for an aesthetic environment. The job opening was for a director of marketing (reporting to the president), which was exactly what I wanted. When I talked to the company president, he assured me that I would be able to run my own show without interference. Since he did not have a background in marketing, nor any great interest in it, I believed him.
>
> Most of the time I spent visiting the company was with him at his home and at a restaurant, but we did meet for about two hours in his office. His office is quite large—about forty by forty feet. It has very functional furniture in it, and it's usually a mess. Outside his office is a smaller office area, twenty by twenty feet, that has five desks in it (yes, five people share that office!). It has the same functional furniture and it's slightly less messy. Off of that area are three other small offices nine by nine feet, each with a functional desk, chair, and grey filing cabinet.
>
> So here we have a setup where his space is clearly dominant, and where his tastes (he has an engineering/manufacturing background) dominate also. I sat in the middle of that for two hours and yet didn't really see it.
>
> When I came on board, I was given one of the nine by nine offices, and for the first month everything was OK. Then the dreary office area began to bug me and when I asked my boss about getting some nice office furniture, he just effectively ignored the request. Each month thereafter, especially as I started to initiate some new marketing programs, we began to clash. After five months it became clear he was not about to give me the autonomy he promised. I quit after six months.

So we encourage you to be alert when you make company visits and to pick out signals that tell you something about the firm.

Goldman, Sachs & Co.

The following pictures simulate a recruiting visit to the New York City headquarters of Goldman, Sachs & Co., a premier investment banking company. Although call-back visits vary, candidates visiting Goldman Sachs for the first time might expect a rigorous interview schedule that includes meeting people from several departments of the company, usually in two-on-one interviews. Often, when the candidate arrives, he or she is hosted by a first year associate whose responsibility it is to arrange the schedule and distribute the candidate's resume and evaluation sheets. Lunch is usually out of the building in the company of two recent associates of the firm, who talk about what the first year at the firm is like. The host associate collects the evaluations from the interviewers at the end of the day. If this first visit is successful, the candidate will return to meet with additional vice presidents and partners in the firm, usually those more closely associated with the probable work place of the candidate.

As you move sequentially through these snapshots of such a visit, be alert for patterns. Then, summarize your observations into tentative inferences as we did in the self-assessment portion of the book. Given these photos, complete the sentence, "Goldman Sachs is a firm that. . . ."

LaGuardia Airport, New York.

Central Manhattan from the Triborough Bridge across Queens.

Southern Manhattan near Wall Street from The Statue of Liberty.

The trading floor of the New York Stock Exchange.

Broad Street, Manhattan.

85 Broad Street, headquarters of Goldman, Sachs and Co.

The front door of Goldman Sachs, and some employees.

Elevators to the offices at Goldman Sachs.

Reception and Security on the fourth floor.

Reception Area, fourth floor.

Reviewing the day's schedule with your host.

Interviewing with a vice president from Research.

Getting an explanation in Operations.

Walking by the Fixed Income floor.

Interviewing with professionals in Equity Trading.

Meeting associates in Mergers and Acquisitions.

Another interview in Mergers and Acquisitions.

Waiting for an interview to begin.

Pearl Street on the way to lunch.

Lunch will often be at the Customs House.

Fourth floor waiting/conference room.

Interview in Global Finance.

An interview in Global Finance.

Passing by a daily meeting in Municipal Finance.

Meeting with vice presidents in Investment Banking Services.

Talking with professionals in Investment Banking Services.

An interview in Real Estate.

Waiting for a meeting with professionals from Fixed Income.

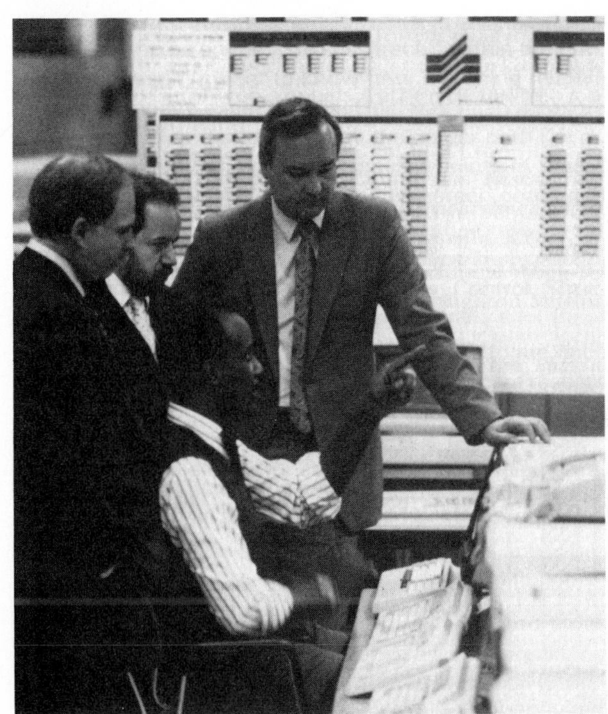

Walking through Operations.

A quick look at the Fixed Income Trading floor.

Coming to an interview in Equity Sales.

Meeting associates in the Data Center.

Observing the Equities Trading floor.

Passing by a Mergers and Acquisitions team at work.

Passing by the mortgage trading floor.

Sharing a ride back to the airport.

Arriving at LaGuardia for the flight home.

29

Managing Your Life During the Job Search

After interviewing for a job, and before a job offer is made (or not made), an interviewee often feels helpless; there is nothing to do but wait and hope. While it's easy to understand why people feel this way—the ball, so to speak, is in the employer's court—passive behavior is not in an interviewee's best interests.

Follow-up Techniques

Systematic follow-up after interviewing can be an important part of successful job hunting.

Keeping in Contact

Keep in contact with potential employers during the waiting period(s). After an initial screening interview, and after a final set of interviews, many successful job hunters will write a letter (or letters) to those with whom they spoke. The letter can communicate your appreciation of the way in which you were treated, your interest, your initiative, and the reasons why you think there may be a good match between your abilities and desires and the job. It can also help keep you visible, even though you're not there.

When visiting a potential employer, if you find that you share some professional interests with someone you meet, you may wish to follow up on that after leaving. Successful job hunters will sometimes stay in contact by letter or in person (if the employer is geographically close by) with a few of the people they met at a particularly interesting potential employer. Such contacts can help produce job offers.

Persisting and Persevering

Recognize that the key to getting what you really want—not your second, or third, or tenth choice—often depends upon your own perseverance. Some people would argue that the key to the whole process of getting job offers is persistence. The following story, while not at all typical, is instructive in this regard.

> Jim Howard began job hunting with a major focus on consumer product management jobs and a minor focus on advertising jobs. Primarily because he had a good understanding of product management jobs, of himself, and of why he would probably make a good product manager, he was enormously successful in his initial interviews with consumer product companies. He contacted ten such companies, got initial interviews with each, and was invited for a second set of interviews at all but one place. His understanding of advertising jobs and how he might fit in, as well as his commitment to an advertising career, was much lower. He contacted six ad agencies, was invited to interview with two, and was invited back to only one. All this occurred in January and February.
>
> During March, while Jim was going through the second round of on-site interviews, he began to learn more about advertising through a course and his own research, and as he did he grew more and more excited about it. It became clearer and clearer to him that he

could be really good at account management and derive a lot of satisfaction from it.

In April Jim found himself in a rather unusual position. He was the envy of all of his friends—for he had seven attractive job offers. Unfortunately, all seven offers were in product management, which he was no longer convinced that he wanted. Worse yet, he had fallen in love with the ad firm in which he had a set of second interviews. And the attraction was not just emotional infatuation. The job and company sounded almost perfect in light of his self-assessment paper.

On April 15, five days before he had promised some employers that he would respond to their job offers, Jim tentatively decided to accept a particular product management job. But it didn't feel right to him. He kept thinking to himself—if you know what you want, why take anything else unless you have to?

The next day he called the one person at the ad firm who had seemed to respond the most favorably toward him when he had visited them six weeks earlier. He invited that person to lunch, saying he needed some advice. At lunch he presented his dilemma, including his detailed analysis of why he would probably do a very good job at that ad firm. He effectively ended by saying that unless he heard very convincing evidence to the contrary, he was going to turn down his offers and pursue the ad firm until it offered him a job. The man he spoke with was visibly impressed.

At 8:30 the next morning his luncheon partner from the previous day called and invited him to come down to the agency that afternoon. Jim spent the afternoon talking to other employees of the firm, much as he did with the first person the day before.

On April 19, one day before he was to respond to his other offers, the ad firm called and offered him a job. He accepted, and when last heard from was doing very well and was extremely pleased with his job and company.

This brief description of Jim's job search, especially his management of his life during the process, illustrates the importance of persevering. But it is difficult to portray in print the emotional ups and downs that one can experience during the job search process. Even more difficult is trying to prepare for the sometimes lengthy periods of anxiety caused by the uncertainty of waiting.

Keeping Things in Control

Managing Anxiety

There are many reasons why people find job hunting anxiety-producing. Serious young students, in particular, often overestimate the stakes involved and then worry about making errors. Many people, who find rejection in any kind of social situation unpleasant, live in daily fear of being rejected by some employer they are beginning to like. The stream of ambiguous information a job hunter receives from potential employers drives some people to despair. The relative success experienced by other job hunters leaves some people feeling like the "ugly child at the orphanage." And the stream of first positive (an invitation to a second set of interviews), then negative (a rejection), then positive (a job offer) stimuli can turn one's life into an emotional roller coaster.

It has been our observation that many of the poor judgments people make while job hunting are due to their own anxiety, or more broadly, to an emotional state that is increasingly out of control. An individual's success at managing his or her own emotional state can be a very important factor while job hunting.

Just knowing that it is not unusual to feel anxious, and knowing the typical events that create anxiety, can help you to reduce and manage your anxiety while job hunting. People become "out of control" when they are surprised and frightened by their own anxiety. When typical human anxiety becomes predictable, it becomes manageable.

A technique our students have found useful in putting the hectic events of job hunting in a rational perspective is to keep a diary. By spending just a few minutes almost every day to summarize job-hunting events, your own thoughts and strategies, and your current feelings, you create a "monitoring system" that can be very useful in keeping things under control. By periodically rereading the entries for the last few weeks or months, one is able to make current decisions based on a more accurate understanding of what has really been happening. Rereading the diary helps put things in perspective. An example of such a diary is the Henry Rock case you encountered earlier (pp. 245).

Managing Time

It should be apparent from our discussion in the past few chapters that job hunting can be a very time-consuming activity. People who have not recently had to search for a job seem invariably to underestimate the time involved. It is not at all unusual for a nonstudent to spend half to all his or her time for three or four months looking for a job. Even students will often spend about a quarter of their time for four months. Some individuals, in both cases, spend up to five times as long.

Because job hunting is time-consuming, it seldom fits very neatly into an already busy life. It causes conflicts with school, work, family, and leisure time. Unless one is prepared for these conflicts and prepared to manage them, they can create a continuing sense of crisis.

Individuals who normally have a busy schedule, and who normally manage it well, tend to be quite successful at managing their time while job hunting. People who do not typically have a busy schedule, or who do not usually manage their time well, often run into problems while job hunting.

For the person who has problems managing time or who normally has an unbusy schedule, we offer two specific recommendations that can help to manage time while job hunting. First, get an appointment book (if you don't already have one). By recording in it all your time commitments (not just appointments) while job hunting, you can make it serve as an effective time-management tool. Second, every time you undertake a task, stop and ask yourself a few questions. Do I really need to do this? Can someone else do it instead? Do I have to do this now? Or is something else a higher priority? What is the most efficient way to get this done? And so on.

Managing the Scope of the Search

As we mentioned earlier, people who are more successful in finding a very satisfying job tend to keep a narrower focus during job hunting. Among other things, a clearer and more structured focus helps one keep one's time demands within reasonable bounds.

Despite its importance and usefulness, however, maintaining a restricted scope while job hunting can be very difficult. Forces exist that push toward a widening of one's focus. For a variety of reasons, people sometimes do succumb to these forces, and they end up facing all the problems associated with an unfocused job search.

For example, most job hunters, at one point or another, begin to worry that maybe they just won't get any job offers. Some try to reduce that possibility by broadening the scope of their search. We've seen students who, after receiving their first rejection letter, panic, and discard any and all focus in their job campaign. Many people, once they have spread the word that they are looking for a job, receive a few unsolicited leads that are not even close to what they are looking for. But if they are attractive in some way, some job hunters will take the bait.

We've seen companies send telegrams to students telling them what wonderful things the company has heard about them and asking them to please sign up to interview with the company when it is on campus. Students who have no interest whatsoever in the firm or its jobs will often sign up for an interview. Maintaining a rational focus in a job search is also difficult when one is around other job hunters whose enthusiasm for a different kind of job can be infectious. Some students seem to change the focus of their search almost daily to whatever the last excited friend they talked to was describing. The "grass-is-greener" phenomenon is very much at work here. Finally, some people expand the scope of their job search after they receive their first job offer. They seem to find their first "valentine" very exciting, want more, and so they go out and collect lots and lots of job offers.

If you feel yourself wanting to broaden your focus while job hunting, don't do it immediately. Examine the idea carefully over a period of time. You will probably decide it is not a good idea.

Managing Pressure

Most job hunters get more than enough advice regarding what they "should" do from friends, professors, parents, spouses—even from a little voice inside them. While this advice is sometimes helpful, often it is not. One of the challenges of job hunting is not to succumb to well-intentioned but inappropriate advice and pressure.

When Fran Kelly's parents learned that she was not looking for a job in banking, they let her know (almost on a daily basis) how terribly disappointed they were that she wasn't following in the family tradition. When John Allen decided he would not interview anyone on campus or even look for a job until after he graduated and moved to the city he wanted to make his home, his peers gave him blank stares and an occasional, "Boy, does that sound like a dumb idea." When Frank Lenaro decided to change his career field after working for ten years, his friends made it a habit of saying (while Frank was present), "Frank's decided to throw out everything he has built up over the past ten years." When Kim Evans decided that she wanted to look for a job in an area seldom entered by graduates from her school, she was greeted constantly with puzzled looks and questions such as, "Why don't you want any of the good jobs?"

The more highly one is integrated into a network of friends, relatives, and acquaintances, the more pressure one is likely to feel from others while job hunting. This short-run pressure can, and sometimes does, push people away from a rational course of action.

Differentiating between inappropriate pressure and good advice can be difficult, especially if you are already out of control, and letting events and feelings direct your behavior. Periodically reviewing your themes and their implications from your self-assessment can be invaluable at this point. So can keeping a job-search diary. Both can help you keep on the right track.

Assignment

Read the vignettes that follow. Then carefully outline how you would handle each situation. Be specific. Outline what you would do, what you would say, where you would go, and what the impact of your actions would likely be.

1. REJECTION After a long and particularly grueling week of classes during which you have been eagerly anticipating a response from your number one company choice, you receive a letter in the mail informing you that, while the company appreciated your interest, it is unable to offer you a position at this time. You still have not heard from the other two companies who have expressed interest, but they are not particularly attractive openings anyway.

2. FATIGUE AND OVERLOAD It is Sunday evening about 7 P.M. You have just returned from a cross-continent recruiting trip and are exhausted from the flight. You have a major paper due the following morning that needs some polishing and one or two additional exhibits. You also have two very stimulating classes scheduled for the following morning in subjects you feel are important to your education, but you have not yet read the cases. The phone rings. An old, close friend from out of town who is here for one day wants to go out to dinner.

3. RESPONSIBILITY Your field project team has scheduled a very important meeting to pull together the data and analysis for your term project for Thursday night. Today is Wednesday, and you have just received a telephone call from your number-one recruiting choice asking you to fly to its city on Thursday evening to be there for Friday morning interviews.

4. LATE You are walking out of class with two of your friends who are excitedly chattering about the job offers they have received, the benefits associated with them, the high salaries offered, and the thrill of being wanted by companies of such prestige. You, however, have not yet received any job offers, and in fact have not yet received any strong expressions of interest.

5. DATA You receive a telephone call from your number one choice. The personnel director on the other end of the line thanks you for your recent company visit and expresses to you how interested they are in you. Then he says that, of course, in the recruiting process they have been interviewing a number of students from the business school, and wonders if you have any observations that may be of help to them on the following three people.

6. LOCATION You have received two job offers, one that seems to fit your career objectives, personality, and skills perfectly, and the second which is less well matched. The first, however, happens to be in a rural community in the Midwest, and the second is located in a major urban center with all its attendant opportunities. While you are eager to accept the position in the Midwest, your partner feels very strongly that he/she would rather live in the urban location.

7. PARENTS You have received three offers from firms in different industries, one of which is clearly more prestigious in the eyes of the world than the other two. Nevertheless, the second option seems to match up more closely with your personal interests and career objectives. When you describe the three options to your parents over the telephone, it is clear that they hope and expect that you will accept the most prestigious offer.

8. SALARY You are sitting in the pub having a snack and a drink with several of your classmates. The talk naturally turns to the job recruiting process, and several of them start talking about the salary offers they have received. The only offer you have received at this point is more than $5,000 less than the lowest offer the others have mentioned.

9. FRIENDSHIPS Your parents are coming for a short visit on Sunday, and you have blocked the day off. You have a major paper due on Monday, and have scheduled Saturday to do the final analysis and writing. On Saturday morning, as you are sitting down to write, your roommate and close friend at the business school calls from a city two hours away to say that his car was stolen with his wallet in it. He wants you to come down, pick him up, and bring him home.

10. HOLDING OUT Your number two choice has made you a reasonable offer and asked for a reply next week. Your number one choice has just called to say that they enjoyed your visit. They also report that since some people are going on vacation, you will not be notified one way or the other for two weeks.

11. CHOOSING You have received two job offers, both of which, although in different parts of the country and with different job descriptions, seem to fit very closely the goals and objectives you had had for a first job. The more you analyze the two alternatives, the more equal they seem. You have promised one of the firms that you would let it know the following morning.

12. PRIORITIES You have received two offers. One includes a salary that is well above last year's

class's mean salary, but is in a location that you find distasteful. The other offer has a salary that is slightly below last year's mean salary, but is in a location that meets your life style objectives well.

13. OTHER SITUATIONS There may be other situations that you could imagine or have heard about that take place during job search and that tend to disrupt one's routine or one's emotional equanimity. Describe one such situation, and how you would feel, and devise a response to it.

30

Analyzing and Choosing a Job Offer

At some point in the job search process, usually in March or April for business school candidates, you will receive some offers for employment. You are then faced with the task of assessing these offers.

To assess job offers rationally, a job hunter needs a considerable amount of information. Although some people would argue that you can't know much about a company or job until you have actually worked in it for six months, evidence from our students suggests otherwise. Clearly, there is a limit to what you can "know" about a job without directly experiencing it, but many people stop far short of that limit during job hunting. Often, because they are so worried about being rejected by potential employers or so flattered by all the attention and offers they are getting, some job hunters neglect to assess their job offers and potential offers seriously and rationally. By neglecting to use all available sources of information, by failing to understand how to utilize their sources properly, and by relying on inappropriate methods to analyze the data they obtain, they consistently make poorly informed decisions on which potential offers to pursue, which to eliminate, and finally which offer to accept.

Job-offer decision making can usefully be thought of as made up of two parts: (1) analysis and (2) choice. To understand this type of decision making, one needs to understand both of these very different parts of the overall process. By avoiding or doing a poor job in either part, job hunters can create serious problems for themselves.

Analysis

The analytical part of decision-making processes is characterized by words such as *cognitive, conscious, rational,* and *objective*. With regard to job selection, it involves the systematic assessment of an individual, the systematic assessment of a number of job options, and the deduction of a set of most probable future events for each option if that option were selected by that individual. Virtually the entire book, up to this point, has been directed at helping you become more aware of this process and more skilled at using it.

Engaging effectively in analysis helps a job hunter more accurately predict the future consequences of accepting each of the available options. It provides a more realistic understanding of the rewards one might receive, and the problems one might encounter, with different options.

For a number of reasons, job hunters sometimes engage in analysis in a superficial and ineffective manner. Many people simply do not have the information, the expertise, or the training to analyze job offers effectively. Others are just not analytically oriented; they neglect serious analysis in almost all their decision making. Still others avoid analysis in this particular case because, at some level, they don't want to have to face the objective reality of their own personal limitations, or the limited future possibilities their current options offer them.

The person who fails to engage effectively in the

analysis of a job decision may end up in a situation where he or she simply cannot do what is being demanded and expected, and is constantly and unpleasantly surprised by obstacles and problems. Typically, the individual who does a poor job of analysis while selecting a job offer will either quit or be asked to leave the job in four to twelve months. The employer will often be disappointed in the person's performance, and the employee will often be disappointed in his or her lack of satisfaction in the job.

Most job hunters we have observed do a fair or good job of analysis before selecting a job offer. A small number do an excellent job of analysis, and an equally small number do a very poor job.

Using the Self-Assessment

We have been developing the means for a job choice analysis all along. You now have a set of life themes and their implications for work. Since these are the criteria that will determine your satisfaction at work, they should also be the criteria that govern your choice of that work. We have been surprised on occasion by students who have diligently and enthusiastically developed a careful self-assessment, but who in the throes of choosing a job have ignored their themes and implications. In those cases, we ask the students to bring their self-assessments to our next meeting. There, we go through each theme and implication one by one to see how each option measures up. That discussion often makes it clear that one or maybe two of the offers they are considering are better than the rest.

Sometimes a student will say, "Yeah, but that theme is not what is *really* important. This [other criterion] is." If you feel this way during your decision-making process, you need to ask yourself two questions. First, ask yourself again (see "Writing Your Self-Assessment") if your self-assessment is accurate. It is intended to be systematic *and* accurate. If your thinking about choosing tells you that something else needs to be added to your self-assessment, do it.

But before you do, ask yourself another question: What forces are influencing you to think the way you are thinking now? Your self-assessment was generated systematically over two or three months of time and utilized a wide variety of tools in the data generation. Are you sure that your desire to change that assessment now is based on something more than impulse or peer pressure or some other transient phenomenon? Only when you have thought about it carefully and convinced yourself that the potential change to your self-assessment is an enduring part of you would we recommend that you go ahead and make the change.

The important, central point is that insofar as your self-assessment is complete and accurate, it reflects the criteria on which you will judge your life and your career. As such, your self-assessment should be used explicitly—theme by theme and implication by implication—in your job offer analysis.

This careful approach will do two things for you. First, it will help to clarify how well each opportunity matches up with the things that are most important to you. Second, it will clarify those dimensions on which the fit is not so good. Rarely does one find a job that is perfect in every way. Almost always there are aspects of a job that one finds less than ideal or even downright irritating. Your themes and implications can help you identify these areas in advance and, in so doing, help you think about how you will manage those aspects of the job so as to reduce the negative impact on you or your work. This will reduce the number of shattered expectations you will experience on the job after the "honeymoon" period is over.

Utilizing Other Information Sources

In addition to using your self-assessment as the basis for assessing the information you have about an opportunity, you may wish to consider the questions in Exhibit 30–1 as a means of stimulating your thinking about the job and the organization and the ways they will affect you.

To recap the previous chapters on written sources, interviewing, and company visits, there are a variety of ways of collecting data that will be useful to you. These are summarized in Exhibit 30–2.

People we have known who have been very successful at job hunting tend to rely extensively on all the information sources we've mentioned. Their less successful peers, on the other hand, do not. And if asked why they do not, they will often complain that they just didn't have the time. The *management of one's time is a very real problem for the job hunter.* In the case of assessing job offers, the dimensions of the problem can be understood if we consider how much time a professional—a consultant or a financial analyst—will typically spend just assessing a single company (not including an assessment of a specific job in it). Forty to 100 hours is typical. If job hunters tried to do a thorough, professional job of assessing each job and organization they were interested in, it would require literally thousands of hours.

Exhibit 30–1

Information Often Useful in Assessing Job Offer or Potential Offer

Regarding the Job Itself

1. What major tasks are involved, and what are their key characteristics?
2. What skills are needed to perform each task?
3. Approximately what percent of the time will the job holder spend on each task? How does this vary (if at all) over time?
4. What time and resource constraints does the job holder have to work within?
5. How many hours per week do people holding similar jobs work?
6. What percent of the time will the job holder be working alone?
7. Who else will the job holder interact with? What are these people like? What percent of the time will the job holder be with them?
8. How much discretion will the job holder have in deciding how to perform the job?
9. How many people and how much money or equipment will the job holder be responsible for?
10. How many people will report to the job holder?
11. Who will be the job holder's boss? What is this person like? How good a coach is he or she?
12. How is performance measured in this job?
13. What type of salary and other rewards are available given what level of performance?
14. Specifically what type of advancement opportunities are available to the job holder?
15. Who makes decisions and how regarding promotions?

Regarding the Organization

16. How large is the organization's industry (employment, number of competitors), and what are its prospects for future growth?
17. Specifically what parts of the industry will probably grow (or decline) at what rates over the next few decades?
18. What are the industry's most important characteristics? (Is business seasonal? What type of organizations do well or poorly?)
19. How is the industry changing now?
20. How old is the organization? What are the big events in its history?
21. How large is the organization (people, assets, sales volume, net income)?
22. What goods and services does it produce?
23. How does it produce these goods and services?
24. Where does it have plants or offices?
25. Does the organization have any particularly important suppliers, customers, or regulators? If yes, who are they, what are they like, and what is their relationship to the organization?
26. What important technologies does the organization use?
27. What are the major parts of the organization, and how are they structured?
28. What are the organization's compensation policies? Performance appraisal practices? Training and development practices? Other important personnel policies?
29. What type of people work for the organization?
30. What do they generally like about the organization? Dislike about it?
31. Does the organization have any important traditions?
32. How are the people and the way in which they interact different from people in other organizations you have known?
33. What are the company's plans for the future?

Since that is impractical, many job hunters simply give up and do a very random and superficial job.

The keys to an effective strategy to assess potential job offers are: (1) *utilizing all information sources,* but systematically emphasizing different ones at different times, depending upon how many organizations and jobs are under examination at the time; (2) *accurate self-knowledge.*

Choice

The process of choice is often much more nonrational, emotional, subjective, and unconscious than the analytic job assessment process. We don't know a great deal about the actual dynamics of job choice, but we do know the function it seems to serve and the consequences of not engaging in it.

Exhibit 30–2

Information Sources and Their Uses

	Library	Informed Nonemployees	Potential Boss and Superiors	Potential Peers and Others	Direct Observation
Industry Characteristics	***	**	*	*	
Major organizational characteristics (what it does, where, etc.)	***	**	*	*	
How the organization functions		***	**	*	**
What it's like to work for the organization		**	*	***	***
Job characteristics			*	***	*
Career possibilities	*	*	***	*	

*** Best source.
** Good source.
* A source.

In the only systematic examination of the job-offer decision-making process we are aware of, Peer Soelberg studied 32 graduate students at the Sloan School of Management (MIT) while they were job hunting.[1] He was surprised to find that the process these students engaged in, especially near the end, was much less rational and analytic than he expected. Among other things, he found that:

1. The students tended to reduce their options to two (precisely two in almost every case) using a pragmatic, although not very elegant, analytical process.
2. They would then often agonize while deciding which of the two options to take.
3. Significantly, before the average student would announce that he had reached a decision, Soelberg found he could predict which option would eventually be chosen.
4. Upon announcing a decision, the average student could then provide an elaborate "justification" for his choice, the details of which sometimes clashed with what he had said earlier.

These findings are entirely consistent with what we have observed less systematically over the past few years. Even people who have done an excellent job at analytically assessing themselves and their options typically go through an emotional phase of varying lengths and intensity during which they seem unconsciously to: (1) create a situation of choice (usually between two options); (2) try to come to grips emotionally with the implications of each option; (3) choose one of the options; and (4) find some rationale for rejecting the option not chosen.

The Importance of Choosing

No matter what the exact dynamic of this process is, it seems to be important, or needed, because it serves two important functions. It helps the decision maker develop an emotional commitment to one of the options. It also helps the decision maker cope with feelings of loss associated with cutting off the other option.

To follow through on a major life decision with the energy and vigor needed to ensure its successful implementation, people seem to need some emotional commitment to the direction the decision will take them. Among other things, that commitment seems to help them overcome obstacles when they encounter them. But the very process of choosing, and emotionally committing oneself to one option, means that another must be cut off. The feeling of loss associated with such cutting off can be very powerful and troublesome to people. To help cope

[1]See Peer Soelberg, "A Study of Decision Making: Job Choice" (dissertation, Sloan School, 1967), and "Conclusion from a Study of Decision Making" (MIT Working Paper 173–66).

with these feelings, people tend to find some "rational" reason that minimizes the loss.

People sometimes avoid choosing, or engage in it only minimally. They allow others, or "fate," to choose for them. Or they simply deny that they have a choice. (How often have you heard someone say, "I had no choice"?) Some people always behave this way in their decision making, just as some others always avoid serious analysis. Sometimes it seems they just can't accept the responsibility of cutting off what might be a "good" option. The loss of what "could be" is too painful for them.

The Consequences of Not Choosing

The consequences of not engaging in choice can be as serious as the consequences of not engaging in analysis. Without the emotional commitment to a particular direction, it is often very difficult to mobilize one's energies and overcome the inevitable obstacles. Without effectively dismissing the other options, and suffering the loss, one can often be plagued by thoughts of their continuing availability. These thoughts can paralyze a person.

One student we observed, a very bright and highly analytic young man, devised an elaborate mathematical formula to help him select one among four job offers. He announced that he did so to help him make a rational decision, "not an emotional one like so many people seem to." The formula gave option one 110 points; option two 85 points; option three 118 points; and option four 96 points. He aggressively defended his formula against occasional jokes from friends. ("What does an eight-point difference mean, Larry? One less ulcer every 8.0 years?") He accepted option three, even though he didn't feel entirely sure it was right.

After eight months on the job, a downturn in company sales and layoff of personnel put everyone in Larry's division under some pressure. He thought there must be better opportunities elsewhere and quit. Five months later, he started to work in another job. When his boss was promoted six months after that and the person who replaced his boss was not "as easy to work with," Larry quit again. He was also to get still another job within three months. When we talked to him last, he expressed concern that his career did not seem to be progressing as well as those of some of his less able classmates. We are left wondering whether his seeming inability to really choose an option, and to commit himself to it, might not underlie his lack of career progress.

Assignment

The Mike Downer case which follows raises several of the issues introduced in this chapter. Read the case and prepare your answers to the following questions.

1. What tools did Mike Downer use to evaluate and analyze his choices? Do you think they were useful or effective? Why or why not?
2. As Mr. Reese, what, if anything, would you say to Mike?
3. As Mike Downer, what would you do? Why?
4. How would *you* go about making the decision between two job offers?

MIKE DOWNER

> I feel lousy. I can't sleep. I can't eat. I can't concentrate on my classes. My whole life is being affected. This is the fourth and last semester of business school and I have two good, firm offers. Most people would welcome either offer. I should be enjoying myself, but I still feel lousy.

Mike Downer, a second-year MBA student, sat and stared out the window. He was tired and emotionally drained. His job search had been a long and exhausting process, especially when considering his efforts were in addition to normal classroom work. In an attempt to sort out his thoughts, Mike had sought the advice of his organizational behavior professor, Mr. Reese.

Mr. Reese was attentive as he listened. Mike appeared to be confused and bewildered as he

This case was prepared by Kent Guichard under the direction of Associate Professor James G. Clawson. All names have been disguised. UVA case OB-227.

searched for words to express himself. Mr. Reese watched and waited. Still gazing out the window, Mike began to speak again.

> I've got to make a decision. I promised Mammoth Foods a decision by Friday. That gives me just four days to make up my mind.
>
> What infuriates me is that this should be the easy part. The hard part is all done. The preparation, the interviews, and the waiting for offers is all behind me. All I have to do is choose one of two offers. Both offers are good opportunities with excellent firms. Both offers have advantages, both have disadvantages. It's so hard to choose.
>
> I'm in trouble. I haven't smiled in four days. I'm in the deepest depression I have ever experienced during two years of business school. At this point, I'm not very popular with too many people. Even my friends tell me that I'm a mess. I feel lousy. Is this normal? What should I do?

Background

In preparation for his job search, Mike Downer had enrolled in the fall elective on career management. Mike felt that he came out of the course with a good view of himself and with a solid plan of action for his job search. While he knew that the job search would be strenuous, Mike felt that he was well prepared for the challenge.

As a course requirement, Mike made a list of life themes (see Exhibit 30–3). He felt the themes were a strong and accurate assessment of what he considered important. Mike expanded the themes into twenty-one career implications (see Exhibit 30–4). These implications described the characteristics of the type of job he wanted. It was from these implications that he developed his action plan. Mike briefly outlined his plan as follows:

> The main focus of my job campaign was people oriented (selling/persuading) positions within the financial services industry. At one time, I believe that my choice would have been very segmentable along the lines of investment Banks, Commercial Banks, Insurance Companies, and Real Estate Firms. However, the distinctions between these industries are diminishing, creating the opportunities I was seeking among all four.
>
> One of my toughest assignments in my job search was to determine whether I wanted to be on the selling side (Institutional Sales, Loan Officer) or client side (Investment Management) of the financial services industry. However, I viewed the job hunt as a unique opportunity to gain valuable insight into the industry.
>
> In determining which companies I contacted, I used two main vehicles as the focus of my efforts: the placement office and firms which I contacted on my own initiative. The following is the method I used to select companies through the placement office:
>
> 1. Read the placement job descriptions for each position that was interviewed for on campus.
> 2. Check each position against my themes and implications for suitable fit.
> 3. Rank each position on a scale of 0 (no interest) to 5 (high interest). Allocate my interviewing time to firms ranked 5 to 1 in descending order.
>
> By using this method, I felt that I would be focused, but at the same time would have a sufficient number of interviews to satisfy my job search goals.
>
> Outside contacts were the other source of my interview prospects. Whenever possible, I contacted an alumnus or key contact in a firm by telephone to introduce myself and express my interest in a company. When I was unable to make contact by telephone, I contacted the company in writing. I developed my letters along the following format:

Exhibit 30–3

Mike Downer's Life Themes

Most Important

1. Meeting people is important/people-oriented
2. High value placed on variety/diversity/change
3. Enjoy leadership/controlling positions
4. Want to be in on what's going on/dislike isolation
5. Motivated by money as a reward for work
6. Place a high value on self-reliance/independence
7. Achievement-oriented
8. High value on learning new things
9. High value on being recognized for efforts

Very Important

10. Dislike of detailed work/repetitive tasks
11. Action-oriented/like to be doing a lot
12. High value on receiving guidance and support
13. Emphasis on the practical
14. Enjoy politics
15. Enjoy persuading/selling
16. High value on tackling a challenge
17. Like physically demanding activities/keeping in shape

Important

18. Self-starter/entrepreneurial
19. Want to have time for my own benefit
20. Desire to be close to people
21. Strong sense of likes/dislikes/priorities
22. Enjoy traveling
23. Active/passive involvement with sports activities

Important Minor Theme

24. Underlying sense of ethics/fairness

Exhibit 30–4

Implications of Life Themes

	Implications	*Theme Support*
1.	A job that offers a high degree of people interaction	1,4,12,20
2.	A job that offers an opportunity to experience a changing environment with a minimum of detailed and repetitive tasks.	2,8,10,16,22
3.	A job that offers some flexibility as far as being able to leave the office when desired (not chained to a desk from 9 to 5).	6,17,18,21
4.	A job that offers the independence to take an idea, design its implementation, and implement it.	3,6,15,18
5.	A job that offers a tangible feeling of accomplishment.	5,7,9,13,15,16
6.	A job that offers visibility, quick feedback on and support for efforts.	4,9,12
7.	A job that keeps me busy—where I don't have to wait for work.	11,16
8.	A job that relies on some understanding and interest in the political process.	13
9.	A job that offers the opportunity to persuade others to my viewpoint.	3,15
10.	A job that offers enough free time for me to pursue outside interests like keeping fit.	17,23
11.	A job that offers the opportunity to become financially independent.	5,6,18
12.	A job that deals with a subject matter I truly enjoy (i.e. investments, politics, real estate).	21
13.	A job that offers the opportunity for travel within the work setting and time to travel on my own during leisure hours.	2,8,19,22
14.	A firm that keeps its promises to its employees and also requires employees to practice high ethical standards.	24
15.	A firm that places a high value on employees' physical well being.	17,23
16.	A firm that rewards performance with good monetary increases.	5
17.	A firm that has the resources available for me to draw on in order to constantly improve my professional abilities.	6,8,12,13,16,18
18.	A city that offers a lot to do.	2,8,11,23
19.	A place that offers facilities so that the opportunity to keep in shape is available.	17,23
20.	A place where the local political scene is active.	14
21.	A place that has an open social system to get to know people.	1,20

1. Who I was, why I was writing
2. What I wanted
3. What I could offer
4. Asked for a specific action

I enclosed in each letter a copy of my résumé (see Exhibit 30–5).

My planned approach to interviewing was simple. I was prepared. I looked at company reports, talked to classmates, explored alumni contacts, and scanned the business press. I also planned to be ready for some standard questions.

To assist me in my final choice, I developed an evaluation form (see Exhibit 30–6). The evaluation went into a notebook that I kept on each company. The notebook contained all the pertinent information about the company.

I realize my choice is not all rational. Therefore, after all is analyzed, I am also trying to choose a job I can build the most emotional commitment to.

The Job Search

Mike went through the interviewing process almost exactly according to his action plan. He saw every firm he wanted to see. Most of his interviews were in three areas: banking, institutional sales of stocks and bonds, and investment management. In addition, Mike also interviewed for product management positions with three large consumer goods packaging companies. Mike explained the reasoning behind the product management interviews to Mr. Reese:

The three interviews with consumer goods packaging companies were out of my original plan. I had made a change in my job focus sometime during the fall semester. Originally, my job objective was for a position in marketing in consumer goods and/or financial services.

The first brief contacts with the investment banks caused me to do some thinking about my objective. They reacted very negatively to the consumer goods part of my résumé. In fact, the inclusion of consumer goods would probably have eliminated me in the first round weeding-out process. So, I decided to narrow my focus in the plan to just financial services.

But I still wanted to talk to some consumer goods companies. I received excellent grades in marketing courses and wanted to find out what it was really like outside the classroom environment. I tried to select three companies that had a reputation of being good teaching firms. One company, Mammoth Foods, I picked out because of a good fall presentation at school.

Exhibit 30–5

Mike Downer's Résumé

Michael Downer
P.O. Box 000
Central States, USA
Phone: (100)234-5678

Employment Objective	Seek position in marketing of financial services leading to general management responsibilities.
Education	Candidate for MBA degree in May 1982, The Graduate School of Business.
	Bachelor Degree Magna Cum Laude, East Coast College. Outstanding Young Men of America, Dean's List, President of the local chapter of the National Business Society, Vice President of Sigma Chow Fraternity.
Experience	NEW YORK BANK Summer 1981. Full-time summer intern responsible for a project in the marketing department on how to serve small business customers better.
	MIDATLANTIC BANK 1979 to 1980. Marketing Representative responsible for marketing checking and savings accounts, cash management services, investments, and loans to businesses and individuals.
	NATIONAL SAVINGS AND LOAN ASSOCIATION 1978 to 1979. Business Development Representative marketing a pilot program for investment and retirement plans to both individuals and businesses.
	U.S. STOCK BROKERS, INC. 1978. Account Executive involved in the marketing of financial instruments. Successfully completed the New York Stock Exchange examination.

Mike experienced a very high success rate in his first-round interviews. All his interviews went smoothly. In fact, Mike almost had too many callbacks. There wasn't enough time to get back to all the firms that had invited him for a second interview. The commercial banks were all very impressed with Mike and felt even more comfortable with him because of his previous banking experience. The investment banks were equally impressed; Mike received four callbacks out of five companies. In the product management area, he received one callback, from Mammoth Foods.

Mike had a total of nine job offers. Five offers were in commercial banking. These positions were mostly in business development and credit management. One offer was in commercial banking product management. Two more offers were in sales and trading with two investment banks. And finally, Mike received an offer from Mammoth Foods.

From Nine Down to Two

After the offers started coming in, Mike continued to follow his plan. With each company

Exhibit 30–6

Company Evaluation Form

Company Name________________________ Interviewer________________________

Address________________________ Date ________________________

Phone ________________________

Implication	Rank (1 to 5)	Comments
People-oriented		
Changing environment		
Detail/repetition		
Office flexibility		
Tangible accomplishment		
Visibility		
Feedback/support		
Workload		
Politics		
Selling/persuading		
Free time		
Financial independence		
Subject matter		
Travel		
Fairness/ethics		
Physical well-being		
Monetary incentives		
Training		
City attributes		
Recreational facilities		
Political scene		
Open social system		
Total	________	

Overall impressions:

Office appearance (visual data):

Things to remember:

visit, he wrote down his impressions and compared them to the criteria listed in his life themes and job implications. Then he compared and rated the companies against each other.

Mike managed to eliminate six of the nine offers fairly quickly. He narrowed it down to three choices from three different areas: First Commercial Bank in business development; Madison and Monroe, an investment bank, in stock and bond sales; and Mammoth Foods in product management. Two of the offers, First Commercial Bank and Madison and Monroe, were in areas of Mike's original plan. The Mammoth Foods offer was not in the plan, but Mike considered the company unique and wanted to pursue the opportunity.

First Commercial eventually began to drop out

of the picture. Part of the reason was that Mike had left commercial banking to get his MBA. Returning to basically the same type of position and doing much of the same type of work would, in a way, be almost like saying that his MBA was not worth the effort it took to get it. Mike gave some additional reasons to Mr. Reese for eliminating First Commercial:

> The job content itself looked questionable. The office was great. The perks associated with the position were fine. But the work looked terrible. I would go through company after company after company doing the same thing over and over again. After a while, they would all look the same.
>
> I also began to wonder about my fit with the "banking" mentality. The people I met were cynical people. They were also very, very risk adverse. If a company was highly successful, they were always trying to find out how it was going to fail and fall. I just didn't like that atmosphere.

Mike eliminated First Commercial in his selection process. Now there were only two left: Mammoth Foods, and Madison and Monroe.

Mammoth Foods

Mammoth Foods is one of the largest consumer goods packaging companies in the world. The company is headquartered in Kansas City, Missouri. Mike and Mr. Reese discussed the recruiting trips to Kansas City:

> My first visit is what really made me start to seriously consider joining the company. I had pretty much ruled out product management because of the amount of detailed work involved and because of my dislikes for the electives that I had taken in the MBA program. The visit changed my view.
>
> I liked what I saw. I had six interviews in all levels of the organization. I liked the people. They were truly professionals. It seemed like a healthy work atmosphere.
>
> There were some negatives. The company places people in product areas almost at random. You have very little to say as to where your first job assignments are. Where they need you is where you go. Also, the management style of the company is to provide a limited number of positive strokes for a job well done. Finally, I talked to several "East Coast" people who said that they went through a tough adjustment period living in the Midwest.
>
> Thinking back, the positives of my first visit outweighed the negatives. They made me an offer on the spot and that was good. I knew where I stood.
>
> My second trip to Kansas City continued to increase my evaluation of the Mammoth Foods opportunity. My reservations about the city, the people, and the job content were all effectively reduced.
>
> I really like the city. I am surprised at how much there is to do. The city has sports and culture. The entire area has a positive feeling.
>
> I was also reassured about the people. I was especially impressed with many of my peers. There is a lot of positioning and image building during the first six months. The organization is so large that you want the management to notice you right from the start. My peers are competitive as a result, but not cutthroat. There is a mentality that everyone is working through the system together. It is like an extension of the business school environment.
>
> The job content is still a stumbling block. There is detail upon detail. The initial year is full of detailed work, but it does get less and less as time goes on.
>
> After two visits to Kansas City and Mammoth Foods, I had two overall impressions. First, I had a good feeling that said I would fit in. Second, it seemed like a very nice place to live and work.

Madison and Monroe

Madison and Monroe is one of the leading investment banking firms on Wall Street. The firm is engaged in a wide variety of financial services for a broad range of clients. Mike had a very different experience at Madison and Monroe than he had at Mammoth Foods.

> The first round visit at Madison and Monroe was a little on the impersonal side. Impersonal in the sense that the process dictated events. They set aside eight Fridays for the partners to interview MBAs who had received callbacks. Each Friday they had six or seven people come in. We all went through six one-on-one interviews on the Friday we visited.
>
> The interviews were not typical investment banking interviews. There was not as much stress and I considered most of the questions to be better than average. I enjoyed the interviews.
>
> I also enjoyed the people. They were serious, but fun. They were competitive, but not cutthroat. The firm had an air of competence about it. The people were top-notch and their personalities blended together well.
>
> After the first visit to Madison and Monroe, I felt that it would be a good fit if I decided to go into investment banking. At this point, I felt Madison was convinced that I could handle the job content. The remaining question was one of fit.
>
> My second visit to Madison and Monroe gave me a real flavor of investment banking. I spent most of the day with three people. The first was a Graduate School of Business alumnus from last year. I don't know how well he was doing, but I don't think that he was very happy. He answered my questions for over an hour and I think I got some valuable insights.
>
> The second guy was an equity sales trader who had an MBA. I didn't like his attitude. It was like, "I'm here and you're not" and "I'm bigger on this block than

you are.'' He sat back and made me force the conversation. The exposure to him was marginally helpful.

The third guy was in equity research sales and had been with Madison for about three years. He was extremely helpful and I was lucky enough to spend two hours with him. We discussed what he did, how he felt about the firm, and the pros and cons of the whole investment banking situation.

After visiting Madison and Monroe twice, I continued to be impressed. The whole operation is first class. They are a top firm, and I believe I would fit in.

Which One?

At this point, Mike had managed to narrow down his choice between two strong opportunities. He had visited each company twice and had spoken to several people in each firm. Mike set out systematically to evaluate the two alternatives.

Both offers were firm. Madison and Monroe had offered Mike $33,000 a year plus unspecified, but negotiable, extras. Mammoth Foods was offering $31,000 and a nice, neat package of attractive benefits. Neither firm had put a time restriction on Mike, but he had promised Mammoth Foods a decision by the coming Friday.

Mike explained his process up to this point in evaluating the offers:

I started by listing the pros and cons of each offer. I went through different career paths, flexibility, job content, people and the rest of the criteria that I had set up in the beginning. I ended up with a whole set of reasons for and against each offer (see Exhibit 30–7).

I looked at the lists and found that they weren't much help. The idea was good and the list looked good, but it really wasn't much help.

I went back and reread my original plan. I had pretty much executed it exactly, with the exception being that one of my final two choices was in product management. My original negative feelings about product management weren't that strong now that I think about it.

After my first attempt to evaluate the offers, I was leaning towards Mammoth Foods. It was a nice situation. I already had the selling experience that was the primary function in the Madison position.

Mammoth Foods would give me the planning and policy side of marketing. Put that together with my selling, and in five years you've got a full marketing executive.

My second attempt to evaluate the offers was also on a pro and con basis. But this time, I positioned Mammoth Foods against Madison and Monroe. This time Madison came out on top, but the two were still so close (see Exhibit 30–8). As far as I was concerned, I had gotten absolutely nowhere.

Yesterday morning I sat myself down and said, ''Look Mike, this is ridiculous. Look at both offers. Evaluate

Exhibit 30–7

First Evaluation of the Alternatives

Mammoth Foods

Pros:	*Cons:*
1. Good fit with people	1. Structured work atmosphere
2. Exposure to the other side of marketing	2. Time-oriented promotions and raises
3. Career flexibility	3. Less financial independence
4. Flexible start time	4. Team play (I'm a doer)
5. Pleasant city to live in	5. Grunt work
6. Fair amount of variety	6. City is out of the way
7. Some travel	7. Slow-moving organization
	8. Confined to desk
	9. Past work experience with this type of work was less than satisfactory

Madison and Monroe

Pros:	*Cons:*
1. Money potential	1. Limited management support
2. Capitalize on existing selling skills	2. Nontransferable skills
3. Job variety	3. Heavy rejection factor
4. Relies on doer skills	4. Will be doing the same thing for at least 5 years
5. Would lead to a career in financial planning	5. Everyone is fairly cynical
6. Immediate satisfaction from work	6. Alcoholism is an occupational hazard
7. East Coast location	7. Confined to desk
8. Some travel	8. Past experience in this atmosphere was not enjoyable
9. Working with investments	9. Limited chances to be a consultant to clients

Exhibit 30–8

Second Evaluation of the Alternatives

Mammoth Foods		*vs.*		*Madison and Monroe*
Promotion on time		vs	**	Promotion on merit
Strengthen weaker skills	**	vs		Use existing skills
Skills to run my own business	**	vs		Money to start my own business
Structured atmosphere	**	vs		Little management support
Less interesting work		vs	**	Work in investments
Delayed feedback		vs	**	Immediate feedback
Midwest location		vs	**	New York location
Career flexibility	**	vs		Specialization
Good fit with people	**	vs		Intimidated by people
Group work		vs	**	Doer role
Number crunching at first		vs	**	Verbal skills
Minimum control of destiny		vs	**	Major control of destiny

Note: ** indicates the stronger offer.

Scorecard: Mammoth Foods: 5
Madison and Monroe: 7

them. Make a decision." Simple as that. So I read over all my notes. I read "Confessions of a Brand Manager" again. And I rescored the two jobs. This time I used my evaluation sheet. Madison won again, barely. Well, call it even (see Exhibit 30–9).

I feel that there is a war raging inside me. When I sit down and analyze the situation, Madison seems to come out ahead "on points." Yet emotionally I am still drawn to Mammoth Foods. I like the people. I enjoy Kansas City. My salary would go further. Product management is new and unknown. But then, I didn't know much about sales and I loved it once I tried it.

I feel lousy.

Mike needed to make up his mind. He felt that his whole life was being consumed by the decision. It almost haunted him. Mike recognized that he was tired and confused, that he needed new

Exhibit 30–9

Third Evaluation of the Alternatives (RANKED 1 = WORST TO 5 = BEST.)

Implication	*Mammoth Foods*	*Madison and Monroe*
People orientation	4	4
Environment	3	4
Detail/repetition	2	3
Flexibility	2	2
Tangible accomplishment	3	4
Visibility	3	3
Feedback	3	2
Workload	2	3
Selling	3	4
Free time	3	3
Financial independence	2	4
Nature of work	2	4
Travel	3	3
Ethics	4	2
Monetary incentive	2	4
Training	4	2
Social system	4	2
City attributes	3	4
Recreational facilities	3	3
Physical well-being	4	2
Total	59	62

information. Information from a different perspective. It was for this reason that Mike sought out Mr. Reese.

What Now?

Mike Downer sat and stared out the window. Mr. Reese had been listening for over an hour now. Mike was almost through.

What is wrong with me? This is simple. I've got this nice, neat package from Mammoth Foods and I can get to be a marketing director or I can go with Madison and Monroe and cash in on a competent sales skill, make a lot of money, and go from there.

It should be simple, but I just can't decide. Both offers are equal. What should I do?

31

Negotiating and Accepting a Job Offer

Sometime in the later stages of your choosing process or perhaps even after you have chosen your favorite firm but before advising the firm that you have accepted the offer, you will be considering and assessing the various job-related characteristics of the offer. In some cases, you may be satisfied with the offer; in other cases, you may not be satisfied. These situations bring the need to negotiate the terms of employment. A number of dimensions may be the object of your negotiations. (See Exhibit 31–1 for a sample list).

While the characteristics of a job offer may or may not change as a result of negotiations, we believe it is important in the process of selecting a job that matches your self-assessment as well as possible that you take into consideration each of these characteristics and in so doing reduce the number of surprises you will have on the job. It is important to negotiate or discuss the specifics of these various characteristics before you accept an offer. Some corporations have policies for some of these characteristics that cannot be negotiated; generally, when you raise the question, they will advise you of this. Other corporations may be much more willing to meet your needs. In either case, before you accept a position, it is important that you understand the details of the offer clearly. Again, this will reduce the likelihood of both positive and negative surprises after you have already committed yourself.

Gentlemanly Agreements

The first thorny issue around receiving and accepting a job offer relates to the desire of everyone not to be rejected. This is also true of organizations. Many firms will not make a job offer until they are reasonably sure that it will be accepted. This motivation will become apparent to you in your conversations with interviewers at the company. In fact, in some cases they may say: If you received an offer, would you accept it? This kind of approach puts the candidate in an uncomfortable position, and in reality may create additional problems for the recruiting organization because people who otherwise might have accepted offers later on might not be given the opportunity.

One student, after a day of interviews at her first-choice company, felt very confident that she was about to receive an offer. In the last interview of the day with the person charged with the responsibility for making offers, she was asked if she were to receive an offer, would she accept it. She had not yet learned all the details of that position, nor had she heard from her number two and number three choices. She did not know how the specifics of those offers might stack up against what appeared to be her primary interest. Her response was that she liked the company, but wanted to hear what a couple of other alternatives would have to say before she made her decision. She sensed an immediate change in the attitude of the recruiter and felt as though she could almost see the offer being withdrawn.

In that case, this person, if made a firm offer, probably would have in the longer run accepted the company's offer. But the company's reluctance to extend that offer with anything less than 100 percent certainty made it difficult for her to make a commitment on the spot.

One way to deal with this problem is to express to the corporation your sincere and genuine interest in the company and in the position you have been discussing. Then go on to say that many of the details, not only of the job but of the life style associated with it, require further investigation in your mind, and that a real decision is only possible once all the details have been collected. Nevertheless, from all current indications your interest in that company is extremely strong and the probability is very high that if extended an offer you would accept it. This approach expresses sincere interest in the corporation and yet leaves the candidate the option of choosing another alternative if in some unforeseen way it should be more attractive.

Exhibit 31–1

Negotiable Characteristics of Job Offers

- Job content and activities
- Supervisor
- Title and its review period and likely next steps
- Location and office space
- Salary level, bonuses, and additional compensatory perquisites like stock options
- Starting time—that is, beginning work
- Vacations, holidays, sick leave
- Travel
- Overtime work
- Flexibility of working hours
- Moving expenses
- House hunting expenses
- Medical, life, and other forms of insurance
- Maternity leaves
- Educational participation programs
- Pensions
- Company expectations for performance in the first year of employment

Buying Time

During the course of your analysis and choosing process, you may have looked at the details of job offers and know exactly what it is that you want. In many cases this will not be true, so that when you receive an offer you will need to buy yourself some time to consider the details. One response to a telephone offer is to say that it is very attractive and that you are appreciative of the company's expression of confidence, but that you would like to take one or two days to consider some detailed questions relating to the offer and get back to the individual to talk about some of those additional characteristics. You may at this point say that in principle the offer seems satisfactory, and you are very likely to accept it.

Then you can refer to Exhibit 31–1 and your self-assessment to develop specific questions about your activities, compensation, and the parameters that will constrain you when you join the organization. The question of how much to ask for depends upon the importance of the money criterion to you in your experiencing of the work and to the urgency of gaining employment. If you're low on funds and need work immediately, you may be more willing to sacrifice some of the details than if you are determined and have the means to wait for a more attractive and better-matching alternative.

Most employers will leave a job offer open for a particular period of time. Frequently this period is two weeks, but it may extend up to several months. On occasion, companies will demand an immediate response. This they do at least in part because they want to feel that they are in the candidate's first choice, and are reluctant to hire people who would accept them only as their second or third choice. Unless you are very sure that the company that has extended you an offer is the right fit and that the details of job offers have been considered carefully, we do not recommend that you allow yourself to be pressured into making a commitment in the same moment that you receive an offer.

Again, the strategy employed above seems to provide an acceptable and usually effective alternative approach. Express your appreciation at the offer, and say that although it is extremely likely that you will accept it, you want a day or two to consider it carefully before you respond. In many cases, a day or two is insufficient time, and you may ask for a week to two weeks to consider the offer. This is not unusual in industry, and you should not feel embarrassed or unique for asking for this time. You might also make a point to the recruiter that it is in their best interest as well as your own that both parties have the opportunity to consider the match carefully.

Assignment

Read the vignettes that follow. For each one, write down your specific plans for dealing with each of the situations. What would you say? What would you do? Where would you go? With whom would you talk?

1. Salary Differentials

You have just received an offer from Company XYZ, which is high on your priority list. During the day you discover from friends that other people have been given offers $5,000 above yours. Knowing the people and the jobs they would be taking in the company, you do not understand the difference in salary, since you are at least as well qualified as they and the position you are being offered is at least as responsible as theirs.

2. Moving Expenses

You have just been offered a position in a distant city but do not have a lot of excess funds in savings and personal bank accounts. You have learned from other people who have been given offers by the company that the company does not pay moving expenses.

3. House Search Expenses

You have a house, but have just been offered a position with a company in another city. You are to leave within the month. You are concerned about the time and expense of selling your own home and the time and expense involved in purchasing a new one in the city to which you're moving.

4. Starting Work

You feel mentally, emotionally, and physically exhausted by the rigors of your academic program. Although the job you have chosen is exciting and stimulating, you are concerned about starting work immediately. You have sufficient money in your savings to spend a month or two on vacation, and even though you've heard the company needs you immediately, you are thinking about negotiating for a later starting date.

32

Decision Making for Couples

In a situation where a job hunter is not a relatively independent individual, but is highly interdependent with another person, such as a spouse or a fiancé, any decisions made will directly affect not just one but two people. The job selection decision-making process, which we have already seen is complex for an individual, becomes even more complex when the decision maker is a part of a couple. But exactly how much more complex it becomes, and in what ways, will vary depending upon the nature of the couple's relationship.

The Spectrum of Relationships

Exhibit 32-1 presents a spectrum of relationships for couples. At the extreme left of the spectrum is the traditional relationship: The husband is the breadwinner and the wife is the homemaker and child-raiser. As one moves from left to right across the spectrum, male and female roles change toward more equal participation in family and career. At the right extreme, both people essentially assume the same role, in terms of careers and homes.

In the case of the traditional couple, the job selection decision-making process usually comes the closest to what we have already seen for individuals. The only additional complication is that the decision maker typically adds to his selection criteria a few constraints related to his perception of his spouse's needs (for example, "She will never move outside the United States, so I won't bother to pursue non-U.S. jobs").

As we move to the right on the spectrum, the job selection decision-making process tends to become more complex. The further right we are, the more we are likely to find not one but two decision makers, both involved in analysis and choice. The additional complexity derives from the need to somehow coordinate two different cognitive *and* emotional processes—which may be very difficult and time-consuming.

Today, most couple relationships are still traditional or semi-traditional. But the trend over the past decade has been movement from left to right in Exhibit 32-1. And, for our purposes, that means movement toward additional complexity in job-related decision making. One might reasonably wonder how well prepared most people are for the increased complexity.

Assignment

The Bradshaw case is of a young couple involved in a job decision. Consider these questions when you study the case:

1. How is the decision being reached?
2. What are the key forces that affected the manner in which they went about reaching a decision?
3. What job do you think Jim accepted? Why?
4. How well do you think subsequent events will work out for the Bradshaws?
5. What generalizations, if any, might you draw from this case regarding job decision making for couples?

Exhibit 32–1

A Spectrum of Relationships for Couples

THE TRADITIONAL COUPLE	THE SEMI-TRADITIONAL COUPLE	THE TYPICAL DUAL CAREER COUPLE	THE EGALITARIAN COUPLE
HE is the breadwinner SHE is the homemaker and child-raiser HE competes and succeeds for both SHE provides child care, social, and maintenance for both	HE is the breadwinner (with some involvement in family and home) SHE is the homemaker and child-raiser but she also works, usually for a specific purpose (such as better vacations for the family, college tuition, braces for someone's teeth, her own personal satisfaction) HE has the dominant career but acknowledges her contribution to their quality of life, and her need for some kind of outside activity SHE works, but neither of them thinks of her as having a "career"	HE is committed to a professional career SHE is committed to a professional career The couple think of themselves as being a dual career family BUT, one of them (almost always the woman) takes on more than 50 percent of the responsibility for housekeeping and child-raising, and provides less than 50 percent of the income	HIS and HER roles vis-à-vis career and home are essentially the same. BOTH work; they have an equal commitment to their jobs. BOTH do 50 percent of the housework. BOTH do 50 percent of the child-raising.

Note: Couples can change their relationships on the continuum. Perhaps the most typical example we see of this today is the couple who in their twenties assume a traditional couple role. In their thirties, after their children are in school, they shift to the semi-traditional role. And in their forties, after the children have left home, they become a dual career couple.

THE BRADSHAWS

Jim and Helen Bradshaw, both in their late twenties, looked tired and somewhat tense as they sat down in the apartment of a close friend on the afternoon of April thirtieth. They had felt the need to talk over their current problems with someone whom they knew to be a good listener. Jim, a second-year MBA student, had promised one company that he would let them know by May first whether he would accept their offer for full-time employment. He and Helen had spent the last few nights talking nonstop about the merits and drawbacks of the two offers they were considering. After lighting a cigarette, Jim launched into the subject.

Jim: A lot of things have been happening lately and it seems like it is happening a little bit too quickly. We have been on the merry-go-round here the last two years with Helen out working and me totally involved in school work. Now all of a sudden we're being confronted with issues that we didn't really spend enough time thinking about or discussing.

The way I see it, there are really two dilemmas. One is the personal dilemma I have regarding job choice, and that can't really be separated from the other dilemma, which is my relationship with Helen.

Helen: I think it would be helpful if we explained to Doug what the two jobs are and the difference between them, since he doesn't really know.

Jim: Well, there are two companies. One is Davidson Manufacturing Company, which is located in St. Joseph, Missouri, and . . .

Helen: Small town—30,000 people.

Jim: . . . on a continuum that would be at one extreme according to my viewpoint, as far as its being the typical MBA opportunity. It has a lot of responsibility and a lot of exposure to top-level management. They have a lot of Harvard MBAs and they push them ahead and give them many opportunities to move around. The big negative is the location. St. Joseph, Missouri, is just out in farm country and it's a small town.

Helen: It's not near a big city and it doesn't have in its immediate vicinity all the nice things about a city that we very much like; theater, museums, galleries, restaurants, etc.

Jim: On a rational level I can say that as an MBA going to work for them I would be on the fast track and it would just be very stimulating professionally, but socially it would leave just an awful lot to be desired. Everyone we talked to who's from that area or works for the company says it's a great place to raise a family.

Helen: Which we have no interest in doing and everybody there does!

Jim: The other extreme is working for Browning Corporation in San Francisco. I would start out as an auditor—an internal consultant type. I would be on my own or working with another person—which really appeals to me—but I would have to travel at least 50 percent of the time. I would be going to all their subsidiaries and operations to find out what their problems are and to make some recommendations. There would be a lot of, I guess what people would term, mechanical work to that as well. A lot of number crunching.

And yet that's a location we both like. We lived there before we came here. We enjoyed the life style out west. Our friends are out west. If we ever wanted to settle in a place, that would be it.

The reason I've said this option is toward the other end of the spectrum is that there aren't many MBAs in the company. There is some uncertainty at this point concerning what I might be doing in the future. It's not clear that in one and a half years I would get this or that type of job. The potential is certainly there, because they are growing at the same rate Davidson is. They are a larger company to begin with, which means that it might be a little faster moving, but it is so difficult to tell based on one visit. The reason Davidson is so attractive is that I worked for them last summer, or rather for one of their distributors (which is an independent business). Anyway I got to meet a lot of the people, and they got to know me and I performed very well and I guess they all liked me.

Helen: Jim's got a couple of friends here at the school who worked with them, and so when we are with them it is very easy to get carried away and become very excited about the possibilities of working for that company.

Jim: There are so many little minor pluses and minuses. You can live very well in St. Joseph, Missouri. It is very inexpensive. You can get a house comparable to something in Boston at half the price. Yet the wages there are higher or equal to Boston and New York. On the other hand, this offer on the West Coast is substantially lower in salary. Now money is not my top priority. I don't think money is that important in the short run or even in the long run. There has to be enough so we can live comfortably, but I don't think I would make a job decision based solely on that. I would make a decision based on the elements of the job.

Helen: If you were just making a decision on money, then the decision would very easily be made.

Jim: Right. I have talked to two firms in New York and one in Boston that I'll probably get offers from at higher salaries. (*Turning to Helen*) Perhaps this is a good time for you to get into the aspect of what you'd like to be doing, and I can talk about those other jobs and the cloudiness as far as my decision goes a little later.

Helen: My problem is I don't know what I want to do. I want to work and I feel a very urgent need to work but I don't have any professional expertise. I don't have any credentials. I went to college and was then married and I have worked as a secretary ever since.

Jim: And part of the reason that took place is we were moving every two years.

Helen: We were never in one place long enough for me to get into anything.

Jim: And there's always been that certainty. We knew when we got to a location that we would only be there as short as six months or as long as two years. That's been part of the problem, I guess.

Helen: But I do want to work. I don't know what I want to do, as I said. In St. Joseph, Missouri, I don't see very many alternatives. I see none in the town itself. It's all unionized and there have been layoffs left and right, and it is not a good time for someone from outside the area to come in and expect to be able to get a job. It is located about 30 miles from Greensville, which is where the University is. I suppose if I wanted to commute, I would look there for either employment at the University or consider going back to school. Neither of those options has an enormous amount of appeal to me right now. In San Francisco there are lots of options. I know several people who are in various businesses that I have some interest in. I see a couple of choices for myself out there. Some things I would like to try. I don't see any in Missouri.

Jim: Another thing about Davidson is that if you survive and do very well with the company, opportunities are pretty much in St. Joseph, Missouri. Certainly there are field operations and international operations, which would be a sidelight for a few years, but if you thought in terms of the long term, that's where we would be. The thought of that kind of scares me, because the things we like to do socially and even athleticwise just don't happen to be in the Midwest. They happen to be on the coasts. The life style itself is something we have always taken for granted because we have always lived in good places. In Georgia we lived not too far from Atlanta. We lived overseas for a couple of years in Japan, when I was in the Navy, and then the West Coast, and then Washington, D.C. These are all places we were very comfortable with—big cities, metropolitan areas, lots of activity. Of course Boston has a lot more to offer also.

Helen: I think that the closest I have ever come to living in what I would call a small-town environment is when we were in the military overseas. The American community was very close-knit and I didn't particularly like that. My idea of living in a foreign country is not spending your life on the base. So I had very few American friends over there and I had many Japanese friends. The thing I disliked about the ugly-American syndrome which went on over there was that U.S. people had nothing better to do than talk about other U.S. people, and I don't like—I am not comfortable in—an environment where everybody knows me, everybody knows when I come and go. I like the city. I have a need for that kind of privacy.

Jim: Because we have always had a lot of the good things that a big city has to offer, it's hard to decide what it is exactly that really attracts us. I did receive what I considered good professional offers in New York City, but the jungle aspect of the city just sort of overwhelmed me.

There's another company which I guess would be a compromise between the two companies we talked about earlier, and that was Johnson Company. It's in Chicago, which is a big city and not a bad place. The company happens to be located in the suburbs. It's not San Francisco, certainly, but it takes away the disadvantages that Davidson has, being in a small town in Missouri, because it has the restaurants, the museums, and what have you. I was really expecting to get an offer from them, and had I received an offer from them, that would have been the best of both worlds. It would have been a professional challenge on one hand, and also it wouldn't have been such a bad place to live. We have never lived in Chicago before, so it would be an adventure for us, and we probably would have really enjoyed it. The program that they had for MBAs was very flexible. You could almost name the area you wanted to start in, and they would guarantee that you have a different job after about 6 to 12 months. There was a lot of mobility, top-management exposure, and good salaries. It just really seemed to be sort of an ideal situation. Unfortunately, I didn't quite make the final cut, and I know why—I had a good set of interviews with the exception of one person and he happened to be the person that they were looking for an MBA to work with. He was a little bit older than everyone else, and I knew he wasn't totally impressed with me. I wasn't totally impressed with him either. I have one trait which sometimes turns out to be a weakness, I am honest. After the day was over, someone asked me what my impression was, and I told them exactly what my impression was. I felt that at that point in the job search I fool myself when I try to fool anyone else, because it can come back and bite me in the ass. I also value very highly a person's honesty and straightforwardness, and that's why I discuss everything the way I see it. I think that's probably the way I cut my throat, although they waited until the very end until they rejected me. I suspect that I wasn't unacceptable, but there were other prople that were more acceptable, so they had to wait until they had everything in.

There was another factor that added to the confusion of the job search. The company I worked for last summer was in Los Angeles and, as I said, was an independent distributor for Davidson Manufacturing. They have on the order of $15 million in sales. When the summer was over I was told by my employer, who was an HBS alumni, that he would be in a position to offer me a job. He was president of a company by the age of 36 or something like that. He was 32 when he got out of the B-School, so he didn't waste much time in going through the hierarchy. He went in as a divisional manager and a year later he was a vice-president and two years later he had his own business. He was in Boston last week, and unfortunately I didn't get to see him. I just talked to him on the phone. He saw Helen before he saw me.

Helen: And so he told me that he couldn't offer Jim a job. . . .

Jim: . . . because of the economy. He said the last nine months had been slow. So he told Helen. I was on an interview trip out in Denver. She called me up on the phone that night before I had my interview with Browning (that's where their headquarters is). . . .

Helen: I thought you'd like to know.

Jim: I'm glad you told me, because prior to that I wasn't too serious about Browning. I got rejected from Johnson at the beginning of the same week, which was last week. Johnson rejected me on Monday morning and on Thursday afternoon I found out that I wouldn't have an offer from the place in L.A. Then—this is the same day—I called Davidson because I hadn't heard from them in a month, and they told me the job I was being considered for initially at Davidson, which was assistant to this Executive Vice-President, and which I was really excited about, was being filled by someone else. So now they had something else in mind for me but they didn't know exactly what it was. I found out just last night when this other vice-president called that essentially it would be a sales rep. I would do that for six months just to learn the product, and that appeals to me. I think that would be the best way to find out about the nature of the business and their customers and deal with the people.

Helen: Well, it's almost a kick in the teeth from them, isn't it?

Jim: Well, in a sense. But then again, when I asked them last night on the phone if they didn't hire me for this job would they hire someone else, they said no, they wouldn't hire anyone. So that sort of rebuilt my ego a little bit by saying that they are interested in me as a long-term investment as a person. The fact that I got rejected from Johnson and the guy I worked for last summer in the same week and I didn't know what my status was has sort of weighed a little bit heavy on me. Now I am getting a little concerned that while the job in San Francisco has so many pluses, there are a lot of question marks.

Helen: Long-term question marks you mean.

Jim: Right. I must admit that the organization and the people I have met in Davidson by and large really impressed me. I got along with them, and it's just a great working environment. But then there is St. Joseph. There would always be other options—I could take no job and just pack up and go out to the West Coast or any other place.

Helen: I don't really see that as beyond the realm of possibility.

Jim: At the same time it is not something that one would like to do.

Helen: It's the riskiest option.

Jim: Right. There's enough uncertainty in our lives already. It costs a lot of money to move, so financially it would be a hardship in the short run. Of course in the long run I am sure we are talking about nickels and dimes. On the other hand, if we did go out to San Francisco, say, no matter what company I would go with, unless it was a small business, chances are that I wouldn't stay in one place.

Helen: To get ahead and have the kind of professional future that we would like, we must move. That's always been our assumption.

Jim: I think I've always enjoyed moving. I love being on the go, and adventure, and new experiences, and new challenges and not doing the same thing year after year. That's been in my blood, but needless to say, that might change. I try to keep an open mind even now.

Helen: In me that is starting to change now. The idea of settling down and staying in one place has more appeal to me today than it used to. Maybe that's because I'm tired out—I'm moved out.

Jim: But the reason that appeals to you is that you were in a place, the San Francisco Bay area, that you really enjoyed. Since you're a little more uncertain about your professional future than I am, you feel that you have to be in a location for longer than just a year so that you can get into a job and get some experience and maybe find out some of the things you'd like to do. I don't think you could say with certainty that a profession you might get into would require that you would stay in one place forever and ever.

Helen: It might not, I'm just saying that, professional considerations aside, I think what I want to do more and more is settle down, have a house, live in a neighborhood.

Jim: That definitely has appeal, but one of my problems is that I'm not ready to say that's what I want to do. (*Pause*).

Going to San Francisco if nothing else has some very good short-term considerations from our point of view, and it could or could not have some good long-term possibilities. But when you look at Missouri, you think that it wouldn't be so bad for a couple of years. Professionally I could do very well, and yet the thought of spending 20 or 30 years in a place like that just leaves us both very cold.

Helen: I keep thinking, well you know it might only be for a year and a half and then we would move someplace else, but the fear that keeps jumping into my head is that someday I am going to wake up 40 and be in the same damn spot that I am right now and I really don't want that to happen.

Jim: I could always say, well a company like Davidson would be a great challenge and give me much more than I could handle, which would push me along and help me. Then after a couple of years if I found I didn't really like St. Joseph, Missouri, I could go somewhere else. It's a good place for corporate headhunters, so there is a lot of visibility there. Yet making a decision to do that scares me a little bit, too, because I have never done anything like that.

When I was in the military for four years, I always got my first choice and I had independent jobs so that people were not pressing their thumbs down on me all the time. I had a lot of flexibility and latitude. I was allowed to become an expert in some areas that nobody else had any detailed knowledge of. It was very rewarding and satisfying. Yet at the B-School here it has been a very painful experience. Certainly there's more work here than any place I have been before, although I am not averse to work. Most of my classmates say they view it the same way. I must admit, it's a real chore to get up in the morning at times.

Two years is a short amount of time, however. I certainly don't regret the decision, and it will be worth it to me. I probably won't realize the benefits fully until I have been gone for several years, because many of the things we acquire at the B-School are intangible. After having been here, I say maybe I'm ready to quit postponing my pleasure.

I don't mind paying my dues. I realize that whatever company I go to work for will have services I'm not totally knowledgeable about, and it will take a little bit of effort in burning some midnight oil to come up to speed and learn the politics of the organization and learn how everything flows. I think that is normal wherever one goes. I think I can be very happy in a place if I have an unpalatable job or if there are some painful things to do for a few months like working late or working on weekends. But when you put together a bad environment with bad working conditions, well, I'd rather dig ditches, I really would.

Helen: You just answered the question then.

Jim: I say that now, but my gut will be gnawing away at me when I go home tonight. I'll be thinking, now wait a minute, am I giving up an opportunity. . . . If I say no I don't want to go to Missouri, am I giving up an opportunity that I might have had otherwise?

Helen: If it were such a great opportunity, it wouldn't be this hard to make a decision, would it?

Jim: Well, probably not.

Helen: (*Looking at Doug and shaking her head.*) We seem to be going back and forth just day in and day out.

Jim: We're very happy about Davidson and that offer, and then not so happy about the other. Then the next day we'll think of San Francisco and some of the possibilities with Browning, and I guess when we do this we rationalize whichever decision we seem to be leaning toward. For instance, the other day we were looking through the St. Joseph local newspaper and looking at the houses. There were some fantastic prices and just really far-out things. We were, I don't know, trying to come up with some good things we could do there that we couldn't do elsewhere. You could play golf cheaply and play it every weekend, for example.

Helen: Somehow all of those very nice little things don't add up to having enough weight to really swing us that way.

Jim: And yet the anxiety about going the other way is that. . . .

Helen: Maybe part of the problem with the Browning job is that you don't have a clear enough picture in your mind as to where you could go with that company, whereas you do have somewhat of a clearer idea of where you would go in Davidson.

Jim: Well, that's part of it. But I'm not averse to that kind of uncertainty—that's what life's all about.

Helen: It's not just a question of uncertainty. You don't even know what options there are.

Jim: Well, I know a little bit about the options. They have a computer subsidiary and they have a leasing subsidiary which leases anything. It is a financial institution. They have many service operations like food service, catering, transportation, and things along that line. While their total sales aren't growing at the same rate that some companies' sales are going, some of their businesses are growing quite a bit. I'm certain that at some point in the future, if I decided I liked the company, I'd be given the advantage of these vacant slots. But there aren't a lot of MBAs in the company and so they look upon this institution as, you know, one of those Ivy League schools which turns out arrogant people. It demands exorbitant salaries for people who don't like to get their hands dirty. Some of it's true. They do hire MBAs, though; in fact what they call an internal audit staff is composed of 26 people evenly divided between career people and MBAs—young guys like myself who come in and go out and see all the businesses and give them a lot of ideas and yet rely on experience that the older guys have. So there is a constant turnover and the average guy maybe takes three years before he goes into a line job. The best guy probably gets out in about 18 months. Now I would consider myself as good as the rest of the competition. I could get out some of the mundane tasks within two years. That doesn't bother me. I think I could learn an awful lot about their business and a lot about just going in and evaluating businesses.

Helen: Now you see, my impression all along has been that that was the part of the offer that you found most unpalatable. I have been thinking all along that you would just be unhappy for the first 18 months and wouldn't like what you were doing. (*Directed to Doug.*) I don't want to ask him to do that.

Jim: Well, if I was with Davidson, my dues-paying period would be shorter, probably about six months. As long as I was learning, that Browning deal wouldn't bother me at all. There is travel involved in the Browning job which would involve a month or two months in one location, where I'd be by myself. That's a little bit of a headache. On the other hand, I don't mind personally at this point in my life traveling around. I think the MBA program really prepares one to adjust to situations like that very rapidly.

We're still not addressing the problem that we as a couple, as a married couple, face. We've avoided the issue very conveniently in the past—realizing that what Helen wants to do and what is best for her growth and what is best for me might not be in the same place. We don't have any children, so that's not a factor, and we don't have aspirations of starting a family now. I still suspect that in a couple of years from now, at most, when I do well, I will be offered an opportunity and it probably won't be in San Francisco. It will probably be somewhere else. It could be in Denver, could be Boston, could be anywhere. Someone will come to me or I will go to them and say, "Hey, I want to get my teeth into a little bigger responsibility," and there will be an offer made. We have no idea what Helen will be into at that point.

Helen: And that's a problem. I don't know how to find answers short of trying a bunch of things, but I have to be in an environment where the possibilities are open so I can try them.

Jim: I realize that it would be unfair for me to expect Helen just to pack up and move wherever the company says they want to send me.

Helen: That's what we call the tag-along syndrome.

Jim: Well, we have been married six years and Helen has had to move along wherever I have gone up until now. I guess there was some hesitancy in the past. You didn't really want to come to Boston because you liked San Francisco. You even applied to Stanford, and in fact I didn't apply to Stanford, even though it probably would have been the easy way out. I probably could have found it a bit easier to get a job on the West Coast when I graduated had I been there. Harvard was unquestionably the best opportunity for me as far as graduate education, and it was really Helen who pushed me toward it.

Helen: That's what I've done all along, encouraged Jim to go after the *best* opportunity available.

Jim: And yet, up to now I haven't pushed her into anything. That is the basic difference in our personalities.

Helen: It's a big difference. It's just the whole way I was raised. I wasn't taught to think. I was always pushed—told I would do this and I would do that. I would go to college. It didn't matter where I went. Nothing mattered but that after a certain number of years the sheepskin. My parents expected that I would then get married and be a housewife just like my mother, and I didn't really quite question that or start thinking about it until the last few years. Now I'm really in a fix because I don't know what to do or how to go about finding out what I'm good at.

Jim: Well, there are two problems in that regard. The first being that I don't have that much confidence in my ability to be objective and to help Helen find out what she wants to do. I certainly don't have any training or experience. By nature, I just don't like to impose my standards or my ideals consciously on someone else, and my perception is that's what I'd be doing if I tried to suggest what Helen should do and. . . .

Helen: And I don't quite see it the same way.

Jim: In fact you see it very differently.

Helen: In fact, I would like to think that Jim would say, you know, well here's the way I see you, here's what I think you are good at, why not check out these possibilities. I want to hear something from him. I want some advice.

Jim: Based on our conversation the other day, I suspect you would also like a little bit of firmness from me, like saying, "Hey, get off your ass and go do this."

Helen: That wouldn't hurt. But that's not what I need. I know full well that nobody can make any decisions for me; I just feel that I'm not aware enough of what sorts of jobs are out there. It sounds incredibly naive, but I don't feel that I have the knowledge of what sorts of positions I could go after and I want some help in trying to find out what they are.

Jim: And since I don't go ahead and fulfill the expectations that she has for help, she looks upon me as being unconcerned, or less concerned, which isn't true.

Helen: Well yes, but you see that's the biggest difference between Jim and me. He's an extremely analytical person and I operate intuitively, almost exclusively. So you can see how he's trying at this level and I'm at another level—and it gets in the way.

Jim: In the past when I have tried to explain things to Helen, it has become very frustrating for me because on my terms she won't understand it. If I can be aware that I should relate to her on her level then perhaps I can be persuasive, but that takes a lot of awareness and a lot of energy as well.

Helen: See, because I am such an intuitive person, I am greatly affected by my environment. If I'm not going to feel happy there, I'm not going to be happy there. I'm not going to feel comfortable or at ease. I'm not going to like it. I mean that's the only way to say it.

Jim: Why, Helen?

Helen: Well, you know when one is talking about intuitive feelings it is very difficult to say why I am not going to like it.

Jim: Since we both make decisions at a very different level, one of the things we know that happens between us is that Helen often has a tendency to overreact or to imagine bad situations as being worse than they really turn out to be, and I on the other hand tend to underestimate the badness. Many times unconsciously and unknowingly we can both make totally different assumptions in a situation. I'm trying to think of a good example that has happened recently. Well, we made a different assumption the other day and we both got upset and started arguing and there was no cause for that.

Helen: We had a conversation and I came away perfectly satisfied that I knew what was supposed to take place. Jim came away satisfied that he knew exactly what was going to take place, but we were thinking different things.

Jim: So in the case of this job decision I made a lot of assumptions about Helen that are just very far off base compared to her assumptions, especially with respect to this job search for her and this uncertainty she has about what she might be doing. So I guess Helen doesn't want to feel that her needs are being imposed on me by saying, "Well, we have to go to San Francisco because that's where I can do my thing." She doesn't want to feel guilty or responsible if I take a job that I don't consider to be the best job for me just to make her happy. Yet I don't want to say, "Hey, Helen, you have to go to St. Joseph, Missouri, and live there for a while," because that would be forcing my structure on her.

So I guess there's another option. She can go to San Francisco, and I can go to St. Joseph, Missouri, which probably creates more problems in the long run than it would solve. Although we certainly have an element of independence. Last summer I spent three months on the West Coast and she stayed here most of the time because that was the best job opportunity. Now I could have stayed here and had a job that I didn't enjoy. After spending nine months at HBS doing work I didn't enjoy I wasn't about to do that. She really couldn't have quit her job because part of the condition of her employment was that she would stay here during the summer.

Helen: Well, I accepted that job and I felt I didn't want to give it up for what was in my mind a ridiculous reason. I have a sense of responsibility about wherever I work even though it might not be the most glamorous job in the world. It was my choice to stay at work.

Jim: In that case, it was a simple decision for both of us. While I was in the Navy I was always away, so it was not a new experience to be separated. Living under the same roof 365 days a year tends to make one nonobjective at times. We all need a rest and a change of pace.

The way we come out is we don't mind sacrificing for the other person, but if you're in that other person's role the knowledge that the other one is giving up something just for you is just not acceptable. That's why if we had another job offer. . . .

Helen: Well, we don't, so that's not another possibility—two jobs or none.

Jim: Well, we can just pack up and start driving around and I can extend my job search for a while longer. (*He pauses and stares at the floor, and then lifts his head suddenly.*) The other thing that is frustrating from my point of view is that I haven't fully thought this out and it's sort of catching up to me. The circumstances are sort of forcing me to think about it. Yet to compare all our awareness of this dilemma we're in now versus what it was two months ago—is just a totally different situation. We've really sort of been complacent, I guess for too long. We can't undo that, of course, so we won't sit here and be anxious about it, but . . .

Helen: I have no doubt that I will eventually find some work which is meaningful to me and satisfying to me and that's not my real problem. My real problem. . . . Six months ago if anyone had said, "What are you going to do in June?" my answer would have been, "Well, we'll go where Jim gets a job." But I took an Interpersonal Behavior course this spring and I began to really think about me and Jim, and now I don't like the implications of simply following Jim around. But now we get down to what's more important. . . . Is it more important for me to be Jim's wife or for me to be an employed member of the work force? Since I'm only just beginning to think about the implications of both, I don't know which direction I am going in. (*Long pause.*) Work is not so important to me that I would do that at the risk of our relationship, however. . . . (*Long pause.*)

33

The Career Development Paper

Purpose

Once a person has developed a job search focus, and anticipated the job search process by working through the previous chapters, what comes next? We have developed a document that will guide you through the actual process. We outline here a career development paper (CDP) that our students have found very useful as a guide during recruiting. The career development paper works similarly to an annual budget in a corporation, so the skills involved in developing, using, and modifying it, and then finishing what it outlines, are very relevant to necessary organizational skills.

The career development paper is designed to help you to use your self-assessment paper—that is, to think through and manage in an active, rigorous way the implications of that paper.

The career development paper is a nuts-and-bolts strategy paper that asks you to outline a job search program and to lay *specific* plans for implementing it. Our experience has been that students who carefully consider and execute the assignment and then implement its components during their job search find that process to be much less difficult than it otherwise could have been (and often is for their peers). The notebooks are *not* to be handed in with the papers. You should hand in a *copy* of your typed paper, *keeping* the original.

Content

The CDP should contain the following elements:

1. A copy of the themes list developed in your self-assessment paper. If, upon reexamination, you wish to refine those thematic labels, you are encouraged to do so. The themes should be listed on one page and *numbered for easy reference*. Whereas the raw data from the various data-generating devices was your data base for the self-assessment paper, your themes will be your basic data base for the career development paper.

2. Implications of your themes for work and career. These implications should (1) be specific; (2) address a variety of dimensions of work; and (3) be referenced to specific themes (again to demonstrate the logic you used to construct them). Some dimensions you might wish to consider would be physical environment, interpersonal requirements, location, tasks and routines, organizational style, rewards. The logic connecting implications to themes should be clear.

3. An analysis rigorously based on your themes and implications of what career opportunities you have elected to pursue in your job search and *why*. Be sure that your assumptions are explicit and that your focus is clearly defined. Note briefly how each alternative could fit into a long-term career path.

4. A statement describing the kind of life style you intend to live next year, including a justification,

based on themes and implications, for that plan. I encourage you to push yourself here to think through the variety of life style issues we have raised throughout the course and at the same time to be realistic. You may wish to include your personal definition of "success," a typical intended weekly schedule, and expected financial allocations.

5. A *detailed* action plan for your job search for the coming year. *What* will you do? Calendar *whom* you will visit, contact. *When? Where* will you go? *What* will you want to learn? *How* will you learn it? What is your time frame/schedule? How will you manage your personal life and school work? These issues (and others) should be addressed carefully. The action plan should be justified clearly by your themes and implications and should consider the topics raised in the career development half of the course. We encourage you to review this plan several times asking yourself these questions: "What am I assuming or taking for granted? Is that reasonable?" and then to be very explicit about the answers.

IF YOU HAVE A JOB OR ARE NOT LOOKING THIS SPRING: Some of you have already accepted jobs for next year or are in joint programs that will keep you off the job market next spring. Those of you deferring your entry to the job market for a year should write the paper as assigned. For those who have already accepted a job, the content of the paper is altered slightly.

A. Write section 3 as a *detailed* justification of your job next year in light of your themes and implications. How well does it fit? What difficulties do you expect to encounter? Specifically, (who, what, how, when, where) how will you manage the joining up process?

B. Substitute for section 5 a discussion of your long-term career strategy (based on themes and implications) and of how the job you have accepted fits into that plan.

Format

Your CPD must be typed. *Maximum* length is twenty-five pages. Hand in *two copies. Keep the original* for yourself. Do *not* hand your notebook in. Do not put your papers in a notebook or cover. Staple in the upper left corner.

Criteria for a Good Career Development Paper

1. Logic of connections between themes and implications
2. Logic of connections between themes/implications and jobs to pursue
3. Logic of connections between themes/implications and intended life style
4. Detailed and specific action plan with attention given to the issues raised in the CD half of course (focus, correspondence, interviewing, support systems, company visits, coping, choosing, and joining up)
5. Reasonable length
6. Clarity of communication
7. You may wish to include various forms you will use to help you organize your job search [contact log, interview questions (tied closely to and referenced to themes and implications), company research form (again, based on themes and implications), list of target companies, a linking chart (a matrix with themes and implications down one side, life style aspects or job demands across the top and comments in the cells), and/or a typical weekly schedule during the second-semester job search (have you realistically allocated enough time to implement your action plan?)].

> **ASSIGNMENT**
>
> We have included here a copy of Steven Taylor's career development paper so that you can see what one might look like and find its strengths and weaknesses. Read through it and identify what it does well and what could be improved. How will you improve on this design in your own paper? What feedback would you give to Steve? Are there any cautions you would pass on to him as he begins his job searches?

Steven Taylor's Career-Development Paper

To rise to a position of such power that we have no one to blame but ourselves is a fearful state of affairs . . . . A very few march unambivalently and unhesitatingly into adulthood, ever eager for new and greater responsibilities. We are accustomed to imagining the conversion or sudden call to grace as an "Oh, Joy!" phenomenon. In my experience, more often as not it is, at least partially, an "Oh, Shit" phenomenon.

—M. Scott Peck, 1978
The Road Less Traveled

Self-Assessment Themes (plus Three)

Steven Taylor is a person who:

1. Requires a balance in both work and personal life.

2. Plays a little fast and loose with traditional customs.
3. Thrives in an unstructured environment.
4. Is demanding of self/a drive for continuous improvement.
5. Has a need for intellectual stimulation.
6. For whom Family is important.
7. Can be pompous, but usually conscious of it.
8. Needs to spend time in outdoor activities.
9. Values independence and self-sufficiency.
10. Cares more deeply about a smaller number of people.
11. Enjoys external confirmation of success.
12. Is demanding of friends.
13. Prefers an active environment.
14. For whom Playing music is missing as a part of my life.
15. Handles crises well.
16. Learns from setbacks.
17. Adapts well.
18. Is restless, I like to get on to the next project.
19. Is willing to take risks to gain greater rewards.

Plus three!

20. Would like to see more of the world and its variety.
21. Senses the emergence of a more contemplative me.
22. Would like to find a place to call home, somewhere I will always come back to.

Implications of Self-Assessment Themes

Professional Aspect

Cognitive:

1. I like to balance intuitive and analytical approaches to solving problems (T4,T7,T8).
2. I enjoy a constant flow of new and challenging situations (T3,T4,T5,T17,T19,T20).

Routines:

3. Predictability of hours is not critical, but relentlessly long hours will be unacceptable (T1,T3,T6,T8).
4. I like to take a break between major projects (T1,T3,T15).
5. A varying daily routine is exciting (T2,T3,T13, T18,T15).
6. I want to commute less than 45 minutes from home to work, and I prefer not to drive (T6,T18).

Tasks:

7. I enjoy making presentations and being challenged to support the analyses (T3,T4,T5,T7,T9,T17, T19).
8. I like to travel in my work and would like to travel internationally. (T3,T5,T9,T13,T17,T20).
9. I thrive on unearthing the difficult questions, the ones nobody likes to answer (T3,T4,T12,T17).
10. I want to be responsible for managing my day (T1,T2,T3,T4,T9).
11. I derive great satisfaction from getting a team to pitch in and push a project to completion (T3,T10,T15,T17).

Organizational Style:

12. If it's not a fun place, then it's not for me (T2,T3,T13,T20).
13. I want to work with people who see excellence as a goal in and of itself and worth the effort (T4,T5,T9,T10,T12).
14. I like to work in an informal environment (T2,T3,T13,T15,T19).
15. I want to work in a firm small enough that I know everyone by name (T1,T9,T10,T19).
16. I want to know if I've done well, and I want to hear about it if I haven't (T4,T11,T16,T19).
17. A little pressure in my work is exciting! (T3,T4,T13,T15,T16,T19).

Rewards:

18. I would like to have an equity interest in my work, or at least a compensation plan that returns some equity (T11,T19).
19. I would like to have enough capital seven years from now to take no salary for a year while starting a business (T2,T19).
20. I will seek at least $50,000 per year as a base salary.

Environment:

21. I would like to work in an office where I can tell whether it is day or night outside (T8).
22. It would be best if I can work with a very organized secretary or support staff (T2,T3,T13,T15,T18, T19).

Social Aspect

23. I would like to live in a place where there is a diverse and international population (T20,T22,T2).
24. I would like to have access to both the ocean and the mountains (T8,T21).
25. I would like to be close enough to theaters and music performance venues to go on a week night (T14,T5,T21,T20).
26. I like having a small group of friends to get together with regularly (T5,T10,T12,T22).

Material Aspect

27. I want to buy a home and a piano to go inside (T22,T14).
28. I would like to begin planning for acquiring a ski house with access to both downhill and cross-country skiing (T6,T8,T22).

Family Aspect

29. I would like to begin a family within the next ten years (T6,T13,T22).
30. I want to give my children the same exposure to natural beauty that I had while growing up (T6,T8,T10,T20,T21).
31. I want my children to have a place they will always think of as home (T6,T22).

Emotional Aspect

32. I need to cultivate a more conscious sensitivity to the effects of my actions on others (T2,T4,T7, T10,T12).
33. I need to come to a better understanding of my own definitions of success, and I need to evaluate myself in those terms and not as much by what others say or do in reaction to my efforts (T2,T9,T11,T17).
34. I need to allow myself greater joy in my successes, lest I exhaust myself through relentless self-criticism (T4,T18,T19,T21).

Careers I Intend to Pursue

Venture Capital

I would like to join a venture-capital firm where there is an opportunity to move up into a partnership position.

Why?

Agreement with implications:

a. Venture capitalists are concerned with seeking out investments in ideas and people that create new products, develop new markets, or exploit market niches that others have missed. (I-2,I-9)
b. A large part of a venture capitalist's time is spent convincing other investors or partners to join him in investments. (I-7,I-11)
c. Firms are generally small (2-20 professionals). (I-14,I-15)
d. The venture business consists largely of listening to and reading about a lot of crazy ideas, and trying to sort out which ones aren't so crazy. (I-9,I-1,I-5)
e. Most firms are organized as partnerships. (I-18)
f. The work tends to be transaction by transaction, so there are peaks and valleys in the intensity. (I-4)
g. Competition in the business has forced investors to expand the geographic range of their work. (I-8)
h. Certain firms are forming alliances and cross-investment pools with foreign venture investors, while an even smaller number have set up overseas offices. (I-8)
i. If I am very good, there is the potential for great financial reward. (I-19)
j. Working environments tend to be open, informal, and collegial. (I-14,I-16)

Why not?

Contradictions with my implications:

a. The business is domestic for the most part. (I-8)
b. Most venture firms have minimal support staff. (I-22)
c. There is a certain objectivity and distance required of professional investors when looking at new opportunities. (I-11,I-12)

Other Factors

The venture business is made up of many very small firms, and the competition for the few jobs available to MBAs is fierce. For jobs with venture firms investing primarily in technology innovations, a technical background is a big advantage, but it is not an advantage I possess. The small size of the firms means that they do not actively recruit new employees, so the amount of effort required to find opportunities is much greater than it would be to look for work as a brand manager or financial analyst. Further, the industry has entered a phase where returns have fallen because of the tremendous amount of new investment funds that have been allocated to venture investing over the past five years.

In spite of all the challenges presented above, if I am interested in the venture business, I feel as though I should give it my best shot.

Fit with Long-Term Career Path

I have to be realistic in acknowledging that I may not find an opportunity, but since I think that I want to start my own business in the long run, the contacts I make in this job search and the knowledge I gain will hold intrinsic value even if I don't find the opportunity I seek.

A position with a venture firm can lead in two directions long term. The first is the obvious upward move into a partnership, and the second is the outward move to join with some of the entrepreneurial ventures the firm has either funded or turned down. I believe that my path lies along the second fork, toward an entrepreneurial venture, but that will depend on how I evolve over the next few years, and I suppose it also would depend on the evolution of any partnership I may join.

Action Plan

Date	Action
12/88	Meet with contact at San Francisco firms, seek additional names, particularly firms with international plans.
1/88	Meet again with summer employer, Smith Group. Seek commitment on permanent hire/no hire decision.
1/88	Generate additional letters and follow-up calls. Plan dates for February S.F. trip if appropriate. Follow up on Wasserella, London opportunity.
2/88	Visits to interested firms in Boston, S.F., D.C.
3/88	Decide!

Questions to Ask

1. What type of investments are you currently pursuing? LBOs, start-ups, work-outs, intermediate stage?
2. What are your plans for expanding investment activity and staff over the next five years?
3. Any plans to seek cross-investment with foreign V.C. firms?
4. What is your general philosophy on compensation and what is required to become an equity participant?
5. What is the working style of the firm? Collaborative, individual, hours, expectations on additional education/training, travel?
6. How are troubled investments handled?

Luce Scholarship

I have applied for a Luce Scholarship to be assigned to work in Asia from August 1989 to June 1990. I have been selected by the University of Virginia for the national competition, but the final selection will not occur until March, three months from now.

Why?

Agreement with my implications:

a. I think that Asian cultures are becoming a major influence on life in the United States, yet I have little understanding of the places or the people. (I-2,I-9)
b. The Luce Scholars are bound to be an extremely accomplished and inspirational group of individuals. (I-13)
c. My life has been greatly enriched by my previous experiences living abroad. (I-2,I-8,I-23)
d. The Luce program is specifically dedicated to developing a cadre of Americans with a sensitivity to Asian concerns. (I-1,I-32)
e. There is a great element of unpredictability to life in a foreign country. (I-2,I-3,I-5,I-17)
f. A year in Asia would provide a clean break from my life to date, and will grant me a rare opportunity to move in new directions upon my return. (I-33)

Why Not?

Contradictions with my implications:

a. A Luce year will delay acquisition of material gains. (I-27,I-28,I-19)
b. The combination of Asian language study and working in a foreign culture will demand tremendous effort. (I-3)
c. I will be far from my current friends and support group. (I-26)
d. I will not know much about my work or location until after I have committed and arrived there! (I-1,I-12, I-14,I-15,I-21)
e. It is uncertain whether my work will be continuous with the work I pursue upon my return. (I-18)

Fit with Long-Term Career Path

I have been working for three years now to expand my hopes and dreams upward from the cynical state I found myself in the summer of 1985 in New York. I expanded the range of geographic possibilities by moving to San Francisco; I expanded the range of intellectual and professional possibilities by coming to Darden and performing well here. The opportunity to work and study in Asia as a Luce Scholar represents a geometric expansion of possibilities beyond those I have achieved, and a chance to challenge myself and grow in ways which I will not realize along any other path.

The Luce in itself would achieve my long-term goal of working internationally (8), but it also fits very well with my hope to be an investor/manager in an international business. In a very real sense, a placement into an Asian country with only a minimum of language training will test my entrepreneurial mettle to the utmost degree.

Action Plan

I have already completed the bulk of the work required for pursuing the Luce Scholarship. This fall I completed an application and submitted a personal statement and several recommendations. The University selection process also included an hour-long interview with four international studies specialists. Additional steps are as follows:

Date	Action
12/12/88	Request a recommendation letter from the Dean to the Luce Foundation endorsing my candidacy.
12/31/88	I should be notified by here about a second-round interview appointment.
1/88	Second-round interview.
2/88	Selection of finalists, day-long interview in Washington, D.C. (if I make the final group).
3/88	Announcement of awards, selection of assignments.

Management Consulting

A good bit of our class discussion this term about the Darden placement process has centered around the career du jour, which in 1989 everyone seems to be saying is management consulting. Well, so be it! The facts of the matter are that I came to the Darden school thinking that consulting was not for me, largely on the basis of having observed a close family friend over the years who has now become a managing partner at a consulting firm. Mr. D. was gone almost all week long when we were growing up, and when he was around, he seemed to be constantly falling asleep on the couch. Now that I've grown older and gotten to know him more as an equal, I see that, while part of his problem is a general selfishness, clearly part of his problem was that his job forced him to constantly be away from home and family.

I have looked at the management consulting field this fall, and there are wide differences in approach and style among these firms. Some of them seem to have an asset-allocation philosophy of personnel management. Others approach their assignments in discrete chunks, consciously attempting to alleviate undue pressures on staff. Nonetheless, the business is a client-service business, and if a client requires a sudden trip to Timbuktu, you *will* be on the plane. At present, I do not have a family, so lifestyle pressures would not be as large a factor, but I expect that once I do find someone to begin a family with, I would find the lifestyle intolerable at many of these firms. So I come to this element of my job search with some skepticism and the knowledge that, while there are certain practices within some firms (small to medium-size companies and international strategy) that I will find appealing, the large bulk of these firms are probably not for me. Let's go to the analysis!

Why?

Agreements with my implications:

a. Consultants tend to be handed the most difficult and prickliest problems their clients face. (I-2,I-7,I-9,I-13)

b. The business requires rapid grasp of new situations. (I-1,I-2)

c. Assignments are generally geographically diverse. (I-5,I-8)

d. Many firms explicitly approve and assist employees to leave for entrepreneurial opportunities. (I-9)

e. The work is project oriented, with definite beginnings and endings. (I-4,I-16)

f. Support and research staff is an essential part of most firms. (I-22)

g. There are few very large firms, although consolidations are occurring. (I-15)

h. Competition for talent is keen, bidding up starting salaries. (I-19,I-20)

Why Not?

Contradictions with my implications:

a. There will be pressures between client demands and personal wishes. (I-10,I-12)

b. Most firms compensate on a salary-only plan up until the partnership level. (I-18)

c. Certain firms *do* take an expendable-asset view of entry-level staff. (I-3,I-10,I-4,I-21,I-24)

Fit with Long-Term Career Path

And now will the compromise be revealed? The long-term career fit lies in the opportunity to develop my skills as a crisis problem-solver and as a creator of solutions that work, not just solutions that look good on camera. The long-term fit also lies in working in a place that doesn't contradict my goal of leaving to start my own business. There is also a sort of backwards fit, in that I have not yet discovered what business I want to start (or buy?), and consulting firms do provide an opportunity to look around at industry trends, and even different industries to some extent. What I would really like to be is a management consultant who invests in his clients or who is paid in equity (see action plan)!

When I argue with myself about the long-term merits of joining a consulting practice, I focus on: How am I going to find the expertise to start a business if my expertise is not going to be in the technical side of a particular business or industry? Shouldn't I be learning a trade if I want to be in business for myself? And what business does a consultant know how to run, save for a consulting business? My reply is that I see myself joining with a partner or a group of partners. I have the finance background and the crisis-management capability, but I need a partner with a technical expertise to figure out how to make the product and a partner with the administrative skills and temperament to keep us all on track and keep track of where we've been.

Action Plan

Date	Action
12/88	Interview at West Coast job fair.
	Meet with [Darden grad consultant] to talk further about consulting practices in S.F.
1/88	Research additional firms working with smaller companies and consulting firms with venture-capital investment arms. Write letters to targets and arrange meetings if possible.
2/88	If possible, combine visits with trips to V.C. firms as outlined above. If not, defer to spring break. Time will be constrained in February by need to complete field project/SBS.
3/88	Additional visits and interviews if necessary.
4/88	Negotiation of offers and decision.

Time Constraints and Personal-Stress Red Flags to Watch for!

One thing which has struck me lately about the Darden placement process is its focus on completing the job search by mid-March or so. The *Self Assessment and Career Development* book does not insist on that schedule, but because the Darden placement office places such a major emphasis on the first three weeks of January, a large proportion of students begin to believe that these three weeks are the only opportunity they have to find the perfect career for themselves. I have been focused on those days as well until the last two weeks, when I have looked at myself in the mirror and realized that the ideal job will probably not emerge for me out of that process. For the job-seeker not targeting the Fortune 500, a large dose of self-confidence and a daily reminder of whose decision this is are going to be of critical importance.

I forecast a scenario where extreme depression will be visited upon those who have not accepted employment offers by spring break, and worse, extreme pressure will descend upon those who have job offers which are not yet what they want but are the last "on the table" at that point.

This fall, I have been through tremendous emotional strain, having been rejected (at least for now) by my girlfriend of three years, and having come to the realization that I would like to point my career toward international opportunities over the long run. My initial inquiries into international opportunities have been almost universally met by "we are only hiring local nationals for overseas slots," which, unfortunately to me, makes a lot of sense when I am in an objective mood. The Luce Scholarship is one step I've taken to combat this frustration.

I have also been somewhat overcommitted in terms of day-to-day activities, with being an officer of two clubs (I must have been crazy last spring!), tutoring two first years, taking days off to join two friends' wedding parties, traveling back and forth to Washington to try to patch things up with Sandi, and working on my field-project team. I have coped with my stress by sticking to a five-day-a-week exercise schedule and deliberately setting time aside for non-Darden reading. This strategy has worked well, and I intend to continue it this spring, but I am still under internal strain. One of my tasks for this Christmas holiday is to begin to discover what else is bothering me and see whether I can return to Darden a more settled individual.

Location Analysis

My life so far

1960–1968	Five cities in eight years: Akron and Newark, Ohio; Baltimore, Maryland; Washington, D.C.; St. Paul, Minnesota
1968–1976	Barrington, Illinois—the formative years
1976–1977	Bloomfield Hills, Michigan

1977–1981	Ithaca, New York—Cornell University Leave terms spent in: Bourges, France Washington, D.C. Michigan
1981–1986	New York City
1986–1987	San Francisco, California
1987 (summer)	London, England
1987–1988	Charlottesville, Virginia
1988 (summer)	Washington, D.C.
1988–1989	Charlottesville

When you look at it this way, my desire to have a place to return to begins to make more sense. I've been a moving target!

Likes and Dislikes

Charlottesville

Likes:	Dislikes:
Access to outdoor sports Convenient gym, pool Blue Ridge Mountains Lots of cultural events at the university Exceptionally intelligent group of friends	Good ol' boys not the most welcoming crowd Heterogeneous population Shopping-center mentality Requirement to drive everywhere Friends all from Darden

San Francisco

Likes:	Dislikes:
Incredible setting for a city! Access to both ocean and mountains Close to running and biking trails Great restaurants and diverse selection Higher quality food in groceries, health consciousness Walk to take care of errands Close to parents (1/2 hour) Fun, outdoor group of friends Cultural events Quiet at night even in city Very clean Friendly feeling	Limited change of seasons Traffic congestion leaving or returning to city Expensive housing (but beautiful views)

New York City

Likes:	Dislikes:
Tremendous diversity of population Very diverse, very bright group of friends Great restaurants Any kind of culture you want Very convenient for errands, services Sky's-the-limit approach to life Long Island beach weekends	Dirty and noisy, even at night Congested Very expensive, lower quality housing Everything is expensive, for that matter Element of danger, defensive feeling Far from skiing

Washington, D.C.

Likes:	Dislikes:
Lots of parks and open space Metro to work Sunny, no tall buildings Good restaurants Fairly diverse population Political arguments everywhere	Everybody lives in the suburbs! Noisy at night (not everywhere) Hot, hot, humid, hot hot Far from skiing, hiking Traffic congestion to ocean and human congestion to beach!

Final Comments

Much as was the case with the Self-Assessment Paper, writing this piece was partially enlightening, partially unnerving. The process of deliberate self-examination and comparison of spoken goals with careful, documented research about how well those goals fit with my needs and abilities is, I think, one of the most difficult tasks I have taken on. I hadn't done it before this class, although I have certainly spent loads of time thinking and writing in a general way about what and where and who I like and don't like. Elevating the realities of managing professional, familial, and spiritual life into one's full consciousness is a key element in the assumption of fully responsible adulthood. The development of a more conscious reality has helped me to take greater responsibility for my life, and I think that it will help me to make more careful life decisions going forward from today. This increased responsibility will probably lead to periods of increased uncertainty, but in the end, I believe it will lead to greater peace and fulfillment. For that I am grateful.

34

Managing the Joining Up Process

The change from student to employee is, in most instances, a great one. Many people, especially those with little or no full-time work experience, tend to underestimate the size and nature of this change. They enter the job with very unrealistic expectations, based mostly on their student experiences. This leads to inappropriate behavior, which sometimes alienates others or is just ineffective at accomplishing given tasks. The end result for the individual is frustration and disappointment.

The Differences between Student and Employee

Consider for a moment a few of the major ways in which the environment of a student and that of a full-time employee differ:

1. *Bosses.* A student at any one point in time will have four, five, or six "bosses" (teachers), who usually change every four months, and who are often selected by the student. An employee usually has one boss, sometimes for years, and has little if any influence over the choice of that superior. These different situations make for very different superior–subordinate dynamics. New workers sometimes continue to behave as if their bosses were professors whom they can ignore, or, at worst, get rid of in a few months. Such behavior causes obvious problems.

2. *Feedback from superiors.* A student learns to expect brief, quantitative performance evaluations (grades) on numerous specific occasions throughout the year. Such a person will often get written feedback on his or her work also. An employee, on the other hand, may *never* get any concrete feedback from superiors outside of pay raises or promotions. It is not unusual for new workers to feel that they are working in a vacuum and that the organization is at fault for not giving them more feedback.

3. *Time span.* A student learns to think in terms of time cycles of one or two hours (a class), one week (after which a sequence of classes repeats itself), and four months (a semester, when classes change). The time span of an employee can be as short as a few hours (in some production/operating jobs) or as long as many years (in some planning jobs). More important, the time cycle can change on the job, often leaving the new employee confused and disoriented.

4. *Magnitude of decisions.* A business student often gets used to making a number of major decisions (hypothetically) every day. At least at first, the new employee will rarely make any major decisions in his or her job. This often leads to feelings of being underused or ignored.

5. *Speed of change.* Because of the pace of academic life and the number of major innovations and changes students are encouraged to consider, they often develop highly unrealistic expectations concerning the ease and quickness of making changes in the real world. Discovery of the realities is often quite frustrating and depressing.

6. *Promotion.* A student with a master's degree and no full-time work experience has lived in an environment where promotion occurred once every twelve months—nineteen promotions in nineteen years. It is no wonder that when a student takes a job five levels below the president, others often complain that "the young hotshot seems to want to be president in just a few years."

7. *The nature of problems.* Schools often carefully select problems that can be solved in a short period of time using some method or theory that is being taught. Such a process is "efficient" by many educational standards. New workers often find it incredibly frustrating when the problems they are given are not as neat and solvable and the information needed for a decision is not available.

We could go on, but the point should be clear by now.

Unrealistic Expectations

Individuals also create a slightly different kind of unrealistic expectation through a poor assessment of themselves and the job while job hunting. The benefits of the assessment processes described in this book go far beyond the job decision. The very process of systematically assessing yourself, your future organization, and your job helps create more realistic expectations about what your initial experiences will be like in that job. More realistic expectations lead to fewer disappointing surprises and to more intelligent, adaptive, problem-solving decisions on your part.

Phil Hammer, for example, learned through his self-assessment how much he tended to overlook detail. He learned through his job assessment that his new job would require some (not a lot of) attention to certain types of detail. When he started work, he took specific actions to avoid a potential problem. First, he managed to rearrange his secretarial assignment so that he was assigned a person who was very detail-oriented. Second, he explained his "problem" to his secretary, and requested that a major aspect of her responsibility would be to keep track of details for him. Finally, he made it a habit to carry a note pad with him at all times and forced himself to make himself notes so that he wouldn't overlook things. After twelve months on the job, Phil had not created one single significant problem because of his personal "weakness."

Regardless of the source, inaccurate expectations cause problems for recent graduates. They cause poor performance, disappointment, frustration, and low morale. In some cases, the organization concludes that the inappropriate behavior reflects a poor employee selection on its part, and the person is let go. In some cases, feeling "had" by the organization for not being warned about what was to come, the employee quits. In still other cases the problems are overcome, but seldom without leaving some bad feelings all around.

Managing One's Own Joining Up

Perhaps one of the most lethal expectations of recent graduates is that, in effect, "It is the organization's responsibility to make sure that the new employee gets the orientation and training needed to be able to do his or her job." Some organizations do try systematically and quickly to help all new employees get "up to speed." They have "orientation programs," "training programs," and "special first assignments." But very few companies do even a fair job of making sure that all new people get the specific orientation, training, and help they need to get "up to speed" quickly and efficiently.

Most people who have an effective, relatively trouble-free year after leaving school explicitly or implicitly take responsibility for their own "joining up." Regardless of whether or not their organization has programs for new people, these people systematically take actions to help themselves get "on board." They recognize that if they don't take the initiative and something goes wrong, they will probably have to suffer the consequences.

In assuming responsibility for their own joining

Exhibit 34–1

Actions That Can Help a Person Get Up to Speed in a New Job

BEFORE STARTING WORK

1. Get on the organization's mailing list.
2. Get your new boss's secretary to send you copies of memos, etc., that you would receive if you had already started work.
3. Request an organization chart and a book of pictures of employees (if one exists) and start learning names and faces.
4. Subscribe to the local paper in the town or city where you will be working.
5. Write to the Chamber of Commerce and real estate agents for information on housing, schools, etc.
6. Open a local bank account.

AFTER STARTING WORK

1. Invite people to lunch to get to know them.
2. Get to know the secretaries (great sources of information).
3. If athletically inclined, join some of the organization's teams (a good way to form relationships informally).
4. Sit down and have a long talk with your boss regarding what he or she expects of you.

up, people typically take a variety of actions both before they start work and immediately afterward (see Exhibit 34–1). While most students do virtually nothing between the day they accept a job offer and the day they show up for work to help their period of adjustment from school to work, others do a number of useful and practical things. By requesting an organization chart and a book of employee pictures (if available), for example, you can start to learn the names and faces of people you will be working with. Knowing who's who, of course, can be enormously helpful to a new employee. It's much easier to do this in a leisurely way over a two- or three-month period instead of trying to learn names and faces in the first few weeks of work, when you are trying to learn so many other things too. As a general rule, the more that you can do before starting work to relieve the burden of your first few weeks on the job, the fewer problems you will face in your first year out.

A variety of actions that people sometimes take once they start work are designed primarily to assist their joining up. By sitting down and having a fairly long and detailed talk with one's boss regarding what he or she expects, for example, you can help minimize the probability that you will inadvertently violate those expectations. Disappointing, surprising, or annoying your new boss during your first few months on the job can prove to be a major impediment, since your boss is usually the key person who can help you during that period or block your way.

Different people will no doubt prefer different specific tactics to help them manage the joining up process. We encourage you to prepare as much as you can for work *before* you walk through the front door on your first day on the job.

Assignment

Read "Cyrus Walker: Making the Transition". Develop from it a list of the things you think you will have to deal with in making the transition from school to work. How will you deal with them?

CYRUS WALKER: MAKING THE TRANSITION

In the spring of 1982, Cyrus Walker graduated from the Darden Graduate School of Business at the University of Virginia. A year later, Cyrus reflected on what it was like for him to move from school to work.

Being in School after Accepting a Job Offer

This is just to give you a feel of some of the things that occur after making a decision, some more practical things that may appear very basic to some people, but which become very relevant.

For instance, the man I was negotiating with called me up one Friday and said he'd get back to me on Monday. I got a call from my alumnus contact on Sunday telling me that my negotiating contact had been fired and that now he, the alumnus, would be doing the negotiating. I found that very uncomfortable. So my contact within the firm was down to an alumnus from the school, who said a senior manager would call me on Monday. He didn't. More anxious moments. He finally called me late Tuesday, explained what had happened with the other guy, and that the offer that he had made would stand and stand alone without any further negotiation. Any ambiguous things like benefits, vacation, moving expenses, starting date, etc., would be handled by the Personnel Department. My response was, I would prove to him that I was worth what I had been asking for, and that I was happy to be joining such a fine firm. The Personnel Department sent down an information package later explaining what was going to happen and that helped.

I made my decision by mid-April, and a ton of

This case was prepared by Associate Professor James G. Clawson as a basis for class discussion rather than to illustrate effective or ineffective handling of a career situation. © 1983 by the Sponsors of the Colgate Darden Graduate School of Business Administration, the University of Virginia, Charlottesville, Virginia. UVA case OB-255.

bricks came off my shoulders. I felt good. I had done all I could to make the right decision, and I got real determined that I was going to implement it. And it's a good thing I did because not all things were going to go my way. Some may have a difficult transition from school to work, but even if you have an easy transition, there are going to be adjustments along the way. Without a mental attitude that you are going to make this thing work, you know, it will be hard.

The basic question was, "Okay, I've made the decision and I'm going to do it. Now what?" The first thing that came to my mind was to enjoy the rest of the year at school. All my friends were there. I had been around these people for two years, and we only had four to six weeks remaining. It was a unique period to just take time to go out, to have the parties, to go to the mountains, whatever. I realized it was going to be very difficult to get these people back together again.

Finals were approaching; I had a few group projects to finish, but I had finished my term project early. I remember being very busy during that time. There were a lot of things to do. At the same time, I was comfortable. I think you reach the point that the pressure has been resolved, and you really have a chance to enjoy. It was a real golden time for us to do all of the things we hadn't been doing for the past two years. After this year, after this season, you realize that you won't be able to see Monticello, or the Blue Ridge, or Ralph Sampson dunk for UVA. Believe me, it takes a lot more time and energy to do those things and keep up, but that's what I did, and I really looked at it as a big plus.

We had a lot of parties. We had the softball game with the sales class. We got together as a group and went out to the lake and just had a lot of cook-outs. There are moments you get depressed. You are trying to enjoy the groups of people that you have gone through this experience with and all of a sudden the realization is that you won't be seeing them anymore.

The B-Bar Ball

I got engaged the night of the "B-Bar Ball" two weeks before graduation. My girlfriend had been in on the job search and choice process all along, so that my job selection was not a surprise to her. Anyway, we had to wait until October to set a date for the wedding because of my training program and the fact that my permanent assignment wasn't going to be made until then.

So, that led to something else. With a significant other involved, as soon as the decision is made, if they're going to work, things should start rolling right then and there. They should make their contacts in that city. I had one employer offer to help out in any way they could to find a job offer for my fiancee. Your significant other needs to contact friends in the area, firms to work for, maybe even use some of the resources in the school to get the job search rolling. It is a virtual time bomb sitting there waiting to go off if nothing is done. You come home from being all hepped up about your job, and they are still struggling to find a job. That is a difficult transition to handle, and it can really try your personal relationships.

As an example, I had a friend whose wife was a teacher. If she hadn't gotten her applications in early, right after he had made his decision, she would not have been considered for employment. These are the deadlines that can pass that you never think about. You've made your decision, but now there are other deadlines that people have to look at. This is a very individualized process. You can't rely on your classmates' timetables or you can run out of time.

So we were at the "B-Bar Ball." Someone had been up in New York the week before and was telling about the apartment crunch: "Hey, it's going to take a lot longer than you think, there is a very tough real-estate market up there." I'm sitting there and all of a sudden I realized, Hey, you better get on the stick! I was having a good time with school over, but I realized I had to go to New York.

We had plans to go to the beach for the week between the B-Bar Ball and graduation. There were three or four people who were getting a house, and we were going to go and relax. We canceled our plans, although without this jolt we probably would've gone. That was what REALLY started the transition period for me. It was like, BOOM, you better get a roof over your head.

So, I got REAL determined to make the transition work. It had been a long process, putting a lot of work into the job search, and I'd made my decision. Then it was time to move on and DO it. I had to get myself psyched up while I was still at school that I was going to MAKE this thing work. It's getting the attitude built up that you've made a decision, and you're going to MAKE it work so that when times get tough, you'll know you've thought about it and you'll know why you're there. Without that attitude, and I've talked to a lot of people who graduated the same time I did, it becomes very difficult and you have a lot of second thoughts.

For me, the first test came in my search for an apartment in New York. I spent the week between the B-Bar Ball and graduation in New York, and that was a tremendous eye-opening experience. I realized that it wasn't as easy in New

York as it was in Charlottesville, where you came for the day and looked at three or four vacant apartments, picked one based on what you liked and what you could afford, and decided. In New York, there is a very tight real estate market. And there are all different kinds of neighborhoods and all different kinds of price ranges and all kinds of conveniences and things to be weighed. And, it is very difficult. At the end of the first week, nothing was resolved and I came back to Virginia for graduation.

Right after graduation, I went back to New York. I tried to settle this thing, and finally it got to be the end of the second week and on the last day I decided I had to find SOMETHING, so I took a furnished summer sublet. Even then it wasn't resolved because it wasn't permanent. But it was a good way to look at the situation, actually. Especially in a city like New York where there are a lot of different neighborhoods, and they offer different things, different commutes, different stores, different people. If you don't know the city, you learn quickly, but it also is good to just live up there on a three-month sublet deal and get a feel for where you want to live.

After School Before Joining

The funny thing is that there was a great contrast within the school. Some people were going to take off the whole summer, going to go to Europe; they don't worry about moving. Others might start the day after graduation, and boom, they have to be up in the City. If you are in that circle of friends who are going to Europe, moving out and starting in late August, then there you are, watching them pack to go off. . . .

I returned to Charlottesville after lining up the New York sublet on a Tuesday. On a Wednesday, one of my friends said that the air fares to the West Coast were the cheapest they were ever going to be. Thursday, we were on a plane to the West Coast planning a twelve-day vacation.

It was the first time we had been to the West Coast. It was a fantastic trip; it met and exceeded all expectations that I ever had. I had never been to the West Coast, but knew two or three other couples from Darden who were going cross country, all doing the same routine. The people who did that seemed to have a much healthier attitude toward work when they finally started. I have pictures of, unbelievable pictures of, five or six rolls, 200 pictures, of the trip that are sitting there on the mantel. It was a nice transition from school back to the city and starting a job. So . . . I took a two-week vacation, you might say, on the spur of the moment.

We only had about $1,000 free cash in my checking account. We didn't have the money—did it on plastic. I'm still paying for the trip; I will be paying for the trip for a long time. When I came out of school, I was heavily in debt. I was as leveraged as I ever want to be. I was on loans; I had stretched financially even to be able to come back to school. I figured it out that, overall, I have, including undergraduate school loans, $19,000 or so to pay back. And I had no cash, very little cash. The trip to California cost us about $1,000. I usually do not use my credit cards. I'm a guy that charges on them and then pays them off, but I used them then. However, the trip was worth it.

There were some financial surprises. First, there was the brokerage fee. If you go through a broker to find an apartment in New York the buyer pays a fee of usually 15% of the annual rent. The company should pick that up; you've got to negotiate hard to make sure that the firm picks that up. You've also got to put down a month's rent for a security deposit, if you're lucky, possibly two months if you're not, and then you've got to have your first month's rent. So, you're looking at about $3,000 on day one in a city like New York. Now, I don't know how many people have $3,000 laying around, but I sure as hell didn't. I was fortunate the firm picked up the broker's fee, but I still had to do the embarrassing thing which was to borrow from my parents. I increased the lines on my credit cards when I got back from the West Coast, so I would have some slack. For the first time in a while, I was very, very concerned about cash flow.

I still do daily and weekly cash flow statements to see where my money's going. Maybe people who move into a non-New York atmosphere don't have to consider it as much. Another thing, you move into an apartment, and you've got to furnish it, draperies, rugs. Even if you've got some stuff, you've still got to buy some things for the apartment. Maybe you got by the interviewing season with one or two suits, and now you're not going to be able to do that, so you've got to go out and buy suits, shoes, shirts, etc. These are some things that hit me a little unexpectedly.

A funny thing looking back: you make a decision in a group environment at the Darden School. You make a decision with their help and advice, but when you make your decision, that support group is gone, and you're living with that decision, and your friends are in Chicago or Atlanta or wherever, and suddenly, it's you all alone. And, you've got to make it work now. You can't call "time-out" and say well, let's meet and talk about it. Those people are GONE. Now, you've got to make it work. It's a subtle thing. Some people don't believe in this positive mental attitude toward it, but you get tested real early.

So, we had about a week before work to settle into the apartment. Then, one day, you wake up and you go to work. It's a funny feeling that first day: Even after all the preparation you're not exactly sure what is going to happen when you walk in the door.

Going to Work

I was part of a training program with 21 other people. I had been in touch with the firm several times: once to nail down moving expenses, another time to nail down what the real starting date was going to be, another time to find out what the training program was like, how it had changed people. I walked in the front door, and here's where I got a break that I'm not sure other people got. They said, Day One, we are going to begin a general introduction to the firm that will last the first week. So many weeks of analytic training, eight weeks of rotation, and you'll see in your booklet that you're going to be at this desk on this day, etc. You will be evaluated every day, and at the end of this we're going to have a draft pick. The firm delivered. The training program was extremely organized. Fifteen weeks. He spelled everything out which was phenomenal. I got a folder, and I knew where I was going to be, to the desk, on a day by day basis.

They spelled out the expectations for the training program right then and there. You see, I came off a 90-day game plan that we did in business policy. I knew that I had three goals in mind because I had been through similar situations. One, I needed to differentiate myself from the rest of the pack. I wanted to be considered among the top people. And two, I wanted to get to know the people who were in my training program very well, because they were a good resource. The third thing is that I wanted to get to know as many people in the firm as I could because this was a once-in-a-lifetime shot to circulate around the whole firm with no job to worry about and just talk with them about what they thought about the firm, what they didn't like, etc. Those were the three goals I took in, and I did get off to a good start.

We had a classroom part of the training in which we had some tests. I scored no. 1 in those. I kept studying and made sure that I came out no. 1. That gave me respect with my peers and the training people. Then the word started to get out that this guy can do the work which later helped out in the draft pick. And it built my leverage around some things that were surprising later on. I had some leverage.

After the first week of training, there were three weeks of classroom work where they give you three volumes of material to study. You had classes during the day and three volumes to review at night and were tested every day or at least at the end of the week on each major volume. It was straight memory work, back to undergraduate days. That's my ballgame. I knew it was my ballgame. I just basically studied the material very hard.

I was working in the evenings, too. There was a Darden student who was in New York for the summer as well; not at my firm, though. He graduated with me, and was spending the summer in New York with his wife. I would come home basically around 4:30 or 5:00 and have a little bit of dinner, study for a couple of hours, and maybe give them a call and meet them somewhere to just get out and walk around. The sublet was in Greenwich Village, and there is always entertainment on the streets in the summer. Then back and study maybe another hour or two, and hit the sack around 11:30. Then on Friday we would have an exam. We did a fair amount of booking it in those three weeks. I was making sure that I was memorizing the material that would help me through the registered representative exam, and I knew that it was a way to differentiate myself from the start.

We went out as a group a lot of times, going out to bars after the exams, you know, finding out where the people are from and what they are like, what their past experience has been. I made an effort to do that. It was a great way to get to know those people. If you're generally interested in getting to know them, then they become interested in you, and you get along very well, and that was important to me.

Plus all this time I was trying to find a permanent apartment. The person that I had talked with in Personnel had agreed to pay my moving expenses on a U-Haul basis. He agreed to fly me back home when I found a permanent place to pick up some stuff I had stored. I had stored some of my stuff at my fiancee's place and some at home. So, he said I could go back down and get it. It was a long, drawn out process. I didn't find a place until late in the summer. The actual move into my own room didn't take place until the Labor Day weekend. On Labor Day I flew back down home, picked up all my stuff, drove back up, unloaded the trailer.

Then we began our rotation. We were on a schedule, so we sat with the same group of trainees. There were four major areas: Equity, Corporate Finance, Municipal Bonds, and Money Market Securities. We spent about two weeks in each area. Each Monday would usually be a lecture day where someone from that area would come in and teach a class and give us the product knowledge. At the end of each day, they evaluated you on such things as interest, attentiveness, and ability to learn. They sat there, and you asked questions. You had to go home and think about what you were going to ask these people. At the same time everybody else was rotating through different parts of the firm. Here's where the contacts that you had made in the first three or four weeks of the classroom session became very helpful because you knew this guy would treat people like dirt, he wouldn't answer questions, or this guy was great, ask him anything you want, he's a good resource. We swapped all of these stories.

We were getting closer to this giant draft pick for final assignment. People, very similar to Darden, were very cooperative, but there is a little competition and as that begins to shape up, people begin to express some preferences. Then the mass of politics starts going, certain people make sure they get known in certain areas. This is what they really want, they try to nail down some kind of commitment for a final assignment.

You have to express three preference areas within the firm, and then you have some time to rearrange those, communicate those to the management in those areas, and they give you feedback whether they liked you or didn't like you in kind of a general way. All through the training area trainees start communicating bits and pieces about their needs and likes.

All this time there are contacts within the firm. All this time you are finding out who you want to work for, what they are like, things you need to do to be good, what the firm likes, the people. It's just a whole socialization process that they use to get to know you.

Then management sits down one day and has a giant draft pick. Like the NFL, I guess. They've got the performance on the classroom part. They've got your evaluation sheets which were all quantified: People skills—one, two, three, four, five, excellent, good, whatever. And then the four heads of the departments sit down, and they deal. They have their political interplay. They all want the best people and certain people do emerge as top candidates. Then a little swapping goes on here and there, and then you are assigned to that area.

Joining Up Again

Then you get your permanent assignment. October 16th. I emerged as one of the top three out of the 21 in the training process. I had expressed some preferences in corporate bond sales and told them that I had wanted to do that. I have to say, there were a lot of interesting positions across the floor; there were a lot of things that I could have done and would have enjoyed very much. Anyway, apparently, I was bid for in all four major areas; they were bidding for my services, and I ended up assigned to an area that I hadn't put on my preference sheet at all.

And here's where I cashed in some chips. I had been a top performer in the training program, everybody had liked me. It just so happened that in the political situation in the wrangling, corporate bonds had ended up with one of the other top three people in the training class. So, then they said they wanted a salesman. All of the other people sort of said, well, okay now you've just got a trader, so you're not going to get one of the top people to be a salesman. So, I ended up assigned to an area I had not chosen. It was a great opportunity as a start-up position, and a great job, a challenging job, a sales job that I liked, but I had ignored the department.

I was called in by the partner of that area and he told me that I had been assigned to that particular job, and I cashed in my chips. I told the person that I had realized what had happened. Then I said in a not-so-controlled voice, "One, I want accounts and I want them early, I don't want to wait. I want to get on with it and perform." He assured me that that would happen, that my immediate manager who reported to him would convey that and that that would happen. "Two, if I produce, I want to be paid." As it worked out, having gone on record for that, it was a smart thing to do.

All along I was making sure that I met those three criteria that I brought in for the first 90 days: (1) try to shape myself as one of the top performers, (2) know the people in the training program very well which has turned out to be great, and (3) make sure a lot of people in the firm, top management, etc., get an exposure to me.

Becoming a Colleague

Now, once I got into the department, I also did something else. I went home the evening of my first day on the job and did some scratch sheet analysis on some bonds. The reason I did that was I said "This is Day #1, and I don't want to be treated just like another person. I am going to go home and do this." The World Series is playing, and I'm punching out on my calculator. I was just doing some averages and some standard deviations which is helpful information. Now, believe me I am not a mathematics buff—I know zippo, just the bears about quantitative analysis, but I worked up some standard deviation numbers on these averages.

They absolutely loved it. All of a sudden, my boss tells me that my name has come up with management and senior management and the president of the company, and my boss is telling the president about this standard deviation analysis, that it was a way that they had not looked at a particular thing before.

I had to explain it to the entire department at a meeting and say this is what is available to you, and I will help you in any way I can. So, now I have positioned myself within the department as somebody. And they're thinking, Okay, this guy knows what he is doing. I am going to respect him. He has a little bit more on the ball than somebody else who has just come on. He is above the average bear.

They said that I would get my accounts around the first of December. On Friday, December 4th, I received my accounts, on schedule and in half the time it took the people in the department from the training class before me. And so far, all indications are that the money will flow if the production is there. I have a very challenging position.

35

The First Year Out

For many people the first year of work after graduating from school is a period of great challenge and excitement. It is a time characterized by considerable changes—a new job, new work associates, a new dwelling, a new city.

The first year out can also be a difficult period. In a recent survey of MBAs six months after graduation, sixty-two percent reported that they were less than happy with either job, employer, career progress, or life style. Only five percent of those sampled reported no real problems since graduation.

Those who have studied the experiences of recent graduates have concluded that people who have a relatively trouble-free first year out tend to be systemically different from those who experience some difficulty. Specifically, those students who make more personally appropriate job choices, who start work with realistic expectations concerning what will follow, and who take an active role in managing their own joining up process, seem to experience significantly fewer problems during their first year out than those students who don't.

The Impact of Job Choice (and Related Decisions)

As one might expect, many of the problems reported by people during their first year out can be traced directly to an inappropriate job selection. For a variety of reasons, some people make job decisions based on an incomplete or inaccurate understanding of themselves, the job, or both. These kinds of decisions invariably lead to problems and often to a change of jobs within a year of graduation.

The same underlying causes that lead people to poor job decisions often lead them to poor decisions in other important areas of their lives. Recent graduates sometimes make inappropriate decisions regarding how to approach a new job, where to live, how to allocate their income, and so on. Again, an incomplete or inaccurate understanding of themselves, the option they are choosing, or both, creates first-year-out problems for them.

Some Examples

Underestimating how much he depends on the proximity of friends for relaxation and support, Bill Jones takes an apartment by himself in an area where he knows no one. Within three months his loneliness seriously affects his work. Helen Johnson, who never commuted more than a few miles to work or school before, finds exactly what she wants in a house about twenty-five miles from work. After moving in, she finds that it takes one hour to drive to or from work. The ten hours-a-week commute eats into both her work and nonwork activities, creating a variety of problems for her. Herb Palmer is not really aware of how slowly he gets up to speed in a new situation, so he bases his decision to "not even think about work" after accepting the job offer on other considerations. The same is the case with his decision to take a six-week vacation and start work on August 1. When October 1 comes, all of Herb's contemporaries are well settled in their jobs and

Exhibit 35–1

A Life System

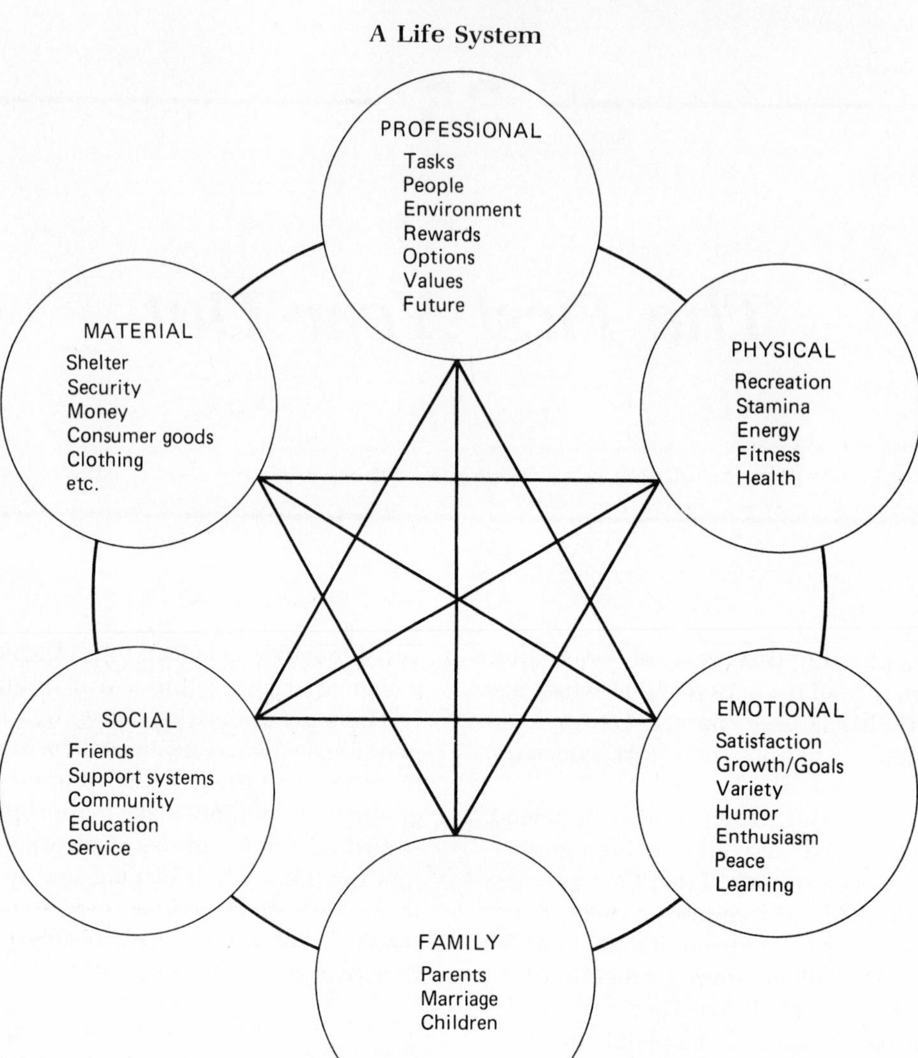

Herb's continuing awkwardness stands out like a sore thumb to him and others, including his boss.

As the above examples suggest, virtually none of the important individual decisions made just before or during one's first year of work are independent of the other decisions. Each decision tends to affect other parts of one's life in small and large ways, now and in the future. Insensitivity to the interdependence among decisions and their consequences inevitably leads to problems for many recent graduates.

Pete and Pam Marsh, for example, really wanted to return to a less urban part of the Midwest after graduation. Their families and many of their old friends were still there. Peter carefully looked for jobs in that area but found nothing really appealing. Bit by bit, he began to search in a wider area. Eventually he landed a job, enviously considered by his friends to be "a find." The starting salary was good and the company would allow a long vacation period and pay moving expenses—to New York City! After a tense and anxiety-producing process, the Marshes agreed to accept the job. They found a decent apartment and put their 6-year-old in school. Pam made some friends and so did their 4-year-old. Pete threw himself into the job. Next came another "find"—a great house, close to the apartment, and at a good price. They moved. But after eight months Pete became increasingly frustrated. The job was not developing, and the company seemed less than supportive as time wore on. After ten months he left. He wanted once again to look for jobs in the less urban part of the Midwest. But what of the child in school, the other child's friends, Pam's attempts to dig in, and the house? He ended up taking another job in the city. Their big-city life style in a short time quite subtly had become the constraint affecting Pete's job choice. It didn't start out that way.

Taking a Life System into Account

Operationally, this means that in making important job and nonjob decisions, one needs to take into account all aspects of one's life. The relevant system to analyze when making a job decision or a life style decision is one's entire life system (see Exhibit 35–1). The critical thing to realize here is that each of the areas of a person's life—job/career, family, psychological and physiological selves, and life style, including where you live, your movement patterns, your use of money, your social life, your recreation, and so on—are affected, inexorably, by career-related decisions.

People occasionally like to deny that these decisions are interdependent. They want to believe that what they do at work and what they do out of work can be totally separated. They want that "freedom." As they soon learn, the world as we experience it today is one big interdependent mass, and the interdependencies are growing, not shrinking. And those who do not understand that, or who refuse to accept it, are in for a tough time.

Exhibit 35–2 presents a list of the issues commonly mentioned by graduates of major business schools when they return to campus a year after graduation to talk with students. The list reveals that many graduates experienced some surprises in their first year of work. Work, and especially work embedded in a particular organizational culture, was not exactly what they expected. Sometimes the work was too fast, sometimes too slow. Often they were surprised by the vagaries of dealing with people—people who moved within or left the organization, people who had different values from theirs, people who weren't as talented as they, people who didn't communicate well, people who sought power, and so on.

One of the major tasks associated with the first year of work is the tentative exploration and establishment of a life style. People test the ways that the six major components of a life system (see Exhibit 35–1) are going to fit together for them.

Exhibit 35–2

Issues Faced by MBA Graduates in the First Year

1. How do I manage my marriage *and* my career? Especially if my spouse is also working—and maybe in a different city?
2. How do I manage the frustration of dealing with a hierarchy? Decisions seem to take so long and to be made as much for political reasons as for analytic conclusions.
3. How do I manage my time and priorities? What should I do next? (These questions were particularly poignant for entrepreneurs.)
4. How little sleep can I get by with?
5. There have been a lot of changes in bosses and colleagues. How do I manage *that* uncertainty?
6. How do I learn about corporate culture, and how much will I have to conform?
7. Where should I live? Where will I find my (our) social life?
8. How long and in what ways will I have to pay my dues? How long will it take until I have established credibility? How long will I have to do junk work?
9. How do I deal with the big changes in seasonal workloads?
10. I am getting virtually no feedback on my performance. How do I find out how I'm doing or learn to live with the lack of feedback?
11. I had the joining up blues. No one wanted to bother with me. Everyone was busy doing their work and I was the low man on the totem pole.
12. How do I find a mentor? Do I need one?
13. Things were more disorganized than I expected.
14. Authority is not always clearly linked to responsibility. People don't respond just because you have a title. Managing relationships is a bigger part of it than I thought. People have their own hidden, but powerful and often irrational, agendas.
15. How do I work for someone who is less capable than I am?
16. Timing goes in fits and starts. Sometimes things move very fast, faster than seems wise. Other times it seems to take forever to accomplish the simplest things.
17. How long can I go on with this pace? It's okay now, but I don't want to be working this hard in five years.
18. I just got married. That took a lot of my time. But now that I've got my social life buttoned up, I can focus on my career.

Assignment

Read the Jewel Savadelis case (pp. 392–398). What should she do, and why? How are the issues she is facing similar or dissimilar to ones you may face? What seems typical or unusual about her first year out?

JEWEL SAVADELIS

On Friday, September 25, Jewel Savadelis pulled slowly out of the parking lot of Atari, Inc., and headed south on Mathilda Avenue toward her home in Sunnyvale, California. Jewel was oblivious to the rush hour traffic. An offer she had received from her boss kept rolling over and over in her mind. Mr. Moon, the president of Atari's Consumer Division, had asked Jewel to be the director of the Software Development Department. The offer presented an exciting opportunity for Jewel at an early stage in her career, but she wondered if it was the right move to make and, if so, under what circumstances.

Atari, Inc.

Atari operated three main lines of business. Coin-operated video games stood in game arcades and high-traffic areas in bowling alleys, supermarkets, and restaurants. Home video games were attached to consumer televisions. Personal computers were designed not only for games, but also for personal data processing applications. Atari was the only company which operated in both the coin-operated and home segments of the growing video game market. By 1980, Atari was generating an estimated $415 million in sales revenues and earning an estimated $77 million in operating profits. Company analysts expected these figures to more than double in 1981.

Atari was founded in 1972 by Nolan Bushnell, a young engineer graduate of the University of Utah. Mr. Bushnell had written a computer game later named "Pong" while working as a research engineer in the area between Palo Alto and San Jose, California, known as Silicon Valley. Mr. Bushnell formed his own corporation, Atari, Inc., to produce and market the game in the coin-operated arcade market, and it became an instant hit.

Mr. Bushnell's love of games and creative, flamboyant style encouraged other Atari engineer/managers to imagine and to create new, increasingly more exciting games. Groups of managers and engineers would go off to local resorts for two- and three-day brainstorming sessions that included "plenty of marijuana and beer."[1] The video games required weeks and sometimes months of painstaking and careful programming. Then the problems of mass producing the programmed chips that were the heart of the video game hardware had to be overcome before attacking the common production and assembling tasks associated with a video game console.

Some games were developed specifically for either the arcade or home video markets, but the company generally tried to apply the considerable development costs to products in both segments. In 1975, the company produced over 100,000 copies of a home version of Pong which was sold out before it reached the Sears, Roebuck outlets. Sears had had to help Atari finance the buildup of the Pong inventory, and it became apparent to the management of Atari that the company would need additional funds in order to pursue its high-growth strategy. In 1976, Mr. Bushnell agreed to sell the company to Warner Communications for $28 million.

With the infusion of cash from Warner, Atari continued to develop and distribute new products. Officials at Atari had realized from their experience during the early years that video games often became repetitive to players and had concluded therefore that the future growth of the industry in both the home and arcade markets would rely on a continuous stream of new and ever more interesting products. Evidence to sup-

[1] Peter W. Bernstein, "Atari and the Video-Game Explosion," *Fortune*, July 27, 1981.

port this conclusion was found in the arcade market where the Space Invaders game, imported from Japan and produced in the United States by Bally Corporation, had become extremely popular. Space Invaders added variations of color, sound, control, and skill development to the relatively simple Pong video game experience. Atari was able to capitalize on the arcade popularity of Space Invaders by introducing to the consumer market in 1977 the Video Computer System, a flexible device that would accept cartridges each programmed with a different game. By 1981, the Atari cartridge version of Space Invaders introduced in 1980 had sold over one million copies. In 1980, Atari also introduced the coin-operated Asteroids. The game quickly became another major seller. Over 70,000 units were sold by the end of the year.

The architect of much of Atari's success in the late seventies and the man who did much to change the operating culture at Atari was Raymond Kassar, who had worked for Burlington Industries for 25 years before coming to Atari. In many ways, Mr. Kassar was a sharp contrast to Atari's founder. Mr. Kassar had been steeped in corporate management philosophy and techniques over the course of his career. When he was made the chief executive officer in 1978, he immediately set about establishing formal control and reporting systems. He expected people to be to work on time and to dress in more formal attire rather than the T-shirts and jeans that were commonplace at Atari and in the industry. Mr. Kassar also proved to the industry that video games were not just a seasonally oriented toy business. His introduction of four new game cartridges in late January created a run on retail outlets and a year-around demand for Atari products. Mr. Kassar's considerable marketing skill and the fact that only 3.5% of American homes had video game players augured well for Atari in 1981.

Jewel Savadelis

These were the fascinating and compelling highlights of Jewel Savadelis's investigation of Atari as she searched for an appropriate position during her last semester in the Harvard Business School MBA program in the spring of 1981. The previous fall, Jewel had taken an intensive course on career management in which she had developed a well-supported list of personal life themes (see Exhibit 35–3) and implications for work (see Exhibit 35–4) that she thought would help guide her in her job search. After careful consideration of her knowledge of herself, of Atari, and of its industry, Jewel had accepted the product manager position, which would play a large role in the marketing activities of the Consumer Division of the company, which produced and sold the home video games.

After graduation, Jewel and her husband took a much-needed vacation, returning in time for Jewel to begin work August 3. As the new product manager for home video games, Jewel had no set job description, no subordinates, and an open mandate to structure the position in light of the company's growing portfolio of video games. Jewel spent the first eight weeks on the

Exhibit 35–3

Life Themes

To facilitate a clearer understanding of the links between my life themes and their implications for work, I'd like to summarize the rationale behind each theme.

Dominant Themes

1. Likes control.
   Likes control over self and work situation. Prefers autonomy and nonauthoritarian boss. Solicits added responsibility. Likes control over others; seeks leadership, is decisive, enterprising, self-motivated. Enjoys persuading people; is manipulative.
2. Has self-confidence.
   Confident in most work-related situations and of ability to deal well with most people. Lacks confidence in technical, quantitative areas.
3. Likes dealing with people.
   Enjoys dealing with people rather than things. Social activities, even if business-related, are relaxing and recharging. Enjoys acting as teacher or mentor. Enjoys diverse types of people.
4. Needs Chuck's support (husband).
   Chuck has always been central to my stability and well being. Experienced conflict between strong feelings of affection for Chuck and lack of time spent with him.

Exhibit 35–3 (continued)

Major Themes

5. Deals well with people.
   Is successful with superiors, peers, subordinates, and clients by understanding motivations. Able to influence and persuade, inspire, handle difficult people, form cohesive group. Varies style with different people. Sometimes, too domineering.
6. Wants to achieve significant ends and to improve self.
   Requires challenging work to feel accomplishment. Driven to accomplish many tasks. Continually seeking personal growth, self-improvement. Perseveres in accomplishing tasks.
7. Is creative and appreciates esthetics.
   Solves problems creatively. Has characteristics of the artist: expressive, original, intuitive, nonconforming, independent.
8. Is risk-loving.
   Has no fear of taking manageable risks. Has ability to move confidently in totally new situation. Has need for constant stimulation in environment. Shows courage.
9. Needs praise and recognition.
   Driving force behind need for achievement is need for recognition.
10. Can get things accomplished.
    Delivers on promises. Attends to details. Handles variety of tasks simultaneously and efficiently. Builds teams and accomplishes tasks through others.
11. Needs self-respect.
    Must stand up for issue I believe in. Demands integrity in others.
12. Likes variety.
    Self-explanatory.
13. Is emotional.
    Exudes enthusiasm. Is not objective in opinions. Has mood swings. Likes periods of extreme activity followed by periods of relative calm.

Intermediate Themes

14. Is flexible.
    Willing to experiment with new approaches. Sees relationships in unrelated fields. Willing to change mind in light of fresh evidence. Ability to improvise (particularly in crisis).
15. Has high material needs.
    Self-explanatory.
16. Needs support of friends and family.
    Support systems permit risk-taking because they provide a secure base.
17. Lacks stamina.
    Self-explanatory.
18. Is self-reliant.
    Tied to need for control (Th 1), confidence in own ability (Th 2), ability to accomplish tasks (Th 10). Depends on self rather than others to get things started (relies on others to carry through, under my direction).
19. Concerned about women's position in life.
    Fights loss of control and dependence on men fostered by discriminatory practices. Interested in promoting equal rights for self and for other women as humanitarian gesture.
20. Is organized.
    Systematically sets goals, uses effective criteria for projects, attends to details.
21. Is intuitive.
    Self-explanatory.

Subordinate Themes

22. Is unconventional.
    Self-explanatory.
23. Is impatient.
    Self-explanatory.
24. Is practical.
    Self-explanatory.

Exhibit 35–4

Summary of Implications

	Company Implications
C1	Renegade
C2	Sufficient leisure time
C3	Personal growth & advancement
C4	Open access to executives
C5	Ethical leadership
C6	Company values employees
C7	Pleasant surroundings
C8	Mainstream industry
	Life Style Implications
LS1	Time for leisure activities
LS2	Preferred geographic location
LS3	Satisfy high material needs
	Task Preference Implications
T1	Low structure & supervision
T2	High variety
T3	Minimum quantitative & technical tasks
T4	Central importance of task
T5	New learning
T6	Use many HBS skills
T7	Deal with people often
T8	High creativity
T9	High risk
T10	Measurable outcome
T11	Organization required
	Co-Workers (People) Implications
P1	Diverse co-workers, few similar to me
P2	Nonauthoritarian supportive boss
P3	Open, informal atmosphere
P4	Co-workers have integrity
P5	Make unique contribution
	Leadership Style Implications
L1	Challenge subordinates and be fair
L2	High expectations of self and others
L3	Achieve organizational goals
	Approach to Tasks Implications
AT1	Use unusual approach & intuition

job familiarizing herself with the company's products and meeting most of the key people whom she would be dealing with in the years ahead. On several occasions during this two-month period, Jewel's boss, Mr. Stringari, had expressed his satisfaction with Jewel's recommendations and work. By the third week in September, Jewel was settling in. That week, Jewel went on a trip to New York with Mr. Edward Jones, director of software development, Mr. Stringari, vice president of marketing, and several other executives. During that trip, Jewel learned that Howard Sels, the last manager in the Software Development Department other than Mr. Jones, had received a job offer from a competitor and had left on one day's notice.

Meeting with Mr. Moon

On Thursday, September 24, shortly after returning from New York, Jewel was called into Mr. Moon's office. The president began by recalling that while Jewel was in New York three of the programmers had gone to Mr. Moon and expressed their dissatisfaction with their supervisor, Mr. Jones. Mr. Moon had already discussed their complaints with Mr. Stringari and Mr. Ebertin, vice president engineering, and had decided to replace Mr. Jones immediately. Mr. Moon said he had advised Mr. Jones that he was to relinquish his position as director of software development and to become the director of special projects. (See Exhibit 35–5 for an organization chart of the division at that time.) He had then called a meeting with the programmers in the software development department. At that meeting, Mr. Moon, knowing that the programmers were a headstrong group, had tested their reaction to his idea that Jewel would make a good director of product development. The programmers had agreed. He asked if Jewel would take the job.

Jewel ended the meeting by asking for a couple of days to think it over. The next morning, Friday the 25th, she went to see the three senior programmers. Her knowledge of the characteristics of that group made her wonder if she would be effective in trying to manage their efforts.

The Programmers

There were 16 video game programmers working for Atari in the Consumer Division's engineering software department. Fifteen of these were men, and they ranged, in Jewel's estimation, from normal to temperamental. Most of them were single, recent college graduates with degrees in computer science. In school, they had been dedicated computer enthusiasts accustomed to working when, where, and how they wanted.

This preference for control over their work habits extended from their appearance to their schedules and activities. Programmers usually wore sandals or sneakers, jeans, and T-shirts to

Exhibit 35–5

Consumer Division Organization Chart as of September 25, 1981

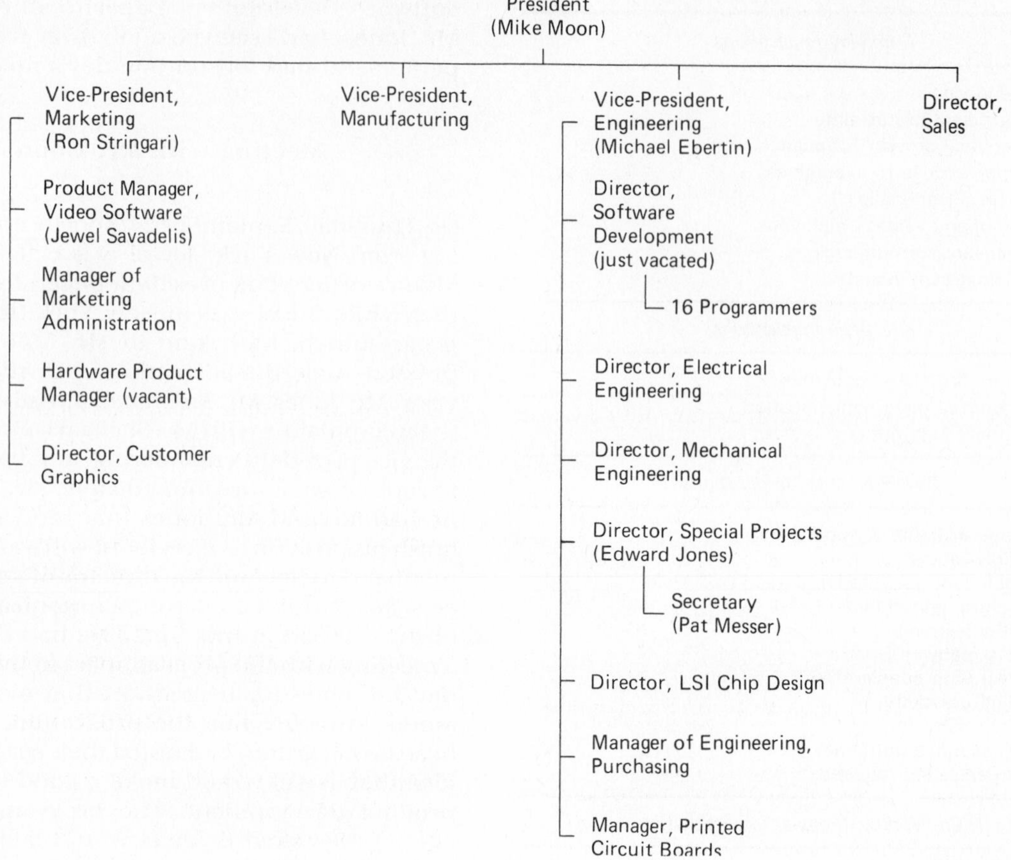

work. Many of them wore longish hair and on occasion would smoke marijuana on the job. They knew little about business, much less about corporate procedures. When disgruntled or dissatisfied, as evidenced by their previous actions, they were used to going "straight to the top" to get satisfaction.

The compensation system in the group called for individual bonuses to be based on the sales of video games created and programmed. If a programmer conceived and produced a game that was successful, he or she could earn large bonuses. Several of the programmers would soon be earning an annual income, including bonuses, well into six figures—more than three times Jewel's salary. This system and the high visibility of the programming department's products gave the programmers a clear sense of their importance to the company's future. Turnover among the programmers was low in comparison to industry standards. The group had lost only four people in the last two years to budding competitors.

Meeting the Senior Programmers

Jewel's meeting with the three senior programmers reconfirmed her concerns. They told her that they would be willing to accept her as their new manager, but that she should understand a few things at the outset. First, they would retain hiring, firing, time allocation responsibilities, and monetary sanctions. Second, they would work three-day weeks only. Third, they were to be permitted to do the cartridges they wanted and to smoke pot on the job. Fourth, they would tolerate no creative suggestions on their cartridges from Jewel. Jewel's responsibilities would consist of filling out the paperwork required of their department by the corporation and to buffering them from other corporate interference. They said that their complaint with the previous manager had been that he was not supporting them enough to senior management when management wanted them to program games that did not fit their current interests. The director's responsibility, they said, was to maintain the freedom of the programmers to work on projects of personal interest. Finally, while they did admit that none of them was prepared yet to assume the position of director of the department, they wondered out loud if Jewel's marketing background did not disqualify her at the start. Programmers simply did not trust the marketing types.

Jewel thanked them for their candor and confidence and said that she was going to think about the offer over the weekend.

Meeting the Former Director and His Secretary

After meeting with the programmers, Jewel went to see Mr. Jones. Edward received her in a restrained way, and said that he would have resigned had it not been Jewel who was being tapped to replace him. He offered to help her in whatever way he could and even drew up a list of things needing attention in the department (Exhibit 35–6). Mr. Jones indicated that he wanted to stay in his current office, which was in the middle of the programming area, and that his secretary would be staying with him. Jewel could take a small office down the hall.

Upon leaving Mr. Jones's office, Jewel went next door to see his secretary, Pat Messer. Pat was Jewel's age and had been with Atari for six months. Pat knew extremely well the systems and procedures that were in place in the programming department. When Jewel asked if she would be interested in working for her, Pat gave a cautious answer.

Jewel's Deliberations

As Jewel walked back to her office, collected her things, and drove home, she pondered some other considerations connected with the offer.

She would be doing two full-time jobs working for two different bosses. Ron Stringari, the vice president of marketing and her current boss, had proven in eight short weeks to be a powerful ally and a helpful guide. At 38, he was only ten years older than Jewel. Michel Ebertin, on the other hand, the vice president of engineering, was 45, had numerous years of experience as an engineer at National Semiconductor, and from afar, seemed to be much more "businesslike" and demanding. It was generally known that Mr. Ebertin had high standards and if disappointed would reprimand the offending employee in public meetings. Since Jewel had no programming background and knew virtually nothing of the technical side of the programmers' work, she was concerned about her ability to run the operation to Mr. Ebertin's satisfaction.

Exhibit 35–6

Mr. Jones's List

1. Fix "bug" in already released cartridge.
2. Customer Week preparations.
3. Find assistant.
4. Coordinate requests for carts in development (200 cart requests per month).
5. Devise schedule for carts and their completion dates.
6. Coordinate marketing research projects.
7. Coordinate instruction manual writing.
8. Determine standards for final game design approval.
9. Initiate title selection procedures.
10. Handle personal problems of staff.
11. Coordinate technical support interface.
12. Coordinate activities contracted for interior decoration.
13. Devise de-bug standards.
14. Devise game standards.
15. Define programmer reporting relationships.
16. Devise/initiate on-the-job training for new programmers.
17. Write technical manuals and documentation of operating system.
18. Study manpower/hiring requirements.
19. Fill out copyright information sheets to legal department.
20. Provide legal support for pending lawsuits against competitors.
21. Coordinate interface with hardware department to get correct controllers for new hardware.
22. Do 1982 budget.
23. Customer service interface.
24. Attend Michel Ebertin's meetings: staff—every Tuesday; project review—every Thursday.
25. Address issue of software security.
26. Address issue of programmers unhappy with current cartridges.
27. Pursue job reclassification for tester.
28. Initiate request for fireproofing system for computer room.
29. Engineering—status reports required twice monthly.
30. Set up room with competitors' products.
31. Order coin op games for research.
32. Schedule and announce department meetings.
33. Address design of next generation of video systems.
34. Joint venture with DC Comics on new cartridge.
35. Extended offers in the mill to new programmers—2 are due to arrive within 3 days.
36. Hire department secretary.
37. Order office equipment for new hires.

38–45. Assorted confidential projects.

Jewel also wondered if she would get the support she would need to succeed in the proposed dual position. The programmers tended to be autonomous and freewheeling, and they had all the technical knowledge needed to monitor progress in the department. Mr. Jones seemed supportive, but he was still sitting in the same office with the same secretary, overlooking the software development group. And Mr. Ebertin's style contrasted with that of her current boss, Mr. Stringari.

Finally, although the appointment could clearly be a major expansion of responsibility and therefore a promotion, no one had said anything to Jewel about a change of title or salary. Mr. Jones, as the director of the software department, had been earning much more than Jewel's current salary.

All in all, the opportunity was an exciting one for Jewel, coming as it did so early in her career. She felt that her decision would be an important one. If she accepted it and succeeded (and she was not sure what that meant), she would surely have learned a lot about another critical part of the company, expanded her general managerial skills, and built her reputation with senior management. If she accepted and failed, she would have a major black mark on her record in the first year of employment. If she declined the offer, management might see her as less capable than they had calculated and her reputation—and future career opportunities—might suffer.

36

Developmental Relationships

In recent years there has been a significant increase in the interest of employers and employees alike in understanding and developing mentor-protégé relationships. Many articles and books have left people with the impression that in order to get ahead in business it is necessary—even critical—to have a mentor. The current research on this question is not so clear. In one study (Roche, 1979), it was determined that over sixty-six percent of the people claimed that they had had a mentor, but the definition was so broad that it left one wondering just what a mentor or a mentor–protégé relationship was. Further, the article did little to help one understand whether or not one has a mentor–protégé relationship, much less how to develop one. What we need is an idea of what a good mentor–protégé relationship (MPR) looks like, and then, more important, an idea of how to go about developing our relationships so that they become more and more like that ideal MPR.

Exhibit 36–1 outlines the characteristics of a full blown mentor–protégé relationship as described in a wide body of literature. As you read the characteristics, you will probably conclude that a "true" mentor–protégé relationship is a relatively rare phenomenon. Most researchers presently conclude that there are a variety of "developmental relationships" that vary along several dimensions in terms of their impact on the development of the younger person. These may involve "coaches," "quasi-mentors" or "partial mentors" or "career mentors," or just plain supervisors.

Exhibit 36–2 presents a grid on which these various relationships can be categorized. The important thing to note is that people learn from a variety of relationships, not just the relatively rare mentor–protégé relationship. "Quasi" or "partial" mentors are senior people who take an interest in a portion of the younger person's life and have a significant influence on them, but who do not have the comprehensive and intimate impact on a protégé's life that Mentor did on Ulysses' son, Telemachus, or that the medieval guild masters did on their apprentices.

Consequently, a much better way to think about developmental issues in relationships on the job is to think about the developmental aspects of the relationships that form naturally. The most common one, of course, is the superior–subordinate relationship. As you begin your career you will no doubt have several superiors who will be charged with the responsibility of supervising, monitoring, and perhaps developing your activities.

As Exhibit 36–3 shows, superior–subordinate relationships take place primarily in the context of an organization, which constrains the relationship in many ways. Organization structure, personnel policies, hiring, promotion, and compensation practices, like the history of relationships within the organization and the philosophy of the current senior management, all tend to affect what superiors and subordinates can do in managing the developmental aspects of their relationship. In addition, the organization and, in part, the relation-

Exhibit 36–1

An Eclectic Profile of Mentor-Protégé Relationships

1. Mentor–protégé relationships (MPRs) grow out of personal willingness to enter the relationships and not necessarily out of formal assignments. Thus, MPRs may not coincide with formal hierarchies.
2. MPRs pass through a series of developmental stages characterized as formative, duration, and fruition. Each stage has a characteristic set of activities and tasks.
3. Mentors are generative—that is, interested in passing on their wisdom and experience to others.
4. Mentors try to understand, shape, and encourage the dreams of their protégés. Mentors often give their blessings to dreams and goals of their protégés.
5. Mentors guide their protégés both technically and professionally; that is, they teach things about the technical content of a career and things about the social organization and patterns of advancement of a career.
6. Mentors plan their protégés' learning experiences so that they will be stretching but not overwhelming, and successful. Protégés are encouraged to accept responsibility, but are not permitted to make large mistakes.
7. Mentors provide opportunities for their protégés to observe and participate in their work by inviting their protégés to work with them.
8. Protégés learn in MPRs primarily by identification, trial and error, and observation.
9. Both mentors and protégés have high levels of respect for each other.
10. Mentors sponsor their protégés organizationally and professionally.
11. MPRs have levels of affection similar to parent–child relationships.
12. MPRs end in a variety of ways, often either with continuing amiability or with anger and bitterness.

ship take place within a broader environmental context. Alternatives for both individuals at other organizations in the environment, the economic demands of the current environment, the supply and characteristics of co-workers coming from the environment, and the set of societal and cultural norms and values supported by the environment all contribute to the set of forces which will affect the growth of the developmental relationship on the job. We can reconstruct this model, as shown in Exhibit 36–4, to indicate the cause and effect relationships among these five elements that produce a series of outcomes from the relationship. Obviously, there are many outcomes, only some of which have to do with development.

In one study of a major insurance company (Clawson, 1979), fifty-one managers involved in thirty-eight different superior–subordinate relationships were examined in regard to the amount of learning perceived by both the superior and the subordinate to have taken place in the subordinate on three different dimensions. Those relationships that were most effective in terms of developing the subordinates were then compared with those that were least effective and the sets of criteria that appear in Exhibits 36–5, 36–6, and 36–7 were developed.

Characteristics of Effective Coaches

As shown in Exhibit 36–5, the coaches whose subordinates learned more tended to be people-oriented and even-tempered. Their subordinates knew how they were going to respond because of the consistency in their behavior. They also had somewhat higher tolerance for ambiguity than their less effective counterparts. This meant that they were able to assign projects and tasks to their subordinates without feeling the need to watch over their shoulders every step of the way. A fourth psychological predisposition that characterized effective coaches was the value they placed on working at and advancing in their organization. This was important because it reflected a sense of loyalty which they passed on to their subordinates.

The effective coaches saw their subordinates as being capable, intelligent, and likable people. They also saw themselves as teachers and accepted as part of their managerial jobs the responsibility for developing and instructing and coaching their subordinates.

These psychological predispositions and perceptions are played out in the behavior of the effective coaches in several ways. They took a lot of time to stay in touch with their subordinates. They walked around the office, maintaining a real and not just symbolic open-door policy. Their communications were characterized by an informal style. They tended to use first names and to be excellent listeners, trying as best they could to understand their subordinates' points of view. They carried out their instructional responsibilities by trying to broaden the perspective of their subordinates. This meant sharing information with regard to their own jobs, setting high but

Exhibit 36–2

Two Essential Dimensions in Classifying Developmental Relationships

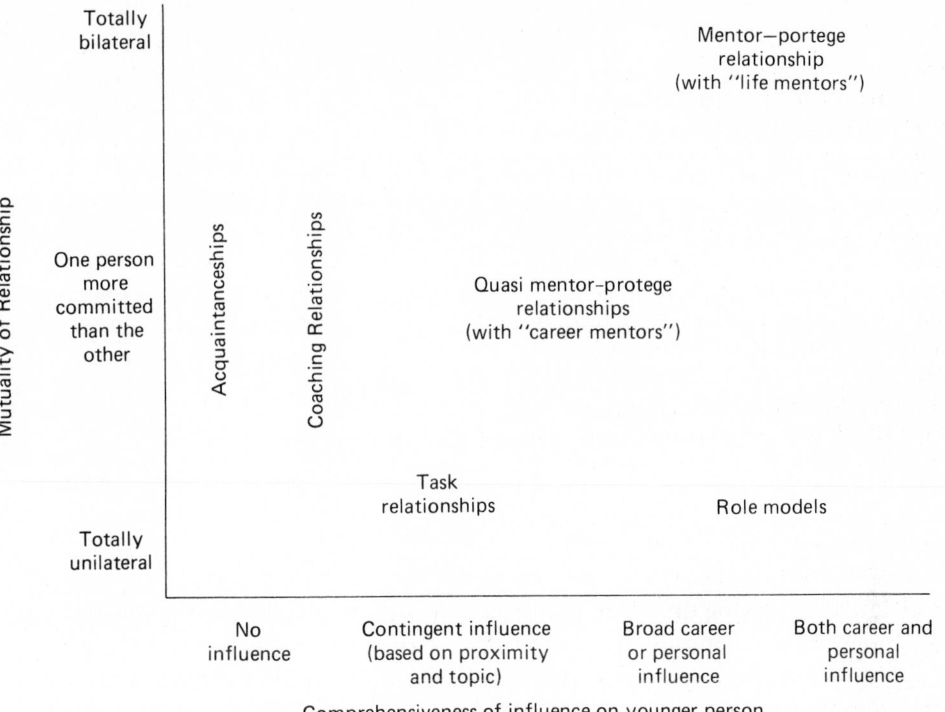

Exhibit 36–3

Basic Elements in Developmental Relationships

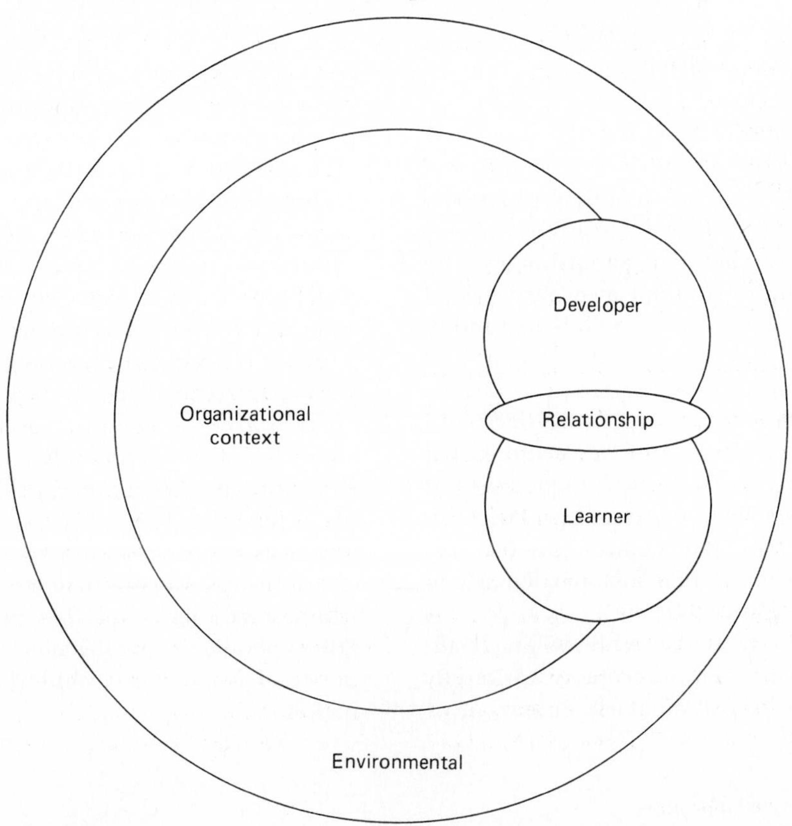

Exhibit 36–4

A Casual Model of Developmental Relationships

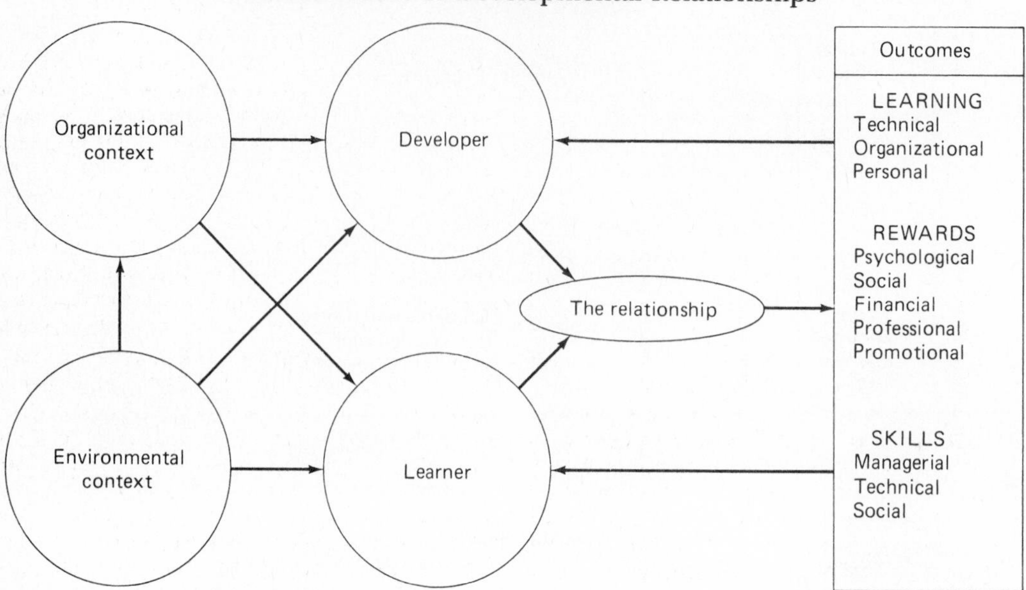

obtainable standards, and giving their own opinions about the way things were accomplished within the confines of the organization. In a sense, this was teaching their subordinates the organization politics of their particular company. Finally, they were willing to sponsor their subordinates to other members of senior management.

Characteristics of Subordinates Who Learned

The subordinates who learned more in the study also had a higher orientation toward people and were somewhat more independent than the subordinates who learned less. This is consistent with the notion introduced earlier that subordinates who took more responsibility for their own learning and for their own joining up tended to do better and to learn more than those who expected managers and bosses to teach them what they needed to know.

The subordinates who learned more liked and respected their bosses, and had perceptions that were consistent with their bosses' high levels of regard for them. They felt appreciated, and they felt liked. Not only that, they saw themselves as learners and were willing to accept that role, particularly in the early stages of their career.

The learning subordinates were also willing to adjust their schedules in order to accept invitations by their bosses to work on particularly important or time-constrained projects. This enthusiastic response to their bosses' requests signaled to their bosses the level of commitment and loyalty they had to their work and to the organization and in turn encouraged the bosses to provide them with additional responsibilities.

Characteristics of Effective Developmental Relationships

Taking these characteristics of the two individuals in developmental relationships together, the characteristics of an effective developmental relationship are in many ways complementary. The superior takes an educational role and the subordinate takes a learning role. There is a great deal of mutuality of trust and respect in the relationship. The effective developmental relationships had a higher frequency of interaction than those which were ineffective. They also had a higher number of "perspective discussions," discussions in which the superior asked open-ended questions about the subordinate's view of the world and in turn shared his or her own. These discussions considered many topics that were not work-related. And finally, the relationships were much less formal than those which were ineffective: The two individuals could talk as people on a first-name basis about important personal as well as technical and organizational matters.

Exhibit 36–5

Characteristics of Effective Superiors

The Interpersonal Learning Ladder

One thing that emerged from this study was the importance of mutuality of trust and respect in a highly effective developmental relationship. Consider the diagram in Exhibit 36–8. When a person learns from another person, that learning is based upon respect for the first person's expertise. If there is no respect for the coach's expertise, the subordinate is not likely to be open to what that superior has to say.

The respect may be in a variety of areas. It may relate to technical parts of the job, to organizational parts of the job, to personal characteristics, or to other specialized areas of expertise. The broader the subordinate's respect for the superior's expertise, the more likely the superior is to have a broad influence on the subordinate's life and career. Unless the respected areas are ones the trainee wants to develop, however, the respect will play a passive role. If the area of respected expertise is one the younger person wants to develop, he or she is likely to be motivated to act on that respect by emulating the coach's behavior in that area, by listening to the coach talk about that area, and by striving to become involved in the coach's activity in that area.

The third and fourth rungs in this ladder of learning revolve around the question of safety for the subordinate when he is in relationship with the superior. If the superior has two characteristics—first a concern for the general well-being of the subordinate, and second a consistency in behavior—the subordinate will begin to develop trust for the superior. The first trust is a "defensive trust" in the sense that the subordinate can rest

Exhibit 36–6

Characteristics of Subordinates Who Learned More

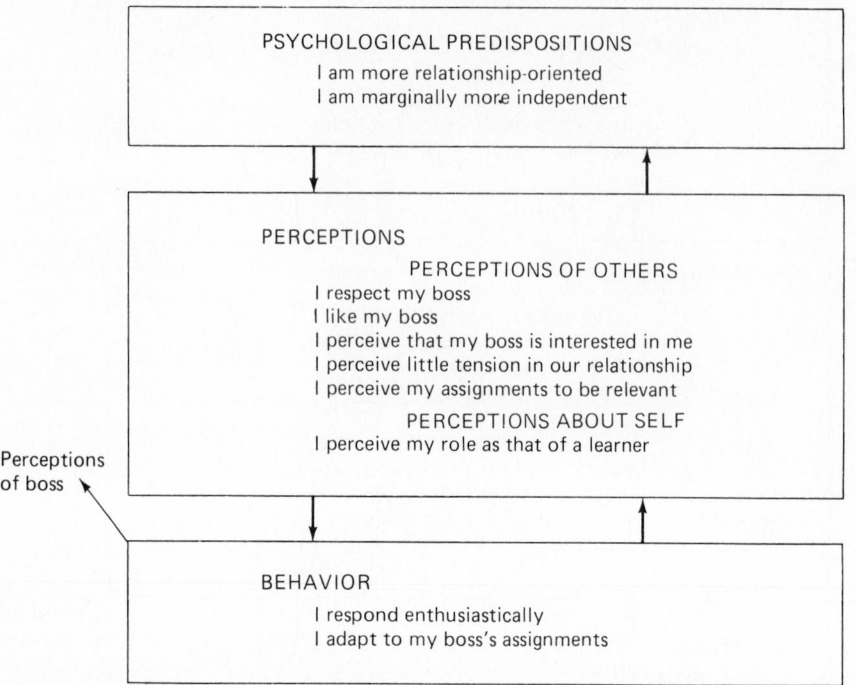

assured that the boss will not do anything to harm the subordinate intentionally. If one adds to that a "protective trust" for the superior's interpersonal skills—that is, a reassurance that the boss will not only not intentionally harm the subordinate, but also is skilled enough to avoid unintentionally harming the subordinate—then the subordinate is likely to lower his defense mechanisms and be open to the influence of the superior.

This takes us to the fifth rung of the interpersonal

Exhibit 36–7

Characteristics of Effective Developmental Relationships

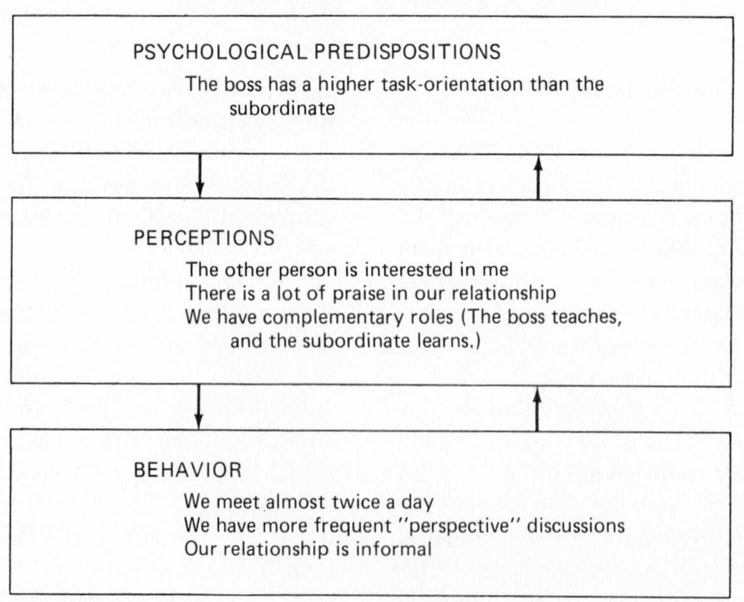

Exhibit 36–8

Interpersonal Learning Ladder

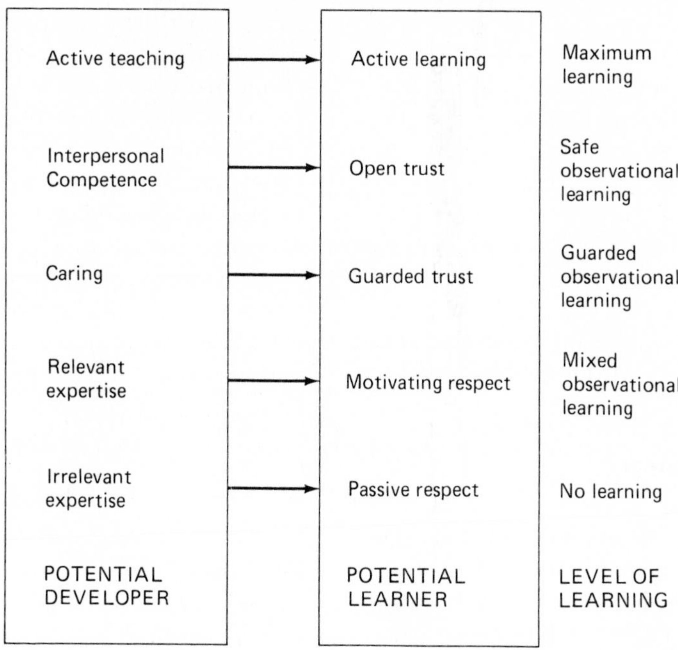

learning ladder, where the superior exerts some positive teaching influence on the subordinate who, because of the respect for his expertise and his trust in the superior's motivations and interpersonal skills, responds to those activities and is now most able to learn from what the superior has to offer.

Developing the Characteristics of Effective Developmental Relationships

The characteristics of effective developmental relationships are not necessarily natural ones. In cases where the superior and the subordinate have a natural fit, this may be the case. But there is much a subordinate and a superior can do to manage the development of these characteristics and their relationship.

Let's consider the case of the subordinate. Many new employees, particularly those with graduate degrees in business administration, feel that the strength of their education is wasted in the early months and years of their careers. Sometimes they see themselves working for people they judge to be less competent than themselves. They often do not hide their opinions and evaluations well. What they fail to realize is that in the history of business management careers in the United States and in the history of the people working above them in the organization are embedded values based on experience and proven track records that relate to credibility. In order for a senior manager to strive to develop a subordinate by giving him or her additional responsibility and instruction, the superior must first have confidence in the subordinate's capacities and abilities. In some cases, as we have mentioned above, this confidence comes naturally to the superior. In other cases it may not be so, and the subordinate bears much of the responsibility for building that confidence.

Perhaps the first and most important step in building this confidence is communicating to your boss that you have his or her best interests at heart. Letting your superior know that in any way that you are able, you will strive to make the superior look good and be successful will go a long way toward reassuring the superior as to your basic motivations and attitudes.

The next step is to demonstrate your own expertise and ability at doing this. A fundamental guideline here is avoiding surprises. Few managers enjoy surprises, even if they are positive ones. A key in business management is being able to anticipate results and to manage one's activities accordingly. In the same way that a boss's dependability and consistency in dealing with a subordinate fosters the relationship, your consistency and dependability in dealing with your superior goes a long way toward developing your superior's respect for you and sense of safety in dealing with you.

If you can add to that the excellent discharge of your current duties, even though they may be "dues-paying" responsibilities, and an additional perspective on the demands facing your boss's position, he or she will be reassured as to the commitment you have for making him or her look good. If your analysis and comments regarding the problems and decisions facing your boss's office are accurate and consistent with his or her own thinking, you probably will be invited to participate more in the formulation of those problems and their solutions.

Summary

Subordinates can do a great deal to manage their learning in the early stages of their careers. They would do well to consider the managing of developmental aspects of their current relationships, rather than constantly seeking for some mentor or sponsor elsewhere in the organization.

Developmental relationships are characterized by high degrees of learning, trust, and respect, and the subordinate can do much to develop those characteristics by accepting the role of a learner, by being as dependable and consistent and concerned about his superior as he would like his superior to be about him, and by looking for ways to demonstrate expertise in areas that are relevant to the superior and his job. This process requires a multifaceted assessment of the subordinate, of the superior, and of their relationship. It requires the subordinate to refrain from making snap judgments, and to consider all the reasons why a superior might be in the position he or she is in in the first place, and to accept the possibility there is much to learn from that experience and background.

Assignment

Read the Karen Harper case (starting below). What should Karen do? Why? What are the pitfalls she should avoid? What are the potential consequences of your recommendations?

KAREN HARPER

> I've got to know by tomorrow morning, Karen. I've got two MBAs from Harvard bugging me every ten minutes on the phone about whether or not they're going to get the job. If you say no, it goes to one of them. Besides, I'm beginning to feel a little uncomfortable around Harry when I see him in the hall—if you leave Fund Management to come work in Investment Advisory, he'll be all over me. I can handle that, but I'd like to get things settled.

Those had been Steve Ackerman's words to Karen Harper this afternoon. As she rode home on the train she began to once again make a list of pros and cons.

The Last Six Years

Karen was 28 years old and had spent the last six years in the Fund Management Group at Hingham Investment Co. Like so many other English Lit grads, she had graduated from college with absolutely no career preparation. She moved from New England to Chicago without a job and into a crowded apartment with three roommates.

On the first day of her job search she registered with a personnel agency as a junior secretary. Right now all she wanted was a job that promised a paycheck every week—she would think about a career or graduate school later. All that mattered was that she survive in Chicago. The agency sent her to Hingham Investment Co., a large, well-known investment management firm whose offices occupied a 20-story older building in the financial district. Karen was well-dressed, attractive, and articulate and didn't think she'd have any trouble getting a job fast.

Her interview took 20 minutes. She was offered an entry-level marketing slot in the Retail

Marketing Department. Her boss (and interviewer) was Harry Rosenberg, the vice president and manager of the department. Harry, who had been with Hingham for the past five years, was a modishly dressed man in his early fifties. He had started the Retail Marketing Department at Hingham, which was a departure from Hingham's traditional business of investment advisory services for large institutional and retail clients.

Karen and Harry liked each other right away. Karen saw Harry as a father-type figure who was very interested in her, both professionally and personally. He told her that she was selling herself short as a secretary and that the marketing slot was a great opportunity to learn the business. He was very concerned about her adjustment to Chicago and invited her to join him for dinner that evening. Karen was flattered and grateful. After pinching pennies for so long, it was great to go out in style. Harry talked a lot about the business and treated Karen like an old friend. Harry's general philosophy seemed to be that hard work really pays off, and since Karen was bright and willing, the sky was the limit.

The next six years seemed to prove Harry's theory. Karen worked hard, often until nine in the evening. After two years in marketing, Harry promoted her to the most prestigious and highly paid area—securities acquisition. Until Karen assumed this role, Harry had done it himself. Karen was viewed by the other members of the department as Harry's favorite. This was undoubtedly true, since no one else spent as much time with Harry, nor did he brag to outsiders about anyone else. When Karen decided to get an MBA and was considering applying to Harvard and Stanford, Harry convinced her to remain in her job and get her MBA by doing evening course work at Northwestern which the firm paid for. Karen's salary increased from $8,000 at her time of hiring to $40,000 plus a sizeable bonus six years later. Harry told her she had it made.

At times Karen believed him. She made plenty of money to support herself in a comfortable apartment. No more roommates. Her job was lots of fun and was coveted by others in the department. Harry allowed her considerable fringe benefits—expense account, free cabs home after a late night at work, after a big project she was free to take a day off. But still she always felt vaguely uneasy—why was Harry doing all this for her? Was it all in her best interests? What did the rest of the firm think? Now she had an MBA—why weren't any other MBAs attracted to Retail Marketing? There were plenty of them in Investment Advisory.

Karen knew the answer to this last question—it was because of Harry. General opinion in Hingham was that Harry was a real eccentric. Karen had to agree that Harry had a rather unorthodox management style and didn't know the first thing about delegating authority. Harry had started Retail Marketing at Hingham and could do all the functions better than anyone else in the department. He loved his work and had to get his hands in everything. Subsequently, no one in the department had much autonomy and the general feeling was that Harry was "on everybody's back" all the time. Karen found that her working relationship with Harry was smoothest when she didn't try to take over things, but instead checked every so often with Harry to keep him informed and ask his advice. Usually she didn't mind this, since it made for the most tranquil atmosphere, but sometimes she felt angry about having to ask Harry's advice on something she felt perfectly able to handle herself. Waiting to see Harry slowed things down considerably and often created problem situations.

The real zinger about Harry was that in spite of all his yelling and meddling, he paid his people exceedingly well and always gave them a sizeable bonus at the end of the year—much bigger than those given out in Investment Advisory to nonpartners. He was always ready to help out an employee in an emergency or problem situation—with either money or time off or whatever. Those who worked for him often said that "just as they were feeling real good about hating Harry for being such a tyrant, he'd go and do something really great out of the blue and totally screw up their heads."

The Investment Advisory Division

Karen's opportunity was to start out as an associate in the Investment Advisory Division. Providing investment management advisory services to clients had always been Hingham's main business. The associate position had been created in order to give young, talented individuals an introduction to money management by working closely with a variety of senior investment managers. Associates were considered to be part of a "resource pool" that was available for work on different projects as they came up. If a large pension fund, for example, requested Hingham to make a presentation on fixed income management, a senior manager in the Fixed Income area of Investment Advisory would select a group of Fixed Income specialists and an associate from the "pool" to work on the presentation. Senior managers also called on associates to assist on day-to-day work with existing clients, which could involve gathering research on a particular industry or providing market information. After a year or so of being in the "pool," the associate has the opportunity to indicate his/her preference for where he/she would like to be placed—whether it be Fixed Income, Equities, Foreign Currency, Research, etc. If this preference coincides with the firm's needs, the associate moves into the desired area. After initial placement, an individual often decides that he/she would like to try another area. If he/she has developed a strong reputation, this movement is usually easy to accomplish.

At the present time, nearly all the associates in the "pool" were recent graduates of top business schools. Investment management was generally regarded as a prestigious field, and the possibility of being made a partner lured many MBAs who were eager to earn big dollars over a period of time. Hingham had recruited at the top business schools for many years for the Investment Advisory Division. No MBA had ever been hired to enter any other area of the firm, including Fund Management.

Associates were expected to work long hours in the first few years. Most associates stayed until early evening at least and were often in the office on weekends. The hours one put in were viewed with a certain degree of pride and indicated how committed one was to the firm and to getting ahead. Associates were often called upon to travel with senior managers to clients' offices. Often this travel was on very short notice. You never really knew where you were going to be the next day.

The Retail Marketing Department

Retail Marketing seemed to be viewed as an amusing curiosity by the rest of Hingham and the investment community. The product was portfolios of securities which were assembled and sold through a broker network to small individual investors and were subsequently not managed. They were sold on the basis of providing steady income and safety through diversification. Its very nature was in contrast to Hingham's traditional business, which was to provide expert advisory service to very wealthy clients and institutions on managing their investment portfolios. By its design, Retail Marketing was a very profitable department for Hingham. Although other firms had tried to imitate the Hingham product, none had been as successful. Most observers attributed Hingham's success to their high-quality and long-standing reputation in the investment community and access to extensive brokerage sales networks. But Harry Rosenberg, the partner in charge of Retail Marketing, insisted that it was his genius that was responsible for the success and that he could do the same at several other firms.

Only about 40 people worked in the Fund Management Department—of these about 10 could be considered to be professionals, either in buying, marketing, or research. The majority of the staff had been there for several years—several had come to Hingham with Harry about 11 years ago when he had joined the firm. Hingham employed close to 500 people, of whom about 100 were professionals and 28 were partners.

The major part of Karen's job was selecting securities for the "packaged pools" of securities Hingham marketed. The purpose of the "pools" was to allow small investors to participate in the attractive yields offered to institutional investors without having to select their own individual portfolios. The product was very successful—popular with both investors and securities brokers and very profitable for Hingham. In fact, during the bad times of 1974–75, it was Retail Marketing which kept Hingham in the black.

Due to the Fund's popularity, there was an almost constant need to accumulate more securities for the pools. Karen bought about $50 million each week. The process of buying securities involved following credit market rates, checking with the department's research team on the current creditworthiness of individual issuers, maintaining a balance of different types of issues in the portfolio, and most important, trying to get the best price on every security purchased. Karen bought stocks and bonds from a wide variety of brokerage firms—she had direct phone lines to eight of the largest firms. Every day involved taking phone calls from about 20 different bond salespeople—mostly aggressive, smooth-talking salesmen. These people worked on commission and had a vested interest in keeping Karen happy, since she was such an important customer. They were continually offering theater tickets, dinners on the town, party invitations, etc. Although they could be a nuisance, Karen enjoyed this part of her job a lot—most of them were reasonably bright and funny. She had to keep reminding herself, however, that their attentiveness was due solely to her buying power, not her personal charms.

Because of her close relationship with Harry, Karen was involved in all the strategic decisions of the department—something which was not a strict function of her job. In the past Karen had helped develop new concepts for pools to expand on the theme. Harry valued Karen's opinions very highly and often designated her as his spokesperson at meetings both inside and outside the company.

When Karen tried to analyze her feelings about the job, it boiled down to the old joke about "not wanting to join any club that would have me as a member." She suspected this might be silly, but she had learned this job almost five years ago without any MBA or financial background—how difficult could it be? Harry made such a big deal about it—in moments of hyperbole he called her the "most important woman on Wall Street." She really enjoyed the job itself, but she didn't feel that she was really "growing" any more, and wasn't growth supposed to be essential? Karen's doubts were exacerbated by the fact that Hingham was practically unique in both the size and the activity of its Retail Marketing Department—no other firm offered a position similar to hers, so there was no way of comparing herself with others. She got a lot of attention from salesmen, but nobody else really knew anything about the pools—it wasn't a well-known glamour position like investment advisory or investment banking. She was worried that she would become a high-priced but "illiquid" commodity. If something went really wrong with the department, where would she go? To sum up, she felt like a very large fish in a very small pond.

The atmosphere in Retail Marketing could best be described as "chaotic." Harry Rosenberg's personality definitely contributed to this situation. His moods seemed to determine the group mood. He involved himself in all areas of the department and delegated very little authority but much responsibility.

Harry Rosenberg

Harry usually arrived in the office at ten or eleven in the morning after calling his secretary and key people at least once by phone from home. Everyone knew when he arrived and there was always a "mood check"—is he in a good or bad mood?—which would be relayed verbally throughout the department. Harry spent most of the day in meetings and on the phone and always left the office at one o'clock for a two-hour lunch. Since so little authority was delegated, workers in the department had to consult Harry before making important decisions and this resulted in a line of people outside his office all day. Once you did get in to see him there were constant interruptions—phone calls, secretaries (three of them) walking in and out to extricate papers from his jumbled desk, urgent questions from underlings who didn't know what Harry wanted done about this or that. Harry liked to stay in the office late—often until eight or so, and several people regularly stayed late in order to get to talk to him without the constant interruptions. Often Harry would take an employee out to dinner to continue these discussions. He expressed great disdain for "nine-to-five-ers" and commented that they would "never get ahead in his department."

Harry had a very controversial management style. If something or someone displeased him, he would let the offender know exactly how he felt. He had a violent temper which didn't last very long. He seemed to explode only with those workers from whom he expected a lot and had disappointed him. In spite of all his noise, he had never fired anyone. There was a continual rumbling in Retail Marketing that Harry was "absolutely nuts" and that he was "driving everybody crazy." Key people would threaten to leave from time to time, but actual turnover was very low.

Harry gave the impression of having absolute authority in his department and gave little indication that he was concerned about any hierarchy at Hingham that was above him. The partnership structure at Hingham was actually quite stratified, and Harry was several rungs down from the top of the partnership group. He found this structure exceedingly frustrating and was very critical of top management. The senior partners tended to stay away from Retail Marketing—it was not the mainstream of the firm's traditional business and, though it was extremely profitable, was not fully understood by many of the older partners. Most of the professional staff in Retail Marketing had had limited, if any, exposure to the partners above Harry's level.

Most sources attributed Harry's managerial autonomy to the profitability of the product. General sentiment was that "as long as Harry brings in the dollars, nobody's going to tell him what to do." Harry enjoyed running the department as a little profit center and did many things which were not "standard Hingham policy."

> I like to think of Retail Marketing as my little family and I'd do anything for my people. I pay them much more than they'd get anywhere else and they feel they're working for me, not Hingham and Company. Yeah, I know I don't do things by the book but I don't want this place to be just a regular department of a stuffy, impersonal firm where everybody gives 50% of their energy and ability and gets a raise every year and a vacation. People here know that if they put out the maximum effort, they'll get rewarded—and that any job in the department, including mine, is open to anyone who shows me they can do it.

Karen's Dilemma

I know Investment Advisory *seems* to be appealing to Karen, but it's dead wrong for her. She's got it made here if she'd just wise up and realize it. That's the trouble with young people in business today—they think they've got to keep moving all the time—get titles, etc. If they'd just plug away at something and be patient they'd be a lot better off. Look, I've been in business for 30-odd years and I've seen just about all there is to see. If Karen just sticks with me and accepts the fact that I've got her best interests at heart and have the experience to know what's the best course for her, she'll be fine. She's a bright kid, but when she gets all this MBA rhetoric in her head, she's dangerous. What happens if she goes to Investment Advisory? She'll be just one MBA in a sea of them—and they're all after the same thing—to be a partner. Well, the existing partners would have to be hit by the plague for spots to open up fast enough to please these kids. She'd be working her ass off for a whole bunch of people, none of whom would be able to give her the kind of close direction and support I can. I'm not going to be alive forever; I'm 57 years old—somebody's got to take my spot—and Karen's the obvious choice if she doesn't lose her head and do something stupid.

Karen had heard Harry's thinking a million times. She thought he was sincere, but seriously doubted that if she stayed in Retail Marketing a senior partnership would ever open up for her. The rumor mill had it that the senior partners were concerned about Harry's management style and were just waiting until he retired to put someone into that spot who was "one of them"—someone who could integrate Retail Marketing better into the Hingham mainstream. Karen felt sure that no matter how competent a manager she was, she would always be viewed as "Harry's girl" and would be considered suspect. She thought a lot about how she could stay in Retail Marketing and get more visibility with top management, but was at a loss as to how to accomplish this. Day-to-day business did not put her in much contact with the rest of the firm and it was Harry who met with the partners at the weekly luncheon and planning sessions. She knew that he always spoke highly of her but didn't know if that was a positive or negative fact, given the partners' general reaction to Harry.

Maybe she should grab at the associate's spot while it was available. She had known Steve Ackerman, the junior partner in charge of the training program, for several years and they had always been cordial. After a particularly frustrating day last week, she had called him on an impulse and asked to meet him for lunch. She had guardedly confided her frustration in working with Harry to Steve. He seemed to understand completely and said that he himself could never work for someone like Harry. This made Karen wonder if there was something wrong with her—why was she putting up with this situation? The more she thought, the madder she got. Before lunch was over, Steve had offered her the chance to enter Investment Advisory as an associate. He warned her that initially it might seem like a step down—taking orders from everyone and doing grunt work after she had been largely on her own, not counting Harry's influence, for the past few years. The move would mean an initial pay cut of $5,000, which would still make her the most highly paid associate. Steve explained that this was the best he could do, since he didn't want the newly hired MBAs to think that someone doing the same job, although experienced in another area, was being paid $10,000 more than they. Besides, Steve had explained, the salary would increase over time and her chances of making a partnership were definitely enhanced.

Karen felt depressed and confused. The idea of entering the competitive world of an associate in Investment Advisory really didn't appeal to her. She felt she had proven her ability and didn't want to go through the initial stages of having to make a big impression again. Besides, Harry was her mentor, wasn't he? And from all she'd read about women in business, wasn't the mentor system supposed to be an essential ingredient in helping women move to the top? Was she looking a gift horse in the mouth and just being a spoiled brat? After all, without Harry's guidance and support, she might be still typing somewhere.

The flip side of this argument was that Karen felt that she was getting too old to be involved in the paternalistic relationship with Harry. If she didn't stand on her own now, when would she? She knew that some of the partners had definite opinions as to the nature of Harry and Karen's relationship. Even though Karen knew that their insinuations were unfounded, she still felt a little embarrassed. The rumor mill also postulated that the reason why Harry was so supportive of Karen was that she was a woman—and in Harry's macho mind that meant "nonthreatening." Why had Harry never taken a bright young *male* under his wing and pushed him along?

Karen knew she had to decide tonight. She didn't want to throw a great thing away—but she didn't want to get trapped in a childlike relationship either.

37

The Early Career

In the early phase of their careers, usually when they are between twenty and thirty-five, people make and deepen initial commitments to a type of work, an organization, and a nonwork life style. Professionals, in particular, expend considerable energy to become competent (and recognized as such by others) in their chosen trade. It is usually an exciting period, in which one begins to try to fulfill expectations about the "professional me" that have been developing (through education) for two decades.

Four general sets of issues seem to be particularly important if one is to try to understand this early phase, the obstacles encountered, and the methods typically used to deal with them. One set of issues relates to adapting to being an employee in a complex human organization. A second has to do with getting established in one's work or organization and achieving some initial success. A third has to do with establishing some type of a workable relationship between one's career and the nonwork aspects of life. The fourth relates to a period of questioning of initial career and noncareer choices, which most people go through around age thirty.

Adapting to the Realities of Complex Organizations

Most professionals start their careers within an established organization. Having been students in an educational setting for anywhere from sixteen to twenty-two years, they suddenly become employees inside what are usually noneducational organizations. This change can create some serious problems for people in their first year of work. Beyond that, the ability to grasp quickly the more subtle realities associated with human organizations often makes the difference between a very successful and an ordinary early career. Some of the more important of these realities are discussed below.

Distribution of Rewards

Simply doing what you think is a good job, or even a very good job, is no guarantee that you will receive the rewards you desire.

For a number of complex reasons, most established organizations do not have performance evaluation systems that (1) completely define what "good performance" is for each job, (2) make sure that employees are aware of those performance criteria, (3) systematically collect data on employees' performance, (4) feed those data back to employees so they can monitor how they are doing, and (5) use those data as the basis for distributing rewards (such as interesting assignments, promotions, money, discretion).

Considerable evidence exists that such a system would be very beneficial for employees, especially during the early career. But because "good" performance is often difficult and expensive to define and measure, and because creating such systems where they don't exist is expensive and time-consuming, good performance appraisal systems are very seldom found in organizations.

Instead, rewards are distributed in most organizations based on the "judgments" of a number of people (a person's immediate superior is usually the key judge), some of whom may have only secondhand information on many of the people they are asked to judge.

People who are successful in their initial careers are those who perform well on the criteria used by the judges, and whose performance record is known by the judges. It is for these reasons that the better "how to" books on building a successful career stress (a) learning what your bosses' expectations are concerning your work and (b) getting involved in some highly visible projects.

Development of Potential

Most organizations have no coherent system to make sure that people in their early careers get the experience, training, and human contacts needed to really develop their potential for their own benefit and the organization's.

Although the development of people is an important goal for most organizations, it is a *long-range goal.* In most organizations, long-run objectives receive a priority lower than short-run concerns. For this and other reasons, employee development is seldom given anything close to the resources needed to do a uniformly good job. Even in companies where resources have been allocated to employee development, and where training programs and job rotation systems have been created, numerous individuals seem to end up coping with short-run demands at the expense of their future development.

We have seen many former students who seem to learn more in their first five years of work than others learn in fifteen years or more. The fast-learning group appear to be different from others in that they proactively take responsibility for their own learning. They seek out role models and mentors, recognizing that one relationship with a highly talented and successful senior person can be enormously instructive. They don't stay in any one job for more than a few years, taking advantage of the fact that almost all the learning associated with most jobs comes in the first two years. They don't wait to be assigned to new projects and jobs by others; they nominate themselves. In this and other ways, they actively manage their own careers.

Dependency on Others

Most professional jobs in organizations, especially managerial jobs, make an individual dependent on numerous others, who often have different or conflicting objectives. Complex interdependencies and conflict are facts of life in most organizations. Individuals who cannot (or will not) find a way to manage their own dependencies are in for a hard time.

Younger people in particular often feel their dependence on others who know more than they do about the job, the organization, the people, and how to get things done. Young managers will often find themselves dependent on the cooperation of subordinates, a boss, other senior officials, various service departments, and possibly even outside suppliers, customers, and regulators. All these individuals and groups have limited time and talent, and their objectives sometimes clash with cooperation. Students are seldom if ever trained in how to manage this type of dependence network.

Managers use a wide variety of techniques to cope with their complex dependencies. Their techniques are sometimes aimed at reducing dependence, sometimes at influencing those on whom they are dependent to cooperate in certain ways, and sometimes at gaining power over the dependencies (which makes influencing them much easier). The faster a young employee learns to use these techniques effectively, the more successful he or she will generally be in the early career.

The larger and more complex the organization, the more time people end up having to spend managing interdependencies. For example, the following is excerpted from a twenty-nine-year-old manager's description of what he does in a typical day at a moderately large manufacturing company:

> When I arrive in the morning I normally read the paper for 15 minutes or a half hour to catch up on the latest news. Randomly throughout the month I will call my boss before working hours actually begin, to let him know that I'm there and on the job, and he can reach me whenever he wants me. This is an important game to play in my situation, because he is located in a different building eight miles away, and sometimes he feels a little insecure as to whether all of his people are working full time and are doing the kinds of things he would like to have done.
>
> I spend about one-fourth of the day actually here in my office. The table in the center of the office is the major working area, and it's round. I don't have a standard desk. This was something that I designed when I was promoted six months ago. The average age of my direct reports was about 47–48 years old, and I felt that it would be very difficult for me, being only 28 at the time, to sit behind a big desk and give these guys orders. They had 20 years of experience and knew the company backward and forward. There wasn't any way I could effectively tell them what to do. So I decided to get in a round table and to make sure that all the chairs

around the table were of the same type and description so there wouldn't be any overt status difference between anyone in the office, so that we could build a teamwork relationship among all members of the group.

After reading the morning paper I would normally attend several meetings. I spend almost 70 percent of my normal day in meetings. By the way, that drives a lot of people nuts, and it bothers me too, but most of our meetings really are necessary. My peers and I have got to know what each other and top management are doing or we trip all over each other. Meetings are often the best way to get the information across. Meetings are also useful when I need the commitment from other divisions for some action, and when we have a problem but not all the expertise to solve it.

This would take me normally till about 10:30 or 10:45, at which point I would come back to the office and handle the mail. The mail comes in a stack of about 4 to 6 inches each day. I would quickly sort it and deliver messages to my staff to work on the projects and various assignments that came through the mail. I would delegate all the assignments with the exception of *politically* sensitive issues. Those I would discuss with the appropriate manager and handle them together with him. Normally it would take me 10 to 15 minutes to sort the mail and another 15 to 20 discussing the various sensitive issues.

This would bring me to around 11:30–11:45, where I would work on my personal mail, which includes salary and merit reviews, expense accounts, purchase requisitions, etc. This would take me right up to lunch.

After lunch, the schedule of activities changes, depending on what part of the year it is. During the first half of the year the work load is not as heavy as during the last half. During the first half of the year I would spend most of the afternoon in meetings of the type described earlier. In the latter part of the year I spend a great deal of time working on the annual long-range plan. This is a very extensive effort and requires hundreds and hundreds of man-hours of work to put together the details, schedules, and plans that support the strategies of this division. One of the reasons that this effort takes such a great deal of my personal time is that my boss' incentive salary depends on the achievement of many specific goals.

Parenthetically, this young man has had a very successful and satisfying early career.

Achieving

For most professionals, the early career is a period directed toward personal achievement. Considerable time and energy are invested in work and in establishing themselves as credible professionals with proven "track records."

In most of the cases we have observed personally, or heard others report, those people who achieved the most professionally in their early careers were people who were able to generate what Doug Hall has called a "success syndrome."[1] As we have observed it, this process can be described as follows:

1. The new employee does not usually have a traumatic first year and is able to adjust rather quickly to organizational realities. As a result of careful selection or luck, the individual fits well with the organization and its work.
2. The individual gets some challenging initial assignments which, because of the lack of adjustment problem and the generally good fit, he or she performs well on.
3. This initial success bolsters the individual's self-confidence and helps him or her get challenging, more important (and visible) assignments.
4. The person's self-confidence, on top of everything else, helps him or her to do well in these next assignments.
5. These successes continue to bolster the individual's self-confidence and provide access to additional human and technical resources that are needed to continue to quickly grow and handle more important work.
6. The cycle continues, more or less dramatically, throughout the early career period. Success continues to breed success.

The "high flyers"—those who achieve more success in less time than ninety-five percent of their peers—seem to be people who position themselves to have opportunities come their way, and then take advantage of most of these opportunities. Eugene Jennings had studied this process in managerial careers,[2] which he calls developing mobility, and has identified the types of underlying rules associated with it. Those rules are:

1. Never become overspecialized. Get broad experience in a number of areas and always maintain your options.
2. Become a "crucial" subordinate to a very mobile and successful boss. If you find yourself working for an immobile superior, move.
3. Make yourself highly visible. Make sure your superiors know about your accomplishments and your ambitions.
4. If you are blocked and can't find a way out, leave the organization, but do it in a way that allows you to part

---

[1]Douglas T. Hall, *Careers in Organizations* (Pacific Palisades, Calif.: Goodyear, 1976).

[2]Eugene Jennings, *The Mobile Manager* (New York: McGraw-Hill, 1967).

as friends. Never allow a showdown to occur, and don't quit work with an emotional parting shot.

Both moderately and very successful people seem to reach a point late in the early career period where continued growth in their achievements requires that they be put "in charge." It is not unusual for professionals around age thirty-five to abandon their mentors and begin to feel frustrated because they don't have the power to continue producing even larger achievements. For many, this period doesn't last long, because they are soon put "in charge."

Establishing a Workable Relationship Between a Job and Other Aspects of One's Life

Most professionals develop two key commitments during their twenties—a commitment to get a job (or organization) and a commitment to an off-the-job life style (with or without a spouse, with or without children). The demands made on an individual by these two commitments periodically change in ways that conflict and put strain on the individual.

The following example, reported by a twenty-eight-year-old man who had established a successful initial career at a bank, is not atypical:

> I usually get home by 6:00 P.M. My wife and I have got until at least 7:30 P.M. before we really have any time to exchange more than a "Hi, how are you?" By 7:30 we get the kids to bed. Sometimes we eat with Bobby, sometimes we don't. After dinner we do get some time together, even though we're both a little bit tired. Alice complains, with some reason, that I read magazines and newspapers during the little free time that we have together. We find that time is more precious than it was before. Ever since the baby came, we haven't been able to go to bed before 11 P.M. because that's when Alice completes her last nursing. Normally, we would try to get to bed earlier than that. We hope to resume our normal schedule as soon as the baby starts sleeping through the night.
>
> We're thinking of moving out to the suburbs soon. There's not much for kids to do in the city. There are a lot of other reasons, though. One of our biggest problems is that it is just too damn expensive to live in the city. So we might buy a house—we're really looking into it now—but with a lot of mixed feelings.
>
> Kids, I don't know, we didn't realize until after we had them how much time they require of you. They are just so damn dependent upon you. There's so much work involved with younger children that you've just got to reorder your life a bit. We found the change from being young marrieds without kids to being young marrieds with kids to be something more than we expected.
>
> We have no real desire to go to the suburbs. It's just that it costs so much less to live in the suburbs than in the city. We can own a house, save money, and build up equity at the same time. But in the suburbs I would have a 45-minute commute. I don't like the thought of that very much. On the other hand, I should get to play a little more tennis out there. I have let myself go; I've gotten a little soft. The extra commuting will make time even more precious than it was before though. It's a rough choice . . .

Young professionals whose spouses also are pursuing careers often find it even more difficult to establish and maintain a workable relationship between their two jobs and an off-the-job style. "Dual career" couples who also have children usually find that their time and energy are very scarce resources.

The work vs. off-the-job strains that develop during the early part of a career are not confined to married couples or couples with children. Single people often run into difficulties, too. Witness the comments of these two young men:

> We're having a meeting next week out at St. Georges. This is the fifth week out of the last eight that I have been at one of these conventions. Many of these conventions are executive oriented, and many of the executives bring their wives. This creates an interesting situation for a bachelor like myself, particularly when most of the women are middle-aged and older. You see, they don't appreciate seeing me show up at each convention with a different attractive young woman.
>
> I'm in a rather tough situation right now, and I don't see any relief in sight. I was given a promotion six months ago, and at 31 I am now the company's youngest plant manager—which, of course, is terrific. But, the promotion moved me from Chicago to Panto Flats, Texas, which has a population of about 6000. I would like very much to establish a permanent relationship with a woman, but unlike in Chicago, there just aren't many unmarried women around here. My nonwork life style, at this point, is very unsatisfactory.

There are three ways in which people generally deal with a work-nonwork conflict. Some people make changes in their nonwork lives that, in effect, reduce their commitment there. Many successful young executives take this option. One *New Yorker* cartoon captures this response well. A thirty- to thirty-five-year-old manager in a posh office holds a phone in his hand and displays a very annoyed expression. The caption reads: "Martha, how many times have I told you not to bother me while I'm on the way up?"

A second option some people choose is to take actions that reduce their commitment to work. Individuals who receive a great deal of satisfaction from their nonwork lives, and individuals who are disappointed in the amount of satisfaction they are getting from their work, both often select this option.

A third option people sometimes choose attempts not to reduce the commitment to either work or other activities, but simply to allow the conflict to exist and to absorb the strain personally. The young plant manager from Panto Flats "solved" his problem by jetting to Houston and back an average of two or three nights per week, where he eventually did meet a young woman and got engaged. In the interim, he lived with less sleep and a special variety of jet lag.

Pace

People in the early career stages are working hard even without the special demands faced by this young plant manager. In the early stages of a career, people are experimenting with, among other things, the *pace* of their lives. Pace is a widely variable and individually specific feature of life style. Some people work and live faster than others. Although many organizations value efficiency (speed) in their employees, faster is not always better. Sometimes doing more faster can mean doing more in a mediocre fashion.

Another potential pitfall of rapid pace is burnout. Exhibit 37–1 highlights the commonly observed symptoms of burnout. These symptoms can arise from very rapid-paced life styles in which the person comes to one of two conclusions. The first is, "Is that all there is?" Here, the emotional sense is one of disappointment—that I've worked too hard and achieved so much, but somehow it's not satisfying. The second conclusion that can lead to burnout is resignation. This is the sense of having worked so hard and still not having been able to keep up. Effort is no longer seen to produce rewards and so much energy has already been expended in the search for those rewards that there is none left. One becomes exhausted.

In her book, *Living with Stress,* Nancy Gross makes the following statement:

> ... You owe yourself the indulgence of a sense of humour through which you can cut ... annoyances down to size. You owe yourself the indulgence of the patience that permits you to ignore pressures and delays. ... You owe yourself the indulgence of vacations, of aspirin when you are coming down with a cold, of hours of peaceful privacy, of relaxation, of occasional bursts of the extravagance ... that give[s] color to life. You owe yourself the responsibility of using your body and your mind in the interests of the constructive realities and aspirations that mean the most to you. You owe yourself a pace ... which meets your temperamental needs, which neither hurries you nor holds you back.

Exhibit 37–1

Symptoms of Burnout

Low morale	Exhaustion/chronic fatigue
Depression	Frequent headaches
Absenteeism	Nervous stomach
Increased anxiety	Ulcers/colitis
Overly critical	Weight loss
Disenchantment	Rapid, irregular heartbeat
Mental rigidity	Poor appetite
Loss of sense of humor	Loss of sexual interest
Easily discouraged	Change viewed as a threat
Bored	Not enjoying time off
Easily angered	Feeling out of control
Negative attitude	Overuse of alcohol
Withdrawn from people	Making everything a problem
Cynicism	Postponing decisions
Difficulty in concentrating	Not recognizing limitations
Unwillingness to ask for help	Perfectionism

Adapted from "Burn Out" by Marvin Fogel, *DM* Magazine, August 1979, and "Burn Out in Academia" by Gib Akin, *Exchange: The Journal of the Organizational Behavior Teaching Society,* Vol. V, no. 2, 1980, p. 5.

We believe this is true and encourage you to find the pace that fits you and that will sustain you and your enthusiasm for life throughout your career and lifetime. Indeed, part of the individual–organization matching process involves matching the paces at which each desire to operate.

Balance

Another characteristic of early career work-nonwork experimentation is balance—that is the proportion of time and energy to be allocated to each aspect of a person's life. Balance does *not* imply, in this case, equal proportions; rather, it simply refers to the proportion of time and energy chosen by an individual. One person's "balanced" life may seem "out of balance" to another.

A common such phenomenon in the business world is the workaholic's life style. Workaholics balance their lives heavily in favor of their careers. They typically exhibit the characteristics outlined in Exhibit 37–2. To many people, a workaholic's life is out of balance. To the workaholic, says Marilyn Machlowitz, author of the book *Workaholics,* life is as it should be. Whether or not workaholics *choose* their life styles or are *driven* to them, many seem to enjoy and thrive on them. Regardless of the workaholic's predispositions, though, living and working with workaholics creates some special problems that need to be managed carefully. We refer you to Machlowitz's book for a detailed discussion of these. The important point for our purposes here is that regardless of the particular balance between work, family, self, and life style you choose, you should try to consider the short-run and long-run consequences of that balance in each component and for the people in it. If you are able to do this, you are less likely to be surprised or disappointed by your choices later on.

Exhibit 37–2

Characteristics of Workaholics

Spend most of their time working
Seldom take vacations
Get up early regardless of how late they go to bed
Read or work while they eat
Make lists of things to do each day
Have a hard time doing nothing
Are fiercely competitive
Work on weekends and holidays
Dread retirement
Really enjoy working
Have strong self-doubts and fear their own inadequacy
Strive to get the most out of their time
Make little distinction between work and play
Pursue everything with vigor, enthusiasm, and intensity

Adapted from *Workaholics* by Marilyn Machlowitz, Addison-Wesley, Reading, MA, 1980.

Not everyone, of course, experiences the same amount of work-nonwork conflict during the early career. The people we have observed who have experienced the most conflict, and who tend to "solve" this problem in ways that eventually create even more conflicts and problems, make decisions in one aspect of their lives without considering the implications for the other parts. That is, they ignore, to some degree, the interdependence that exists between the various aspects of a life. We have even seen people who tend to be planning-oriented create problems for themselves by planning only *within* their careers. People who behave this way are often able to survive during their early career, but the lack of total life planning and decision making eventually catches up with most of them—often in the midlife period between thirty-five and forty-five.

There are at least four ways to characterize different approaches to balance in one's life. These are shown in Exhibit 37–3 and are a career focus, a family focus, a pendulum focus, and a do-it-all-now composite focus. The exhibit lists the basic dominant values, the critical demands, the potential rewards, and the potential consequences for each focus. We encourage you to stop and think a moment about your balance, to identify which of these four seems closest to yours, and then to write down your feelings and observations about the values, demands, rewards, and consequences as they might apply to you. How will you manage the consequences? Will the rewards be sufficient? Do you have the skills to meet the critical demands?

Questioning Initial Choices

Most professionals seem to go through a period of questioning their initial work, organization, family, and life style choices after about five to ten years. For some this is a mild period, while for others it can be fairly difficult and traumatic. As a result, some people abandon their initial commitments and make new ones; they sometimes change organiza-

Exhibit 37–3

Approaches to Balance in Life

	Career Person	*Family Person*	*Pendulum Person*	*Composite Person*
Basic Values	Success is getting ahead.	Success is love at home.	Success is getting ahead and then having love at home.	Success is having it all at once.
Critical Demands	Singular focus. Large amounts of time on the job. Political skill. Suppression of "softer" desires. Supportive partner.	Large amounts of time at home. Suppression of "harder" desires. Sharing partner.	Ability to reconstruct from neglect. Ability to change habits. Sense of timing. Patient partner.	Large amounts of time. Ability to plan time, not projects. Ability to manage stress. Sense of timing. Ability to shift focus and to learn quickly. Supportive partner.
Potential Rewards	Power. Money. Prestige. Satisfaction.	Peace. Love. Friendships. Satisfaction.	Sense of quick growth (career). Changing satisfactions.	Power, money, prestige, and love at home. Peace, fulfillment, and satisfaction.
Potential Consequences	Loss of love at home. Sense of hollowness of rewards. Desensitization. Stressful life.	Loss of power, money, and prestige. Loss of impact, sense of contribution.	Loss of love at home. Loss of pinnacle achievements (in order to deal with other focus). Desensitization.	Mediocrity. Sense of being out of control. Stressful life.

tions, go back to school, start over in a new line of work in a new city, or get married or divorced.

People who make poor initial decisions—who start work with very unrealistic expectations, who have serious problems adapting to their new environments, or who have trouble creating a workable arrangement between their work and nonwork lives—often find around age thirty that the satisfaction they are getting from the various aspects of their lives is less than they expected or desired. This leads them to a period of reexamination. A few are forced into reexamination and change. Some are fired. Others lose a key promotion they expected. The spouses of a few walk out on them. Even people who are fundamentally satisfied with their lives seem at least to pause and ponder their life situation around age thirty. Is this what life is really all about? Have I really made the right choices? Am I responding too much to what I think I "should" do?

Those who actually make major changes as a result of this period of questioning are a minority, no doubt partly because of the difficulties associated with change. Unless one is in a highly unsatisfying position, change usually increases the pain one feels in the short run. Finding a new job or breaking off a marriage relationship can be a traumatic experience.

After the period of questioning is over, or after a change has been made, people generally plunge back into their careers with increased dedication and energy. For five to ten years, they focus again on achievement in their chosen profession.

Assignment

Read the Ben Jerrow case (pages 418–422). Be prepared to describe Ben's life style and the events which caused him to review his life style. What kind of events would (will) cause you to reexamine your life style? What are Ben's options? What do you think Ben should do? Why? What would *you* do? Why?

BEN JERROW

At age 36, Ben Jerrow was the youngest full partner in C. B. Kline and Company, one of the world's most prestigious management consulting firms. Jerrow, his wife, and three children led a very comfortable life on his $65,000 salary.

Except for a slight cold, May 12 (1974) was in many ways a very typical day for Jerrow. He left his Westchester home at 6:30 A.M. and arrived at his office in Manhattan at 8:00. At 3:00 in the afternoon he took a cab to La Guardia, then flew to Pittsburgh for what was scheduled to be a short planning meeting with one of his clients. Instead of ending at 8:00, however, the discussion dragged on until 12:30, at which point Jerrow headed back toward the airport in his rented car. At 1:15 A.M., about three miles from the airport, Jerrow fell asleep at the wheel and drove his car at 50 miles per hour into the back of a truck parked on the side of the road. At 2:12 A.M. Nancy Jerrow received a call from the Woodlands Community Hospital informing her that her husband was in critical condition in their emergency room.

* * *

Benjamin Jerrow was born and raised in Chicago, the second son of a behavioral science professor at a local college. His father served as a consultant to a number of organizations in the Chicago area, and Ben actually worked with him during his summers while going to school at Northwestern. After getting his BS in economics, Ben attended a midwestern business school, getting both an MBA and a doctorate. While in graduate school he married Nancy McKenzie. They had their first child soon after he began work at Kline in the Chicago office.

"I started work at Kline," Ben had said to others, "thinking I'd transform the place in a couple of years into something more competent and exciting. I suppose almost everyone who is attracted to Kline is that way: the five letter men, the superstars, who just look at a problem and it gets solved. Which is to say, they are all very egocentric."

> I remember my first assignment well. The old Buttersworth College was taken over by the Board of Regents for higher education in Illinois. They were going to transform a 3,500-student technical school into a 30,000-student university in the course of five years, and ours was the mission to figure out how the hell to do it; how should you organize, how should you staff, and on and on and on. I remember thinking, well that looks easy enough.
>
> What I didn't know at the time was that the study was badly negotiated, and even more poorly managed.
>
> Jim Welch was the study manager. He's about 5′6″ and had a mind that went about 400 miles an hour and a mouth that went about 500. Unfortunately they weren't quite in sync. Jim was very very bright, but he could piss off the Good Humor Man. He was just unbelievable. We'd go up to Jim and say, "Here are the five different organizational alternatives we've got," all laid out on charts. He'd say, "Where's the date." "What do you mean, where's the date?" "Well, there's no date on the organization chart." Half an hour later after a lecture as to why dates are important, you grab the thing and say, "All right Jim, I'll put a fuckin date on it." It was just interchange after interchange like that. In all fairness, every time he'd come up with things like that, there would be a message in it. You just had to pull the skin over your head to make sure it didn't absolutely destroy you.
>
> About halfway through the study, or what we thought was halfway through it, Jim ended up crossing irons with the head of the Board of Regents commissioned by the governor to get this college going. We had laid out the economic analyses and what the organizational and staffing alternatives were, etc. In that meeting, the chairman said, "No, no, that isn't what I really want. I want to know what the University of Illinois, the University of Chicago, Northwestern and a half a dozen other universities are organized like and I'll decide which type of organization we want." That isn't the way Kline operates. To make a long story short, it ended up Jim pissing off the chairman and we got pulled off the study. It just ended right there. An absolute disaster.

Jerrow's second assignment at Kline was not a disaster, but his performance, as rated by the project manager, was close to being unsatisfactory.

> I didn't know what the hell I was doing and I wasn't thinking very clearly. That was a phenomenal ego blow. It isn't that it hadn't happened previously in sports or whatever. Part of my game has always been that of the street fighter—I may not start out winning but by the time the thing is over I will. And it was clear

at that point in time that I not only wasn't winning, but it wasn't all that clear that I ever would. I had serious doubts about whether I was smart enough to be able to do it. I knew I worked hard enough to be able to get it done. I began to wonder whether I fit with them from a personal chemistry point of view, and so forth. In fact, I started looking a little for a job. I figured, screw this, I just gotta do something else. I got a couple of offers, none of which really seemed very exciting, but they did help my wounded feelings at that point in time.

Six months after joining Kline, Jerrow began his third assignment. He ended up traveling five days a week for the next six months with almost no break. His performance, as judged by more senior employees, rose to "average" during this period.

It was then I got my first little view of political infighting. I found ideas on this or that which we traded over cocktails or dinner circling back and being presented to the engagement director and the engagement manager by some people as their own neat new idea. I found that happened two or three times and it ended up pissin me off a little bit. So I decided at that point in time, all right, I'll set you up with one that will give you 80% of the answer and when you get shot out of the saddle I'll come in with the other 20% and make it clear who the hell's idea it was anyway. Well, one guy got cut up pretty badly on that one. It was good clean fun.

After one year with Kline, Jerrow decided he probably wasn't ever going to "make it" there. He seriously considered taking a job offer as a VP for a $80 million a year industrial firm. The offer, however, came from a longstanding client of his Dad, and it wasn't ever clear to Jerrow whether the offer was made because of that relationship or because of his demonstrated abilities. He turned it down.

It got to the point where I didn't really give a damn whether I stayed at Kline or not. And that really helped in a way, because I started to be a bit more bold. I decided to take a number of calculated risks.

In July on a plane from Montreal to Chicago, John Michaels (the head of the Chicago office) asked Ben if the project teams that he had seen since joining the company were different in any ways from what he had expected. Ben said yes, that they were about one-half as effective as he would have expected. A month later, Michaels sent Ben a note asking him to take on the administrative assignment of looking into the effectiveness of their project teams. In September Jerrow put together an effort that included a questionnaire survey of all people in the Chicago office concerning the effectiveness of project teams and the methods by which they usually operated. He analyzed the results, gave them to Michaels, along with suggestions for corrective action. Michaels agreed with Jerrow's report and told him to go ahead with his improvement program. By December, almost everyone in the office agreed that the working climate had changed considerably for the better. Michaels was clearly impressed.

By early December, while I was far from being out of trouble, the bleeding had stopped and it looked like I was at least not going to be fired. By January this was virtually assured.

In February, Jerrow was asked to come and do a similar survey in the San Francisco office. In April, he was asked by the New York office (headquarters) to work with virtually every Kline office to evaluate and improve their effectiveness. By April, Jerrow was beginning to establish a positive reputation throughout the firm.

Kline had been anxious to make headway into the market for organization, manpower planning, and compensation studies, but had been relatively unsuccessful for the previous three years. With Jerrow's new visibility and reputation, principals in New York began to solicit and then listen to his ideas about how to get into these areas. They also began to ask his advice regarding the two or three cases in that area which they did have.

On May 10, Jerrow received a call from the managing director in New York asking him to take a look at a questionnaire they had developed as a part of a large manpower planning project they were doing for one of the 10 largest industrial companies in the United States.

A couple of weeks later, I finally got the questionnaire. I looked at it, called them back and said it's dog meat. It's just not going to work. It's poorly designed. I don't understand really what you're trying to do, and so on. To make a long story short, they asked me to come to New York to help. I went, and found the way they were trying to go about the case didn't make any sense at all. I ended up spending five days a week there for the next two months—the Monday morning special going out and Friday night or Saturday morning coming back. We ended up completely changing the thrust of the study from one in which we were going to provide answers to one where we were going to provide questions. It served as the first real personnel diagnostic I think the firm had done.

With great effort, we finished just before we were scheduled to present the findings. Our presentation wasn't going to give the chairman the answers he was looking for. In fact it was going to raise questions that would make him as well as the whole personnel function, look awfully bad. And I probably was a little overly aggressive on that one. I showed the presentation to the managing partner on the case (Bob Jordan) the day before the meeting, and he turned white. He said, "Oh, shit, we're dead. The chairman isn't going to like this even a little." But he didn't have time to change the presentation and he didn't really want to cancel the meeting or postpone it, so he made one of the other guys (George Elms) give the presentation with me there. It was one of those things where you figure, "That's it baby. I better get the résumé polished up." The chairman sat there for 45 minutes or so just stone-faced. There wasn't a word that came out of anyone in this whole entourage of his. About three-quarters of the way through the presentation there was one specific piece of data that a personnel guy picked up on and started to blast. Elms couldn't answer the question and immediately passed it to me. I came up with one quick fact that put it all back into perspective again while the personnel guy sat there smoking. He started to interrupt one other time and the chairman told him to shut up and quit trying to cover his ass and that he wanted to hear the whole story. That was when I knew we were in pretty good shape.

I pulled one other coup on that one which was unbeknownst to either Bob or George. I suspected the question that was going to come out of it was, "All right, what do we do from here? You've pointed out that things are in total disarray, how do we fix them?" I had half a dozen slides prepared the day before showing how to proceed from there. The chairman asked the question at the end of the session, Bob turned white and George turned red. We took a five minute break and I gave the slides to George and—bang—we were right in for another 200,000 bucks or so with a new project.

In June, Jerrow was asked to come permanently to the New York office, with a healthy increase in pay. They moved in July, to the chagrin of his wife.

Nancy was thoroughly pissed off with me for being away too much and moving to New York didn't really help any.

Kline began getting more contracts in the areas of Jerrow's interests, and he succeeded in developing a few techniques that were considered technical breakthroughs. One of his clients offered a VP job at a 75% increase in pay, but he turned it down on the basis that he was having a good time and learning a lot at Kline. When the annual spring announcement of new partners at Kline came, Jerrow expected to be named one. He wasn't.

It was a legitimate decision. The screw is that I had been led to believe I was going to be made a partner that year. And one other person made it whose track record wasn't as good as mine. I was clearly disappointed, and went out looking for job offers. I got two or three attractive ones, but each had some fatal flaw. And I began to think it would be smarter to wait a year and leave after being elected partner so there would be no questions at all about whether I cut it or not.

I learned later that Jerry York, a very influential partner in the New York office, had real trouble supporting my candidacy. Jerry is a silver-spoon type of guy, very bright, very good. I managed to finagle my way into doing a project with him, which was the first study we had ever done for this fairly complex client organization. The chairman was an old school buddy of Jerry's. It turned out to be a very interesting study and the beginning of a long-standing relationship—five years now—with the firm. Jerry was directing it and I was managing it. (For all intents and purposes, I was directing it too.) I got very close with the president of their major subsidiary as a result of our compensation work. It was clear that there were sticky problems of communications, trust, and direction between New York, which is where the headquarters were, and Los Angeles, where the sub-headquarters were. This subsidiary represented 60% of their sales and about 90% of their growth potential.

The chairman of the corporation (Ted Young) knew there were problems but wasn't really fully aware of the magnitude. We had an intriguing session with him. I guess I had met with him twice prior to that meeting. The last item on a four or five point agenda was something innocuously worded like "closing the gap between Los Angeles and New York." I went through a brief academic description of what I saw were some of their problems, communications-wise, without really suggesting what the source of the problem was. Jerry began to get a little uncomfortable. Ted has a style of listening in which he will give you his undivided attention while you're talking and won't think about the thing until you stop. Then there will be a massive pregnant pause as he considers a reply. And he has a complete poker face all the time. You'd get absolutely no response—no laughter, nod, shake of the head. I was convinced that I wasn't getting through to him, and Jerry meanwhile didn't know what the hell was going on. He kept confusing the issue with general management platitudes about this, that and the other thing. About ten minutes into it, I said, "Let me try and put it as crisply and clearly as I can in terms of this last specific event we were talking about. You fucked up." Jesus, I thought Jerry was going to crawl under the table. He started talking about 84 different things at 100 miles an hour.

Ted is sitting there with an absolute poker face. Five minutes later Jerry stops. Ted just sat there. There had to be what felt like a 10-minute pause, although it was probably 30 seconds or so. Jerry couldn't stand it any longer, so he started back into it again. When he stopped, another 30-second pause and he started again. Ted broke in and said, "Jerry, you're covering old ground. Ben, why did you tell me I fucked up?" I said, "Two reasons: one, you did, and two, I didn't know any other way to get your attention." And then we started into it. Jerry was obviously sweating armpits through the whole thing. We made some major strides in terms of helping Ted understand what the problem was, and what he could be doing about it.

Jerry and I have been good friends ever since. That was the turning point in my relationship with a number of the powers that be at Kline. If it was still a bit unclear whether I was going to make it at Kline, after that it wasn't.

Within six months Jerrow was elected a partner.

* * *

The 12-room Westchester home owned by the Jerrows sits on 3 acres of land overlooking a small valley. Approaching it from the road, all one sees at first is a large driveway bordered by woods on one side, and by grass and flower gardens on the other.

A friend of Ben's from Harvard Business School stopped by on July 2, 1974, to see how well he was recovering. He found Jerrow in very good spirits, despite still being confined to a bed or a wheelchair. The doctors had concluded a week earlier that there would be no permanent damage, but that he still needed a few more months of rest.

Nancy's been an absolute savior the last two months—especially just after the accident. She got in touch with Kline the day after the accident and gave my secretary the 48-item agenda I had planned for the next day and worked with her to notify people, and so on. She made it VERY clear that "No conversation with him is allowed. I don't care what your problem is, he just is not available." Two or three days after the accident, when I could see that projects were going down the tubes, my reaction would have been to start calling people from the hospital and setting up shop by the bed.

Three or four days after I got home, as we were getting ready for a medical progress review, about a dozen guys from Kline showed up. And I can remember just sitting out there thinking, "Well, you son of a bitch, I guess you're really going to have to die before you are going to get these guys off your back."

That started me thinking. All right, if you're going to stay with Kline for any extended period of time, you're just going to have to do some things to cut down on the workload, especially the physical demands. My average workday had been 10 or 12 hours, and then I'd have a 3½ hour commute on top of that. I'd spend some time with Nancy and yet have very little time with the three kids. So it would mean I'd get four or five, or if I was lucky six, hours of sleep.

I suppose if Nancy was less effective and less strong then this thing may well have been precipitated a lot earlier. She's doing a super job raising the kids. We've always assumed that, you know, her job is to raise the kids and my job is to go out and raise the money. Now we're beginning to realize that really wasn't the way to operate.

Anyway, in the past week I've been trying to think out what my alternatives are. So far I've identified six. I could try to cut back my responsibilities at Kline. Right now I'm responsible for all training activities for our U.S. offices, for secretarial and support services for the New York office, for three firm research projects, as well as a full client load. And that's insane. If I could just cut off a few things, to get the 65-hour work week down to say 45-50 hours, I think I could manage.

I'm unquestionably in a good position right now to go to the people at Kline and get them to take some of these things off me. What I'm afraid of is that because of the way Kline is, they won't stay off. Other things will come up and I guess I'm afraid that in a place where: (1) there is an unending amount of work to be done, and (2) the norm is for everyone, or at least all the young stars, to work until they drop, that it might not be possible to work a 50-hour week.

A second obvious option is to try cutting down the commute time. There are seven of us from the New York office that live within a 5-mile radius of here, so why not open an office up here. It would be a working office—not for clients. Even if we still had to go into the city two days a week, that would save 10½ hours. And it would be so nice to be able to drive home for lunch.

This idea just might not be practical. Economically it's no problem. And I talked to two of the Kline people who live nearby and they think it's a good idea. But I don't know.

Of course, I could leave Kline. The thought has crossed my mind before. I've got one offer and two potential offers floating around right now. All three are for VP jobs in very large companies. The money in all three cases is very nice, as much as double what I get now. All three of them have the major drawback of being in New York City, which brings us back to the problems of the commute. In two of these there is substantially less travel involved. In the other there is about as much travel. I think in all three cases I could cut the work week back considerably. But I'm not sure. I've always had itchy fingers to run something and all three offer that. But I'd frankly just as soon not get bogged down in a bunch of administrative trivia. It's all I can do to screw up my courage to pay our personal household bills; and, the fewer administrative things I have to worry about, the better I feel about it. In terms of types of people to interact with, it's one of the real negatives in leaving Kline. They are very bright, talented, creative kinds of people. You look at any of the corporate alternatives and, boy, they get very thin on talent very quickly in terms of stimulating your own thinking.

The final obvious option is to leave Kline and start my own consulting company. I really do think I've got some concepts and ideas that are unique and for which there is a huge market. And I've only begun to develop this business at Kline.

We can afford a lower income while I get started. I could set up an office somewhere here near the house.

Unlike the other situations, I'd be in control. One of the beauties about consulting on your own is that if you get cross wired with a client, or you don't like what he's doing or whatever, you can say screw you.

You can afford a hell of a lot more risk. So I take a 10 or 15 or 20% cut in pay—big deal. Once you get to a certain level, an extra buck doesn't mean that much. Yet, if I do well, I could make a bundle at consulting.

One of the problems in sorting out these options is that I'm still not sure how important money is to me. Our family really never had a hell of a lot of money, but we were always reasonably well off. I can still remember selling Christmas cards and cutting lawns, caddying and working in the local gas station and all of that sort of thing. I guess I was 10 when I started selling Christmas cards. I sold vegetables around the neighborhood. The next-door neighbor had a big garden and I would go out and pick his vegetables. He knew that I was picking part of them. I don't know if he knew I was picking all of them. I would just go peddle them to all the neighbors. It was always one of those jokes—what's Ben going to be selling next? I got a job working in a gas station in the summers when I was 13 and 14. The summer when I was 15 years old my dad got me a job as a laborer in a plant. I did the playboy kind of thing between 16 and 17, starting as a lifeguard at the country club swimming pool and ending up as manager of the pool. And there was always, you know, one kind of outside extracurricular deal or another like getting the flower concession and hamburger truck at college. I often say to myself that money isn't really important, but then, I look at my behavior pattern and I say—who are you kidding?

When I first joined Kline, Nancy and I sat down and tried to specify what an idealized life style would be in terms of how we would like to live. Then we translated that into dollars and totaled it up. And then we made an estimate of what that meant in terms of yearly income. We passed that figure three or four years ago. I'm doing everything I want to do. I'm not driving a Ferrari and no, I don't have an airplane, but shit I don't have enough time to fly one anyway. No, I don't have a yacht, but I decided I don't like sailing that well either. I'd rather play golf. So maybe the money doesn't really mean a hell of a lot other than as a scorekeeping thing.

There's one other factor that's probably important here. Nancy is the only child of a guy that runs one of the largest privately held real estate development companies in the world. So, she and the kids are going to come out all right financially. Her dad and I have never really talked about it, other than to say that they are in pretty good shape, and I don't really need to worry a hell of a lot about that.

Jerrow paused and stared out the living room window at the valley below.

I don't know. I wish one of the options looked very good and clearly better than the rest.

38

Managing a Career Over Time

A professional is called on to make decisions related to job and career throughout his or her life. From the time we leave school until the time we retire, we are faced with a continuous string of questions:

- How should I approach my new assignment?
- Should I try to get the marketing research job when it becomes available next year?
- Am I spending sufficient time on my job now, or am I spending too much?
- Should I quit my job soon and go into business for myself?
- If the vice president asks me to go to Europe to open up a new plant, should I accept?

The career of Ben Jerrow rather clearly illustrates that the quality of the answers to these questions is directly related to the quality of our lives.

The approach to making these job and career decisions so far is summarized graphically in Exhibit 38–1. The alternative life style systems shown in the exhibit are extensions over time of the snapshot model introduced earlier in Exhibit 35–1. The elements in the system are, clockwise from the top, professional (P), physical (Ph), emotional (E), family (F), social (S), and material (M). In this final chapter we will discuss how this approach can be used not only to make one or two important initial career decisions, but to manage a career effectively over time.

The Decision-Making Model

The approach to job or career decision making shown in Exhibit 38–1 begins with a self-assessment process characterized by:

1. The use of multiple sources of data, which have been carefully selected
2. Thematic analysis, based on explicit logic

This type of process can generate the accurate self-awareness that is the cornerstone to our whole approach. Self-understanding makes systematic and effective opportunity assessment, option generation, and option analysis possible.

The approach to identifying, securing, and understanding opportunities shown in Exhibit 38–1 can be characterized as highly proactive and based on a reasonable understanding of the realities of job hunting, career development over time (career stages, adult development), and your own character. These processes can generate options that you will find attractive, and that you will understand.

The approach to the actual decision-making process shown in Exhibit 38–1 is made up of two components—analysis and choice. The analytical process is characterized by the rational examination of each option in terms of its impact on the various interdependent parts of one's life, and the projec-

Exhibit 38–1

Career and Job Decision Making

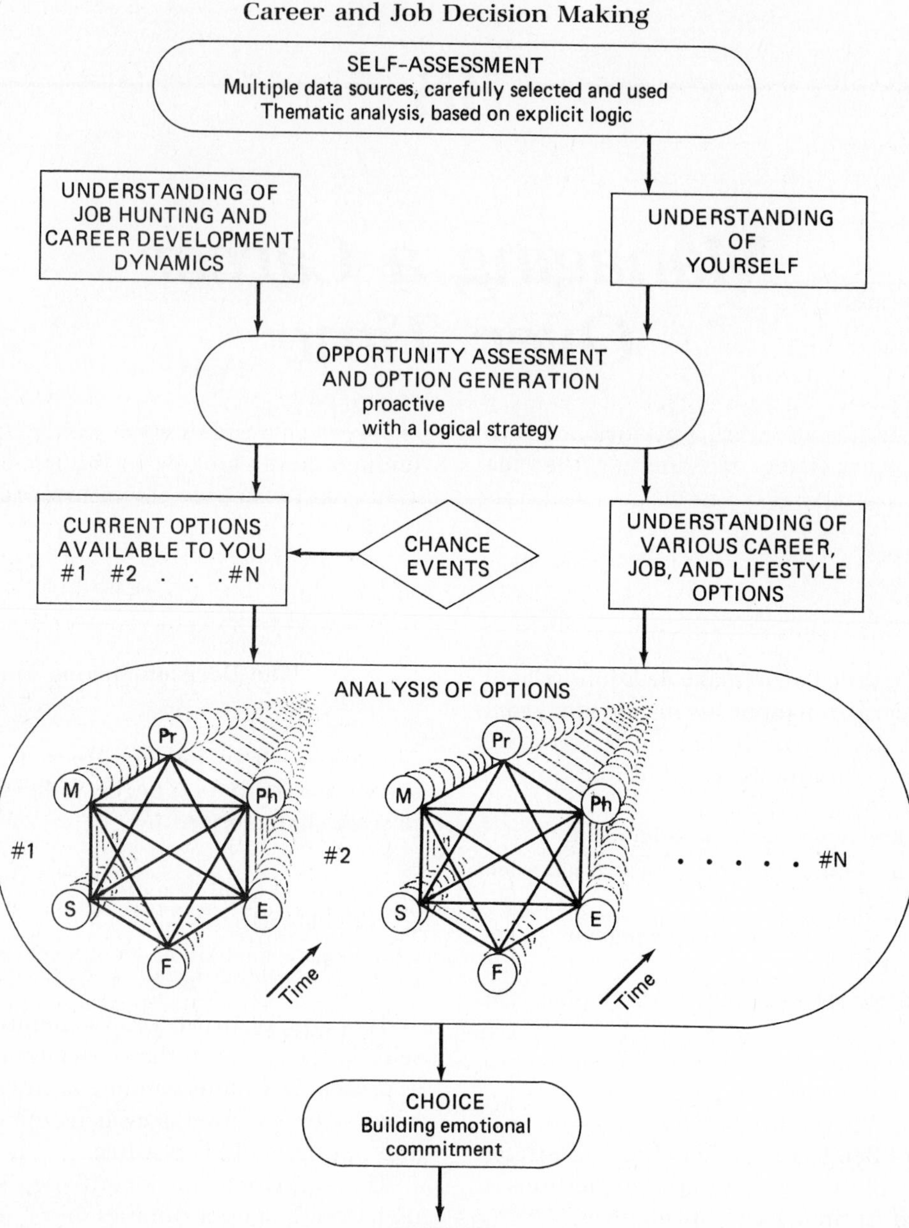

tion of the most probable events into the future for each option.

The choice process is characterized by coming to grips emotionally with each of the options and then choosing one and building emotional commitments toward it. Together these processes lead to a rational decision that one is prepared to implement.

With one modification, this systematic approach to making job- and career-related decisions can be used throughout your career. And that modification relates to the self-assessment and opportunity-assessment processes.

It obviously is not necessary, every time you wish to make a job- or career-related decision, to do the type of self-assessment outlined in Part One of this book or the type of opportunity assessment and option generation described at the beginning of Part Two. Those processes are designed to give you self-awareness and understanding of opportunities in general that can support decision making over a period of time. Only when those understandings grow to be out of date do the processes need to be repeated, in whole or in part.

Reassessment

Keeping an up-to-date assessment of yourself and your opportunities requires periodic reassessment. Our observations of people who seem to manage their careers effectively suggest that at least three different types of reassessments are needed (see Exhibit 38–2).

At least once a year it seems useful to sit down to review your performance, the satisfaction gained from work and other parts of your life, and any indications of problems that are not being addressed. This one- or two-day review might usefully be scheduled soon after a formal job performance review if your organization has a performance appraisal and feedback system. If it does not, then the ball is squarely in your court to seek out this information.

Once every three to four years, a more detailed analysis of how you and the world around you are changing can be very useful. The questions you address here are: Do any of the assumptions about myself and my opportunities used in my last complete reassessment need to be altered because of changes in the last few years? If yes, what are the changes? Do they call for some type of change in my current career or life situation?

This type of assessment takes more than a day. In structuring it, three-day to one-week career planning seminars that are offered by some companies to employees and by some consulting firms to the general public can be very helpful.

Finally, about every seven to ten years, one needs to take the time to do a complete reassessment of the magnitude described in this book. Setting aside the time to do any of these reassessments and structuring them is extremely difficult, but this one is probably the most difficult of all. Assessment centers of the type some companies are now developing can be helpful. So can professional career counselors and structured sabbaticals (such as to a three- to four-month program at a university).

The Challenge

Many professionals get on a track during their twenties as a result of carefully made choices or of chance events and then chug along that track for a lifetime, never looking to the left or right or up. They don't ever stop the train to reevaluate their situation, even if they recognize that the ride is not as much fun as it used to be. Some people go through life this way. Others, like Ben Jerrow, have their trains derailed by a sudden boulder from the sky and are forced to do some reassessment. As you might expect, being forced into a major reassessment and change during one's mid or late career can be a very painful experience.

It's amazing how many excuses people can invent to avoid reassessment exercises. And this tendency is exacerbated by most professions and organizations, which provide people with little or no help or encouragement for reassessment. Often both individuals and organizations avoid the subject of individual career reassessment out of uneasiness—let well enough alone, don't open up Pandora's box.

Exhibit 38–2

ACTIVITY	INTENSITY	FREQUENCY	SOURCES OF INPUT AND HELP
General evaluation of year's performance and of satisfaction with various aspects of life. Any problems?	One or two days' worth of work.	Once a year	Organization-initiated formal performance appraisal. Conversations with important others in your life.
Analysis of changes in you and your opportunities. Are changes needed?	Up to a week's worth of work, at one time or spread out over a few months.	Every three or four years.	Three- to seven-day career planning seminars.
Major reassessment of self and opportunities.	Of the magnitude described in this book.	Once every seven to ten years.	Assessment centers. Career counselors. Three- to four-month university programs.

One of the biggest challenges you face in your career is to use the tools and knowledge you now have regarding career management and not to let yourself slip into a self-induced career coma. Dealing with the challenge requires awareness and self-discipline on your part, because while you may receive some help from elsewhere (more and more organizations are providing career planning workshops, assessment centers, and counselors each year, but the total amount of such services is very low), the burden rests mostly with you.

Although the amount of available support for career management is not as great as we might like it from the point of view of society, it does make career planning in one sense even more attractive for the proactive individual. Today a person who is willing and able to use the ideas presented in this book to manage his or her career has a real competitive advantage. In a world that currently supplies considerably less money and fewer interesting jobs than people would like, competitive advantage is very important. The ideas here can give you an edge. Use them!

Assignment

Read the case material that follows, "Adult Life and Career Stage." Then read "The Life and Career of a Chief Executive Officer," (pp. 433–444). Which career and/or adult life stage model or pieces of models helps you to best understand Harold Clawson? Pick one model and, using it, be prepared to describe Harold's life. How would you summarize Harold's career and its impact on him, his family, and his life style? What do you learn from the case about managing your own career development?

ADULT CAREER AND LIFE STAGES

We all have many sides to our lives. The most obvious are the physical, the emotional, and the mental. But we also have social, familial, marital, recreational, and spiritual sides as well. Exhibit 38–3 outlines a starting list of our many facets. Each of these aspects develop and evolve over time. In some of these areas, the development seems to follow fairly consistent patterns; in other areas, it does not. Research conducted over the past three decades, for instance, shows that people's careers tend to follow predictable patterns of development. Various researchers have characterized the stages in this development in different terms, but there are a lot of similarities. On the other hand, although there is still much to learn about it, emotional development seems to be much less predictable. We don't have time to discuss all the current knowledge about the developmental processes observed in each of life's aspects, but we can consider the more common ones.

As we do, keep in mind the two-dimensional framework of the various aspects on the vertical scale and the developmental stages outlined below on the horizontal one. The image, then, is like a musical score, with each melody line representing an aspect of our lives and each bar representing a developmental stage. From bar to bar, some are in crescendo, others diminishing. But whether the melodies are salient or not, they are there and together comprise the symphony of one's life.

Exhibit 38–3

Aspects of Our Lives

Physical
Emotional
Mental/intellectual
Spiritual/philosophical
Recreational
Social
Familial
Marital
Parental
Professional
Educational
Financial
Organizational
Political
Societal

This note was written by James G. Clawson to provide a basis for class discussion. UVA case OB-224.

We will first present three of the major theories on adult life development and then turn to the professional aspect of our lives and the development of identifiable career stages.

Adult Life Stages

Although the changes in activity, interest, ability, and tasks that humans experience over a lifetime have been the subject of literary pieces for millennia, modern social scientists have not paid much attention to the topic until relatively recently.

Erikson's Theory

The most influential early adult life stage theoretician was Erik Erikson. In his book *Childhood and Society,* published in 1950, he identified stages of human development in terms of several psychological dilemmas that confront all individuals. The dilemmas common to young people built on the work of Sigmund Freud, the first person to begin to describe human development in terms of predictable stages. Freud left off before addressing adult development; Erikson continued to hypothesize. He believed that:

1. From early adolescence to early middle age, the key psychological task a person faced was one of *intimacy* vs. *isolation.* One had to learn to care for and be concerned for another person without fear of losing one's self. If one did not learn to do this, then life became a series of experiences in which the individual felt isolated from the rest of society.

2. In middle age, the key issue was *generativity* vs. *self-absorption.* In this dilemma, the individual had to choose between developing concern for individuals beyond one's own family, including colleagues at work and people in society, or remaining absorbed in self. Failure to develop a generative approach to life would, he said, leave one feeling stagnated and bitter.

3. Finally, in old age, Erikson saw a battle between *integrity* and *despair.* Integrity was the sense that life and all its choices and experiences had "come together," become whole and integrated. Despair was the feeling that things had not turned out as one would have liked, that one had missed a lot of opportunities—and that it was too late to do anything about it.

Again, not much was done in the field of adult development for many years. Then in the late 1970s several social scientists began publishing the results of their observations from clinical practice and formal research projects.

Gould's Theory

Roger Gould was a California psychologist who began to notice common patterns in the issues clients of similar age groups would bring to him. In his book, *Transformations,* he presents a series of assumptions which people learned in their formative years and which must be reconciled in later life, typically at predictable stages. He outlines the following adult life development themes:

16–22 *Leaving the parents' world.* False assumption: "I'll always belong to my parents and believe in their world." During this period young people move from a set of beliefs that revolves around their parents' teachings and support to developing confidence in their own ability to care for themselves and to make decisions that will affect their lives. They feel half in, half out of the family. They wrestle with learning about their independence, their own opinions, their own ability to provide, and relying on people other than family members.

23–28 *I'm nobody's baby now.* False assumption: "Doing things my parent's way, with willpower and perseverance, will bring results. But if I become too frustrated, confused or tired or am simply unable to cope, they will step in and show me the right way." Although people in this period are feeling their autonomy, they are still learning what "works" in the world, and confront the notions that people who play the game by the rules do not always get rewarded, that there is no one best way to do things, that others cannot do for us what we cannot do, and that rationality does not always win. They also are learning about commitment to spouses, to children, to work—and the responsibilities that all these carry—and in so doing, are learning many new roles they will play in society.

29–34 *Opening up to what's inside.* False assumption: "Life is simple and controllable. There are no significant coexisting contradictory forces within me." Having spent nearly a decade establishing oneself in a family and work, an individual now begins to look internally and to question whether or not the commitments and responsibilities assumed were really independently chosen or were mere extensions of parental guidance. People in this period typically begin to confront the difference between the intellectual (rational) and the emotional; they realize that in some ways they did not want to be like their parents; they learn that others are not so neatly understood as they once thought; and they realize more fully than before that their security depends upon them alone.

Marriage and career lives are established. Children are growing.

35–43 *Midlife decade.* False assumption: "There is no evil or death in the world. The sinister has been destroyed." Gould believes that this period is centered on the question of vulnerability. In it, he says, we work to come to grips with the reality of our own mortality and with the illusion that safety can last forever. We also, he says, work to face the notion that we are not "innocent," but that we, like others, invite others to play complementary roles to the ones we assume. That occurs most obviously in marriage, and in this period we examine these "unhealthy conspiracies" to make our own roles and our relationships more comfortable. Gould notes: "It is always unhealthy to sacrifice our identity for the stability of the relationship" (p. 280).

44–50 *Post-midlife period.* Realization: "That's the way it is, world. Here I am." In this period, finite time is resigned to as reality; one feels that "the die is cast." We become more actively involved with young adult children. We depend on our spouses for sympathy and affection. We may regret "mistakes" we made in raising our children. Money becomes less important. We attempt to reconcile what is with what might have been. Life settles down, becomes even. We accept the new ordering of things.

50+ *Meaning making.* The false assumptions of childhood have been encountered, if not all proved false. It is a period of mellowing, of making within us sense of the things that have happened both within and without. Children are seen as potential sources of comfort and satisfaction. We value spouses more. We have greater self-acceptance. There is little concern for past or future; the present is emphasized. We renew our questioning of the meaningfulness of life. And as we are concerned about our health, we hunger for personal relationships. We realize that we cannot do things as well as we once did.

Levinson's Theory

Daniel Levinson, a psychiatrist at Yale University Medical School, and his colleagues studied the lives of fifty men from five different walks of life. His theory concludes that there are a series of transitions and periods of relative stability in adult life. Each transition examines the life structure that preceded it and evaluates its appropriateness for the next era. Transitions are often times of turmoil and stress. The stable periods are often ones of renewed commitment and focus. Levinson's cyclical stages look like this:

17–22 *Early adult transition (EDT).* This is a critical transition in which the young man is half in and half out of his parental family. He is faced with necessity of leaving his family, but is not yet sure how to enter the adult world before him. His choices in this transition begin to form his adult self, both as he and as others will see it.

22–28 *Entering the adult world (EAW).* In this period, the young man attempts to establish a link between his view of himself and adult society. He seeks assistance, often, in doing this and may become a protégé. He begins to engage in adult relationships and explores what that means to him. He attempts to establish a life structure that will at the same time be flexible, leaving him options to change, and sufficiently stable to allow him to get on with his initial choice of means for making something of himself.

28–33 *Age thirty transition (ATT).* The young male adult now feels that if changes are to be made, he had better begin, for time is passing. The life structure initiated in the twenties is reevaluated. Once fondly held dreams are reassessed in the light of several years of adult experience. Some continue on rather smoothly, but for many it is a time of stress—one struggles with how to make the changes one desires. These three periods—EDT, EAW, and ATT—together form the early adulthood or novice stage.

33–40 *Settling down (SD).* In this period, the male adult attempts to consolidate his experience and efforts to build a life structure that will allow him to invest heavily in the things most central to him. Becoming an expert and a valued member of society are key objectives. He is no longer a novice, but is now a full adult determined to "make it." At the end of this period, he looks for a sense of becoming his own man—a male adult with seniority and respect. As one becomes more of one's own man, the need for active mentors begins to wane.

40–45 *Midlife transition (MLT).* Now the reexamination focuses not on where one is going, but where one has been. One becomes concerned about his accomplishments and whether or not they have fulfilled his dreams and ambitions or been less significant diversions. Aspects that have been suppressed during the early adulthood period bubble up for reassessment. One wonders if the path taken thus far is really the one that is right for him. One begins to sense physical declines and being no longer young. For some, these quesetions bring reconfirmation, for others great turmoil and perhaps drastic changes—in career, in relationships, in activities, in the attempt to resurrect long-neglected but valued parts of the self.

45–50 *Beginning of middle adulthood (BMA).* This is a period of consolidating the reassessments conducted during the MLT. Old relationships receive new attention, and new ones are developed more consciously. One settles into his new or reconfirmed view of himself and savors it. Some sense that a middle adulthood of decline and constriction have arrived; others begin to feel a deep sense of fulfillment in their lives and a mature sense of creative ability. For some, this is the most satisfying season of life.

50–55 *Age fifty transition (AFT).* In this period, the issues which were brushed over or not fully treated in the ATT and MLT are brought forcefully to the fore. Levinson does not believe that it is possible to escape at least a moderate transition crisis in either the MLT or the AFT.

55–60 *Second middle adult structure (SMAS).* Similar to SD, this period is one of completion and settling into. One must prepare for the next transition from middle adulthood into late adulthood. For some this is a time of rejuvenation and realization, filling out the structure outlined in the AFT.

60–65 *Late adult transition (LAT).* This transition anticipates the change in structure from SMAS to late adulthood in which career changes are likely to have a significant effect on one's self and relationships. It is often a period of deep reflection. For some, this is a particularly painful change which they try to avoid.

65+ *Late adult era (LAE).* One must now decide not only the meaning to one's previous existence, but also begin to establish the new structure formulated in LAT. Much more needs to be learned about this period.

Career Stages

Four very useful and comprehensive theories of career stage development were identified by Miller and Form; Super; Schein; and Dalton, Thompson, and Price. We will outline these theories and then ask you to consider them in the life of a person who has lived through them all.

Miller and Form

In 1951 these two pioneering researchers identified five career stages and attempted to describe career development patterns throughout a person's lifetime. They found it useful to think of career development in these terms:

0–15 *Preparatory work period:* From the time we are born, we are socialized by our parents, by our schools, and by the experiences we are exposed to in our immediate environment into a set of views about the world of work. These views and values tend to follow us into our adult working careers. Young people develop their attitudes as they do their first work (chores and homework) in limited doses. Not only do parents and teachers affect this formation, but so do one's peers and social cliques. One of the main features of this preparatory socialization was the American cultural injunction to "make good." They note that most young people were socialized with what they call the four main values of Puritanism: (1) It is man's duty to know how to work and how to work hard; (2) success in work is evidence of God's favor; (3) the measure of success is money and property; and (4) the way to success is through industry and thrift.

15–18 *Initial work period:* This period is a temporary one consisting of the time when one gets the first part-time job until one accepts full-time, year-round employment. One knows that the initial jobs are temporary and therefore there is a lack of commitment to each position. The common goals are to make "spending money" and to "prepare oneself" for something else. Psychologically, they note, the common agendas are to manage the transition from school to work, to gain independence, to demonstrate an ability to work hard, to learn how to get along with people, to get money as a symbol of independence, and to get a good track record. Most of the occupational frustration comes from work values held as a result of social class membership, expectations of reward based on educational achievement, a decline in the generally accepted intrinsic value of work (see Puritan value 1 above), and expectations of specific monetary rewards for work.

18–34 *Trial work period:* The trial period begins when one takes the first "permanent" job—and yet the period is marked often by considerable changing of jobs. Finally, after trying several different jobs, one "finds himself," "steadies himself," or perhaps just "resigns himself" to a more long-term position. Miller and Form characterize six distinct types of career orientation that begin to form in this period: (1) the ambitious worker who has confidence he can move up; (2) the responsive worker who fulfills the career expected of him by others; (3) the fulfilled worker who has attained his occupational goal; (4) the confused worker who is uncertain about past and future decisions and whose career pattern is erratic; (5) the frustrated worker who feels thwarted; and (6) the defeated worker who views himself as a failure. Common to all these is the cultural imperative they call the "American career stereotype" of a young, ambitious man who with average intelligence, but high character, unbounded determination, initiative, and hard work climbs from the "lowliest jobs" to higher income levels which signify "success."

35–65 *Stable work period:* This period is characterized by long-term commitment to "the kind of work that I've always wanted" or to the resignation that one will not find it. Not everyone, Miller and Form state, will continue in one stable work period throughout the rest of their careers. There are many reasons why one stabilizes in one company or job: (1) realization or rationalization of the trial period goal, (2) advantages gained by seniority; (3) age; (4) higher levels of income; (5) family responsibilities; (6) home ownership; (7) friendship ties; (8) institutional ties; (9) identifying with the company and community. The emotional tasks faced in this period relate to redefining occupational goals that may have been achieved or will never be achieved, to waiting for promotions in informal seniority systems, to doing work for which one is overqualified which no longer is stimulating, and to changing personal and family interests which may no longer fit the job. Some will enter another trial period, although Miller and Form say little about why.

65+ *Retirement period:* Anthropologists claim that the elderly have four common psychological goals: (1) to live as long as possible until the troubles of old age exceed the benefits of living; (2) to remain active in personal and group affairs; (3) to protect the privileges accumulated over the career; (4) to withdraw from life honorably with high prospects for the next life. Some do not accept the withdrawal in the fourth goal and hence develop a negative attitude toward retirement.

Super's Theory

Six years later, in 1957, Donald Super and his colleagues published an expanded career theory that built on the earlier work of Eli Ginzberg, his colleagues, and of several other researchers and psychologists. Eli Ginzberg and his colleagues had outlined an occupational choice sequence they felt was an irreversible process. Each stage in this process was influenced, they said, by four factors: (1) the reality of the occupational environment, (2) a person's educational experience, (3) certain personal and emotional characteristics, and (4) a person's values. These four factors, especially the tradeoffs between the first two factors and the last two, shaped the decisions a person would make in the *fantasy, tentative,* and *reality* stages of career development. Super expanded Ginzberg's theory as follows:

0–14 *Growth stage:*
Fantasy substage (4–10): fantasy, role-playing
Interests substage (11–12): emphasizes likes
Capacity substage (13–14): emphasizes abilities

15–24 *Exploration stage:*
Tentative substage (15–17): makes tentative choices
Transaction (18–21): enters labor market
Trial (22–24): begins working

25–44 *Establishment stage:*
Trial substage (25–30): may change occupation
Stabilization substage (31–44): tries to settle down

45–66 *Maintenance stage:*
Holding on to what one has

65+ *Decline stage:*
Deceleration (65–70): beginning to retreat from work
Retirement (71–): moves out of career

Super's theory outlined activities characteristic of periods covering one's entire lifetime, but most of his work and focus was on the exploration stage.

Schein's Theory

Ed Schein of MIT finds the following theoretical framework most useful:

1. *Preentry and entry:* The person prepares for work by exploring the possibilities and making a choice.
2. *Basic training and initiation:* One is socialized by the people in the organization into the formal and informal rules and norms of behavior in the organization.
3. *First assignment and promotion:* One establishes one's reputation as probable managerial material or as one who will "level off."
4. *Second assignment:* One either continues toward further advancement or continues to level off.
5. *Granting tenure:* One is admitted to the inner circles of the organization as a permanent member.
6. *Termination and exit:* One withdraws from the organization.
7. *Postexit:* One tries to come to grips with a life style in which the career plays a very reduced or very different role.

Perhaps the most distinctive characteristic of Schein's scheme is the conical view of organization structure which he takes to describe the movement of individual careers within organizations. There are, he says, three directions of movement: (1) *up,* which approximates the conventional notion of promotion up a heirarchical ladder; (2) *in,* which describes the movement of a person from the outer circles at entry to the inner circles later on; and (3) *around,* in which person moves from one functional area to another in job rotation assignments. Each promotion, of course, may involve one, two, or all three of these kinds of movement.

Dalton's, Thompson's, and Price's Theory

These three researchers from Brigham Young University have studied the careers of thousands of people, many of them engineers, and report the following typical pattern:

> *Stage One: Apprentice.* The individual must learn how to make the transition from school to organizational life, how to be an effective subordinate, and how to live within the informal and formal social system of the organization. This stage is critical because the novice learns values, beliefs, and habits of organizational and interpersonal life that he will use throughout his career.
>
> *Stage Two: Independent specialist.* One begins to work without supervision. In order to develop one's abilities to contribute and one's reputation, one works hard to build competence, often by specializing. One of the main tasks of this stage is to take the initiative for one's own work so that one is no longer dependent upon supervision for decisions about what needs to be done.
>
> *Stage Three: Mentor.* One becomes concerned not only about one's own work, but also about the work of those who follow. One of the main tasks here is to move from a frame of mind that focuses on doing to one which focuses on managing the work and development of others—to coaching and directing rather than producing.
>
> *Stage four: Sponsor.* One becomes involved not only with the objectives and activities of face-to-face subordinates, but also with the goals and work of large groups or systems of groups of people. Sponsors begin to ask about the goals of the organization or how the organization fits into the rest of society—and to take initiative for answering those questions.

One way to summarize the work of Dalton and his colleagues is to note that each stage in their theory describes an increasingly broad perspective of the work that needs to be done and of the people involved in doing it. In stage one, for instance, the apprentice focuses on his boss and the demands he places on the new employee. In stage two the full-fledged employee is now interested primarily in his own work. In stage three, his view expands to include the activities of those immediately around him. And in stage four, the sponsor is concerned about the work of hundreds, thousands, perhaps hundreds of thousands of people.

These researchers also note that individuals do not necessarily move through all the stages. Some people (probably Driver's steady-state types) prefer to remain in the independent specialist stage, and others may not move from the mentor to the sponsor stage.

Summary

This case has introduced very briefly the main points of several major adult life stage and career development theories. You may have noticed similarities in them (see Exhibit 38–4). We would expect this of theories that attempt to describe similar phenomena. For instance, Erikson's generativity vs. self-absorption dilemma may be viewed as a psychological task facing a person near the end of the Dalton independent specialist stage. The individual who opts for "generativity" is likely to move on to Dalton's mentor stage, while the person who chooses "self-absorption" is likely to remain an independent specialist. Similarly, Levinson's EAW stage has many of the same characteristics of Super's establishment trial period stage.

One relatively common feature of the theories we have reviewed is a cyclical pattern. Levinson, for instance, holds that adults experience alternating periods of stability and transition. Miller and Form agree that many careers are characterized by alternating trial and stable work periods.

We believe that people have a basic internal tension between stability and variety. Although we all vary in our personal preferences for a balance between these two psychological states, we all tend to reexamine the current state (whether it be variety or stability) with an eye toward moving toward the other one. Thus, if our lives and/or careers have been stable and orderly for a while, we begin to get bored and to think about introducing some change or variety. If our lives have been filled with change, we may seek periods of stability to consolidate our perspectives and feelings. Perhaps you can identify additional steps in a cyclical pattern of adult life and career stage development. We encourage you to do this, and to note how they relate to the development of the various human aspects outlined in Exhibit 38–3.

Exhibit 38–4

A Brief Comparative View of Selected Major Adult Stage Theories

Theorist	Age 10	20	30	40	50	60	70
Adult Life Stages							
Erikson		Intimacy vs. isolation			Generativity vs. self-absorption		Integrity vs. despair
Gould	Break away	Mastery		Resigned		Mellowing	
			Questions				
Levinson (Stable)		EAW	SD/BHOM	BMA	SMAS	LAE	
(Transitions)	EAT		ATT	MLT	AFT	LAT	
Career Stages							
Miller and Form	Preparation	Trial	Stable ⟶	⟶	⟶	⟶	Retirement
		Initial					
Super	Growth		Establishment				Decline
		Exploration			Maintenance		
Schein		Entry	Promotion	Tenure	Termination		
	Preentry	Initiation		Watershed (Up or level)			Postexit
Dalton et al.		Apprentice	Independent specialist	Mentor	Sponsor		

References

DAVIS, JOHN. "Theories of Adult Life Stages and Their Relevance for the Management of Human Resources." Unpublished subfield examination, Harvard Business School, 1980.

ERIKSON, E. H. *Childhood and Society,* 2d ed. (New York: Norton, 1963).

GINZBERG, E., J. W. GINSBERG, S. AXELROD, and J. L. HERMA. *Occupational Choice* (New York: Columbia University Press, 1951).

LEVINSON, DANIEL J. *The Seasons of a Man's Life* (New York: Knopf, 1978).

MILLER, D. C., and W. H. FORM. *Industrial Sociology* (New York: Harper and Row, 1951).

OSIPOW, S. H. *Theories of Career Development* (New York: Appleton-Century-Crofts, 1973).

SUPER, D., J. CRITES, R. HUMMD, H. MOSER, P. OVERSTREET, and C. WARNATH. *Vocational Development: A Framework for Research* (New York: Teachers College Press, 1957).

THE LIFE AND CAREER OF A CHIEF EXECUTIVE OFFICER

> My first goal was to be a school teacher. There were very few jobs in Cache Valley, and Salt Lake City wasn't much better. Ninety percent of the people were engaged in agriculture or manual labor. If one didn't have land that meant he worked as a farmhand for somebody else. Without capital, one couldn't own land.
>
> There were ten children and fifteen acres in my family, so what was I to do? I had to prepare for something. The most lucrative job in those days, other than farming, was school teaching, unless one could get to the very rare jobs in a bank. The banks seldom had turnover. School teaching, while it was not lucrative, really, was a white collar job and it had something more in it than muscle work. The best job I could hope for at teaching was $65 a month.

So began James Harold Clawson as he reflected at age 80 on his life and career as an auditor, manager, and chief executive officer of one of the United States' major private utilities. That statement was perhaps the best simple summary of the motivation that propelled Jack Clawson from a modest and isolated farm community to the paneled boardrooms of corporate America. His story is neither unique nor common; it reflects the imprints of great individual drive and of serendipitous luck. It also reflects the subtle and intricate ways in which career can become life and life become career. Mr. Clawson's family knew him as Harold; his business associates called him Jack. Yet in spite of this superficial separation of roles, whenever he was asked about his life, the dilemmas he faced, or the emotions he felt, Mr. Clawson always began to explain by describing what was happening at the company. He was loyal yet independent; demanding yet understanding, intense yet calm. By almost any standard, he was successful.

The Early Years

Harold Clawson was born in 1899 in Providence, near Logan in the northern, mountainous part of Utah. Automobiles were still in their infancy; airplanes were yet to fly. William McKinley was president, the Spanish-American War barely ended. Harold was the second in what was to be a family of ten children—eight boys and two girls. His father had 15 acres of land, but could not make a living out of them alone. So he worked at a variety of odd jobs, working now as freighter hauling stone by wagon team from the local quarry, then as laborer, always doing his farming on the side. His mother was hardly educated at all, but worked hard and had a great love for her children.

Harold grew up farming, milking cows, and attending a small rural school. In the summer of his twelfth year he contracted an unusual fever that refused to go away. He felt weak and lethargic; he could not walk more than a half-mile without resting. When the Scouts went off hiking, they took a horse for Harold to ride. From that summer on, he did not feel physically strong. He did not grow so tall as his brothers and tired more quickly at physical labor. Some foods did not sit well in his stomach, and he began to have abdominal pains.

Consequently, Harold began to spend more time reading and thinking. His favorite uncle, Leo, attended Utah State University and then became a local school teacher. He brought books home from the school library for Harold to read—a new book each week.

> I was under his influence for about five years. He got me started in seeking an education and in doing well in my studies. He was a teacher for awhile in the school to which I went, and so that he wouldn't show any favoritism, he really held me to a higher standard than the others. When I was 15 he unfortunately died from the bad effects of sickness contracted during his youth.

In his local high school (an academy that included two years of college work), Harold did very well. He was outgoing and popular. He took up tennis, and in his junior year won an oratorical contest. His senior year, he defeated the high-status and well-to-do candidate from Logan in the student body presidential election by talking quietly to all the students from the various small farming towns that surrounded Logan, collecting their support for a rural ticket.

This case was written by Assistant Professor James G. Clawson as a basis for class discussion rather than to illustrate effective or ineffective handling of an administrative situation. Harvard Business School case 9-480-036.

Harold worked during his summer vacations as a laborer at the local sugar factory. He remembered clearly the advice of Mr. Campbell, the foreman:

> He came up to me where I was working, sweating it out—I wasn't too strong physically—and he said, "Harold, my boy, it's a lot easier pushing a pencil than it is pushing these shovels. It pays better, too!" That impressed and encouraged me quite deeply.

While Harold was at the academy, the nation entered World War I. Expecting to be drafted, he enlisted voluntarily and was sent to Officer's Training School in Waco, Texas, in the fall of 1918. He took correspondence courses at the academy to add to his credits while he was gone. The war ended a few months later, and Harold returned to school. By virtue of his earlier work and the correspondence courses, he was able to complete the six-year course for teacher certification in five years.

He no longer intended to teach, but thought it wise to have the training and credential just in case. In the meantime, his thoughts had turned to law so much that the academy yearbook predicted he would become a judge.

> In the fall I enrolled at Utah State. There I met Parley Peterson and George B. Hendricks (professors of accounting and finance). Both of them were very strong on postgraduate work. I was in a formative stage as to what I was going to do. I didn't have any money and thought mostly of getting a job. If somebody had offered me a hundred dollars a month I probably would've postponed or given up going off to Harvard.

Peterson and Hendricks dissuaded young Clawson from going into law ("there were too many starving lawyers") and encouraged him to think about the Harvard Business School. Harold's older brother Charles had gone there that year, so the idea was not altogether new. He applied and was accepted. About that time, Harold also applied for a Rhodes scholarship, but did not receive the appointment.

After finishing his college program at Utah State in June 1920, Harold went to southern Idaho to work on a dry farm and to prepare for Harvard. He took with him the accounting and finance texts (acquired from his brother) written and used by Business School faculty and read them line by line, underlining as he went.

> I spent the summer growing and harvesting wheat on a big farm. All my spare time I spent reading these first-year books and some of the reports that had been written by students for the management classes. I went to HBS well prepared. I figured I had to dig because Utah State at that time was not rated too high academically.

The Harvard Business School and First Job

Harold Clawson went to the Harvard Business School in the fall of 1920, and having read many of the texts used at the school, he did well his first year. He was often able to quote and argue the professor's point of view, since the texts he had read the previous summer were written by the same faculty that he had as instructors. No particular professor was influential in Jack's development, though he had very high respect for all of them.

Jack did not have a lot of time for extracurricular activities at the Business School. He focused his studies on finance, accounting, and auditing and was consistently at the top of his classes in these areas. Jack dated only occasionally (usually a girl from the New England Conservatory of Music) and took trips to Marblehead beach, the theater, or the symphony. One of Harold's classmates noticed that Harold's initials were J.H. and took to calling Harold "John Harvard." Another friend shortened that to "John" and later "Jack," the nickname that stayed with him throughout his professional life.

Jack financed his degree with a mixture of funds—summer jobs, part-time work at Widener Library, and borrowing from his father and other sources. The library work was ideal for him because he was able to study at work and was also able to see what books his classmates were checking out and later read them. During the summer between his first and second years, Jack lived in the campus dorms for about $6 per month. He earned his living expenses and savings by working first in a packing house and then as the editor for the Camp Devens Citizens Military Training Camp newspaper. When he finished school, Jack had about $2,000 in education debts.

Jack began his job search with the usual campus recruiters. He interviewed with one of the Big Eight public accounting firms that came, and it first appeared that he would go to work for them, but they delayed their decisions until after graduation. So Jack followed up on interest expressed by the engineering, management, and investment firm of Stone and Webster of Boston. Jack had a great interest in traveling, so when Stone and Webster recruiters described the company's far-flung holdings and the job of a traveling auditor, Jack accepted their offer. He went home for a month and then reported to his senior traveling auditor in Houston, Texas, to begin work.

Jack and his senior companion traveled the country auditing the company's electric, gas, and street car system holdings. He learned "the ABCs" of these businesses in those early assignments, but he felt his performance reviews were mixed:

> One senior man I went out with said I wasn't much good, but another said I was a humdinger. So I went to the head of the department and asked which one of these men was right. He said I was doing just fine, excellent in fact. So I was okay.

On the auditing circuit, Jack occasionally dated women in the towns where he was working. In one midwestern city he met a banker's daughter who was eager to get married, but their religious backgrounds were so different that Jack decided not to pursue the relationship in spite of his fondness for the lady.

After two years of heavy traveling and extremely long hours, Jack was exhausted. He told the company he was going home for the summer to regain his health. Harold spent a month in Logan chopping wood and farming. By then, he felt renewed enough to return to work on the auditing circuit. He established a regular program of exercise and health care which he followed rigorously thereafter.

> After a year and a half I got a call which said that our team of auditors out in Seattle needed another man, would I leave the circuit I was working on and go to Seattle? So in January 1924, I left Columbus, Georgia (where I was working), crossed the snow-covered plains and mountains and came down into Seattle, where the roses were still blooming.

Leora Gibbs

On his way to Seattle, Harold stopped off in Logan and had his first date with Leora Gibbs. Leora was the second of three daughters of a struggling family in Cache Valley. She was very outgoing and full of spunk—qualities which Harold liked and felt complemented his own quietness and reserved manner. Leora was teaching school near Logan at the time.

Harold came to see her during his summer vacation the following year, and they were engaged. The next year, 1925, Harold was reassigned to Boston. On his way east, he stopped in Logan and married Leora. They honeymooned across the country.

Harold spent one week in Boston, found his wife an apartment, enrolled her in a finishing school, and went to Florida and Texas on a three-month auditing trip. He had become a senior auditor himself, and his new circuits included the entire United States, Nova Scotia, and Puerto Rico.

> I left her alone. I told her she was just a young girl and needed to learn more about the world and to get a little Boston culture. So she went to a finishing school. It was a choice experience and she learned a great deal, including expression, oratory, and social graces. She mixed with some very fine people.
>
> Having gone to college and studied to be a teacher with the idea of helping people to learn and to excel in all things, and having been through fine colleges and a good education, I had a high sense of the responsibility and the opportunity to help my wife to excel in those things. I got her interested in going to school in Boston, and later in Seattle I encouraged her to take a class here at the University of Washington from an excellent professor in child training. She took copious notes, and we both read them and studied them together. I wanted my wife to be able and capable in all things. I wanted her to have her own personality, to do the things in life that *she'd* like to do. She sometimes feels like she's been treated *too* independently, but I think that the woman *should* have a real degree of independence. I believe that couples can help each other and be useful to one another.

In the fall of 1926, Jack (in Boston) was about to begin a six-month tour of companies in the southern states. Their first child was soon to be born. Leora felt that six months was too long to be alone, so she decided to return to Utah. They were packed and scheduled to leave on diverging trains in the early afternoon. At eleven o'clock the phone rang. A man for whom Jack had worked in the South was now in Seattle, needed help, and wanted Jack to come out. Sudden though it was, the change in plans was more than appealing to both Jack and Leora, so they changed his tickets and headed west.

> In Seattle they had an audit force of five men and needed another senior man to work with the other senior man for about six months. So, in an hour we were on the same train and headed in the same direction. Instead of a sad parting, it was a celebration traveling west together.

Moving to Seattle

Jack's first boss in Seattle left shortly thereafter and was replaced by a man who was unfamiliar with the work. Jack was in the uncomfortable position of having to work for a man who knew less than he. Jack was asked to stay beyond his six-month assignment. Then in 1928, Stone and

Webster put Jack in charge of that small but permanent auditing operation. He was responsible to the company for all the audits of the West Coast holdings including the principal one, Puget Sound Power and Light Company (PSPL).

> That (auditing work) was very interesting, because it included innovative processes of suggesting improvements. It was not merely seeing if everything was in order and that all the money was accounted for. It was more finding shortcuts, things that were taking up too much time or wasting money and that sort of thing. The reports were all, "what can be done to better performance, reduce costs and improve profits?"
>
> When we came to Seattle I had reached a point where being away from home for long periods of time, two or three months at a time, was distasteful. I didn't intend to stay with the traveling when I got married. I had figured I would continue traveling for two or three years. Leora and I had agreed on that. I missed her terribly. It makes me almost weep to think about it, some of those long weeks away from her. (*Tears.*) I don't want to think about it. It wasn't easy.
>
> It was hard on our marriage. Lorie had to take care of the boys, but she was good about it. We used to talk about it. When we came to Seattle, I traveled some, but seldom on weekends.
>
> We recognized, looking ahead, that there were many people in the accounting department, but that there were only a few people in the auditing department of which I was head. Both roads led to the top of the company. In auditing, one had only a few competitors. Plus the work was a fine learning process. Those people in the accounting office had their daily routine work, and seldom saw the whole picture as the auditors did. I highly recommend the auditing approach for an ambitious person.
>
> The public library was very close to my office. At five o'clock when work was over, instead of going home I would go right over to the library and stay there until ten o'clock when the library closed, then take a street car home. I'd leave the house about seven (A.M.) and get home after ten. I did this every weekday for about two years. I went through *every* accounting book and auditing book in the Seattle Public Library. I also obtained the questions on every Washington State CPA examination for the previous ten years, and without reference to the answers (which were available in other books) I worked the answers to all the questions and compared my work with the suggested answers.
>
> At one time, I signed up in a coaching class for CPA examinations. After listening to two lessons and the students who didn't know very much what it was all about—asking simple questions about things that I knew backwards and forwards—wasting my time, I just gave up the fee I'd paid to join the class and went back to the library. By the time I sat for the examination I had it cold.

The big depression of the 1930s caused a heavy (20%) reduction in staff, but that did not have a debilitating effect on PSPL. The Holding Company Act of 1935, however, had a much greater impact on Stone and Webster. As a result of that act, the company had to divest itself of most of its holdings. The reduction in holdings meant the elimination of the auditing department to which Jack Clawson was attached.

> The man who was the head of the department was one whom I liked very much, a Mr. Bissell. He was a high-type individual who encouraged improvement and growth. The other men in the department, who were my seniors, were rather ordinary people. I had realized that I was every bit as capable as any of the thirty of them and perhaps more so. I was a CPA and had a Harvard Business School background, which none of them had.
>
> It looked like I would shortly be out of a job, so I went to Mr. Bissell and said: "You have a highly qualified auditing force here. Why don't we set up a public accounting firm specializing in auditing public utilities around the United States?" He was not a CPA, and couldn't quite see hanging his hat on a single CPA to put up a firm as I had proposed. I wanted to go out and take a swing at it because I knew we were really good at auditing public utilities.

In the meantime, however, the treasurer of PSPL argued successfully with his management, over the course of three or four months, that they needed a senior auditor, and so Jack became an employee of Puget Sound Power and Light Company.

Opportunities for Career Advancement

One year later, the treasurer of PSPL instructed his head accountant to draft a plan to centralize the accounting systems for all its companies. The accountant spent about four months on the project, but when he brought in his report the treasurer felt that it was inadequate. Furthermore, he disagreed with its recommendations. He handed the assignment to Jack. The other man failed, Jack believed, because he did not have an overall perspective of the company. Jack knew that his Stone and Webster experience had given him that perspective. He wrote up the plans in one month, including the use and assignment of various personnel, and took it in to the treasurer's office. The treasurer thought the plans and proposals were "just great," and then asked Jack to go ahead and implement them. Jack, at 37, was made the assistant treasurer, in charge of the Auditing Department.

It was that little knowhow from auditing that helped me. There's a little saying, "An expert is a man eighty miles from his home." When one goes out and audits companies one after another all over the country, he is keeping up on all the latest procedures and practices. I saw a little benefit here, or a little better way there.

Pretty soon one can say in an office, "Well, you could be doing this." And they say, "Well, you're sure smart to think of that." You're just learning and copying from the places you've been. Pretty soon I came to know all of the best practices in the utility industry, and had become an "expert" in the judgment of others.

That operation focused the attention of the company on me. First, there had been the dilemma whether or not to keep me. Then when I put this reorganization together, the president and the treasurer both were very pleased. I took over the whole financial system then, making a big jump from just being kind of an "outsider" into head of all the departments underneath the treasurer. I had about 150 people working for me.

That same year a Public Utility District (PUD) law was passed granting any county the power to condemn private utility companies and to take over their operations. Almost immediately, about two-thirds of the counties in the northwestern part of Washington formed PUDs and initiated a struggle for the electric power business that was to last over 25 years. During the course of that struggle, PSPL lost about a third of its holdings to municipal and various PUDs, but was able to forestall the complete dismantling of the company and a proposed merger with another Washington company. During this struggle there was a competition with the City of Seattle during which services were duplicated—power lines and poles ran down both sides of the streets. In Jack's words, "It was really a mess."

When World War II began, Jack, an officer in the Naval Reserve, received a "critical industry" deferral from serving and continued working. In 1942 he was approached by a CPA friend on behalf of Boeing, then a fast-growing airframe manufacturer, with a proposal to become a special assistant to the president. The job held the allure of being a steppingstone to any number of positions at Boeing.

I was at that time third or fourth from the top at Puget and with all of the condemnation suits (by the PUDs), it looked like the company was hanging by a thread. One local newspaper had been running cartoons with the company depicted as a big corpse being hacked to pieces. It looked like I was going to be out of a job. I was invited to dinner with the president of Boeing, his financial vice president, and my CPA friend. We had a nice discussion and the president was all for employing me. Later, I talked further with my friend who was the go-between about terms. It was about double the salary I was getting, but the war was just starting and I told him, "I don't like to leave a job I've had for twenty years to work for two to three years in an industry that will decline drastically after the war." I told him I'd take it, but that I would need some assurance that I would be continued on with Boeing in some capacity after the war. The president of the company didn't like that and chose the other candidate. It was a big setback for me, and I could hardly live for about a week. It looked like my company was going out of business and I had insisted on something hard and sure. I should have taken my chances on my own abilities rather than ask for assurances.

However, it wasn't too long after that that another individual came to me and wondered if I'd be interested in taking a high financial position in Weyerhaeuser, about the largest timber company in the world. I said, "And how!" even though it would have meant moving to another city and it was a family company. Everything was being set up and then all of a sudden I got word that the deal had died cold. I feel sure that Weyerhaeuser decided not to disturb their close relationships with Puget.

I had missed both jobs, and it looked like Puget was going out of business for sure. I felt very low. I didn't have much appetite for about three months. I thought I'd made a big mistake, especially in fouling up the Boeing offer.

Another inquiry came from Seattle-based General Insurance Company looking for a potential top executive. In this case, the president of PSPL called me in and told me that General Insurance had inquired of him about me, and he had dissuaded them from making me an offer. So I settled down to work it out with and for Puget.

In about a year, the man in line to succeed the treasurer of PSPL died suddenly of a heart attack and I moved into second place. Only two years later the treasurer retired because of illness. I took over as treasurer, working with the president of the company.

The affairs of the company began to brighten. The PUDs had failed to take over and I was happy that the Boeing deal had not worked out. The war was over and Boeing was having a rough time adjusting to drastic reductions and cutbacks.

Financial Strategy

Jack had saved vigorously throughout his life. When he was traveling, he lived on an expense account and so was able to pay off his education debts within two years. He established his financial strategy early:

1. Save enough cash to cover unforeseen emergencies.
2. Carry as much life insurance as possible.
3. Protect wife and family with trusts as fast as possible.

4. Save enough to invest in income assets to cover retirement without relying on pensions.

I set goals for myself and made plans on which I was always working, revising and extending them from time to time, and by preparation, training and fortuitious circumstances succeeded considerably beyond my expectations. The main hope and goal in my occupation was to become the chief financial officer of a major corporation. I achieved it and went considerably beyond it to become the top executive of such a corporation, as well as a director in two other large corporations.

My personal financial goal was to earn and save sufficient that by wisely investing I could build up a personal estate to protect my family financially and to provide well for the time when I would no longer be employed. I continually studied and looked for promising investments with these essentials:

1. A basic, sound, noncyclical industry
2. Young, capable, aggressive management
3. Good growth prospects
4. High earnings on investment mostly retained in the business (little or no dividends, but compounding investment value)

In an unspectacular way I worked at this over my early years with a fair modicum of success. Some of my investments were good, a few were rather sorry. In fact, I almost lost my "shirt" on three really bad ones. They could have been disastrous except for special diligence on my part.

About 1950, a close, relatively young friend for whom I had done some favors and who had been an outstanding, successful businessman was asked to take over the management of a relatively small, struggling drugstore chain. He discussed the matter with me and a couple of other friends and subsequently agreed to take over the business, provided he and (we) his associates would acquire a controlling interest. The plan was to plow back all the earnings into the opening of new stores. It appeared to have all the elements for success and be very much in line with my investment purposes. I liquidated all of my investments, borrowed 25% more than that, and put it all into the business.

From the modest beginning of three small stores in the Seattle area, the company has grown to over 200 stores (in all the far western states including Alaska and Hawaii), generating over a half billion in annual sales. The original stores required an investment of around $50,000 each; present stores, which now include not only a drug division but hardware, soft goods, nurseries, sporting goods, require an investment of over $500,000 each. No dividends were paid for about the first ten years. However, expansion became so great that it became necessary to go public and begin to pay dividends—which at first were only stock dividends. The result of this compounded reinvestment of earnings plus inflation has produced a remarkable—not to say fantastic—increase in the market price of the original stock over the 30 years. The stock, allowing for splits, is now selling for about 75 times its original cost. Cash dividends, which are a payout of only about 20% of earnings, are annually 200% of the cost of the *original* stock; that is, an *original* stockholder now gets back in cash *double* the cost of his investment *every year*. Of course, there were only a few in that position, but subsequent investors have done very well.

In 1965, when I was approaching retirement in PSPL (I remained on the board of directors for some years thereafter), I realized that I was building up a rather large estate which would be subject to very heavy state and federal inheritance taxes. I therefore began an orderly divestment of my holdings by liberal donations to educational, religious, civic and other organizations and to hard-pressed relatives, but principally by gift to my three sons to permit them to establish businesses or other investment pursuits, and also educational trust funds for each of our 21 grandchildren and a few other needy and worthy young relatives, retaining sufficient to assure taking care of all of our own possible needs, including such travel (mostly to our scattered family) as we may enjoy, as well as further modest contributions to family, relatives, and worthy causes.

Family Strategy

When asked about his children, Jack said: "Just ask Leora what you want to know, and she'll tell you." But when pressed gently, he continued:

I have had some rather basic principles for guiding, inspiring, and helping my children make the most of their talents and get all the education and training they possibly could. The country needed it, the church needed it, and the children needed it to have a fulfilling life. They needed knowledge and understanding and wisdom. The way to get that, of course, is to pursue a logical course of training and education and to give their best to it. However, you just don't push them into it.

Leora: And he worked with his boys on this *all the way along*, and I may say, very successfully.

Jack: You have to *lead* them so that they want to do it. Nothing is more sorry than pounding on the backs of children to get them to do this or that. The better way is to set before them patterns and inspiration to understand their natures so that they will grab a line of action and go with it. This was a very conscious effort on our part. From the time they were small, we were determined that they would make the most of their talents and abilities.

Leora was most helpful. She did a tremendous job with those little kids. As they got older my influence began to have a larger bearing on it, but in those early stages she was magnificent.

Leora: However, in those early stages, let me tell you, he'd come home from work in the evenings and after dinner he'd gather those little ones around him and sit on the sofa and tell them stories. They weren't the stories from the story books. They were stories he made up in his own mind, often as he went along, and they always had a point. They would sit there enthralled, listening to his stories.

Jack: Well, I had read a tremendous amount and knew so many stories that it was not difficult to improvise. I would remember the main plot or theme and would be able to tell it to them in an interesting way. There was always a helpful or learning point to the stories—not a heavy moral, not preachy.

We took a deep interest. We gave them full backing in Scouting and in other activities and they loved it. Along with it was always this view of developing their talents. There were many things that we encouraged them to do without ever forcing them. One boy saved his money for a long while until he could buy his own bicycle. He's now a capable businessman doing very well—partly, we think, because he went through that period of saving to buy a bicycle when money was hard to get. At an early age, they chose their own life insurance policies and kept them up.

Jack's father died in 1940, his mother in 1954. During the years in between their deaths, Jack contributed heavily to the support of his mother. His two sisters, who lived in Logan, took care of her comfort and physical needs.

Reaching the Top

Jack's belief had always been that he should use imagination and careful thought before he acted. This included for him a continuous attempt to do his own job well and to understand the demands and perspective of his boss' job. This was not always easy, since many managers in the company were not inclined to discuss their jobs with their subordinates. Jack, however, encouraged his own employees to consider and reflect on the problems that faced the treasurer's office.

During the mid-1950s, Jack, as treasurer, was traveling with the president of PSPL making presentations to stock analysts and fighting off merger attempts. The Eisenhower administration defused the furor over the PUD takeovers so that the company no longer had to worry so much about that threat. Repeated questions about the nature of Harold's personal life and disposition during this period were always answered with descriptions of what was happening at the company. It was as if his personal life had merged into his corporate life.

While on one of the eastern trips, the president of PSPL was advised by one of the financial institutions that unless he soon made provisions for his succession, the firm would withdraw its very substantial investment. It was not apparent to the analysts who would provide the leadership of the company in the future. This was a "bolt" to both the president and to Jack. Jack had never thought of being president of the company before, and he realized for the first time that he was one of the few people in the company who was capable and familiar enough with the job to handle it.

The result of the investment firm's statement was a period of active review by the president. As the word that a successor was being selected got around, there was a lot of politicking among the senior officers of PSPL. In Jack's terms, this was characterized by a great deal of secrecy and game playing, but Jack's approach was to avoid that and to continue to attend to the financial affairs of the business.

Puget often used consultants on matters of major importance, and the succession to the presidency was no exception. At least two firms were retained to evaluate top management and their skills. The president of Puget agreed with their conclusions, and made Jack senior vice president in 1959. This promotion was an interim one designed to prepare Jack and ease the shock to the two or three people who considered themselves in line between Jack and the presidency. Jack was made president of the company in 1960. A year later, he was elected chairman of the board and chief executive officer.

Chief Executive Officer

During his incumbency as CEO, Jack felt that his most important contribution was to change the nature of executive management in the company from one of relative secrecy and authoritarianism to one of mutual participation. He felt that the other top executives, as a result of his efforts, enjoyed their work better, were happier, and performed better.

> The atmosphere and work became one of mutual cooperation rather than one of hard discipline and dictatorship. That was the first big job that I saw I had to do. I was not there long enough to carry out fully the long-range planning required by the physical operations of the utility business, but we set the stage for that to go on.

When faced with difficult problems, Jack would frequently lie awake at four or five in the morning and mentally probe various alternative means of solving them. This was a very important time for him in which he could explore these action plan scenarios without the interruptions of the office routines. The pressures of his job were demanding but not debilitating to Jack.

> Yes, there is a lot of stress, but there's another aspect of it. The executive who works hard and carries lots of responsibility and concerns . . . it isn't necessarily *that* which causes him to have ill health and break down as many do. It's more a matter of their personal nature or state of mind. It is true that "hard work never hurt anybody." Stress itself won't hurt you unless you let it. I don't think that the stress hurt me. I liked challenges and when I had problems that were really serious, I labored over them very hard. There were many problems where decisions had to be made. There were a lot of decisions that whichever way you went, you were partly wrong. It was as they say, "Like being caught between a rock and a hard place."
>
> There are a lot of people who evaluate what distinguishes a successful executive by his decisions. With all of the tough ones he has to make, if the majority of them are right, he's a good executive. No executive makes them all right. He is going to make some wrong, and then he is going to have to work to straighten them out. If you've made the wrong decision, and you know you've made the wrong decision, you have to know how to reverse your field and still not lose face in your organization. The best way to do it is to be frank about it and not start covering up, or somebody will find out. Then you lose faith, which is worse than being wrong and correcting your mistake.

Jack's concern with his mental agility and education focused on another aspect of working as a CEO:

> As a chief executive officer, you are waited upon. You can lose touch with the normal activities of life. May I tell you what happened to me? When I was chief executive, I had secretaries and assistants to do practically everything. Before that I used to take care of all my own financial affairs, write my own letters, and checks, and everything. When I was CEO they did everything for me. I didn't do any arithmetic. Didn't need a computer, didn't even know how to use one. At one time, having been an accountant, I could add up a string of figures like nothing at all. By the time I retired, would you believe it, I could hardly remember a telephone number long enough to dial it! I hadn't kept accustomed to the relationship of numbers. I could feel it, and it was just enough of a warning to me. From that point on, I began to practice with figures and writing. I *felt* that slippage. It GOES. You get away from your skills a few years, and they leave you.

In 1965, Jack reached retirement age and stepped down from the top job. He retained a seat on the board of directors for several years and took an active role in the planning and implementation of management changes over the next five years.

Retirement

Jack had few reservations about retiring:

> Look at it this way. I went through some really tough years when I was working with the president of the company. I practically had no vacations. Something was always coming up. He'd call me from New York on a Saturday evening about ten o'clock and want me to get on a plane at eleven and be back there Sunday at noon. In those days it took fourteen hours by plane to get back to New York.
>
> That was all right. I didn't mind; it was the nature of my job, but it *was* strenuous work. There was a lot of travel. One year, I was in New York staying in a hotel for eleven out of the twelve months. It was not easy. There were lots of early and long hours.
>
> So, having been successful in my financial strategy, I looked forward to retirement so that I could engage in other activities that were more enjoyable.
>
> I've had no problems keeping busy. The first year we took a little vacation and rest in Europe. We spent the summer over there. Then I had lunch with the president of one of the local television/radio stations here. We became good friends, and he invited me to be on the board of directors and on the management committee of the television station.
>
> One day the telephone rang while I was out in the garden, and I was asked if I would like to go to Iran. And I said, "Fine." The caller said, "I am speaking for the U.S. State Department, and we have a team of experts going to Iran to study its national electric system to determine what sources of energy should be used to produce electricity. They've got oil, gas, and water power. They also need to know what kind of transmission and distribution lines to put in. The team will study what the growth of the country's going to be, how big a system should be built, and related matters."
>
> I was invited to head up the team. They needed a name and a position to deal with the cabinet-level officials in Iran. When I got over there it was more than that. I was paid well, but it was darn hard work. It was interesting, and I got a lot out of it, but it was very hard on me and Leora. It was so hot in that 119-degree weather at an altitude of 4,000 or 5,000 feet.
>
> The following year we made a trip of about a month to South America for the Chamber of Commerce. About that time, we also made a swing with another official group for a couple of months to Japan, Hong Kong, Manila, and then down to Australia. I came back

all bugged out from that. I mean, we went so *much*. We had a whale of a good time and enjoyed it.

During these years, the drugstore business was expanding rapidly, and it went public. The owner, my friend, had tried to keep it a family business. Since he and I were very close, he asked me to be on the board of directors so he would not have to take an outsider. So, I was on the board of directors there.

Then a local hospital asked me to be on the advisory board. I was involved in Boy Scouts, too. I was active in my church work, business, and community activities. After awhile I had to begin gradually unloading some of these responsibilities so I could have a little time for my family and myself. I began playing golf once a week. So I have been as busy as I ever was at the office.

Leora: If he had retired as treasurer of the company, he still would have enjoyed retirement and doing the things he likes to do. He loves the garden. He loves his golf. He loves being active.

Jack: He loves spending time with his wife a little bit, too! (*Laughter.*)

Leora: No matter what happened, that man would be busy. He'd be doing something. And he'd be enjoying it.

His sons call him for advice when they have a problem, a business deal, a decision or something. They ask him, "Hey, Dad, what about this?" And they spend an hour talking on the telephone. That's awfully nice. It's good for the relationship between father and son, and it keeps him thinking about things. And it's good for the boys because they have respect for his years of experience.

In 1979, Jack returned to his alma mater, Utah State University, to accept an honorary doctor's degree in business management. This was a rewarding and satisfying experience for him.

As the Clawsons continued to reflect on their fifty years of marriage and career, Jack was asked how he would describe himself:

One thing I have, I reckon, is a pretty fair mental capacity and ability. I do not learn very rapidly. There are a lot of people who can learn faster than I, but I'm persistent and orderly in it so that in the long run I will probably come out even or on top. I may not be the first, but I am thinking about difficult problems and I can stick with it for a long time until I get an answer. A lot of others may get lost in the complexity of the problems.

Leora: He says he doesn't learn rapidly, and yet I've seen him take a thick book, receive it at 5:00 P.M. and go and give a report on it at a meeting the next morning. He doesn't learn rapidly??!

Jack: Most executives have to be able to do that. I learned that in making presentation to a superior, you have to get to the vital point at once and supply the additional data if you are asked for it. When I was chief executive, each day I'd get a stack of reports, business magazines, and papers to go through on my desk every morning. But I'd have people coming in for long conferences, discussing very serious problems all day long. Come five o'clock, the stack of papers was still there. Then I would have to bring that stack home at night to go through them. If you want understanding, you have just got to look at the reports yourself.

As a student journalist, I learned that in writing a newspaper article one has to say in the first paragraph what the whole story is about because a lot of people just read the first line or two. The first sentence of every paragraph normally is the essential point. The rest is secondary information regarding that particular idea and if you don't need it, you go to the next one and on down. That is a kind of speed reading that I've done a lot of and still do because I want to cover a lot of information.

Beyond this matter of my mental capacity, the next thing is I think I have imagination. Looking ahead and visualizing events and problems in the future, and solving them in advance or planning steps to be taken. I have solved a great many problems the first hour of the day when I wake up at 4 or 5 o'clock. It's surprising how looking at all the angles of a particular problem at that hour would bring out things I'd never thought about. When I was a kid, I read many of Horatio Alger's talks. I began thinking about accomplishing things in life—right from the start. Even when I was 8 or 10 years old, I began imagining myself doing what the Horatio Alger boys did. As I continued on in life I could always visualize myself doing things. I think I have done this all of my life—this projecting of myself. In doing so, I have visualized the problems in advance, before they happened or had to be settled. This has been a great help. Having done that early in my life—first it was to be a teacher, then it was to be a lawyer, then it was to be a businessman—at each stage I was using my imagination and saying: "What do I do so I'll be the best or at least good at it?" And then I would begin to do those things.

I had serious setbacks and times when it looked as though I were a failure and not making the grade, very off-base with serious shortcomings. I think this is a common experience, psychological ups and downs. Little things will set us back, but somehow the sun will shine, next month anyway, and better things will come up to get us going. Sacrifice comes before miracles—sometimes you have to go through the hardships in order to achieve your goals. We often learn more from our mistakes and our bad times than we do from all our successes. I have had confidence that there's always another side beyond the dark times.

I've made a lot of mistakes, but I don't dwell on them. I don't think it's wholesome, I don't think that helps any except to recognize that most of them have been very good for us. I can't conceive of anybody getting on without setbacks of various kinds. You learn from them.

I have a good sense of responsibility. My first motivation was unhappiness with a life in which I was born and raised, rural people with low incomes and virtually no prospects of employment in the area. This disturbed me, and I had a feeling that I wanted something better. This became a source of great motivation to me. I was determined to achieve something better. From reading and observing, I knew it was available. There had to be a way, and I was going to find it.

I was very awkward and self-conscious in dealing with people, especially groups. I didn't have that natural inclination.

I've been described as, "He is not able to accept compliments graciously. He's embarrassed by it." When I was growing up, I had a feeling of inadequacy. An inability to deal with people. I didn't feel at ease. Not in school or classes where I had a feeling of ability with effort to match anybody, even at the Harvard Business School. However, I always felt I lacked personality. I just didn't seem to have the personality to feel at ease with other people.

When I was made president of the company, I attended a meeting of top executives in a big hotel. I found it difficult to go up to some of them and find anything intelligent to talk about. For one thing, I hadn't been brought into it gradually. I also felt, "Here's the head of Boeing over here, a billion-dollar business, and here are all these top bankers. They're top men in their businesses. I'm top man in mine, but heck I'm just an old country boy." That took time to get over. I worked hard to develop the ability to be gracious and to get along with everyone. I did, and that made a big difference. I found that they were just men, talking little talk like you and me.

Leora: This seems like a contradiction to me. I've never seen him with a person or a group that he hasn't been able to carry on a fine conversation. He's said that for years but I never see it—it's never evident.

Jack: Here's another thing. I have an innermost urge to take over and run things in directions in which I am interested or feel I have an ability. In Boy Scouts, I wanted to be the troop leader, and became a troop leader. In school, when there was a question, I didn't mind holding up my hand. I have to hold myself down in groups because when I think I know more about it than anybody else, I want to tell them. I want to give them another point of view. I try to stimulate their thinking.

I am also curious. I can't sit down where there's any kind of a book without having to pick it up and see what it is about—whether it's a women's magazine, a magazine in a dentist's office, whatever it is. I want to pick it up and read it and see what it's about. I have a lot of mental curiousity.

Leora: That all got in the way a little bit. Especially when he was so loaded with responsibilities—both company and church. I felt very neglected. I felt that I had to do something about it. It couldn't continue the way it was. There was always somebody calling him for time and attention, so I had to work it out.

There's one thing that I might change in him, though I might be sorry if I did.

Jack: Besides, now it's fifty years too late!

Leora: I'd try to have him be more aware of other people's feelings, moods, needs. He's very aware of his own, and the need to work and to do and to deliver (*pause*), but I wonder sometimes if he even *sees* my needs.

Jack: Some people have thin "insulation," and they are very sensitive to everything that people do and say and think. Other people have a thick insulation mentally, spiritually, and physically. They're built that way, and no matter what they do they'll never be as thoughtful as those who are naturally sensitive. In my personal drive, I become insensitive and hurt her. She thinks it's because I don't care. *She* feels it through her whole system. To me, I feel I'm going quite a ways with my level of sensitivity. Often, I'm thinking more in terms of what I'm doing than of the feelings that are involved. I'm thinking of the programs, aspirations, and that sort of thing—the management of affairs, not of the feelings. In thinking about what needs to be done all the time, I am not so careful about managing the feelings.

It's very difficult for a person who is thin-skinned to be running the management of a business without getting into trouble, because one cannot be that sensitive. On the other hand, one has to be considerate, but if you get *too* sensitive, you're in trouble.

Leora: Well, that's very true. I've never been in business, but I've been in management positions (in the church) where you don't get paid for the job but where you have to manage well. I've been an executive in that sense for twenty-five years. It's been my sensitiveness, not touchiness (and there's a difference) that has kept people coordinating with good feelings. I think some say, "This is the way I am, so just take it or leave it. This is me." I know I'm extremely aware and sensitive, and many times I tell myself, "That's just none of my business, just stay quiet and don't let your feelings take over."

We recognize these characteristics in ourselves and in recognizing them, we have to know also that there are advantages and disadvantages. We can't play it always just the way we want it. We have to discipline ourselves to try to know, and in all integrity, to do what we feel is the right thing to do. If you don't have feelings, if you don't see these things, and you just tell yourself that's not one of your characteristics, you build and build and build this indifference rather than saying, "Now, for one hour today I'm just going to watch and do whatever I can and to help. . . ." I mean you can justify yourself in being inconsiderate.

But, too, there isn't a day that goes by that he doesn't come up and put his arms around me and tell me how sweet I am and how much he loves me, and what could he have done without me. Sometimes, I say to him in humor, "You have a hell of a way of showing it!" Words alone are not enough.

Jack: For me, even if I do it, I don't feel so deeply as she does. When I'm working with people, I try to be mindful of the things they're interested in, so I can inspire them to move ahead. I may not be quite as sensitive in some of the things I say to them and perhaps even offend some of them because I am not so sensitive. Lorie does it spontaneously. I cannot change completely, but I can change my ways of doing things but it's like teaching my muscles to do something that doesn't come naturally.

I don't mean to offend. But quite often I'm so set on accomplishing something that I think is more important than maybe hurting their feelings a little bit. Actually on rare occasions, I have deliberately shocked or startled someone a little bit in order to impress them—which is a different thing than Lorie might do by loving them into doing it—perhaps both ways get results.

Having finished his self-description, Harold volunteered his view of his wife:

> Among Leora's qualities, and constant endeavors, let me list a few—not necessarily in any order of importance:
>
> Deep concern for other people, including especially her own family.
>
> Constantly seeking improvement.
>
> Outgoing friendliness and *helpfulness* to every one. Everyone who knows her, loves her.
>
> Generous to a fault, really!
>
> Indefatigable, sets highest standards of performance for herself—encourages others in same direction.
>
> Considerate and highly sensitive to the needs and feelings of others.
>
> Constantly striving to improve in cultural things and refinement, and encouraging others in that direction.
>
> Inveterate "student" (reader) to improve and increase in knowledge, particularly in all phases of life—health, activities, as well as cultural things.
>
> A competent teacher, speaker and leader—confident and winning.
>
> Tremendous supporter of family *and* friends.
>
> Constantly holding to highest standards in goals, performance, conduct *ideals*.
>
> Well-liked and admired wherever she goes, with a multitude of friends.

During the latter part of his administration, Jack had begun having even more serious abdominal pains. He had lived with them for 55 years, excusing himself at times to go lie down and massage his stomach. Leora had made it her crusade to ease that burden and had researched diet and exercise programs constantly over the years. Jack described Leora's help in one sentence: "I could *not* have achieved what I did without the help, advice, counsel and support Leora gave me in every way, nor would I even be alive today, I am sure, without her tremendous interest and concern in everything having to do with health, and personal concern in all matters." About five years after he had retired, though, the pain was too much, so the doctors advised exploratory surgery. They found, to their surprise, that Jack's intestines had fused almost shut in several places—the result of bovine tuberculosis contracted in Jacks' tenth year. After corrective surgery, Jack regained his strength and felt better than he had for his entire working career.

After the interview, Jack arose, and motioning to the casewriter, ambled down to the lake by his home, climbed in his 17-foot runabout, and said: "Let's go waterskiing!" And they did.

ASPECT CARDS

FINANCIAL (Money)	INTELLECTUAL
FAMILIAL (Parents, siblings)	EMOTIONAL
RECREATIONAL	PHYSICAL
SOCIAL (Friends, parties, meeting people)	POLITICAL (Campaigns, public office)
MARITAL (Spouses, live-in partners)	SPIRITUAL (Meaning of life, God, cosmos)

ASPECT CARDS

PROFESSIONAL (Occupation, career)	MATERIAL (Possessions)
SOCIETAL (Community service)	ECCLESIASTICAL (Church work)
PARENTAL (Children)	IDENTITY (Clarity of self-image)

VALUES CARDS

BEING INDEPENDENT	BEING CLOSE TO OTHERS
BEING PRAISED BY COLLEAGUES AT WORK	GAINING PUBLIC RECOGNITION
ACHIEVING A GOAL	FINISHING A TASK
BEING PRAISED BY SPOUSE	GETTING REWARDED FAIRLY FOR MY EFFORTS
BEING PRAISED BY PARENTS	HAVING AS MUCH (MANY) AS POSSIBLE

VALUES CARDS

ENJOYING THE ACTIVITY	USING MY ENERGY AND RESOURCES WISELY
CONCENTRATING ON ONE THING	DOING BETTER THAN THE NEXT PERSON
FOLLOWING DIRECTIONS	DIRECTING THE NEXT PERSON
DECIDING WHAT TO DO NEXT	CHANGING ACTIVITIES DAILY
MOVING QUICKLY	CHANGING ACTIVITIES WEEKLY

VALUES CARDS

MOVING SLOWING	CHANGING ACTIVITIES MONTHLY
ORGANIZING THINGS	LOOKING AHEAD
BEING ENCOURAGED	PLANNING AHEAD
CREATING NEW THINGS	LOOKING BACK
FEELING EXPERT (especially at ___)	THE TRANQUILITY

VALUES CARDS

WORKING ON DETAILS	TACKLING A CHALLENGE
WORKING ON THE BROAD ISSUES	BEING SEEN AS AN EXPERT (especially at ___)
GETTING AHEAD	ADMIRING THE BEAUTY OF IT ALL
LEARNING NEW THINGS (especially ___)	BEING FREE
MEETING PEOPLE	FEELING A PART OF THE GROUP

VALUES CARDS

HELPING PEOPLE	TAKING RISKS
TEACHING PEOPLE	BUILDING THINGS
EXPANDING INFLUENCE	WATCHING PEOPLE GROW
HAVING A SET SCHEDULE OR ROUTINE	RELAXING
BEING ABLE TO ___	HAVING ___

VALUES CARDS

FEELING ___	BEING ___